Life and Health Insurance Law

THE IRWIN/McGRAW-HILL SERIES IN FINANCE, INSURANCE, AND REAL ESTATE

Stephen A. Ross
Sterling Professor of Economics and Finance
Yale University
Consulting Editor

FINANCIAL MANAGEMENT

Benninga and Sarig
Corporate Finance:
A Valuation Approach

Block and Hirt
Foundations of Financial Management
Eighth Edition

Brealey and Myers
Principles of Corporate Finance
Fifth Edition

Brealey, Myers and Marcus
Fundamentals of Corporate Finance

Brooks
PC FinGame: *The Financial Management Decision Game*
Version 2.0—DOS and Windows

Bruner
Case Studies in Finance:
Managing for Corporate Value Creation
Second Edition

Chew
The New Corporate Finance:
Where Theory Meets Practice

Grinblatt and Titman
Financial Markets and Corporate Strategy

Helfert
Techniques of Financial Analysis: *A Modern Approach*
Ninth Edition

Higgins
Analysis for Financial Management
Fifth Edition

Hite
A Programmed Learning Guide to Finance

Kester, Fruhan, Piper, and Ruback
Case Problems in Finance
Eleventh Edition

Nunnally and Plath
Cases in Finance
Second Edition

Parker and Beaver
Risk Management: *Challenges and Solutions*

Ross, Westerfield, and Jaffe
Corporate Finance
Fourth Edition

Ross, Westerfield, and Jordan
Essentials of Corporate Finance

Ross, Westerfield, and Jordan
Fundamentals of Corporate Finance
Fourth Edition

Schall and Haley
Introduction to Financial Management
Sixth Edition

Smith
The Modern Theory of Corporate Finance
Second Edition

White
Financial Analysis with an Electronic Calculator
Third Edition

INVESTMENTS

Ball and Kothari
Financial Statement Analysis

Bodie, Kane, and Marcus
Essentials of Investments
Third Edition

Bodie, Kane, and Marcus
Investments
Third Edition

Cohen, Zinbarg, and Zeikel
Investment Analysis and Portfolio Management
Fifth Edition

Farrell
Portfolio Management: *Theory and Applications*
Second Edition

Gibson
Option Valuation

Hirt and Block
Fundamentals of Investment Management
Fifth Edition

Jarrow
Modelling Fixed Income Securities and Interest Rate Options

Lorie, Dodd, and Kimpton
The Stock Market: *Theories and Evidence*
Second Edition

Morningstar, Inc. and Remaley
U.S. Equities OnFloppy Educational Version
Annual Edition

Shimko
The Innovative Investor
Version 2.0—Lotus and Excel

FINANCIAL INSTITUTIONS AND MARKETS

Flannery and Flood
Flannery & Flood's ProBanker: *A Financial Services Simulation*

James and Smith
Studies in Financial Institutions: *Non-Bank Intermediaries*

Johnson
Financial Institutions and Markets: *A Global Perspective*

Kohn
Financial Institutions and Markets

Rose
Commercial Bank Management: *Producing and Selling Financial Services*
Third Edition

Rose
Money and Capital Markets: *Financial Institutions and Instruments in a Global Marketplace*
Sixth Edition

Rose and Kolari
Financial Institutions: *Understanding and Managing Financial Services*
Fifth Edition

Santomero and Babbel
Financial Markets, Instruments, and Institutions

Saunders
Financial Institutions Management: *A Modern Perspective*
Second Edition

INTERNATIONAL FINANCE

Eun and Resnick
International Financial Management

Kester and Luehrman
Case Problems in International Finance

Levi
International Finance
Third Edition

Levich
International Financial Markets

Stonehill and Eiteman
Finance: *An International Perspective*

REAL ESTATE

Berston
California Real Estate Principles
Seventh Edition

Berston
California Real Estate Practice
Sixth Edition

Brueggeman and Fisher
Real Estate Finance and Investments
Tenth Edition

Corgel, Smith, and Ling
Real Estate Perspectives: *An Introduction to Real Estate*
Third Edition

Lusht
Real Estate Valuation:
Principles and Applications

McLoughlin
Principles of Real Estate Law

Sirmans
Real Estate Finance
Second Edition

FINANCIAL PLANNING AND INSURANCE

Allen, Melone, Rosenbloom, and VanDerhei
Pension Planning: *Pension, Profit-Sharing, and Other Deferred Compensation Plans*
Eighth Edition

Crawford
Life and Health Insurance Law
Eighth Edition (LOMA)

Hirsch
Casualty Claim Practice
Sixth Edition

Kapoor, Dlabay, and Hughes
Personal Finance
Fourth Edition

Kellison
Theory of Interest
Second Edition

Lang
Strategy for Personal Finance
Fifth Edition

Skipper
International Risk and Insurance

Williams, Smith, and Young
Risk Management and Insurance
Eighth Edition

LIFE AND HEALTH INSURANCE LAW

Muriel L. Crawford, J.D., FLMI, CLU, ChFC, CEBS
Member of the Illinois and California Bars
Formerly Associate General Counsel and Secretary
Washington National Insurance Company

Published for the FLMI Insurance Education Program
Life Management Institute—LOMA
Atlanta, Georgia

Irwin
McGraw-Hill

Boston, Massachusetts   •   Burr Ridge, Illinois   •   Dubuque, Iowa
Madison, Wisconsin   •   New York, New York   •   San Francisco,
California   •   St. Louis, Missouri

Irwin/McGraw-Hill

A Division of The McGraw·Hill Companies

LIFE AND HEALTH INSURANCE LAW
Originally published as *Law and the Life Insurance Contract*

This book is printed on acid-free paper.

2 3 4 5 7 8 9 0 DOC/DOC 9 0 9 8

ISBN 0-256-16699-4

Vice president and Editorial director: *Michael W. Junior*
Publisher: *Gary Burke*
Associate editor: *Shelly Kronzek*
Editorial coordinator: *Holly K. Zemsta*
Senior marketing manager: *Katie M. Rose Matthews*
Project manager: *Kimberly D. Hooker*
Production supervisor: *Scott Hamilton*
Senior designer: *Crispin Prebys*
Compositor: *Shepard Poorman Communications*
Typeface: *10/12 Times Roman*
Printer: *R. R. Donnelley & Sons Company*

Library of Congress Cataloging-in-Publication Data

Crawford, Muriel L.
    Life and health insurance law / Muriel L. Crawford.—8th ed.
      p. cm.
    "Published for the FLMI Insurance Education Program, Life
Management Institute—LOMA, Atlanta, Georgia."
    Includes index.
    ISBN 0-256-16699-4
    1. Insurance, Life—Law and legislation—United States.
2. Insurance, Health—Law and legislation—United States.   I. Life
Office Management Association. Life Management Institute. FLMI
Insurance Education Program. II. Title.
KF1175.C73   1998
346.73'08632—dc21   97-20964

http://www.mhcollege.com

To Barry, with gratitude for his constant support and encouragement

This book and its predecessor, *Law and the Life Insurance Contract*, have been used to educate students of life and health insurance law for almost 40 years. Of the eight editions of the book, I have had the privilege of coauthoring two and authoring two.

In this book I have attempted to present the major principles of life and health insurance law in a manner that will allow students without legal training to readily understand them. I have defined legal terms as they occur and have tried to explain legal concepts in everyday English. I have given an example whenever I thought it might clarify the legal concept being discussed. I have retained the illustrative case at the end of each chapter, because I believe that a firsthand acquaintance with the reasoning of the courts is essential to the student's understanding of law.

The purpose of this book is to educate students to recognize legal problems so they can seek advice from legal counsel. This book is not intended to provide solutions to individual legal problems because laws vary from jurisdiction to jurisdiction and are subject to change. Moreover, if a fact situation differs slightly from a similar fact situation presented in the book, the action that should be taken could vary materially from that suggested in the book.

Although the general organization of earlier editions has been retained, I have incorporated much new material into this edition. Some of this new material concerns court oversight of lawyers, market conduct, the new NAIC Life Insurance Illustrations Model Regulation, genetic information, the constitutionality of punitive damages, state statues limiting punitive damages, the federal Health Insurance Portability and Accountability Act of 1996, minimum premium plans, self-funded plans, stop-loss contracts, managed care organizations, utilization review, case management, health care fraud, the NAIC Model Variable Contract Law, qualified assignments of liability, Internet advertising, race discrimination, and age discrimination. I have reorganized some chapters and have added many new examples and definitions. I have, of course, deleted discussions of laws that have been repealed, reversed, or overruled and have in other ways brought the book up to date.

I have had assistance from a number of people in producing this edition. The lawyers who reviewed the manuscript and gave me many excellent suggestions are Harriett E. Jones, J.D., FLMI, Senior Associate, Educational Programs, LOMA; David W. Perez, J.D., FLMI, Assistant General Counsel, Northwestern Mutual Life Insurance Company; and Julia Davis, J.D., Associate General Counsel, Independent Life & Accident Insurance Company.

James R. Ruegg, FLMI/M, CLU, Assistant Vice President, Amica Life Insurance Company, and Edward E. Graves, CLU, ChFC, Associate Professor of Insurance, The American College, both of whom have taught insurance law courses for many years, gave me their valuable perspective on the manuscript. Daniel J. Burnside, Ph.D., R.I.A., a financial consultant located in Binghamton, New York, reviewed the seventh edition and made a number of helpful suggestions for changes in and additions to this eighth edition. Linda Tirdel, R.N., who is one of the country's leading experts on structured settlements, provided me with a wealth of information about structured settlements and reviewed the chapter entitled Annuity Contracts. Law librarian Joyce M. Dahlberg, M.A.L.S., did much of the research for this edition. My husband, Barrett Crawford, read the entire manuscript twice and gave me his wise counsel. My daughter, Barbara Crawford, M.L.I.S., whose education and expertise are in computers and information science, gave me essential technical advice. Washington National Insurance Company and Provident Mutual Life Insurance Company of Philadelphia allowed me to reproduce their policy forms, using fictitious applicants, in the appendix. My thanks to all who have helped me so generously.

Muriel L. Crawford

BRIEF CONTENTS

C O N T E N T S

14 Assignments and Other Transfers   276

15 Lapse and Reinstatement   294

16 Equitable Remedies   307

1 INSURANCE AND THE LAW

Chapter Outline

The student of life and health insurance needs a basic understanding of the law for four reasons. First, an insurance policy describes a *contract,* which is an agreement enforceable in a court of law. For this reason, an understanding of contract law is a necessary part of insurance education. Second, a study of contract law inevitably leads to many other areas of law. A familiarity with the law of agency, property, wills, trusts, community property, equitable remedies, and torts is necessary to an understanding of contract law and of the insurance business. Third, insurance is heavily regulated by a body of insurance law that is becoming more complex every day. Insurers must work continually to ensure that they are complying with these laws. Fourth, insurers must conduct their businesses in accordance with many laws that do not directly involve insurance. For example, as employers they must deal with employment laws and, as corporations selling their corporate stock (securities) to the public, with securities laws. The purpose of this chapter is to explain the structure of law and the way the laws governing insurers fit into that structure.

Structure of Law

When people speak of a law, they usually mean a statute enacted by a legislature. However, law is a great deal more than a collection of statutes. The structure of law is highly complex.

In its broadest sense, the term *law* can be defined as a system of rules governing human conduct, rules that are enforceable by a controlling authority. Included in the concept of law are the broad philosophies and principles of constitutional law, agreements in treaties between nations, congressional enactments, state statutes, rules and regulations of the numerous administrative agencies of the federal and state governments, decisions of federal and state courts, and many general principles of custom and public policy, some dating back so far that no one can say accurately when they began.

The laws of a society are shaped by and tailored to the needs of that society. A law appropriate to and necessary for one society might be intolerable in another. Even within a country, different regions require different laws. In the United States, no two states have identical sets of laws. Moreover, a federal law that applies to the entire country might be readily accepted by people in some states and not so readily accepted by people in others. Such was the case with the federal law requiring vehicles to limit their speed to 55 miles per hour. Many people in the western states, where it is often necessary to travel great distances, found this law difficult to accept, while people in small eastern states accepted it more readily. A lack of public acceptance will often cause a law to be ignored, unenforced, modified, or repealed.

Some laws are old and others new. The age of a law does not govern its validity. A court decision handed down two centuries ago may still regulate the actions of people today. Nevertheless, as society changes, some laws lose public acceptance. For example, at one time, a state could lawfully deny women the right to practice law.[1] Social changes made this law obsolete, and it was eliminated. Social changes also necessitate new laws. For example, when computers came into general use, the legislatures and courts had to begin developing a body of computer law.

---

[1]Bradwell v. Illinois, 83 U.S. (16 Wall.) 130 (1872).

Common Law

The United States is often said to be a common-law country. The term *common law* has a number of different meanings. Some of the most important meanings are given below.

General Principles of Law.   In one sense, the ***common law*** is a heritage of general principles involving customs, public policy, and ideas of justice that are followed by courts of common-law countries, states, and provinces. The common law originated in England and was brought to the United States by the early English settlers.

Common Law and Civil Law.   ***Common law*** also means the legal systems of England and of nations, states, and provinces that derive their law from English law. *Common law* is often used in this sense to contrast legal systems derived from English law with legal systems derived from the law of the Roman Empire.

England, Canada (except Quebec), and most of the states in the United States are common-law jurisdictions. By contrast, France, Spain, Italy, Quebec, and some states in the United States derive their legal systems in whole or in part from the law of the Roman Empire. These countries, states, and provinces are said to be civil-law jurisdictions.[2] Perhaps the most important distinguishing characteristic of the ***civil law*** is that it attempts to bring together all the general principles of law and to organize them into a relatively complete written code. Court decisions then are made only with reference to principles that have been made a part of that code. In common-law jurisdictions, there is no attempt to codify all the principles that will be used, although such principles often are enacted into statutes.

Case Law.   The term *common law* is sometimes used to distinguish case law (court decisions) from statutory—that is, legislative—law. In this sense, the ***common law*** of a jurisdiction is made up of the decisions of the courts, but not the enactments of the legislature.

Civil Law and Criminal Law

In the discussion of common law above, we defined the term *civil law* to mean a system of law derived from the law of the Roman Empire. Another meaning of the term ***civil law*** is "the body of law that determines private rights and liabilities." In this sense, civil law is distinguished from ***criminal law,*** which prohibits and punishes conduct causing harm to the public. Thus, civil law is private, whereas criminal law is public. Under civil law, a private person sues another private person for the enforcement of the first person's rights. In contrast, the state or nation (represented by the public prosecutor) brings criminal proceedings on behalf of the public against a violator of criminal law.

A single act can, in certain circumstances, violate both civil and criminal laws. For example, a person who has been assaulted might sue the person who committed the assault and be awarded damages (money), because assault is a violation of the victim's rights under civil law. The state might also prosecute the offender under the state criminal assault laws. If convicted, the offender might be imprisoned or fined or

---

[2]Louisiana comes closest to being a civil-law state. Texas is sometimes said to be a civil-law state. Many states have some laws that have been influenced by civil law.

both. The state would imprison the offender, and any fines would go to the state, because assault is a violation of criminal law, a harm to the public.

A civil case and a criminal case arising from the same act are independent of each other. For example, after the close of the well-known criminal case in which O. J. Simpson was acquitted of murder, the families of the victims sued Simpson for damages in a civil action, claiming that he had wrongfully caused the victims' deaths.

The title of a court decision often indicates whether the court was dealing with a civil or a criminal matter. Examples of civil case titles are *Higgins v. McCulloch, Markham Manufacturing Co. v. Johnson Bolt Co.,* and *Stillson v. Prudential Insurance Co.* These titles indicate that one private party sued another private party. Criminal cases, on the other hand, are styled as follows: *People v. Henderson, United States v. Robel, Commonwealth v. Root, City of Chicago v. Gregory,* and *State v. Lehigh Valley Railroad Co.* In these cases, the state or nation prosecuted a person or other entity for violation of the criminal law.

A *crime* is usually either a felony or a misdemeanor. A *felony* is a serious crime for which the punishment can be imprisonment in a state or federal penitentiary or even death. Murder, treason, robbery, and kidnapping are examples of felonies. A *misdemeanor* is a less serious crime, usually punishable by fine or by imprisonment in a facility other than a penitentiary, such as a county jail. A parking violation is an example of a misdemeanor.

Substantive Law and Procedural Law

Each area of law is considered to be either substantive or procedural. An area of *substantive law* creates rights and duties. Contract law is an area of substantive law. Other areas of substantive law that are discussed in this book include tort law, the law of wills, trust law, property law, and criminal law.

Procedural law provides both a structure and set of rules for the enforcement of the rights and duties created by substantive law. Procedural law is usually divided into civil procedure and criminal procedure—that is, law governing procedure in civil matters and law governing procedure in criminal matters. Much of the material in this chapter deals with civil procedure. Jurisdiction of the courts, pleadings, motions, discovery, presumptions, the prima facie case, the burden of proof, and application of law are aspects of civil procedure.

Courts of Law and Courts of Equity

In the early days of the English common law, a person seeking justice applied for a royal order, or writ, which authorized a judge to hear the case. During the 13th century, these writs became highly formalized and applicable only to certain kinds of cases. In order to ask a court to enforce a right or redress a wrong—that is, to provide a *remedy*—a person had to fit the case into one of the writs that were available. Often, this was not possible, and, as a result, there was no remedy at law. In those situations, special appeals were often made to the king himself. He, in turn, would refer the question to his adviser, the chancellor. By the 15th century, in cases in which the remedy at law was unavailable or inadequate, the chancellor issued special decrees. These decrees were said to be obtained *in chancery* and provided *equitable remedies.* Thus, courts of chancery are also called *courts of equity.* An *equitable remedy* is a court of equity's enforcement of a right or redress of a wrong.

Law and Equity Today.   Although the distinction between courts of law and courts of equity was preserved in the court systems of the United States for many years, it has been abolished by statute in the federal courts and in the courts of most states. Ordinarily, the same court now has jurisdiction over both legal and equitable matters. Both legal and equitable remedies are available in the same suit. Nevertheless, equitable remedies continue to be distinguished from those available at law, and the basic principles of equity have not changed.

Equitable Remedies.   Because equity courts arose out of the inadequacy of ordinary legal remedies, remedies available in equity courts historically have been considered extraordinary in nature. For instance, in a suit on a contract the legal remedy for breach of contract (failure to perform as promised in the contract) is damages. *Damages* means the sum of money that the law awards as compensation for a legal wrong (also called an *injury*). In contract actions where money does not adequately compensate the person seeking redress, that person can pursue an equitable remedy known as *specific performance*. If granted, this equitable remedy will require that the contract be carried out as promised. For example, if one person contracts with another to buy land, and the person holding the land refuses to perform the contract by conveying the land to the buyer, an equity court might decree that the land must be conveyed and will enforce the specific performance of the contract.

Other remedies that developed in equity include interpleader, rescission, reformation, and declaratory judgment. These remedies are frequently used in connection with problems arising under insurance contracts. They are discussed in Chapter 16, "Equitable Remedies."

Sources of Law

Sources of law include constitutions, statutes, administrative rules and regulations, and case law. This section contains discussions of these sources of law as well as of model laws and of legal research.

Constitutions

A *constitution* sets forth in general terms the principles that form the legal foundation of a government. Because of a constitution's importance as an instrument of government, drafting and adopting a constitution is an especially serious undertaking. Constitutions are intended to be changed less often than statutes. Therefore, most constitutions include safeguards designed to prevent frequent or ill-considered amendments. A constitution ordinarily meets the needs of a changing society through interpretation by the courts rather than by amendment. Its general language makes this flexibility possible.

The Twofold Purpose of a Constitution.   A federal or state constitution in the United States has a twofold purpose. First, a constitution describes the structure of the government, defining the extent of its powers and outlining the principles on which it is to operate. A constitution provides for three branches of government—*legislative, executive,* and *judicial*—and establishes a system of checks and balances to guard against any branch becoming too powerful. Second, a constitution guarantees to citizens certain basic human rights, such as freedom of speech, freedom of worship, and the right to assemble peaceably.

The Dual Constitutional System of the United States.   In the United States, there are two kinds of constitutions: the federal Constitution and the state constitutions. The basic difference between the federal Constitution and a state constitution is that power is delegated by the federal Constitution to the federal government, whereas a state constitution defines and limits the already existing power of the state government. The federal government has no power that is not given to it by the federal Constitution. A state government has all powers that are not prohibited to it by the federal Constitution or by the constitution of that state.

The Federal Constitution.   Early in our history, each of the 13 colonies was a well-defined political unit and exercised its own governing powers. When representatives of the colonies met to frame a constitution for a proposed federal government, they delegated authority over certain areas to the new federal government. The states kept all other powers. The 10th Amendment of the federal Constitution states: "The powers not delegated to the United States by the Constitution, nor prohibited by it to the States, are reserved to the States respectively, or to the people."

The federal Constitution gives to the federal government, specifically to Congress, various enumerated powers. For insurance law purposes, the most important of these is the power to regulate interstate commerce that the Commerce Clause gives to Congress. This power is discussed in the section entitled "Insurance Regulation" that appears later in this chapter.

The federal government has direct authority over the people themselves to the extent of the governing power delegated to it. The U.S. Supreme Court has the final power to decide whether the federal government has exceeded the limits of its constitutional authority. However, over the years, the Court has broadened the authority of the federal government by holding that many powers not explicitly granted to the federal government are implied in the Constitution.

Once it has been established that a power is properly exercisable by the federal government, any acts by the federal government in that particular area take precedence over the acts of any state or subdivision of a state with respect to the same subject matter. The federal Constitution, the laws of the United States that are enacted under its provisions, and all treaties made under the authority of the United States are declared by the federal Constitution to be the "supreme law of the land." Accordingly, any law, whether federal or state, that violates a provision of the federal Constitution is unconstitutional and therefore void.

The State Constitutions.   A state constitution performs some of the same functions for the state that the federal Constitution performs for the United States. That is to say, it outlines the framework of the government and spells out guarantees of fundamental human rights. However, a state constitution does not grant the state the power to govern. Instead, it functions as a limitation of the power that is inherent in the state. The governing power of a state exists whether there is a state constitution or not.

Thus, while the federal Constitution enumerates delegated powers, a state constitution limits powers already acknowledged to exist, powers that in all other respects are unlimited. The practical effects of this concept are significant. An act of Congress must be based on some affirmative provision of the federal Constitution and will be constitutional only if it is the exercise of a power delegated to the federal government. By contrast, an act of a state legislature will be constitutional unless the state constitution or the federal Constitution prohibits it.

Under the federal Constitution, some of the powers that otherwise would be exercisable by the states were given up and delegated to the federal government. In all other areas, however, the state constitution represents the supreme law of the state. Thus, the Constitution of the United States and the constitutions of the various states, each operative in its own respective sphere, together provide the fundamental principles on which the government of the United States is based.

Statutes

A *statute* is "an act of the legislature declaring, commanding, or prohibiting something; a particular law enacted and established by the will of the legislative department of government."[3] Thus, another word meaning *statute* is *act*. Statutes enacted by Congress are called either *federal statutes* or *acts of Congress*.

Both Congress and the state legislatures enact statutes. Statutes are apt to be changed more often than constitutions, and, ordinarily, statutes are expressed in more specific terms as rules and standards of conduct. In areas of power granted to the federal government, Congress enacts the statutes. In areas that are the concern of the individual states, the legislatures of the respective states enact the statutes. If it is not clear whether Congress or the state legislatures have the power to legislate in a given area, the question can be referred to the courts for decision. In fact, that is how the landmark insurance case *United States v. South-Eastern Underwriters Association*[4] arose. The right of the individual states, as opposed to the federal government, to regulate insurance was challenged. The question was decided by the U.S. Supreme Court. This subject will be discussed more fully in the section entitled "Insurance Regulation" later in this chapter.

The published statutes of a jurisdiction, arranged in systematic form, are often referred to as a *code*. A collection of a jurisdiction's statutes that all relate to the same area of law may also be called a code. Thus, an insurance code is a collection of the insurance statutes of a given jurisdiction, a criminal code is a collection of statutes relating to crimes, and so on. The term *revised statutes,* as in, for example, *Oregon Revised Statutes,* denotes a code based on a prior code with alterations and additions necessary to bring the code up to date.

Administrative Rules and Regulations

In the United States, both federal and state governments operate under a doctrine called separation of powers. *Separation of powers* means that a government is divided into departments or branches, each of which primarily performs a distinct function. A branch of government performs a primarily legislative function when it enacts, or makes, laws; a primarily executive function when it enforces, or carries out, laws; and a primarily judicial function when it interprets laws and adjudicates disputes under the law.

An *administrative officer* is part of the executive branch. Under a strict separation-of-powers approach, a rule made by an administrative officer would not be effective. However, the complexities of modern business have necessitated some overlap among

---

[3]BLACK'S LAW DICTIONARY 25 (6th ed. 1990).
[4]322 U.S. 533 (1944).

the three branches. Highly technical businesses require highly technical knowledge for appropriate regulation. Legislators cannot have the necessary technical knowledge about every business that must be regulated. Consequently, they have adopted the practice of enacting regulatory statutes in general terms. They then authorize the administrative officer having the duty of executing the law to fill in the details by enacting administrative rules and regulations that have the force and effect of law. This delegation of rule-making power to administrative officers has been upheld by the courts as constitutional, as long as the rules so made are within the scope of the delegated power, are made following specified procedure, and are subject to judicial review.

Administrative officers also perform judicial functions. They hold hearings, make decisions, and impose penalties. Thus, administrative officers function in all three spheres—executive, legislative, and judicial.

The commissioner, director, or superintendent of insurance is a state administrative officer. Today, state legislatures have authorized the commissioner, director, or superintendent of insurance to adopt appropriate rules and regulations implementing the provisions of the state insurance statutes. Such administrative rules and regulations constitute a major part of the regulatory law governing the life and health insurance industry.

Model Laws

A *model law* is an act or regulation proposed by experts in a particular field for adoption by the states. The National Association of Insurance Commissioners (NAIC) has proposed many model acts and regulations for adoption, some of which are discussed in this book.

A model act or regulation itself is not a law and does not have the force or effect of law. It is merely a pattern on which a state legislature might base a statute, or on which an administrative officer, such as an insurance commissioner, might base a regulation. Sometimes a statute or regulation is patterned exactly on a model law, but often various changes are incorporated.

Another name for model law is *uniform law*. The term *uniform law* is sometimes used because an important purpose of a model law is to promote uniformity among state laws.

Case Law

A court applies laws to resolve the controversies brought before it. In so doing, a court interprets those laws and thus creates more law. In the United States, federal and state court decisions form a vast and growing body of law called *case law*. State case law consists of state intermediate and supreme court decisions, because most state trial court decisions are not published. Federal case law is made up of federal trial court decisions, federal intermediate court decisions, and U.S. Supreme Court decisions. Sections later in this chapter describe the organization of the courts and the procedural rules by which lawsuits are conducted.

Legal Research

Finding the entire applicable body of law on any given subject often requires searching a number of sources. Constitutions, statutes, rules and regulations of administrative agencies, and court decisions may have to be examined. Treaties between nations or executive orders might also bear on the question under consideration.

The constitutions of the federal government and of each state government are available in published form. Federal and state statutes are arranged, or codified, alphabetically by subject matter and indexed, so that they can be found easily. Each code has a title indicating its jurisdiction, as *United States Code, Nevada Revised Statutes,* or *Massachusetts General Laws Annotated.*

The decisions of courts of appeals, also called appellate courts, and of some trial courts are published in bound volumes called reports or reporters. Reporters occupy many shelves in any law library, and detailed systems have been devised for indexing the court decisions contained in these volumes. A standard form of reference for these published court decisions has been developed. The title of the case as it appeared on the court docket is written thus: *Smith v. Jones.* Then follow the volume number, the abbreviation for the reporter system referred to, the page on which the case begins, and, in parentheses, the year in which the case was decided. Thus, the landmark insurance case of *United States v. South-Eastern Underwriters Association,* 322 U.S. 533 (1944), will be found in volume 322 of the *United States Reports,* beginning at page 533. This case was decided by the U.S. Supreme Court in 1944. Only U.S. Supreme Court cases are reported in the *United States Reports.*

Cases decided by the state courts are often reported in a state reporter as well as in a regional reporter. The state court cases that are cited in footnotes in this book are cited to the regional reporters. The regional reporters include the *Atlantic Reporter,* the *Northeastern Reporter,* the *Southeastern Reporter,* the *Southern Reporter,* the *Northwestern Reporter,* the *Southwestern Reporter,* and the *Pacific Reporter,* among others. Thus, the 1977 Louisiana Court of Appeal decision of *Provident Life & Accident Insurance Co. v. Carter,* 345 So. 2d 1245 (La. Ct. App. 1977) is reported in volume 345 of the *Southern Reporter,* Second Series, beginning on page 1245.

Lawyers also make frequent use of treatises on various aspects of the law. These treatises appear in general reference series, such as the **American Law Reports Annotated (A.L.R.), Corpus Juris Secundum (C.J.S.), American Jurisprudence 2d (Am. Jur. 2d),** *Williston on Contracts,* and *Couch on Insurance,* to mention only a few. Such treatises help lawyers gain a general understanding of the law, and some have influenced the development of legal principles.

Lawyers can now use computers to assist them to do fast, thorough, accurate legal research, because much of the law has been put into electronic law libraries. LEXIS and WESTLAW are two well-known on-line electronic law libraries. Their databases are large and are continually being expanded. In addition, reporters, statutes, regulations, and treatises are available on CD-ROM. Finally, some of the law is available on the Internet.

Organization of the Courts

Because there are federal and state governments in the United States, there are many court systems. There is a national system of federal courts, and each state has its own court system.

The Federal Court System

The federal Constitution itself established the U.S. Supreme Court. Congress, under Constitutional authority, enacted laws establishing the lower federal courts.

There are three levels of federal courts: ***district courts*** on the lowest level; *courts of appeals,* also called ***appellate courts,*** on the intermediate level; and the U.S.

Supreme Court at the top of the hierarchy. Most cases involving subjects over which the federal courts have jurisdiction are brought first in one of the district courts. Each district court is a ***court of original jurisdiction***—that is, a trial court. Each state has one or more U.S. district courts. The losing party can appeal a district court decision to the appropriate court of appeals. There are 13 U.S. courts of appeals. Finally, the U. S. Supreme Court will review some court of appeals decisions. However, the U. S. Supreme Court grants a hearing in only a small percent of the cases brought to it for review.

The U.S. Supreme Court consists of nine justices. Most of the cases it hears come to it on appeal from a lower court. However, a few types of cases can be taken directly to the Supreme Court. These include controversies to which a state is a party and cases affecting foreign ambassadors, ministers, and consuls. For these rare cases, the Supreme Court functions as a trial court.

In addition to the district courts, the courts of appeals, and the Supreme Court, there are several special federal courts that have limited jurisdiction. These special courts include the U.S. Claims Court, the U.S. Tax Court, and the U.S. Court of International Trade.

The State Court Systems

The courts of most states have the same type of three-level organization that the federal courts have, although one-fifth of the states do not have intermediate-level appellate courts. However, every state has courts of original jurisdiction and a higher court, usually called a supreme court, to which lower court decisions can be appealed.

All cases begin in a court of original jurisdiction, and most end there, as few are appealed to a higher court. There are state courts of general original jurisdiction and state courts of limited original jurisdiction. The courts of general original jurisdiction have the authority to decide almost all types of cases, both civil and criminal. These courts are usually called circuit courts, district courts, or superior courts. Courts of limited original jurisdiction have authority to decide only certain types of cases. For example, probate courts handle only cases relating to wills and estates. Juvenile courts handle only cases involving delinquent, dependent, or neglected children.

From the court of original jurisdiction, the losing party can appeal the case to an intermediate-level appellate court if the state has courts on the intermediate level. An appeal from the intermediate court decision can then be made to the state supreme court. The decisions of the state supreme court are final with respect to interpretations of the state constitution and state and local laws. However, appeals may be taken from a state supreme court to the U.S. Supreme Court on questions involving the federal Constitution or federal laws and treaties.

Court Oversight of Lawyers

A lawyer is an officer of the courts. Thus, the ultimate authority over lawyers is vested mainly in the courts. A state supreme court has the power to grant licenses to practice law in that state. The court also adopts the rules governing the professional conduct of lawyers practicing in the state, although statutes, case law, and state bar associations also govern lawyers' professional conduct.

The rules of professional conduct that the state supreme courts have adopted are many and complex. Generally speaking, these court rules are patterned on model rules of professional conduct drafted by the American Bar Association (ABA), but the court rules vary somewhat from state to state. Under the court rules, a lawyer must not engage in conduct that is dishonest or prejudicial to the administration of justice. A lawyer must perform legal services competently and diligently, keep client confidences, and avoid conflicts of interest.

Insurers employ lawyers as advisers, negotiators, and advocates. Large insurers have law departments and employ many lawyers full time. These lawyers are called *in-house counsel* to distinguish them from lawyers who work in law firms, called *outside counsel.* Insurers that employ in-house counsel usually also employ outside counsel to do special legal work. A small insurer might not employ any lawyers as in-house counsel, but rather hire law firms to do all its legal work. All lawyers, whether employed as in-house counsel or by a law firm, are officers of the courts and must conform to the court rules governing professional conduct.

When an organization, such as an insurer, employs a lawyer, the organization itself is the lawyer's client, not the organization's officers, directors, shareholders, or employees. Court rules patterned on the ABA Model Rules of Professional Conduct require that the lawyer advise any officer, director, shareholder, or employee whose interests become adverse to the interests of the organization that the organization itself is her client and that her duty of loyalty must be to the organization. Moreover, if the lawyer becomes aware that a person within the organization intends to violate a law or a legal duty to the organization, and that such violation is likely to result in substantial injury to the organization, the lawyer has a duty to protect the organization by asking the person to reconsider the matter, by advising the person to seek a separate legal opinion, or by referring the matter to higher authority in the organization.

Jurisdiction of the Courts

In a system involving many different courts, there must be rules for determining which cases are properly heard by each court. These rules are called ***rules of jurisdiction***.

Jurisdiction of the Subject Matter. A court has ***jurisdiction of the subject matter*** in a case if the constitutional or statutory provisions that establish the court give it the power to hear and render an enforceable decision in that type of case. For example, a tax court has jurisdiction of the subject matter in tax cases but not in divorce cases.

Often, the amount of money in controversy will be a governing factor. For example, small claims courts do not have jurisdiction in cases involving more than a small amount of money—$1,500 to $5,000, depending on the state statute. On the other hand, the U.S. district courts do not have jurisdiction in some kinds of cases unless the amount of money in controversy is in excess of $50,000.

Jurisdiction over the Person. It is not enough that the court have jurisdiction over the subject matter. In addition, the court must have ***jurisdiction over the person*** being sued if that person is to be bound by the decision of the court. To obtain jurisdiction, a summons must be issued by the court and must be served upon the defendant, usually personally, although, in some cases, publication is sufficient. *Publication* of a summons means advertising the summons in a newspaper as a means of notifying a defendant who cannot be served with the summons personally.

Where Jurisdictions Overlap.   Often, more than one court has jurisdiction in a given kind of case. This is particularly true of insurance cases because they frequently involve diversity of citizenship.

Diversity of citizenship means that the parties on opposite sides of a lawsuit are domiciled in different states. Diversity of citizenship is a basis for invoking the jurisdiction of a U.S. district court, provided that the controversy also involves a claim for more than $50,000. The purpose of diversity of citizenship is to provide out-of-state litigants with a hearing in a federal court, which may be more impartial than a state court located in the domiciliary state of one of the litigants. Alternatively, the lawsuit could be tried in a state court. Thus, many cases involving life or health insurance contracts can be brought either in a U.S. district court or in a state court.

The Applicable Law

The discussion thus far might seem to imply that state courts always apply the law of their respective states and that federal courts always apply federal law. Such is not the case. A court often must apply the law of another jurisdiction. For example, the activities of persons in one state can become the subject of a lawsuit in another state, requiring the court hearing the case to decide which state's law should apply. Conflict of laws rules are used to resolve this problem.

Conflict of Laws.   *Conflict of laws* has been defined as "that part of the law of each state or nation which determines whether, in dealing with a legal situation, the law of some other state or nation will be recognized, be given effect, or be applied."[5] Each jurisdiction has its own conflict of laws rules.

Conflict of laws problems often arise in lawsuits on life insurance policies because the laws of more than one jurisdiction frequently are involved. Often, a person who applies for insurance on her life lives in one state when the policy is delivered and in another state at the time of death. The beneficiary may bring a court action against the insurer in yet another state. In such instances, the laws of several jurisdictions could be involved in resolving such questions as the rights and obligations of the parties to the life insurance contract, interpretation of specific policy provisions, and the proper procedure for bringing the action.

In one life insurance case,[6] brought in a Texas state court, the beneficiary's assignees contended that the laws of Texas applied because the beneficiary and the assignees of the policy were Texas residents and the insurer was doing business in Texas. The insurer contended that California law applied because the insured was a resident of California and had applied for and taken delivery of the policy in California. If the Texas court applied Texas law, the assignees would win the lawsuit. If it applied California law, the insurer would win.

The Texas court, applying the Texas conflict of laws rule, determined that California law should apply to the issues in the case. The court stated:

> [N]o part of the transaction leading up to the consummation of the original contract, or to the reinstatement thereof, or to the maturity of any right accruing thereunder, occurred or transpired within the State of Texas. . . . [W]e have concluded that the validity, interpretation, and obligations of the contract in suit must be determined and controlled by the

---

[5]BALLENTINE'S LAW DICTIONARY 246 (3d ed. 1969).
[6]Washington Nat'l Ins. Co. v. Shaw, 180 S.W.2d 1003 (Tex. Civ. App. 1944).

laws of California and not by the laws of Texas, insofar as the laws of the former state may be shown to be different from the laws of the latter.

This case illustrates the application of the traditional conflict of laws rule regarding contracts. This traditional rule is that the laws of the state in which a contract is made determine the validity and effect of the contract, unless the parties have agreed otherwise. The contract is generally considered to be made in the state where the final act necessary to complete the contract is done. The last necessary act might be acceptance of the application by the insurer, payment of the premium, or delivery of the policy, depending on the circumstances.

The modern conflict of laws rule, used in a growing number of states, is the **center of gravity rule**. This rule is also called by other names. These are *grouping of contacts, principal contacts, most significant relationship, governmental interest analysis,* and *paramount interest*. States that use this rule apply the law of the state most concerned with the outcome of the litigation.

Application of Law in Federal Courts. If there is no constitutional provision or statute on a given question, courts ordinarily will apply previous case law on the subject. In a federal court, the case law of the state in which the court is sitting will be applied where the question involves state law.

The federal courts did not always apply state case law. There has long been a federal statute requiring that, in cases involving diversity of citizenship, a federal court must apply state law. Nevertheless, in 1842, the U.S. Supreme Court decided in *Swift v. Tyson*[7] that the word *law* in this federal statute meant state statutory law but not state case law. For almost a hundred years thereafter, each federal court applied the statutory laws of the state in which it was sitting, but if there were no applicable statutory laws, the federal court applied its own version of the common law.[8] In this way, a body of federal case law was built up that was often advantageous to insurers.

The *Swift v. Tyson* decision was followed in the federal courts until 1938. Then, in the case of *Erie Railroad Co. v. Tompkins,*[9] the U.S. Supreme Court overruled *Swift v. Tyson* and held that both the statutory and case law of the state in question must be applied by the federal courts. This is the procedure that is followed today.

Lawsuits

Most disputes are resolved without recourse to the courts. However, when other efforts to resolve a dispute have failed, one of the parties to the dispute sometimes brings a lawsuit or a suit in equity. As discussed in the subsection above entitled "Substantive Law and Procedural Law," the procedures that must be followed when bringing a lawsuit or a suit in equity constitute civil (as opposed to criminal) procedural law. This section deals with civil procedural law.

Procedures vary in different jurisdictions and for different types of courts. The following discussion is in general terms because of the wide variation in terminology and practices among jurisdictions. Moreover, the following discussion mentions only lawsuits because the terminology pertaining to suits in equity often differs, although

[7]41 U.S. (16 Pet.) 1 (1842).
[8]*Common law* was defined and discussed earlier in this chapter. Application of the common law is discussed in a later subsection.
[9]304 U.S. 64 (1938).

many procedural aspects of law and equity are the same. Suits in equity will be discussed in Chapter 16, "Equitable Remedies."

Pleadings

Lawsuits—also called legal actions, actions at law, suits at law, or cases—usually begin with pleadings. *Pleadings* are the parties' formal written statements of their respective claims and defenses. Complaints, answers, counterclaims, and cross-claims are examples of pleadings.

The Complaint.   Ordinarily, a lawsuit begins when the person suing—the *plaintiff*—files a complaint. A *complaint* is a formal written statement of the plaintiff's cause of action. For example, in a contract case the plaintiff will set forth the provisions of the contract, allege that the person being sued—the *defendant*—has failed to perform a promise in the contract, and state the amount of damages that the plaintiff is seeking. The complaint tells the plaintiff's version of the dispute.

When a complaint has been filed, the court issues a summons that the sheriff or other designated officer serves on the defendant. The *summons* is a notice to the defendant that an action has been filed against him and that a judgment will be granted unless an answer is filed within the specified time. Attached to the summons is a copy of the complaint. The time allowed for answering the complaint is ordinarily 20 to 30 days from the date of service of the summons and complaint. Therefore, the defendant should promptly seek the advice of an attorney. If no answer is filed within the allotted time, the court might grant the plaintiff a default judgment. A *default judgment* is a judgment, usually in favor of the plaintiff, entered without the defendant's being heard in his own defense, because of the defendant's failure to answer the complaint or to appear at trial.

The Answer.   The defendant answers the complaint in a formal written statement, usually termed an *answer,* in which he admits or denies the facts alleged by the plaintiff. The defendant might admit what the plaintiff says but contend that the admitted actions do not constitute a wrong on which a legal action can be based. Or the defendant might admit the plaintiff's contentions but allege that his own conduct was excusable under the law. On the other hand, the defendant might deny the plaintiff's contentions.

Other Pleadings.   Other pleadings sometimes follow the complaint and answer. For example, the defendant might file a counterclaim against the plaintiff, stating that the defendant has a cause of action against the plaintiff based on the same set of facts. If proved, the counterclaim will defeat or diminish the plaintiff's claim. Or, in a lawsuit involving two defendants, one defendant might file a cross-claim against another defendant, stating that the second defendant is liable for all or part of the money that the plaintiff is demanding. There are other types of pleadings in addition to the four described in this subsection.

Motions

The parties are permitted to make motions before, during, or even after trial. A *motion* is an application made to the judge for a ruling favorable to the applicant. For example, the defendant might challenge the sufficiency of the complaint by filing a motion to dismiss the lawsuit for failure of the plaintiff to state a claim on which a legal action can be based. Or the defendant might file a motion for a more definite statement if the complaint is vague or ambiguous. There are many types of motions. Often, a lawsuit will end before or during trial because the judge grants a motion made by one of the parties.

Discovery

Under modern court procedures, the process by which the parties gather information relevant to the lawsuit is called *discovery*. Discovery consists of the devices used by each party to obtain information from the other party or from witnesses. Depositions, interrogatories, and subpoenas requiring the production of documents (*subpoenas duces tecum*) are discovery devices.

Depositions.   A *deposition* is the oral testimony under oath of a witness, taken somewhere other than the courtroom. Typically, each party's lawyer calls the other party's witnesses to depositions in order to find out what the witnesses know. The deposition ordinarily will be taken in one of the attorney's offices, and the plaintiff's attorney, the defendant's attorney, a court reporter, and the witness will be present. The court reporter will swear in the witness and record the proceedings. The witness will be examined by the plaintiff's attorney, by the defendant's attorney, or by both.

Interrogatories.   *Interrogatories* are a series of written questions drawn up by one party and given to the other party, or to a witness, to answer within a fixed period of time. Written answers to the interrogatories are given under oath. The person answering the interrogatories signs a sworn statement, usually before a notary public, that the answers are true.

Subpoenas Duces Tecum.   A *subpoena* is a command to a witness to appear at a certain time and place to give testimony. A *subpoena duces tecum* requires that the witness provide specified documents or other physical evidence to the court or to the lawyer for one of the parties. Frequently, the appearance of the witness will not be required if the witness produces the documents or other physical evidence.

Insurance claim files are sometimes the subject of a *subpoena duces tecum*. For example, suppose that Sarah Kramer had purchased a health insurance policy from the Adams Insurance Company. Kramer was crossing the street with the green light when she was struck by a speeding automobile. She was taken to the hospital, where she incurred hospital and medical expenses. She submitted the bills and her medical records to the Adams Insurance Company, where the claims adjuster put them in a claim file. Kramer then filed a lawsuit against the driver of the automobile. In the course of the lawsuit, Kramer's attorney, as an officer of the court, issued a *subpoena duces tecum* directing the Adams Insurance Company to produce the claim file. Depending on the number of insureds it has, an insurer might receive dozens, or even hundreds, of *subpoenas duces tecum* each year.

Trials

A *trial* is a judicially supervised investigation and determination of the issues between the parties to a lawsuit. Trials are costly in both time and money. For this reason, most lawsuits are settled before the lawsuit actually goes to trial. When a lawsuit does go to trial, the trial process is governed by a multitude of procedural concepts that have developed over the centuries. In a jury trial, the judge will instruct the jury on the procedural concepts that they need to know.

The following subsections describe various concepts associated with trials. These concepts are (1) issues; (2) three important procedural concepts governing the proof of facts—presumptions, the prima facie case, and the burden of proof; (3) oral testimony; and (4) the application of case law and of common law to the facts proved.

Issues.   An *issue,* also called a question, is a material point that is affirmed by one party and denied by the other. An issue can be deduced by comparing the complaint with the answer.

There are two types of issues: issues of fact and issues of law. *Facts* are actions that were taken, events that occurred, or circumstances that existed. If the plaintiff alleges a fact in the complaint and the defendant denies in the answer that such is a fact, there is an *issue of fact* to be decided. In a jury trial, the facts are determined by the jury. In a nonjury trial, also called a bench trial, the facts are determined by the judge. Thus, in a jury trial the jury is the trier of fact, whereas in a bench trial the judge is the trier of fact. The determination of the trier of fact is called a finding of fact.

In some cases, plaintiff and defendant agree on the facts but disagree on the application of the law to those facts. When this occurs, there is an *issue of law* for the judge to decide in what is called a summary judgment proceeding. The judge always decides issues of law.

Often, there are issues of both fact and law to be decided. When such is the case in a jury trial, the jury will decide issues of fact and the judge will decide issues of law. In a nonjury trial, the judge will decide both issues of fact and issues of law.

Presumptions.   A *presumption* is a conclusion that the law requires to be drawn from a given set of facts. A presumption will stand until adequate evidence to the contrary is presented to the court. For example, every person is presumed to be capable of making a valid, binding contract. In a case where a person's contractual capacity is challenged, the challenging party has the right to present evidence that the person lacks contractual capacity by reason of minority, mental incompetence, and so on. If the challenging party cannot present adequate evidence of a lack of contractual capacity, the presumption that the person has contractual capacity will stand.

The Prima Facie Case.   *Prima facie* means "at first sight" or "before closer inspection." A *prima facie case* is a set of facts established by evidence sufficient to entitle the party presenting the evidence to a verdict in her favor if the other party does not refute the evidence. For example, the plaintiff who introduces in evidence the provisions of a contract, and establishes failure on the part of the defendant to carry out the terms of the contract, has presented a prima facie case of breach of contract. It is then the defendant's responsibility to introduce evidence disproving the facts as stated by the plaintiff or to show that there was an acceptable excuse for nonperformance (for example, that the agreement was not a valid contract or that the plaintiff made performance impossible). If the defendant produces no evidence disproving the facts as shown by the plaintiff, or presents no excuse, the decision ordinarily will be in the plaintiff's favor.

Burden of Proof.   The term ***burden of proof*** includes two related concepts: the burden of producing evidence and the burden of persuasion. The party with the burden of producing evidence on a particular issue must produce the first evidence on that issue. The party with the burden of persuasion must convince the jury (or the judge in a bench trial) to resolve a disputed issue in his favor.

The plaintiff ordinarily bears the burden of producing evidence as to the elements of the prima facie case applicable to her theory of recovery. The defendant bears the burden of producing evidence as to any affirmative defenses. An affirmative defense is a defense that amounts to more than a mere denial of the plaintiff's allegations. For example, if a beneficiary sues a life insurer for a death benefit and the insurer in its answer contends that the insured committed suicide during the period when the suicide exclusion was operative, the insurer has stated an affirmative defense. The burden is on the insurer to produce evidence proving its contention.

The party with the burden of persuasion must convince the trier of fact to find in his favor according to the applicable standard of proof, or that party will lose the lawsuit. The standard of proof in civil trials is usually a preponderance of the evidence. This means that the party with the burden of persuasion must produce evidence at least slightly more convincing than the evidence produced by the other party. A higher standard of proof sometimes used in civil trials (usually where the issues are particularly serious, such as fraud) is clear and convincing evidence. Where clear and convincing evidence is the standard of proof, the party with the burden of persuasion must convince the trier of fact that there is a high probability that the evidence in her favor is true.

In a criminal trial, the party with the burden of persuasion—that is, the public prosecutor—must convince the trier of fact beyond a reasonable doubt that the accused is guilty or the accused must be acquitted. The standard of proof in criminal trials—beyond a reasonable doubt—is more difficult to meet than the standard of proof in civil trials.

Oral Testimony.   *Oral testimony* is spoken testimony given under oath, either in a deposition or at trial. It is not unusual for an insurer's employee or agent to be called on to give oral testimony for the insurer, especially an employee working in the claims area. Giving oral testimony either in or out of court can be an intimidating experience. Some companies hold seminars designed to train employees to be effective witnesses. In any event, the trial lawyer representing the insurer in a lawsuit will prepare the insurer's witnesses to testify.

The lawyer will remind the witness that he will be under oath and must tell the truth. The lawyer will likely also instruct the witness to dress neatly and conservatively and to maintain a serious, polite demeanor. The witness will be instructed to listen to the question carefully and to answer only *that* question without excess verbiage or rambling. If the witness does not understand the question or does not know the answer, the lawyer will instruct him to say so. If the witness gives an incorrect answer, he will be told that he should say he made a mistake and correct his testimony. Some trial lawyers prepare a witness by holding a mock examination and cross-examination before the witness testifies at trial.

When the insurer's witness testifies at trial, the insurer's lawyer will examine the witness and the lawyer for the other party to the lawsuit will cross-examine the witness. The purpose of cross-examination is to bring out any inconsistencies or fabrications by the witness. If the witness has carefully followed the instructions he was given, the cross-examination is likely to be less rigorous.

Application of Case Law.   When an issue reaches a court for decision, constitutional or statutory law will be applied if there is any such law on the subject. If there is none, or if such law is unclear, courts that follow the common-law system—which includes most of the courts in the United States—decide cases on the basis of principles established in previous decisions called *precedents*.[10] A **precedent** is a previous decision by that same court, or by a higher court of the same jurisdiction, on the same issue and involving the same general set of facts. If there is such a decision, it will be followed unless there is a strong reason to depart from it.

In deciding an issue in accordance with precedent, the court is following the doctrine of *stare decisis*. **Stare decisis** means the practice of following previous decisions on the same issue. *Stare decisis* helps give certainty and stability to the law.

Application of Common Law.   Sometimes there is no precedent governing an issue. In such an instance, the court will decide the issue before it in accordance with the common law. In this sense, the common law means a body of general principles and ideas of justice followed by courts in jurisdictions that derive their law from English law.

Authorities differ as to whether there is a common law for every jurisdiction or one body of common law that includes all common-law jurisdictions. It is generally agreed, however, that the meaning of the term *common law* for any jurisdiction is defined by the courts of that jurisdiction. In deciding a case in accordance with the common law, the court is making case law and establishing a new precedent that will be followed in later cases involving essentially the same set of facts.

Appeals

A small minority of trial court decisions are appealed to a higher court. With some exceptions, the rule is that only final judgments of the trial court can be appealed. A final judgment disposes of the case in full.

The appeals court will examine the decision of the trial court for errors made in applying the law. If the appeals court finds a reversible error, it will reverse the judgment of the trial court. If the appeals court does not find a reversible error, the judgment of the trial court will stand, unless a successful appeal is made to a yet higher court.

Ordinarily, the appeals court will not review the trial court's determination of facts. This is because the appeals court does not hear the testimony of witnesses or examine other evidence but rather confines itself to examining the written record of the trial proceedings. Therefore, the appeals court cannot judge the credibility of witnesses or other factual evidence and must accept the judgment of the trial court as to the facts.

Insurance Regulation

State governments regulated the first insurance companies in the United States, just as state governments regulated other corporations. Very little was involved then except the details of incorporation and some taxation. Later, however, as insurance

---

[10]This is possible because appellate courts and some trial courts support their decisions with written opinions that are published and made available to the public. Court decisions are of interest primarily to lawyers and judges, but they are available to anyone who is interested.

companies began operating in states other than those in which they were incorporated, the question arose as to whether the transaction of an insurance business across state lines should subject the business to federal regulation as interstate commerce.

Congress has the power to regulate interstate commerce by reason of the ***Commerce Clause*** in the federal Constitution. The Commerce Clause is found in Article I, Section 8, which reads in part as follows: "The Congress shall have Power . . . To regulate Commerce with foreign Nations, and among the several States, and with the Indian Tribes."

As the result of this provision, Congress has the sole power to regulate commerce "among the several States." Exactly what constitutes commerce and when it is transacted among, rather than within, the several states are not easy questions. This has been true especially in regard to the business of insurance. Until 1944, however, these questions were consistently resolved in favor of state regulation of insurance on the ground that the business of insurance was not commerce.

In 1868, the question of whether it was proper for the states to regulate the business of insurance reached the U.S. Supreme Court in the case of *Paul v. Virginia*.[11] In reaching its decision that the State of Virginia had the right to regulate the business of insurance, the court stated:

> Issuing a policy of insurance is not a transaction of Commerce . . . in any proper meaning of the word. . . . They [insurance policies] are governed by the local law. They do not constitute a part of the commerce between the States.

This view—that issuing contracts of insurance is not commerce and thus cannot constitute a part of the commerce among the several states—prevailed for the next 75 years. Other cases presenting essentially the same question followed, but in each of them the court made it clear that insurance was not commerce and therefore could not be interstate commerce, which is subject to federal regulation. The last important case using this reasoning was *New York Life Insurance Co. v. Deer Lodge County*, decided in 1913.[12] After the *Deer Lodge County* case, there seemed little reason to question the regulation of insurance by the states.

As a result of this unbroken line of decisions, the states developed extensive systems of laws to regulate the business of insurance and provided special administrative departments to supervise insurance companies operating within their respective jurisdictions. This was the situation in 1944 when the *South-Eastern Underwriters*[13] decision was handed down by the U.S. Supreme Court.

The *South-Eastern Underwriters Decision*

The facts of the *South-Eastern Underwriters* case are as follows: the South-Eastern Underwriters Association and its nearly 200 private stock insurance company members had been indicted for alleged violations of the federal Sherman Antitrust Act.[14] Their defense was that the federal act did not apply because insurance was not commerce and thus not a proper subject for regulation by the federal government.

---

[11]75 U.S. (8 Wall.) 168 (1868).
[12]231 U.S. 495 (1913).
[13]United States v. South-Eastern Underwriters Ass'n, 322 U.S. 533 (1944).
[14]The Sherman Antitrust Act prohibits contracts, combinations, and conspiracies that unreasonably restrain trade or commerce. Price-fixing and monopolization are examples of actions that the Sherman Antitrust Act prohibits.

The federal district court had held, in effect, that even though an insurance company conducts a substantial part of its business transactions across state lines, it is not engaged in commerce among the states within the meaning of either the Commerce Clause or the Sherman Antitrust Act. The U.S. Supreme Court took a different view.

The Supreme Court pointed out that cases prior to *South-Eastern Underwriters* had concerned the power of the states "to regulate and tax specific activities of foreign insurance companies which sell policies within their territories."[15] In *South-Eastern Underwriters,* the Court considered a different question—the effect of an act of Congress on insurance transactions conducted across state lines. In its analysis of prior cases, the Supreme Court stated:

> Not one of all these cases, however, has involved an Act of Congress which required the Court to decide the issue of whether the Commerce Clause grants to Congress the power to regulate insurance transactions stretching across state lines. Today for the first time in the history of the Court that issue is squarely presented and must be decided.

The Supreme Court held that insurance is commerce. Therefore, when insurance business is conducted across state lines, it is interstate commerce and subject to regulation by the federal government. The gist of the decision is found in the following passage:

> Our basic responsibility in interpreting the Commerce Clause is to make certain that the power to govern intercourse among the states remains where the Constitution placed it. That power, as held by this court from the beginning is vested in the Congress, available to be exercised for the national welfare as Congress shall deem necessary. No commercial enterprise of any kind which conducts its activities across state lines has been held to be wholly beyond the regulatory power of Congress under the Commerce Clause. We cannot make an exception of the business of insurance.

Thus, the landmark *Paul v. Virginia* decision of 1868 was overruled by the U.S. Supreme Court in 1944 in the *South-Eastern Underwriters* decision. Insurance *was* subject to regulation by the federal government.

The *McCarran-Ferguson Act*

The *South-Eastern Underwriters* decision presented a serious problem for the insurance industry. For 75 years the industry had assumed that the question of federal regulation was settled. Insurance had been regulated by the states exclusively, and no federal statutes were applicable. Because the situation could have become chaotic, Congress almost immediately enacted the McCarran-Ferguson Act.[16] The McCarran-Ferguson Act declared that continued regulation and taxation of insurance by the states "is in the public interest." Under the McCarran-Ferguson Act, acts of Congress are not to be construed to invalidate, impair, or supersede state law regulating insurance, unless the acts of Congress relate specifically to the business of insurance. The Sherman Act, Clayton Act, and Federal Trade Commission Act[17] are applicable

---

[15]A foreign insurance company is a company that is not incorporated in the state. For example, a company incorporated in Illinois is a foreign company in Georgia even though it does business in Georgia.

[16]15 U.S.C. §§ 1011–1015 (1994).

[17]The Clayton Act, 15 U.S.C. §§ 12–27 (1994), an amendment to the Sherman Act, 15 U.S.C. §§ 1–7 (1994), prohibits certain kinds of price discrimination and other practices that lessen competition. The Federal Trade Commission Act, 15 U.S.C. §§ 41–58 and 7 U.S.C. § 610 (1994),

to the business of insurance under the McCarran-Ferguson Act, but only "to the extent that such business is not regulated by State law." One exception to this general rule is that the Sherman Act applies to agreements to, or acts of, boycott, coercion, or intimidation.

Immediately after passage of the McCarran-Ferguson Act, a committee made up of various kinds of insurance companies (property, liability, life, etc.) began the work of drafting model laws designed to guide the state legislatures in their enactment of state laws that would prevent application of the federal antitrust acts to the insurance industry. Rate-making laws were the first to be developed and adopted. An unfair trade practices law was enacted by all the states. Most states have also enacted antitrust laws that apply to insurance companies.

During the mid-1980s, state regulation of insurance came under attack, as proponents of federal regulation attempted to repeal or amend the McCarran-Ferguson Act. The proponents of federal regulation argue that the federal antitrust law immunity contained in the McCarran-Ferguson Act should be eliminated to enhance competition within the insurance industry. They claim that the availability and affordability of commercial liability insurance has been adversely affected by a lack of competition.

The insurance industry and other proponents of state regulation argue that repealing or restricting the McCarran-Ferguson Act would not enhance competition in the insurance industry, which is already highly competitive, and would not solve the problem of availability and affordability of commercial liability insurance. They cite the unique nature of the insurance industry and the necessity for such cooperative activities as collection of industrywide loss data and pools for jumbo risks as sound reasons for the McCarran-Ferguson exemption from federal antitrust laws. They also argue that repeal of the McCarran-Ferguson Act would lead to duplicative and conflicting regulation of insurance.

Federal Regulation Today

The McCarran-Ferguson Act does not entirely exempt insurers from federal regulation. To the extent that the insurance business is not regulated by state law, federal law will apply. As previously noted, the Sherman Act will apply to agreements to, or acts of, boycott, coercion, or intimidation. Moreover, other federal laws, notably securities laws, have been held to apply to certain insurance activities. Finally, federal laws govern insurers in many areas not specifically related to the insurance business itself.

Interstate Advertising.   Because a state cannot regulate beyond its own borders the advertising of insurers domiciled within it, the Federal Trade Commission contended that an area existed that could not be governed effectively by state laws. In 1960, the U.S. Supreme Court upheld this position.[18] The Court held that the Federal Trade Commission can regulate the interstate mailing of unfair or deceptive advertising material by an insurer for solicitation except in the case of states that have adopted laws sufficient to control the mailing of such material into the state.

---

created the Federal Trade Commission, an agency of the federal government, the function of which is to restrain unfair methods of competition such as price-fixing, false advertising, and illegal combinations of competitors.

[18]FTC v. Travelers Health Ass'n, 362 U.S. 293 (1960).

Variable Annuities and Variable Life Insurance.   Because of their similarity to investment contracts issued by equity investment trusts (mutual funds), variable life insurance contracts and variable annuity contracts are governed by federal securities laws as well as by state insurance laws. This topic is discussed in Chapter 7, "Structure of the Life Insurance Policy," and in Chapter 21, "Annuity Contracts."

Federal Regulation of Non-Insurance Activities.   Federal laws govern insurers in many areas not specifically related to the business of insurance. For example, when stock insurance companies offer their securities for sale to the investing public, those companies are regulated by the federal securities laws as are other corporations. As employers, insurers are subject to federal employment laws such as the National Labor Relations Act, the Fair Labor Standards Act of 1938, the Employee Retirement Income Security Act of 1974, and the Civil Rights Act of 1964. However, most of the laws regulating the insurance business itself are state laws.

State Regulation Today

Insurance is heavily regulated by the states primarily because of the size and importance of the industry. Insurance affects so many people that the mismanagement or failure of an insurance company has serious social and economic effects. For this reason, courts and legislatures speak of insurance as a business "affected with a public interest." This means that insurance is of such importance to so many people that it is in the public interest to enact whatever laws are necessary to assure that the great trust vested in insurers is not abused. As a result, a detailed system of insurance laws strictly regulates the insurance industry. Safekeeping of funds; company solvency; representation by qualified, ethical agents; and contracts that safeguard the rights of policyowners and beneficiaries—almost every aspect of the insurance business has been acknowledged as a proper subject for regulation. Thus, every year, many new insurance bills are introduced into state legislatures and enacted into law.

The states also regulate insurers in areas not specifically related to insurance. Many state and local non-insurance laws govern insurers just as such laws govern other businesses.

Summary

The United States is generally said to be a common-law country rather than a civil-law country. In this sense, the term *common law* means the law of countries, states, and provinces that derive their law from English law, rather than from the law of the Roman Empire. The term *common law* also means general principles of law and case law.

The term *civil law* can also mean the body of law that determines private rights and liabilities, as distinguished from criminal law, which prohibits and punishes harm to the public. Some acts that are violations of civil law are also crimes. A crime is usually either a felony or a misdemeanor.

Equity courts developed hundreds of years ago in England because of the inadequacy of ordinary legal remedies. For many years, law courts and equity courts were separate. However, modern courts usually have jurisdiction over both legal and equitable matters. Several equitable remedies are important to insurers.

Law comes from many sources: constitutions, statutes, rules and regulations of government agencies, and court decisions, among others. Constitutions set forth in general terms the principles that form the legal foundation of a government. Constitutions tend to be changed little. In the United States, federal and state constitutions define the extent of governmental powers and outline the principles on which the government is to operate. They provide for an executive, a legislative, and a judicial branch of the government. They also guarantee human rights. The federal and state constitutions in the United States differ in that the federal Constitution delegates power to the federal government, whereas state constitutions limit the inherent power of state governments.

Statutes are apt to be changed more often and are more specific than constitutions. A statute is a law enacted by a legislature. Statutes are arranged in codes so that they can be found easily.

Administrative officers, such as a state's commissioner of insurance, are members of the executive branch of government but also perform legislative functions. That is, they adopt rules and regulations to assist them in executing laws. In addition, they perform judicial functions when they hold hearings, make decisions, and impose penalties. Thus, although administrative officers are a part of the executive branch of government, they perform legislative and judicial as well as executive functions.

In the United States, there is a federal court system and each state has a court system. Each court system has courts of original jurisdiction and a high court, usually called a supreme court. The federal court system and many of the state court systems have intermediate appellate courts as well.

State supreme courts have oversight of the lawyers practicing law in the state. These courts grant licenses to practice law in the state and adopt court rules governing those lawyers' professional conduct.

In order to render a binding decision, a court must have jurisdiction of the subject matter and jurisdiction over the person of the defendant. Often, more than one court has jurisdiction in a case. A court, especially in insurance cases, sometimes must apply the law of another jurisdiction. Conflict of laws rules are used to determine which jurisdiction's law applies.

The rules for bringing a lawsuit are part of procedural law. Lawsuits usually begin with a complaint filed with the court by the plaintiff. The court then issues a summons to the defendant. The defendant ordinarily files an answer. The issue (or issues) can be deduced by comparing the complaint with the answer.

In order to discover facts related to the lawsuit, a party might use one or more discovery devices, such as a deposition, interrogatories, or a *subpoena duces tecum*. Facts are proved at trial using various procedural devices. Among these devices are presumptions, the prima facie case, and the burden of proof. In a jury trial, the jury decides the facts, but if there is no jury the judge decides the facts (a bench trial). The judge then applies the law to the facts decided.

The judge will apply appropriate constitutional or statutory law, and if there is none, or if such law is unclear, the judge will usually follow precedent. If there is no precedent, the judge will decide the issue in accordance with the common law—that is, in accordance with general principles of law.

In the early years of the insurance industry, no serious challenge arose to the right of the states to regulate insurance. In 1868, the U.S. Supreme Court held that insurance was not commerce and hence that the insurance industry was not subject to federal regulation under the Commerce Clause of the federal Constitution. Then, in 1944, the Supreme Court reversed itself and held that insurance is commerce. Congress passed the McCarran-Ferguson Act shortly thereafter. This act declares that state regulation and taxation of insurance is in the public interest. Therefore, most insurance regulation is performed by the states.

Insurance is heavily regulated because of the size and importance of the insurance industry. Insurance is important to so many people that it is said to be a business affected with a public interest.

Illustrative Case

The following case is included in this introductory chapter because it illustrates the use of presumptions, the presentation of a prima facie case, and the burden of proof. Explanatory footnotes have been added where the legal terminology may not be clear.

Robinson, as executor of the estate of the deceased, J. R. Creighton, brought the suit against the life insurer. In the lower court, therefore, Robinson was the plaintiff and the insurer was the defendant. The decision was in favor of Robinson, and the insurer appealed. In the court of appeals, therefore, the insurer was the appellant and Robinson was the appellee. This information is conveyed in the title of the case by referring to Robinson as "plaintiff-appellee" and the insurer as "defendant-appellant."

WM. HEDGES ROBINSON, JR., EXECUTOR OF THE ESTATE OF
J. R. CREIGHTON, DECEASED, Plaintiff-Appellee
v.
NEW YORK LIFE INSURANCE COMPANY, Defendant-Appellant[19]
Colorado Court of Appeals

COYTE, Judge.

This is an action on the double-indemnity clause of an insurance contract which provides for double recovery of benefits in case of death by accident. However, double recovery is not provided in the policy where death occurs because of suicide. The company claimed the insured committed suicide whereas the estate maintained that his death was accidental, thereby entitling it to recover under the double-indemnity clause. From a jury verdict favoring the estate, the company appeals.

The alleged error is that the verdict is unsupported by the evidence, and that the trial court should have directed a verdict in the company's favor or granted it a new trial.[20]

The insured in this case was a man in his fifties, suffering from a variety of ailments, including a blood disorder, congestive heart failure, and partial paralysis which affected his speech. He was under medication and was being cared for by a private nurse.

The decedent, together with his wife and nurse, went to Hawaii for a vacation. While there, they rented a suite of rooms on the twentieth floor of a hotel. Adjacent to the suite was an outside balcony, the outer perimeter of which was surrounded by a wall and railing. There was a wooden platform in one corner of the balcony upon which the decedent had stood on occasion to view the scenery.

The following evidence was given concerning the death of decedent. On the night of his death, the decedent and his wife had dinner in the hotel restaurant. Both consumed alcoholic beverages and had been quarreling during dinner. The nurse helped both back to their rooms after dinner. She helped the decedent to bed after giving him his medication and a sleeping pill. Some time after 3:00 AM the wife awoke and found her husband had left the bed. She went to the balcony and saw him just before he plunged to his death, but had no other recollection of the event.

The police investigated the occurrence but did not question the wife upon their arrival because she was unresponsive and appeared to be in deep, heavy sleep.

Later in the day, in the afternoon, the wife was questioned concerning her husband's death. The police investigator testified that at that time she stated to him that she went to the balcony and found her husband standing there; that she asked him if he wanted a drink; that he apparently became angry and pushed her away and then went to the platform and began to climb over the wall and railing; that she went to him and attempted to hold him, but again he pushed her away, and went over the side to his death.

This testimony of the officer as to the statement given to him by decedent's wife was the only evidence presented to the jury concerning the precise manner in which the decedent met his death. Whether he accidentally fell or deliberately jumped was the question to be answered by the jury, which found that death was the result of an accident.

The certificate of death, duly authenticated and admitted into evidence, listed death as being "accidental." The certificate showing death to be accidental was prima facie evidence of "accidental death."[21] Defendant maintains that the notation on the death certificate was placed there as a routine matter by the medical officer who signed the certificate and that he had no basis for placing the words "accidental death" on the certificate. The certificate would still be prima facie evidence of its contents, but its weight depends upon the information upon which it is based, the source of that information, and the manner in which it is obtained.

In any event, there is no dispute that defendant met his death as a result of a fall from the balcony. Death by suicide is not a natural occurrence, and is never presumed. The burden is on the company to prove by a preponderance of the evidence that the insured committed suicide.

It is the contention of the insurance company that the statement made by the wife to the investigator is direct evidence as to how and why the fall occurred and is conclusive proof of the fact the decedent took his own life, and that the court erred in refusing to direct a verdict in the company's favor. We disagree.

After the death certificate was introduced into evidence showing the fact of death to be "accidental," the plaintiff had established a prima facie case and the defendant company then had the burden of proving that death

---

[20]The court is said to "direct the verdict" when it makes the decision for the jury because the evidence is so clear that there is no fact question to be decided by the jury.

[21]In the case as published in the reporter, the court here referred to a statute that declares that a death certificate shall be prima facie evidence of the cause of death. Following the statutory reference, a list of cases was cited to support or explain the point just given. In order to simplify this illustrative case, such statutes and cases will be omitted.

determine the actual state of mind of any contracting party. State of mind is best evidenced by the words and actions of the persons concerned. Ordinarily, mutual assent, or agreement, is evidenced by the making of an offer by one party and the acceptance of the offer by the other party.

A life or health insurance or annuity contract is a legally enforceable agreement between an applicant and an insurer. Ordinarily, an insurance agreement is set forth in a policy, but this is not essential. If the actions of the parties and the documents involved otherwise satisfy the legal requirements of an informal contract, an insurance contract might be held to be effective, even though no policy has been issued. Conversely, if the legal requirements of an informal contract have not been met, the insurer might not be legally obligated, even though a policy has been issued and delivered.

The elements that are necessary to form an enforceable informal contract are (1) an offer; (2) an acceptance; (3) legally adequate consideration; (4) legally competent parties; (5) a form required by law, if any; (6) no statute or rule of law declaring a contract of that kind of no legal effect; and (7) parties not under duress or undue influence. A large body of law has been developed in connection with each of the elements of an informal contract. Much of this chapter is devoted to a discussion of these elements and of the law pertaining to them.

Offer

An *offer* is a proposal that, if accepted by another according to its terms, will create a binding agreement. The person who makes an offer is the *offeror*, and the person to whom the offer is made is the *offeree*.

It is impossible for a person to make a binding contract with herself, even though that person may act in a representative capacity. A person acts in a representative capacity when she acts as an executor, an agent, a trustee, the officer of a corporation, or in any other capacity in which she is empowered to act for another. For example, an offer made in one's individual capacity to oneself as executor is void—that is, the offer has no legal effect. The concept of offer and acceptance, therefore, demands that in addition to an offeror who makes the offer, there must also be an offeree to whom the offer is made.

In considering an offer, the offeree has several choices. The offeree usually can ignore the offer[2] unless a prior course of conduct would justify the offeror in interpreting the silence as acceptance. If the offeree wishes to reply, she has the following choices: (1) the offeree can reject the offer; (2) the offeree can make a counteroffer, which in legal effect is a rejection of the original offer and the making of a new offer; or (3) the offeree can accept the offer according to its terms and thus form a contract.

A Promise or an Act

An offer can be in the form of a promise or of an act. It can be in the form of a promise to do or refrain from doing something. For example, an offer can be in the form of a promise to pay a sum of money if the offeree performs an act or makes a promise that the offeror requests. If the offeror requests the performance of an act in exchange for his promise, the contract when completed will be a unilateral contract, as it will involve a promise by the offeror only. If the offeror requests and receives a

[2]As will be explained in a later section, an insurer-offeree might incur liability if it ignores an applicant's offer.

promise from the offeree in exchange for the offeror's promise, the resulting contract is bilateral.

An act may be offered in exchange for a promise. This is often the case with life and health insurance. The act is submission of the application for insurance and payment of the initial premium. One treatise gives the following example:

> A makes written application for life insurance through an agent for B Insurance Company, pays the first premium, and is given a receipt stating that the insurance "shall take effect as of the date of approval of the application" at B's home office. Approval at the home office in accordance with B's usual practice is an acceptance of A's offer even though no steps are taken to notify A.[3]

Thus, the life or health insurance or annuity contract, like any other informal contract, is created when one party makes an offer and the other party accepts the offer.

Requirements for a Valid Offer

A valid offer creates a power of acceptance in the offeree. The recipient of a valid offer has the power to create a contract by accepting the offer. An expression of intent to enter into negotiations is not an offer and will not create a power of acceptance in the offeree. However, a person must take care that such an expression of intent does not appear to be an offer, or the court might construe it as an offer.

A Definite Commitment.   The offeror must manifest a definite commitment to be bound by the offer. A court is properly reluctant to construe a person's words or acts as an offer unless the court can reasonably conclude that the person had made a definite commitment. That is to say, a court will not determine that the person created a power of acceptance unless he clearly manifested an intent to do so. Moreover, an offer must be sufficiently definite in its material terms (or must require such definiteness in the acceptance) that the terms of the contract can be ascertained.

Communication to the Offeree.   An equally important requirement is that the offeror must communicate the offer to a person, or persons, with whom the offeror is willing to contract. An offer is made when an offeree receives it.

A basic principle in the law of contracts is that a person may choose those with whom he is willing to contract. For this reason, communication of an offer requires that the offeror intentionally and actually bring the offer to the notice of a person, or persons, with whom the offeror wishes to contract. If the offer is sent by mail, it must be received by the offeree to be effective.

Duration of the Offer

The offeror can, if she wishes, specify the length of time the offer will be held open. The offer will then terminate automatically at the expiration of the stated period without further action on the offeror's part. Any attempt to accept the offer after it has expired will be ineffective, because one of the conditions stated in the offer—that it be accepted within the time specified—will not have been met.

---

[3]RESTATEMENT (SECOND) OF CONTRACTS § 56 (1981). This is technically a reverse unilateral contract. JOHN D. CALAMARI & JOSEPH M. PERILLO, THE LAW OF CONTRACTS 70 (3d ed. 1987).

If the offer contains no mention of an expiration date, it is presumed to remain open for a reasonable length of time. What constitutes a reasonable length of time is a question of fact[4] that depends on the circumstances. An offer to buy stock on the floor of a stock exchange when stock prices are fluctuating rapidly might create a power of acceptance that lasts only a few minutes. On the other hand, a court might hold an offer of a reward for the capture of a criminal to have a reasonable duration of years.

Withdrawal of the Offer

Unless the offer includes an enforceable promise that it will be kept open only for a specified period of time,[5] the offeror ordinarily has the privilege of withdrawing the offer—that is, revoking it—at any time as long as it has not been accepted. After an offer has been accepted, it cannot be withdrawn.

Generally, the offeror must notify the offeree of the withdrawal. However, if an offeree knows of acts of the offeror that are inconsistent with a continuance of the offer, the offer is revoked, even though the offeror did not give express notice of withdrawal to the offeree. For example, if the offeror sells the property that is the subject of the offer to a third person, and the offeree knows of the sale, the offer is revoked even though the offeree was not expressly notified of the revocation.

Rejection and Counteroffer

The offeree can reject the offer. If this is done, the offer terminates immediately. That particular offer cannot be revived by the offeree, even if the offeree later wishes to accept it in accordance with its original terms.

If the offeree is unwilling to accept the offer as it stands but would be willing to contract on different terms, the offeree can reject the original offer and make a *counteroffer*. In fact, under such circumstances the offeree need not state specifically that the offer is being rejected. Words or actions that are not in themselves definite rejections, but that reasonably imply that the offeree does not intend to accept the offer, will be considered rejections. Thus, any attempt to substitute new terms or modify the original offer will be considered a rejection of the offer and the making of a counteroffer.[6]

For example, suppose James Bloch offers to paint Thomas Davenport's house for $3,500 and Davenport replies, "I would pay $3,000 for the paint job if you also paint the fence." Legally, this is a rejection. The offeree has clearly indicated an unwillingness to contract on the terms set forth in the offer. In this situation, therefore, the original offer lapses, and the original offeror becomes an offeree. The original offeror, who is now the offeree, can accept or reject the counteroffer.

---

[4]If the question reaches a court of law, in a jury trial it, like all questions of fact, will be decided by the jury.

[5]Such an offer is called an option. The optionee (offeree) must have given something of value (consideration) in exchange for the optionor's (offeror's) promise to keep the offer open for a specified period of time, or the offeror will not be bound to his promise to keep the offer open. The option itself is a separate contract, distinct from the contract it contemplates.

[6]Article 2 of the Uniform Commercial Code, which is law in all states except Louisiana, modifies this principle of contract law as to sales of goods. The Uniform Commercial Code states that "additional terms are to be construed as proposals for addition to the contract." U.C.C. § 2-207(2) (1977).

Death or Incapacity of Offeror or Offeree

The death of the offeror prior to the offeree's acceptance of the offer terminates the offer. Death of the offeree, assuming there was only one offeree, precludes the possibility of acceptance.

At one time, the insanity of either the offeror or offeree was considered to have the same legal effect as death. More recently, some courts have recognized the legal capacity of insane persons to create binding contracts under some circumstances. However, if the insanity of the offeror or offeree has been established in a court action, the offer is still generally held to terminate. If the insanity has not been judicially established, the person's legal capacity to complete the contract is a question of fact to be decided in the light of all the pertinent circumstances of the particular case.

Acceptance

The general rule is that the offeree's **acceptance** must be positive and unconditional and must manifest assent to the offer. An acceptance must be sufficiently positive to indicate a clear assent to the exact terms proposed by the offeror. If an act is requested, that act must be performed. If a promise is requested, that promise, and no other, must be given.[7] Acceptance must be unconditional. As previously pointed out, any attempt to impose new conditions will be construed as a counteroffer.

Although it is sometimes said that the offeree must have an intent to accept, the actual intent of the offeree is ordinarily not important if there is an adequate manifestation of assent to the offer. For example, a secret intent not to be bound is of no significance if the person's actions or words are such as to justify a reasonable belief that the person intended to enter into a contract.

Unless the offeror requires the acceptance to be in a specified form, any words or actions on the part of the offeree indicating assent to the offer will constitute acceptance. The simple statement "I accept" is sufficient if made with reference to the offer and if the offeror has requested a promise in return. Performance of the act requested in an offer for a unilateral contract is a legally sufficient acceptance.

Only the person to whom the offer is made can accept it. However, an offer need not be directed to one person only. It may be made to any member of a large group as in the case of an offer of a reward. Regardless of the number of persons who may be eligible to accept, one person must manifest assent to the offer in accordance with its terms, or there will be no contract. For this reason, as a general rule, silence on the part of an offeree will not be construed to be an acceptance.

Despite this general rule of contract law, the majority of courts that have considered the point have held that an insurer must act with reasonable promptness when it receives an application. In those jurisdictions, silence or delay in acting on the application may result in liability for the insurer. Fortunately, the general practice of issuing premium receipts that provide temporary coverage before the policy is issued has made liability for delay less likely. Moreover, courts in a substantial minority of jurisdictions have denied that an insurer has any duty to act promptly on an application.

---

[7]This rule has been modified by the Uniform Commercial Code as to the sale of goods. See footnote 6.

It would seem that a manifestation of mutual assent would require that acceptance, like the offer, be communicated. However, this is not always true. There are some instances in which acceptance does not have to be brought to the attention of the offeror for a binding contract to result. For example, when an applicant for life insurance submits an application and the initial premium to an insurer, that act is usually an offer. The insurer communicates its acceptance by delivering the policy applied for to the applicant. However, if the insurer states, in the premium receipt or otherwise, that the insurance shall take effect upon approval of the application, communication to the applicant of the insurer's acceptance is not necessary in order to form a binding contract. The insurer will be bound to the contract as soon as its underwriters approve the application, even though the applicant does not yet know of the approval.

Consideration

Long before the doctrine of consideration arose, formal contracts were effective by reason of their form alone. Historically, therefore, the doctrine of consideration was not applicable to formal contracts. The doctrine of consideration *is* applicable to informal contracts such as insurance contracts.

Consideration is the thing of value the promisor requested that is given to him in exchange for his promise. Consideration involves a bargained-for exchange. Informal contracts must include legally adequate consideration given in exchange for a promise in order for a court to enforce the promise. This means that the person who seeks to enforce the promise of another must have given something of value for it. This thing of value, or consideration, might have been another promise, a sum of money, or something else of value. The person giving the consideration might have performed an act or refrained from doing something she was legally entitled to do. However, in some way this person must have promised or given something the promisor requested. In the case of a life insurance contract, the consideration is the application and the initial premium that the applicant gives to the insurer in exchange for the insurer's promise to pay the death benefit under circumstances specified in the policy.

Legally Adequate Consideration

As a general principle, the law does not inquire into the adequacy of the consideration given in exchange for a promise. If there was consideration and if it was what the promisor requested, the courts will not substitute their own judgment of value for that of the parties to the contract. The classic statement is that under such circumstances "even a peppercorn" will be considered legally adequate consideration. After all, adequacy and value are subjective concepts. Something that has great value to one person often has little or no value to another. In the absence of fraud, the courts take the position that the parties knew what they were doing and that the promisor knew what she wanted in return for the promise.

A Requested Act or Promise.   There are two generally accepted approaches for determining the adequacy of consideration. The approach the courts use more frequently is that adequate consideration is any act or promise that the promisor requested and received in exchange for his promise. Thus, if A requests an act on the part of B in exchange for A's promise to pay a specified sum of money, and if B performs the act, the performance of that act is adequate consideration for A's promise. It is what A requested and received in return for A's promise.

A Benefit or Detriment.   Consideration is also defined as "any benefit to the promisor or detriment to the promisee." However, a legal detriment need not operate to the promisee's actual disadvantage. The classic illustration of this point concerns an uncle who promises his nephew a sum of money on the nephew's 25th birthday if the nephew abstains from smoking until that date. Here, the consideration for the uncle's promise—the nephew's abstention from smoking—is not actually detrimental to the nephew and, indeed, is probably beneficial. However, in legal theory, the voluntary forgoing of a legal right—the right to smoke—is a detriment. In this sense, there is a detriment to the nephew and thus legally adequate consideration given in exchange for the uncle's promise.

A Promise for a Promise.   Generally speaking, mutual promises constitute legally adequate consideration for each other. In other words, in a bilateral contract, each promise is consideration for the other, as each is the thing requested and received in exchange for the promise of the other party to the contract.

A Conditional Promise.   A conditional promise will be legally adequate consideration for another promise or for an act. For example, a promise to pay an insurance benefit is conditional, because it is conditioned on the occurrence of a loss. Payment will be made only if the loss insured against occurs. Many term life insurance policies expire without the payment of a death benefit. The insurer promises to pay a death benefit but only *on the condition* that the insured dies during the term of the policy. If the insured does not die during the term of the policy, no payment will be made. This does not mean that the contract was not valid or that the promise was not binding. It means only that the specified condition did not occur.

Legally Inadequate Consideration

There are two situations in which courts ordinarily hold that consideration is inadequate. These situations involve past consideration and preexisting legal duty.

Past Consideration.   If a promisor says, "In consideration of your not smoking last year, I promise to pay you $500," there is no consideration for the promise and therefore no contract. Such past consideration usually is not adequate to create a binding contract, because past consideration did not induce the promise and was not given in exchange for the promise. Adequate consideration requires a bargained-for exchange.

Preexisting Legal Duty.   Ordinarily, the promise to perform or the performance of a preexisting legal duty will not be adequate consideration to create a binding contract. For example, suppose A has contracted to build B a house for $100,000, but, in the middle of construction, A demands that the contract price be raised to $110,000. B agrees to pay the extra $10,000. B's promise to pay the extra $10,000 will be unenforceable because A has a preexisting legal duty to build the house for $100,000, and there is no consideration for the promise to pay the additional $10,000.

Competent Parties

A person of legal age, without mental or other incapacity, is legally ***competent*** to enter into a contract. Such a person is said to have contractual capacity.

Generally speaking, a person is presumed to be legally competent to enter into a valid contract. However, the contractual capacity of certain classes of persons is limited. These classes include minors, mentally infirm persons, intoxicated persons, convicts, aliens, and corporations. Some contracts of such persons are void or voidable.

Valid, Void, and Voidable Contracts

Contracts are valid, void, or voidable. A ***valid contract*** is a contract that either party can enforce by court action. The requirements relating to offer, acceptance, competence of the parties, and legality must be met if an agreement is to be a valid informal contract.

Some contracts of persons with limited contractual capacity are void or voidable. A ***void contract*** is an agreement that is unenforceable by court action. To say that a contract is void is actually a contradiction in terms, as the term *contract* means "an agreement enforceable at law." It would be more exact to say that no contract was created. However, the term *void contract* is in general use and will be used in this book.

A ***voidable contract*** is enforceable until a party who has the right to disaffirm the contract takes some action to disaffirm it. In a situation in which a contract entered into by a legally incompetent person is voidable, that person may disaffirm the contract and avoid the legal duties created by it. However, if she does not disaffirm the contract, the contract will remain in effect. The power of some persons of limited contractual capacity to disaffirm—that is, to avoid—a contract after having entered into it is important to anyone contemplating making a contract with such a person. The competent party will be bound, while the person of limited contractual capacity has the privilege of deciding whether to carry out the contract or disaffirm it.

Minors

At common law, a minor, also called an infant, was any person under the age of 21. However, most states have passed legislation terminating infancy, for contractual purposes, at a younger age, usually 18.

As a general rule, a few kinds of contracts made by a minor are valid, and all others are voidable (but not void). This means that with respect to most contracts the minor can decide whether he wishes to be bound by the contract. If the other party's own contractual capacity is unimpaired, the other party is bound by the contract unless and until the minor decides to disaffirm it.

A minor disaffirms a voidable contract simply by declaring that thereafter he will not be bound by its terms. Minors are free to disaffirm voidable contracts at any time during their minority and within a reasonable time after they attain the age of majority.

Disaffirmance of a voidable contract on the ground of minority requires that the minor return any consideration he received if it is still in his possession. However, as a general rule, if the minor no longer has the consideration, the minor can still avoid the contract and recover whatever money or objects he parted with without restoring the other party to the position the other party had prior to the making of the contract.

The law accords minors the power of avoiding certain contracts as a protection from unscrupulous persons who might otherwise seek to take advantage of young people. For this reason, if there is no statute to the contrary, the power is almost absolute. It applies to everyone who has not yet attained the age of majority, regardless of how nearly of age she may be. Even minors who are engaging in business for themselves or who have married[8] usually retain the power to disaffirm their contracts.

Although it might appear that a minor has an additional privilege and not a contractual disability, this is not the case. A minor cannot give legal assurance that he will not disaffirm a voidable contract. Therefore, competent parties often refuse to contract with a minor. This puts the minor at a disadvantage.

Contracts That the Minor Cannot Avoid.   Federal or state statutes relating to banking, military enlistment, educational loans, marriage, and insurance may modify a minor's power to avoid a contract. Also, at common law there are certain kinds of contracts that a minor may not disaffirm. Agreements in fulfillment of a minor's legal duty are binding. For example, a minor's agreement to support the minor's illegitimate child will be binding on the minor, as minors have a legal duty to support their children.

Minors are also liable for the reasonable value of necessaries they purchase for themselves or their dependents. Note that they are not liable for the contract price but rather for the *reasonable value* of the goods. *Necessaries* are "those things which are reasonably necessary for the proper and suitable maintenance of the minor in view of his social position and situation in life, the customs of the social circle in which he moves, and the fortune possessed by him and his parents."[9] *Necessaries* is a broader word than *necessities*, for *necessaries* includes not only those items essential to subsistence but also other things that are reasonably required for the minor's maintenance, considering his social position and financial status. Food, shelter, clothing, medical services, and education are necessaries. Legal services are often a necessary. Many other articles may be necessaries, such as an automobile needed to transport the minor to her place of employment. Questions involving which kinds of food, shelter, clothing, and other goods or services are necessaries for a particular minor are questions of fact for the jury to decide. Luxury articles usually will not be found to be necessaries, but an expensive article, such as an automobile, could be a necessary if the minor is in actual need of it.

The Minor as Insurance Applicant.   The courts have held that insurance is not a necessary. Therefore, in the absence of a special statute, minors can disaffirm a contract of life insurance. Moreover, the majority rule is that, upon such disaffirmance, the minor can recover the entire amount of the premiums paid for the insurance. In such a situation, the minor will have had the insurance protection without paying anything for it.

Statutes have been enacted in many states authorizing minors above specified ages to enter into valid life or health insurance contracts under certain conditions. A typical statute of this kind reads as follows:

> Any minor of the age of fifteen years or more may, notwithstanding such minority, contract for life, health, and accident insurance on his own life for his own benefit or for the benefit of his father, mother, husband, wife, child, brother or sister, and may exercise all

---

[8]In a substantial minority of states, marriage will confer contractual capacity upon a minor.

[9]BALLENTINE'S LAW DICTIONARY 836 (3d ed. 1969).

such contractual rights and powers with respect to any such contract of insurance as might be exercised by a person of full legal age, and may exercise with like effect all rights and privileges under such contract, including the surrender of his interest therein and the giving of a valid discharge for any benefit accruing or money payable thereunder. Such minor shall not, by reason of his minority, be entitled to rescind, avoid, or repudiate such contract, or any exercise of a right or privilege thereunder.[10]

This statute permits a minor 15 years of age or older to insure "his own life." Note, however, that the beneficiary must be the minor's estate (as indicated by the words "for his own benefit") or a person closely related to the minor. Statutes of this kind sometimes permit the minor to insure the life of a child or spouse as well as the minor's own life.

Mentally Infirm Persons

A person can be mentally infirm because of insanity, retardation, disease, injury, or advanced age. Degrees of mental infirmity range from very slight retardation to the deep and permanent coma that sometimes occurs when a person receives a severe head injury. The contractual capacity of a mentally infirm person depends on whether a court has judged the person to be mentally incompetent and has appointed a guardian of the person's estate or, if not, whether the person can reasonably understand the nature and effect of the agreement.

If a Guardian Has Been Appointed.   If a court has judged a mentally infirm person incompetent and has appointed a guardian of the person's estate, usually any contract attempted by the mentally infirm person will be void. The purpose of appointing a guardian is to preserve the mentally infirm person's property from his own improvidence, and this purpose would be defeated if the mentally infirm person had the power to contract. The guardian has control over the mentally infirm person's property, subject to court supervision. The court proceedings establishing incompetency and guardianship are considered public notice of the mentally infirm person's status.

If No Guardian Has Been Appointed.   If no guardian has been appointed, then the mentally infirm person's ability to understand and the complexity of the agreement usually will determine whether the contract is void or voidable. For example, a mentally infirm person might be able to understand what is involved in buying a bicycle but not what is involved in buying stock in a corporation.

If a mentally infirm person totally lacks understanding of the nature and effect of the agreement, then the contract is void from its inception. However, if the mentally infirm person does not totally lack understanding but does not reasonably understand the nature and effect of the agreement, the contract will be voidable. The mentally infirm person, or a guardian who is later appointed, can disaffirm a voidable contract.

Necessaries.   As with minors, mentally infirm persons, whether or not they are under guardianship, will be liable for the reasonable value of necessaries they purchase. Insurance is not a necessary, and therefore insurance contracts of the mentally infirm will be void or voidable. A mentally infirm person can disaffirm a voidable insurance contract and recover the total amount of premiums paid.

---

[10]215 ILL. COMP. STAT. ANN. 5/242 (Michie 1993).

Intoxicated Persons

A contract is voidable if one of the parties was so much under the influence of alcohol or drugs at the time that the contract was made as to be unable to understand the nature and effect of the contract. Upon recovery, the party who was under the influence of alcohol or drugs can affirm or disaffirm the contract. However, she will be liable for the reasonable value of any necessaries she purchased.

Convicts

Convicts are limited by contractual disabilities, which vary from state to state. In the absence of a statute to the contrary, a convict does not totally lack capacity to contract. A convict will be liable for the reasonable value of necessaries in some states. In some states, a convict can contract with respect to his own property.

Aliens

Citizens of different countries frequently make contracts with each other. These contracts are ordinarily valid and enforceable. However, an attempted contract between citizens of two countries at war is void.

Corporations

The contractual capacity of a corporation is determined by the provisions of its charter and the statutes of the state in which it was incorporated, that is, its domiciliary state. A corporation has the express powers granted in its charter and the laws under which it was created. A corporation also has the implied and incidental powers necessary to the exercise of its express powers.

Insurers are ordinarily corporations. The charter of a life and health insurer states that the insurer is authorized to transact life and health insurance business. The insurer's domiciliary state must also issue the insurer a certificate of authority—that is, a license—before the insurer can enter into life and health insurance and annuity contracts in the domiciliary state. To qualify to do business in another state, the insurer must apply to the proper official of that state for permission to conduct insurance business there. If the insurer meets the necessary requirements, it will be granted a certificate of authority to do business in that state.

The contractual capacity of an insurer therefore depends on two things. First, under its charter and the laws under which it was incorporated, the insurer must be empowered to issue contracts of insurance of the kind desired—life, health, fire, automobile, and so forth. Second, it must be authorized to do insurance business—to enter into contracts of insurance of the type desired—in the state where the contract becomes effective. The power to enter into a contract incidental to the conduct of an insurance business is implied—for example, a contract to purchase a building to house the insurer's corporate headquarters.

The legal effect of an insurance contract issued by an unlicensed insurer depends on state law. The majority of states have laws similar to the National Association of Insurance Commissioners Nonadmitted Insurance Model Act, which specifies that such a contract will be enforceable by the policyowner or beneficiary according to the terms of the contract. In other states, there are no applicable statutes. In the absence of an applicable statute, the majority of courts uphold the rights of the policyowner or beneficiary if the policyowner entered into the contract in good faith and without knowledge of the insurer's legal incompetence. In most states, the laws provide for penalties upon an insurer that does business in the state without being licensed. An insurance agent who sells the policy of an unlicensed insurer can incur penalties also.

Contract Form

There are a number of practical reasons for expressing informal contracts in writing. Memories are often unreliable, and it is convenient for the parties to have a written contract to which to refer. It is also easier to prove the terms of a written contract than of an oral contract. Nevertheless, in the absence of a statute to the contrary, an oral informal contract is valid.

Oral Informal Contracts

The principle that informal contracts need not be in writing to be valid applies to insurance contracts as well as to other informal contracts. Oral, or partly oral, temporary insurance contracts are commonplace. When a premium receipt incorporating a temporary life insurance contract is issued to a life insurance applicant, a life insurance contract is created that is partly oral and partly written. Some terms of the temporary insurance contract will be in the premium receipt, but many other terms will be governed by a life insurance policy that has not yet been issued and, indeed, will never be issued if the insurer rejects the application or if the proposed insured dies before the policy can be issued. Moreover, it has been held that a temporary insurance contract that is entirely oral is enforceable. In one case, the neglect of a life insurance agent to give the applicant a premium receipt incorporating a temporary insurance contract did not make an otherwise valid oral contract of temporary insurance invalid.[11]

Although oral, or partly oral, temporary insurance contracts are enforceable by the applicant or beneficiary, it is highly desirable that the written contract be issued at the earliest possible time. The many and complex terms of an insurance policy necessitate the policyowner's receiving the policy in order for the policyowner to have an opportunity to review those terms.

Insurers usually do not permit oral life insurance contracts, other than those for temporary insurance. Life insurers do not ordinarily grant their soliciting agents the authority to make insurance contracts, other than temporary insurance contracts. The applicant will be on notice of the agent's lack of contractual authority, as a statement to that effect will be in the application.

The Statute of Frauds

Some contracts are required by law to be in writing. Formal contracts, such as negotiable instruments, must be written to be valid. In addition, state statutes require that certain informal contracts be evidenced by a writing. The ***Statute of Frauds*** is the most important of these statutes. The Statute of Frauds does not ordinarily apply to

---

[11]Overton v. Washington Nat'l Ins. Co., 260 A.2d 444 (1970).

life and health insurance contracts, but an explanation of the Statute of Frauds is nevertheless necessary to an understanding of life and health insurance laws.

The Statute of Frauds was originally enacted in England in 1677 and expressed as its purpose the "prevention of many fraudulent practices." Some form of this statute has been enacted in nearly all the states. In its most common form, the Statute of Frauds enumerates the following five classes of contracts[12] that must be evidenced by a writing:

1. A promise by an executor, or administrator, to pay a claim against the decedent's estate out of the executor's or administrator's own funds.
2. A promise to be legally responsible for the debt or default of another.
3. A promise made in consideration of marriage.
4. An agreement to sell, or a sale of, any interest in real property.
5. An agreement that cannot be performed within one year after the contract is made.

As enacted in most states, the Statute of Frauds lists at least these five classes of contracts and provides that any oral agreement falling into one of these classes will be unenforceable unless it is evidenced by some note or memorandum signed by the party to be charged with performance of the contract. This means that a person who sues another for breach of a contract falling into one of these classes can prove the existence of the contract only if it is in writing or if she has some note or memorandum identifying the parties, subject matter, and essential terms of the contract signed by the other party to the contract. The contract itself does not have to be in writing; a written note or memorandum evidencing the promise is all that is required.

Only the fifth class of agreements listed above is of significance in a discussion of life insurance contract law—namely, an agreement that cannot be performed within one year after the contract is made. Since many life insurance contracts remain in force for many years, the contention has sometimes been made that life insurance contracts must comply with the Statute of Frauds and that oral contracts of life insurance cannot be proved except by a written note or memorandum. This contention is not supported by the Statute of Frauds, as it has been enacted in most states, because the insured could die and the life insurance contract could be performed "within one year after the contract is made." Many life insurance contracts are performed within the first year, and an agreement that can be performed within one year from the date it is made usually does not fall within the Statute of Frauds. Thus, an oral contract of life insurance ordinarily does not have to be proved by a written note or memorandum.

An exception to this general rule is found in the New York statute[13] that reads in part as follows:

Agreements required to be in writing. Every agreement, promise or undertaking is void, unless it or some note or memorandum thereof be in writing, and subscribed by the

---

[12]The English Statute of Frauds also included a section dealing with the sale of "goods, wares, or merchandises" for a price in excess of a specified sum. This provision was included in the Statute of Frauds as it was originally adopted by many of the states, but it has since been replaced in many states by provisions of the Uniform Commercial Code. One provision, U.C.C. § 2-201(1), states that a contract for the sale of goods in excess of $500 is not enforceable unless there is a sufficient writing to indicate a contract for sale was made between the parties, and signed by the party or her agent, to be charged with performance of the contract.

[13]N. Y. Gen. Oblig. § 5-701 (McKinney 1989 & Supp. 1996).

party to be charged therewith, or by his lawful agent, if such agreement, promise or undertaking:

    1. By its terms is not to be performed within one year from the making thereof *or the performance of which is not to be completed before the end of a lifetime.* . . . [Emphasis added.]

As it includes any contract "the performance of which is not to be completed before the end of a lifetime," this New York statute specifically includes life insurance contracts. Therefore, in New York, a life insurance contract does have to be evidenced by a writing under the Statute of Frauds.

Illegal Agreements

A contract is an agreement enforceable in a court of law. Because the courts will not enforce an illegal agreement, a contract cannot be illegal.

An agreement may be illegal because it is unconstitutional, forbidden by statute, against an express rule of common law, or against public policy as expressed by the courts.[14] Agreements in restraint of trade, usurious agreements, many wagering agreements, and agreements to commit torts[15] or crimes are illegal.

Ordinarily, the law will not aid either party to an illegal agreement. Neither party can compel the other to perform the contract or obtain damages from the other.

However, sometimes a statute is written to protect one of the parties and is directed against the other party. In such a case, the protected party can enforce the contract. For example, statutes concerning the validity of life insurance contracts issued by unlicensed insurers are meant to protect the citizens of the state. For this reason, these statutes often do not declare such contracts void and unenforceable but instead permit the policyowner or beneficiary to enforce them against the insurer at fault.

Aleatory Contracts

In an **aleatory contract**, the promise by one party is conditioned on the happening of an uncertain event. Some aleatory agreements are illegal, whereas others are not. Wagering agreements are aleatory agreements that are often illegal. Insurance contracts are also aleatory agreements, but insurance contracts ordinarily are legal and will be enforced by the courts.

The uncertain event on which the promise in a wagering agreement is conditioned could be that one horse will run faster than another in a race or that a certain number of black dots will appear on the tops of dice when they are thrown. One person promises to pay money to another if a certain horse wins the race or a certain number of black dots appears on the tops of the dice.

The uncertain event on which the promise in an insurance contract is conditioned could be a fire, an automobile accident, a death, a sickness, and so forth depending on the type of insurance contract. The insurer promises to pay money on the occurrence of the event insured against.

---

[14]BALLENTINE'S LAW DICTIONARY 1023 (3d ed. 1969).

[15]A tort is the breach of a noncontractual legal duty to another person resulting in injury to that person. Assault, slander, and negligent operation of a motor vehicle resulting in injury to another person are examples of torts.

Many contracts are not aleatory. For example, a contract between two people in which one agrees to sell a plot of land to the other, and the other agrees to pay a specified amount of money for the land, is not conditioned on the happening of an uncertain event and thus is not an aleatory contract.

Wagering Agreements Compared to Insurance Contracts

Wagering agreements are often illegal. In the earliest days of the English common law, wagering agreements were not prohibited, but laws were later enacted declaring certain kinds of wagers to be against public policy. Statutes to this effect are now in force in most states.

Unlike wagering agreements, insurance contracts are considered to be in the interests of society. However, this issue has not always been so clearly settled. An insurance contract obligates one party to pay another a specific sum of money on the happening of an event that is presumably not within the control of either. Such an agreement bears more than a passing resemblance to a wager. Obviously, an unscrupulous person standing to gain from the destruction of an insured piece of property or an insured life might feel a strong temptation to implement the whims of chance in his own favor. Therefore, if life insurance contracts were issued indiscriminately, they could pose a threat to the public welfare by creating a motive for murder in the minds of unscrupulous people. The requirement that the beneficiary have an insurable interest in the life of the insured helps avoid these problems. Insurable interest is such an essential concept in life insurance law that it will be discussed at some length in Chapter 6, "Formation of the Life Insurance Contract."

Duress and Undue Influence

The contracting parties' freedom of will is essential to the validity of a contract. Therefore, duress or undue influence exerted on one of the parties may make the contract unenforceable. *Duress* occurs when the wrongful act or threat of one person induces another to enter into a contract against his will. *Undue influence* often involves misuse of a position of confidence or dominion by one person to overcome the will of another person. Undue influence also occurs when one person takes advantage of another's weakness of mind, necessity, or distress. Often, undue influence involves both a position of confidence or dominion on the part of one person and weakness of mind, necessity, or distress on the part of the other.

Duress or undue influence may nullify the modification of a contract, as well as its formation. Sometimes a person who was originally named the beneficiary of a life insurance policy claims that duress or undue influence was exerted on the policyowner to make a change of beneficiary. The insurer will not ordinarily be liable to the original beneficiary if it paid the benefits to the new beneficiary without knowledge of the claim of duress or undue influence. If the insurer receives notice from the original beneficiary of the claim of duress or undue influence before the insurer has paid the policy benefits, an interpleader[16] action might be in order. Interpleader is discussed in Chapter 16, "Equitable Remedies."

---

[16]Interpleader is an equitable remedy whereby a stakeholder, such as an insurer, with no claim to the fund that the stakeholder holds, and confronted by rival claimants, can pay the money into court and be dismissed from the suit. The court will then decide which claimant is entitled to the money.

Rules of Contract Construction

There are a number of general rules that a court will apply when it interprets a contract. These are called rules of contract construction. The word *construction* comes from the word *construe*, which means "to interpret." Rules of contract construction assist the court in interpreting a contract. The most important rules of contract construction are discussed below.

Clear and Unambiguous Language

Generally, a court will give effect to clear and unambiguous contract language. A court ordinarily is not permitted to rewrite a contract under the guise of interpreting it. However, as to insurance contracts, this traditional rule of contract construction has been modified by the reasonable expectations doctrine discussed below and in Chapter 18, "Performance of the Insurance Contract."

Unclear Language Construed against the Writer

Where the language in a contract is unclear, a court will interpret the unclear language against the party who selected the language and wrote the contract; that is, the court will interpret the unclear language to benefit the other party. This rule applies particularly to the interpretation of insurance policies, which are adhesion contracts written by the insurer.

Adhesion contracts are standard contract forms offered on a "take it or leave it" basis. The other party cannot bargain as to the terms of the contract. Adhesion contracts differ in this respect from contracts in which the terms result from mutual negotiation and concessions of the parties. Thus, when an insurer selects policy language, writes a policy, and sells it to a policyowner, if the policy contains unclear or ambiguous terms, a court will interpret those terms in favor of the policyowner or beneficiary and against the insurer.

There is an exception to the rule that unclear or ambiguous terms will be interpreted against the party who wrote the contract. Sometimes, that party is required by law to include specific language in the contract. In this situation, some courts will not interpret the required language against the party who wrote the contract if the required language is unclear or ambiguous.

Construed as a Whole

The court will *construe*—that is, interpret—the contract as a whole. The court will gather the contract's meaning from the entire context and not from detached portions of the contract. The contract's general intent will supersede any conflicting specific clauses.

Ordinary Meaning of Words

Generally, the court will give the words in a contract their ordinary meaning. However, if a party shows that certain words were meant to be used in a technical sense, the words will be given their technical meaning.

Construction in Favor of Validity

If it is possible to do so, the court will give an interpretation that makes a contract valid rather than one that makes it invalid. Generally, the court presumes that the parties intended to make a valid contract and tries to interpret the contract according to the parties' intent.

Printed, Typed, and Handwritten Matter

Many contracts consist of a printed form to which the parties have added typed or handwritten matter. When the text of such a typed or handwritten addition is inconsistent with the text of the printed form, the typed or handwritten addition will control. The reason for this general rule is that ordinarily the parties chose such typed or handwritten matter, whereas the printed form was developed for general use. Thus, a court will deem the typed or handwritten matter to indicate the parties' intent. Furthermore, if a contract contains both typed and handwritten matter that are inconsistent with each other, the handwritten portion will control.

The Parol Evidence Rule

The term *parole* in French means "speech." French terms are often used in English law, and in laws that derive from English law, because French was used in the English courts after the Norman Conquest of England in 1066.

Parol evidence is oral evidence—that is, testimony given by witnesses in court. Under the *parol evidence rule*, when parties put their contract into a writing, all previous agreements merge into the written contract. Parol evidence ordinarily is not admissible to add to, detract from, or alter the contract as written.

Life insurance policies, as written contracts, are subject to the parol evidence rule. Oral evidence ordinarily cannot be admitted to contradict the provisions of a life insurance policy. However, courts recognize a number of exceptions to the parol evidence rule. Oral evidence can be introduced in the situations described in the following subsections.

Formation Defects

The parol evidence rule does not prohibit testimony indicating that no contract was ever formed, because the parol evidence rule does not become effective until a binding contract exists. For example, where a party asserts that there was an oral agreement that the contract would not become effective until a certain event occurred, the court can hear oral evidence of such an agreement. Formation defects due to fraud, duress, mistake, lack of consideration, illegality, or certain other causes may also be shown by parol evidence.

One court permitted the introduction of parol evidence in a life insurance case to show that no contract was ever formed because someone other than the proposed insured took the medical examination. The court noted the general rule that parol evidence cannot be introduced "for the purpose of contradicting, changing, or adding to the terms incorporated into and made a part of a written contract." Nevertheless, the court allowed oral testimony, saying:

In a case such as the instant one, where the defense of fraud is invoked, in that the named insured never knowingly made application for insurance and where a person other than the named insured was substituted for the medical examination, we are of the opinion that the Parol Evidence Rule cannot be invoked to preclude the medical examiner from giving testimony as to the facts and circumstances connected with and surrounding the parties at the time of such examination. The purpose of such testimony is not to vary or contradict a contract, but to show that the alleged contract never came into existence.[17]

Incomplete Contract

If the face of the written contract shows that the writing is incomplete, parol evidence can be used to show those provisions that the parties had previously agreed to but that they failed to incorporate into the written contract.

Interpretation of the Contract

If there is ambiguity in a written contract or if the parties disagree as to the meaning of words in the contract, parol evidence will be admissible so that the contract can be interpreted. In addition, where words used in a contract have a special trade meaning or a special meaning by reason of the locality in which the contract was drawn up, parol evidence can be used to explain the meaning.

Reformation of the Contract

Reformation is an equitable remedy by which a written contract is revised to express the original intent of the parties.[18] Reformation of the contract will be granted when it is proved that the contract as written does not reflect the actual agreement of the parties because of mistake. The parol evidence rule will not be applied if a party to a written contract alleges facts that would entitle him to a reformation of the contract.

For example, suppose that a buyer and seller had agreed that the purchase price of a painting was $1,000. If the person who drafted the contract wrote $100 by mistake, the seller could have the contract reformed to reflect the parties' original intent. The parol evidence rule would not prevent the introduction of oral testimony regarding the price agreed upon.

The Reasonable Expectations Doctrine

If a court applies the reasonable expectations doctrine, the court will honor the reasonable expectations of a policyowner or beneficiary even though the strict terms of the insurance contract do not support those expectations. In such a case, parol evidence may be admitted to establish a policyowner's or beneficiary's expectations as to the contract terms. The reasonable expectations doctrine is discussed in Chapter 18, "Performance of the Insurance Contract."

---

[17]Obartuch v. Security Mut. Life Ins. Co., 114 F.2d 873 (7th Cir. 1940).

[18]Reformation is discussed more fully in Chapter 16, "Equitable Remedies."

Subsequent Modifications of the Contract

The parol evidence rule applies only to negotiations occurring prior to the time a contract is put into writing. The parties may present parol evidence to prove the existence of modifications of the contract agreed upon after the contract was put into writing.

Contract Performance and Breach of Contract

When a contract has been formed, one or both of the parties has promised to do something. If a party who promised to do something fails to act when his duty to perform arises, that party has committed a breach of contract. As might be expected, contract performance and breach of contract have been the subject of many lawsuits and comprise a large part of the law of contracts.

Contract Performance

A contract is performed when the act or acts required by the contract are completed. In the case of a bilateral contract, both parties have promised to do something. For example, in the case of a bilateral contract for the sale of a computer, the seller has promised to deliver the computer to the buyer and the buyer has promised to pay the agreed-upon price. The contract will be performed when the seller has delivered the computer to the buyer and the buyer has paid the money to the seller.

In the case of a unilateral contract, only one of the parties has promised to do something. Under an insurance contract, which is a unilateral contract, the insurer promises to pay money under conditions specified in the policy. The contract is performed when the insurer has paid the money.

When a contract is conditional, the condition or conditions must be satisfied before the duty to perform the contract arises. An insurance contract is conditional. For example, in order for an insurer to have a duty to pay an accidental death benefit, a number of conditions must be satisfied. First, the insured must have died. Second, the insured must have died from injury sustained in an accident rather than from disease or suicide. Third, the policy must have been in force at the time of the insured's death. Fourth, the insurer must have received timely notice and proof of the insured's death.

Because the insurance contract is conditional, the insurer's duty to perform the contract might never arise. For example, if the insurer issues a five-year term life insurance policy, and the insured is living when the policy expires at the end of the term, the condition that the insured die during the term of the policy has not been satisfied. Therefore, the insurer's duty to perform the contract by paying the death benefit will never arise.

An insurer's claims department deals with performance of the insurer's contracts. Chapter 18, "Performance of the Insurance Contract," explores this subject in more detail.

Breach of Contract

A **breach of contract** is the failure of a party to perform a contract according to its terms without a legal excuse. The breach of contract can be either total or partial. For example, suppose an insured died from injury sustained in an accident and the policy provided both a death benefit and an accidental death benefit. If the insurer refused to pay both the death benefit and the accidental death benefit without a legal excuse, the insurer would have committed a total breach of contract. If, however, the insurer paid the death benefit but refused to pay the accidental death benefit without a legal excuse, the insurer would have committed a partial breach of contract. In either case, the beneficiary could maintain a suit for damages against the insurer.

Third-Person Beneficiaries

In order to maintain a legal action, a person must have *standing to sue*. A person has standing to sue when he has a legally protectible interest at stake in the controversy.

In the past, there have been conflicting views as to whether a third person who is not a party to a contract could maintain an action for damages for breach of the contract. It is now settled in the United States that when a contract is for the direct benefit of a third person, that person has standing to sue and can maintain an action on the contract. When a life insurance contract is not payable to the policyowner or to her estate, it is a contract for the benefit of a third person. The third-person beneficiary of a life insurance contract therefore has standing to sue for damages for breach of the contract. The beneficiary, rather than the personal representative of the insured, is the proper party to bring the suit. A *personal representative* is the executor or administrator of a deceased person's estate.

Liberty of Contract

It has been noted in this chapter that an offeror can include what terms he wishes in the offer and choose the persons with whom he wishes to contract. The offeree can ignore, reject, or accept the offer. The adequacy of the consideration will ordinarily be left to the judgment of the parties. The freedom to contract as one wishes is known as *liberty of contract*.

Liberty of contract prevails unless other laws limit it. Because insurance is affected with a public interest, there are many laws limiting an insurer's liberty of contract. Nevertheless, the basic principle of liberty of contract should be borne in mind. An insurer is free to contract as it wishes unless some law limits that freedom.

Constitutional Protection of Existing Contracts

The Contract Clause of the U.S. Constitution[19] provides that "No state shall . . . pass any . . . law impairing the Obligation of Contracts." Because of the Contract Clause, states cannot enact statutes that materially change the rights of parties to contracts already in existence at the time the statute is enacted unless the statute serves a significant and legitimate public purpose.[20]

In addition, rights under existing contracts are protected by the Due Process Clauses of the 5th and 14th Amendments to the U.S. Constitution. These amend-

---

[19]Art. I, § 10.
[20]Energy Reserves Group, Inc. v. Kansas Power & Light Co., 459 U.S. 400 (1983).

ments prohibit governments from depriving people of life, liberty, or property without "due process of law." Contract rights are valuable property, as will be discussed in Chapter 9, "Property Rights in the Life Insurance Policy."

Insurance Contract Law

The law of life and health insurance and annuity contracts rests on the general principles of contract law discussed in this chapter. Therefore, in many respects, life and health insurance policies and annuity contracts are governed by the same rules that apply to any other type of contract.

Nevertheless, for a number of reasons, a large body of special insurance contract law has developed. For example, there are laws requiring that the beneficiary have an insurable interest in the life of the proposed insured. These laws are designed to prevent insurance contracts from being used for wagering in human life. Legal safeguards also prevent the unscrupulous from collecting premiums without observing the necessary accounting and investment practices that will enable them to pay claims as such claims are presented. Special unfair claims practices laws regulate the contract performance of insurers. As a result of the large body of insurance law that has been developed, some general principles of contract law have been modified as they apply to insurance contracts.

Summary

A contract can be defined as a binding promise or as an agreement enforceable at law. Contracts can be unilateral (that is, containing promises by one party only) or bilateral (containing promises by both parties). A life or health insurance or annuity contract is unilateral, because only the insurer makes a promise.

A contract is either formal or informal. A formal contract is binding because of its form. An informal contract is binding because the parties have met requirements that relate to the substance, rather than to the form, of the transaction. Insurance contracts are informal contracts.

An informal contract is created when an offer by one person, the offeror, is accepted by another person, the offeree. The offer can be in the form of a promise or of an act. The offer must indicate a definite commitment to be bound by the contract and must be communicated to the offeree.

The offer will last for the period of time that the offeror specifies or for a reasonable period of time if no period is specified. The offeree can reject the offer, in which case the offer terminates. Or the offeree can make a counteroffer. A counteroffer is a rejection of the offer and a proposal of a new offer. If the offeror or offeree dies, the offer automatically terminates.

Only an offeree can accept the offer. The offeree's acceptance according to the terms of the offer creates the contract. The acceptance usually must be positive, unconditional, and the manifestation of an assent to enter into the contract. Performance of a requested act is a legally sufficient acceptance in the case of a unilateral contract.

Consideration is necessary to the formation of a binding informal contract. Consideration is the thing of value requested and given in exchange for a promise. It is "any benefit to the promisor or detriment to the promisee." As a general rule, the law does not inquire into the adequacy of the agreed-upon consideration. Mutual promises are adequate consideration for each other. A conditional promise is adequate consideration.

A person of legal age and without mental infirmity or other incapacity is competent to contract. Minors, mentally infirm persons, intoxicated persons, convicts, aliens, and corporations have limited contractual capacity. Contracts of those with limited contractual capacity are often void or voidable.

A minor's contracts, except for contracts for necessaries, are generally voidable by the minor. If the minor avoids a contract, the minor can recover the consideration she gave. Life insurance contracts are not necessaries and, unless there is a statute to the contrary, are voidable by the minor, allowing the minor to get back the amount of the premiums she paid.

The contractual power of a corporation is determined by the provisions of its charter and the statutes of the state in which it was incorporated. An insurer is ordinarily a corporation. An insurer must have a certificate of authority (license) from each state in which it does business.

Informal contracts can be oral unless there is a statute to the contrary. The Statute of Frauds requires some types of informal contracts to be evidenced by a writing, but in most states the Statute of Frauds does not apply to insurance contracts.

An illegal agreement will not be enforced by the courts. Some aleatory agreements are illegal. Under an aleatory agreement, the promise of one party is conditioned on the happening of an uncertain event. Wagering agreements are aleatory agreements that are often illegal. Insurance contracts are aleatory agreements that are legal.

Contracts are interpreted by a court according to certain rules. If the contract language is plain and unambiguous, ordinarily there will be no interpretation by the court, but ambiguities will be interpreted against the writer of

the contract. The contract will be interpreted as a whole, and its words will be given their ordinary meaning. The contract will be given an interpretation that makes it valid rather than invalid. Typed and handwritten matter will control over printed matter.

Parol evidence, that is, oral testimony given by witnesses, will not be admissible to alter the terms of a written contract, as a general rule. However, the parol evidence rule does not apply to contracts that have formation defects or ambiguities, that are incomplete, or that do not reflect the original intent of the parties. If a court follows the reasonable expectations doctrine, oral testimony to establish the expectations of a policyowner or beneficiary as to the terms of an insurance contract may be permitted. The parol evidence rule applies only to negotiations occurring prior to the time a contract is put in writing but not to subsequent modifications of the contract.

A contract is performed when the act or acts required by the contract are completed. Where a contract is conditional, the condition or conditions must be satisfied before the duty to perform the contract arises. A breach of contract is the failure of a party to perform a contract without a legal excuse.

ILLUSTRATIVE CASE

The following case has been selected because it illustrates two important principles, offer and acceptance, in connection with the life insurance contract.

JOHN HANCOCK MUTUAL LIFE INSURANCE COMPANY
v.
DONALD H. DIETLIN et al.[21]
Supreme Court of Rhode Island

JOSLIN, Justice.
This is a bill in equity[22] to declare null and void a policy of life insurance issued by the complainant [the insurer] insuring the lives of Donald H. and Charlotte R. Dietlin, husband and wife, and their minor children, Donna J., Paula R., and Patricia A. Dietlin, all of whom are respondents,[23] as well as the life of Kathleen B. Dietlin, de-

ceased. After appointment of a guardian ad litem[24] to represent the interests of the minor respondents, the cause was heard on bill, answer and proof[25] by a justice of the superior court who entered a decree declaring the policy to be null and void, ordering the respondents to surrender it to the complainant for cancellation, and granting the complainant other incidental relief. In addition the com-

---

[21]199 A.2d 311(1964).

[22]A written complaint addressed to a court of equity; the remedy sought is an equitable remedy—rescission (cancellation) of the policy.

[23]Literally, those who respond (to the complaint).

[24]A guardian appointed by the court to represent a minor or minors who are parties to the proceedings.

[25]"The cause was heard on bill, answer and proof" means that the case was heard on a basis of the bill in equity filed by the insurer, the answer that was filed by the respondents, and the proof presented in support of the various contentions. Here the decree or decision in the lower court was in favor of the insurer, and the Dietlins appealed.

plainant was directed by the decree to refund to the respondents the sum of $14.60, being the amount of the premium paid at the time of the execution of the application for the policy. From that decree the respondents have appealed to this court.

The material facts are not in dispute. The application for the policy was made by Donald H. Dietlin, hereinafter sometimes referred to as the "insured," and is dated February 28, 1959. Listed therein for inclusion as insured lives in the policy were all of respondents as well as Kathleen, and in reference to the latter the application states that "About 2 months ago Kathleen had pneumonia after which her heart was impaired & has been treated at St Josephs Hosp. Prov RI since then." In the course of the preparation of the application, James R. Lockett, complainant's soliciting agent, questioned whether in the light of her condition Kathleen would be covered in the policy. He told the insured and his wife that Kathleen's name and those of the other minor children were required to be listed on the application, but that he could not assure them that the company would include her as an insured family member.

In the course of the processing of the application by complainant, there was stapled to it a company form designated "Underwriting Data Sheet" on which, under a heading entitled "Company's Action On Application," appear the notations "3-16 Delete Kathleen" and "Deleted Kathleen," the latter having been approved on March 24, 1959.

Thereafter a life insurance policy designating the insured, his wife, and all of their minor children as insured family members was received by Lockett from complainant. Attached to it was a copy of the application and a document designated "Amendment To Application," the former document having been affixed apparently pursuant to clause 19 of the policy which provided in part that "The entire contract between the Company and the applicant consists of the policy and the written application, a copy of which is attached at issue." That amendment, which required the signature of the insured, provided that Kathleen be deleted from the list of the proposed family members on the application and that no coverage should be provided under the policy for her.

Not being able to contact the insured who was not at home when he called, Lockett left the policy and attached documents with the insured's wife and requested that she have her husband execute the amendment. Although the version given by Mrs. Dietlin on this phase of the cause differed slightly from that of Lockett, respondents make no contention that the acceptance by the trial justice of the Lockett version was either clearly wrong or that in accrediting that account he overlooked or misconceived any evidence. In those circumstances in accordance with our well-settled rule his finding on that issue is conclusive.

The amendment had not been signed by the insured when Kathleen died on April 2, 1959 and subsequent refusals so to do resulted in the instant suit being brought.

The only question is whether the insurance policy is in effect.

In the formation of a contract of insurance as in other contracts there must be a manifestation of mutual assent in the form of an offer or proposal by one party and an acceptance thereof by the other. Ordinarily, the application for a policy is the offer and before a contractual relationship can come into being the offer must be unconditionally accepted. An acceptance which is equivocal or upon condition or with a limitation is a counteroffer and requires acceptance by the original offeror before a contractual relationship can exist.

In this case the application or original offer was for a policy insuring the lives of all respondents as well as of Kathleen. The complainant was not required to nor did it accept that offer. Instead it attached the amendment to the contract of insurance, thereby proposing to the insured that there be deleted from the policy one of the lives included in the original application. This constituted a counteroffer and required the unequivocal assent of the insured as a prerequisite to a completed contract. By the terms of such offer that assent could be manifested only by the insured affixing his signature to the amendment. Because that signature was not obtained the counteroffer was not accepted and the policy did not take effect as a contract of insurance.

The respondents' appeal is denied and dismissed, the decree appealed from is affirmed, and the cause is remanded to the superior court for further proceedings.[26]

---

[26]The case was sent back (remanded) to the superior court for the procedures necessary to carry out the original decision.

Questions for Review

1. Briefly explain what a contract is.

2. How do a bilateral and a unilateral contract differ? Explain why a life insurance contract is a unilateral contract.

3. Define an offer. What are the requirements of a valid offer? How can an offer be terminated?

4. What is meant by a counteroffer? What is the legal effect of making a counteroffer?

5. Define and briefly discuss the meaning of consideration as it applies to informal contracts. Would a contract to sell a family heirloom for approximately twice its fair market value be supported by a legally adequate consideration?

6. If a mentally infirm person makes a contract, what are the possible legal effects?

7. What is meant by the legal term *minor?* What is the general law concerning minority and the capacity to contract? What types of contracts can a minor *not* disaffirm?

8. Many states have statutes relating to the minor as an applicant for insurance. Describe the common characteristics of these statutes.

9. Must a life insurance contract always be in writing to be enforceable?

10. Why does the Statute of Frauds, as it is commonly enacted, not apply to the life insurance contract?

11. Briefly summarize the parol evidence rule. Why is this rule important in connection with the life insurance contract? What are some of the exceptions to the parol evidence rule?

3   AGENCY

Chapter Outline

The term *agent* is broadly defined as a person who acts for another person, the agent's **principal**. The term *person* here includes organizations, such as corporations and partnerships, as well as human beings (natural persons). This broad definition of agency includes employer-employee and employer-independent contractor relationships.[1] Thus, an insurer's vice presidents, typists, programmers, maintenance workers, soliciting agents, and actuaries are all its agents under the broadest definition of the word *agent*.

The fundamental rule of agency law is that acts of an agent, within the scope of the agent's power, are acts of the principal. Courts frequently state this rule in Latin: *Qui facit per alium facit per se*, which means "He who acts through another acts himself."

Generally, a person can appoint an agent to perform any act that the person might have performed.[2] However, a person cannot appoint an agent to vote in a public election, make a statement under oath, or sign a will. If a contract calls for personal services, such as those of an artist or a surgeon, the artist or surgeon cannot properly delegate the work to an agent. Similarly, a fiduciary cannot delegate to an agent the performance of matters in which the fiduciary must use judgment.[3] A person can delegate almost everything else to an agent.

By its very nature, a corporation must carry on all its business through agents. A corporation is an artificial being—invisible, intangible, and existing only in contemplation of law.[4] It has a legal, but not an actual, existence. It is a legal entity, separate and distinct from its owner, or owners, authorized by law to transact a specific kind of business. Ordinarily, an insurer is a corporation authorized to transact an insurance business. All the work of a typical insurer is carried on by the natural persons who are its agents.[5]

It has been said that "most of the world's work is performed by agents."[6] This is true under the broad definition of *agency* noted above.

However, **agent** can also be defined more narrowly to mean a person who acts for another person, a principal, in contractual dealings with third parties.[7] Under this definition, an agent is a person who creates, modifies, performs, or terminates contracts for another person. Thus, under this definition, the soliciting agent is an agent of the insurer, but the typist, programmer, and maintenance worker are not agents. In this book, we are concerned primarily with contract law. Therefore, the term *agent* will hereafter be confined to this narrower definition unless otherwise noted.

Power and Authority

The essence of agency is power. The agent has the power to subject the principal to contractual liability and to create contractual rights for the principal. For example, if Priscilla appoints Amos to be her agent to sell some corn, and Amos contracts on

---

[1]Employer-employee and employer-independent contractor relationships are discussed in Chapter 24, "Insurers and Agents as Employers."

[2]Although a *contract* to commit a crime or tort is unenforceable, there can be an *agency* to commit a crime or tort. This is because the law wishes to hold the principal liable for a criminal or tortious act that the principal directs another to do.

[3]A *fiduciary* is a person who occupies a position of special trust and confidence in handling the affairs or funds of another person.

[4]Ballentine's Law Dictionary 275 (3d ed. 1969).

[5]Such natural persons are subagents in some cases, as where a corporation hires another corporation as its agent.

[6]Harold Gill Reuschlein & William A. Gregory, The Law of Agency and Partnership 3 (2d ed. 1990) [hereinafter Reuschlein].

[7]Unfortunately, terminology in the law of agency is sometimes inconsistent or overlapping.

Priscilla's behalf to sell the corn to Theodore, a contract has been created between Priscilla and Theodore. Amos had the power, and in this case the actual authority, to create a contract for Priscilla. Both Priscilla and Theodore are contractually bound exactly as if Priscilla herself had negotiated the contract with Theodore. Amos is not a party to the contract.

Although power is sometimes confused with actual authority, power is broader than actual authority. An agent sometimes has power to bind a principal to a contract when the agent has no actual authority to do so. This will be explained below in the subsection entitled "Apparent Authority."

Capacity of Principal and Agent

The capacity necessary to be a principal differs from that necessary to be an agent. This difference results from the dissimilar roles of principal and agent.

Capacity to Be a Principal

As a general rule, any person who has the capacity to contract can appoint an agent and be a principal. Most natural persons have the capacity to contract and therefore can be principals. Organizations that are legal entities have the capacity to contract and can be principals. A corporation is a legal entity and can be a principal. However, its capacity to contract, and hence its capacity to appoint agents, is limited. It can appoint agents only for those purposes within its corporate powers.

The contractual capacity of partnerships, on the other hand, is not so well settled. One view is that partnerships cannot be principals because they are not legal entities and therefore do not have the capacity to contract. According to this view, an agent of a partnership is actually the agent of the individual partners. Another view is that the partnership *is* a legal entity and thus can be a principal. Whether or not a partnership is a legal entity, the partners will be individually liable on the contract.[8]

Persons without capacity to contract cannot be principals. An incompetent person cannot cure his incapacity, or enlarge a limited capacity, by appointing someone with contractual capacity to act as an agent. Modern courts hold that a minor can contract through an agent for necessaries. Other contracts a minor makes through an agent will be voidable by the minor.

Mentally infirm persons who have no contractual capacity cannot appoint agents. A person who is so intoxicated or drugged that his reason is impaired cannot appoint an agent, although such a person might do so when not intoxicated or drugged.

Capacity to Be an Agent

Almost any person can be an agent. An agent need not have contractual capacity because the contract that the agent forms is the principal's contract, not the agent's. Therefore, a minor, a mentally infirm person, or a person under the influence of alcohol or other drugs can act as an agent if she can receive and convey ideas. A principal with contractual capacity cannot avoid a contract completed by an agent who lacks contractual capacity on the ground of the agent's incapacity.

---

[8]REUSCHLEIN, *supra* note 6, at 264–65.

Partnerships and corporations can act as agents. The general rules of agency law apply whether the agent is a natural person, a partnership, or a corporation.

If the law requires an agent to have a license, the agent cannot legally act without one. Insurance and real estate agents, attorneys-at-law, and other agents whose activities involve the public must be licensed before they can represent others.

Creation of the Principal-Agent Relationship

An agency relationship can be created in several ways. First, a principal can give express authority to an agent to act on the principal's behalf. Second, the agent will have incidental authority to do the things normally incident to performing the agency. Express authority and incidental authority are two types of actual authority. Third, an agent will have apparent authority if the principal's conduct has led a third person to believe that the agent has express authority when, in fact, the agent does not. Finally, an agency will be created if a principal ratifies the unauthorized act of a purported agent.

Actual Authority

Actual authority is the authority to act on the principal's behalf that the agent reasonably believes the principal has given him. Note that it is what the agent *reasonably believes* that controls and not what the principal actually might have intended. As with offer and acceptance in the formation of a contract, it is the manifestation of the intent of the parties that the court will examine to determine whether an agency was created.

As noted above, there are two types of actual authority, express authority and incidental authority.

Express Authority.   A principal can, orally or in writing, appoint an agent to act on the principal's behalf. If the principal communicates this appointment to the agent, and the agent consents to the agency, the agent will have actual *express authority* to act. Consideration is not necessary. An agent can act with or without being paid.

Incidental Authority.   When an agent has express authority to perform an act, the agent also has *incidental authority* to do all the things normally required in order to perform the act. Such incidental authority is implied. Although incidental authority is implied, it is a type of actual authority. Incidental authority is necessary because it is often impossible to specify in detail everything the agent must do to carry out the agency. Therefore, unless the principal directs otherwise, the agent will have the incidental authority to act in accordance with the general customs of the business. For example, a life insurance soliciting agent usually has incidental authority to accept a check in payment of the initial premium for a life insurance policy. The agent would not have incidental authority to accept a motorboat in payment of the initial premium because this would not be in accordance with the general customs of the insurance business.

Apparent Authority

Ordinarily, a principal must consent to the agency relationship if he is to be bound by the acts of an agent. Nevertheless, if the principal's conduct has led a third party to reasonably believe that a purported agent has actual authority when the purported agent does not, the purported agent's contractual dealings with the third party will bind the principal. The purported agent will have ***apparent authority***, and hence the power, to bind the principal. However, the third party cannot disregard irregularities in the purported agent's behavior if the irregularities should have aroused suspicion in the mind of a reasonable person. In other words, the situation must have been such that the principal's actions would have actually misled a reasonable person. A third party attempting to establish apparent authority has the responsibility of proving that he did, in fact, believe that the agent was acting within the scope of the agent's authority and that the facts were such as to justify the third party in that belief.

Apparent authority can arise in a situation in which the agent has no actual authority. The agent may be an imposter who, through carelessness on the part of the principal, appears to a third party to be the principal's agent. In one case, a hotel desk was left unattended, and an imposter, posing as the desk clerk, was given money and jewelry by a guest to put into the hotel safe. The imposter gave the guest a receipt and absconded with the money and jewelry. Carelessness in leaving the desk unattended made the owner of the hotel liable for the loss that the guest suffered. The imposter had apparent authority.[9]

In other cases, the principal has forbidden the agent to exercise the incidental authority that is customary in the particular business, but third parties are unaware of this limitation of authority. Apparent authority will be created if the agent exercises the customary incidental authority, because a third party could reasonably believe that the agent had actual incidental authority. For example, as noted above, it is customary in the life insurance business for soliciting agents to collect the initial premium. Suppose that a life insurer told its soliciting agent that he lacked authority to collect the initial premium but did not mention this on the application. If an applicant paid the initial premium to the soliciting agent, who absconded with it, the applicant would not have to pay again because the agent had apparent authority to collect the premium. Payment to the agent would be payment to the insurer.

An agent whose agency is terminated may still possess lingering apparent authority. Third persons who have dealt with the agent may be justified in believing that the agent still retains actual authority. The principal must make certain the third persons have notice of the termination of authority, or the agent will have lingering apparent authority. For example, suppose that for several years Prince, who manufactures jewelry, employed Ajax to buy diamonds for Prince. Ajax bought the diamonds from Thurmond. Prince later fired Ajax, terminating Ajax's actual authority, but failed to notify Thurmond of the termination. Ajax then wrongfully bought diamonds from Thurmond, telling Thurmond to bill Prince, and absconded with the diamonds. Prince is bound by the contract because Ajax had lingering apparent authority; Thurmond reasonably believed that Ajax was still Prince's agent.

Lingering apparent authority might also result if the agent is permitted to retain indicia of authority. ***Indicia of authority*** means indications, signs, or evidence of authority. For example, if an insurer discharges an agent but permits the agent to retain credentials or documents that had been used in carrying out the agency, these credentials or documents may create the appearance of authority to third parties. Thus, if Phyllis Hayes had been the duly authorized soliciting agent of the XYZ Life Insurance Company, and if she still possesses a supply of life insurance application forms and a rate book after her agency has terminated, a client would have no reason to doubt that Hayes continues to represent that insurer as an agent. For this reason,

---

[9]Kanelles v. Lock, 12 Ohio App. 210 (1919).

insurers usually require the surrender of all such indicia of authority at the termination of an agent's contract.

The principal can maintain a suit for damages against an agent whose use of apparent authority has caused the principal to suffer a loss. However, there are often practical problems in trying to recover damages from such an agent. For example, an agent might have absconded with money or other property that he obtained from the third party, and the principal might not be able to locate the agent. Or the agent might have spent the money and have no other property from which he can pay the damages. Because of these practical problems and the costs of litigation, a principal is wise to avoid conduct that will cause agents to have apparent authority.

Ratification

Sometimes, an agent who is authorized to represent a principal in one line of business makes a contract in the name of that principal in an entirely different business. For example, an agent authorized to sell the principal's automobiles might sell one of the principal's trucks even though the agent was not authorized to sell the truck. Or a person who has no agency authority whatever might purport to make a contract for another person. In either situation, the transaction will not have any binding effect on the purported principal if the purported principal's conduct has not led the third party to reasonably believe that the purported agent had actual authority. However, if the transaction would be advantageous to the purported principal, the purported principal may wish to adopt it as his own by ratifying it.

Ratification is a purported principal's validation of a purported agent's unauthorized act. Generally speaking, if a principal can authorize an act before it is done, he can ratify the same act after it is done. The latter relationship is agency by ratification.

Requirements for Ratification.   An effective ratification must meet certain requirements. First, the person who performed the unauthorized act must have purported to have acted on behalf of the principal. The person must have represented himself as an agent. The third person must have reasonably believed he was dealing with an agent.

Second, no one except the person in whose name the contract was made can ratify the act. Thus, if Alice Anderson purports to make a contract for Paul Putnam, then Marilyn Bauer cannot ratify that act. No one except Paul Putnam can ratify that act.

Third, if the ratification is to be effective, the ratifier must know all the material facts about the transaction at the time of ratification. If the ratifier was not aware of all the material facts, he can, on learning the truth, avoid the ratification.

Fourth, a principal can ratify only an entire transaction. A principal cannot select those parts of a transaction that are beneficial to him, ratify them, and reject other parts.

Fifth, intervening events sometimes nullify the power of ratification. For example, the third person with whom the purported agent dealt is free to withdraw before the ratification. If the third person withdraws, an attempted ratification will be ineffective. Moreover, the death or loss of contractual capacity of the third person will destroy the purported principal's right to ratify.

A change in the circumstances of the transaction will also nullify the right to ratify. For example, if a purported agent sells the purported principal's cow to a third person, and the cow dies before ratification of the transaction, the purported principal's right to ratify is lost.

The lapse of time can destroy the right to ratify. The ratification must be made within a reasonable time.

Form of the Ratification.   Ordinarily, any conduct indicating approval of the purported agent's act is sufficient to constitute an effective ratification. Thus, ratification can consist of express words, spoken or written, or it can be implied from conduct by the purported principal clearly indicating that she ratifies the act of the purported agent and accepts the act as her own.

Even if the principal does not intend to ratify the purported agent's act, ratification will be the legal effect if the principal accepts the benefits of the purported agent's act. For example, if a soliciting agent collects a renewal premium on a life insurance policy, without authority to do so, and remits the premium to the insurer, the insurer's acceptance of the premium will constitute ratification of the soliciting agent's act.

Furthermore, a principal will ordinarily be held to have ratified a purported agent's act if, with full knowledge of the facts, the principal fails to repudiate the act within a reasonable time.

Effects of the Ratification.   An effective ratification binds the principal exactly as if the agent had acted according to the principal's directions. When a person ratifies the act of another, the ratification becomes effective as of the date of the purported agent's act.

Ratification of an unauthorized contract will usually relieve the agent of liability to the principal for acting without authority. It will also, ordinarily, relieve the agent of liability to the third party. Moreover, the agent will be entitled to the customary commission or other compensation.

Subagents

A *subagent* is a person employed by an agent to assist in performing functions for the principal. The principal must empower the agent to appoint the subagent. The agent must agree with the principal to be primarily responsible for the subagent's conduct. The subagent is an agent of both the principal and the appointing agent.[10]

Soliciting agents of insurers are often subagents. For example, when an insurer appoints a general agent for a specified territory and both parties agree that the general agent shall hire and be primarily responsible for the conduct of soliciting agents, then the soliciting agents are subagents. Even if the insurer does not give the general agent express authority to hire such soliciting agents, the general agent may have incidental authority to do so. In either case, the soliciting agents are subagents and, as such, are agents of both the insurer and the general agent.

Limitations of the Agent's Authority

A principal can limit the authority of her agent. Such limitations will be binding on parties with whom the agent deals if the limitations are properly communicated to those parties and if the limitations themselves are proper. Proper limitations are reasonable, legal, and not against public policy.

---

[10]RESTATEMENT (SECOND) OF AGENCY § 5 (1957).

One improper limitation is a statement in a life insurance policy attempting to make the soliciting agent the applicant's agent for the purpose of taking the application. Ordinarily, this limitation will not be effective. Another limitation that is ineffective in most states is one that stipulates that the knowledge of the agent will not be imputed to the insurer. This limitation goes against the rule of agency law that knowledge of the agent is knowledge of the principal. This rule is discussed in the section below.

A statement in an insurance policy that no agent can exercise certain powers except in a manner spelled out in the policy is effective as to some agents but not as to others. This limitation can be effective as to agents with limited contractual powers, such as a life insurer's soliciting agents, but ineffective as to agents who have full authority to contract, such as the insurer's senior officers. For example, a policy clause might effectively prohibit the waiver of any condition in the policy except in writing by specified officers. However, this clause itself could be deleted by an agent with full contracting authority.

Proper communication to applicants of limitations on the soliciting agent's authority is essential if those limitations are to be effective. The applicant usually is not on notice of limitations of the agent's authority contained in the policy before the policy has been delivered. The applicant, therefore, is not bound by such policy limitations as to acts of the agent occurring before delivery of the policy if the applicant could reasonably assume that the agent has authority to do such acts. For this reason, insurers often put notice of limitations on their soliciting agents' authority in the application. Such notice of limitations is ordinarily binding on the applicant who signs the application.

Knowledge of the Agent

A rule of agency law is that knowledge of the agent concerning business transactions that the agent conducts for the principal will be considered knowledge of the principal. This rule applies whether or not the agent actually tells the principal what the agent knows.

Life and health insurance soliciting agents usually fill in the application for the applicant, and the insurer's medical examiner fills in the medical certificate. These agents of the insurer sometimes include incorrect statements. If the insurer's agent knowingly has written in an incorrect statement, courts in a majority of states have held that the knowledge of the agent is the knowledge of the insurer. Thus, in these states, if the insurer's underwriters issue a policy that they would not have issued had they had the actual knowledge of the soliciting agent, the insurer will nevertheless be bound on the contract. That is, the contract will be valid despite the incorrect statements in the application and the insurer cannot maintain a suit for rescission of the contract. *Rescission* is an equitable remedy in which a court declares a contract void because of material misrepresentation or mistake.

However, a rule of contract law is that a person who accepts a written contract is presumed to know and assent to its contents. Thus, in the minority of states, the applicant, upon receiving the policy and the attached application, has a duty to read the application and inform the insurer of any incorrect statements. The insurer can then maintain a suit for rescission of the contract if the incorrect statements are material. Thus, in a minority of states, the rule of agency law that knowledge of the agent is knowledge of the principal will not prevent the insurer from rescinding the contract even though the agent had actual knowledge of a material misrepresentation in the application.

Payment to the Agent

Payment to the agent, where the agent has express or incidental authority to collect payment, is payment to the principal. However, the general rule is that an agent authorized to sell has no incidental authority to collect payment. On the other hand, an agent sometimes has apparent authority and therefore power to collect payment.

If a third party has made payment to an agent who has express, incidental, or apparent authority to receive such payment on behalf of the principal, the third party will not have to pay again if the agent does not turn the money over to the principal. The principal cannot win in a lawsuit against the third party for the money. For example, suppose Agnes, an agent who has express authority to receive payments, collects a large sum of money owed to Preston, the principal, from Debra, the debtor. If Agnes then loses the money while gambling at the race track, Preston cannot recover a second payment from Debra. Payment to Agnes is payment to Preston. The authority of an insurance agent to collect premiums is discussed in Chapter 4, "Agency in Life and Health Insurance."

Principal and Agent

In agency relationships, it is the principal's business that is transacted. Therefore, the agent has a duty to respond to the wishes of the principal in regard to that business. The principal has control over the conduct and activities of the agent.

Control by the Principal

The degree of control that the principal exercises over the agent and the agent's acts depends on whether the agent is an employee-agent or an independent contractor-agent. The principal exercises control over the means and method of doing the job if the agent is an employee-agent. An independent contractor-agent follows his own discretion in carrying out the job. For example, an attorney who works in a law firm is ordinarily an independent contractor-agent of his client. Independent contractors are discussed in Chapter 24, "Insurers and Agents as Employers."

Agent's Duties

The agent has duties that spring from the agent's fiduciary role, from the agency relationship, and from any contract between the agent and the principal governing their rights and duties.

Duty of Loyalty.   An agent is a fiduciary. A *fiduciary* is a person who occupies a position of special trust and confidence in handling the affairs or funds of another person. All fiduciaries have a duty of loyalty. A trustee is a fiduciary with a duty of loyalty toward the trust beneficiary, and an agent is a fiduciary with a duty of loyalty toward the principal. A duty of loyalty means that the agent must act solely for the benefit of the principal in every matter connected with the agency. The agent must exercise the utmost good faith and integrity in dealing with the principal.

An agent must not deal for himself when he should be dealing for the principal. For example, in a case in which an agent was sent to purchase a parcel of land for his principal but took title in his own name, the court held that the agent had breached his duty of loyalty and that the land belonged to the principal.[11]

If the agent has an interest that is adverse to the principal's interest, the agent must reveal his interest to the principal. For instance, if the agent's personal dealings with a third person might affect the agent's judgment when dealing for the principal, the agent must tell this to the principal.

An agent must not serve two principals whose interests are adverse unless both principals consent. A contract negotiated by an agent acting for both parties to the contract is voidable by a party who did not know that the agent was also acting for the other party.

The agent must be scrupulously honest in all her dealings with the principal. Agency funds or property held by the agent must be used for agency purposes only. Any use of such funds or property for a nonagency purpose will subject the agent to liability to the principal for the funds or property and for profits made from their use.

If the agent receives anything of value from a third party with whom she is dealing on behalf of the principal, the agent must account for it to the principal. Such items of value belong to the principal.

Duty of Obedience.   The agent has a duty to follow the principal's lawful and reasonable instructions. Moreover, the agent has a duty to act within the bounds of the authority given by the principal. Even if the principal's limitation or termination of the agent's authority breaches an agency contract, the agent must obey the principal (although the agent can maintain a suit against the principal for the breach).

Duty of Reasonable Care and Skill.   An agent has a duty to carry out the agency with reasonable care. The agent must exercise the skill ordinarily possessed by persons in the same business. The agent has a duty not to undertake business that the agent is incapable of performing properly.

Principal's Remedies

A principal has a variety of legal and equitable remedies against an agent who violates his agency duties. For example, in some circumstances, if a third person sues the principal as a result of the agent's wrongful acts, and the principal loses the lawsuit, the principal can recover from the agent the money paid to the third person.

The principal can also recover from the agent for conversion of the principal's property. *Conversion* is an unauthorized act that deprives an owner of his property. Conversion is a tort. A *tort* is a violation of a duty to another person imposed by law, rather than by contract, causing harm to the other person and for which the law provides a remedy, often damages. For example, if a third person pays to the agent money belonging to the principal, and the agent does not give the money to the principal, the principal can maintain an action for conversion against the agent.

---

[11]Krzysko v. Gaudynski, 242 N.W. 186 (Wis. 1932).

The agent may also be liable to the principal for damages in tort if the agent causes loss to the principal by exceeding the authority given by the principal. Furthermore, the principal can maintain a suit in equity against the agent for an accounting if the accounts are complicated.

The principal can deny the agent compensation for services that the agent has performed if the agent is guilty of fraud, disobedience, or other misconduct. Finally, the principal has a right to dismiss the agent before the termination date of an employment contract if the agent has breached an agency duty of loyalty, obedience, or reasonable care.

Principal's Duties

The principal sometimes has a duty to provide the agent with an opportunity to work. This is true in the case of a selling agent who works on a commission basis. The principal must provide the necessary goods to sell.

In most instances, the principal has a duty to compensate the agent. The principal must also reimburse the agent for authorized payments that the agent made and indemnify her for liabilities incurred in acting for the principal, unless their contract indicates otherwise.

The principal has a duty to keep accounts of what he owes the agent. The principal often has statutory obligations to deduct various amounts from the agent's compensation for remission to government agencies, as for example, income tax payments. In addition, the principal may have other duties toward the agent under workers' compensation laws, unemployment compensation laws, pension laws, and other employment laws.

Agent's Remedies

The agent can maintain a suit for damages against the principal if the principal breaches the agency contract. However, the agent usually cannot sue for specific performance of the agency contract. Specific performance is an equitable remedy requiring that a contract be carried out according to its terms. Because both principal and agent must consent to the agency relationship, the remedy of specific performance, which would require the principal to continue the agency relationship against her will, would be inappropriate. In addition, the court will usually grant specific performance only if both parties have a right to this remedy. The principal does not have a right to specific performance of the agency contract because to force the agent to continue the agency relationship would be to force him into involuntary servitude (slavery). The U.S. Constitution forbids involuntary servitude.

The rule that a court will not require the principal to specifically perform an agency contract—that is, continue the agency relationship—does not always apply if the agent proves that the principal unlawfully discriminated against him or wrongfully discharged him. Employment discrimination and wrongful discharge are discussed in Chapter 24, "Insurers and Agents as Employers."

The agent sometimes has a right to a lien on property belonging to the principal that is in the agent's lawful possession. A *lien* is a right to retain another person's property as security for a debt. Unless otherwise agreed, an agent in lawful possession of property belonging to the principal has a lien on that property for money due her from the principal as a result of the agency relationship. The agent can keep possession of the property until the principal pays her the money.

Principal, Agent, and Third Persons

A principal becomes a party to an informal contract made for him by his agent if such transaction was within the agent's power. The principal's liability to the third person is spelled out in the contract.

Principal's Liabilities to Third Persons

The principal will be bound by a contract made by an agent just as if the principal had made it personally. The principal will also be bound by a contract formed by the unauthorized act of a purported agent if the principal later ratifies the act.

The third person will ordinarily have all the remedies available to any contracting party. However, if the agent acted with an improper motive, and the third person knew this, the principal will not be bound by the contract.

The principal can be liable to third persons for torts committed by the agent in the scope of her employment. This subject will be covered in greater detail in Chapter 24, "Insurers and Agents as Employers."

Principal's Rights against Third Persons

The principal can enforce a contract made by his agent. A contract created by an agent on behalf of a principal binds the third person to the contract just as if the principal had negotiated the contract.

The principal has a cause of action against a third person who knowingly induces or assists the agent to violate fiduciary duties to the principal. A third person who bribes, coerces, or fraudulently induces the agent to act contrary to the principal's interests will be liable to the principal for the harm that results.

Agent's Liabilities to Third Persons

A person who represents herself as an agent makes an implied promise to the third person that she has authority to act for the principal. If a person purporting to act as an agent actually has no authority, the principal is not bound and no contract is formed. The purported agent will be liable for any harm caused to the third person.

An agent will also be liable for other misrepresentations made to a third person if the third person reasonably relied on the misrepresentation to his detriment. Such a misrepresentation is a tort against the third person. An agent has a duty not to injure third persons, regardless of agency status.

Agent's Rights against Third Persons

The agent who negotiates a contract for a principal is not a party to the contract and is not entitled to maintain an action on the contract. The causes of action that agents have against third persons ordinarily arise from unlawful interference with the agency itself, as when a third person improperly prevents the agent's employment or causes the agent to be fired.

General Agents and Special Agents

Agents are often classified as *general agents* or *special agents*. Unfortunately, the courts have been inconsistent in their definitions of these terms. The definitions used in the life and health insurance industry are also inconsistent. Moreover, the legal definitions are not the same as the life and health insurance industry definitions. Finally, the terms *general agent* and *special agent* are not used consistently throughout the insurance industry. These terms may mean one thing when applied to life and health insurance agents and another when applied to agents for other types of insurance.

Legal Definitions

Although the courts have been inconsistent in their definitions of *general agent* and *special agent,* the definitions in the American Law Institute's *Restatement (Second) of Agency* are most commonly used. The *Restatement* defines a general agent as "an agent authorized to conduct a series of transactions involving a continuity of service," whereas a special agent is "an agent authorized to conduct a single transaction or a series of transactions not involving continuity of service."[12] Thus, continuity of service is the hallmark of the general agent. Continuity of service gives the general agent power to bind the principal in situations where the special agent would not have power. The courts distinguish between general agents and special agents because of the difference in their power to bind the principal.

Life and Health Insurance Industry Definitions

In life and health insurance terminology, a general agent is ordinarily a person holding a franchise to develop an insurer's business within a certain geographical area. The general agent hires soliciting agents and clerical staff to help run the general agency. Soliciting agents find prospects for insurance sales, determine the prospects' needs, and sell the insurer's products. Soliciting agents are sometimes called special agents to contrast them with general agents.

The imprecision with which the terms *general agent* and *special agent* are used often creates confusion. However, the title of the agent does not govern the agent's authority. Rather, the facts of the situation will determine whether the agent has either actual or apparent authority to do a particular act.

Termination of the Agent's Power

An agent's power terminates when the agent's actual and apparent authority terminate. Actual authority terminates by agreement, by act, or by operation of law. Apparent authority ends when third persons no longer have reason to believe that the agent has authority to act for the principal.

Termination of Actual Authority

An agent's actual authority can terminate by agreement between principal and agent, by an act of the principal or of the agent, or by operation of law.

---

[12]RESTATEMENT (SECOND) OF AGENCY § 3 (1957).

Agreement between Principal and Agent.   Sometimes, the principal and agent agree that the agency is to last for a specified period of time. In such a case, the agent's actual authority will terminate at the end of this period. In other cases, the agency agreement specifies that the agent will have authority until the accomplishment of some objective. When that objective is accomplished, the agent's actual authority will terminate.

Act of Principal or Agent.   Either the principal or the agent can terminate the agency relationship; the principal can dismiss the agent, or the agent can resign. The power to terminate exists even if the termination breaches the agency contract. If such a breach occurs, the injured party usually can recover damages from the other party.

Operation of Law.   If certain events occur, the agent's authority terminates by operation of law. *Operation of law* refers to the determination of rights and obligations through the automatic effects of the law and not by any direct act of an affected party. As a general rule, the death of the principal will cause the agent's authority to terminate by operation of law, even if the agent and third persons with whom the agent is dealing are unaware of the death. Death of the agent also terminates the agency by operation of law.

The principal's permanent loss of contractual capacity (for example, by reason of a major stroke that renders the principal permanently comatose) will usually cause the agent's authority to terminate by operation of law. Although an agent does not need contractual capacity, the agent's authority terminates when the agent loses capacity to perform the authorized act. For example, in one case, an insurance agent's authority terminated when paralysis made it impossible for the agent to handle the business.[13] If the agent loses her license or fails to qualify for a required license, the agency will terminate.

A change of circumstances sometimes causes the agency to terminate by operation of law. For example, bankruptcy of the principal can cause the agency to terminate. Bankruptcy of the agent will cause the agency to terminate if the agent's financial condition affects the principal to such an extent that, with knowledge of the facts, the principal would have revoked the agent's authority.

War ordinarily suspends commercial activities between citizens of enemy countries. Therefore, if war makes an agent the enemy of the principal's country, the agency usually terminates by operation of law.

Termination of Apparent Authority

If a third person knows that the agency has terminated, the agent will no longer be able to bind the principal in dealings with that person. However, the agent will have lingering apparent authority, and hence power to bind the principal, if third persons are unaware of the termination. Ordinarily, the principal must give direct notice of the termination to parties who have dealt with the agent if the principal wants to avoid the problems that sometimes occur when an unscrupulous agent has apparent authority.

---

[13]Citizen's Home Ins. Co. v. Glisson, 61 S.E.2d 859 (Va. 1950).

Effect of Termination

When the agent's authority terminates, the agent's right to act for the principal ends. However, the agent still has the duty to account to the principal for acts done prior to termination of the agency.

Summary

An agent is a person who acts for another in contractual dealings with third persons. The essence of agency is power. The agent has the power to subject the principal to contractual liability and to create contractual rights for the principal. Acts of the agent, within the scope of the agent's power, are acts of the principal. Knowledge of the agent concerning business she transacts for the principal is usually considered knowledge of the principal.

A person must have contractual capacity to be a principal, but an agent need not have contractual capacity. Corporations can be principals or agents.

An agency relationship can be created by the principal's express grant of authority to the agent. The agent will have incidental authority to do the things normally incident to carrying out the agency. Apparent authority also creates an agency relationship. Apparent authority results from conduct of the principal that causes a third person to reasonably believe that a purported agent has authority to contract for the principal. Finally, an agency relationship can be created by ratification. Ratification occurs when a purported principal validates a purported agent's unauthorized act. An effective ratification binds the principal exactly as if the agent had acted according to the principal's directions.

A principal can limit the agent's authority. Proper limitations, properly communicated to third persons, will be binding on the third persons.

The agent is a fiduciary with duties of loyalty and obedience toward the principal. The agent also has a duty to carry out the agency with reasonable care and skill. The principal can take legal action against an agent who violates her agency duties.

In some instances, the principal has a duty to provide the agent with an opportunity to work. In most instances, the principal has a duty to compensate the agent and to keep accounts of what he owes the agent.

The principal is liable to a third person if the agent acts within his power in contracting with the third person. The principal also has the right to enforce the contract against the third person. A principal has a cause of action against a third person who knowingly induces or assists the agent to violate fiduciary duties.

A person who represents that he is an agent when such is not the case will be liable for harm resulting to a third person to whom the misrepresentation is made. An agent will also be liable for certain other misrepresentations made to third persons.

An agent's actual authority can terminate by agreement of principal and agent, by an action of the principal or of the agent, or by operation of law. Death of the principal usually terminates the agency. Death of the agent always terminates the agency. The principal's loss of contractual capacity or the agent's loss of a necessary license will cause the agency to terminate. Bankruptcy of principal or agent can also cause the agency to terminate. When the agency terminates, the agent no longer has the right to act for the principal, but the agent has the duty to account to the principal for actions taken prior to the termination.

ILLUSTRATIVE CASE

In this case, an insurer, through its chief claims consultant, was held to have ratified an unauthorized act of the insurer's soliciting agent.

THE PRUDENTIAL INSURANCE COMPANY OF AMERICA,
Plaintiff-Appellee

v.

WILLIAM D. (BILL) CLARK and MARGARET CLARK,
Defendants-Appellants[14]
United States Court of Appeals, Fifth Circuit

---

[14]456 F.2d 932 (1972).

Before THORNBERRY, MORGAN, and CLARK, Circuit Judges. CLARK, Circuit Judge.

This appeal requires that we review a case tried to a jury on disputed evidence. . . . We will consider the facts in the light most favorable to the jury's findings.

Steve Clark (Steve), a young single man residing with his parents, who are the defendants and appellants here, enlisted in the Marine Corps in January 1966 and thereafter purchased a 10,000 dollar life insurance policy with the World Service Life Insurance Company (World Life). This policy has no war risk and aviation exclusion clauses. In late 1966, Steve was contacted by Robert Brumell, an agent employed by Prudential Insurance Company of America (Prudential) to sell its insurance policies, who urged Steve to drop the World Life policy and to permit Prudential to replace it with one of its life insurance policies. Brumell advised Steve that he could obtain a 10,000 dollar policy similar to the World Life policy without any limiting war risk or aviation exclusion clause. An application was completed and mailed to Prudential for approval. Steve, meanwhile, in reliance upon Brumell's representation, dropped his World Life policy. Subsequently, Prudential mailed the application back to Brumell in order to secure some additional, minor information. The jury found that Prudential issued this initial 10,000 dollar policy when the application was returned to Brumell. The policy, however, was never delivered to Steve because when Brumell received the policy and the request for additional information Steve had already left for Marine training in California. Brumell contacted a Prudential agent in California and asked him to go out to the Marine base and secure the requested information from Steve. The California agent balked because he wanted to share in the commission which would be paid to the writing agent. It took six weeks before Brumell and Prudential's California agent could reach an agreement as to how they would divide these funds. By this time, Steve had been shipped to Viet Nam. We have no way of knowing the contents of that first Prudential policy. Presumably it was destroyed pursuant to Prudential's internal procedure of eliminating all records over thirteen months old.

A year later, in early May 1968, Steve returned from Viet Nam and was again contacted by Brumell. Brumell told Steve what had happened and requested that he submit another application. This second application also sought a 10,000 dollar policy without the war risk and aviation exclusion clauses. Brumell explained that he thought it would be possible to obtain such a policy in view of the prior events. Another application was completed and, along with Steve's prepaid premium, mailed to Prudential. The jury found that Brumell wrote an accompanying letter asking that the policy be issued without the exclusion clauses. On May 20, 1968, Steve returned to Viet Nam. Thereafter the policy issued effective June 1,

but unfortunately, Prudential did not comply with Brumell's letter request. However, Steve never had a chance to protest. The policy was not delivered to him, and no one told him that it contained war risk and aviation exclusion clauses. Brumell either had no chance to communicate this information, or remained silent in the hope that these exclusions would not become material; but this was not to be.

On July 28, Steve was killed in Viet Nam when his helicopter crashed and burned. Thereafter, Brumell assisted the defendants in preparing a claim against Prudential. He also wrote an accompanying letter asking Prudential to pay the claim despite the fact that the current policy contained the exclusion clauses. He urged this course of action in view of the above described circumstances, the position of the defendants in the community, the impairment of Prudential's image, and the possibility of legal action being taken against Prudential.

The claim was submitted to Raymond Thomas, the Chief Claims Consultant, who had the ultimate authority for approving or rejecting claims. Thomas approved the claim, and 10,000 dollars was disbursed to the defendants. The policy was then sent to the home office of Prudential in New Jersey for actuarial studies and statistical analyses but not for further review. An employee in the actuarial office noticed the exclusion clauses and Thomas was notified that the claim should not have been paid. Demand was then made upon the defendants for the return of the money. When they refused, this suit ensued.

Thomas testified that he paid this claim through oversight and mistake. The jury, however, refused to credit this testimony because it found that Prudential, by paying the face amount of the policy, intentionally waived the exclusionary clauses. Since the instructions to the jury correctly defined waiver as the voluntary, intentional relinquishment of a known right, and since Thomas was the ultimate authority for approving claims, it follows that the jury must have found that Thomas was cognizant of the exclusion clauses and Steve's war death, but deliberately and knowingly relinquished Prudential's right to rely upon those clauses and paid the claim, not under the policy, but to honor the commitments made to the deceased by the company's representative. There is abundant evidence to support this finding of the jury. First of all, Prudential knew what Brumell knew. He was the company's representative. His "twisting" to further Prudential's business caused Steve to drop the other policy and to prepay a premium to Prudential. Second, the claims department had Brumell's letter detailing all of the circumstances. Their correspondence discloses that they in fact knowingly dealt with this claim as one resulting from the operation of a military aircraft, because they would not accept the burial permit tendered by Steve's parents but insisted on the Marine Corps' Official Casualty Report listing the death. This report showed he met his death as a crew member of a helicopter on a Marine combat supply mission in Viet Nam. Third, Thomas testified that he personally knew a war death was involved when he reviewed the claim. Fourth, a notice that the policy contained the exclusion clauses is conspicuously stamped across the face of the policy.

* * * * *

[T]he non-contract theory of ratification is fully applicable here. When a principal, with full knowledge of the facts, chooses to approve and adopt an unauthorized act of an agent, he is bound by that action as fully as if it had been preauthorized. Assuming *arguendo*[15] that Brumell's promise to obtain a policy of insurance without war risk or aviation exclusion clauses was unauthorized, the act of payment by Prudential constituted a ratification of the agent's promise to obtain the form of policy the deceased applied for rather than the one actually issued. Certainly the jury could have found and did find that Prudential was fully cognizant of the facts and circumstances involved contemporaneously with its payment. Indeed, Prudential not only paid the defendants in accordance with Brumell's representations but, in calculating the amount of their debt to them, deducted a premium to cover the month of July 1968, which had not yet been paid to them by Steve's Marine Corps allotment.

Prudential argues that under no theory may this Court take cognizance of the agent's promise and its inequitable conduct because of the Florida rule that any matters transpiring prior to or contemporaneous with the signing of an application for insurance are waived or merged into the application. This argument highlights the basic error of Prudential's position in the court below and here. The jury's verdict found that Prudential did not part with its monies because of a mistaken supposition that they were owed on the policy of insurance it issued to Steve. Rather, this verdict recognized a duty of Prudential, dehors the writing,[16] to act in an honorable and upright way in accordance with its agent's promise. Thus, application of promissory estoppel in no way trammels upon the parol evidence rule. Involved here is a separate enforceable promise and not a variance or modification of the terms of the policy. Additionally, Prudential's act of payment, which ratified its agent's commitment, and thereby recognized its duty to honor this action which had enriched the company and misled Steve to drop the World Life policy to the detriment of his beneficiaries, could not have been merged into the document since it did not occur until after the instrument was in being. The Florida "merger" rule is wholly inapplicable to either legalism which would support the jury's verdict.

The judgment of the court below is reversed and the cause is remanded with directions to enter judgment on the jury verdict for the defendants, and to include therein an award for attorneys' fees.

Reversed and remanded.

---

[15]*Arguendo* means "by way of argument."

[16]*Dehors* means "outside of."

Questions for Review

1. Define *agency*.
2. Two fundamental rules of agency law relate to acts of the agent and knowledge of the agent. Describe each of these rules.
3. Distinguish between the power of an agent and the authority of an agent. What kinds of authority can an agent have?
4. Distinguish between the actual authority and the apparent authority of an agent. What is lingering apparent authority?
5. What is ratification? What are the requirements for an effective ratification?
6. What are subagents? Describe the legal relationship (*a*) between a subagent and the agent and (*b*) between a subagent and the agent's principal.
7. Describe the effectiveness of limitations upon the powers of an agent (*a*) as between the agent and the principal and (*b*) as between the agent and a third person.
8. What are the duties that an agent owes to the principal? What are the duties that a principal owes to the agent?
9. What are a principal's liabilities to third persons? What are a principal's rights against third persons?
10. What are an agent's liabilities to third persons? What are an agent's rights against third persons?
11. How can an agency relationship be terminated?

4   AGENCY IN LIFE AND HEALTH INSURANCE

Chapter Outline

People who solicit the sale of insurance policies must comply with general agency law as described in Chapter 3. They must also comply with laws specific to their business. This chapter is concerned with statutory, regulatory, and case law governing life and health insurance agents, brokers, and consultants. These laws often vary considerably from state to state. Nevertheless, patterns occur among the state laws, and certain general principles apply in most or all states. These patterns and principles will be discussed in this chapter.

In recent years, the improper sales practices of some agents soliciting the sale of life insurance has cost insurers millions of dollars in damages awards, settlements, and fines. The bad publicity that resulted has diminished public trust in the life insurance industry and put insurers' market conduct in the public spotlight. Insurance agent compliance with state and federal laws, as well as with company and agency policies, is critically important if the life insurance industry is to regain public trust.[1]

Both the insurance industry and its regulators, the state insurance commissioners, have acted to deal with market conduct problems. The American Council of Life Insurance (ACLI), an insurance industry association, recently approved its Principles and Code of Life Insurance Ethical Market Conduct that the ACLI's president called "a common sense, consumer-oriented approach to marketplace practices."[2] The ACLI also worked to create a market conduct organization. A life insurer that wants to be a member of the market conduct organization must undergo internal and external reviews of its current market practices. To maintain membership, an insurer will have to undergo periodic reassessment. The new market conduct organization will accredit the market conduct assessors who will conduct the external reviews.[3]

In December 1995, the National Association of Insurance Commissioners (NAIC) adopted the Life Insurance Illustrations Model Regulation. Agents use life insurance policy illustrations in selling life insurance. The purpose of the model regulation is to provide rules for life insurance policy illustrations that will protect consumers and foster consumer education. Some states have adopted regulations patterned on the model. The model regulation is discussed in Chapter 22, "Life and Health Insurance Advertising."

In 1996, the NAIC approved the development of a Producer Information Network. The Producer Information Network is an electronic database containing information about soliciting insurance agents. The Network is designed to help insurers hire agents with good compliance records and avoid those with poor records.[4]

---

[1]Dennis M. Groner, *Compliance: Making Lemonade Out of Lemons,* NAT'L UNDERWRITER, LIFE & HEALTH/FIN. SERVICES EDITION, April 29, 1996, at 37.

[2]Stephen Piontek, *ACLI Board Approves Ethical Market Conduct Code,* NAT'L UNDERWRITER, LIFE & HEALTH/FIN. SERVICES EDITION, Nov. 20, 1995, at 2.

[3]Diane West, *ACLI Eyes Criteria for Market Conduct Assessors,* NAT'L UNDERWRITER, LIFE & HEALTH/FIN. SERVICES EDITION, June 24, 1996, at 9.

[4]L. H. Otis, *NAIC Agent Network Gets Tentative O.K.,* NAT'L UNDERWRITER, LIFE & HEALTH/FIN. SERVICES EDITION, June 10, 1996, at 1.

This chapter deals with many aspects of market conduct and compliance: agent and broker licensing, disclosure to clients, misrepresentation to clients, policy replacement, rebating, defamation, forgery, timely and competent service, the unauthorized practice of law, the agent's duty to inform the insurer, and the agent's duty regarding premiums that the agent collects.

Insurance Agents and Brokers

Both state and federal laws govern insurance agents and brokers. As with other aspects of the insurance business, state laws are predominant, but federal laws such as the Employee Retirement Income Security Act of 1974 (ERISA) and the Securities Exchange Act govern some acts of insurance agents and brokers.

An insurance agent ordinarily is a person or an organization appointed by an insurer to solicit applications for insurance on its behalf. Usually, the agent and insurer have signed a written agency contract. The agent ordinarily obtains a license from a state to solicit applications for the insurer in that state.

In many instances, a person obtains a license to sell insurance for more than one insurer. The term *broker* is sometimes incorrectly applied to such a person. Legally, in most cases, such a person is an agent of each insurer but is not a broker.

A **broker** is a person whose business is to bring buyers and sellers together. An insurance broker is ordinarily a person who procures insurance for people who request this service. An insurance broker is usually the agent of the applicant for purposes of procuring the insurance or making the application, although the broker may be the agent of the insurer for other purposes, such as collection of the initial premium or delivery of the policy. Life insurance brokers sell the policies of a number of life insurers. They often sell other types of insurance as well.

Half the states recognize and license life and health insurance brokers.[5] In those states, an insurer can accept applications from, and pay commissions to, a licensed broker. Before accepting an application from a person claiming to be a broker, an insurer usually requires proof that the person has a valid broker's license. This is necessary because an insurer cannot lawfully accept an application that was not lawfully solicited.[6]

Insurance Consultants

An **insurance consultant** is a person who receives fees from clients for rendering advice about insurance contracts. Insurance consultants are also called insurance analysts, advisers, specialists, or counselors. Many states require insurance consultants to be licensed as such. State laws governing insurance consultants vary considerably from one state to another. The following are examples of such state laws.

California calls insurance consultants *insurance analysts*. California will grant an insurance analyst license to a California resident who has worked as a life insurance

---

[5]Arizona and California recognize and license health insurance brokers but not life insurance brokers.

[6]Some states have licensing exemptions that permit an insurer to accept an application from an agent licensed with another insurer. These will be discussed later in the subsection entitled "Licensing Exemptions."

agent, broker, or solicitor for at least the five years preceding the date of the license examination. The applicant must be of good general and business reputation and have a thorough knowledge of life or health insurance (health insurance is called *disability insurance* in California) as proved by the successful completion of the state's license examination. All fees an insurance analyst charges a client must be based on a written agreement that the client has signed. An unlicensed person who acts as an insurance analyst is guilty of a misdemeanor and a public nuisance. Certain classes of persons, including attorneys, actuaries, and bank and trust company employees, are exempt from the licensing law.[7]

Connecticut law allows a person who has attained the age of 18 to be licensed as a *certified insurance consultant* upon passing the required state examination. The examination may be waived if the applicant has been awarded a Chartered Life Underwriter (CLU) designation or has been a licensed certified insurance consultant within the preceding two years.[8] Maryland requires an examination for an insurance adviser license unless the applicant has attained an insurance designation, such as the CLU designation, and is a member in good standing in a related society, such as the American Society of Chartered Life Underwriters and Chartered Financial Consultants. Maryland will issue insurance adviser licenses to nonresidents who are licensed as insurance advisers in their state of residence.[9]

Some states mandate continuing education for insurance consultants. Arkansas requires a licensed insurance consultant to satisfactorily complete courses equal to 16 hours of instruction during each consecutive two-year period while the license is in effect.[10] Nebraska law states that licensed consultants shall complete 24 hours of continuing education in insurance subjects and 6 hours of continuing education in insurance industry ethics in each two-year period.[11]

Statutes of both California and Texas specifically state that insurance consultants also can be licensed as insurance agents. However, in California the insurance consultant may not receive both agent's commissions and consultant's fees for work regarding the same policy[12] or, in Texas, regarding the same client.[13]

Both of the model licensing acts adopted by the NAIC—the Agents and Brokers Licensing Model Act and the Single License Procedure Model Act—require that insurance consultants be licensed. Under both model acts, an insurance agent or broker can act as an insurance consultant without an insurance consultant license.[14] Some states have followed the model acts in this regard.

Financial Planners

In recent years, many insurance agents and brokers have become financial planners. The American College, which offers the course of study leading to the CLU designation, also offers another course of study for financial planners leading to a Chartered Financial Consultant (ChFC) designation.

---

[7]Cal. Ins. Code §§ 1831–1849 (West 1993).
[8]Conn. Gen. Stat. § 38a–786 (West Supp. 1996).
[9]Md. Code Ann., Ins. § 10–204 (Michie Supp.1995).
[10]Ark. Code Ann. § 23–64–301 (Michie Supp. 1994).
[11]Neb. Rev. Stat. § 44–3904 (Supp. 1994).
[12]Cal. Ins. Code § 1848 (West 1993).
[13]Tex. Ins. Code Ann. art. 21.07–2(4a) (West 1981).
[14]Agents and Brokers Licensing Model Act § 7 (Nat'l Ass'n of Ins. Comm'rs 1990); Single License Procedure Model Act § 3 (Nat'l Ass'n of Ins. Comm'rs 1990).

Financial planning typically involves providing advice to individuals or families regarding management of financial resources based on an analysis of each client's needs. The financial planner elicits information from the client, develops an overall financial plan, and assists in implementing the plan. The financial planner then periodically reviews the plan to be certain it is still appropriate, making changes where necessary.

Insurance agents and brokers who are also financial planners will often involve the client's attorney and accountant in the implementation of the plan. This is necessary because the insurance agent or broker cannot draft wills or trust documents for the client or give the client detailed legal or accounting advice. The client's securities broker might also be involved.

Registration under the Investment Advisers Act

An insurance agent or broker who is also a financial planner ordinarily must register under the federal Investment Advisers Act of 1940.[15] A person must register as an investment adviser if she "(1) provides advice, or issues reports or analyses, regarding securities; (2) is in the business of providing such services; and (3) provides such services for compensation."[16]

The Securities and Exchange Commission (SEC) has asserted that a financial planner who provides even nonspecific advice that concerns securities is an investment adviser under the act. This is true even if the financial planner merely provides general information concerning the relative advantages and disadvantages of investing in securities as compared to other investment media.[17]

Investment advice need not constitute the financial planner's principal business or any specified portion of it but need only be given on a regular basis in order for the financial planner to be considered an investment adviser.[18] The financial planner does not have to receive a separate fee for investment advice as long as the advice is considered part of the total services rendered. Moreover, the compensation does not have to come from the financial planner's client. The SEC has stated that "a person providing a variety of services to a client, including investment advisory services, for which the person receives any economic benefit, for example, by receipt of . . . commissions upon the sale to the client of insurance products . . . would be performing such advisory services 'for compensation.' "[19]

Once the financial planner has registered under the Investment Advisers Act, he must comply with the duties of registered investment advisers set out in the act. These duties involve delivery of disclosure statements to clients, record keeping, compliance with advertising and fee restrictions, and fiduciary responsibilities.[20] In addition, a financial planner is not permitted to use the initials RIA after his name, although the financial planner can use the words *registered investment adviser.*[21]

---

[15]15 U.S.C.A. § 80b–1, et seq. (West 1981 & Supp. 1996); Applicability of Investment Advisers Act to Financial Planners, Investment Advisers Release No. 1092, 52 Fed. Reg. 38,400 (Oct. 8, 1987) [hereinafter Release No. 1092].

[16]Release No. 1092, *supra* note 15, at II A.

[17]*Id.* at II A1.

[18]*Id.* at II A2.

[19]*Id.* at II A3.

[20]15 U.S.C.A. § 80b–4, –5 & –6 (West 1981 & Supp. 1996); Kelvin, *Post RIA Registration Responsibilities Facing the Financial Services Professional,* J. AM. SOC'Y CLU & CHFC, Nov. 1987, at 76.

[21]Securities & Syndication Review, SEC No-Action Letter [1984 Transfer Binder] Fed. Sec. L. Rep. (CCH) Par. 77,602 at 77,813 (Jan. 17, 1984).

There are also restrictions on the use of the term *investment counsel* under the act.[22]

State statutes also regulate investment advisers. Thus, in many states financial planners must register with the state as well as under the federal act.

Continuing Education for Financial Planners

Many financial planners have earned the ChFC designation from the American College or the Certified Financial Planner (CFP) designation from the College of Financial Planning. In order to keep these designations, ChFCs and CFPs must, with some exceptions, fulfill continuing education requirements. The American College requires that ChFCs who earned the designation after July 1989 complete 60 hours of continuing education every two years. ChFCs who earned the designation before July 1989 can volunteer to participate in the continuing education program. Once such a ChFC has volunteered, the continuing education program becomes mandatory for that ChFC. CFPs must complete 30 hours of continuing education courses every two years to keep the designation.

Licensing of Agents and Brokers

The power of a state to regulate the insurance business includes the power to license and control persons who solicit the sale of insurance. All states and the District of Columbia have licensing laws. As with other state laws regulating agents and brokers, these laws are not uniform. The NAIC adopted the Agents and Brokers Licensing Model Act in 1973, but as of this writing only four states have based their licensing laws on it.

In 1988, the NAIC adopted the Single License Procedure Model Act, which is designed to streamline agent and broker licensing laws. It is a "one license" model act. Under laws patterned on the new model act, agents and brokers, called *producers,* no longer have to secure separate licenses for each type of insurance they sell and for each insurer they represent, nor do they have to maintain separate agent and broker licenses. A single license listing the types of insurance that the producer is authorized to sell is sufficient. Under the producer concept, the contractual relationship between the insurer and the producer, rather than the license, determines whether the producer is acting as an agent or as a broker. Two states have enacted laws based on the new model act and six states have enacted related legislation.

Some patterns do exist among the licensing laws currently in force. An idea of the diversity and similarities of these laws can be obtained from the following comparisons.

The Texas statute defining *life insurance agent* reads as follows:

> The term "life insurance agent" for the purpose of this Act means any person or corporation that is an authorized agent of a legal reserve life insurance company, and any person who is a sub-agent of such agent, who acts as such in the solicitation of, negotiation for, or procurement of, or collection of premiums on, an insurance or annuity contract with a legal reserve life insurance company.[23]

---

[22]15 U.S.C.A. § 80b–8(c) (West 1981).
[23]TEX. INS. CODE ANN. art. 21.07–1 § 1(b) (Vernon Supp. 1996).

This definition goes on to exclude home office or agency employees who do not receive commissions, persons operating employee benefit programs who do not receive compensation from the insurer, banks involved in collecting and remitting premiums, ticket agents selling travel accident insurance, and certain credit insurance agents. Texas does not recognize the term *broker*. Subagents must have regular agent licenses.

The NAIC Agents and Brokers Licensing Model Act, on which licensing laws of Colorado, North Dakota, Oklahoma, and Vermont are based, defines the term *insurance agent* as follows:

> An individual, partnership or corporation appointed by an insurer to solicit applications for a policy of insurance or to negotiate a policy of insurance on its behalf.[24]

The model act defines the term *insurance broker* as follows:

> [A]ny individual, partnership or corporation who, for compensation, not being a licensed agent for the company in which a policy of insurance is placed, acts or aids in any manner in negotiating contracts for insurance or placing risks or effecting insurance for a party other than himself or itself.[25]

Under the model act, regularly salaried officers and employees of insurers or insurance agencies are exempted from the licensing requirements if such persons' duties do not include the negotiation or solicitation of insurance. Also exempted are persons involved in the administration of employee benefit plans, group creditor policies, or other group plans if they receive no commissions or compensation from the insurer, and certain persons representing fraternal organizations.[26]. Thus, under the model act, home office employees are exempt from licensing only if they do not solicit or negotiate contracts of insurance, whereas, under Texas law, receipt of commissions is the test for determining which persons are exempt from licensing. The model act further provides for the licensing of limited insurance representatives. These persons can sell certain types of insurance, such as travelers' baggage insurance, which do not require the professional competence of a licensed agent or broker. Limited insurance representatives do not have to pass an examination to receive a license.[27]

People Who Must Be Licensed

As a general rule, all persons soliciting the sale of insurance or annuity contracts must be licensed in the state, or states, in which they do business. As was noted above, consultants who merely advise on insurance purchases without selling insurance or receiving commissions must have a consultant license in many states. A person who sells variable annuities or variable life insurance must have two licenses: a license to sell insurance from the state and a license to sell securities from the National Association of Securities Dealers. Both licenses are required because variable annuities and variable life insurance policies are considered to be securities as well as insurance. Moreover, some states require a person to have a special type of insurance license to sell variable annuities or variable life insurance.[28]

---

[24]Agents and Brokers Licensing Model Act § 2A (Nat'l Ass'n Ins. Comm'rs 1990).

[25]*Id.* § 2B.

[26]*Id.* § 4G.

[27]*Id.* § 4A(b).

[28]*E.g.,* Tex. Ins. Code Ann. art. 3.75 § 7 (Vernon Supp. 1996).

Doing Business

As stated above, agents and brokers must receive a license from each state in which they do business. However, the state in which an agent or broker is doing business is not always readily apparent. Obviously, if an agent is a resident of a state selling to other residents of the same state, the agent is doing business there and must be licensed in her state of residence. Other selling situations are not so clear-cut. For example, an agent selling in New York may have clients who live in Connecticut or New Jersey.

A state sometimes makes an extraterritorial application of its licensing statute. That is, a state might require an agent selling to a resident of that state to have a license from the state, even though the agent sold and delivered the contract in another state. For example, a Kansas statute reads in part as follows:

> [I]t shall be unlawful for any insurance company to effect contracts of insurance in this state on the life or person of residents of this state . . . except through persons duly licensed and certified in accordance with the insurance laws of this state.[29]

The Kansas Department of Insurance takes the position that an insurer may not effect insurance contracts on the life or health of Kansas residents except through persons duly licensed in Kansas. If a Kansas resident travels to another state, meets with an insurance agent, fills out an application for insurance on her own life, pays the premium, receives the policy, and returns to Kansas, the department requires that the out-of-state agent selling the policy to a Kansas resident have a Kansas license or that the policy be countersigned by an agent with a Kansas license. The department puts more emphasis on the involvement of a Kansas resident than on the place of contracting. Court cases uphold the right of a state to regulate contracts that are made outside its borders if the risk insured is located within the state.

Because state laws are so diverse, the question of when and where an agent or broker is doing business cannot be answered without careful scrutiny of the laws of the states involved. Generally speaking, an insurance agent or broker will be subject to licensing in all states in which he solicits or negotiates insurance sales, delivers contracts, collects premiums, or has an office for the conduct of an insurance business. Prudent agents and brokers obtain nonresident licenses if they have any doubts.

Requirements for Licensing

A natural person can, of course, be licensed as an agent. State statutes also list various organizations that may be licensed. These include partnerships, corporations, and associations.

A natural person who applies for a license often must be over a certain age, usually 18. Ordinarily, the person must meet required educational standards. Many states require a certain number of hours of classroom instruction in insurance-related subjects. For example, a New Jersey statute requires that the applicant "[h]ave completed a course of education as the commissioner may provide by rule or regulation."[30] State law ordinarily mandates an examination conducted by the insurance commissioner. However, the course of study or the examination is not always

[29]KAN. STAT. ANN. § 40-214 (1993). Enrollment of individuals under a group policy and the inclusion of insurance in a credit transaction are excepted.
[30]N. J.STAT. ANN. § 17:22A–4(c) (West 1994).

required if the applicant has previously been licensed to sell insurance; is a Chartered Life Underwriter;[31] has worked for an agent, broker, or insurer; or intends to sell only certain types of limited insurance, such as travel insurance.[32]

An applicant for an agent's or broker's license must be of good character. California, for example, will deny an agent's license to a convicted felon or to a person convicted of certain misdemeanors. California will also deny a license to an applicant who has had a license denied, suspended, or revoked within the prior five years.[33] New Jersey requires that the applicant not have been convicted of a crime of moral turpitude.[34] ***Moral turpitude*** means "baseness, vileness or depravity in the private or social duties which a [person] owes to [other people] or to society in general."[35] The Agents and Brokers Licensing Model Act stipulates that an applicant "must be deemed by the Commissioner to be competent, trustworthy, financially responsible, and of good personal and business reputation."[36]

Some states require that an applicant for a license is to be actively engaged in the insurance business. In Illinois, "[n]o insurance producer license shall be granted . . . if the Director has reasonable cause to believe . . . that during the 12 month period . . . following the issuance . . . of the license . . . the aggregate amount of premiums on controlled business would exceed the aggregate amount of premiums on all other insurance business of the applicant. . . ." *Controlled business* is insurance procured by a person on his own "life, person, property or risks, or those of his spouse" or of "his employer or his own business."[37] In other words, the applicant for a license in Illinois must intend to sell insurance to the public, not merely to procure insurance for himself or his associates.

Nonresident Licenses

A state issues a ***nonresident license*** to an agent who is a resident of another state to authorize the agent to sell insurance in the licensing state. The agent must represent an insurer that is authorized to do business in the licensing state.

States differ in their treatment of nonresident applicants. In Illinois, a nonresident agent can receive a license only if her state of residence grants nonresident licenses to Illinois producers. Illinois will waive examination requirements for a nonresident applicant if her state of residence waives examination requirements for Illinois residents.[38]

Massachusetts requires nonresident agents of foreign companies to "transact business in the commonwealth only through the lawfully constituted and licensed resident agents of such company in the commonwealth."[39] Some states will license as agents natural persons who are nonresidents but will not license foreign corporations.

---

[31]*E.g.,* Mass. Gen. Laws Ann. ch. 175, § 163A (West 1987); Tex. Ins. Code Ann. art. 21.07–1 § 5(a)(3) (Vernon Supp. 1996). The Agents and Brokers Licensing Model Act, § 6, exempts persons previously licensed and CLUs from examination, except that CLUs must study the laws of the licensing state and take the part of the examination relating to those laws.

[32]Cal. Ins. Code § 1755 (West 1993).

[33]*Id.* § 1669.

[34]N. J. Stat. Ann. § 17:22A–4(i) (West 1994).

[35]Ballentine's Law Dictionary 815 (3d ed. 1969).

[36]Agents and Brokers Licensing Model Act § 5E(4) (Nat'l Ass'n Ins. Comm'rs 1990).

[37]215 Ill. Comp. Stat. Ann. 5/504.1 (Michie 1993).

[38]*Id.* 5/497.1

[39]Mass. Gen. Laws Ann. ch. 175, § 163 (West Supp.1996).

Aggrieved parties can sue nonresident agents and brokers in the licensing state. Some state laws provide that an agent or broker, by receiving a license, has appointed the commissioner of insurance as agent to receive the summons and complaint.[40]

Some states require the countersignature of a resident agent. A countersignature is an additional signature required to be put on the application or policy. West Virginia requires that all life, accident, and sickness policies issued as a result of solicitation by nonresident agents "shall be reported, placed, countersigned and consummated by and through a duly licensed resident agent of the issuing insurer."[41] Wyoming requires the signature of a resident agent for accident and health policies but not life policies and annuity contracts. The amount of commission that the countersigning resident agent must receive is spelled out in the Wyoming statutes.[42]

Most states do not have countersignature requirements. The only purpose of a countersignature requirement seems to be to guarantee that a local agent will share in the commission on a policy sold by a licensed nonresident agent. The trend is toward elimination of countersignature requirements. The Agents and Brokers Licensing Model Act specifically states:

> Notwithstanding the provisions of this chapter, or any other laws of this State, there shall be no requirement that a licensed resident agent or broker must countersign, solicit, transact, take, accept, deliver, record, or process in any manner an application, policy, contract, or any other form of insurance on behalf of a non-resident agent or broker and/or an authorized insurer; or share in the payment of commissions, if any, related to such business.[43]

Temporary Licenses

Temporary licenses serve several purposes.[44] In some states, a temporary license allows an applicant for a permanent license to sell insurance while he is pursuing the required course of study for the permanent license.[45] Some states issue a temporary license (1) to a relative or guardian of a disabled agent or broker, (2) to a relative or personal representative of a deceased agent or broker,[46] or (3) to a person designated by an agent who is entering military service.[47] These temporary licensees are allowed to renew the business of the absent agent or broker and perform other acts necessary to assure continued operation of the agent's or broker's business. Such temporary licensees do not have to pass an examination. In addition, some states issue temporary licenses to enable individuals to collect home service insurance premiums pending permanent licensing.[48]

The statutes usually specify the maximum time that a temporary license will remain in effect. The Agents and Brokers Licensing Model Act specifies a 90-day maximum,[49] and this period is often found in state statutes.

---

[40]N. J. Stat. Ann. § 17:22A–9(c) (West 1994).

[41]W. Va. Code § 33–12–8(a) (1996).

[42]Wyo. Stat. §§ 26–3–127, –128 (1991).

[43]Agents and Brokers Licensing Model Act § 13 (Nat'l Ass'n Ins. Comm'rs 1990).

[44]Temporary licenses are sometimes called *certificates of convenience*.

[45]*E.g.,* Tex. Ins. Code Ann. art. 21.07–1 § 10(a) (Vernon Supp. 1996); Cal. Ins. Code §§ 1685, 1689 (West 1993).

[46]*E.g.,* Cal. Ins. Code §§ 1685–1686 (West 1993); Mass. Gen. Laws Ann. ch. 175, § 174D (West 1987); N.Y. Ins. Law § 2109 (McKinney 1985).

[47]*E.g.,* Cal. Ins. Code § 1685 (b) (West 1993); N.Y. Ins. Law § 2109 (McKinney 1985).

[48]*E.g.,* Cal. Ins. Code §§ 1685, 1688 (West 1993).

[49]Agents and Brokers Licensing Model Act § 14 (Nat'l Ass'n Ins. Comm'rs 1990).

Limited Licenses

Licenses for limited purposes are available in some states. The Agents and Brokers Licensing Model Act reads as follows:

> **Limited Insurance Representative**. A limited insurance representative is an individual, partnership or corporation who is authorized by the Commissioner to solicit or negotiate contracts for a particular line of insurance which the Commissioner may by regulation deem essential for the transaction of business in this State and which does not require the professional competency demanded for an insurance agent's or insurance broker's license.[50]

California issues limited licenses as travel insurance agents to employees of airlines, railroads, steamships, and other common carriers.[51] Some states provide limited licenses for other types of selling, including undertakers' sales of burial insurance and financial institution employees' sales of credit life and disability insurance. Under some state laws, a person need not pass an examination in order to receive a limited license.[52]

Solicitor licenses are available in some states. The solicitor works for a licensed agent or broker. Under Washington State law, a licensed solicitor must "make the soliciting and handling of insurance business under his license his principal vocation" and "is to represent and be employed by but one licensed agent or broker."[53]

Licensing Exemptions

About one-third of the states have licensing exemptions that permit an insurer to accept a policy application from an agent licensed with another insurer or insurers if certain conditions are met. Some of these states permit such solicitation if the agent knows that no insurer with which the agent is licensed would accept the policy application. Some states will permit solicitation if an application for appointment as agent for the issuing insurer accompanies the policy application.

Continuing Education

Insurance agents, like other professionals, need to keep abreast of the changes in their field. In recognition of the need for continuing education, in the 1970s the states began to pass laws requiring licensed agents and brokers to take a certain minimum number of insurance-related courses each year.

In 1978, the NAIC adopted an Agents Continuing Education Model Regulation. This model regulation applies to resident agents or brokers engaged in the sale of those lines of insurance that require the agent or broker to take an examination to be licensed.[54] Under the model regulation, new licensees must "satisfactorily complete courses or programs of instruction or attend seminars equivalent to a minimum of 25 classroom hours of instruction" each year for four years.[55] All licensees must complete at least 15 classroom hours of instruction each year.[56] Among the courses

---

[50]*Id.* § 2D.

[51]CAL. INS. CODE § 1752 (West 1993).

[52]*Id.* § 1755.

[53]WASH. REV. CODE ANN. § 48.17.280 (West 1984).

[54]AGENTS CONTINUING EDUCATION MODEL REG. §§ 3 & 4 (Nat'l Ass'n of Ins. Comm'rs 1990).

[55]*Id.* § 5A(1).

[56]*Id.* § 5A(2).

that can be used to satisfy the requirement are Chartered Life Underwriter courses, Life Underwriter Training Council life courses, Certified Insurance Counselor Program courses, and college or university insurance courses.[57] Each licensee must furnish the state's insurance commissioner with a certificate of compliance with the education requirement.[58] About one-fourth of the states have laws based on the model regulation.

Over three-fourths of the states have continuing education laws. Unfortunately, many states do not agree on the standards for continuing education. This has created a difficult situation for nonresident agents, who must comply with the continuing education requirements of two or more states.

Denial, Suspension, or Revocation of License

Felony convictions or violations of the insurance code can result in denial, suspension, or revocation of an insurance agent's or broker's license. Agents and brokers are, of course, subject to the general body of criminal law applicable to all persons. Crimes such as embezzlement of funds, larceny, fraud, forgery, and conspiracy are punishable by imprisonment or fine under the general criminal laws and ordinarily will result in forfeiture of the license as well.

In addition to the general criminal laws, there are criminal laws specifically governing insurance agents and brokers. For example, Massachusetts statutes provide the following:

> An insurance agent or broker . . . who receives any money or substitute for money as premium for . . . a policy or contract from the insured or holder thereof, shall be deemed to hold such premium in trust for the company. If he fails to pay the same over to the company after written demand made upon him therefor, less his commission and any deductions to which, by the written consent of the company, he may be entitled, such failure shall be prima facie evidence that he has used or applied the said premium for a purpose other than paying the same over to the said company and upon conviction thereof he shall be guilty of larceny.[59]

Among the insurance code violations that can result in loss of a license are rebating,[60] twisting,[61] solicitation made without authority from the insurer, solicitation for an unlicensed insurer, delinquency in premium remission, and misrepresentation in the license application. These violations may also be punishable as misdemeanors or felonies.

The Contract between Insurer and Agent

An agency relationship between an insurer and a selling agent is created in the same way that other agency relationships are created. Ordinarily, the insurer gives the agent actual authority to perform the agency—that is, express authority as well as

---

[57]*Id.* § 5B.

[58]*Id.* § 6E.

[59]Mass. Gen. Laws Ann. ch. 175, § 176 (West 1987).

[60]Rebating occurs when an agent gives something of value, usually a percentage of the agent's commission, to a prospect to induce the purchase of insurance.

[61]Twisting is the effort of an agent to induce a person to drop his existing insurance and buy insurance the agent is selling when such effort is characterized by misrepresentation.

incidental authority to do things normally required to perform the agency. The agency can also exist because of apparent authority, although an agent should not act without actual authority and will be liable if he does so.

The agency contract between the insurer and the agent can be oral if no law, or corporate charter or bylaw, forbids an oral contract. However, an agent almost always has a written agency contract with an insurer or a general agent. The agency contract describes the agent's compensation and, in some instances, grants exclusive rights to represent the insurer in a certain geographic area. If the agent agrees to work for the insurer exclusively, that agreement would also appear in the agency contract. The agency contract spells out the agent's duties and authority.

The agency contract, not the agent's license, controls the extent of the agent's authority to act for the insurer, although the agent must not act in areas where he is not licensed. For example, if an agent's license gives the agent authority to sell both life and health insurance, but the agency contract gives the agent authority to sell only life insurance, the license itself does not confer the further agency authority to sell health insurance. Authority from the state under the license and agency authority from the insurer under the agency contract are both necessary.

The agency contract will usually specify the manner in which the contract will terminate. Generally speaking, unless the agency contract says otherwise, either the insurer or the agent can terminate the contract without breaching it. If the insurer discharges the agent in violation of the terms of the agency contract, the agent can maintain an action for the wrongful discharge. However, the insurer can rightfully discharge an agent who has breached a duty to the insurer, lost his license, or committed a crime.

Solicitation of Business

After studying insurance, passing an examination, entering into an agency contract, and receiving a license or licenses, the typical life or health insurance agent begins soliciting insurance business from the public. The general rules of agency law apply to the agent's actions. In addition, other laws apply specifically to the solicitation of business by insurance agents. Indeed, a large body of statutory, regulatory, and case law applies to the agent's role in the making of insurance contracts. This section will deal with some of the most significant of these laws.

Unlicensed Insurers

An agent or broker must make certain that the life or health insurer that is to issue the policy has a certificate of authority—that is, a license—admitting it to do business in the state where the solicitation occurs. An insurer must comply with detailed requirements bearing on many phases of its business before a state will license it to conduct business. An insurer might be licensed to do business in one state, a number of states, or all states.

It could be a serious matter for an agent to solicit insurance applications for an insurer that does not have a license to do business in the state of solicitation. In *Robertson v. California,*[62] the U.S. Supreme Court upheld the conviction of an agent

---

[62]328 U.S. 440 (1946).

who violated a provision of the California Insurance Code that prohibits a person from acting as an agent for an unlicensed insurer. Other states have similar laws. The South Carolina statute reads as follows:

> No person may in this State act as agent for an insurer not authorized to transact business in this State or negotiate for or place or aid in placing insurance coverage in this State for another with an unauthorized insurer.[63]

Unapproved Policy Forms

The policy form must have approval from the state insurance department in the state where the agent or broker sells the policy. If the state insurance department has not approved the policy form, the insurer that issues such a policy could be fined or have its license revoked. Therefore, the insurer will ordinarily refuse to issue such a policy. In cases in which an insurer has issued an unapproved policy, the policy is usually enforceable by the policyowner or beneficiary as long as the applicant did not intend to circumvent the law.

Misrepresentations

The agent or broker who sells a policy must truthfully present the policy coverage. For example, it is a misrepresentation to overemphasize the investment element of a life insurance policy to the extent that the client does not realize he is buying life insurance. The states have statutes providing penalties for agents and brokers who make false statements about the insurance they are selling. For example, in California, the statutes provide that an agent or broker who misrepresents the terms, benefits, or dividends of a policy is "guilty of a misdemeanor and punishable by a fine not exceeding two hundred dollars or by imprisonment not exceeding six months."[64] In addition, the agent's or broker's license may be suspended for up to three years.[65] An agent's or broker's misrepresentation to an insurer to induce issuance of a policy is specifically forbidden under the statutes of some states.[66] Misrepresentation to an insurer is also a breach of the agent's fiduciary duty.

An agent's attempt through misrepresentation to induce a policyowner to replace his policy is called *twisting*. The laws of almost all states specifically forbid twisting.

An agent or broker must not misrepresent to a client the financial condition of a proposed insurer. If an agent or broker makes misrepresentations as to the financial ratings, financial strength, or solvency of a proposed insurer and the insurer later becomes insolvent, causing loss to the client, the agent or broker could be liable for the loss.[67]

Some agents and brokers use the financial strength of the insurer, as reflected in financial rating reports by A. M. Best Company, Standard & Poor's Corporation, Moody's Investors Service, Duff & Phelps Credit Rating Company, or other respected rating firms, as a selling point for the insurance.[68] If the agent or broker uses

---

[63]S.C. CODE § 38–25–120 (1989).

[64]CAL. INS. CODE §§ 780-82 (West 1993).

[65]*Id.* § 783.

[66]PA. CONS. STAT. ANN. tit. 40, § 518 (Purdon 1992).

[67]Bertram Hartnett, *Life Insurer Insolvency: Liability Concerns of Agents and Brokers,* J. AM. SOC'Y CLU & CHFC, May 1992, at 60, 65.

[68]Rich Wilner, *Reassuring Clients: Agents Put Ratings' Prestige to Use,* FIN. SERVICES WK., July 22, 1991, at 1.

the insurer's financial rating as a selling point, she should provide the client with the financial rating report on the insurer and the rating firm's explanation of the meaning of the financial rating so that the client has complete information.

Disclosure

Concern among insurance regulatory officers and other interested persons about the consumer's lack of understanding of the technicalities of life insurance has led a number of states to require that the insurer give the policyowner a period of time, usually 10 days, in which to examine the policy. If the policyowner is not satisfied, he can return the policy for a refund of the premium. The laws requiring a "free look" period are discussed in Chapter 7, "Structure of the Life Insurance Policy."

Concern over the consumer's lack of understanding has also led many states to require that the life insurer provide the insurance applicant with a buyer's guide and a policy summary to help the applicant make an informed choice of policies. A *buyer's guide* contains simple descriptions of term insurance, whole life insurance, and endowment insurance. It also explains the use of cost comparison indexes. Cost comparison indexes assist those purchasing life insurance in comparing the costs of similar policies.

A *policy summary* discloses detailed financial data with respect to a particular policy. These data include a listing of premiums payable, death benefit, additional benefits, cash surrender values, estimated cash dividends, guaranteed endowment amounts, and loan interest information. Cost comparison indexes are also included.[69]

The NAIC has encouraged the states to require that insurers provide buyer's guides and policy summaries to policy applicants. In the 1970s, the NAIC adopted model regulations concerning deceptive practices and life insurance cost comparison requirements. In 1984, the NAIC adopted a Life Insurance Disclosure Model Regulation that superseded those earlier regulations. Most states now have statutes or regulations requiring an insurer to deliver to a buyer of life insurance information that should improve his ability to select the plan of life insurance most appropriate for his needs, evaluate the relative costs of similar plans of life insurance, and understand the basic features of the policy that is under consideration. However, not all of these laws are patterned on the NAIC Life Insurance Disclosure Model Regulation.

Laws patterned on the NAIC Life Insurance Disclosure Model Regulation and the NAIC Universal Life Insurance Model Regulation require that the agent or broker selling a universal life insurance policy furnish the applicant with policy information in a specified form.

Replacement

Replacement of one policy with another is sometimes in the best interests of the policyowner, but often it is not.[70] The NAIC has adopted a Replacement of Life Insurance and Annuities Model Regulation. The purpose of this model regulation is to protect life insurance and annuity purchasers by making certain that they receive information with which they can make replacement decisions that are in their best

---

[69]The illustrative policy form in the Appendix, Figure 2, contains a policy summary with cost comparison indexes. Figure 10 in the Appendix contains a life insurance buyer's guide.

[70]Donald R. Dann et al., *Replacement in the Context of a Need for New Life Insurance,* J. Am. Soc'y CLU & ChFC, Mar. 1989, at 36; John S. Moyse, *The Ethics of Replacement,* J. Am. Soc'y CLU & ChFC, Nov. 1991, at 76.

interests. Most states have adopted replacement regulations patterned on the model regulation.

Replacement regulations patterned on the model regulation require that the agent or broker give the applicant a Notice Regarding Replacement, which encourages the applicant to compare the existing and replacement life insurance policies or annuity contracts and to confer with the existing insurer or its agent. The agent or broker selling the replacement coverage must inform the replacing insurer of the replacement. The replacing insurer must in turn send to the existing insurer notice of the replacement and specified replacement policy data. This gives the existing insurer an opportunity to conserve the existing coverage. Finally, the replacing insurer must give the applicant a refund of premium if the applicant so requests within 20 days from the date of delivery of the replacement policy.

Replacement regulations ordinarily do not apply to certain types of policies. These include credit life insurance policies, group life insurance policies, group annuity contracts, conversion policies, and temporary insurance contracts under premium receipts.

Rebating

Rebating occurs when an agent gives a purchaser part of his commission or some other thing of value to induce the purchase of insurance, or when an insurer makes a deduction from the stipulated premium to induce such a purchase. Rebating was a common practice early in this century, but now laws in nearly all states forbid it.

There has been a widespread debate over whether or not rebating should be allowed.[71] The insurance industry generally opposes rebating, whereas some consumer groups and agents favor it.

Opponents of rebating argue that the practice would harm policyowners, agents, and insurers. They say that purchasers of small policies might pay more per $1,000 of face value for their life insurance because purchasers of large policies could negotiate lower prices. The opponents argue that rebating can encourage frequent replacement of existing policies with new policies with a consequent increase in price for all policyowners. They say that commissions would have to increase if rebating by agents were allowed, resulting in increased insurance costs to the public. They also argue that rebating would make accurate cost comparisons among policies more difficult for the insurance purchaser.

Furthermore, opponents of rebating argue that newer agents would not be able to compete against agents with a large, established clientele if the practice were allowed and that this would lead to monopolistic domination by a few large agencies. Some oppose rebating because they fear it would create an undignified insurance marketing atmosphere in which agents would give away such items as television sets and food mixers to induce sales.

Insurer insolvency is another concern of opponents of rebating. They argue that policyowners would replace their policies more frequently to obtain rebates. Because the first-year life insurance commission of an agent is often 100 percent of the first-year premium, a policy must stay in force for several years before the insurer can generate a profit. Thus, opponents of rebating argue, frequent replacement could threaten insurer solvency.

---

[71]Deanne Sherman, *Rebating: Consumerism Causes a Resurgence,* Soc'y Page, Am. Soc'y CLU & ChFC, June 1991, at 5.

The major argument of those who favor rebating is that it would drive down insurance prices by permitting more competition. Those who favor rebating also argue that a policyowner should be aware of the charge made for the agent's services (the commission) and be allowed to negotiate that charge.

Both the state and federal levels of government have seen efforts to repeal state antirebating laws. In 1986, the Florida Supreme Court declared the Florida antirebating statute unconstitutional under the Florida state constitution.[72] California repealed its antirebating laws in 1988.

Defamation

A *defamation* is a false communication that tends to harm the reputation of the defamed person so as to lower the defamed person in the estimation of others and to deter others from associating or dealing with him. *Slander* is spoken defamation. Other types of defamation, such as written or pictorial defamation, are called *libel*. Defamations by insurance agents, or against insurance agents by other persons, occur occasionally. Corporations such as insurers, as well as natural persons, can be defamed. Defamation is a tort for which the defamed person can recover damages. Defamation may also be a crime.

Note that a statement is not defamatory unless it is false. If a person accused of defamation can prove that the statement she made is true, she will not be liable for defamation because truth is an absolute defense.

Under some circumstances, one person can defame another without liability. Persons involved in judicial proceedings have absolute immunity from liability for defamation. Judges, lawyers, plaintiffs, defendants, jurors, and witnesses involved in judicial proceedings have such absolute immunity. Legislators and executive officers of the government in the performance of their duties also have absolute immunity in most instances.[73]

In certain instances, persons who make defamatory statements are protected by a qualified, rather than an absolute, privilege. For example, in *Pierce v. Northwestern Mutual Life Insurance Co.*[74] an insurer made allegedly defamatory statements about an agent in a report required by an insurance department. The court held that the insurer had a qualified privilege to do so, because the insurer had acted without ill will or malice.

Many states have a statute providing that certain required communications regarding agents' activities made by insurers to the state insurance department are privileged. Even if such a statement is defamatory, the statute will protect the insurer if the agent sues the insurer for defamation. Some of these statutes provide that the statement cannot be used as evidence in a court action. Others simply state that such statements are privileged or absolutely privileged. The Connecticut statute provides that the agent shall not have a cause of action against the insurer unless the required statement "is false and was known by such company to be false when made."[75] Under any of these statutes, the insurer is protected in making the required report unless the insurer acts in bad faith.

---

[72]Department of Insurance v. Dade County Consumer Advocate's Office, 492 So. 2d 1032 (Fla. 1986).

[73]W. PROSSER & W. KEETON, THE LAW OF TORTS 816–23 (5th ed. 1984).

[74]444 F. Supp. 1098 (D.C.S.C. 1978).

[75]CONN. GEN. STAT. ANN. § 38a–708 (West Supp. 1992).

Because defamation is a tort, an insurer could be liable for damages for its agent's defamation under the doctrine of **respondeat superior**. *Respondeat superior* means "Let the master answer" and stands for the principle that an employer is responsible for a tort that an employee commits in the course of his employment. Thus, the insurer's liability will usually depend on whether or not the defamation was made in the course of the agent's employment.[76] Some courts have held an insurance agent, an insurer, or both liable for the agent's defamatory statement.[77] These cases ordinarily involve defamation of a rival agent or insurer.

Some states have insurance statutes forbidding defamation. Louisiana's statute reads as follows:

> The following are declared to be unfair methods of competition and unfair or deceptive acts and practices in the business of insurance:
>
> * * * * *
>
> **Defamation**. Making, publishing, disseminating, or circulating, directly or indirectly, or aiding, abetting or encouraging the making, publishing, disseminating or circulating of any oral or written statement or any pamphlet, circular, article or literature which is false, or maliciously critical of or derogatory to the financial condition of an insurer, and which is calculated to injure any person engaged in the business of insurance.[78]

Forgery

Forgery ordinarily occurs when one person signs another person's name to a document with the intention of deceitfully and fraudulently presenting the signature as genuine. Forgery is a crime punishable by fines and imprisonment. It is therefore extremely inadvisable to sign another person's name to a document without clear evidence of that person's permission.

Some agents have signed an applicant's name to an application where the original application has been lost or improperly completed. This is a practice that can create serious problems, even if the issue of forgery does not arise. For example, the insurer might blame the agent for misrepresentations the applicant made on the original application.

False signatures on change of beneficiary forms can also create serious problems. If a former beneficiary can prove that the signature on a change of beneficiary form is not genuine, a court might hold the change to be ineffective. The intended beneficiary might then take legal action against the person who made the false signature.

Timely and Competent Service

A life or health insurance agent or broker can be liable to an applicant for the breach of an implied contract to procure insurance. For example, an insurance agent who takes an application will be liable to the applicant if the agent unreasonably delays in submitting the application to the insurer and this delay harms the applicant.[79] The proposed insured could become uninsurable or die before obtaining the insurance if

---

[76]H. D. Warren, Annotation, *Liability of Insurance Company for Libel or Slander by Its Agents or Employees,* 55 A.L.R. 2d 828 § 3 (1957).

[77]*Id.*

[78]La. Rev. Stat. Ann. § 22:1214(3) (West 1995).

[79]Talbot v. Country Life Ins. Co., 291 N.E.2d 830 (Ill. App. 1973).

the agent does not act promptly. The agent also has a duty to promptly notify the applicant if the insurer rejects the application so that the applicant can try to obtain insurance elsewhere. The agent will be liable for harm to the applicant resulting from a breach of this duty.[80]

In giving advice to a client, an agent or broker has a duty not to harm the client. Numerous cases hold agents and brokers liable to policyowners or beneficiaries for improper advice. An agent or broker who holds himself out as an expert is legally bound to exercise the expertise claimed.

Courts have held agents and brokers liable for convincing a client to adopt an insurance plan that the agent knew to be inappropriate to the client's needs,[81] for improper advice or conduct regarding the preparation of an application that resulted in lack of coverage,[82] and for failure to point out that a suicide period would run anew under a new policy that replaced a policy the client already owned.[83]

A purported agent who lacks authority from the insurer can also be liable to the applicant.[84] In some states, an agent who acts for an insurer where the insurer has no capacity to contract will be personally liable for harm caused to the applicant.

An agent or broker might be liable for damages to a beneficiary or intended beneficiary, or cause the insurer to have liability, because of the agent's or broker's careless acts. In one case, an agent who failed to include on the application all the intended beneficiaries named by the policyowner created a liability of the insurer to those not included.[85]

Unauthorized Practice of Law

The professionals who may be involved in planning a person's estate are accountants, trust officers, lawyers, stockbrokers, and insurance agents. Laws permit only lawyers to practice law. Nonlawyers face sanctions for the unauthorized practice of law. The problem arises in determining exactly what constitutes the practice of law. The drafting of wills, trust agreements, and pleadings for others is clearly the practice of law. So is the representation of others in court.[86] At the other end of the spectrum, it is not practicing law to remind someone of a generally known legal principle. A parent who reminds a child to drive under the speed limit to avoid breaking the law, or a life insurance agent who points out that death benefits are not taxable income to beneficiaries under the federal tax law, is not practicing law. Between those two extremes lies a gray area in which it can be difficult to ascertain whether the act in question is the practice of law. However, whenever a nonlawyer gives advice requiring legal knowledge, skill, and judgment, and applies the advice to specific factual situations, or such advice is a substantial part of the service rendered, the nonlawyer may be involved in the unauthorized practice of law.

---

[80]Thomas R. Trenkner, Annotation, *Liability of Insurance Broker or Agent to Insured for Failure to Procure Insurance,* 64 A.L.R. 3d 398 (1975).

[81]Anderson v. Knox, 297 F.2d 702 (9th Cir. 1961), *cert. denied,* 370 U.S. 915 (1962).

[82]Miller v. Union Cent. Life Ins. Co., 33 N.Y.S. 112 (1895).

[83]Larson v. Transamerica Life and Annuity Ins. Co., 597 P.2d 1292 (Ore. App. 1979).

[84]Brawner v. Welfare Finance Corp., 104 N.E.2d 203 (Ohio Ct. App. 1950).

[85]Sovereign Camp, W.O.W. v. Nash, 36 S.W.2d 284 (Tex. Civ. App. 1931).

[86]Haberkorn v. Sears, Roebuck & Co., 427 P.2d 378 (Ariz. App. 1967); *In re* Unauthorized Practice of Law, 192 N.E.2d 54 (Ohio 1963), *cert. denied,* 376 U.S. 970 (1964), *reh'g denied,* 377 U.S. 940 (1964).

Courts regard an act calling for the skill and learning of a lawyer as being the practice of law.[87]

A case involving the unauthorized practice of law by insurance brokers involved in estate planning is *Oregon State Bar v. John H. Miller & Co.*[88] In that case, the Oregon Supreme Court commanded the defendant insurance brokers to stop "preparing estate plans embodying legal analysis either as a separate service or as an incident to carrying on the business of selling insurance."

The court held that the brokers were engaged in the unauthorized practice of law when they performed the following activities:

  a. Suggesting, recommending or advising on the form or contents, in whole or in part, of legal documents, and particularly wills and trusts.

  b. Directly or indirectly preparing, construing or drafting legal documents, including wills and trusts.

  c. Rendering any legal opinion or advice, particularly as to the tax consequences of any activity or asset except life insurance or annuity plans.

  d. Preparing any estate plan except that part of the plan which directly concerns life insurance or annuities.

  e. Holding themselves out as persons who prepare legal documents, give legal advice or prepare estate plans whether by use of business names or otherwise.

  f. Employing any person, firm or corporation to give legal advice to customers of defendants.

The court further held that the defendant brokers were not engaged in the unauthorized practice of law when they performed these activities:

  a. Collecting information on customer or potential customer's financial affairs, including kind and value of assets.

  b. Questioning customers as to the customer's desires as to the amount of estate to be left in the case of death.

* * * * *

  e. Preparing the policies of insurance.

The court went on to say that "an insurance salesman can explain to his prospective customer alternative methods of disposing of assets, including life insurance which are available to taxpayers *generally* . . . [and] may inform his prospect in general terms that life insurance may be an effective means of minimizing his taxes." The court would prohibit an insurance agent from giving advice with respect to a prospective purchaser's "*specific* need for life insurance as against some other form of disposition of his estate unless the advice can be given without drawing upon the law to explain the basis for making the choice of alternatives." This Oregon case has been cited with approval by the courts of several other states. However, the definition of the unauthorized practice of law varies from state to state, and each state regulates the practice of law within its own borders.

---

[87]*In re* Baker, 85 A.2d 505 (N.J. 1951).
[88]385 P.2d 181 (Or. 1963).

In another case, a court held that an advertisement by an insurance agency that mentioned "trusts" and "wills" violated a statute prohibiting nonlawyers from advertising legal services.[89] The defendants in this case asserted that they did not prepare trusts or wills but only intended to advise clients to seek the services of a lawyer. This argument did not prevail.

The federal Employee Retirement Income Security Act enacted in 1974 has created further problems for insurance agents in avoiding the unauthorized practice of law. ERISA is a complex law administered by multiple agencies. Agents who wish to sell insurance to employee benefit plans need a good grasp of the basic features of the law so that they can serve their clients competently. On the other hand, such agents must be wary of the unauthorized practice of law in this area.

Agent's Duty to Inform the Insurer

An insurance agent, like any agent, has a fiduciary duty to act in the best interests of his principal, the insurer. Part of this duty consists of the agent's full disclosure to the principal of facts the agent knows that the principal needs to know. For example, a life or health insurance agent has a duty to inform the insurer of material facts regarding a proposed insured's health. A ***material fact*** is a fact that would influence the insurer's decision as to whether to issue the policy. A negligent failure to inform the insurer of a material fact could result in the the agent's being held liable for any harm resulting to the insurer. An intentional concealment of such a material fact can be a criminal matter as well.

The agent also has a duty to the insurer to relay applications promptly and to advise the insurer of the issuance of premium receipts. If an insurer or agent does not act upon an application promptly, either or both may be liable for any resulting loss to the applicant. The agent must promptly inform the insurer when the agent has issued a premium receipt so that the insurer can take the appropriate underwriting action. This is especially important if the agent issues a binding premium receipt because the insurer bears the risk of the insured's death upon issuance of the receipt.[90]

Malpractice Insurance

Malpractice insurance coverage for life and health insurance agents and brokers has become commonplace as the complexities of selling insurance and the number of lawsuits against agents and brokers have increased. These malpractice policies are similar to those covering physicians, lawyers, accountants, dentists, and other professionals.

Malpractice policies provide protection from liability caused by acts, errors, or omissions of the agent or broker while performing professional services. In fact, they are often called errors and omissions policies. These policies typically exclude liability for damages caused by an agent's or a broker's dishonest or malicious conduct.

---

[89]Burch v. Mellor, 43 Pa. D. & C. 597 (1942).

[90]Paul G. Reiter, Annotation, *Liability of Insurance Agent, for Exposure of Insurer to Liability, because of Failure to Fully Disclose or Assess Risk or to Report Issuance of Policy,* 35 A.L.R. 3d 821 (1971).

Ordinarily, the malpractice insurer has a duty to defend a covered agent or broker who is sued for negligence and to pay the damages if the agent or broker loses the suit. The malpractice insurer also may have a duty to defend an agent or a broker who is sued for an intentional tort—intentional libel, for example. However, the malpractice insurer will not have to pay the damages if the court determines that the agent or broker did intentionally libel the plaintiff. On the other hand, if the court were to determine that the libel was negligent, rather than intentional, the malpractice insurer ordinarily would have to pay the damages. A body of case law interpreting insurance agent and broker malpractice policies has been building since the first reported case was decided in 1961.[91]

Collection and Remission of Premiums

An insurer might authorize its agent to collect the initial premium only, or to collect initial and renewal premiums. Payment to an insurance agent within the scope of the agent's authority is payment to the insurer. Ordinarily, a broker who collects a premium is the agent of the insurer for this purpose, not the agent of the applicant or policyowner.[92]

Often, a life insurance agent has authority to collect only the initial premium. If the policy states that the policyowner is to pay renewal premiums only at the home office or to an authorized agent in exchange for a special receipt, payment to an unauthorized agent is not payment to the insurer.[93] Payment to an unauthorized agent is payment to the insurer if the insurer accepts and retains the payment from the agent—that is, if the principal ratifies the agent's act of collection. If the insurer has ratified an unauthorized agent's act of collection in the past and thus conferred upon the agent apparent authority to receive renewal premiums, payment to the agent is payment to the insurer.[94]

Duty of the Agent Regarding Premiums Collected

An insurance agent has a duty to account to the insurer for premiums collected. In some instances, the agent holds the premium payments as debtor of the insurer. In other instances, the agency contract or a state statute declares that the agent holds the money in trust. A *trust* is a fiduciary relationship in which one person, the trustee, holds legal title to property subject to a duty to manage the property for the benefit of another person. Missouri law states:

> Any person who shall be appointed or who shall act as agent for any insurance company within this state, or who shall, as agent, solicit applications, deliver policies or renewal receipts and collect premiums thereon, or who shall receive or collect moneys from any source or on any account whatsoever, as agent, for any insurance company doing business in this state, shall be held responsible in a trust or fiduciary capacity to the company for any money so collected or received by him for such company.[95]

---

[91]Otteman v. Interstate Fire & Casualty Co., 111 N.W.2d 97 (Neb. 1961).

[92]Johnson v. Schrapferman, 119 N.E. 494 (Ind. App. 1918); Aetna Life Ins. Co. v. Harris & Reichard Fur Dyers, 270 N.Y.S. 543 (1934).

[93]Gordon v. New York Life Ins. Co., 60 S.W.2d 907 (Ark. 1933).

[94]Huber v. New York Life Ins. Co., 63 P.2d 318 (Cal. App. 1936); Elizabeth T. Tsai, Annotation, *Person to Whom Renewal Premium May Be Paid or Tendered so as to Bind Insurer,* 42 A.L.R. 3d 751 (1972).

[95]Mo. Ann. Stat. § 375.051 (Vernon 1991).

Premium Payment with the Agent's Own Funds

An agent sometimes has an agreement with the insurer, the policyowner, or both regarding premium payment with the agent's own funds. The rights and liabilities of the agent, insurer, and policyowner will depend on their agreements.

In some instances, the agent and insurer agree on conditional payment of the premium by the agent. Conditional payment means that the insurer will charge the agent with the premium, but if the policyowner or applicant does not pay, the insurer will credit the agent for that amount. The policy will not bind the insurer if the policyowner or applicant does not pay unless there was an agreement between the agent and the policyowner or applicant for the agent to pay the premium.

As a general rule, an agent or broker has no duty to pay or loan money for premiums. However, agents and brokers do sometimes pay premiums with their own funds. The agent sometimes pays the premium and receives a promissory note from the policyowner in return. The insurer then considers the premium paid, and the agent can collect or sue on the promissory note.

If the agent pays the premium under the terms of an agreement between the agent and the policyowner, the agent is entitled to repayment and can maintain an action against the policyowner if the policyowner does not pay.[96] However, the agent must be able to prove that the parties entered into such an agreement. If the court deems the agent a volunteer—that is, a person who paid the premium without the policyowner's request or authorization—the court might not allow the agent to recover the premium payment.[97]

Commissions

Insurers calculate commissions as a percentage of the premium paid. As a general rule, only a licensed agent or broker who produces a signed application and a premium can receive a commission. Most states have statutes forbidding payment of commissions to unlicensed persons. The Texas statute reads as follows:

> No insurer or licensed insurance agent doing business in this State shall pay directly or indirectly any commission, or other valuable consideration, to any person or corporation for services as an insurance agent within this State, unless such person or corporation shall hold a currently valid license to act as an insurance agent as required by the laws of this State; nor shall any person or corporation other than a duly licensed insurance agent, accept any such commission or other valuable consideration; provided, however, that the provisions of this Section shall not prevent the payment or receipt of renewal or other deferred commissions to or by any person solely because such person or corporation has ceased to hold a license to act as an insurance agent.[98]

The *agent* (or *broker*) *of record* is the person whom the insurer recognizes as having earned the commission. If more than one agent or broker dealt with the client, the client's designation of one of them as agent or broker of record is usually the deciding factor.

The agency contract spells out the commission arrangement between the insurer and the agent. An agent who has faithfully performed the duties that the contract

---

[96]A. G. Barnett, Annotation, *Right of Insurance Agent to Sue in His Own Name for Unpaid Premium,* 90 A.L.R. 2d 1291 (1963).

[97]Parsons v. John Hancock Mut. Life Ins. Co., 20 App. D.C. 263 (1902).

[98]TEX. INS. CODE ANN. § 21.07(1) (b) (Vernon 1981).

requires is entitled to the compensation that the contract provides.[99] However, an agent can lose the right to commissions if she breaches any of her agency duties.

Renewal Commissions

The agency contract also determines an agent's right to commissions on renewal premiums. Some agency contracts provide that renewal premium commissions cease on termination of the agency contract. Other agency contracts provide that the renewal premium commissions will belong to the agent who obtained the business unless the insurer terminates the agency relationship for cause.[100] Usually, the agency contract specifies that either the agent or the insurer can terminate the agency relationship on notice to the other. The courts ordinarily uphold these agency contract provisions.

Sharing Commissions

In some states, statutes specifically permit licensed agents to share commissions. For example, the statutes of South Carolina provide that:

> [A]gents licensed under this title may write insurance at the request of other licensed agents or licensed brokers or licensed nonresident brokers and allow the licensed agents or licensed brokers or licensed nonresident brokers not exceeding one half of the commissions which they receive on the business written.[101]

The agency contract ordinarily entitles the agent to commissions on insurance placed by her subagents. These commissions are called "overrides."

Records and Reports

Agents and brokers must keep careful records of their business. State statutes and regulations sometimes spell out in detail exactly how agents and brokers are to keep records and set up bank accounts.[102] These statutes or regulations sometimes forbid commingling of premiums with personal funds in bank accounts.[103]

An insurer must file reports regarding agents and brokers with the state insurance department. Agents and brokers must file reports also. Each state has its own requirements. Most states require notification of broker and agent address changes and of agent appointments or terminations. Some require that agents selling variable life insurance or annuity contracts report disciplinary actions that securities agencies have taken against them.[104] Under some state laws, agents must keep various records and make them available to the state insurance department on request. Agents and brokers must carefully comply with state statutes regarding record keeping to avoid loss of license or other sanctions that these statutes provide.

---

[99]44 Corpus Juris Secundum *Insurance* § 205 (1993).

[100]*Terminated for cause* usually means *terminated for misconduct*.

[101]S.C. Code Ann. § 38–43–200 (b) (1989).

[102]*E.g.,* Ill. Admin. Code tit. 50, §§ 3113.40-3113.50 (1994).

[103]Wash. Rev. Code Ann. § 48.17.600 (West Supp. 1996); Ill. Admin. Code tit. 50, §§ 3113.40/ 3113.50 (1994).

[104]La. Ins. Dept. Reg. 28 (1969); Kan. Admin. Regs § 40-7-9 (b) (1995).

Summary

Although the general laws of agency govern persons who solicit life and health insurance, additional laws in each state apply specifically to these persons. State laws governing life and health insurance agents and brokers vary from state to state, but there are certain similarities. All states have licensing laws that govern life and health insurance agents. Some states recognize and license brokers also. Insurance consultants must be licensed in some states.

Generally speaking, persons soliciting life and health insurance must obtain a license in each state in which they do business. An agent who does business in a state in which he is not a resident must obtain a nonresident license. Some states issue temporary licenses for certain purposes spelled out in the state's statutes. Some states issue limited licenses to permit certain types of solicitation, such as the sale of travel accident policies. In some states, an agent licensed with one insurer may submit an application for insurance to another insurer with which she is not licensed.

Solicitation of insurance requires that an agent obtain a license and have an agency contract with an admitted insurer. The state insurance department must have approved the policy form. It is illegal for the agent to misrepresent coverage. In most states it is illegal to give rebates. Agents and brokers must also observe laws regarding disclosure, replacement, and timely and competent service. Agents and brokers must avoid the unauthorized practice of law. In addition, agents and brokers must keep accurate records and make reports in accordance with state laws. Malpractice insurance protects agents and brokers in a selling environment that has become increasingly complex.

The agent or broker of record is entitled to commissions on sales. The agency contract usually spells out the commission arrangement. Agents sometimes share commissions.

ILLUSTRATIVE CASE

In the following case, a named beneficiary brought an action against a life insurer and its soliciting agent because the agent failed to take action on the insurance application within a reasonable time. The court decided the case in favor of the beneficiary.

SUZANNE TALBOT, Plaintiff-Appellant

v.

COUNTRY LIFE INSURANCE COMPANY and ROY MELODY,
Defendants-Appellees[105]
Appellate Court of Illinois, Third District

DIXON, Justice.

This is an appeal from a judgment of the Circuit Court of Rock Island County dismissing, for failure to state a cause of action, an amended complaint filed by Suzanne Talbot, the plaintiff, against Country Life Insurance Company, the defendant in Count I and against Roy Melody, the defendant in Count II.

Count I of the amended complaint alleges in substance that, on September 13, 1969, Larry L. Talbot the husband of plaintiff applied in writing to the company's agent, Roy Melody for a life insurance policy in the amount of $15,000.00 on his own life, designating plaintiff as beneficiary; a first premium was then and there paid; on Feb. 19, 1970 Larry Talbot died; defendant retained the first premium and made no attempt to return it until Feb. 21, 1970; between the time of application and death Larry L. Talbot was in good health, his life was an insurable risk; he would have been able to obtain and would have obtained a policy from another company if it had not been for the representations of defendant; that defendant failed to take action on the application within a reasonable time; failed to issue a policy in accordance with the application and; failed to give notice of the action, if any, taken on the application and; that as a direct and proximate result the plaintiff was damaged.

One of the steps necessary to effecting an insurance policy is the filing of an application by the prospective insured; the application, being a mere offer or proposal for a contract of insurance, is not a contract. The existence of a contractual relationship between the parties (absent a

---

[105]291 N.E.2d 830 (Ill. App. 1973).

binder) depends upon the acceptance by the insurer of the application. In the instant case the appellant concedes that she has no action ex contractu[106] (the original complaint was on that theory). Neither the application nor the premium receipt provisions, if any, were pleaded, no binder is claimed; so the issue (Count I) is whether an insurer may be liable in tort for damage resulting from unreasonable delay in passing on an application for insurance.

There are divergent views on the question. On the one hand, it has been said that the failure of an insurer to act upon an application for insurance within a reasonable time, with resultant damage is a breach of the insurer's duty subjecting the company to liability for negligence. On the other hand, it has been said that an application for insurance is a mere offer and the insurer is under no duty to act on the offer.

* * * * *

Appleman[107] . . . states in Sec. 7232, "The better rule is to the effect that where application was made for a life policy with a beneficiary being designated to receive the proceeds, a cause of action lodges in such beneficiary, upon the applicant's death, for unreasonable delay on the part of the insurer, in accepting or rejecting such application."

Count II charges the agent Roy Melody with having failed to take action on said application within a reasonable time and failing to give notice of any action taken on the application. The complaint clearly alleges that Roy Melody was the agent of Country Life Insurance Com-

---

[106]*Ex contractu* means arising from or out of a contract.

[107]*Insurance Law and Practice* by John Alan Appleman and Jean Appleman is a multi-volume treatise on insurance law.

pany (as distinguished from being a broker). Brokers as distinguished from soliciting agents have long been held liable in tort. The agent here is not the agent of the applicant. He is the agent of the company and his primary responsibility is to the company.

It has been suggested that the duty of an agent to use care in dealing with the application may be based on the principle, familiar in negligence cases, that one who enters upon an affirmative undertaking, to perform a service for another, is required to exercise reasonable care in performing it, to avoid injury to the beneficiary of the undertaking. Insurance agents who take applications, particularly where they receive premiums, may be said to have entered definitely upon a course of affirmative conduct, and be liable for misfeasance if they unreasonably delay. This appears to us to be a salutory rule. The thought it stands for is that the agent or company owes an applicant for insurance what amounts to be a legal obligation to act with reasonable promptness on the application, either by providing the desirable coverage or by notifying the applicant of the rejection of the risk so that he may not be lulled into a feeling of security or put to prejudicial delay in seeking protection elsewhere. Those engaged in the insurance business understand perfectly the peculiar urgency of the need for prompt attention in these matters, and in fact many premium receipts provide for delay by inserting an express provision that if the application is not accepted within a definite time it shall be deemed to have been rejected; others provide for a definite termination date (where conditional [*sic*] insurance is expressly given from the date of the application provided the applicant is then insurable for the plan and amount and at the premium rate applied for).

For the above reasons the judgment of the Circuit Court of Rock Island is reversed.

Reversed.

Questions for Review

1. What are some of the objective evidences that a life or health insurance agent is doing business in a given state? Why is it necessary to determine the states in which such an agent is doing business?

2. What are the usual requirements for a person to obtain a license as a life insurance agent?

3. What are countersignature laws? What appears to be their chief purpose?

4. What are some of the grounds on which an agent's license can be suspended or revoked?

5. What is defamation? Under what conditions might an insurer be held liable for defamatory statements of an agent?

6. What are the probable legal effects of a life insurance agent's collecting a renewal premium without the authority to do so?

7. What is meant by the term *agent of record*?

8. Why is the subject of unauthorized practice of law important to life insurance agents?

9. What are some of the grounds on which a life or health insurance agent can become liable to the applicant? To the the insurer?

10. What is rebating? Twisting?

5 WAIVER AND ESTOPPEL

Chapter Outline

The words or actions of an insurer's agents sometimes give rise to a waiver or an estoppel. For this reason, students of life and health insurance law need an understanding of the legal doctrines of waiver and estoppel. In this chapter, waiver and estoppel will be defined, compared, and illustrated.

The rules governing waiver and estoppel are not consistent from state to state. Therefore, this book deals primarily with the most important rules that the majority of states have recognized.

Waiver and Estoppel Defined

A *waiver* is the voluntary and intentional giving up of a known right. Thus, a waiver requires knowledge of one's right coupled with an intention not to assert the right. For example, an insurer knows that if it does not receive the renewal premium by the end of the grace period, it has a right to declare the policy lapsed. If the insurer tells the policyowner at the end of the grace period that it will not declare the policy lapsed at that time but will give the policyowner an additional 10 days to pay the premium, the insurer has waived its right to declare the lapse at the end of the grace period. However, the insurer will be able to declare the lapse at the end of the additional 10 days.

There are several types of *estoppel,* including estoppel by record, estoppel by deed, and equitable estoppel. An estoppel by record precludes a person from denying the truth of matters set forth in a judicial or legislative record.[1] Estoppel by deed bars a party to a deed from denying the truth of material facts set forth in the deed.[2] In this book, we will be concerned only with *equitable estoppel,* as this is the kind found in insurance cases. Therefore, whenever the word *estoppel* is used in this book it will mean equitable estoppel. As its name implies, equitable estoppel developed in the equity courts. However, courts of law have adopted equitable estoppel. Courts frequently invoke equitable estoppel in legal actions based on contracts.

To *estop* means to stop, bar, prevent, or preclude. *Estop* is a word that derives from French and is now a legal term only. *Estoppel* occurs when a court bars a party from exercising a right or from asserting a fact because of something the party said or did that misled a second party to act so that harm resulted to the second party. For example, in order for Michael Gold to establish an estoppel in a court action against Otis Black, Gold must prove the following: (1) that Black's words or conduct misled Gold into believing that certain facts existed when they did not exist; (2) that Gold was ignorant of the facts; and (3) that Gold, relying reasonably and in good faith on the words or conduct of Black, acted to Gold's harm. If Gold can establish an estoppel against Black, Black will not be able to use the facts—that is, the truth—in his own defense.

For example, in *Boggio v. California-Western States Life Insurance Co.,*[3] an insurer, through its agent, told an applicant that the applicant did not have to disclose on the application a head injury incurred while the applicant was in the military. Evidence showed that, at the time the agent and the applicant filled out the application, the applicant discussed this with the agent, who said, "Well, as long as you do not have a medical discharge they don't care about all this. As long as you have an honorable discharge and not a medical discharge you can sign this application." Therefore the application did not mention the head injury. The insurer later denied the death claim because the application had not mentioned the head injury. In the ensuing lawsuit, the court said:

> The question presented is whether a binding insurance contract arises when the application of the insured contains misstatements of fact occurring because a soliciting agent of the insurer wrongfully represents to the applicant that certain facts (which were fully disclosed to the agent) need not be included in the application and the application is

---

[1] 28 AM. JUR. 2D *Estoppel and Waiver* § 2 (1966).
[2] *Id.* § 4.
[3] 239 P. 2d 144 (Cal. App. 1952).

signed in good faith by the applicant who relies on the agent's superior knowledge of insurance matters. . . .

To allow the insurer under these circumstances to place the responsibility upon the insured would not only be manifestly unjust but would allow it to profit by its own wrong. In such cases the courts have uniformly held the insurance company to be estopped to assert the defense of material misrepresentations.

Thus, the insurer, through its agent, misled the applicant into believing that the insurer did not require information revealing the applicant's head injury in the application when, in fact, the insurer did require such information.The insurer was therefore estopped to assert the defense of material misrepresentation, even though the application contained a material misrepresentation. The court estopped the insurer from asserting the defense of material misrepresentation in order to protect the applicant, because if the applicant had known that the insurer would not have insured him, he could have sought other insurance, perhaps at substandard rates. Had the court not estopped the insurer, the insurer would have misled the applicant into relying on this insurance to the applicant's harm.

Express and Implied Waivers

The waiving party can expressly make a waiver. Also, the waiving party's words, conduct, or, in some circumstances, silence, can imply a waiver. This section contains a comparison of express and implied waivers. It also contains an explanation of the reasoning some courts have used to equate implied waivers with estoppels. Finally, it describes those situations in which silence can result in an implied waiver.

Express Waivers

Express waivers can be either oral or written. An oral express waiver would occur if an insurer's authorized agent tells a policyowner or beneficiary that the insurer is willing to waive a right. For example, if an authorized agent of the insurer told a beneficiary over the telephone that the beneficiary need not submit proof of loss within the time specified in the policy, the insurer would have made an oral express waiver of its right to require timely submission of proof of loss. The insurer could not then deny liability for payment of the policy proceeds based on the beneficiary's failure to submit proof of loss within the time specified in the policy.

A written express waiver can occur in the policy itself or in a writing outside the policy. When insurers first included incontestable clauses in life insurance policies, these clauses were express waivers written in the policy. The incontestable clause stated that the insurer waived its right, after a specified period of time, to contest the validity of the policy because of a material misrepresentation in the application. Because incontestable clauses are no longer voluntary on the insurer's part, but are statutory requirements, they are not true waivers today.

Insurers can also make express written waivers outside the policy. For example, if an insurer states in a letter to the policyowner its intention to accept a premium after the expiration of the grace period, the insurer makes an express written waiver, outside the policy, of the insurer's contractual right to lapse the policy if the renewal premium is not paid before the grace period ends.

Implied Waivers

A party creates an ***implied waiver*** when that party does not express an intention to waive a right but that intention can be clearly inferred from the party's words or conduct. For example, if an insurer repeatedly accepts premium payments from a policyowner 60 days after the end of the grace period, a court usually will hold that the insurer has waived its right to lapse the policy if the premium is not paid on time. If the insured should die 40 days after the grace period has expired and before the premium has been paid, a court likely would hold that the contract was in effect at the time of death and that the death benefit is payable.[4] The only reasonable explanation for the insurer's act of repeatedly accepting late premiums is that the insurer wished to waive its right to declare the policy lapsed if the premium is not paid on time.

According to the courts of some jurisdictions, a party can also make an implied waiver in a second, quite different, situation. These courts hold that a party will create an implied waiver where the party has, in fact, no actual intention to waive a right, but the party's conduct has led the other party into acting on a reasonable belief that the first party has waived a right. This type of implied waiver is inconsistent with the usual definition of waiver, which requires that the waiving party intend to make the waiver. Furthermore, this definition of implied waiver is so similar to the definition of estoppel that the courts of some jurisdictions have declared that there is no difference between a waiver and an estoppel.[5] However, the courts of other jurisdictions have said that waiver and estoppel are different concepts.[6] In the author's opinion, this is the better view. Among the myriad of fact situations in which a court can apply either waiver or estoppel, some fact situations lend themselves to waiver analysis and others to estoppel analysis. In some borderline cases, a court can use either waiver or estoppel analysis equally well.

Waiver by Silence

A person's silence will not create an implied waiver of his rights unless the person has a legal duty to speak. For example, if, before a loss occurs, an insurer learns of a ground on which the insurer can ask a court to rescind the policy, in most jurisdictions the insurer has a duty to notify the policyowner within a reasonable time that it intends to have the policy rescinded. If the insurer does not do this, the court might hold that the insurer has waived, by silence, its right to a rescission of the policy.[7]

For example, suppose an insurer learns, three months after it issued a life insurance policy, that the policyowner-insured had made a material misrepresentation in the application regarding her health. If the insurer makes no attempt to rescind the policy, and the insured dies six months later, a court would probably hold that the insurer has waived its right to rescind. The courts in a majority of jurisdictions have held that it is unfair to allow the insurer to lull the policyowner into a false sense of security, and that the insurer must promptly inform the policyowner of its intent to rescind the policy. However, some courts have disagreed with this view and have held that they will not infer a waiver if the insurer remains silent after learning of facts that give the insurer a right to a rescission of the policy.[8]

---

[4]Hoffman v. Aetna Life Ins. Co., 22 N.E.2d 88 (Ohio App. 1938).

[5]*E.g.*, Liberty Mut. Ins. Co. v. Cleveland, 241 A.2d 60 (Vt. 1968).

[6]*E.g.*, American Ins. Co. v. Nationwide Mut. Ins. Co., 270 A.2d 907 (N.H. 1970).

[7]Swedish-American Ins. Co. v. Knutson, 72 P. 526 (Kan. 1903).

[8]44 Am. Jur. 2d *Insurance* § 1640 (1982).

Intent to Waive

One of the key elements in the definition of waiver is the intent on the part of the waiving party to create a waiver. Even if an insurer expresses in the policy its intent to waive a right, difficult legal questions can arise. The legal questions that have arisen in connection with waiver of premium because of disability constitute one example. Some of these questions are discussed in Chapter 8, "Added Benefits and Limitations."

The greatest number of problems as to the insurer's intent arise in connection with implied waivers. Some acts clearly create implied waivers. For example, as noted above, an insurer's repeated acceptance of overdue premiums creates an implied waiver of its right to lapse the policy if the premium is not paid on time. However, many other acts have an uncertain meaning, and the courts often must determine whether the insurer intended to waive a right. In one case, an insurer received notification of the insured's death, but rather than sending proof of loss forms to the beneficiary, the insurer requested that the beneficiary send a newspaper account of the accident causing the death. The court held that the insurer had waived the right to require that the beneficiary submit proof of loss forms. The court stated:

> The receipt and retention by the company of informal notice and proofs, without objection, or demand for further or more definite notice and proofs, constitute a waiver of objections as to their regularity.[9]

The act of the insurer in accepting the newspaper account implied its intent to waive its right to receive formal proof.

Knowledge of the Insurer

One presumption of contract law is that a party to a written contract knows and assents to the contract's contents. Courts hold that an insurer has knowledge of its rights under the policy.

However, sometimes the insurer does not know of a situation that would give it the right to avoid a particular contract. The insurer's acts will not create a waiver or estoppel if it does not know the pertinent facts.[10] For example, suppose an insurer, not knowing of a misrepresentation in the policy application that gave it a right to a rescission of the policy, accepted a premium payment. The insurer's acceptance of the premium payment would not create an implied waiver of its right to a rescission of the policy, because it did not know of its right. The decisions in many cases in this area hinge on whether or not the insurer knew the material facts.

Knowledge of an Agent Imputed to the Insurer

Often, a soliciting agent or medical examiner has knowledge that the court will impute to the insurer under the general rule of agency law that knowledge of an agent, acquired while in the performance of the agent's duties, is knowledge of the principal. Soliciting agents or medical examiners, who are agents of the insurer, frequently fill in questions on the application for the applicant. If such an agent knows the truth

---

[9]Barstow v. Federal Life Ins. Co., 242 N.W. 862 (Mich. 1932).
[10]Gardner v. North State Mut. Life Ins. Co., 79 S.E. 806 (N.C. 1913).

about a proposed insured's health but fills in answers that are false, without the applicant's knowledge or consent, the court will impute the agent's knowledge to the insurer in the majority of jurisdictions.[11] In these jurisdictions, if the insurer issues a policy, the knowledge of its agent will bind the insurer so that the insurer cannot rely on material misrepresentations in the application in seeking to avoid liability under the contract. In some of these cases, the courts have held that the insurer waived its right to avoid such liability. In others, the courts have held that the insurer was estopped from asserting the defense of material misrepresentation.

However, in the minority of jurisdictions, the courts have held that the applicant is responsible for the truth of statements in an application that he signs and that is part of the policy the insurer delivers to him. In these jurisdictions, the applicant must read the application to be certain that the answers are correct. If the answers are false, the insurer can avoid liability on the contract within the contestable period.[12]

This rule is summarized in the case of *Theros v. Metropolitan Life Insurance Co.*[13] as follows:

> [A]n insured is under a duty to read his application before signing it, and will be considered bound by a knowledge of the contents of his signed application. This is merely an application of fundamental contract law. While courts generally are inclined to treat insurance contracts as special and do not always vigorously apply all the principles of contract law, that tendency should not be allowed to overrun the bounds of legitimate exception.

The court noted that there was no evidence to show that the insured was prevented from reading the application before signing it by fraud, accident, misrepresentation, imposition, illiteracy, artifice, or device. Therefore, the court said, the insured is, by law, conclusively presumed to have read the application and his beneficiary is bound by its contents.

Thus, some courts will not estop an insurer from denying the truth of answers its own agent recorded, because these courts presume that the applicant had knowledge of the false answers and yet did not inform the insurer.

Sometimes the special facts of the case will overcome the presumption that the applicant has read the application. In one case,[14] the evidence showed that the applicant gave correct information concerning the diabetic condition of her daughter (the proposed insured), but the agent recorded incorrect answers that made it appear that the daughter's health was good. After the daughter's death, the company denied the claim on the ground of misrepresentation of material facts in the application. The insurer contended that even if the agent inserted false answers, the applicant was presumed to have knowledge of the false statements, since the insurer had attached a copy of the application to the policy. The mother testified that the policy the insurer delivered did not include a copy of the application. The court found for the mother and held the insurer liable for payment of the policy proceeds.

In another case (*Boggio v. California-Western States Life Insurance Co.*, cited above), the soliciting agent told the applicant that the applicant did not have to

---

[11]*E.g.*, Pannunzio v. Monumental Life Ins. Co., 151 N.E.2d 545 (Ohio 1958); Progressive Life Ins. Co. v. Dooley, 192 S.W.2d 128 (Ark. 1946).

[12]B. H. Glenn, Annotation, *Insured's Responsibility for False Answers Inserted by Insurer's Agent Following Correct Answers by Insured, or Incorrect Answers Suggested by Agent,* 26 A.L.R. 3D 6 (1969).

[13]407 P.2d 685 (Utah 1965).

[14]Hart v. Prudential Ins. Co., 117 P.2d 930 (Cal. App. 1941).

disclose on the application his head injury received in military service because he had an honorable, rather than a medical, discharge from military service. Of the insured's duty to read the application under these circumstances, the court said:

> Defendant correctly states that when the insured has a copy of the application in his possession he is presumed to have read it and to be aware of any misstatements therein even though they were not due to his own fault. . . . The rule would not apply here to charge Boggio with knowledge he did not have when he signed the application unless he could have ascertained that his statements were false in the sense that they withheld information sought to be elicited by the questions contained in the application. This was not he case. He relied on Angelino's [the soliciting agent's] statement that the questions did not call for information as to the injury received in the service unless it had led to medical discharge. Having had the question interpreted for him in this manner, repeated reading of the questions and answers would not have led him to believe that his service injury was material. He knew at all times that his answers were literally untrue but not that they would be deemed untrue by the company in determining whether he was an insurable risk.[15]

Collusion between Agent and Applicant

Collusion is a secret agreement between two or more persons to do some act to defraud a third person. Where an applicant and an agent agree to write false answers in an application in order to defraud the insurer, collusion exists between the applicant and agent. A court will not allow either the applicant or the beneficiary to benefit from the collusion. If there is collusion, the rule that knowledge of the agent is knowledge of the principal is not applicable.[16] A court will not estop the insurer from asserting the material misrepresentation in the application in defending a lawsuit for the death benefits.

In one case, the soliciting agent knew of the applicant's diabetic condition and recent hospitalization. The agent inserted false answers in the application for insurance on the applicant's life with respect to the diabetes and hospitalization. The applicant knew that the agent had inserted the false answers. The court held that the insurer had properly canceled the policy under these circumstances. The court said:

> As to the question of waiver and estoppel appellant [the beneficiary] earnestly contends that the knowledge of Jones [the agent] concerning the status of Gardner's [the insured's] health was imputed to appellee insurance company and therefore it, with such knowledge, issued the policy and can now not be heard to complain or assert the defenses presented. Such is not the law.[17]

Authority of the Agent

An authorized agent can waive a principal's rights. In the case of a corporate insurer, waiver is always by agent, because agents perform all of a corporation's acts. The term *agent* here includes not only soliciting agents but also officers, medical examiners, underwriters, and others whose actions affect the insurer's contractual relationships.

---

[15]239 P.2d144 (Cal. App. 1952).

[16]Gardner v. North State Mut. Life Ins. Co., 79 S.E. 806 (N.C. 1913); Commonwealth Life Ins. Co. v. Spears, 294 S.W. 138 (Ky. 1927); Aetna Life Ins. Co. v. Routon, 179 S.W.2d 862 (Ark. 1944).

[17]Bennett v. National Life & Acci. Ins. Co., 438 S.W.2d 438 (Tex. Civ. App. 1969).

In many waiver cases, the authority of the agent to make the waiver is in question. An agent's waiver of the conditions of an insurance policy becomes binding on the insurer only if the agent has power to make the waiver. If the applicant or policyowner knows that the agent lacks authority to make a waiver, the applicant or policyowner cannot claim that the agent had apparent authority to waive. The applicant or policyowner is bound by limitations on the agent's authority of which she has notice.

Notice to applicants of limitations on the agent's authority is usually contained in the application, as well as in the policy. This notice is often called a ***nonwaiver clause***. The nonwaiver clause in the application form in the Appendix, Figure 1, reads in part as follows:

> No agent is authorized to make or modify contracts, to waive any of the Company's rights or requirements or to bind the Company by making or receiving any promise, representation or information, unless the same be in writing, submitted to the Company, and made a part of such contract.

The word *agent* in this clause pertains to soliciting agents. Other agents of the insurer at the home office will determine whether to permit a soliciting agent's written request for a waiver.

The policy itself in the Appendix, Figure 2, contains the following nonwaiver clause:

> Only our President, one of our Vice Presidents, our Secretary or our Actuary has the authority to modify or waive any provision in this policy, and then only in writing. No Agent or other person has the authority to change or waive any provision of this Policy.

The court decisions regarding the effectiveness of nonwaiver clauses are conflicting. First of all, one rule, as stated above, is that limitations on the authority of an agent bind the applicant or policyowner, if the applicant or policyowner has notice of those limitations. Moreover, most courts deem that the applicant or policyowner has notice of the nonwaiver provision, especially where it appears in the application as well as in the policy.

On the other hand, there are limitations on the effectiveness of the nonwaiver clause. First, certain agents can waive the nonwaiver clause itself. The nonwaiver clause will not prevent an agent who has full authority to make contracts, such as a senior officer of the insurer, from effecting a waiver.

Second, several jurisdictions follow a rule that nonwaiver provisions apply only to waivers made after issuance of the policy. The reasoning here is that a policy provision the policyowner has not seen cannot bind her. For this reason, insurers frequently put a nonwaiver clause in the application also.

Finally, there is a rule in the majority of jurisdictions that a nonwaiver clause does not apply to conditions that a beneficiary must fulfill after a loss has occurred. That is, a nonwaiver clause will not affect waivers of the insurer's rights under policy provisions requiring notice or proof of loss. Agents of the insurer can waive such provisions despite the nonwaiver clause.

Forbidden Waivers and Estoppels

The general rule is that a party to a contract can waive any right that was inserted in the contract solely for that party's benefit. However, neither party can waive some rights under insurance policies because those rights do not solely benefit one party or the other but partly benefit the public. A party cannot waive other rights because such a waiver would create coverage that the policy does not provide. Moreover, a party cannot invoke an estoppel to create such coverage. Finally, a party may release a right to receive a sum of money but cannot waive it.

Rights That Are Partly for the Public Benefit

No party to a life insurance contract can waive a right that is partly for the public benefit. For example, in some jurisdictions, the insurer cannot invoke the doctrine of waiver to validate a policy if there is no appropriate insurable interest in the life of the proposed insured. Public policy requires that there be such an insurable interest. The right to require an insurable interest is not for the insurer's sole benefit but is also for the benefit of the public.

The policyowner may not be able to waive certain rights. For example, it has been held that a policyowner cannot waive rights under statutes that require notice of premium due, because these rights are for the benefit of the public as well as for the policyowner's benefit.[18]

The policyowner ordinarily cannot waive rights under nonforfeiture statutes, because these statutes have been enacted for the benefit of the public. One court said the following in regard to nonforfeiture statutes:

> The benefits conferred by these statutes cannot be abrogated, waived, or contracted away, either by agreement in the policy or by agreement made between the parties prior to default. . . . The public policy involved overrides the freedom of contract of the parties.[19]

Creation of Coverage

The rule in the majority of jurisdictions is that neither party can invoke waiver or estoppel to create coverage.[20] If the policy does not include a risk, or specifically excludes it, waiver or estoppel will not bring the risk within the policy coverage.

For example, in *Pierce v. Homesteaders Life Association,*[21] the policy provided that the insurer would pay the death benefit only if the insured died prior to attaining age 60. The insured attained age 60 on March 3 and died on March 11, but the premium had been paid through September. After the insured's death, the insurer tendered back the excess premium. In a lawsuit for the benefits, the beneficiary argued that, because the insurer had accepted premium payment for a period beyond the insured's 60th birthday and beyond her death, the insurer had waived the expiration of the insurance. The court held that the insurer did not owe the benefits. The court stated the following: "It has been repeatedly held that while a forfeiture of benefits contracted for may be waived, the doctrine of waiver or estoppel cannot be successfully invoked to create a liability for benefits not contracted for at all." However, exceptions to this rule exist, as will be shown in the illustrative case at the end of this chapter.

---

[18]Reynolds v. Metropolitan Life Ins. Co., 185 P. 1051 (Kan. 1919).

[19]Fayman v. Franklin Life Ins. Co., 386 S.W.2d 52 (Mo. 1965).

[20]Kaminer v. Franklin Life Ins. Co., 472 F.2d 1073 (5th Cir. 1973), *cert. denied,* 414 U.S. 840 (1973); Garland v. Jefferson Standard Life Ins. Co., 101 S.E. 616 (N.C. 1919).

[21]272 N.W. 543 (Iowa 1937).

Releases

If one person has a right to receive a sum of money from another person, the first person can release this right but cannot waive it. A **release** is the giving up of a right or claim and is therefore similar to a waiver. However, a release ordinarily requires that the person receiving the release give consideration for it. For example, an insurer gives the death benefit as consideration in exchange for a release from the beneficiary of the beneficiary's right to receive the death benefit.

A release is usually made in the form of a creditor's written statement that the creditor (for example, a beneficiary) has discharged the debtor (for example, an insurer) from his obligation. The creditor gives the written release to the debtor, which provides the debtor with a defense if the creditor should later claim that the debtor still owes the debt. Insurers often include a release on the back of a check given in payment of a claim. When the beneficiary endorses the check, he is also signing the release.

Revocation of Waiver

If an insurer acquires a right to avoid a contract or to set up a defense to payment of benefits because the other party has breached a condition of the contract, the insurer usually can waive its right if it wishes to do so. Once it waives its right it cannot revoke the waiver. The contract is as binding as before the breach of the condition.[22]

For example, suppose a policyowner breached a condition of the contract by failing to pay the premium before the end of the grace period. If the insurer told the policyowner it would not lapse the policy but would allow an extra 10 days for payment of the premium, the insurer would have expressly waived its right to declare the policy lapsed as of the end of the grace period. If the insured died five days after the end of the grace period, with the premium unpaid, the insurer could not then revoke the waiver and declare the policy lapsed as of the end of the grace period.

Nevertheless, an insurer may give express notice that it will, in the future, insist that the policyowner fulfill the contract conditions, even though it has waived strict compliance with those conditions in the past. For example, suppose an insurer has repeatedly accepted late payment of premiums. Its actions can give rise to an implied waiver of its right to lapse the policy if the premium is not paid on time. However, if the insurer notifies the policyowner before a premium due date that it will no longer accept late payment, this notification will revoke the implied waiver of the insurer's right to lapse the policy. In that case, the policy will lapse if the policyowner does not pay the premium on time.

Election of Remedies

The doctrine of **election of remedies** has elements of both waiver and estoppel. It is sometimes called estoppel by election. The courts apply the doctrine of election of remedies when a person has two or more inconsistent remedies available for the redress of a single wrong. The person must elect one of the remedies. This necessarily means she must forgo, or waive, her right to pursue other inconsistent remedies.

For example, in one case, an insurer canceled an insurance contract that provided disability income benefits.[23] The policyowner-insured, Rhame, sued the insurer for

---

[22]State Life Ins.Co. v. Finney, 114 So. 132 (Ala. 1927).

[23]Pacific Mut. Life Ins. Co. v. Rhame, 32 F. Supp. 59 (E.D.S.C. 1940).

breach of contract because of the cancellation, and the court awarded him damages. Later, Rhame claimed continuing disability benefits. The insurer filed a suit for declaratory judgment asking the court to rule on whether or not Rhame had a right to sue for the disability benefits.[24] The court held that Rhame had already chosen his remedy and that the courts could not "permit repeated actions of a nature inconsistent with that already adopted by the insured with reference to the contract in question." Quoting from another case, the court noted:

> By the weight of authority, where an insurer wrongfully cancels, repudiates, or terminates the contract of insurance, the insured may at once pursue either of three courses: (1) He may elect to treat the policy as still in force, and let the test of the validity of the cancellation or repudiation await until the policy is payable and is sued on; (2) he may sue in equity to set aside the cancellation, and to have the policy declared to be valid and in force; or (3) he may maintain an action at law to recover damages for the wrongful cancellation or repudiation.[25]

The court pointed out that in the *Rhame* case,

> Rhame unquestionably chose as his remedy the alternative of treating the contract at an end and instituting an action at law to recover damages for its wrongful cancellation or repudiation. The allegations of his complaint, which has been exhibited, do not in any manner indicate that he regarded the policy as still in force, or seek to base recovery on the provisions of the contract.

The court further said, quoting from yet another case:

> The doctrine of election of remedies is regarded as being an application of the law of estoppel, upon the theory that a party cannot in the assertion of his right occupy inconsistent positions in relation to the facts which form the basis of his respective remedies; it is based on the proposition that, when a party has two remedies proceeding upon opposite and irreconcilable claims of right, the one adopted excludes the other.[26]

Thus, Rhame was bound by his first choice of remedy, the award of money damages for wrongful cancellation of the contract, and could not proceed with the second suit for the payment of disability benefits under the contract. In other words, he could not treat the contract as canceled in one suit and later sue for disability benefits as if the contract were still in force. If a person carries an action for one remedy through to judgment, he cannot thereafter elect to pursue a second, inconsistent remedy. The doctrine of election of remedies prevents this. As one authority has pointed out, the doctrine of election of remedies is a legal version of the idea that a person "cannot have his cake and eat it too."[27]

Estoppel and the Parol Evidence Rule

Estoppels were originally equitable remedies and therefore applied only in courts of equity. When the common-law courts adopted estoppels, they did not fit in well with all of the common-law rules.

---

[24]A declaratory judgment is an action in which one party asks the court to declare the rights and duties of the parties to the action, but it involves no direct relief by the court as a consequence of the judgment. Declaratory judgments are discussed in Chapter 16, "Equitable Remedies."

[25]Schuler v. Equitable Life Assur. Soc., 193 S.E. 46 (S.C. 1937).

[26]McMahan v. McMahan, 15 S.E. 293 (S.C. 1922).

[27]Dan B. Dobbs, Law of Remedies § 9.4 (2d ed.1993).

Conflict between estoppel and the parol evidence rule of the common-law courts was inevitable. The parol evidence rule forbids introducing into court oral testimony of the words or actions of the parties to a written contract before the contract was signed if that testimony would contradict the written contract. If a party brought a lawsuit in which an alleged estoppel was based on words or actions of the parties *after* the contract became effective, this action did not conflict with the parol evidence rule. However, lawsuits involving alleged estoppels based on a party's words or actions *before* the policy was in force did conflict with the parol evidence rule.

In 1872, in *Union Mutual Insurance Co. v. Wilkinson,*[28] the U.S. Supreme Court held that such evidence was admissible to establish an estoppel. In the *Wilkinson* case, the proposed insured signed an application for a life insurance contract. By the terms of the policy, the policy became void if any of the representations in the application proved to be untrue. The statement in question concerned the age of the mother of the insured at the time of the mother's death. Alleging the untruth of the age represented, the insurer denied the claim for the death benefit.

In the trial that followed, the beneficiary offered evidence to show what actually took place at the time the application was taken. Witnesses testified that the agent asked the insured the age of her mother at the mother's death, and the insured said she did not know. Someone else who was present volunteered an answer, and the agent inserted it in the application. The insurer later found that the answer was incorrect. If admitted in the trial, this evidence would support an equitable estoppel against the insurer. The issue was whether the parol evidence rule would preclude the admission of this oral testimony.

The Court held that the oral testimony was admissible to establish an estoppel and that the insurer was estopped from pleading the misrepresentation. The Court said:

> It is in precisely such cases as this that courts of law in modern times have introduced the doctrine of equitable estoppels, or, as it is sometimes called, estoppels *in pais*. The principle is, that where one party has by his representations or his conduct induced the other party to a transaction to give him an advantage which it would be against equity and good conscience for him to assert, he would not in a court of justice be permitted to avail himself of that advantage. And although the cases to which this principle is to be applied are not as well defined as could be wished, the general doctrine is well understood and is applied by courts of law as well as equity where the technical advantage thus obtained is set up and relied on to defeat the ends of justice or establish a dishonest claim.
>
> * * * * *
>
> This principle does not admit oral testimony to vary or contradict that which is in writing, but it goes upon the idea that the writing offered in evidence was not the instrument of the party whose name is signed to it; that it was procured under such circumstances by the other side as estops that side from using it or relying on its contents; not that it may be contradicted by oral testimony, but that it may be shown by such testimony that it cannot be lawfully used against the party whose name is signed to it.

The courts of most states have followed this holding, although some exceptions do exist.

---

[28]80 U.S. (13 Wall.) 222 (1872).

Common Waiver and Estoppel Situations

A number of common situations in the insurance business can result in a waiver or an estoppel. This section will deal with waivers and estoppels that are apt to occur in connection with application submission, premium payment, and claim examination.

Application Submission

Many waivers and estoppels have resulted from the application process. Some of these waivers and estoppels have resulted from words or actions of the soliciting agent or the medical examiner. Others have resulted from words or actions of other agents in the home office, such as underwriters.

Fraud, Misconduct, or Negligence of an Agent.   Collusion between a soliciting agent and an applicant to insert false answers in the application will not result in an estoppel of the insurer to defend on the basis of the misrepresentation. However, as previously discussed, if the applicant gives the insurer's agent true answers, but the agent writes in false answers, the courts in the majority of jurisdictions impute the agent's knowledge to the insurer. These courts will hold that the insurer has waived its right to rescind the policy on the ground of material misrepresentation. In this situation, the insurer will have a cause of action against the agent for breach of the agent's fiduciary duty.

If the soliciting agent, while preparing an application, incorrectly interprets to the applicant the meaning of a question, an incorrect answer is binding on the insurer unless the applicant should reasonably suspect that the agent's interpretation is incorrect. For example, if an applicant tells an agent of a health problem, but the agent assures the applicant that the health problem need not be stated in the application, the insurer might be estopped if it tries to deny benefits on the ground that the information was not included. The *Boggio* case cited earlier in this chapter is an example of this principle.

Insurer's Failure to Inquire about Incomplete Answers.   If an insurer receives at its home office an application that has a missing or incomplete answer but does not make further inquiry of the applicant before issuing the policy, the insurer will have waived its right to a complete answer. The insurer cannot afterward rely on the incomplete application to deny benefits.[29]

Premium Payment

An insurer, eager to keep the policy in force, often does not insist that the policy-owner strictly abide by the terms of the policy in paying the premiums. As a result, waivers and estoppels are sometimes invoked in connection with premium payments. Waiver of the insurer's right to lapse the policy if the premium is not paid on time has been discussed above. Other waiver and estoppel situations in connection with premiums are discussed in this section.

Acceptance of a Check rather than Cash.   An insurer that has an established practice of accepting checks rather than cash in payment of premiums cannot declare

---

[29]Franklin Life Ins. Co. v. Bieniek, 312 F.2d 365 (3rd Cir. 1962).

a policy forfeited if the policyowner submits a check in payment. This is true even when the policy requires payment in cash. A court will hold that the insurer has waived its right to receive payment in cash.

Dishonored Checks.   If a policyowner pays a premium with a check, the insurer ordinarily accepts the check on the condition that the financial institution on which the check is written will honor the check.[30] If an insurer returns a dishonored check to the policyowner, the insurer will not have waived its right to declare the policy forfeited. However, if the insurer attempts to collect on the dishonored check, a court might hold that the insurer has waived its right to declare the policy forfeited.[31] This is because an attempt to collect on the dishonored check is inconsistent with the position that the insurer had accepted the check on condition that it be paid on presentation. If the insured dies while the insurer is attempting to collect on the dishonored check, and the court holds that the insurer has waived its right to declare the policy forfeited, the death benefit, minus the unpaid premium, will be payable to the beneficiary.

Premium Due Notices.   Often, the policyowner comes to rely on premium due notices sent by the insurer to remind him to pay the premium. When the insurer, without notifying the policyowner that it intends to cease sending such notices, fails to send a premium due notice, the policyowner will not forfeit the policy if he does not pay on time. The insurer will be estopped from asserting such a forfeiture because the insurer has misled the policyowner into believing that a premium due notice would be sent.

Moreover, if an insurer has customarily sent an agent to collect renewal premiums, the policyowner has a right to rely on this kind of notice also. If the insurer stops sending an agent to collect the premiums but does not notify the policyowner that it intends to stop, the policyowner will not forfeit the policy if she does not pay the premium on time.

Claim Examination

In many situations, the words or actions of an insurer during examination of a claim have resulted in a waiver or an estoppel. Some of the most common of these situations are described in this subsection.

The general rule here is that if the insurer knows of the breach of a condition that will cause a forfeiture of benefits but nevertheless enters into negotiations with the beneficiary, and those negotiations cause the beneficiary to incur trouble or expense in the belief that the insurer will pay the benefits, a court would probably hold that the insurer has waived its right to defend on the ground of the breach of condition or that the insurer is estopped from asserting the breach.

Proof of Loss.   If an insurer requires a beneficiary to submit completed proof of loss forms but does not inform the beneficiary that the insurer disputes his claim, the courts of many jurisdictions will infer that the insurer has waived the breach of condition that is the basis of the dispute. To avoid the possibility that a court will infer

---

[30]Kansas City Life Ins. Co. v. Davis, 95 F.2d 952 (9th Cir. 1938).
[31]Stewart v. Union Mut. Life Ins. Co., 49 N.E. 876 (N.Y. 1898).

such a waiver, the insurer must notify the beneficiary of the breach of condition and state that the insurer does not intend to waive the breach. The insurer can also protect itself in two other ways: (1) by inserting a specific nonwaiver clause in the policy or in the proof of loss form saying that the insurer does not waive the breach of a condition by examination of the claim; or (2) by obtaining an agreement with the beneficiary that the beneficiary's submission of proof of loss will not constitute a waiver by the insurer of the breach of a condition.

If an insurer receives a defective proof of loss but does not object to the defect in a timely manner, a court ordinarily will hold that the insurer has waived its right to proof of loss without defect. The insurer cannot then claim that the beneficiary should forfeit the policy proceeds because of the defect.

If a beneficiary notifies the insurer of a loss and requests proof of loss forms, but the insurer does not promptly send the forms, the insurer will have waived its right to require the beneficiary's timely submission of the completed forms. Moreover, as previously pointed out, if the insurer fails to send proof of loss forms when the beneficiary requests them but instead asks for other information, such as a newspaper account, a court might hold that the insurer has waived its right to require the beneficiary to submit proof of loss forms.

Delay of Claim Investigation.   If an insurer asks a beneficiary for additional time for investigation of a claim, and the investigation goes beyond the time in which the policy allows the beneficiary to bring a lawsuit, the insurer will have waived its right to the limitation of time in which the beneficiary can sue. The beneficiary will have a reasonable additional time in which to bring suit.

Promise to Pay.   The majority rule is that if the insurer promises to pay a claim where it knows of the breach of a condition that could result in a forfeiture of benefits, it has waived its right to defend a suit for benefits on the ground of the breach of the condition. On the other hand, the insurer's offer to compromise coupled with its denial of liability will not ordinarily result in such a waiver. An actual payment in full of the claim, where the insurer knows of the breach of a condition, implies a waiver of the insurer's right to defend on the ground of the breach.

Denial of Liability on One of Several Known Grounds.   In most jurisdictions, the courts apply the principle that an insurer that denies liability on less than all grounds for denial known to it will have waived any ground it has not specified. This is true especially when the beneficiary was put to trouble and expense in trying to collect the benefits before he knew of the additional grounds for denial. Therefore, an insurer that knows of more than one ground for denying liability under a contract should state all known grounds in its denial. If it fails to do so, and the beneficiary files suit to recover the benefit, the court will deem that the insurer has waived any unstated grounds for denial.[32]

Note that the court will deem that the insurer waived only its right to those defenses it knew of at the time of its denial of liability. If the insurer does not know of its right to defend a suit for benefits on a certain ground, the courts will not infer a waiver if the insurer did not specify that ground in its denial of liability.

---

[32]Craddock v. Fidelity Life Ass'n, 285 N.W. 169 (Iowa 1939).

Summary

A waiver is an intentional and voluntary giving up of a known right. A court will invoke estoppel in a situation in which person A has by words or conduct caused person B in reasonable reliance on those words or that conduct, to act so that harm results to B. A court will estop, that is, forbid, A to use the facts (the truth) in A's own defense. Waivers may be express, implied, or even, in some cases, implied by silence. The courts of some jurisdictions say that implied waivers are the same as estoppels.

A waiver requires that the waiving party have an intent to waive, express or implied, as well as knowledge of the pertinent facts. Estoppel also requires that the party estopped have knowledge of the pertinent facts. However, the knowledge of an insurer's agent often is imputed to the insurer. Such imputed knowledge has resulted in waivers by, or estoppels against, insurers.

Some waivers are forbidden. A person cannot waive a right that is partly for the public benefit. The rule in the majority of jurisdictions is that neither waiver nor estoppel can be invoked to create coverage for which the parties did not contract. The right to receive a sum of money can be released but not waived.

The legal doctrine of election of remedies is a special application of waiver and estoppel. Election of remedies means that a person, having chosen one remedy for the redress of a wrong, cannot later choose another, inconsistent remedy to redress the same wrong. The person has waived the right to pursue the inconsistent remedy and will be estopped to assert it.

The doctrine of estoppel, which had developed in courts of equity, conflicted with the parol evidence rule of the common-law courts when those courts adopted estoppel. Most courts have held that parol evidence is admissible to establish an estoppel.

ILLUSTRATIVE CASE

In the following case, the court pointed out the general rule that waiver and estoppel cannot create coverage beyond that stipulated in the contract. The court then decided that, under the extreme circumstances of this case, a decision contrary to the general rule was equitable.

MARGARET B. PITTS, Respondent

v.

NEW YORK LIFE INSURANCE COMPANY,
Appellant[33]
Supreme Court of South Carolina

LEGGE, Acting Justice.

Action by the beneficiary of a policy of insurance on the life of her husband to recover double indemnity by reason of his accidental death. The case was tried before the Honorable Clarence E. Singletary, Presiding Judge, without a jury; appeal is from his judgment in favor of the plaintiff.

On July 1, 1920, appellant insured the life of Reuben B. Pitts under a ten-year term policy for $10,000, or $20,000 in the event that his death should result from accident. On July 30, 1925, this policy was converted into an ordinary life policy, with like provision for double indemnity in case of death by accident, and with provision for payment of disability benefit of $100.00 per month if the insured should become disabled before age sixty. As so converted, its annual premium was $405.20, of which $10.00 was stated to be for the double indemnity coverage and $28.20 for the disability coverage, with the provision that after the insured should reach the age of sixty years the premiums to become due would be reduced by the amount of the premium charged for the disability coverage. It excluded the double indemnity coverage in case of death resulting from certain causes, among them "engaging, as a passenger or otherwise, in submarine or aeronautic operations."

On January 27, 1933, pursuant to application by the insured and the beneficiary, the double indemnity provision was amended by endorsement reading as follows:

In accordance with the request of the insured, the double indemnity benefit is hereby modified to permit the double indemnity provision to apply if the insured's death occurs as

---

[33]148 S.E.2d 369 (S.C. 1966).

the result of riding as a fare-paying passenger in a licensed passenger aircraft provided by an incorporated passenger carrier and operated by a licensed pilot on a regular passenger route between definitely established airports.

It is also understood and agreed that the entire provisions for double indemnity as included in the policy will apply only if death occurs prior to the anniversary of the policy on which the insured's age at nearest birthday is 65.

Any premium due on and after the anniversary on which the age of the insured at nearest birthday is 65 will be reduced by the amount of premium charged for the double indemnity benefit.

In 1942, when the insured reached age sixty, appellant reduced the annual premium by $28.20, the amount charged for the disability coverage. The insured became sixty-five years of age in 1947, but in that year and each year thereafter appellant continued to bill him without reduction of the premium by the amount ($10.00) charged for the double indemnity benefit; and the insured continued to pay the premiums as thus billed until his death, at the age of eighty-one, on March 25, 1963.

That the insured's death resulted from accident is not disputed. Appellant paid the face amount of the policy, $10,000 but refused to pay under the double indemnity provision. Its offer to refund the double indemnity premiums paid subsequent to August 1, 1947, together with interest on each such payment, was rejected.

In her complaint respondent [the beneficiary] alleged that appellant, having failed and neglected, after the insured had reached the age of sixty-five, to reduce the premium by the amount charged for the double indemnity benefit as it was obligated to do by the terms of the 1933 endorsement before mentioned, "has waived its right to rely upon the provisions of the said endorsement and is now estopped" to deny liability for such benefit. In its answer appellant alleged that its failure to note that the premium should be reduced in 1947 was the result of a clerical error, and that the continued payment by the insured and acceptance by it of the unreduced premium after the insured had reached the age of sixty-five were the result of inadvertence and mutual mistake and were contrary to the express terms and conditions of the policy.

It appears undisputed that appellant did not discover the error in its records, and the resulting erroneous billing of premiums, until after the insured's death.

The trial judge held that by having billed the insured for the full premium and accepted payment of the same each year for sixteen years after the insured had reached the age of sixty-five years appellant had waived a right to deny coverage under the double indemnity provision of the 1933 endorsement; and he accordingly ordered judgment for the plaintiff for $10,000.00, with interest from the date on which the face amount of the policy was paid to the beneficiary. That ruling is here challenged by several exceptions.

Policy provisions under which an insurer may assert non-coverage fall into two classes: (1) those providing for forfeiture; and (2) those limiting or excluding coverage. The former may be waived; with regard to the latter, the weight of authority is said to support the view expressed in 29A Am. Jur., Insurance, Section 1135, Page 289, as follows:

> The rule is well established that the doctrines of implied waiver and of estoppel, based upon the conduct or action of the insurer, are not available to bring within the coverage of a policy risks not covered by its terms, or risks expressly excluded therefrom, and the application of the doctrines in this respect is therefore to be distinguished from the waiver of, or estoppel to assert, grounds of forfeiture. Thus, while an insurer may be estopped by its conduct or its knowledge from insisting upon a forfeiture of a policy, the coverage, or restrictions on the coverage, cannot be extended by the doctrine of waiver or estoppel.

To the same effect is the following, from 16 Appleman, Insurance Law and Practice, Section 9090, page 629:

> It has been broadly stated that the doctrines of waiver and estoppel cannot be used to extend the coverage of an insurance policy or create a primary liability, but may only affect rights reserved therein. While an insurer may be estopped, by its conduct or its knowledge or by statute, from insisting on a forfeiture of a policy, under no conditions can the coverage or restrictions on coverage be extended by waiver or estoppel.

* * * * *

The essential elements of equitable estoppel are: (1) ignorance of the party invoking it of the truth as to the facts in question; (2) representations or conduct of the party estopped which mislead; (3) reliance upon such representations or conduct; and (4) prejudicial change of position as the result of such reliance. The presence of these elements is not essential to the establishment of implied waiver, which results merely from conduct of the party against whom the doctrine is invoked from which voluntary relinquishment of his known right is reasonably inferable. But the two doctrines are related, and have this in common: that the applicability of each in a particular situation results from conduct of the party against whom it is invoked which has rendered it inequitable that he assert a right to which, in the absence of such conduct, he would be entitled.

Whether an insurer, by accepting and retaining the premium for a coverage that by the terms of the policy is excluded or terminated, may be estopped to deny such coverage, must of course depend upon the circumstances of the particular case. For estoppel is an equitable doctrine, essentially flexible, and therefore to be applied or denied as the equities between the parties may preponderate. . . . Where the insurer over a long period of time after the date prescribed by it for the termination of a particular coverage has continued to demand, accept and retain the premium fixed by it for that coverage, it may reasonably be inferred that the insured, who in the normal course of things relies upon the insurer's billing, has been misled by such conduct to believe that the insurer has continued to accept the coverage. Upon the same premise, excusable ignorance on the part of the insured as to the true fact, i.e., that the insurer has made a mistake in its billing, may likewise be inferred.

In the present case, as has been noted, the premium for the double indemnity coverage, $10.00, was separate and distinct from, and in addition to, that charged for the normal coverage, $367.00. Although by the terms of the policy the double indemnity coverage was to expire in 1947, when the insured became sixty-five, the undisputed fact that appellant continued for sixteen years thereafter to bill him for such coverage, and to collect and retain it, in our opinion furnished sound and adequate basis for the three elements of estoppel—ignorance, misleading, and reliance—before mentioned. The fourth element, prejudicial change of position, is also present. For not only did the insured expend the amount of such premium, in response to the erroneous billing, during each of the sixteen years between 1947 and 1963, but the insurer's claim for relief from the consequences of its error comes not until after the death of the insured and therefore, we think, too late.

We need not, and do not, decide whether the rule of non-waiver is applicable in the present case, for we think that under the facts apparent in the record here the insurer is estopped to deny the coverage in question. The issue of estoppel was before the Court; it was one of law, the essential facts being undisputed; and the result reached was the just and correct one. Affirmance in that result is proper in such case. . . .[34]

Affirmed in result.

---

[34]The appeals court agreed with the decision of the trial court, which was in favor of the beneficiary.

Questions for Review

1. Define the term *waiver*.
2. Discuss revocation of waiver.
3. Under what conditions is an attempted waiver ineffective? What are some rights that the policyowner cannot waive?
4. What is the nonwaiver clause in an application or policy? Discuss its effectiveness.
5. Describe the doctrine of election of remedies.
6. Define the term *equitable estoppel*.
7. Discuss the conflict between equitable estoppel and the parol evidence rule.
8. Describe some situations involving insurance transactions in which a court might hold that an insurer has waived a right or is estopped to assert the truth.

6 FORMATION OF THE LIFE INSURANCE CONTRACT

Chapter Outline

Many of the rules that govern the formation of informal contracts in general also govern the formation of life insurance contracts. Rules unique to life insurance contracts also govern the formation of these contracts. The rules unique to life insurance contract formation are the subject of this chapter.

Life Insurance Offer and Acceptance

As with other informal contracts, life insurance contracts are created by the making of an offer by one party—called the offeror—and its acceptance by the other party—the offeree. Under some circumstances, the life insurance applicant makes the offer; under other circumstances, the insurer makes the offer.

Offer and Acceptance

The traditional life insurance offer and acceptance theory is that the applicant makes the offer and the insurer accepts the offer. This is true in many instances, but in others it is not. The wording of the application usually governs. Usually, too, the initial premium must accompany the application if the applicant makes the offer.

If the initial premium does not accompany the application, submission of the application is ordinarily an invitation to the insurer to make an offer. The insurer can make the offer by issuing and delivering the policy. The applicant can then accept the insurer's offer by paying the initial premium.

One court held that a direct-response insurance advertisement for accidental death insurance, with application attached, was a complete offer by the insurer.[1] Direct-response insurance solicitation is done by direct mail or media advertisement, without the involvement of a soliciting agent. Thus, no agent was available to discuss the coverage with the applicant. The advertisement contained all the information that the applicant needed to make a decision regarding purchase of the insurance. The applicant did not have to answer any medical questions, and the insurer was not likely to reject the application. The advertisement indicated that the insurer would issue the insurance on receipt of an application and the premium from any member of a certain automobile club. Therefore, the court held that when the applicant sent in the application and the premium, she accepted the insurer's offer.

In the case of life insurance marketed by a soliciting agent, ordinarily when the applicant submits an application and the initial premium, the applicant makes an offer. The insurer can accept the applicant's offer by issuing of a policy in accordance with the terms of the application. If the insurer's acceptance occurs during the lifetime and continued good health of the proposed insured, a contract results.

Counteroffers

If, in the situation just described, the insurer chooses to issue a policy with different terms than the policy applied for, it is rejecting the applicant's offer and making a counteroffer. The general rule of contract law regarding acceptances is that they must be in accordance with the offer. A purported acceptance that differs from the offer is

---

[1]Riordan v. Automobile Club, 422 N.Y.S.2d 811 (1979).

actually a rejection of the offer and a ***counteroffer***. For example, if an applicant applies for a policy with a standard premium, and the insurer issues the policy with a higher-than-standard premium, the insurer has rejected the applicant's offer and made a counteroffer.

The applicant must accept the insurer's counteroffer, or the parties will not have created a contract. Therefore, if the proposed insured dies before the counteroffer has been accepted, there is no contract and no death benefit will be payable.[2]

In one case the court summarized the law in counteroffer situations as follows:

> The company reserved the right to accept or reject the proposition contained in the application.
>
> "The application being a mere proposal to the company, it can either accept the proposal, decline it altogether or impose such conditions as to the making of the contract, as it may choose." McCully's Admr. v. Phoenix Mutual Life Insurance Co., 18 W. Va. 782. . . .
>
> In this case the insurance company's reply to the application was the sending of a policy, differing in essential terms from that applied for, to the Wheeling Branch Office. This amounted to a counter-proposition and there was no contract, no meeting of the minds of the parties on the new terms, without acceptance thereof by [the applicant].[3]

Withdrawal of the Application

Until the offeree has accepted the offer, the offeror has the right to withdraw the offer. Therefore, if an applicant tells the insurer that he withdraws the application before the insurer has accepted the applicant's offer, the offer terminates. If the applicant has submitted the initial premium, the insurer must return it.[4]

Rejection of the Application

An insurance contract, like other contracts, rests on the assent of the parties. An insurer ordinarily does not have a duty to accept an application. It can reject the application for any reason or even without a reason. As with most general rules, this rule has exceptions. Statutes or regulations may prohibit denial of insurance on the basis of mental or physical impairment, sex, marital status, or sexual preference.

Signature on the Application

Usually, the insurer requires that the applicant sign the application. When the applicant's signature is required, his failure to sign the application precludes the making of a contract. Ordinarily, the applicant must sign personally. However, if another person has signed the applicant's name at the applicant's direction, and the insurer's agent knows this, the insurer will usually be bound on the contract.

---

[2]There could be a death benefit payable under a contract of temporary life insurance in a premium receipt, but not under the policy applied for. Temporary life insurance contracts are discussed below.

[3]Kronjaeger v. Travelers Ins. Co., 22 S.E.2d 689 (W. Va. 1942).

[4]Wheelock v. Clark, 131 P. 35 (Wyo. 1913).

Delay in Acting on the Application

A general rule of contract law is that a court will not interpret silence on the part of an offeree as an acceptance. Nevertheless, as to insurers, many courts that have considered the point have held that an insurer must act with reasonable promptness when it receives an application.[5] In a few states, a Court will impose contract liability if the insurer does not act promptly. In nearly one-third of the states, a court will impose tort liability.

Contract Liability for Unreasonable Delay

The weight of authority is that an insurer's silence or inaction will not result in an acceptance of the applicant's offer. Some courts have stated that the applicant should infer that a delay constitutes a rejection and should act accordingly.

However, a few courts have held that an insurer's unreasonable delay in passing on an application gives rise to an implied acceptance. A few others have held that if the applicant submits the initial premium along with the application, and such a delay occurs, the insurer's retention of the premium is inconsistent with rejection of the risk. For this reason, these courts will infer that the insurer accepted the risk.

Illustrative of this point of view is the discussion of the Michigan Supreme Court in *Wadsworth v. New York Life Insurance Co.*[6] That case dealt with an application for life insurance submitted by a captain in the U.S. Air Force who paid the first full premium in cash at the time of application. He was lost in action in the Korean War before the insurer approved the application. The court discussed the effect of the insurer's delay in considering the application as follows:

> Appellant [the beneficiary] contends in her second issue that a contract arose as a matter of law through defendant's [the insurer's] unreasonable delay in acceptance or rejection of the application filed by the deceased. . . .
>
> Michigan, it appears, is among the minority of States in holding that there is a duty on the part of the insurance company to act with reasonable promptness. In Robinson v. United States Benevolent Society, 132 Mich. 695, at page 699, 94 N.W. 211, at page 212, this Court stated:
>
> "In insurance contracts of this character it is the duty of the company to act with reasonable promptness. Failing to reject within reasonable time, the law implies an acceptance. . . ."
>
> We do not know what other facts may be shown on retrial but where, as currently shown in the record before us, substantial delay in accepting or rejecting is coupled with retention of the first and succeeding premiums, the question of whether or not there was such unreasonable delay on the part of the defendant or its agent as to imply acceptance would be a question of fact for the jury.

Although the court phrased this discussion primarily in terms of contract law, the statement that the insurer has a duty to act with reasonable promptness brings an element of tort liability into the analysis.

Since delay can mislead the applicant to his harm, the insurer has been estopped to deny acceptance in some circumstances. For example, if an insurer induced an applicant to believe that the insurer would accept his application and in reliance on

---

[5]Kristine Cordier Karnezis, Annotation, *Liability of Insurer for Damages Resulting from Delay in Passing upon an Application for Life Insurance,* 1 A.L.R. 4th 1202 (1980).

[6]84 N.W.2d 513 (Mich. 1957).

the representations made to him the applicant then refrained from obtaining other insurance, the insurer might be estopped to deny that it had accepted the application.[7]

Tort Liability for Unreasonable Delay

An unreasonable delay in acting on an application can subject the insurer to tort damages for negligence in some jurisdictions.[8] A tort is a wrongful act or omission, not arising out of a contractual relationship, causing harm to another person and giving the other person a cause of action for damages. A suit of this kind is called an action in tort. It is based on a legal duty of the defendant, the defendant's violation of that duty (usually through negligence), and resulting harm to the plaintiff. For example, where A negligently operates an automobile and collides with an automobile driven by B, A can be liable in tort for any harm to B's car or person. A has a legal duty to drive with reasonable care.

A tort liability doctrine for an insurer's unreasonable delay in acting on an application has developed in nearly one-third of the states. This doctrine is based on the premise that when an insurer receives an application, it has a duty to act on the application with reasonable promptness. If the insurer does not act with reasonable promptness and the proposed insured dies without insurance coverage, the insurer can be liable in tort damages up to the amount that the beneficiary would have recovered under the life insurance policy. Courts that take this position concede that most business organizations have no comparable duty but maintain that, because insurance is a business affected with a public interest and insurers operate under a state franchise, an insurer has a duty to accept or reject an application within a reasonable time.

A nearly equal number of states have rejected this tort liability doctrine on the ground that insurers are not public utilities and therefore courts should not impose a duty on insurers to consider applications promptly. One of the earliest rejections of the tort liability doctrine was voiced in 1929 by the Supreme Court of Mississippi in the case of *Savage v. Prudential Life Insurance Co.*[9] The court said:

> The fact that the insurance companies are granted a franchise to do business in this state does not and should not impose upon them the duty to consider promptly all who offer to them the risk of insuring their lives, no more than would be required of a bank to lend money promptly to all who should make application and suffer loss while the bank was negligent in determining whether or not it would accept the offer and enter into a contract.

Many insurance spokespeople and lawyers have criticized the theory that imposes tort liability on insurers for delay in acting on an application. Although the tort theory became popular in the 1920s, this popularity has since diminished, and, in recent years, few states have adopted or rejected it. The widespread use of premium receipts providing temporary life insurance has no doubt played an important part in

---

[7]Zielinski v. General Am. Life Ins. Co., 96 S.W.2d 1059 (Mo. Ct. App. 1936).

[8]*E.g.*, Continental Life & Acci. Co. v. Songer, 603 P.2d 921 (Ariz. Ct. App. 1979); Smith v. Minnesota Mut. Life Ins. Co., 195 P.2d 457 (Cal. App. 1948); Duffy v. Banker's Life Ass'n, 139 N.W. 1087 (Iowa 1913); Boyer v. State Farmers' Mut. Hail Ins. Co., 121 P. 329 (Kan. 1912); Witten v. Beacon Life Ass'n, 33 S.W.2d 989 (Mo. Ct. App. 1931); Fox v. Volunteer State Life Ins. Co., 116 S.E. 266 (N.C. 1923), *later appeled* 119 S.E.172 (N.C. 1923); Peddicord v. Prudential Ins. Co. of Am., 498 P.2d 1388 (Okla. 1972).

[9]121 So. 487 (Miss. 1929).

slowing what once appeared to be a popular trend. Nevertheless, benefits under a temporary life insurance contract are sometimes not payable, or are payable in a smaller amount than the policy applied for would have provided. In such a situation, if the insurer has unreasonably delayed in acting on the application, some states impose tort liability. Moreover, in 1979, an Arizona appellate court said that a court need not restrict the amount of damages for negligent delay in passing on an insurance application to the amount that would have been paid if the contract had existed, but could include damages for emotional distress and punitive damages.[10] Because of these various theories of liability, insurers are well advised to act on applications with reasonable promptness.

Temporary Life Insurance Contracts

An applicant for life insurance receives a premium receipt when she submits the initial premium along with the application. Usually, such a receipt includes a contract providing temporary life insurance. This section contains a description of various types of temporary life insurance contracts included in premium receipts and the law governing these contracts.

Almost always, some time elapses between the date the applicant submits the application and the date the policy is effective. During this period, the insurer ordinarily will not cover the death of the proposed insured without a premium receipt providing temporary life insurance, even if the applicant paid the initial premium. It is apparent that it would be to the advantage of the applicant and beneficiary if the insurer provided temporary life insurance during the period in which the insurer is completing its underwriting procedures. It is just as clearly to the advantage of the agent and the insurer to provide such insurance. If the insurer does not provide temporary life insurance, the applicant has no compelling reason to pay the initial premium before the insurer delivers the policy. If the applicant does not prepay the premium, the agent frequently has to make the sale twice—once when taking the application and later when delivering the policy. Often, it is difficult or impossible to make the sale the second time. Moreover, when the applicant has submitted the initial premium, he is less likely to continue to shop around for life insurance. The use of a premium receipt providing temporary life insurance gives the soliciting agent a strong argument in her attempt to persuade the applicant to pay the initial premium at the time that the agent and applicant complete the application.

Without a premium receipt providing temporary life insurance, a difficult situation arises for the agent if the applicant pays the initial premium with the application and the proposed insured dies before the policy becomes effective. The agent is then in the unhappy position of having to tell the beneficiary that, although the insurer had the premium in its possession at the time that the proposed insured died, no life insurance was in force.

For these reasons, life insurers began at an early date to experiment with ways to provide temporary life insurance during the period that they were considering an application. This made life insurance practices more consistent with practices followed in other lines of insurance where coverage often is effective immediately, subject to the insurer's right to cancel it later if the insurer finds that the risk is not acceptable.

---

[10]Continental Life & Acci. Co. v. Songer, 603 P.2d 921 (Ariz. App.1979).

If the premium receipt provides for temporary life insurance, the agent is authorized to extend the insurer's offer to make the temporary life insurance effective on a date prior to the effective date of the policy, as long as any conditions specified in the premium receipt are met. The applicant accepts this offer by performing the act that the insurer requests—that is, by paying the initial premium at the time the applicant submits the application.

Ordinarily, a premium receipt states that the temporary life insurance contract is subject to the terms of the applied-for policy. Thus, for example, if the applied-for policy includes a suicide exclusion, and the proposed insured commits suicide while the temporary insurance contract is in effect, the insurer would not have to pay benefits. A material misrepresentation in the application will allow the insurer to avoid liability under the temporary life insurance contract, just as it will under the policy itself.

If terms in the temporary life insurance contract conflict with the terms in the policy, the terms of the temporary life insurance contract control. For example, if the temporary life insurance contract limits the benefits to $75,000, and the proposed insured dies while the temporary life insurance contract is in effect, no more than $75,000 will be payable. It will not matter that the policy applied for provides higher benefits.

Although the wording of temporary life insurance contracts in premium receipts varies a great deal, most premium receipts fall into one of three categories: the approval premium receipt, the insurability premium receipt, or the binding premium receipt. The approval premium receipt and the insurability premium receipt are often called **conditional premium receipts**. That is, they will not provide temporary life insurance unless certain conditions occur. Two types of conditions—conditions precedent and conditions subsequent—are discussed below. All premium receipts providing temporary life insurance involve one or the other.

Conditions Precedent and Conditions Subsequent

The word *precedent* means "coming before." A **condition precedent** is an uncertain event that must occur before a right arises. For example, the death of the insured while the policy is in force is an uncertain event that must occur before the beneficiary's right to the death benefit arises. Other uncertain events (conditions) also must occur before the beneficiary has a right to the death benefit. For example, the beneficiary must provide notice and proof of death to the insurer.

Another way to view a condition precedent is that it is an uncertain event that must occur before the duty to perform a promise arises. Thus, the death of the insured while the policy is in force is a condition precedent to the duty of the insurer to pay the death benefit.

The word *subsequent* means "following after." A **condition subsequent** is an event that cancels an existing right. For example, if a policy contains a provision that the beneficiary cannot bring suit on the policy after two years from the date of loss, the expiration of the two-year period will ordinarily cancel the beneficiary's right to maintain an action on the policy. The expiration of the two-year period is the occurrence of a condition subsequent.

Simply stated, the occurrence of a condition precedent gives rise to a right; the occurrence of a condition subsequent cancels an existing right. The relationship of conditions precedent and conditions subsequent to premium receipts will be explained in the following analyses of conditional and binding premium receipts.

Approval Premium Receipts

The **approval premium receipt** is one type of conditional premium receipt. If an agent issues an approval premium receipt, and the proposed insured dies after the agent gives the applicant the receipt but before the insurer approves the risk, no temporary life insurance will exist. The temporary life insurance contract in the approval premium receipt gives the applicant very little protection because it provides temporary life insurance only from the date of approval of the risk until the date the policy takes effect. At one time, the approval premium receipt was probably the most commonly used conditional premium receipt, but because it unnecessarily restricts temporary insurance coverage insurers have largely replaced it with the insurability premium receipt.

The effectiveness of temporary life insurance under the approval premium receipt is subject to the occurrence of a condition precedent. That is, before the right to temporary life insurance arises, the insurer must approve the risk.

Insurability Premium Receipts

An **insurability premium receipt** is the other type of conditional premium receipt. If the agent issues an insurability premium receipt, and the proposed insured dies after the receipt is given but before the insurer issues the policy, benefits under the temporary insurance contract will be payable if the insurer determines that the proposed insured was insurable on the date of the receipt, of the application, or of a required examination, depending on the language in the receipt. The language of insurability premium receipts varies from one insurer to another.

If the insurer has not determined the insurability of the proposed insured at the time that the insurer learns of the proposed insured's death, ordinarily the insurer must determine it afterward. The insurer must make the determination in good faith and according to the insurer's own insurability rules. Thus, a proposed insured can have coverage for a significant period of time under an insurability premium receipt, although the amount that the insurer will pay is usually limited. An illustrative insurability premium receipt appears in Figure 6–1.

As with the approval premium receipt, the effectiveness of the insurability premium receipt is subject to the occurrence of a condition precedent. Before the right to temporary life insurance arises, the insurer must have determined that the proposed insured was insurable on the date specified in the premium receipt. The temporary life insurance will then be effective as of that date.

To illustrate, suppose James Diebold completes and signs an application for a $100,000 policy insuring his life from the Ajax Life Insurance Company and submits the initial premium along with the application to the soliciting agent. The soliciting agent, Ellen Wong, gives Diebold an insurability premium receipt identical to the premium receipt in Figure 6–1 and forwards the application and the initial premium to the home office. She then orders an inspection report and a medical examination.

If the Condition Precedent Occurs.   The home office receives the inspection report and the medical examiner's report. Risk appraisal personnel review these documents and find that Diebold meets their standards as an insurable risk. An authorized officer then approves the issuance of a policy on the exact plan and in the amount for which Diebold applied. Suppose that this officer has just approved and is about to initial the application when the telephone rings. It is agent Wong calling long

FIGURE 6–1

Insurability premium receipt

A. The face of the receipt

Name of Proposed Insured if other than Applicant _____.

RECEIVED FROM _____, APPLICANT, $_____
IN CONNECTION WITH THE INITIAL PREMIUM FOR THE PROPOSED INSUR-
ANCE FOR WHICH AN APPLICATION IS THIS DAY MADE TO THE AJAX LIFE
INSURANCE COMPANY.

   Life Insurance and any additional benefits in the amount applied for, but not exceeding a
maximum liability of $75,000, including all additional benefits on all pending applications to
the company combined, shall be deemed to take effect as of the date of this receipt, subject
to the terms and conditions printed on the reverse side hereof.

   The amount received shall be refunded if the application is declined or if a policy is issued
other than as applied for and is not accepted. Any check, draft, or moneyorder is received by
the company subject to collection.

Date of Receipt _____   Signature of Agent _____

B. The back of the receipt

Subject to the limitations of this receipt and the terms and conditions of the policy that may
be issued by the company on the basis of the application, the life insurance and any additional benefits applied for shall not be deemed to take effect unless the company, after investigation and such medical examination, if any, as it may require, shall be satisfied that on the
date of this receipt the person proposed for insurance was insurable for the amount of life
insurance and any additional benefits applied for according to the company's rules and practice of selection; provided, however, that approval by the company of the insurability of the
Proposed Insured for a plan of insurance other than that applied for, or the denial of any
particular additional benefit applied for, shall not invalidate the terms and conditions of this
receipt relating to life insurance and any other additional benefit applied for.

(Not to be detached unless issued under the requirements for using Conditional Receipt)

distance to say that on the previous day an automobile struck and killed Diebold. The
determination that Diebold was insurable—the condition precedent—will put the
temporary insurance contract into effect as of the date of the premium receipt. Thus,
the death benefit under the temporary insurance contract will be payable.

If the Condition Precedent Does Not Occur.   Suppose now that agent Wong mails
the application and the premium check to the insurer, orders an inspection report, and
arranges for a medical examination. Suppose also that the risk appraiser reviews the
documents and finds that Diebold does not meet the insurer's requirements in accordance with its standard practices of risk selection. The risk appraiser is about to make
that notation on the application file when the telephone rings, and agent Wong reports
Diebold's fatal accident.

   In this instance, Diebold is not insured under the terms of the temporary insurance contract. The condition of insurability has not occurred. Even though the insurer
has not yet sent a notice of disapproval, this can follow the death of the proposed
insured. However, the insurer must be prepared to support its decision as to the

proposed insured's lack of insurability and to set forth the controlling language of the insurability premium receipt in a court of law if necessary. Even if the insurer succeeds in doing this, the insurer's liability will depend on the jurisdiction involved, because an increasing number of courts find that there is coverage under an insurability premium receipt even where the proposed insured was not eligible for the applied-for insurance policy. This topic will be discussed in the subsection below entitled "Premium Receipts in the Courts."

Binding Premium Receipts

Many insurers use a premium receipt that is appropriately termed a **binding premium receipt**. Under a binding premium receipt, temporary life insurance always becomes effective on the date the applicant receives the receipt. No conditions need be fulfilled. Typically, as with conditional premium receipts, the insurer limits the amount that will be payable under the temporary life insurance contract in the receipt.

The temporary life insurance continues for the maximum period of time that the binding premium receipt specifies or until the insurer acts on the application, whichever happens earlier. An illustrative binding premium receipt is shown in Figure 6–2.

A binding premium receipt is subject to a condition subsequent. That is, the applicant's right to temporary life insurance coverage arises at the time the applicant submits the application and initial premium in exchange for the binding premium receipt. This right will be canceled if the insurer notifies the applicant that the proposed insured is uninsurable, or if a specified period of time elapses. This right will also be cancelled if the policy is approved, but thereafter there will be coverage under the policy itself.

Binding premium receipts are more advantageous to applicants than are conditional receipts, because the coverage under a binding receipt is effective immediately on payment of the initial premium, without conditions. The courts of some jurisdictions have interpreted premium receipts that insurers meant to be conditional as if they were binding receipts. For this reason, some insurers have abandoned conditional receipts and now use binding receipts instead. This avoids the legal problems that are often associated with the use of conditional receipts. It also has the advantage that binding receipts are easier to explain and more appealing to applicants than conditional receipts. The following subsection contains a discussion of court cases interpreting premium receipts.

Premium Receipts in the Courts

Binding premium receipts have not presented the significant legal problems for life insurers that conditional premium receipts have presented. This is true because binding receipts make temporary insurance effective immediately on payment of the initial premium, and thus some insurance is usually in effect if the proposed insured dies prior to issuance of the policy.

Binding receipts are subject to a condition subsequent. That is, they provide that the right to temporary insurance coverage, which is effective on issuance of the receipt, will be canceled after a specified period or when the insurer takes action on the application, whichever is earlier. Conditional receipts, on the other hand, are subject to a condition precedent. The right to temporary insurance coverage arises only on the occurrence of a condition—approval of the application in the case of an approval

FIGURE 6–2

Binding premium receipt

A. The face of the receipt

Received $_____ from the Applicant in connection with the life application made this day to the Ajax Life Insurance Company for insurance on the life of _____ (proposed insured). Any check or draft is received subject to collection, and, if it is not honored when presented for payment, this receipt is void.

Effective with the date of the application and subject to the terms and conditions on the front and reverse of this receipt, all death benefits applied for shall take effect for death as a result of accidental or natural causes originating after the date of the application. HOWEVER, THE TOTAL DEATH BENEFIT FOR ANY PERSON INSURED UNDER THIS AND ALL OTHER BINDING RECEIPTS AND PENDING APPLICATIONS COMBINED SHALL NOT EXCEED $100,000. IF SUCH PERSON IS UNDER THE AGE OF 15 DAYS AT DEATH, THE TOTAL DEATH BENEFIT SHALL NOT EXCEED $3,000.

Date of application _____   Signature of agent _____

B. The back of the receipt

Coverage under this receipt shall continue until terminated by the earliest of (*a*) approval of the application, (*b*) notification of disapproval of the application, or (*c*) expiration of a 60-day period beginning with the date of the application. The company reserves the absolute right to disapprove the application by offering to issue a policy with an extra rating or other than as applied for, or by declining to issue a policy. Notification of disapproval of the application shall be given to the proposed insured or to the applicant, if other than the proposed insured, by either (*a*) personal notification or (*b*) mailing of such notification to the last known address, in which case the termination of coverage is effective upon mailing.

Monies received with the application will be refunded if a policy is offered and is not accepted or if the coverage under this receipt is terminated by either (*a*) notification of disapproval without offer of any policy or (*b*) the expiration of the 60-day period beginning with the date of the application.

Coverage under this receipt shall be void if the application contains any material misrepresentation.

NO AGENT OR OTHER COMPANY REPRESENTATIVE MAY WAIVE OR MODIFY THE ANSWER TO ANY QUESTION IN THE APPLICATION OR MODIFY THE TERMS OR CONDITIONS OF THIS RECEIPT.

premium receipt and a determination of insurability in the case of an insurability premium receipt.

Sometimes, an insurer intends a premium receipt to be subject to a condition precedent, but a court interprets the receipt to be subject to a condition subsequent instead. In other words, sometimes a court interprets a receipt as binding when the insurer meant it to be conditional.

Until relatively recently, a clear majority of the courts that had considered questions involving conditional receipts had upheld the conditions that the insurer intended. Unless the wording was definitely ambiguous, the court usually held that the conditional receipt expressed a condition precedent with the result that the temporary life insurance was not effective unless the condition had occurred.

Indeed, many courts still take this position. For example, in a 1971 Maryland case, the court held that an applicant must meet the insurer's objective test of insurability to have coverage under a conditional premium receipt.[11]

However, many other courts now interpret conditional premium receipts as if they were binding. The courts that have done so have based their decisions on ambiguity in the premium receipt in some instances. In other instances, they have based the decision on the doctrine that the insurer must honor the reasonable expectations of the applicant and that an average applicant would expect temporary life insurance coverage to be immediate and unconditional. In still other instances, the court has based its decision on unconscionability or on public policy.

For example, the Nevada Supreme Court took a harsh view of conditional premium receipts in a 1967 case.[12] There the court said:

> A conditional receipt tends to encourage deception. We do not mean to imply affirmative misconduct by the soliciting insurance agent. We suggest only that if nothing is said about the complicated and legalistic phrasing of the receipt, and the agent accepts an application for insurance together with the first premium payment, the applicant has reason to believe that he is insured. Otherwise, he is deceived.

In 1971, the Idaho Supreme Court declared that the use of conditional premium receipts "borders on the unconscionable."[13]

Statutes and Regulations Governing Premium Receipts

Some states have statutes or regulations governing premium receipts. For example, California has sought to reduce conditional premium receipt problems by enacting a statute requiring that the insurer pay the claim if the proposed insured dies prior to the date that the insurer approves the application, if the proposed insured was insurable and if the initial premium was submitted with the application. It does not matter whether or not the agent issued a premium receipt. However, the insurer can limit the amount for which it may be liable prior to the date that the policy is in effect.[14]

Risk Classification and Selection

Risk classification means the insurer's identification of people with similar loss potential and placement of those people in the same risk group for the purpose of setting premium rates. Age, sex, health, occupation, and hobbies are criteria insurers use to classify risks.

Risk selection means the insurer's choice from among its proposed insureds of those persons it is willing to insure. Underwriters in the insurer's home office ordinarily select life insurance risks. Soliciting agents do not have the authority to determine the insurability of the proposed insured because life insurers, unlike other

[11]Cannon v. Southland Life Ins. Co., 283 A.2d 404 (Md. 1971).
[12]Prudential Ins. Co. of Am. v. Lamme, 425 P.2d 346 (Nev. 1967).
[13]Toevs v. Western Farm Bureau Life Ins. Co., 483 P.2d 682 (Idaho 1971).
[14]CAL. INS. CODE § 10,115 (West 1993).

insurers, ordinarily cannot cancel life insurance contracts. Therefore, life insurers must select risks with great care.

Discrimination

One meaning of the word *discriminate* is "to note differences." All risk classification involves discrimination in this sense of the word. Insurers charge young people less than they charge older people for insurance on their lives. Healthy people pay less than those with impaired health, and those few with very impaired health may not be insurable at all. Persons in hazardous occupations pay more than persons in safe occupations. Women, who as a group live seven years longer than men, pay less than men for insurance on their lives but more for annuities. Each person pays according to the risk he or she presents. Classifying and pricing risks is the very essence of insurance.

Nearly all the states have passed laws prohibiting unfair discrimination. For example, the New York insurance law, which is typical, provides that no life insurer "shall make or permit any unfair discrimination between individuals of the same class and of equal expectation of life" in premiums, terms, benefits, or dividends.[15] Note that this law prohibits *unfair* discrimination, not discrimination itself. Under these laws, fairness means equal treatment for equal risk.

Unfair Handicap Discrimination.   In 1978, the National Association of Insurance Commissioners adopted the Model Regulation on Unfair Discrimination on the Basis of Blindness or Partial Blindness. In 1979, the NAIC adopted the Model Regulation on Unfair Discrimination in Life and Health Insurance on the Basis of Physical or Mental Impairment. All but a few states have laws patterned on the first of these model laws, and about half the states have laws patterned on the second or have related laws. All of these laws prohibit discrimination against applicants or insureds solely because of blindness or physical or mental impairment. The laws allow an insurer to refuse to insure, to limit the coverage, or to charge a different rate if such action "is based on sound actuarial principles or is related to actual or reasonably anticipated experience."[16]

Unfair Sex Discrimination.   In 1976, the NAIC adopted the Model Regulation to Eliminate Unfair Sex Discrimination. The purpose of the model regulation is to give men and women equal access to insurance by prohibiting insurers from denying insurance coverage on the basis of sex or marital status. Some states have patterned their regulations on this model regulation; others already had regulations similar to the model. The majority of states now prohibit unfair discrimination based on sex through insurance statutes or regulations, equal rights provisions in their constitutions, or other laws.

Laws patterned on the Model Regulation to Eliminate Unfair Sex Discrimination do not mandate unisex insurance rates. The preamble to the model regulation notes that "since the business of insurance is built upon the ability of the insurance company to evaluate risk and assign a price tag to that risk, any attempt to tamper with the pricing mechanism of the insurance business must be approached with great

---

[15]N.Y. Ins. Law § 4224(a) (McKinney Supp.1996).

[16]Model Regulation on Unfair Discrimination in Life and Health Insurance on the Basis of Physical or Mental Impairment, § 3 (Nat'l Ass'n of Ins. Comm'rs 1979).

care." As noted below, there have been attempts, mostly unsuccessful, to impose unisex rates for insurance and annuities.

Limitations on Liberty of Contract

Under the general law of contracts, each person has the right to choose the contracts into which he is willing to enter and the persons with whom he is willing to contract. Therefore, generally speaking, an insurer has the right to accept or reject an applicant's offer to contract and the right to insure a proposed insured at a standard rate, to offer to insure at a substandard rate, or to decline to insure altogether. However, this general rule of liberty of contract as it applies to insurers is limited. As noted above, an insurer cannot decline to insure on the basis of physical or mental impairment, blindness, sex, or marital status.

Two limitations on insurers' liberty of contract that have been of concern to the insurance industry are mandatory unisex insurance rates and restrictions on the right of insurers to determine if a proposed insured has been infected with the AIDS virus. In addition, a debate has arisen about the right of insurers to use genetic testing to determine the insurability of applicants.

Mandatory Unisex Rates.   In 1983, the U.S. Supreme Court in *Arizona Governing Committee v. Norris*[17] ruled that the use of gender-based actuarial tables in a life annuity option of an employer's pension plan violates the federal Civil Rights Act of 1964. Title VII of the Civil Rights Act of 1964 forbids unfair discrimination in employment. Natalie Norris, a female employee of the state of Arizona, received a smaller life annuity on retirement than a male would have received in identical circumstances. Arizona pointed out that all the insurers through which it could offer a life annuity used gender-based actuarial tables in determining benefits under annuity contracts and that the state did not intend to discriminate. The state had provided the same amount of money to purchase the annuity that it would have provided for a male. Nevertheless, the U.S. Supreme Court ruled in favor of Natalie Norris.

The *Norris* case involved only an employment practice. It does not prevent insurers from using gender-based tables of mortality rates. Shortly after the Supreme Court decided *Norris,* the NAIC adopted a model regulation that permits insurers to use sex-blended tables of mortality rates. Most states have regulations patterned on this model regulation. Insurers now provide products with unisex insurance rates to enable their employer-clients to comply with the *Norris* decision.

Prior to the *Norris* decision, a few states mandated that automobile insurance be priced the same for men and women. After *Norris,* Congress and the legislatures of many states considered mandatory unisex rates for all insurance lines. Montana has actually enacted such a statute.[18] The Pennsylvania Supreme Court has upheld unisex insurance rates in that state. The court affirmed a lower court ruling that the use of different rates for men and women is in violation of the equal rights amendment of the Pennsylvania constitution.[19]

Most insurers have steadfastly opposed unisex insurance rates. Insurance industry spokespersons argue that the use of gender for classifying insureds is not unfair discrimination, but rather allows insurance costs to more accurately reflect risks.

---

[17]463 U.S. 1073 (1983).

[18]Mont. Code Ann. § 49-2-309 (1995).

[19]Bartholomew v. Foster, 563 A.2d 1390 (1989), *aff'g* 541 A.2d 393 (Pa. Commw. Ct. 1988).

Statistical and actuarial data have clearly established that, as a group, women live significantly longer than men. A mortality table is a display of death rates by age. It can be much refined by taking gender into consideration also.

Underwriting for AIDS.   Health is one of the principal risk factors that insurers take into account in pricing individual life insurance. The life insurance application ordinarily contains questions about the proposed insured's history of such illnesses as cancer, heart disease, hypertension, diabetes, and stroke. The insurer also might require an attending physician's statement, hospital records, a physical examination, various blood and urine tests, and an electrocardiogram. Nevertheless, in the 1980s various groups lobbied state legislatures and insurance departments to pass laws that would prohibit insurers from testing for the antibody to the human immunodeficiency virus (HIV), the virus that causes AIDS. Although all states allow insurers to test for the HIV antibody, most have laws regulating such testing. These laws govern the notice of AIDS testing that must be given to applicants; the content of consent forms that applicants who are to be tested must sign; the types of tests that insurers are permitted to use; confidentiality of the test results; the questions about AIDS that insurers are permitted to ask on applications for insurance; and counseling that the law may require insurers to provide.[20]

Persons with the HIV antibody are ordinarily uninsurable because of the high risk of morbidity and early mortality that they present. Moreover, those who learn that they have the HIV antibody are apt to seek insurance. If insurers could not test for the HIV antibody or ask questions aimed at determining whether the applicant is infected with the virus, antiselection would occur, resulting in a dramatic rise in premiums for all insurance applicants. Antiselection, also called adverse selection or selection against the insurer, is the tendency of persons who are poor risks to seek insurance to a greater extent than persons who are better risks.

Genetic Information.   The National Center for Human Genome Research in the United States and researchers in Europe are engaged in a massive effort to map and decode all of the approximately 100,000 human genes. A large number of diseases have a genetic cause. It is now possible to determine a person's genetic predisposition to a number of diseases, among them cystic fibrosis, Huntington's chorea, and hereditary forms of Alzheimer's disease and breast, ovarian, and colon cancer. The number of diseases for which it is possible to determine a person's genetic predisposition continues to grow as the gene decoding effort progresses.

One commentator has called genetic testing by insurers "the next underwriting frontier."[21] Although at present insurers rarely do genetic testing themselves, they would like to use any existing information about proposed insureds' genetic predisposition to disease in selecting risks. Lobbying for and against insurers' use of genetic tests has been occurring for several years.[22] In 1992, Wisconsin prohibited

---

[20]Muriel L. Crawford, Eugene Jacobs, & Kathleen Schwappach, *Insurance and Employee Benefits Issues,* in LEGAL ASPECTS OF AIDS (Donald H. J. Hermann & William P. Schurgin, eds., 1990 & Supp. 1995).

[21]Brian Cox, *Genetic Tests become Next Underwriting Frontier,* NAT'L UNDERWRITER, LIFE & HEALTH/FIN. SERVICES EDITION, July 27, 1992, at 3; *Will Genetic Mapping Change the Insurance Industry?,* SOC'Y PAGE, AM. SOC'Y CLU & CHFC, Oct. 1991, at 9.

[22]Frederick Schmitt, *Aetna Official Presents Case for Genetic Testing to NAIC,* NAT'L UNDERWRITER, LIFE & HEALTH/FIN. SERVICES EDITION, June 24, 1996, at 8; Myk Cherskov, *Fighting*

health insurers from using genetic tests to select risks, and a number of states have since followed suit.[23] Moreover, legislation limiting insurers' right to and use of genetic information has been introduced in Congress.

Nonsmoker Premium Discounts

There is proof that cigarette smoking substantially increases the risk of early death, by as much as eight years for people who smoke two packages of cigarettes a day for many years. Therefore, many life insurers offer nonsmoker premium discounts to persons who have not smoked for some period of time, usually a year. The lower premium that insurers charge nonsmokers may tempt some proposed insureds to lie about their smoking habit. For this reason, some insurers test for by-products of smoking, often by measuring nicotine in urine, in addition to asking about smoking on the insurance application.

In 1988, the U.S. Court of Appeals for the Second Circuit ruled in *Mutual Benefit Life Insurance Co. v. JMR Electronics Corp.*[24] that a misrepresentation concerning the proposed insured's history of cigarette smoking, made in an application for a non-smoker policy, was material as a matter of law and entitled the insurer to rescind the policy. In 1985, JMR Electronics Corp. (JMR) had applied for a key man life insurance policy on the life of its president, Joseph Gaon. Gaon represented in the application that he had never smoked cigarettes, and the insurer issued a life insurance policy at nonsmoker rates. Gaon died within the policy's contestable period. In the course of investigating the claim for the death benefits, the insurer discovered that Gaon had smoked half a pack of cigarettes a day for at least 10 years. The district court ordered rescission of the policy and the return of the premiums paid by JMR, with interest.

In affirming the district court's decision, the court of appeals rejected the contention of the beneficiary, JMR, that the proper remedy would have been to allow JMR to recover the amount of benefits that the premiums would have purchased at the smoker rate. The court stated the following:

> There is no doubt that Mutual was induced to issue the non-smoker, discounted-premium policy to JMR precisely as a result of the misrepresentations made by Gaon concerning his smoking history. That Mutual might not have refused the risk on *any* terms had it known undisclosed facts is irrelevant. Most risks are insurable at some price. The purpose of the materiality inquiry is not to permit the jury to rewrite the terms of the insurance agreement to conform to the newly disclosed facts but to make certain that the risk insured was the risk covered by the policy agreed upon. If a fact is material to the risk, the insurer may avoid liability under a policy if that fact was misrepresented in an application for that policy whether or not the parties might have agreed to some other contractual arrangement had the critical fact been disclosed. As observed by Judge Sweet, a contrary result would reward the practice of misrepresenting facts critical to the underwriter's task because the unscrupulous (or merely negligent) applicant "would have everything to gain and nothing to lose" from making material misrepresentations in his application for insurance. Such a claimant could rest assured not only that he may demand full coverage

Genetic Discrimination, 78 A.B.A.J. 38 (June 1992); Jennifer Landes, *Sides Drawn Up on Genetic Testing,* Nat'l Underwriter, Life & Health/Fin. Services Edition, Dec. 10, 1990, at 2.

[23]Wisc. Stat. Ann. § 631.89 (West 1995); Colo. Rev. Stat. § 10–3–1104.7 (West Supp. 1995); Ohio Rev. Code Ann. § 3901.49 (Anderson Supp. 1995); Va. Code Ann. § 38.2–508.4 (Michie Supp. 1994); Ga. Code Ann. §§ 33–54–1 to –8 (1996); Or. Rev. Stat. § 746.135 (Supp. 1996); Md. Ann. Code art. 48A, § 223.1 (1990 & Supp. 1995); Minn. Stat. Ann. § 72A.139 (West Supp. 1996).

[24]848 F.2d 30 (2d Cir. 1988).

should he survive the contestability period, . . . but that even in the event of a contested claim, he would be entitled to the coverage that he might have contracted for had the necessary information been accurately disclosed at the outset. New York law does not permit this anomalous result.

Insurable Interest

The requirement of an *insurable interest* goes back to the 18th century in England. At that time, the persons whose lives were to be insured did not apply for life insurance policies. Rather, third persons applied for the policies. The insureds were merely subjects of the insurance. Often, an insured did not know the person who had obtained the insurance or that an insurer had issued a policy insuring her life.

Naturally, this arrangement was subject to abuses. At one time, it was a sport to wager that public figures would or would not live for even a few days. Thus, people who were not even acquainted with public figures took out insurance on the public figures' lives. The vicious nature of this wagering shocked the conscience of an 18th-century public not noted for its squeamishness because such wagering provided an inducement for the beneficiary to murder the insured.

In 1774, the English parliament took action to end such "a mischievous kind of gaming." It enacted a statute that made null and void all life insurance policies "wherein the person or persons for whose use, benefit, or on whose account such policy or policies shall be made, shall have no interest, or by way of gaming or wagering."[25] Thus, the objective of the insurable interest requirement is to prevent people from wagering on the lives of others.

The insurable interest requirement was adopted early in the United States. In most states, the insurable interest requirement has been enacted into statutory law. In a minority of states, it has been expressed as case law. However, all states require that either the applicant or beneficiary, depending on the circumstances, have an insurable interest in the insured's life at the inception of a life insurance contract.

Today, most insurance applicants insure their own lives. The insurable interest rules that apply when the proposed insured is the applicant differ from those that apply when another person is the applicant. This discussion of insurable interest will therefore address these two situations separately.

Insurable Interest in a Person's Own Life

Generally speaking, a person has an unlimited insurable interest in her own life. A person ordinarily can apply for as much insurance on her own life as the insurer is willing to issue and can name anyone as beneficiary. The beneficiary of such a policy need not have an insurable interest. The reason for this rule is that the insured presumably will not name as beneficiary anyone who would be more interested in the insured's demise than in her continuing to live. Thus, persons who apply for insurance on their own lives ordinarily do not need to be concerned with the question of insurable interest.

U.S. Supreme Court Justice Oliver Wendell Holmes described the reasoning behind this rule in a famous case, *Grigsby v. Russell*,[26] as follows:

---

[25]14 Geo. III, ch. 48.
[26]222 U.S. 149 (1911).

The danger that might arise from a general license to all to insure whom they like does not exist. Obviously, it is a very different thing from granting such a general license, to allow the holder of a valid insurance upon his own life to transfer it to one whom he, the party most concerned, is not afraid to trust.

Insurable Interest in Another Person's Life

An **insurable interest** in another person's life has been defined as "any reasonable expectation of benefit or advantage from the continued life of another person."[27] Such a benefit or advantage need not be monetary. It may also arise from natural affection.

The Maine Insurance Code, quoted below, contains language typical of insurable interest statutes.

2404. Insurable Interest—Personal Insurance

"Insurable interest" as to such personal insurance means that every individual has an insurable interest in the life, body, and health of himself, and of other persons as follows:

  A. In the case of individuals related closely by blood or by law, a substantial interest engendered by love and affection;
  B. In the case of other persons, a lawful and substantial economic interest in having the life, health or bodily safety of the individual insured continue, as distinguished from an interest which would arise only by, or would be enhanced in value by, the death, disablement or injury of the individual insured;
  C. A party to a contract or option for the purchase or sale, including a redemption, of an interest in a business proprietorship, partnership or firm, or of shares of stock of a corporation or of an interest in these shares, has an insurable interest in the life, body and health of each individual party to that contract or option, and for the purposes of that contract or option only, in addition to any insurable interest which may otherwise exist as to that individual.[28]

The courts have tried to identify the relationships that create an insurable interest, but the list is incomplete and sometimes inconsistent. The U.S. Supreme Court has described insurable interest in another's life as follows:

It is not easy to define with precision what will in all cases constitute an insurable interest, so as to take the contract out of the class of wager policies. It may be stated generally, however, to be such an interest, arising from the relations of the party obtaining the insurance, either as creditor of or surety for the assured, or from ties of blood or marriage to him, as will justify a reasonable expectation of advantage or benefit from the continuance of his life. It is not necessary that the expectation of advantage or benefit should always be capable of pecuniary estimation, for a parent has an insurable interest in the life of his child, and a child in the life of his parent; a husband in the life of his wife, and a wife in the life of her husband. The natural affection in cases of this kind is considered as more powerful, as operating more efficaciously, to protect the life of the insured than any other consideration. But in all cases there must be a reasonable ground, founded upon the relations of the parties to each other, either pecuniary or of blood or affinity, to expect some benefit or advantage from the continuance of the life of the assured. Otherwise the contract is a mere wager, by which the party taking the policy is directly interested in the

[27]BALLENTINE'S LAW DICTIONARY 642 (3d ed.1969).
[28]ME. REV. STAT. ANN. tit. 24A, § 2404(3) (1990 & Supp. 1995).

early death of the assured. Such policies have a tendency to create a desire for the event. They are, therefore, independently of any statute on the subject, condemned, as being against public policy.[29]

An applicant for insurance on another's life can name herself as beneficiary or name another person as beneficiary. Usually, an applicant for insurance on another's life names herself as beneficiary. For example, a wife might apply for insurance on her husband's life, naming herself as beneficiary. However, sometimes in modern practice the applicant names someone else as beneficiary. A husband might apply for insurance on his wife's life and name their children as beneficiaries. Some states have therefore enacted statutes that make it clear that, in such a situation, the beneficiary must have an insurable interest in the life of the insured. The New York Insurance Law states the requirement as follows:

> No person shall procure or cause to be procured, directly or by assignment or otherwise any contract of insurance upon the person of another unless the benefits under such contract are payable to the person insured or his personal representatives, or to a person having, at the time when such contract is made, an insurable interest in the person insured.[30]

Ordinarily, one person has an insurable interest in the life of another if they are closely related by blood or marriage, or if they have a business relationship that will cause the beneficiary to profit from the continuance of the life insured or to suffer a loss on the premature termination of that life. In addition, if one person is dependent for financial support on another person, the dependent has an insurable interest in the life of the person supporting him.

Relationships by Blood.   According to the majority rule, a parent has an insurable interest in a minor child's life, and the child has an insurable interest in the life of the parent. It is also the majority rule that a grandchild has an insurable interest in the life of a grandparent and that a grandparent has an insurable interest in the life of a grandchild.

The modern cases support the position that brothers and sisters have an insurable interest in each other's lives because of their close blood relationship.[31] An uncle or aunt and niece or nephew do not have an insurable interest in each other's lives arising out of their relationship alone, according to the majority rule. The same is true of cousins. However, a dependency or business relationship can confer an insurable interest upon such relatives.

Relationships by Marriage.   A husband and wife have an insurable interest in each other's lives. Moreover, some courts hold that persons who are engaged to be married have an insurable interest in each other's lives.[32] Relatives by marriage, other than spouses, ordinarily have no insurable interest merely because of the relationship. For example, a stepchild has no insurable interest in the life of a stepparent, or vice versa, unless there is financial dependency. For example, if a stepson is dependent on his stepfather for financial support, the stepson will have an insurable interest in his

---

[29]Warnock v. Davis, 104 U.S. 775 (1882).

[30]N.Y. INS. LAW § 3205 (b)(2)(McKinney 1985).

[31]Carl T. Drechsler, Annotation, *Insurable Interest of Brother or Sister in Life of Sibling,* 60 A.L.R. 3d 98 (1974).

[32]J.T.W., Annotation, *Insurance; Insurable Interest of Fiance or Fiancee,* 17 A.L.R. 580 (1922).

stepfather's life. However, this would be true whether or not there was a relationship by marriage. Foster children and other dependents have an insurable interest in the life of a person who supports them, by reason of the dependency.[33]

Business Relationships.   There are many business relationships that, if severed by the premature death of one of the parties, could mean serious financial loss to the survivor. In such a situation, the person who would suffer a financial loss by the death of the other has an insurable interest in the other's life.[34] For example, an employer has an insurable interest in the life of a key employee. An application of this principle is found in *Theatre Guild Productions v. Insurance Corporation of Ireland.*[35] The Theatre Guild had procured five policies providing that the insurer would pay $1,500 for each performance that the star of its play, Gertrude Berg, missed by reason of death or disability. Berg became ill, and the show closed 11 days later. The court said that the Theatre Guild's "insurable interest derived from its employment of Gertrude Berg as the star of its production. . . . The economic success of the production depended on the effective appearance and performance of Gertrude Berg."

A corporation ordinarily has an insurable interest in the lives of its directors, officers, and managers. This is because the success of the corporation's business is usually dependent on the continued existence of these persons.

A person who expects economic benefit from the continued life of his partner has an insurable interest in that life.[36] The partnership also has an insurable interest in the life of a partner if it expects to realize economic benefit from the partner's continued life. In *Connecticut Mutual Life Insurance Co. v. Luchs,*[37] the U.S. Supreme Court said:

> Certainly Luchs had a pecuniary interest in the life of Dillenberg on two grounds: because he was his creditor and because he was his partner. The continuance of the partnership, and, of course, a continuance of Dillenberg's life, furnished a reasonable expectation of advantage to himself. It was in the expectation of such advantage that the partnership was formed and, of course, for the like expectation, was continued.

A creditor has an insurable interest in the life of her debtor. The amount of insurance must bear a reasonable relationship to the amount of the debt plus the insurance premium. If the amount of insurance taken out by a creditor is disproportionately higher than the amount of the debt, the contract will be a wagering contract and therefore void.

Creditor policies fall into two classes. In one class are policies creditors take out on their debtors' lives, and in the other class are policies that debtors take out on their own lives and that name their creditors as beneficiaries or assignees. If the debtor applies for the insurance, the insurer will pay the excess over the amount of the debt to a beneficiary named by the debtor, or to the debtor's estate. However, if the creditor takes out the policy, the courts often hold that the creditor is entitled to the proceeds in full, even if they are greater than the amount of the debt.

---

[33]R.E.H., Annotation, *Insurable Interest of Foster Child or Stepchild in Life of Foster or Step Parent, or Vice Versa,* 25 A.L.R. 1547 (1923).

[34]J.T.W., Annotation, *Insurable Interest of Employer in Life of Employee,* 125 A.L.R. 408 (1940).

[35]267 N.Y.S.2d 297 (1966), *aff'd* 225 N.E.2d 216 (1967).

[36]J. H. Cooper, Annotation, *Insurable Interest of Partner or Partnership in Life of Partner,* 70 A.L.R. 2d 577 (1960).

[37]108 U.S. 498 (1883).

Consent of the Insured.   As a general rule, a policy taken out on the life of another person is void without the consent of that person, even though the beneficiary has an insurable interest in the proposed insured's life. One court pointed out that

> [i]t is certainly against public policy for one to procure a policy of insurance on the life of another without such one's knowledge or consent. The wife has an insurable interest in the life of the husband; yet she could not obtain insurance upon his life without his knowledge and consent. Neither should the husband be allowed to procure a policy of insurance on the life of the wife without her knowledge and consent. If such practice was indulged, it might be a fruitful source of crime.[38]

Courts ordinarily make an exception to the consent rule for minor children. A parent can insure a minor child's life without the child's consent, since a minor child does not have legal capacity to give consent.

Insurable Interest: A Question of Fact.   The basic rules concerning insurable interest are always subject to exceptions, especially if the facts show that the application for the insurance was not made in good faith. For instance, it is often stated that partners have an insurable interest in each other's lives. This general rule is ordinarily borne out by the facts, but not always. In one case, two partners were involved in a fatal hunting accident. The victim was insured for $25,000 in favor of his partner. The court decided that the beneficiary did not have an insurable interest in his partner's life. The court said, in part:

> While it is true that partners usually, and perhaps in most cases, have an insurable interest in the life of a copartner, it is the existence of circumstances which arise out of or by reason of the partnership, and not the mere existence of the partnership itself, that give rise to an insurable interest. The legal relationship of one partner to the other does not, and should not, necessarily create an insurable interest as does the relationship of husband and wife.

> * * * * *

> The better rule, and the one based on sound reasoning, is that an insurable interest does not necessarily arise by virtue of the mere partner relationship alone. Therefore, the showing by appellant [the surviving partner] that he and Hankinson were partners did not of itself establish the existence in him of an insurable interest in the life of Hankinson. We must therefore look to the circumstances arising out of or by reason of the partnership to determine whether an insurable interest existed in this case. Appellant's evidence conclusively establishes that Hankinson made absolutely no financial or capital contribution whatever to the alleged partnership, and that he did not in any way obligate himself to do so; that he had no technical knowledge, skill or ability as a worker or manager to add to the partnership; that he did not have any experience in the type of work he was to do or in the business of the alleged partnership; that appellant had no legal claim for his continued services; and that Hankinson did not purchase or acquire an interest in the business or the tools and equipment used in the business. Also there is nothing to indicate that Hankinson brought or could be expected to bring any business to the partnership, or that his presence as a partner increased or favorably affected the partnership good will.

> * * * * *

---

[38]Metropolitan Life Ins. Co. v. Monohan, 42 S.W. 924 (Ky. 1897).

Therefore, we are constrained to and do conclude that appellant's evidence affirmatively establishes that as a matter of law he had no insurable interest in the life of Hankinson.[39]

Insurer's Tort Liability.   An insurer has a legal duty to use reasonable care to determine whether the requisite insurable interest exists and to procure the consent of the insured. If the insurer breaches this duty, the insurer could be liable for tort damages for any resulting harm. The leading case in this area is *Liberty National Life Insurance Co. v. Weldon.*[40]

The beneficiary in the *Weldon* case was a nurse who visited her brother-in-law and his family one afternoon in 1950 and gave his two-year-old daughter a soft drink in a cup. The child died before evening. An investigation showed arsenic in the cup, in the child's body in a sufficient quantity to cause her death, and in the clothes of the child and her aunt-in-law, the nurse. The aunt-in-law was charged with murder, convicted, and executed.

In the course of the murder trial, evidence revealed that three life insurers had issued policies on the applications of the aunt-in-law, insuring the life of the child and designating the aunt-in-law as beneficiary. These policies had face amounts of $500, $5,000, and $1,000. The child's parents had not given their consent to the issuance of any of these policies.

The parents brought suit against the life insurers under a wrongful death statute. A wrongful death statute gives the executor, administrator, or heirs of a deceased person a cause of action for injuries to the deceased that resulted from the wrongful acts of another. The plaintiffs' theory in the *Weldon* suit was that the insurers were under a duty to use reasonable care not to issue a life insurance policy in favor of a beneficiary who had no interest in the continuation of the insured's life and that issuance of the policies was a breach of that duty that resulted in the child's death by murder.

The verdict was for the parents. The Alabama Supreme Court quoted a basic rule of tort law that every person has a duty to exercise reasonable care not to injure another. It said that a life insurer has a duty to use reasonable care not to issue a life insurance policy to someone who has no interest in the continuation of the insured's life. "Policies in violation of the insurable interest rule are not dangerous because they are illegal," the court said, "they are illegal because they are dangerous." The opinion continued:

> We cannot agree with the defendants [the insurers] in their assertion that we should hold as a matter of law that the murder of the young girl was not reasonably foreseeable. This created a situation of a kind which this court and others have consistently said affords temptation to a recognizable percentage of humanity to commit murder.

The jury had held that the issuance of the policies was the proximate cause of the murder of the child and awarded damages to the parents in the amount of $100,000. The reviewing court reduced the award to $75,000, but even so it was the largest wrongful death award to have come out of that court. This case illustrates the importance of the insurable interest requirement.

---

[39]Lakin v. Postal Life & Cas. Co., 316 S.W.2d 542 (Mo. 1958).
[40]100 So. 2d 696 (Ala. 1957).

Conscientious life insurers carefully examine every application to make certain that the legally required insurable interest standards have been met. Moreover, many life insurers impose stricter insurable interest standards than those required by law.

Consideration

In the case of an informal contract, such as an insurance contract, the promise to be enforced must be supported by a legally sufficient consideration. Consideration is the value requested and given in exchange for the promise.

The initial premium and the application constitute the consideration that the applicant exchanges for the insurer's promise. Most life insurance policies specifically state that the insurance shall not be effective until the applicant pays the first premium. The courts have upheld the validity of this stipulation.

Competent Contracting Parties

The parties who create an insurance contract are the insurer and the applicant. The offer is always made by either the insurer or the applicant and accepted by the other, thus creating the contract. Once the parties have created the contract, the applicant becomes the policyowner, unless the applicant has designated someone else to be the policyowner.

A life insurer is considered competent to issue life insurance contracts if the terms of its charter or articles of incorporation authorize it to issue such contracts and if it has a certificate of authority in the state in which it makes the contracts. The various states in which an insurer does business certify the competency of the insurer each year.

The applicant is the other party who creates the insurance contract, and therefore the applicant must have contractual capacity. As was discussed in Chapter 2, "Contracts," a minor or a mentally infirm person with limited contractual capacity can enter into an insurance contract that will be binding on the insurer and voidable by the minor or mentally infirm person.

The beneficiary, as such, is not a party to the contract. In some instances, the beneficiary does not know of the existence of the contract. A person need not have contractual capacity to be a beneficiary. However, if a policyowner makes a person without full contractual capacity, such as a minor, the *irrevocable* beneficiary, the policyowner ordinarily will be unable to exercise ownership rights in the policy (for example, the right to take out a policy loan) because the beneficiary cannot give consent to the exercise of those rights.

The insured, as such, is not a party to the contract, either. If one person takes out insurance on the life of another, the insurer will require the insured's consent, but the insured is not thereby made a party to the contract. For example, a wife may apply for insurance on the life of her husband, who must give his consent to the contract. The insurer and the wife are the parties to the contract. The husband, who is the insured, is not a party. However, an insured must have capacity to give consent to the contract unless the insured is a minor child and a parent gives consent.

Delivery of the Policy

Most life insurance applications expressly provide that the policy shall not become effective until the insurer (1) approves the application, (2) issues a policy, and (3) delivers the policy, and the applicant pays the initial premium during the proposed insured's continued good health. If there is no agreement to the contrary, the parties must fulfill each of these conditions before the policy becomes effective. Thus, all of these are conditions precedent.

The effectiveness of the policy itself should not be confused with the effectiveness of a temporary life insurance contract under a premium receipt. Issuance and delivery of the policy are not conditions precedent to the right to such temporary insurance.

As to the policy itself, once the applicant has paid the initial premium, the contract is completed when the agent delivers the policy as applied for. The agent can deliver the policy by handing it to the applicant. This is actual delivery.

Constructive Delivery

The insurer's agent does not have to actually hand the policy to the applicant to make a valid delivery. In some situations, a court will say a delivery has occurred even though the insurer's agent did not actually hand the policy to the applicant. Such a delivery is called a *constructive delivery*.

Ordinarily, a policy is constructively delivered when the insurer has parted with control of it with the intention to be bound by it as a completed instrument.[41] That is, the courts will construe the policy to be delivered the moment the insurer relinquishes possession of the policy by mailing it to the agent if nothing further remains to be done but the ministerial act[42] of seeing that the applicant receives the policy. For example, suppose the applicant pays the initial premium at the time he submits the application and that the insurer accepts the application, issues the policy as applied for, and mails it to the agent with the intention that the agent deliver it to the applicant. If the insured dies while the policy is in the mail or in the hands of the agent, most courts would hold that the policy was constructively delivered and that the death benefit is payable.

Delivery for Inspection

Occasionally, an insurer delivers a policy to the applicant for inspection. That is, the insurer permits the applicant to keep the policy for a few days for inspection without the insurance being in force. Neither party intends to be bound by the contract at that time.

In such cases, the applicant customarily signs an inspection receipt specifying the conditions under which the policy was left with her. If the insurer had no signed inspection receipt, and the proposed insured died while the policy was in the applicant's possession, it could be difficult for the insurer to establish that the parties did not intend to enter into a binding contract. The inspection receipt is evidence that no

[41]J.P.M., Annotation, *What Amounts to a "Delivery" or an "Actual Delivery" to Insured within Express Provision of Insurance Policy,* 53 A.L.R. 492 (1928), *supp. by* 145 A.L.R. 1434 (1943).

[42]A ministerial act is an act that does not require discretion on the part of the person performing the act.

delivery, in the legal sense of the word, has occurred and that the insurance is not in force.

Delivery for inspection should not be confused with the "free look" period that many states' laws mandate. In the case of the free look period, the policy is in force at the time of delivery, but for a specified period of time the policyowner has the right to cancel it and have the insurer return the initial premium.

Effective Date of the Policy

Factors that can affect the date on which a policy becomes effective are (1) an effective date agreed upon by the insurer and policyowner, (2) backdating, (3) the date of payment of the initial premium, and (4) the delivery date.

Generally, if the insurer and policyowner agree on an effective date, that date will be binding. This will be the case even though the policyowner paid the initial premium on a different date.

The insurer and policyowner can agree on an effective date some time in the past. Thus, backdating a policy is permissible if done within limits established by state law. Six months is the usual limit on the length of time the parties can backdate a policy.

Life insurance policies often require that payment of the initial premium and delivery of the policy occur before coverage takes effect. This requirement sometimes conflicts with another provision regarding the date from which the insurer will calculate the premium due date. The majority rule is that the insurer may calculate the premium due date from the date stipulated in the policy. A minority of courts have held that the insurer must calculate the premium due date from the date coverage began.

Summary

The general rules of contract law govern the formation of life insurance contracts, as do special rules that apply only to life insurance contracts. Either the applicant or the insurer can make the offer to contract, depending on the circumstances. An applicant's offer may evoke an acceptance, rejection, or counteroffer from the insurer. In some states, the insurer must act on an application with reasonable promptness, or it might incur contract or tort liability.

A premium receipt, which the soliciting agent gives to the applicant when the initial premium is submitted with the application, usually contains a contract providing temporary life insurance. There are three types of premium receipts: approval premium receipts, insurability premium receipts, and binding premium receipts. Approval premium receipts and insurability premium receipts are conditional premium receipts requiring that certain conditions be met before the temporary life insurance becomes effective. The binding premium receipt provides temporary life insurance from the time the agent gives it to the applicant in exchange for the initial premium. There is a trend for the courts to treat conditional receipts as if they were binding receipts.

Risk classification means the insurer's identification of people with similar loss potential and placement of those people in the same risk group for the purpose of setting premium rates. Risk selection means the insurer's choice from among proposed insureds of those persons it is willing to insure. Underwriters at the insurer's home office, rather than the soliciting agent, ordinarily perform life insurance risk selection.

Nearly all states have laws prohibiting unfair discrimination in insurance. Some have laws specifically prohibiting unfair handicap or sex discrimination. A few states have laws mandating unisex insurance rates. Most states have laws governing the manner in which insurers test for the antibody to the AIDS virus. Some state laws restrict an insurer's use of information about a proposed insured's genetic predisposition to disease.

Public policy requires that either the applicant or beneficiary, depending on the circumstances, have an insurable interest in the life of the proposed insured, in order to prevent people from wagering on the lives of others. Because a person usually has an unlimited insurable interest in her own life, insurable interest is ordinarily of concern only when the applicant applies for insurance on the life of another. Usually, one person has an insurable interest in the life of another if they are closely related by blood or marriage, or if they have a business or dependency relationship in which the beneficiary expects economic benefit from the continued life of the insured. An insurer must use reasonable care not to issue a policy if the required insurable interest does not exist, or the insurer may incur tort liability.

A life insurance contract, like any informal contract, requires consideration and competent contracting parties. The consideration given by the applicant, in exchange for the insurer's promise, is the application and the initial premium. The applicant is one party creating the contract, and the insurer is the other. The insured and the beneficiary, as such, are not parties to the contract. Only the insurer and the applicant must have contractual capacity.

Delivery of the policy is ordinarily required before the policy becomes effective. However, actual delivery by placing the policy in the applicant's hands is not necessary. Constructive delivery is sufficient. Ordinarily, the policy is constructively delivered when the insurer has parted with control of it with the intention to be bound by it as a completed instrument.

ILLUSTRATIVE CASE

This case deals with a father's insurable interest in the life of his son. The court held that the father (the plaintiff-appellee) had such an insurable interest. The insurer also raised a question of material misrepresentation in the application for the life insurance policy. The court decided in favor of the father. Material misrepresentation is discussed in Chapter 16, "Equitable Remedies," and in Chapter 17, "Policy Contests and the Incontestable Clause."

T. J. BOWMAN, FATHER OF JAMES BOWMAN, DECEASED,
Plaintiff-Appellee
v.
ZENITH LIFE INSURANCE COMPANY, Defendant-Appellant[43]
Appellate Court of Illinois, First District, Third Division

McNAMARA, Justice.

Plaintiff, T. J. Bowman, commenced this action to recover as the beneficiary under an insurance policy purchased by him on the life of his son, James Bowman. After a trial without a jury, the court entered a judgment in favor of plaintiff for $3,000, the face value of the policy. Defendant appeals. Its principal contention in the trial court and in this court is that plaintiff had no insurable interest in the life of his son and, therefore, that the policy was void at its inception.

On February 4, 1974, plaintiff applied to defendant for the policy in question through one of defendant's agents, and the policy was issued. The son was unaware that plaintiff had applied for the insurance. The son lived with his mother most of his life and not with plaintiff. Plaintiff did not know if his son was working prior to his death which occurred on March 3, 1974.

The trial court specifically found that "[t]he defense urged by the defendant that the plaintiff had no insurable interest in the life of his son is without merit in that the father had a reasonable expectation of receiving financial support from his son in his declining years, if needed."

Defendant argues that the trial court erred in holding that plaintiff had an insurable interest in the life of his son. The requirement that one obtaining a policy of insurance upon the life of another must have an insurable interest therein is founded upon a public policy which "forbids one person who has no interest in the continuance of the life of another from speculating on that life by procuring a policy of insurance." The lack of an insurable interest renders the policy "a pure wager that gives the insured a sinister counter interest in having the life come to an end." (*Grigsby v. Russell* (1911), 222 U.S. 149, 154, 32 S.Ct. 58, 56 L.Ed. 133). In the present case, we cannot say that the policy of insurance procured by plaintiff upon the life of his son was a pure wager. We believe the face amount of the policy is not grossly disproportionate to the

---

[43]384 N.E.2d 949 (1978).

extent of plaintiff's interest. This factor is an indication that plaintiff acted in good faith in obtaining the policy. The trial court correctly held that plaintiff did have an insurable interest in his son's life.

Defendant further argues that certain statements in connection with the policy were not answered truthfully by plaintiff and thereby the policy was voided. Defendant's agent came to plaintiff's home to prepare the latter's application for the insurance policy. At that time, plaintiff was asked the following questions, the answers to which the agent recorded on the application:

1. Are you now in good health and free from impairment or disease? Answer—Yes.
2. Are you now receiving or contemplating any medical attention or surgical treatment? Answer—No.
3. Have you during the past five years consulted any physician or other practitioner or been confined to any hospital, sanitarium or similar institution? Answer—No.

At trial, it was stipulated that plaintiff's son had a pre-existing diabetic condition. Defendant's claims manager testified that defendant would not have issued the policy had it known this fact at the time the application was made.

Defendant maintains that the foregoing answers were not truthful. It urges further that, even if the answers were given in good faith, such conduct amounted to a misrepresentation which materially affected defendant's decision to issue the policy. Plaintiff's testimony, which is uncontradicted by any other evidence, was that he believed defendant's agent was inquiring into his own health due to the manner in which the questions were phrased. Since plaintiff himself signed the application, the completed application supports plaintiff's belief. In completing the application, plaintiff was required to disclose only such facts as were responsive to the questions asked.

The trial court correctly found that plaintiff was not guilty of any misrepresentation which would entitle defendant to void the policy.

For the foregoing reasons, the judgment of the circuit court of Cook County awarding judgment to plaintiff in the amount of $3,000 is affirmed.

Judgment affirmed.

SIMON, P. J., and JIGANTI, J., concur.

Questions for Review

1. Under what conditions is the applicant considered to be making an offer to the insurer? If the applicant is not making an offer, what is the legal significance of his submission of the application?
2. How do offer and acceptance in relation to life insurance contracts differ from offer and acceptance in relation to most other business contracts with regard to a delay in acting on the application?
3. Explain the difference between a condition precedent and a condition subsequent. What are some conditions precedent in relation to the life insurance contract?
4. The applicant does not have to pay the initial premium until after the insurer has issued the policy. Describe how the applicant may benefit from paying the premium in advance.
5. What are the two types of conditional premium receipts? How do binding premium receipts differ from conditional premium receipts? Why are more insurers issuing binding premium receipts now?
6. Why do life insurers not give their soliciting agents power to complete a contract for life insurance?
7. In relation to life insurance:
   a. How is insurable interest defined?
   b. When must the required insurable interest exist?
   c. What is meant by the statement "A person has an unlimited insurable interest in his own life"?
   d. Who must have the required insurable interest in the life of the insured?
8. What is meant by constructive delivery?
9. Describe the conditions under which an inspection receipt is used and tell why it is used.

7 STRUCTURE OF THE LIFE INSURANCE POLICY

Chapter Outline

Although the insurer drafts the life insurance policy, it cannot write the policy in any manner it wishes. There are many legal constraints on the form and content of life insurance policies. Many states require that policies be written in simplified language.

They must contain various specified provisions and must not contain certain other provisions. An insurer must file its policy forms with the insurance department in each state in which it will sell the policies. The state's insurance department must approve each policy form that will be sold in that state. Finally, the courts will consider legally required provisions that are omitted from a policy form to be part of the contract exactly as if those provisions were written in the policy. This chapter contains a review of the form and content of life insurance policies and a discussion of the required filing and approval of policy forms.

Simplified Language

The consumer movement has resulted in laws requiring that the writers of many types of legal documents simplify the documents' language so that consumers can more readily understand them. A majority of the states have laws or regulations requiring that life and health insurance policies be written in simplified language. Most of these laws or regulations are patterned on the National Association of Insurance Commissioners Life and Health Insurance Policy Language Simplification Model Act, which was adopted by the NAIC in 1978.

Simplified language laws usually require policies to meet a specified minimum score on the Flesch reading ease test or a comparable test. Psychologist Rudolph Flesch invented the Flesch reading ease test and explained it in his book, *The Art of Readable Writing*.[1] The Flesch test is also described in the NAIC Life and Health Insurance Policy Language Simplification Model Act.[2]

The Flesch test is based on the relationship between reading ease and the length of words and sentences. Shorter words and sentences are more easily understood. To compute a Flesch readability score for a policy clause, a person counts the sentences, words, and syllables in the clause and runs the totals through a formula. The higher the score, the more readable the clause. State laws patterned on the model act require that a policy have a minimum score of 40. Some state laws require other minimum scores. Medical terms, words defined in the policy, policy language required by law, the insurer's name and address, the policy title, and certain other printed matter do not have to be tested. Under the model act, the commissioner of insurance can allow the use of other reading ease tests that are comparable to the Flesch test.

Laws patterned on the model act also require that policies be "printed, except for specification pages, schedules and tables, in not less than 10-point type, 1-point leaded." This eliminates fine print that makes policies difficult to read. This book, for example, is printed in 10-point type, 2-point leaded.

The style, arrangement, and overall appearance of the policy must "give no undue prominence to any portion of the text of the policy or to any endorsements or riders." The policy must contain a table of contents or an index of its principal sections if the policy has more than 3,000 words or more than three pages.

The drafters of the model act were aware that technical terms cannot be eliminated completely from insurance policies. In a drafting note, they stated the following:

---

[1]R. FLESCH, THE ART OF READABLE WRITING (rev. 1974).
[2]LIFE & HEALTH INS. POLICY LANGUAGE SIMPLIFICATION MODEL ACT § 5B (Nat'l Ass'n Ins. Comm'rs 1978).

In establishing minimum standards, it is recognized that certain terminology used in policies is difficult or impossible to restate in simplified language. This is because there are no suitable alternatives to necessary medical terminology, other insurance words of art, and statutory or regulatory language requirements. It is not the intention of this Act to preclude the use of such terminology or to penalize insurance companies for its continued use.

A whole life policy written in simplified language appears in the Appendix, Figure 2.

Policy Contents

The typical individual life insurance policy contains a face page followed by numerous provisions, both required and optional. A modern policy probably will contain a table of contents and a section containing definitions of technical terms used in the policy. There will be a section providing for designations and changes of beneficiary. A settlement options section will spell out the various options and provide tables showing monthly amounts payable under each option. A policy providing cash values will contain a nonforfeiture section that describes the options available if the policyowner decides to discontinue paying premiums before the policy is paid up.

Provisions that are ordinarily required include the free look provision, the grace period provision, the incontestable clause, the entire contract provision, the misstatement of age provision, the divisible surplus provision (required in participating policies), the policy loan provision, and the reinstatement clause. These required provisions will be discussed in this chapter.

Laws prohibit insurers from including certain provisions in life insurance policies. Provisions that curtail payment of the face amount are forbidden under less value statutes in some states. Forfeiture of the policy for failure to repay a policy loan is specifically forbidden under the laws of some states. Finally, statutes in some states forbid a statement that the insurer's agent shall be the agent of the applicant or policyowner. These prohibited provisions also will be discussed in this chapter.

Optional benefits or limitations are often included in the policy or added by rider. These added benefits include accidental death benefits, disability benefits, guaranteed insurability benefits, accelerated benefits, and backdating, ownership, assignment, and contract change provisions. Added limitations include suicide exclusions, war and aviation hazard exclusions, and time limit on legal or equitable action clauses. These optional benefits and limitations will be discussed in Chapter 8, "Added Benefits and Limitations."

Policy Face Page

The face page of an illustrative individual life insurance policy appears in the Appendix, Figure 2. The face page contains the insurer's basic promise. Insurers state this promise in various ways. The illustrative policy, which is written in simplified language, contains the following promise:

> If the Insured dies while this Policy is in force, we will pay the Sum Insured to the Beneficiary, when we receive at our Home Office due proof of the Insured's death, subject to the provisions of this Policy.

In most older policies, as well as some newer ones, the basic promise is in the form of a statement that in consideration of the application and the payment of premiums as they become due, the insurer promises to pay the policy proceeds to the beneficiary on receipt of satisfactory proof of the insured's death. Legally, however, the application and payment of the *initial* premium constitute the consideration for the insurer's promise. The promise will remain in effect only if a required condition, the payment of renewal premiums, occurs.

Officers' Signatures

Below the insurer's promise are the signatures of company officers, usually the president and secretary. These officers may personally write their signatures on each policy, but usually facsimile signatures are preprinted on the policy form for convenience. Whether signed by hand or preprinted, the signatures are evidence that the insurer has put the policy into force. Thus, the signatures are essential to the completion of a written contract of insurance.[3]

Policy Description

The bottom of the face page contains a brief policy description. One of the objectives of legislation governing life insurance policy provisions is to assure that the policyowner understands the basic features of the policy. For that reason, state statutes commonly require that a brief description be included on the face page of every policy. For example, one insurer describes its whole life policy as follows:

WHOLE LIFE INSURANCE POLICY

Premium Payable for a Stated Period

or Until Prior Death of Insured

Sum Insured Payable at Death

Non-Participating

Free Look Provision

Many states have adopted a statute or regulation requiring insurers to include a provision on the face page of a life insurance policy permitting the policyowner to return the policy within some specified period of time, usually 10 days, after receiving it and obtain a full refund of the premium paid. If the policyowner returns the policy within the specified period, the policy will be deemed void from the beginning. These provisions are called free look provisions, or trial examination period provisions. Insurers often allow a longer free look period than that required by law.

The free look provision in the illustrative policy in the Appendix, Figure 2, reads as follows:

---

[3]Coen v. American Surety Co., 120 F.2d 393 (8th Cir. 1941), *cert. denied,* 314 U.S. 667 (1941); Prudential Ins. Co. v. Connallon, 154 A. 729 (N.J. Eq. 1931).

Right to Examine and Return Policy within 20 Days
You may, at any time within 20 days after receipt of this Policy, return it to us at our Home Office or to the Agent through whom it was purchased, and we will cancel it. The return of the Policy will void it from the beginning and any premium paid will be refunded to the owner.

Required provisions that do not appear on the face page of the policy are analyzed in the next section.

Required Policy Provisions

The insurance laws enacted in New York in 1906, as the result of the 1905 Armstrong Investigation of insurance practices, prescribed uniform policy forms for straight (ordinary),[4] limited pay, endowment, and term life insurance policies. These laws required life insurers to issue policies in exactly those forms. When this legislation proved too rigid, in 1910 the New York state legislature replaced it with a law specifying certain provisions that must be included in life insurance policies but permitting insurers to use their own wording as long as the substance was essentially the same as that prescribed in the law and the language used was not less liberal to the policyowner and the beneficiary. This is the New York standard policy provisions law. Considerably more than half the states have adopted similar laws. Accordingly, most insurers now include such provisions in their policies. The following is an analysis of these required provisions.

Introductory Statutory Language

A state's standard policy provisions law is usually introduced with a paragraph similar to the following excerpt from the New York law:

> All life insurance policies, except as otherwise stated herein, delivered or issued for delivery in this state, shall contain in substance the following provisions, or provisions which the superintendent deems to be more favorable to policyholders.[5]

The phrase *in substance* indicates that an insurer need not state a policy provision in the exact words of the statute. Whether the policy's actual provisions are more favorable to policyowners than the provisions outlined in the statute is left to the opinion of the superintendent of insurance.[6]

The New York law excludes from the standard provisions requirements such policies as single-premium policies, nonparticipating policies, and term policies, to the extent that any required provision is not applicable. Thus, a nonparticipating policy would not be required to include dividend provisions, and a single-premium policy would not be required to contain provisions relating to the payment of renewal premiums. Furthermore, the standard policy provisions law does not apply to group life insurance.

---

[4]Straight life insurance is whole life insurance with premiums payable until death, or until some advanced age such as 100 if the insured is still living at that age.

[5]N.Y. Ins. Law § 3203(a) (McKinney 1985 & Supp. 1996).

[6]*Superintendent* is a title given to the head of the New York Insurance Department. In other states, this official may be referred to as commissioner or director.

Settlement Options Tables

Settlement options in a life insurance policy allow the policyowner or beneficiary to have the death benefit paid out over a period of time, rather than in a lump sum. Settlement options are discussed in detail in Chapter 11, "Settlement Agreements, Trusts, and Wills."

The New York standard policy provisions law and the standard policy provisions laws of other states require policies that provide settlement options to include settlement options tables. The New York statute requires the following:

> [A] table showing the amounts of the applicable installment or annuity payments, if the policy proceeds are payable in installments or as an annuity.[7]

The illustrative policy in the Appendix, Figure 2, shows several settlement options tables.

Nonforfeiture Provisions

The owner of a level premium whole life insurance policy contributes more in the early policy years than is required to meet her proportionate share of the insurer's current mortality cost. State laws require that if a level premium whole life insurance policy lapses after it has been in effect for a minimum stated period, usually three years, the insurer must provide a cash surrender value. As alternatives to surrender of the policy for cash, the insurer must offer either paid-up insurance for a reduced amount or extended term insurance for the net face amount, or both, in whatever amounts the net cash value of the policy can purchase.

A newer type of policy, the flexible premium whole life insurance policy, has different rules governing the buildup of a cash surrender value. The cash surrender value under flexible premium policies equals premiums paid minus mortality charges, expenses, service charges, loans, and withdrawals. Flexible premium policies are discussed in the section below entitled "Universal and Variable Life Insurance Laws."

Nonforfeiture laws and policy provisions are discussed at length in Chapter 13, "Policy Loans and Nonforfeiture Benefits." An illustrative nonforfeiture section appears in the level premium whole life policy in the Appendix, Figure 2.

Grace Period Provision

As with some other standard provisions, insurers first included the grace period provision in life insurance policies on a voluntary basis. By the time of the Armstrong Investigation, most insurers used grace period provisions. Thus, the standard policy provisions laws required all insurers to follow a practice many insurers had already adopted.

The grace period provision gives the policyowner an additional period of time in which to pay a premium after it has become due. During that period, the policy continues in force and the premium continues to be payable. Therefore, if the insured dies during the grace period and prior to payment of the premium, the insurer must pay the policy proceeds but can deduct the amount of the premium. If the insured does not die during the grace period, and the policyowner does not pay the premium

---

[7]N.Y. Ins. Law § 3203(a)(9) (McKinney 1985).

by the end of the grace period, the policy lapses, but the policyowner owes nothing for the additional days of protection.

A grace period provision from the illustrative life insurance policy in the Appendix, Figure 2, reads as follows:

> **Grace Period**
> We will allow a period of 31 days after the premium due date for payment of each premium after the first. This is the grace period. If the Insured dies during the grace period before the premium is paid, we will deduct one month's premium from the death proceeds of this policy.
>
> If any premium is not paid on or before its due date, that premium is in default. If that premium is still unpaid at the expiration of the grace period, the Policy terminates except for any nonforfeiture benefits.

Length of the Period.   Most life insurance policies provide a grace period of 31 days. If the last day of grace falls on a nonbusiness day, the premium ordinarily is payable on the following business day.

A late remittance offer does not extend the grace period. An insurer sometimes makes a late remittance offer after a policy has lapsed. The late remittance offer allows the policyowner a limited period of time after the expiration of the grace period in which to reinstate the policy without providing evidence of insurability, as long as the insured is alive when payment is tendered. A late remittance offer form is illustrated in the Appendix, Figure 12.

Interest Charge.   If a policyowner pays the premium at the end instead of at the beginning of the grace period, the insurer will have lost the investment value of the premium for one month. For this reason, state laws often permit the insurer to deduct the amount of interest from policy benefits if the insured dies during the grace period.[8] For competitive reasons, and because such losses are not significant, most insurers do not make this interest charge, as the policy provision quoted above illustrates.

Incontestable Clause

Most standard policy provisions laws require that an individual life insurance policy contain an incontestable clause. An incontestable clause typically provides that, after the policy has been in force for two years during the lifetime of the insured, the insurer will not contest the policy's validity. In the absence of an incontestable clause, years or even decades after issuing the policy the insurer might be able to have it rescinded or successfully defend a suit for the death benefit, on the grounds that the policy was invalid.

A thorough explanation of the incontestable clause, its history, and its relationship to other policy provisions would be too lengthy for this chapter. Chapter 17, "Policy Contests and the Incontestable Clause," covers this topic.

Entire Contract Provision

Entire contract statutes vary from state to state. Some states require that an entire contract provision disclose that the policy, together with the application if attached, constitutes the entire contract. Statutes in other states declare directly that the policy and the application constitute the entire contract.

---

[8]*E.g., id.* § 3203(a)(2).

The requirement that a life insurance policy include an entire contract provision grew out of the practice of incorporation by reference. ***Incorporation by reference*** is a rule of contract law that permits contracting parties to incorporate into a written contract another document simply by referring to it in the contract. The document to be incorporated must be in existence at the time the contract is made. The reference to the document must be express and made in such a way that the document can be identified. Incorporation by reference greatly simplifies contract drafting in many instances.

However, as applied to life insurance contracts, incorporation by reference can be subject to abuse. For example, provisions in the insurer's charter and bylaws could be made an effective part of every life insurance contract that the insurer issued simply by adequate reference to them in the contract. The insurer could limit the privileges and benefits under the contract in that way, yet policyowners might never see the charter or bylaws and, in most instances, would be unaware of their provisions. The entire contract provision assures the policyowner that the policy includes every document affecting the privileges and benefits, as well as the duties and conditions, of the contract.

The application could also be incorporated into the policy by reference if the state did not require an entire contract provision. An important purpose of entire contract statutes is to require the insurer to provide the policyowner with a copy of the application, rather than allowing the insurer to hold it and incorporate it into the policy by reference. This eliminates uncertainties for the policyowner about the contents of the application and allows the policyowner to inform the insurer of necessary corrections. It also prevents the policyowner from contending that he was not aware of statements made in the application. The insurer almost always attaches a copy of the application to the policy. If a copy is not attached, ordinarily the insurer cannot use any misstatements in the application to contest the validity of the policy.

The entire contract provision of the illustrative policy in the Appendix, Figure 2, reads in part as follows:

Entire Contract
We have issued this Policy in consideration of the application and payment of the premiums. A copy of the application is attached and is a part of this Policy. The Policy with the application makes the entire contract. All statements made by or for the Insured will be considered representations and not warranties. We will not use any statement in defense of a claim unless it is made in the application and a copy of the application is attached to this Policy when issued.

Two further points are important in regard to entire contract statutes. First, entire contract statutes do not prevent inclusion of a legally required policy provision that has been omitted. If any legally required provision has not been included in a policy, a court will interpret the contract as if such a provision were included in it.

Second, an entire contract statute or clause refers to the contract at the time it is made. It does not ordinarily prohibit later agreements relating to the contract. For example, an insurer can enter into a valid written agreement with the policyowner to extend the time for premium payment, on condition that the policyowner's failure to comply with the terms of the agreement shall lapse the policy without further action on the part of the insurer.[9]

---

[9]Lincoln Nat'l Life Ins. Co. v. Hammer, 41 F.2d 12 (8th Cir. 1930); Keller v. North Am. Life Ins. Co., 133 N.E. 726 (Ill. 1921).

Misstatement of Age Provision

The age of the proposed insured is of such importance with respect to the degree of risk the insurer will assume that a misstatement of age can make a significant difference in the amount of the premiums. In other words, the statement of the age of a proposed insured is a material representation. Yet misstatements of the age of the proposed insured have been common from the outset of the life insurance business. Thus, some equitable method of adjusting the amount of the premiums paid or the amount of insurance payable has been necessary from an early date.

Misstatement Discovered before the Insured's Death.   If an error as to the insured's age is discovered before the insured's death, the insurer can make an adjustment in either premiums or coverage. If the insured's age was understated, the insurer can issue to the policyowner a policy for a reduced amount or can allow the policyowner to pay the difference in premiums with interest and keep the original policy. If the insured's age was overstated, the insurer will usually refund the excess premiums paid.

Mistatement Discovered after the Insured's Death.   The New York standard policy provisions law requires that life insurance policies contain a provision stating

> that if the age of the insured has been misstated, any amount payable or benefit accruing under the policy shall be such as the premium would have purchased at the correct age.[10]

A majority of states have a similar misstatement of age statute.

The misstatement of age provision assures the policyowner that the insurer will uniformly adjust all death claims where the insured's age has been misstated and the insurer discovers the misstatement after the insured's death. In the absence of such a provision, the insurer could adjust either the amount of the benefit or the amount of premiums paid. There could be certain inequities in allowing premium adjustments rather than benefit adjustments. For example, if the age of the insured had been understated, the beneficiary could pay the difference in premium after the insured's death and, in effect, buy more insurance than the premium paid before death would have provided.

The misstatement of age provision generally applies only if there is an innocent mistake and not if there is fraud or collusion.[11] In one case, where the insurer's agent and the beneficiary had collusively represented the insured to be 30 years younger than her actual age, the court allowed the insurer to deny payment of the death benefit.[12]

Misstatement of Sex.   In life insurance policies for which the insurer charges lower premiums for women than for men, the misstatement of age provision sometimes includes a reference to misstatement of sex. The statutes of a minority of states require a reference to misstatement of sex. The illustrative policy in the Appendix, Figure 2, contains the following reference:

---

[10]N.Y. Ins. Law § 3203(a)(5) (McKinney 1985).

[11]Lucas v. American Bankers' Ins. Co., 141 So. 394 (La. Ct. App. 1932). *See also* dicta in Smith v. National Life & Acci. Ins. Co., 39 S.W.2d 319 (Ark. 1931).

[12]Lucas v. American Bankers' Ins. Co., 141 So. 394 (La.Ct. App. 1932).

Incorrect Age or Sex

This Policy is issued at the age shown on page three, which should be the age attained by the Insured on the last birthday prior to the Policy Date. If the Policy Date falls on the Insured's birthday, the age should be the Insured's attained age on the Policy Date.

If the Insured's age or sex is incorrectly shown on page three, we will adjust the proceeds payable under this Policy to the proceeds the premium would have purchased at the correct age and sex based upon our rates in effect when this Policy was issued.

Divisible Surplus Provision

The 1905 Armstrong Investigation of insurance practices included an investigation of the dividend practices of some of the large mutual life insurance companies. Instead of paying policyowner dividends each year under participating life insurance policies, as is ordinarily done today, life insurers at that time customarily accumulated surplus funds for long periods of time, often 20 years or more. Only those policyowners whose policies were still in force at the end of the period shared in the funds so accumulated. The others forfeited their shares. These forfeitures increased the amounts paid to those who did receive dividends.[13]

Legislation resulting from the Armstrong Investigation required insurers to ascertain and apportion divisible surplus to the policyowners of participating policies at frequent intervals and to express this requirement in a policy provision. Accordingly, the present New York Insurance Law requires participating policies to include a provision stating that the insurer shall annually ascertain and apportion any divisible surplus accruing on the policy.[14] Over three-fourths of the states have laws requiring frequent apportionment of divisible surplus. One divisible surplus policy provision reads as follows:

> Annual dividends such as the company may apportion shall be payable at the end of each policy year after the first while this policy is in force other than as extended term insurance.

No divisible surplus provision appears in the illustrative policy in the Appendix, Figure 2, because it is a nonparticipating policy that does not provide for the payment of dividends. The Appendix, Figure 3, includes a dividend section from a participating policy.

A few states specify optional methods of applying dividends and require that these options be included in the contract. These requirements are discussed in Chapter 12, "Premiums and Dividends."

Policy Loan Provision

The policy loan provision benefits the policyowner who does not wish to surrender the policy and yet has a present need for cash. Insurers first made policy loans available voluntarily, and later by statutory requirement.

Policy loans are not actually loans from a legal standpoint. That is, a policy loan does not create a debtor-creditor relationship between the policyowner and the insurer. A true loan creates a debtor-creditor relationship. Policy loans are actually advances. An **advance** is money paid before the stipulated time of payment. A

---

[13]This is the tontine system, so called because it was devised by Lorenzo Tonti.
[14]N.Y. INS. LAW § 3203(a)(6) (McKinney 1985).

policy loan is an advance of the cash surrender value or of the death benefit. The insurer will deduct the amount of the policy loan and unpaid interest from the cash value if the policyowner surrenders the policy before repaying the loan and interest. If the policy is in effect at the time of the insured's death and the policy loan and interest have not been repaid, the insurer will deduct the amount of the loan and unpaid interest from the death benefit.

Policy loans and automatic premium loans are discussed at length in Chapter 13, "Policy Loans and Nonforfeiture Benefits."

Reinstatement Provision

In the United States, reinstatement provisions in life insurance policies came into general use in the 1890s. Until 1905, however, no laws required them. At the present time, most of the states have laws requiring that any individual life insurance policy issued for delivery in the state must include a reinstatement provision.

A reinstatement provision allows the policyowner to reinstate a lapsed policy. Such a provision ordinarily requires that the policyowner apply for reinstatement within three years from the date of policy lapse. The policyowner must produce satisfactory evidence of the insurability of the insured and pay unpaid premiums with interest. The policyowner must also pay any policy loan with interest or have the insurer reinstate the loan. The policyowner must not have surrendered the policy for cash. Finally, any extended term insurance must not have been exhausted.

Reinstatement provisions provide a valuable contractual right to the policyowner. Reinstatement provisions are discussed at length in Chapter 15, "Lapse and Reinstatement."

Prohibited Policy Provisions

In addition to requiring that certain provisions be included in life insurance policies, the insurance laws of most states also specify some provisions that insurers cannot include in policies issued or delivered in the state. These prohibited provisions are considered to be against the public interest. Prohibited provisions are discussed in this section.

Less Value Statutes

The less value statutes that many states have enacted are intended to prevent the insurer from promising benefits on the face of the policy that are curtailed or extinguished in the body of the policy. The practice of excluding the hazards of war, aviation, and suicide has created a direct conflict with less value statutes, as has the misstatement of age provision.

The Illinois law partially avoids the problem by prohibiting

> [a] provision for any mode of settlement at maturity after the expiration of the contestable period of the policy of less value than the amount insured plus dividend additions, if any, less any indebtedness to the company on or secured by the policy, and less any premium that may by the terms of the policy be deducted, except [for war and aviation hazard exclusions].[15]

---

[15]215 Ill. Comp. Stat. Ann. 5/225 (1)(c) (Michie 1993).

The less value statutes of some states do not include a phrase referring to hazards that can be excluded in the policy, but usually the state will have other statutes relating to suicide exclusions, war and aviation hazard exclusions, and misstatement of age provisions. The courts can take those statutes into consideration in interpreting the state's less value statute.

Forfeiture for Failure to Repay a Policy Loan

Illinois law forbids

> [a] provision for forfeiture of the policy for failure to repay any loan on the policy, or to pay interest on such loan, while the total indebtedness on the policy, including interest, is less than the loan value thereof.[16]

This prohibition implements the required policy loan standard provision. One-fourth of the states have such a prohibition.

Agent of the Insured

Courts generally have held that an insurer's attempt to make its soliciting agent, by policy provision, the agent of the insured for the purpose of taking the application is legally ineffective. The Illinois legislature has enacted this into statutory law by prohibiting

> [a] provision to the effect that the agent soliciting the insurance is the agent of the person insured under the policy, or making the acts or representations of such agent binding upon the person so insured under the policy.[17]

The purpose of this and similar laws is to make certain that the insurer is responsible for its soliciting agent's acts. These laws prohibit the insurer from transferring that responsibility to the applicant or policyowner by policy provision. For example, suppose that the applicant pays the initial premium to the soliciting agent and the soliciting agent absconds with the initial premium. The insurer cannot claim that the initial premium has not been paid. Payment to the insurer's authorized agent is payment to the insurer. However, if the insurer were allowed to transfer responsibility for the soliciting agent's acts to the applicant, the applicant would have to pay the initial premium again to form a binding insurance contract.

Universal and Variable Life Insurance Laws

Insurers developed universal, variable, and universal variable life insurance policies to counter a trend to "buy term insurance and invest the difference." Sales of these policies increased rapidly during the1980s, when interest rates were high. The laws governing universal and variable life insurance are so varied and complex that this book can provide only a brief outline of them.

---

[16]*Id.* 5/225 (1)(d).
[17]*Id.* 5/225 (1)(e).

Universal Life Insurance Regulations

There are three basic types of life insurance policies: whole life insurance, term life insurance, and endowment insurance. Universal life insurance is a type of whole life insurance. Insurers developed it during the early 1980s to capitalize on the high interest rates prevalent at that time. Under a *universal life insurance* contract, the insurer first deducts mortality and expense charges from the premium, and then puts the remainder of the premium into the cash value portion of the policy, where it earns current interest rates. The insurer holds different investment portfolios for universal life policies than for its other whole life policies. The policyowner shares some of the risks of lower current interest rates. There is usually a low guaranteed rate of interest, such as 3.5 percent.

Although the structure of universal life insurance policies differs from insurer to insurer, some features frequently found are death benefits that are level or increasing, at the policyowner's option, and flexibility in the amount of the premiums and in the timing of payment of the premiums.

In 1984, the NAIC adopted the Universal Life Insurance Model Regulation. The model regulation defines a universal life insurance policy as "any individual life insurance policy under the provisions of which separately identified interest credits and mortality and expense charges are made to the policy." The model regulation has sections governing valuation, nonforfeiture values, policy provisions, disclosure to policyowners and prospective policyowners, and filing with the state insurance department. About one-fourth of the states have adopted universal life insurance regulations based on the model regulation. Others have various guidelines that apply to universal life insurance policies.

Variable Life Insurance Laws

Variable life insurance was first developed in the 1960s, but real interest in it began in the 1980s. Generally speaking, *variable life insurance* is a level premium, cash value, whole life insurance contract with premiums that are credited to investment accounts separate from the insurer's other investment accounts. The policyowner has two or more investment accounts from which to choose. One of these accounts might contain growth stocks, another long-term corporate bonds, another intermediate-term government bonds, and so forth. The insurer credits the policyowner with the actual return on the money in the accounts chosen. There is no guarantee of principal or interest. The cash value may increase or decrease on a daily basis. Likewise, the death benefit will increase or decrease depending on the performance of the investment accounts. Most variable life insurance policies guarantee that the face amount will not fall below a specified minimum. The insurer adjusts the death benefit annually.

Variable life insurance is considered a security, as well as an insurance contract. Those selling variable life insurance must obey federal and state securities laws as well as life insurance laws. Variable life insurance policies must be registered under the federal Securities Act. Those selling variable life insurance policies must register as broker-dealers under the federal Securities Exchange Act. The insurer or other entity providing investment advisory services to the separate accounts must comply with the Investment Advisors Act. State securities laws also apply to variable life insurance policies.

Over two-thirds of the states have enacted statutes patterned on the NAIC's Model Variable Contract Law. Nearly all the rest have other variable contract statutes. Statutes patterned on the model law provide for the establishment of separate accounts by insurers domiciled in the state. The model law is discussed in more detail in Chapter 21, "Annuity Contracts."

The NAIC's Variable Life Insurance Model Regulation contains detailed provisions governing insurers' qualifications, policy content and filing, reserves, separate accounts, information to be given to applicants and policyowners, and agent qualifications. More than half the states have regulations based on this model.

Variable Universal Life Insurance Laws

Variable universal life insurance policies are similar to universal life insurance policies, except that with variable universal policies the amount in the policy account can go up and down with the investment experience of the separate account. By contrast, under a universal life insurance policy, the insurer credits a minimum guaranteed interest rate to the policy account and the insurer can declare higher rates periodically. Insurers issuing variable universal life insurance policies are subject to federal and state securities laws as well as to insurance laws.

Policy Filing and Approval

To assure compliance with the policy provisions laws, each state gives its insurance commissioner responsibility for policy forms, although the nature of this responsibility varies from state to state. Insurers must not issue or deliver a policy within a state until the form has been filed with and approved by the state's insurance commissioner. In half of the states, the insurance commissioner is required to notify the company within a stated period, usually 30 days, if the policy form does not comply with the statutory requirements. If the insurer does not receive such notice, the insurer can assume that the insurance commissioner has approved the form. Other states require that the insurer wait until it receives actual approval before using the form.

If an insurer issues a policy without the required approval of the insurance commissioner, the policy is generally held to evidence a valid contract, enforceable by the policyowner or beneficiary. The statutory approval requirements are for their benefit, and therefore the courts usually consider such contracts binding on the insurer. The courts construe these contracts as if they included any required provisions that are more favorable to the policyowner or beneficiary than those actually included in the policy.

Usually, a penalty can be imposed on an insurer for issuing a policy that the insurance commissioner has not approved as the state statute requires. The penalty can be a fine or even the revocation of the insurer's license to do business in that state.

Summary

Many states require that life insurance policies be written in simplified language. State laws also ordinarily require that life insurance policies contain certain standard policy provisions, such as settlement options tables, nonforfeiture provisions, a grace period provision, an incontestable clause, an entire contract provision, a misstatement of age provision, a divisible surplus provision (in the case of a participating policy), a policy loan provision, and a reinstatement provision.

The law prohibits certain other provisions. Less value statutes prohibit an insurer from reducing benefits promised on the face of the policy. Some states have statutes forbidding forfeiture of the policy for failure to repay a policy loan, or interest on the loan, while the total indebtedness is less than the loan value. Statutes in some states prohibit an insurer from stating in the policy that the soliciting agent is the applicant's agent.

Special regulations govern universal life insurance policies. Those selling variable life insurance policies must obey state and federal securities laws and state insurance laws, including special insurance laws governing variable contracts.

The insurance commissioner of the state where a life insurance policy will be sold must approve the policy form. Usually, a penalty can be imposed on the insurer for issuing a policy that the commissioner has not approved.

ILLUSTRATIVE CASE

The following case illustrates the interpretation of the provisions of a life insurance policy by a court.

GRACE L. SUGGS
v.
THE LIFE INSURANCE COMPANY OF VIRGINIA[18]
Supreme Court of Appeals of Virginia

EGGLESTON, Chief Justice.

* * * * *

These are the material facts: On July 1, 1955 the Company issued its policy insuring the life of William Durwood Suggs, III, who was born on February 16, 1942, became twenty-one years of age on February 16, 1963, and died on April 16, 1963. The plaintiff was named as beneficiary in the policy and at the time of the death of the insured all of the premiums had been paid.

Under the terms of the policy the Company contracted to pay $3,000 as "Initial Insurance" "in the event of the death of the Insured during the initial insurance period," or to pay $15,000 as "Ultimate Insurance" "in the event of the death of the Insured after the initial insurance period." The policy defined the "Initial Insurance Period" as "the period between the policy date and the policy anniversary nearest the Insured's 21st birthday excluding such policy anniversary."

On the back of the policy and at the bottom of the first page the following was printed:

"JUNIOR ESTATE BUILDER

"Insurance Payable at Death of Insured—Increased After Age 21

"Premiums Payable to Age 65 or Until Prior Death

"—Non-Participating—"

---

[18]147 S.E.2d 707 (Va. 1966).

It is agreed that these notations are printed on the policy pursuant to Code, Section 38.1–403, which provides: "On the face and on the back of each such policy there shall be placed a title which shall briefly and accurately describe the nature and form of the policy."

The question presented is whether the plaintiff is entitled to the initial insurance of $3,000, payable during the initial insurance period as defined in the policy, or the ultimate insurance of $15,000 payable after the initial insurance period.

The plaintiff does not question that under the policy definition of the initial insurance period, standing alone, she is entitled to recover only $3,000. It is clear that the death of the insured on April 16, 1963 occurred within the initial insurance period which is defined as "the period between the policy date [July 1, 1955] and the policy anniversary nearest the Insured's 21st birthday [February 16, 1963]." But she contends that the Junior Estate Builder endorsement is a part of the insurance contract; that since the death of the insured occurred after he had reached 21 years of age, under the provision in the endorsement—"Insurance Payable at Death of Insured—Increased After Age 21"—she became entitled to the increased amount of insurance, or $15,000. She further contends that there is an inconsistency as to when the ultimate insurance is payable under this language in the endorsement and that in the body of the policy, and that this inconsistency creates an ambiguity which under familiar principles should be resolved against the Company and in her favor.

The lower court held that the Junior Estate Builder endorsement, which it characterized as a "Title" description, is not a part of the insurance contract, nor is it the purpose and intent of the statute . . . to make it a part of the contract. It further held that if such endorsement be deemed a part of the insurance contract, the language therein is not inconsistent with the provisions in the policy fixing the time for the payment of the initial insurance and the ultimate insurance, respectively, and that the plaintiff was entitled to recover the initial insurance of $3,000.

There is a conflict of authority as to whether an endorsement on an insurance policy, designating its kind and type, is a part of the insurance contract.

The obvious purpose of Section 38.1–403 is to require an insurance company to display on the face and on the back of a policy a description of its nature and form in order that a prospective purchaser may know what type of insurance he is purchasing. Such requirement is for the benefit of the prospective purchaser and he is entitled to rely on it. While it may not be strictly accurate to say that such an endorsement is a part of the contract of insurance, in construing the contract the policy must be considered as a whole and the endorsement read in connection with the remainder thereof, as an aid in arriving at the intention of the parties.

The contention of the plaintiff that she is entitled to increased amount of insurance under the language of the endorsement is based upon the premise that the word "After" in the phrase "Increased After Age 21" means "immediately after," "upon," or "as soon as." She argues that as soon as such event occurred she became entitled to the increased amount of the insurance—$15,000. We do not agree with this contention.

When the contractual terms and the provisions of the policy including those in the endorsement, are read in their entirety it is clear that the word "After" as used in the phrase "Increased After Age 21" means "subsequent in point of time" to, or "later in time" than, the insured's attainment of his 21st birthday. This is in accord with the commonly accepted definition of the word after. The language indicating that the amount of insurance payable at the death of the insured is "Increased After Age 21" obviously refers to the provision in the policy that upon the happening of that event the amount of the insurance is increased as therein provided.

Such interpretation removes any question as to the inconsistency between the language of the endorsement and that of the other provisions of the policy and brings them into complete harmony. It accords with the principle that all of the provisions of a contract of insurance should be considered and construed together and seemingly conflicting provisions harmonized when that can be reasonably done, so as to effectuate the intention of the parties as expressed therein. . . . Thus, while the insured's death was "After Age 21," it was also within the initial insurance period.

We agree with the holding of the lower court that there is no inconsistency or ambiguity in the provisions of the policy and that since the insured died "After Age 21" but within the initial insurance period the plaintiff was entitled to recover the amount of the initial insurance—$3,000.

Affirmed.

Questions for Review

1. What are some requirements found in simplified language laws?
2. List the various provisions that state laws usually require to be included in an individual life insurance policy. What is the significance of the words *in substance* in relation to these required provisions?
3. What is the purpose of the free look provision?
4. How do the laws governing the cash surrender value of level premium whole life insurance policies differ from laws governing flexible premium whole life insurance policies?
5. Describe the grace period provision in life insurance policies and the way in which it operates if the insured dies during the grace period.
6. Briefly describe the incontestable clause.
7. Show the relationship between the principle of incorporation by reference and the entire contract provision in a life insurance policy.
8. Within recent years, the word *sex* has been incorporated into the misstatement of age provision of some policies. Tell how this change affects the operation of the provision.
9. Among life insurance policy provisions that are prohibited is a provision relating to the soliciting agent. Describe this prohibited provision.
10. Suppose that an insurer issues a policy without the required approval of the commissioner of insurance. What is usually the legal status of such a contract?

8 ADDED BENEFITS AND LIMITATIONS

Chapter Outline

In the previous chapter, required and prohibited individual life insurance policy provisions were discussed. In this chapter, optional benefits and limitations that the insurer is permitted to add to the policy will be examined.

Added Benefits

Early life insurance contracts provided one benefit, payable at the death of the insured. Today, it is common practice to make additional benefits available, sometimes as an integral part of the policy and sometimes by means of separate, added sections called *riders*. The practice of adding benefits by appropriate riders permits flexibility in adapting basic plans to individual needs.

Benefits often provided in addition to the death benefit are the accidental death benefit and disability benefits (waiver of premium and disability income). In addition, life insurance policies often contain optional provisions that, while strictly speaking not benefits, are beneficial to the policyowner in various ways. Such optional provisions include the guaranteed insurability option, the accelerated benefits provision, the backdating provision, the ownership provision, the assignment provision, and the contract change provision. These added benefits and optional provisions will be discussed in this section, along with the more important legal problems associated with their use.

Accidental Death Benefit

An accidental death benefit is often added to life insurance policies. It is an integral part of some policies. As a general rule, however, the accidental death benefit is available only on application and for an additional premium and is added by rider. The proposed insured ordinarily must meet some underwriting requirements.

Typically, the amount of the accidental death benefit equals the amount of the death benefit. Thus, if the policy provides a $100,000 death benefit, the accidental death benefit will provide an additional $100,000. For this reason, the accidental death benefit is often called *double indemnity*. For losses due to certain types of accidental deaths, some insurers offer triple or quadruple the amount of the death benefit.

Although this subsection contains a discussion of accidental death benefits in life insurance policies, most of the principles stated will also apply to other types of policies insuring against accidental death, such as health insurance policies with accidental death and dismemberment provisions or travel accident insurance policies. Many of the principles will apply as well to coverage of accidental injury in health insurance policies.

Accident and Accidental Defined.   The courts will interpret the terms *accident* or *accidental* according to their ordinary definitions unless a statute or policy provision requires otherwise. According to the ordinary definition, an **accident** is an unusual event that the insured does not foresee. The event happens suddenly, unexpectedly, and without the insured's intent. There is usually an element of force or violence in an accident. The term *accidental* means "occurring by accident."

Accidental Means and Accidental Result.   Thus far, this text has used the term *accidental death benefit* as a generic term encompassing all types of life insurance policy clauses providing an additional benefit where the insured's death involves an accident. Actually, some courts have recognized two categories of clauses: accidental means clauses and accidental result clauses. Both accidental means clauses and accidental result clauses have many variations in wording. However, some patterns do recur.

Under one fairly typical accidental means clause, the insurer promises to pay the specified amount

> upon receipt of due proof that death of the insured resulted from bodily injury effected directly and independently of all other causes by violent, external, and accidental means.

One insurer's accidental result clause reads in part as follows:

> The Company agrees to pay an Accidental Death Benefit upon receipt at its Home Office of due proof that the death of the Insured resulted, directly and independently of all other causes, from accidental bodily injury.

Under an *accidental result clause,* only the result must be accidental, whereas under an *accidental means clause,* both means and result must be accidental if benefits are to be payable. Coverage under an accidental result clause is therefore broader than that under an accidental means clause. For this reason, a distinction between the two can mean the difference between payment or nonpayment of benefits.

In recent years, the courts of a growing number of states have rejected the distinction between accidental means and accidental result. These courts treat accidental means clauses as if they were accidental result clauses. They have said that the distinction is too technical to be readily understood by policyowners.

This is the most favorable interpretation from the policyowner's or beneficiary's viewpoint, as only the result must be accidental rather than both the means and the result.

In 1934, the movement to reject the distinction between accidental means and accidental result clauses was given impetus by a dissenting opinion of U.S. Supreme Court Justice Benjamin Cardozo in *Landress v. Phoenix Mutual Life Insurance Co.*[1] Justice Cardozo asserted that "[t]he attempted distinction between accidental results and accidental means will plunge this branch of the law into a Serbonian Bog."[2] Moreover, most insurers now use accidental result policy language.

Although the courts of many states have ceased to recognize the distinction between accidental means and accidental result clauses, and although most insurers use accidental result policy language, the distinction is still important in many instances. The courts in several jurisdictions have upheld the distinction.[3] The student of life and health insurance law must therefore understand the distinction that the courts have made.

Accidental Means Defined.   *Means* is the same as *cause.* The difference between accidental means clauses and accidental result clauses is the difference between cause and effect. Death is not caused by accidental means merely because the effect, or result, is accidental in the sense that the result is unforeseen, unintended, and unusual. The means or cause itself must also be accidental if benefits are to be payable under an accidental means clause, in a state recognizing such clauses. The accidental means test is thus more difficult to meet than the accidental result test. Some courts have held that deaths that would be accidental under an accidental result clause were not covered if the policy contained an accidental means clause. One court expressed the distinction between accidental means and accidental result as follows:

---

[1]291 U.S. 491.

[2]Referring to Lake Serbonis in Egypt in which, according to Herodotus, whole armies were engulfed. The Supreme Court of Colorado, citing Justice Cardozo's reasoning with approval, said "Whatever kind of bog that is, we concur." Equitable Life Assur. Soc'y v. Hemenover, 67 P.2d 80 (Colo. 1937).

[3]Nicholas v. Mutual Benefit Life Ins. Co., 451 F.2d 252 (6th Cir. 1971); Chelly v. Home Ins. Co., 285 A.2d 810 (Del. Super. Ct. 1971), *aff'd,* 293 A.2d 295 (Del. 1972); Mozingo v. Mid-South Ins. Co., 224 S.E.2d 208 (1976 N.C. Ct. App.); Praetorian Mut. Life Ins. Co. v. Humphrys, 484 S.W.2d 413 (Tex. Civ. App. 1972). In two of these cases, *Nicholas v. Mutual Benefit Life Ins. Co.* and *Chelly v. Home Ins. Co.,* the policy language did not mention accidental means, but the courts nevertheless construed the clauses involved to be accidental means clauses.

[A]ccidental death is an unintended and undesigned result, arising from acts done; death by accidental means is where the result arises from acts unintentionally done.[4]

Thus, if the policy contains an accidental means clause, courts have often held that no benefits are payable if the acts of the insured leading up to the death took place as the insured intended and expected, even though the resulting death was unintended and unexpected. In other words, the cause itself must be accidental.

This principal is easy to state, but, unfortunately, it is difficult to apply. One court said:

A consideration of the literally hundreds of cases where the courts have sought to construe such provisions in policies of insurance and interpret "accidental means" brings one to the sharp realization of the great truth in Justice Cardozo's warning, "The attempted distinction between accidental results and accidental means will plunge this branch of the law into a Serbonian Bog." The cases are in irreconcilable conflict.[5]

Some examples of the way in which the courts have dealt with accidental means clauses may help the reader to grasp the difficulty the courts have had in trying to develop a coherent body of law in this area.

Accidental Means Cases.   In *United States Mutual Accident Association v. Barry*,[6] the insured, a doctor, died from internal injuries after jumping from a platform four feet high. Another doctor who had made the same jump testified that the insured made a heavy, inert sound when he landed. The U.S. Supreme Court upheld, as correct, the following instructions given by the trial court to the jury:

[I]f a result is such as follows from ordinary means voluntarily employed in a not unusual or unexpected way, then, I suppose it cannot be called a result effected by accidental means. . . . [Y]ou must go further and inquire . . . was there or not any unexpected or unforeseen or involuntary movement of the body, from the time Dr. Barry left the platform, until he reached the ground, or in the act of alighting? . . . Did he accomplish just what he intended to in the way he intended to?

The Court further said:

[I]f, in the act which precedes the injury, something unforeseen, unexpected, unusual occurs which produces the injury, then the injury has resulted through accidental means.

Courts frequently rely on this case. It is notable because it has been cited as supporting authority both by courts adhering to a strict interpretation of the term *accidental means* and by those using a moderate approach.

In *Avent v. National Life and Accident Insurance Co.*,[7] the Supreme Court of Tennessee took a strict approach to interpretation of an accidental means clause. There, the insured was receiving treatment for a stiff neck. The treatment consisted mainly of manipulating the insured's head and neck while the insured lay on a table. At the conclusion of one treatment session, the insured was unable to move. Subsequent surgery revealed a chipped bone in his neck, and he died 36 hours later.

---

[4]Pledger v. Business Men's Acci. Ass'n, 197 S.W. 889 (Tex. Civ. App. 1917), *rev'd on other grounds,* 198 S.W. 810 (Tex. Civ. App. 1917), *rev'd on other grounds,* 228 S.W. 110 (Tex. Com. App. 1921).

[5]Thompson v. Prudential Ins. Co. of Am., 66 S.E.2d 119 (Ga. Ct. App. 1951).

[6]131 U.S. 100 (1889).

[7]Life, Health & Acci. Ins. Cas. 2d (CCH) ¶ 506,422 (Tenn. 1954).

The insurer took the position that death was the result of a voluntary and intended act and thus was not caused by accidental means as required by the policy. The beneficiary contended that "excessive force and pressure was unintentionally and accidentally applied . . . and, as a result, a bone in the neck was accidentally broken." The court held that the benefit was not payable, saying:

> It is not sufficient that the injury be unusual and unexpected, but the cause itself must have been unexpected and accidental. . . . The cause of the injury which resulted in the death of Avent was the aforesaid manipulation of his neck. That manipulation was not unexpected or accidental. It was intended by both Avent and the doctor. The means, therefore, producing the injury were not accidental under the rule followed in this State.

The reader likely has a mixed reaction to this case. Is it what the policyowner would reasonably have expected? Could the case not as logically have been decided the opposite way? The difficulty of separating cause and effect that Justice Cardozo pointed out is evident here.

Consider also an Alabama case in which the policy contained an accidental means clause.[8] There, the insured suffered a gash to his lip while he was shaving himself or being shaved. The gash became infected, the infection spread to other parts of his body, and he died. The Alabama Supreme Court stated:

> There was no evidence whatever to show that the insured, or any other person, intentionally cut the gash; but all the evidence shows that the scar, cut, or gash was an accident, and within the risk of the policy.

The facts of this case and the policy language were similar to those in *Avent,* but here the court looked to the intent of the insured or of whoever was shaving him and concluded that the means were accidental and that the benefit was payable.

A court also examined the insured's intent in a Missouri case in which the insured took an overdose of a prescription drug (paraldehyde) and died. There the court said:

> In poison cases, where the poison is mistaken for a harmless substance, there is lack of knowledge of, and intent to take, poison. There is thus unexpectedness with reference to the means. But in the instant case the insured knew he was taking paraldehyde, and the only thing unexpected was the result.[9]

The court therefore held that the means were not accidental, because the insured had done exactly what he intended to do. The court stated:

> If it had been shown that when insured was in the act of drinking from the bottle of paraldehyde, intending to take the dose prescribed, his foot slipped causing him to gulp down an excessive amount, the requirement of accidental means would have been satisfied.

In other words, the court said that if there is a slip or mishap in the action causing the injury, the cause would be accidental, as required by the accidental means provision. In this case, the court held that taking an overdose of the prescription drug was not such a "slip or mishap" as to make the means accidental.

[8]National Life & Acci. Ins. Co. v. Singleton, 69 So. 80 (Ala. 1915).
[9]Murphy v. Western & S. Life Ins. Co., 262 S.W.2d 340 (Mo. Ct. App. 1953).

By contrast, a Kansas court held that taking an overdose of barbiturates was accidental means, and that the insured's death was therefore death by accidental means. The court said:

> There is no evidence that the insured was aware of what amount of the drug would produce death. Without repeating all the evidence as to dosages taken by the insured, we think it such the jury could properly infer that insured was in ignorance that the amount she took was a lethal dose and that her death was by accidental means.[10]

Therefore, whether unintentionally taking an overdose of a prescription drug does or does not constitute accidental means depends on the jurisdiction in which the question arises.

However, the courts generally agree that death results from accidental means if it is caused by taking poison by mistake. A case in which the insured took an arsenic preparation thinking it was a vitamin tonic illustrates this view. In that case, the court held that because of the mistake, the means were accidental, saying, "When death or injury results from taking poison by mistake, the injury or death results from external, violent or accidental means within the terms of a policy of insurance."[11]

External and Violent Means.   Accidental means clauses often state that benefits will be paid

> upon receipt of due proof that the death of the insured resulted directly and independently of all other causes from bodily injuries effected solely through *external, violent,* and accidental means evidenced by a visible contusion on the exterior of the body, except in the case of drowning or of internal injuries revealed by an autopsy [emphasis added].

The term *external means* refers to an agency external to the person. However, the agency may act internally. Poison is an example of an external agency that acts internally.

Violent means signifies a physical force producing a harmful result. The degree of force is unimportant. A very slight force ordinarily will satisfy the policy requirement.

Note that in the clause quoted above the "external, violent, and accidental means" must be "evidenced by a visible contusion on the exterior of the body, except in the case of drowning or of internal injuries revealed by an autopsy." Thus, the provision requires some abnormal bodily manifestation that is observed. The purpose of this requirement is to protect insurers from sham claims. However, the courts have generally been liberal toward the beneficiary in construing the visible contusion requirement. Courts have held that discoloration of the skin, pallor, or slight abrasions will suffice to meet the policy requirement.[12]

Voluntary Assumption of a Known Risk.   Generally speaking, if death is the natural and probable result of the insured's voluntary act, there is neither an accident nor accidental means. A basic legal principle is that a person is presumed to have intended the natural and probable consequences of his own actions. Thus, if a person deliberately exposes himself to what he knows are dangerous circumstances that will

---

[10]Hawkins v. New York Life Ins. Co., 269 P.2d 389 (Kan. 1954).

[11]National Life & Acci. Ins. Co. v. Karasek, 200 So. 873 (Ala. 1941).

[12]Jean F. Rydstrom, Annotation, *Construction and Effect of "Visible Sign of Injury" and Similar Clauses in Accident Provision of Insurance Policy,* 28 A.L.R. 3d 413 (1969).

probably cause his death, it cannot be maintained that his resulting death is either accidental or from accidental means.

For example, in one case, an insured stated that she was going to jump from a car that was being driven around a turn at night at 25 miles per hour. She jumped from the car immediately after making the statement. The court held that her ensuing death from head injuries was not accidental. Even if she did not intend to die, her death was a natural and probable result of her action.[13]

The cases in which the insured voluntarily assumed a risk often turn on whether death was foreseeable. In one case, the court held that the insured's death was foreseeable by him where he had suggested playing Russian roulette. Russian roulette is an act of bravado where a person places one cartridge in a revolver, spins the cylinder, points the gun at his head, and pulls the trigger without looking to see where the cylinder has stopped. The insured died shortly thereafter as a result of a gunshot wound in the head. The court held that the death was not accidental and therefore the insurer was not liable for the accidental death benefit.[14]

In another case, the insured died of a gunshot wound in the head, but evidence showed he had thought the safety was in place when he put the gun to his head. The court held that the death was accidental because the insured did not foresee his death under these circumstances.[15]

Suicide.   Suicide is an intentional act. Therefore, in cases in which the insured, while sane, intentionally takes his own life, the death is not accidental or by accidental means. However, in the absence of a policy provision to the contrary, if an insured is insane at the time of his death by self-destruction and is unconscious of the nature or result of the act, the death is by accident or accidental means.

Suicide is a risk that is often excluded in accidental death benefit provisions or riders, and usually the exclusion will apply to suicide while sane or insane. The accidental death benefit rider in the illustrative policy in the Appendix, Figure 4, states the following:

> Certain risks are not covered. We will not pay the Accidental Death Benefit if the Insured's death results from any of the following causes: (1) Intentionally self-inflicted injury while sane; or (2) Self-inflicted injury while insane; or . . . (10) Suicide, whether sane or insane.

Injury Inflicted by Another Person.   In the absence of a policy provision to the contrary, the general rule is that injury to an insured inflicted by another person results from accident or accidental means if the insured did not foresee the injury. A court determines whether the death is unforeseeable, and hence accidental, from the viewpoint of the insured and not of the other person.[16]

For example, in one case, a robber waylaid and killed the insured. The court held that the death was accidental.[17] In another case, the insured was hanged by a mob; again, the court held that the death was accidental.[18]

---

[13]Zuliskey v. Prudential Ins. Co., 48 A.2d 141 (Pa. Super. Ct. 1946).

[14]Koger v. Mutual of Omaha Ins. Co., 163 S.E.2d 672 (W. Va. 1968).

[15] New York Life Ins. Co. v. Harrington, 299 F.2d 803 (9th Cir. 1962).

[16]Ferdinand S. Tinio, Annotation, *Accident Insurance: Death or Injury Intentionally Inflicted by Another as Due to Accident or Accidental Means,* 49 A.L.R. 3d 673 (1973).

[17]Hutchcraft's Ex'r v. Travelers' Ins. Co., 8 S.W. 570 (Ky. 1888).

[18]Fidelity & Cas. Co. v. Johnson, 17 So. 2 (Miss. 1895).

On the other hand, if the insured provoked an assault or was the aggressor, the insured's resulting death will not be accidental if it was foreseeable and a natural and probable result of his actions. For example, in one case an insured used a deadly weapon to attack police officers. The court held that the insured should have foreseen his death at the hands of the officers and that therefore his death was not an accident.[19]

If the insured assaults a spouse or other family member, the courts are more likely to hold that the insured's death was accidental, particularly if there was a pattern of family fights. Often, the insured could not foresee that death would result from such an altercation. In one case, an insured husband had beaten his wife many times in the past, but she had never violently resisted the beatings. The court held that he could not foresee his death when the wife shot him as he was attempting to beat her again. His death was, therefore, accidental, and the insurer was liable for the accidental death benefit.[20]

Proximate Cause.   The accident must be the proximate cause of the death if an accidental death benefit is to be payable. *Proximate cause* means a cause that is either directly responsible for the death or that initiates an unbroken chain of events, each causing the next, that leads to and brings about the death. The proximate cause of a death is the primary cause. Without the proximate cause, the death would not have occurred. Proximate cause is an especially important concept where accident and disease combine to cause an insured's death.

Accident and Disease.   The accidental death benefit will not be payable if disease is the cause of the death, because ordinarily the risk insured against is loss resulting solely or independently from accident or accidental means. However, in many instances accident and disease are both present. In such cases, the courts will usually look to see whether the accident or the disease was the proximate cause of the death.

If the injury would have caused the death regardless of the insured's state of health, the accidental death benefit will be payable. For example, suppose an insured had an inoperable cancer that was expected to kill him in a month. If he failed to see a fast-moving train and was struck and killed, the insurer would be liable for the accidental death benefit. Moreover, if the accident is the primary cause of the death, the insurer ordinarily will be liable, even if disease has weakened the insured. For example, in one case, an insured had severe cirrhosis of the liver. He fell from a high platform, ruptured his weakened liver, and died from internal bleeding. Even though his chances of survival would have been better if he had had a healthy liver, the court held that the accident, not the disease, was the primary cause of death and that the accidental death benefit was payable.[21]

Conversely, where the disease, rather than the accident, is the primary cause of death, the insurer will not be liable for the accidental death benefit. That is, if an accident would not have resulted in considerable injury had the insured not been afflicted with an existing disease, then the accident is not the primary cause of the resulting harm. For example, in one case, in which the insured had a severely diseased heart, the court held that death caused by a heart attack was not the result

[19]Price v. Business Men's Assur. Co., 67 S.W.2d 186 (Ark. 1934).
[20]Atlantic Am. Life Ins. Co. v. White, 332 So. 2d 389 (Ala. Civ. App. 1976).
[21]Lindemann v. General Am. Life Ins. Co., 485 S.W.2d 477 (Mo. Ct. App. 1972).

of an accident, although the death followed the excitement and exertion generated by a minor incident involving locked car bumpers. The court said the insured was in such bad health that she could have died without there being any noticeable stimulus.[22]

In many cases involving the combined effects of accident and disease, it is difficult to ascertain which was the primary cause of death. These cases are often conflicting.

The courts do agree that if an accidental injury causes a disease and death results from the disease, the accident is the proximate cause of death. There will be coverage under an accidental means clause if injury occasioned by accidental means proximately caused the disease. For example, in one case, in which blood poisoning following an accidental cut on the insured's finger resulted in death, the court held that the accidental death benefit was payable.[23]

Time Limitation Clauses.   Policies containing an accidental death benefit ordinarily include a clause stating that death must occur within a specified number of days after the injury if the accidental death benefit is to be payable.[24] Ninety days is most commonly specified. Such a time limitation clause is primarily intended to reduce problems that arise when the intervening lapse of time makes it difficult or impossible to ascertain whether the injury was the proximate cause of death.

When the time limitation clause originated, medical science was not as far advanced as it is today. The clause therefore causes problems now that it did not cause even a few decades ago. For example, it is not uncommon now for an injured insured to lie in a coma for more than 90 days before dying. Is a 90-day limit realistic in this day of medical skill in prolonging life? Some insurers now issue policies in which the time period has been lengthened to 120, 180, or 365 days.

Moreover, when the circumstances clearly indicate that death resulted from the accident and that only medical skill prolonged the insured's life beyond the specified limit, should the insurer deny the accidental death benefit simply because the death did not occur within the time limit specified? Some insurers waive the time limit requirement under these circumstances. Others waive it if the insured dies within a few days after the expiration of the time limit.

Prior to 1973, the law was well settled that the time limit requirement was enforceable. In 1973, the Pennsylvania Supreme Court held that the time limit requirement is against public policy and is therefore void in Pennsylvania.[25] Lower courts in New Jersey and California have since declared the requirement to be arbitrary and unreasonable in cases in which the accident was clearly the cause of the death.[26]

---

[22]Tix v. Employers Cas. Co., 368 S.W.2d 105 (Tex. Civ. App. 1963).

[23]Central Acci. Ins. Co. v. Rembe, 77 N.E. 123 (Ill. 1906).

[24]Laurent B. Frantz, Annotation, *Validity and Construction of Provision in Accident Insurance Policy Limiting Coverage for Death or Loss of Member to Death or Loss Occurring within Specified Period after Accident,* 39 A.L.R. 3d 1311 (1971).

[25]Burne v. Franklin Life Ins. Co., 301 A.2d 799 (Pa. 1973).

[26]Karl v. New York Life Ins. Co., 381 A.2d 62 (N.J. Super. Ct. 1977); National Life & Acci. Ins. Co. v. Edwards, 174 Cal. Rptr. 31 (1981). The California case extended what is termed *the process of nature rule* from disability cases to accidental death cases in California. Under the process of nature rule, where the death clearly results from the accident, but the processes of nature take more than the specified time to cause the death, the accidental death benefit will be payable.

However, courts in several other states have affirmed the majority position, stating that the requirement is enforceable.[27]

Risks Not Covered by the Accidental Death Benefit Provision.   Insurers customarily list in their accidental death benefit provisions certain risks that the insurers will not cover. One reference source lists 100 exclusions currently in use. Most insurers use only a small fraction of these. The accidental death benefit rider in the Appendix, Figure 4, contains a typical list of risks not covered. The rider states the following:

> Certain risks are not covered. We will not pay the Accidental Death Benefit if the Insured's death results from any of the following causes:
>
> 1. Intentionally self-inflicted injury while sane; or
> 2. Self-inflicted injury while insane; or
> 3. Participation in an assault; or
> 4. Participation in a felony; or
> 5. Travel or flight in or descent from any kind of aircraft; (*a*) on which the Insured is a pilot, officer or member of the crew; or (*b*) on which the Insured has duties aboard; or (*c*) which is being operated for any training or instructional purpose; or (*d*) on which the Insured is being flown for the purpose of descent while in flight; or
> 6. Any bodily or mental infirmity existing before or beginning after the accident; or
> 7. Any infection or disease existing before or beginning after the accident, except a disease or infection as provided in the definition of "accidental death"; or
> 8. Any drug, medication or sedative voluntarily taken unless; (*a*) administered by a licensed physician; or (*b*) taken as prescribed by a licensed physician; or
> 9. Alcohol in combination with any drug, medication or sedative; or
> 10. Suicide, whether sane or insane; or
> 11. Any poison, gas or fumes voluntarily taken, absorbed or inhaled; or
> 12. War or any act of war, whether or not the Insured is in military service. The term "war" includes war declared or undeclared. It also includes armed aggression resisted by: (*a*) the armed forces of any country; and (*b*) any international organization or combination of countries.

Burden of Proof.   A plaintiff suing an insurer for an accidental death benefit has the burden of proving that an accident or accidental means caused the death. If the policy requires that the death result from external, violent, and accidental means, the plaintiff must prove that the means were external and violent, as well as accidental.

If the plaintiff has established the accidental character of the death, authority is split as to whether the plaintiff has to prove that disease was not the proximate cause of death. Some courts have held that the burden of proof is on the plaintiff. Other courts have held that if the insurer wishes to avoid liability on that ground, the insurer has the burden of proving that disease was the proximate cause of death.

---

[27]Hawes v. Kansas Farm Bureau, 710 P.2d 1312 (Kan. 1985); Brendle v. Shenandoah Life Ins. Co., 332 S.E. 2d 515 (N.C. App. 1985); Smith v. Independent Life & Acci. Ins. Co., 346 S.E. 2d 22 (S.C. 1986).

As a general rule, the insurer has the burden of proving that the loss resulted from a risk that was excluded from coverage. Thus, an insurer might have to prove that an accidental death resulted from participation in a felony and that the accidental death policy provision did not cover this risk.

If the plaintiff alleges that the insured's death was accidental, and the insurer alleges that the insured's death resulted from suicide, the majority view is that the burden is on the insurer to prove the suicide. However, a minority of courts have held that under accident provisions the plaintiff's burden of proving death by accident includes proving that the death was not by suicide.

Disability Benefits

Insurers first offered disability benefits in life insurance contracts before the turn of the century. The first disability benefit offered was a waiver of premium during disability. A disability income benefit was added not long afterward.

Generally, insurers offer disability income benefits as a monthly income payable in the event that the insured becomes disabled as defined in the policy. The coverage can be short term or long term. Under short-term coverages, disability income benefits are ordinarily payable for not more than two to five years. Long-term disability income benefits will typically be payable during the continuance of disability until the insured is 65 years old.

Insurers also offer disability income coverages in forms other than as a part of a life insurance policy. Many insurers offer individual disability income insurance contracts, group or franchise disability income insurance, or health insurance contracts covering loss of income along with reimbursement for medical expenses.

Insurers sell the waiver of premium disability benefit as part of a life insurance policy more extensively than the disability income benefit. The waiver of premium disability benefit provision ordinarily states that if the insured becomes disabled, as defined in the life insurance policy, the insurer will waive the payment of premiums that become due on the policy during the continuance of disability, however long the disability may last.[28] The insurer usually will not grant the benefit, however, if the disability begins after the insured has reached a specified age, such as 60 or 65.

Total Disability.   Most policies or riders issued today require that an insured be totally disabled in order to receive disability benefits. Total disability is ordinarily defined in terms of the insured's inability to work and earn an income. This is true for both waiver of premium and disability income coverages.

For example, a definition of *total disability* used by some insurers is that the insured is totally disabled when she is "wholly prevented from performing any work, following any occupation or engaging in any business for remuneration or profit." A few courts have adopted a literal view of this definition—that if the insured is able to work at anything, she is not totally disabled. By far the majority of courts today take the position that total disability does not mean a state of absolute helplessness as would be true under the literal interpretation. Their reasoning is that benefits payable only if the insured is literally "wholly prevented from performing any work, following any occupation or engaging in any business for remuneration or profit" would be

---

[28]In some convertible term policies, if the disability occurs while the policy is still convertible, the insurer will waive payment of premiums until the end of the conversion period and continue the waiver after the conversion of the term policy to a whole life policy as long as the disability lasts.

of limited value. Under this interpretation, an almost complete paralysis would not be disabling, since a person with sufficient gifts and spirit could presumably work at something even under those circumstances.

On the basis that insurers intend a reasonable interpretation of *total disability,* the great majority of courts have taken the position that the insurers could not have intended to require a state of complete helplessness. Instead, the majority of courts interpret the definition in the paragraph above to mean a disability of such a nature as to prevent the insured from performing the substantial and material acts of his own occupation or of any other occupation for which the insured's experience, education, or training reasonably fit him.[29] Most insurers that use this definition follow this interpretation.

Some courts have taken a position even more beneficial to the insured—that if the insured is unable to work at her customary occupation, she is totally disabled within the meaning of this definition. In effect, this rewrites the policy provision. However, most courts do not go this far in their interpretation.

Many companies today use a policy definition of total disability that incorporates the interpretation followed by the majority of the courts. Illustrative of this is the following:

> Total disability is disability of the insured as a result of bodily injury or disease which causes the insured to be wholly and continuously prevented thereby from engaging in any gainful occupation for which he or she is reasonably fitted by reason of education, training or experience.

Some insurers use still another definition, in which the insured will be considered totally disabled if unable to work at any occupation for which he is fitted by training or experience or if the income he is able to earn is reduced to a specified fraction of the income earned before the disability began. Illustrative of this approach is the following policy definition:

> The insured will be deemed to become totally disabled on the Total Disability Date, which is the day when for a period of four consecutive months because of accidental bodily injury or sickness, either (*a*) he or she has been unable to engage in his or her former occupation or in any other occupation for which he or she is suited by education, training or experience; or (*b*) his or her average monthly Earned Income has been reduced to one-fourth or less of his or her former monthly income.

A clause insurers often add to disability provisions defines *total disability* as the total loss of the use of both legs, or of both arms, or of one leg and one arm, or the total loss of the sight of both eyes. Usually, this definition has no reference to whether the insured is able to work or to the amount of his earnings. This clause appears in addition to the clause defining total disability in relation to occupation. The following is typical:

> The total and irrecoverable loss of the sight of both eyes or of the use of both hands or of both feet or of one hand and one foot shall be considered total disability even if the insured shall engage in an occupation.

The disability benefit rider in the Appendix, Figure 5, contains a similar clause.

---

[29]E. L. Kellett, Annotation, *Insurance: "Total Disability" or the Like as Referring to Inability to Work in Usual Occupation or in Other Occupations,* 21 A.L.R. 3d 1155 (1968).

General and Occupational Disability.   Some disability clauses, as noted above, require that the insured be unable to engage in any gainful occupation for which she is reasonably fitted by reason of education, training, or experience. These are general disability clauses. By contrast, occupational disability clauses require only that the insured be disabled from her own occupation.

Combination clauses require the insured to be disabled from her own occupation for a specified period of time and, thereafter, from any occupation. The following is an example:

> Total disability is incapacity as the result of bodily injury or disease, to engage in an occupation for remuneration or profit. During the first 24 months of disability, occupation means the occupation of the insured at the time such disability began; thereafter it means any occupation for which he or she is or becomes reasonably fitted by education, training, or experience.

Permanent Disability.   At one time, it was customary to require that disability be both total and permanent. New policies do not usually require that disability be permanent, although some policies still in effect do contain this language.

It seems relatively certain that, in the early days, the insurers intended the term *permanent disability* to indicate a disability of long-term duration. But how long? And what of the disability from which the insured has already recovered at the time he brings suit for the disability benefits? The literal meaning of *permanent disability,* obviously, is disability that continues until the death of the insured. However, the insurers cannot have meant this. They have long included in their policies provisions relating to the cessation of benefits on recovery of the insured. Therefore, they cannot have contemplated only disability that continues until the death of the insured. Thus, the majority of courts have interpreted *permanent disability* to mean disability expected to last for an indefinite, continuous period of time, without any present indication of recovery.[30]

Insurers usually include a clause requiring that disability must have continued for a specified period, such as four or six months, before it will be considered permanent. A few courts have interpreted this clause to mean that a disability that continues for the specified period is presumed to be permanent in the literal sense of the word.[31] As a general rule, however, the courts have interpreted the specified period to be a mere waiting period, included in the policy for the purpose of relieving the insurer of the expense of having to investigate numerous premature claims.

In permanent disability provisions, insurers usually emphasize that continuous disability throughout the waiting period does not mean that the disability is considered permanent for all purposes. Most provisions contain language such as the following:

> If, and only if, total disability as herein defined has existed uninterruptedly during the lifetime of the Insured for at least six months, it shall be deemed to have been and to be permanent, but only for the purpose of determining the commencement of liability hereunder.

---

[30]E.W.H., Annotation, *"Permanent Disability" within Insurance Policy as Confined to Disability Lasting until Death,* 40 A.L.R. 1386 (1926), *supp. by* 97 A.L.R. 126 (1935).
[31]Heralds of Liberty v. Jones, 107 S. 519 (Miss. 1926); Mitchell v. Equitable Life Assur. Soc'y, 172 S.E. 495 (N.C. 1934).

Risks Not Covered by Disability Benefit Provisions.   As they do with the accidental death benefit provision, insurers usually specify some risks that the disability benefit provision does not cover. Most insurers use only two or three exclusions. Intentionally self-inflicted injury and war hazard exclusions are the most common. Other exclusions insurers sometimes use are "committing or attempting to commit a felony" and "participation in parachute jumping, skydiving, or skin or scuba diving." The waiver of premium disability benefit rider in the illustrative policy in the Appendix, Figure 5, has the following clause:

> Certain risks are not covered. They are as follows. We will not waive premiums if total disability results from:
>
> (1) intentionally self-inflicted injury while sane; or
>
> (2) self-inflicted injury while insane; or
>
> (3) war, or any act of war, whether or not the Insured is in military service. The term "war" includes armed aggression resisted by:
>
> *(a)* the armed forces of any country; or
>
> *(b)* any international organization; or
>
> *(c)* any combination of countries.

Guaranteed Insurability Option

A guaranteed insurability option provides insurance against the risk of becoming uninsurable. It offers the option of purchasing, on specified dates in the future, additional insurance on the insured's life without submitting evidence of insurability. The maximum amount of insurance that a policyowner can purchase is stated in the guaranteed insurability option. Some insurers issue an additional policy each time the policyowner exercises the option to purchase additional insurance. Other insurers amend the original policy to increase coverage.

Until the development of the guaranteed insurability option, a person's only hedge against the risk of becoming uninsurable was to purchase as much insurance as possible as soon as possible. However, in the 1950s this risk was recognized as being insurable. Many insurers now offer a guaranteed insurability option. A guaranteed insurability option rider appears in the Appendix, Figure 6.

The New York legislature has anticipated the possibility of one legal problem with the guaranteed insurability option. This is the operation of the suicide exclusion on the additional insurance provided under such an option. The legislature has therefore enacted a statute that would preclude additional insurance provided under a guaranteed insurability option from having a new suicide period applied to it. The suicide period of the additional insurance must run from the issue date of the original policy—that is, the policy containing the guaranteed insurability option. Thus, the insured not only can purchase additional insurance without evidence of insurability but also, on each option date after the suicide period of the original policy has expired, can purchase additional insurance without a suicide exclusion.[32]

---

[32]N.Y. Ins. Law § 3203(d)(2) (McKinney 1985).

Accelerated Benefits Provision

An accelerated benefits provision, also called a living benefits provision, allows payout of part or all of the death benefit while the insured is still alive if the insured meets the criteria in the provision. These criteria usually include a medical condition of the insured that results in a drastically limited life span, requires extraordinary medical intervention, or requires continuous confinement in an institution for the rest of the insured's life. The face amount and cash value of the policy are proportionally reduced by the amount of the payout.[33] Although the AIDS epidemic spurred the development of accelerated benefits provisions, insureds with other diseases such as severe heart disease, stroke, or end-stage kidney failure also benefit.

Ordinarily, the accelerated benefits provision does not restrict the use of the proceeds.[34] Thus, an insured with AIDS could receive part of the death benefit that his life insurance policy provided and take a trip around the world with the money if he so desired. Often, however, such an insured will simply live out his remaining time more comfortably with funds to pay for living expenses and medical care.

In 1990, the NAIC adopted the Accelerated Benefits Model Regulation as a guideline for the state insurance departments. The model regulation spells out the rights of assignees and irrevocable beneficiaries, the criteria for payout, and the required disclosures, among other things. Almost half the states have regulations or statutes governing accelerated benefits provisions. All states allow the sale of some form of accelerated benefits.[35] Many insurers have added accelerated benefits to their existing policies by rider, often without additional cost to the policyowner, or have included an accelerated benefits provision in newly issued policies.[36] Accelerated benefits are also available in group life insurance policies.[37] An accelerated benefits rider appears in the Appendix, Figure 7.

Backdating Provision

Occasionally, an applicant wishes the policy backdated to "save age." This means that the applicant wants the policy to be backdated to a time when the proposed insured was at a younger age, so that the applicant gets the benefit of a lower premium. However, when a policy is backdated, premiums will be payable for a period in which no insurance was in force. Therefore, many states have enacted statutes making it unlawful for insurers to backdate policies beyond a stipulated period, usually six months prior to the date of the application. Illinois law accomplishes this by prohibiting

---

[33]Linda Koco, *Living Benefits Trends Starting to Clarify,* NAT'L UNDERWRITER, LIFE & HEALTH/FIN. SERVICES EDITION, Oct. 28, 1991, at 27.

[34]Karen Armaganian, *Living Benefits Popular, But Concerns Remain, Bus. Ins.,* Jun. 1, 1992, at 3.

[35]*Pru's Accelerated Benefits Plan Is Now Approved in All 50 States,* NAT'L UNDERWRITER, LIFE & HEALTH/FIN. SERVICES EDITION, June 8, 1992, at 14.

[36]Linda Koco, *Accelerated Benefits Vary by Contract,* NAT'L UNDERWRITER, LIFE & HEALTH/FIN. SERVICES EDITION, Aug. 3, 1992, at 31; *More Insurers Offering Living Benefits Option,* BESTS REV., LIFE/HEALTH EDITION, Apr. 1992, at 7; Matthew Schwartz, *"Accelerated" Benefits Market Is Growing Rapidly: Survey,* NAT'L UNDERWRITER, LIFE & HEALTH/FIN. SERVICES EDITION, Mar. 23, 1992, at 4.

[37]Linda Koco, *Travelers' Small Groups Get Living Benefits—Free,* NAT'L UNDERWRITER, LIFE & HEALTH/FIN. SERVICES EDITION, Oct. 21, 1991, at 13; Steven Brostoff, *Accelerated Benefit Plans Growing Fast,* NAT'L UNDERWRITER, LIFE & HEALTH/FIN. SERVICES EDITION, Feb. 25, 1991, at 3.

[a] provision by which the policy purports to be issued or take effect more than 6 months before the original application for the insurance was made.[38]

Ownership Provision

Insurers issue most policies on the application of a proposed insured who names a revocable beneficiary. The insured has full ownership and control over such a policy. However, most insurers also sell policies that are applied for and issued to persons other than the insured. The insured has no ownership rights under such policies. Most policies owned by a person other than the insured provide coverage for business purposes. In contrast, personal insurance is usually issued on the application of the proposed insured.

The ownership provision indicates the owner of the policy and describes ownership rights. An ownership provision is included in the illustrative policy in the Appendix, Figure 2. Ownership rights are described in Chapter 9, "Property Rights in the Life Insurance Policy."

Assignment Provision

An assignment of a life insurance policy is a transfer by the policyowner of some or all of her rights of ownership. Unless the policy explicitly restricts or prohibits assignment, the policyowner has a right to assign the policy as a matter of law. A policy provision *permitting* assignment is not required. An assignment provision may advise the policyowner of her right to assign the policy and define the insurer's rights and responsibilities in the event that the policyowner elects to exercise the right to assign.

The assignment provision sometimes prohibits or restricts assignment of the policy. An assignment will not be binding on the insurer if the policy prohibits assignment. If the policy restricts assignment, the policyowner must comply with the terms of the assignment provision, or the assignment will not be binding on the insurer.

The assignment provision in the illustrative policy in the Appendix, Figure 2, reads as follows:

Collateral Assignment
You may assign this Policy as collateral for a loan without the consent of any revocable beneficiary. We are not bound by any assignment unless it is in writing and recorded at our Home Office. We are not responsible for the validity of any assignment. The rights of an assignee will at all times be subject to any indebtedness to us at the time the assignment is recorded by us, and, if applicable, to loans granted at any time by us under the automatic premium loan provision of the Policy.

Assignments are discussed in detail in Chapter 14, "Assignments and Other Transfers."

Contract Change Provision

The parties to any contract can, by mutual consent, change their agreement. They can incorporate new terms or effect an entirely new contract. This is true of a life insurance policy as well as of other contracts. A contract change provision is often included in the policy to make this clear. However, the provision does not give the parties any rights they would not otherwise have under the law.

---

[38]215 Ill. Comp. Stat. Ann. 5/225 (1)(b) (Michie 1993).

Added Limitations

An insurer has the option of adding to a life insurance policy a number of clauses that limit the policyowner's or beneficiary's rights under the policy. Limitations that may be added to a life insurance policy include the suicide exclusion, the war hazard exclusion, the aviation hazard exclusion, and the time limit on legal or equitable actions clause.

Suicide Exclusion

If the policy has no clause declaring that suicide is not a risk that the insurer has assumed under the policy, the courts will generally hold that the death of the insured by suicide is a covered risk. However, nearly all modern life insurance policies do contain a provision excluding deaths by suicide. The exclusion will usually be for a specified period of time after the policy's date of issue; one or two years is typical. Some states limit by statute the period of time during which the insurer can exclude death by suicide from coverage. This is reasonable, as most people who commit suicide do not plan the act far in advance. On the other hand, it is also reasonable to exclude suicide for some period of time after the policy is issued. A person who is planning suicide is not an insurable risk, because the event insured against is within his control.

The typical suicide exclusion establishes a compromise between the requirement that the insured be an insurable risk, on the one hand, and the needs of the suicide's beneficiaries, on the other. The exclusion protects the insurer from persons who would take out life insurance intending suicide, while also protecting beneficiaries of persons who die by suicide after the policy has been in effect for a time. The suicide exclusion in the illustrative policy in the Appendix, Figure 2, reads as follows:

Suicide
If the Insured dies by suicide, while sane or insane, within two years from the [date of issue], our liability will be limited to the amount of the premiums paid, less any indebtedness.[39]

The suicide exclusion is discussed at greater length in Chapter 18, "Performance of the Insurance Contract."

War Hazard Exclusion

A war hazard exclusion section or rider limits the liability of the life insurer in the event that the insured dies as a result of war or while in military service. Insurers include this exclusion only in policies issued during periods when war exists or is imminent, and only when the proposed insured is in an age group subject to call to military duty.

It is generally acknowledged that the hazard of war cannot be accurately predicted. It is impossible to predict when a war will occur and equally impossible to predict the death toll of a war. Thus, the statistical studies on which life insurance rates are based generally do not include war deaths. Some underwriting limitations are therefore necessary with respect to war hazards.

---

[39]The phrase *while sane or insane* is explained in the section concerning suicide in Chapter 18, "Performance of the Insurance Contract."

The war hazard exclusion provides a way to issue coverage that would otherwise not be available to a large number of young people in time of war or when war is imminent. Without the exclusion, the insurer might be unwilling to issue any coverage at all. With the exclusion, the insured can be covered for risks other than those excluded in the war hazard section or rider.

One-half of the states have statutes specifically allowing war hazard exclusions.

Status Clauses and Result Clauses.   War hazard exclusion clauses contain a great variety of wording. Nevertheless, the courts recognize two general types of clauses: status clauses and result clauses. *Status clauses* exclude from coverage any death that occurred while the insured was in military service in time of war, regardless of the cause of death. The insured's status as a member of the armed forces is the determining factor. *Result clauses,* by contrast, exclude from coverage only deaths resulting from the insured's military activities.

In cases in which the status of the insured, and not the cause of death, clearly furnishes the basis of exclusion, the courts usually have held that the insurer is not liable if the insured is in the military service in time of war, even though the death did not result from any hazard peculiar to war. Therefore, with a status clause, the insured has no life insurance protection while in the military service in time of war.

Use of the status clause has the disadvantage to the insurer of creating poor public relations by overcompensating for the added risk created by the insured's military service. For example, assume that two young men, both aged 22, are killed in an automobile accident near their homes. One is on leave from the army. The other is a civilian. They have identical life insurance contracts with the same insurer, and each contract contains a status war hazard exclusion clause. Only the civilian's beneficiary would receive the full proceeds. The soldier's beneficiary would receive some lesser amount, ordinarily the amount of premiums paid or the policy reserve, whichever is greater. This outcome is difficult to justify to beneficiaries. For this reason, among others, most insurers have elected to use result clauses.

Some courts have interpreted status clauses as if they were result clauses because the clauses were not clearly written, and the unclear writing created an ambiguity that the court resolved in favor of the beneficiary.[40] In some instances, a statute will control the interpretation.[41]

The status clause does have the advantage to the insurer that it is simpler to administer than the result clause. Ordinarily, under a result clause, the insurer must determine both the status of the insured and the cause of death, whereas, under the status clause, the insurer must determine only the status of the insured.

Under a policy with a result war hazard exclusion clause, if the insured is in the military service in time of war and dies as a result of military activities, the death benefit will not be payable. Ordinarily, the insurer will be liable for either the amount of premiums paid or the policy reserve only. Three questions can arise if the policy contains a result clause. First, was the insured in military service? Second, did the death result from military activities? Third, did the death occur in time of war?

---

[40]A.M.S., Annotation, *Validity, Construction and Effect of Provisions in Life or Accident Policy in Relation to Military Service,* 137 A.L.R. 1263 (1942), *supp. by* C. T. Drechsler, Annotation, 36 A.L.R. 2d 1018 (1954).

[41]*E.g.,* N.Y. Ins. Law § 3203(c) (4)(5) (McKinney 1985 & Supp. 1996).

Military Service.   Ordinarily, both status and result clauses are worded to apply to persons serving in any of the armed forces. The term *in military service* applies to draftees and volunteers, officers and enlisted men and women alike. Courts have held that an army nurse[42] and a member of the military police[43] were in military service. On the other hand, persons in the national guard or naval reserve when not on active duty are not in military service, according to some cases.[44]

Under the wording of some result war hazard exclusion clauses, the status of the insured will not matter, as long as his death resulted from war. A policy will not cover the death from war of a civilian insured if the policy excludes death as a result of war but does not mention military service.

Military Activities.   Result war hazard clauses exclude the insured's death as a result of military activities. Therefore, if the insured dies in combat, the death benefit will not be payable. Even where the insured does not die in combat but dies as a result of military training or maneuvers or other causes peculiar to military service, the death benefit ordinarily will not be payable. By contrast, a policy with a result clause ordinarily will cover death from disease or accidents not related to war or military activities.

Existence of War.   Since 1941, the definition of war has caused problems in regard to war hazard exclusion clauses. On December 7, 1941, some 3,000 people serving in the U.S. Armed Forces were killed at Pearl Harbor in a surprise attack by the Japanese. Congress did not officially declare war until the next day. Most courts ruling on the question later held that war, as insurers used that term in war hazard exclusions, did not exist until Congress officially declared war on December 8, 1941. The beneficiaries were therefore entitled to the death benefit.

The Korean and Vietnam conflicts presented an even more difficult question, because in those instances Congress never officially declared war. The majority of the courts took a position opposite to the position that most courts took in regard to the Pearl Harbor cases. The majority of courts held that *war* meant any actual hostilities between the armed forces of two or more countries. Therefore, even though the war was undeclared, it was war within the meaning of a war hazard exclusion. Many companies have changed the wording of their war hazard exclusions to include war "declared or undeclared."

If actual hostilities have ceased, the courts have held that war no longer exists, even though the hostile nations have not yet signed a peace treaty. Conversely, if there has been a formal surrender, but active hostilities nonetheless continue, a state of war still exists.

War Hazard Exclusion Clauses Today.   In 1991, the Persian Gulf crisis prompted an increased number of insurers to seek approval of war hazard exclusion clauses from state insurance departments.[45] The engagement of the United States in Bosnia and other troubled places gives the war hazard exclusion clause continuing relevance to insurers.

---

[42]New York Life Ins. Co. v. White, 190 F.2d 424 (5th Cir. 1951).

[43]Jorgenson v. Metropolitan Life Ins. Co., 55 A.2d 2 (N.J. Super. Ct. 1947), *aff'g* 44 A.2d 907 (N.J. Ct. Com. Pleas 1945).

[44]*E.g.,* Feick v. Prudential Ins. Co., 62 A.2d 485 (N.J. Super. Ct. 1948).

[45]Jim Connolly, *Companies Seeking War Clause Exclusions,* Nat'l Underwriter, Life & Health/ Fin. Services Edition, Feb. 4, 1991, at 1.

Aviation Hazard Exclusion

Life insurance contracts sometimes exclude from coverage the risk of death as a result of certain aviation activities. As with the war hazard exclusion, an aviation hazard exclusion may appear in the policy itself or be added to the policy by rider. An aviation hazard exclusion appears in the Appendix, Figure 9.

In the early days of aviation, when no statistics were available to measure the added risk of flying, most policy forms excluded aviation deaths. As insurers gained experience, they became able to measure with reasonable accuracy the added risk of flying under various circumstances. As the safety of flying increased, statistics indicated that the added risk was minimal for fare-paying passengers on regularly scheduled commercial airlines. Life insurance policies issued today rarely exclude this type of risk.

Life insurers often insure those engaged in moderately hazardous aviation activities for an extra premium, or provide life insurance coverage if the accidental death benefit provision excludes aviation deaths. Life insurers still use total exclusions for especially hazardous aviation activities, such as military flying, crop dusting, or sports piloting, where an extra premium or an aviation hazard exclusion in the accidental death benefit provision are not practical solutions.

The wording of aviation hazard exclusion clauses is extremely varied. A court will carefully examine an aviation hazard exclusion clause and give the wording paramount importance, although, as with other insurance policy clauses, the court will ordinarily interpret ambiguities in favor of the insured.

Most of these court cases deal with the interpretation of specific terms or phrases in the aviation hazard exclusion clause. For example, courts have held that a glider,[46] a seaplane,[47] and a hang kite[48] are aircraft within the meaning of aviation hazard exclusion clauses. One court held that a parachute is not an aircraft.[49] Some courts have held that the term *fare-paying passenger* does not include a flight attendant[50] or a person traveling on a pass.[51]

Time Limit on Legal or Equitable Actions Clause

Without a clause in a life insurance policy providing for a time limit on legal or equitable actions, the policyowner or beneficiary would be limited in her time to bring suit on the insurance contract only by the state statute of limitations for contract actions. Sometimes, such state statutes of limitations allow a long period of time in which to initiate contract actions. Illinois, for example, allows a party to bring an action on a written contract at any time during the 10 years after the date when the cause of action arose.[52] However, if the policy contains a provision restricting the time for initiating contract actions to three years, as is allowed in Illinois, the time period for initiating such an action would be reduced by seven years.

A delay of many years in the initiation of a contract action could create hardship for the insurer. Key witnesses might die or disappear, or their memories fail, and

---

[46]Spychala v. Metropolitan Life Ins. Co., 13 A.2d 32 (Pa. 1940).

[47]Wendorff v. Missouri State Life Ins. Co., 1 S.W.2d 99 (Mo. 1927).

[48]Wilson v. Insurance Co. of N. Am., 453 F. Supp. 732 (N.D. Cal. 1978).

[49]Clark v. Lone Star Life Ins. Co., 347 S.W.2d 290 (Tex. Civ. App. 1961).

[50]State *ex rel.* Mutual Life Ins. Co. v. Shain, 126 S.W.2d 181 (Mo. 1939).

[51]Krause v. Pacific Mut. Life Ins. Co., 5 N.W.2d 229 (Neb. 1942).

[52]735 ILL. COMP. STAT. ANN. 5/13–206 (Michie 1993).

other circumstances could change so much that the insurer would find it difficult or impossible to support its position with convincing evidence. The majority of states, therefore, permit an insurer to include a provision in its policy that will shorten the time allowed for initiation of contract actions, but not by more than a specified period. State statutes specify periods ranging from one to six years. Periods of three and five years are common. Some states do not allow such policy provisions at all.[53]

The Illinois law regarding time limit on legal or equitable actions clauses is typical of many states. The Illinois Insurance Code states the following:

> After the effective date of this Code no policy of life insurance may be issued or delivered in this State if it includes . . . [a] provision limiting the time within which any action may be commenced to less than 3 years after the cause of action accrues.[54]

The purpose of this statute is to prevent insurers from including a provision in the policy allowing the policyowner or beneficiary an unreasonably short period of time in which to initiate a legal or equitable action against the insurer. Thus the statute does not prohibit time limitation policy provisions. It merely prohibits those that are too restrictive.

The courts will generally uphold contractual limitations on the time that a policyowner or beneficiary is allowed to bring suit, unless a state statute forbids such a limitation. Insurers are not required to include a provision limiting the time in which suit can be brought, however, and many do not. For example, the illustrative policy contains no such limitation.

---

[53]Idaho Code § 41–1925(1)(a) (1991); Mont. Code Ann. § 33–20–121(1)(a) (1995);Wis. Stat. Ann. § 631.83(3)(a) (West 1995).

[54]215 Ill. Comp. Stat. Ann. 5/225 (1)(a) (Michie 1993).

Summary

Insurers often add accidental death benefits, disability benefits, guaranteed insurability options, accelerated benefits provisions, backdating provisions, and ownership, assignment, and contract change provisions to life insurance policies. Suicide exclusions are included in most life insurance policies. War or aviation hazard exclusions sometimes limit coverage. The majority of states permit insurers to include a time limit on legal or equitable actions clause that limits the time a policyowner or beneficiary has to initiate a suit.

Accidental death benefits provide additional payments when the death is accidental. The two types of accidental death clauses are accidental result clauses and accidental means clauses. For benefits to be payable under accidental means clauses, both the cause and the result of the death must be accidental, whereas accidental result clauses require that only the result be accidental.

Accidental death is ordinarily death that was not foreseeable by the insured. An accident, not a disease, must have been the proximate cause of the death. The suicide of a sane person is not accidental. Death that another person inflicted on the insured will ordinarily be accidental if not foreseeable by the insured.

Insurers often include a waiver of premium during disability benefit in life insurance policies. Less frequently, they include a disability income benefit. Most disability benefit provisions today require that the insured be totally disabled either from his own occupation or from any occupation for which the insured has education, training, or experience. Insurers today rarely require that disability be permanent.

The guaranteed insurability option offers the policyowner the option of purchasing, on specified dates in the future, additional insurance on the insured's life without evidence of insurability. The option offers insurance against the risk of becoming uninsurable.

An accelerated benefits provision allows payout of part or all of the death benefit while the insured is still alive if she meets the criteria specified in the provision. These criteria usually include a medical condition that results in a drastically limited life span, requires extraordinary medical intervention, or requires continuous confinement in an institution for the rest of the insured's life.

The backdating provision allows the applicant to have the policy backdated to a time when the proposed insured was at a younger age, so that the applicant gets the benefit of a lower premium. Other optional provisions spell out the policyowner's rights regarding ownership, assignment, and change of the policy.

Most modern insurance policies include a suicide exclusion clause. These clauses ordinarily exclude death by suicide for a specified period after the policy effective date.

War hazard exclusions limit the liability of the insurer in the event the insured dies as a result of war or while in military service. The two major categories of war hazard exclusion clauses are result clauses and status clauses. A result clause, the type more commonly used, excludes from coverage death resulting from the insured's military activities. A status clause excludes death occurring from any cause while the insured is in military service.

Aviation hazard exclusion clauses exclude the risk of death from certain hazardous aviation activities. Ordinarily, today, policies do not exclude death while flying as a fare-paying passenger on a regularly scheduled commercial airline.

ILLUSTRATIVE CASE

In this case, the insured died from a gunshot wound that he received when his assailant discovered him in the act of adultery with the assailant's wife. The question before the court was whether or not the insured died as the result of an accident.

GREAT AMERICAN RESERVE INSURANCE COMPANY,
Appellant
v.
TINA ELIZABETH SUMNER, Appellee[55]
Court of Civil Appeals of Texas, Tyler

MOORE, Justice.

This is a suit for the recovery of proceeds of an insurance policy insuring against accidental death. The policy was issued by appellant Great American Reserve Insurance Company upon the life of Hoyt V. Sumner, deceased. His wife, Tina Elizabeth Sumner, appellee, was named as beneficiary. The policy was in the principal sum of $5,000.00 and provided such sum would be paid to the beneficiary if "(1) loss or disability resulting solely, directly and independently of all other causes from accidental bodily injury sustained during the term of this policy." Section VI of the policy provided: "If such injury shall independently of all other causes and within ninety (90) days from date of accident solely result in any one of the following specific losses, the Company will pay in lieu of any other indemnity payable under this policy: . . . Life—The Principal Sum."

The insurance company pleaded that the insured died as the result of a gun shot wound to the head when he was

confronted by his assailant, David Smith, while the insured was allegedly engaged in an act of sexual intercourse with the assailant's wife. The company denied appellee's claim under the policy on the ground that the deceased should have anticipated death by reason of his adulterous act and did not die as the result of accidental bodily injuries. After a trial before the court sitting without a jury, the trial court entered judgment in favor of the beneficiary-appellee, from which the insurance company perfected this appeal.

The policy in question does not contain any provision which would limit or destroy the insurer's liability for death or injury to the insured as a result of an intentional act of another, nor is there any provision in the policy excluding liability where death or injury results to insured while engaged in the violation of law.

The parties are in basic agreement that the sole question presented by the case in the trial court was whether or not the insured died as a result of an accident. They both further agree that the prevailing law was correctly stated in the case of Releford v. Reserve Life Insurance Company, 154 Tex. 228, 276 S.W.2d 517, at page 518 (1955), wherein the rule is stated:

---

[55]464 S.W.2d 212 (Tex. Civ. App.1971).

As stated in the *Hutcherson* case, the test of whether the killing is accidental within the terms of an insurance policy is not to be determined from the viewpoint of the one who does the killing, but rather from the viewpoint of the insured. If from his viewpoint his conduct was such that he should have anticipated that in all reasonable probability his wife would kill him, his death was not accidental; if from his viewpoint his conduct was not such as to cause him reasonably to believe that she would probably kill him, then his death was accidental.

It seems to be the well settled law in this state that death by gun shot, or by any form of homicide, at the hands of a third person is deemed to be an "accident", even though death was intended by the person doing the shooting. This rule, however is not without exception. If the deceased, prior to death, engaged in some conduct toward his assailant from which he did know, or should have known, the assailant would kill him by violent means, then the death is deemed not to be an "accident".

By its first point as we understand it appellant challenges the legal sufficiency of the evidence to support findings of fact numbers 6 through 8 made by the trial court, whereby the court found that the death was a result of an accident as viewed from the standpoint of the deceased/insured that the deceased/insured had not entered into an affray with his assailant immediately prior to the shooting, and that from the information available to him, the deceased/insured could not reasonably foresee that he would be killed by his assailant. By his third point, appellant says that the deceased, by reason of his adulterous conduct, should have anticipated death and therefore his death did not constitute an accident. Both points will be discussed together.

Under the first point of error it becomes our duty to examine the record and determine whether or not there is any evidence of probative force to support the fact findings of the trial court. No rule is better settled than the one to the effect that if there is any evidence of probative force to sustain the findings of the trier of the fact, the appellate court is bound by such findings. In determining this question we must view the evidence in a light most favorable to the appellee, rejecting all evidence favorable to the appellant. The findings challenged by appellant as being without support in the evidence are as follows:

(6) Viewed from the standpoint of the deceased, it was not reasonably foreseeable to the deceased that by reason of his illicit meeting in a secluded place with assailant's wife that he, the deceased, would encounter the armed assailant, DAVID SMITH, at the place and upon the occasion in question.

(7) After being surprised and confronted by the armed assailant, the deceased did not enter into an affray with the assailant nor engage in any further conduct calculated to invite or provoke the shot which killed him.

(8) Viewed from the deceased's standpoint, with the information available to him at each step of the transaction, it was not reasonably foreseeable to the deceased that any act of the deceased would bring about a fatal gun shot wound.

The only testimony as to what actually occurred at the time and place of the killing was given by the assailant, David Smith; his wife, Birdie Smith, having died prior to trial, there were no other witnesses to the incident. When viewed in a light most favorable to the findings, the evidence shows that the deceased had been acquainted with Smith and his wife, Birdie, for approximately one year prior to his death. During this time he testified that all of his dealings with the deceased had been friendly. On the occasion in question, Smith testified that he became suspicious of his wife when he saw his granddaughter driving his wife's automobile. He testified that immediately thereafter he drove down the Bellview Road, stopped his automobile, took out his 12-gauge shotgun, and walked across the pasture about 300 feet where he discovered his wife and the deceased engaged in sexual intercourse. His purpose, he testified, in taking the gun was to kill his wife. He testified that upon discovering her, he told her "Birdie, haven't I told you I was going to walk up on you." At this point Birdie got up and came toward him attempting to talk to him and he told her not to come any closer. As she continued to approach him, he testified he cocked his gun and threw it on her. At this point the deceased said "Don't shoot her." To which he replied, "I'm not talking to you. I'm talking to my wife." Commencing at this point his testimony appears to be in conflict. On one occasion he testified that the deceased was walking toward him while he had his gun pointed toward his wife and that he shot the deceased. On another occasion he testified that he could not remember just what happened. He also testified that he could not deny the fact that while he was holding the gun on his wife Birdie, it went off and struck the deceased in the head while he was standing some 25 to 30 feet away. He further testified that the deceased was only partially clothed at the time and admitted that he could see that he was not armed with any type of weapon.

The test of whether death is accidental, within the terms of the policy supplement, is a fact question to be determined by the trier of the fact and is to be determined from the viewpoint of the insured and not from the viewpoint of the one that does the killing.

In Hanna v. Rio Grande Nat. Life Ins. Co., 181 S.W.2d 908 (Tex. Civ. App., Dallas, 1944, err. ref.), the court states: " 'Where the effect is not the natural and probable consequence of the means which produce it—an effect which does not ordinarily follow and cannot be reasonably anticipated from the use of the means, or an effect which the actor did not intend to produce, and which he cannot be charged with a design of producing—it is produced by accidental means.' "

Even though we recognize that the act of adultery is morally reprehensible, yet we do not believe death is the usual or expected result of it. In other words, participation in an adulterous affair does not naturally lead to a violent and fatal ending. To hold to the contrary would be to say that the killing of an adulterer, in the absence of any other aggravating circumstances, follows his offense in the ordinary cause of events. Such a holding would appear to be contrary to the relatively few reported cases on the subject. Other than the act of adultery, the deceased did nothing, except taking a few steps toward his assailant, to provoke the deadly assault. He made no threats or threatening gesture and his assailant admitted he could see that he was unarmed. Thus when the evidence is viewed in a light most favorable to the finding, the killing of deceased cannot be said to be the natural and probable consequence of the means which produced it. There is nothing in the crime of adultery, although a violation of the law of the land and a great moral wrong, which in its essence is calculated to produce the death of the adulterer. Under some circumstances it may be the occasion of the death of the adulterer, but his death is not the natural and legitimate consequence of the adultery itself.

The mere fact that Article 1220, Vernon's Annotated Penal Code provides that homicide is justifiable when committed by the husband upon one taken in the act of adultery with the wife does not necessarily mean that every adulterer is bound to anticipate death as the inevitable result of his act. Ordinarily most husbands do not undertake to vindicate such wrongs by homicide but rather lay their problem in the lap of the divorce courts. Therefore we do not believe it can be said that the deceased should have reasonably anticipated such violent consequence by reason of his conduct. As we view the record there is at least some evidence of probative force in support of the trial court's finding that the deceased met death solely as a result of an accident.

* * * * *

The judgment of the trial court is affirmed.

Questions for Review

1. On what grounds have the courts in many states rejected the distinction between accidental means and accidental result?

2. Explain which policy language, accidental means or accidental result, is more favorable to the policyowner or beneficiary.

3. What is meant by the term *proximate cause*? How does proximate cause relate to the accidental death benefit?

4. Describe the typical time limitation clause included in most provisions for accidental death benefits. What is its intended function? Why does this clause cause problems today that it did not cause a few decades ago?

5. With regard to accidental death, tell how each of the following is treated:
   a. Voluntary assumption of a known risk.
   b. Suicide.
   c. Injury inflicted by another.

6. Tell where the majority of courts place the burden of proof when they adjudicate a lawsuit for an accidental death benefit (*a*) if there is no agreement as to the accidental nature of the death and (*b*) when the insurer claims that accidental death resulted from an excluded risk.

7. What are the types of disability benefits available under life insurance policies?

8. Contrast, from the viewpoint of the policyowner, the most liberal and the most restrictive definitions of the term *total disability*.

9. What is a guaranteed insurability option? An accelerated benefits provision?

10. What is the purpose of the suicide exclusion?

11. Contrast war hazard exclusion result clauses with status clauses.

12. Describe the time limit on legal or equitable actions clause.

9 PROPERTY RIGHTS IN THE LIFE INSURANCE POLICY

Chapter Outline

To understand property rights in a life insurance policy, it is necessary to understand property law. This chapter contains a brief outline of property law. It also contains a discussion of property rights under policy terms. Finally, it contains a discussion of property rights in the policy by operation of law.

Property Law

The term ***property*** is popularly associated with anything over which rights of possession, use, control, and disposition are exercised, such as land, buildings, jewelry, or shares of corporate stock. The term is used in this nontechnical sense in modern legal writing and will be so used in many places in this book. The term *property* will, however, be used in its strict legal sense in this section explaining property law.

In the strict legal sense, ***property*** does not mean a thing over which a person exercises rights of possession, use, control, and disposition, but rather these ownership rights themselves. To illustrate the meaning of the term *property*—that is, *ownership rights*—if you own a chair, you can keep it in your house and sit on it. Or you can lend it to a friend, give it as a birthday gift to your mother, will it to your sister, or sell it to a secondhand store. You can put it in storage or chop it up and use it as kindling wood. You can rent it to someone who needs a chair or pledge it as security for a loan. It is your chair, and you have the rights of possession, use, control, and disposition of it. You may use or dispose of it in any legal manner. Your right to do so is protected by the government.

There are two main classes of property: real property and personal property. The terms *real* and *personal* derive from the forms of legal action that the early common law recognized to enforce ownership rights. Laws applying to these two types of property differ in many ways. This discussion will therefore address real property and personal property separately.

Real Property

Real property consists of ownership rights over land and anything that is attached to land. *Real estate* is often used as a synonym for *real property*. For example, suppose that there is a plot of land with a house erected on it, a tree growing on it, a ball lying on the lawn, and an automobile parked in the driveway. A right over the land itself, the house, and the tree is real property. A right over the ball or the automobile is not real property, because they are not attached to the land. However, if the tree is cut down and sawed into firewood, it is no longer attached to the land. A right over the firewood is personal property.

Real property law began to develop in England at the time of William the Conqueror, nearly a thousand years ago. At that time, and for many centuries thereafter, land was the most important thing a person could own. Through the years, a vast and complex body of real property law has evolved. Real property law includes laws relating to landlords and tenants, deeds, mortgages, easements, fixtures, condominiums, and water rights, among many other subjects.

Personal Property

A right over a thing that is not land or something attached to land is ***personal property***. A right over a chair, a bracelet, a racehorse, or money is personal property. A contract right is also personal property. A debt is the creditor's personal property.

The chair, bracelet, racehorse, and money are choses in possession. The word *chose* is French for "thing." A ***chose in possession*** is something tangible of which a person has actual possession. A contract right or a debt, on the other hand, is a chose in action. A ***chose in action*** is a right that can be enforced by a legal action or by a suit in equity. For example, if an insurer breaches an insurance contract, the policy-owner or beneficiary will have a right to recover damages from the insurer. This right is a chose in action. The terms *chose in possession* and *chose in action* are used only in connection with personal property, not in connection with real property.

Rights under Life Insurance Policy Terms

A whole life insurance policy ordinarily confers on its owner a number of valuable prematurity rights. Among these may be the rights to obtain a policy loan, to with-draw dividends or direct their application, and to surrender the policy for its cash value.

It is sometimes advantageous to transfer these valuable rights. As with a chose in possession, such as a chair, these rights can be transferred in many ways. They can be transferred gratuitously as a gift. They can be transferred for value in a sale. They can be pledged as security for a loan. In cases of divorce, life insurance owned by either spouse will often become part of the property settlement. A policy owned by someone other than the insured will pass at the policyowner's death to his per-sonal representative for distribution to his heirs or to those named in the policy-owner's will.

The beneficiary might also have prematurity rights in the policy. The policy-owner often must obtain the consent of an irrevocable beneficiary if the policyowner is to surrender a life insurance policy for cash or to take out a policy loan. Whether the policyowner must obtain an irrevocable beneficiary's consent will depend on the policy provisions and on the laws of the jurisdiction.

At the death of the insured person, the beneficiary has a chose in action. That is, the beneficiary has a right that can be enforced by legal action. The beneficiary can transfer this chose in action to another person. The owner of a chose in action usually transfers it by an assignment. Assignments are discussed in Chapter 14, "Assign-ments and Other Transfers."

Rights by Operation of Law

People other than the policyowner or beneficiary sometimes obtain rights in the in-surance contract by operation of law rather than by the terms of the contract. Wives and husbands in community property states, creditors of the policyowner or benefi-ciary, trustees in bankruptcy, divorced spouses, and others can sometimes assert rights that the life insurance policy itself does not expressly provide. Indeed, these rights are often contrary to policy provisions. The following sections contain a dis-cussion of contract rights by operation of law.

Community Property Rights

The settlers of the United States on the East Coast took their ideas of law mainly from England. Thus, in the United States, the life insurance contract had its origin and most of its development in a legal climate based on English common law.

The early explorers of the South and West, however, brought their ideas of law from the countries of their origin, France and Spain. For that reason, the legal sys-tems of these two countries have influenced the legal systems of some southern and western states. Community property is a legal concept that derives from French and

Spanish law. It is a concept foreign to the English common law. Therefore, state statutes confer community property rights.

Today, the states that have community property laws are Arizona, California, Idaho, Louisiana, Nevada, New Mexico, Texas, and Washington. Wisconsin has enacted a law patterned on the Uniform Marital Property Act. The Uniform Marital Property Act is based on community property concepts.

An understanding of community property law is necessary to students of life insurance because community property laws can affect rights in life insurance policies.

General Rules of Community Property Law

In a community property state, a husband and wife constitute a community. ***Community property*** is certain property owned by a husband and wife residing in a community property state. Each has an undivided one-half interest in the community property because of their marital status.

Property owned before the marriage is ordinarily the separate property of the spouse who owns it. It remains separate property during the marriage. Property a spouse acquires during the marriage with separate property funds is separate property.

Property that the husband and wife acquire during the marriage is community property, with some exceptions. Property that one spouse acquires during the marriage by gift, inheritance, or under a will is the separate property of that spouse and remains separate property.

Property that the spouses acquire with community funds is ordinarily community property, even if title is taken in the name of one spouse only. Ordinarily, if a spouse used both community and separate funds in acquiring property, the husband and wife own the property so acquired as community property and separate property, in the same proportion as the funds that were used to acquire it.

Death of either spouse, divorce, or annulment of the marriage will terminate the husband-wife community. When the death of a spouse dissolves the community, the surviving spouse has a right to one-half of the community property. The deceased spouse's half usually becomes the property of his or her estate.

Until relatively recently, the husband had the right to manage community property, subject to certain limitations. For instance, the husband traditionally had the right to control or sell community property. However, he could not ordinarily make a gift of community property without the wife's consent. Moreover, the husband could not use his management power to defraud his wife.

In recent years, community property states have enacted statutes mandating equal management. That is, the husband and wife now share the management of the community property. Illustrative of such statutes is the following from the California Civil Code:

> (*a*) . . . [E]ither spouse has the management and control of the community personal property, . . . with like absolute power of disposition, other than testamentary, as the spouse has of the separate estate of the spouse.
>
> (*b*) A spouse may not make a gift of community personal property, or dispose of community personal property for less than fair and reasonable value, without the written consent of the other spouse.

* * * * *

(*e*) Each spouse shall act with respect to the other spouse in the management and control of the community assets and liabilities in accordance with the general rules governing fiduciary relationships which control the actions of persons having relationships of personal confidence, . . . until such time as the assets and liabilities have been divided by the parties or by a court. This duty includes the obligation to make full disclosure to the other spouse of all material facts and information regarding the existence, characterization and valuation of all assets in which the community has or may have an interest and debts for which the community is or may be liable, . . . upon request.[1]

Note that paragraph (*a*) provides that either spouse has the right to manage and control the community personal property, including the right to dispose of it. The remaining paragraphs impose certain restrictions on that right. Thus, paragraph (*b*) prohibits either husband or wife from making a gift of community personal property without the written consent of the other. Paragraph (*e*) is especially noteworthy because it summarizes an important rule of community property management: "Each spouse shall act with respect to the other spouse in the management and control of the community property in accordance with the general rules governing fiduciary relationships."

Most of the cases that are mentioned in the following discussion of community property and life insurance were decided at a time when only the husband had rights of management. Therefore, they concern the wife's challenge to her husband's actions as manager. Under present-day statutes, the husband could challenge his wife's actions in managing the property.

Community property laws vary from state to state. The general rules stated in the following discussion of community property laws as applied to life insurance will not always apply in every state.

The Policy or Proceeds as Community Property

A life insurance policy can be either separate property or community property. Likewise, the proceeds can be either separate property or community property.[2]

When a person is issued a life insurance policy before marriage, the policy is separate property at the time of issue. In most community property states, it remains separate property, even if the policyowner pays premiums on it after marriage out of community funds.[3] However, in some states, if the spouse is not the beneficiary, at the death of the insured the community is entitled to part of the proceeds if the policyowner used community funds to pay premiums.[4]

When a person applies for and is issued a policy of life insurance on his or her life during marriage and pays the premiums with community funds, the policy is community property. The proceeds also are community property if the beneficiary is the estate of the insured. However, if the beneficiary is the insured's spouse, the proceeds are ordinarily the spouse's separate property. The theory behind this rule is that the policyowner-insured made a gift of the proceeds to the beneficiary-spouse.

---

[1]CAL. FAM. CODE § 1100 (West 1994).

[2]A.M. Swarthout, Annotation, *Application of Community Property System to Problems Arising in Connection with Life Insurance Policies,* 114 A.L.R. 545 (1938), supp. K.A. Drechler, Annotation, 168 A.L.R. 342 (1947).

[3]Aetna Life Ins. Co. v. Schmitt, 404 F. Supp. 189 (D.C. Fla. 1975).

[4]McCurdy v. McCurdy, 372 S.W.2d 381 (Tex. Civ. App. 1963).

A Third Person as Beneficiary

A policyowner in a community property state sometimes names someone other than her or his spouse as beneficiary. This is the same as making a gift to that person if that person gives no consideration in exchange for being named beneficiary. If the policyowner's spouse does not consent to the gift, the spouse could be entitled to half of the proceeds[5] or, in some cases, to all of them.[6]

Some courts have held that the policyowner acted in fraud of the spouse's rights in these cases. For example, in an Arizona case, the insured husband had purchased the insurance policy after marriage and had paid the premiums with community funds. He changed his life insurance beneficiary designation from his wife to his niece without the wife's knowledge or consent. The husband died, and the wife and niece both claimed the policy proceeds. The court ruled that the husband's action in changing the beneficiary without the wife's consent "worked as a constructive fraud" on her community property right to half of the proceeds.[7]

However, if the policyowner owes a legal duty to provide for a third person who is the named beneficiary, such as a child from a prior marriage, in some jurisdictions the policyowner's spouse will not have a right to the proceeds.[8]

If a policyowner changes the beneficiary from the spouse to a third person in exchange for a valuable consideration, no gift is involved. In such a case, the third person might be entitled to the full proceeds.[9] For example, in a California case, the insured owed a sum of money to his sister. He changed the beneficiary designation from his wife to his sister in payment of the debt. The court held that the sister was entitled to the full proceeds.[10]

If the beneficiary-spouse consents to the beneficiary change, the change ordinarily will be valid, although state law may require that the consent be in writing.[11]

Termination of the Community by Divorce

The community property belonging to the husband and wife will be divided on divorce, either by agreement of the parties or by the divorce court. The question of whether the cash surrender value of a life insurance policy is community property has arisen in connection with divorce. The courts of several states have ruled that the cash surrender value of a life insurance policy is community property if the policyowner has paid the premiums with community funds.[12]

For example, the Supreme Court of Texas held that the cash surrender value of four life insurance policies purchased with community property funds was community property to be divided between the divorcing spouses. Three of the policies insured the life of the husband and had a total cash surrender value of $1,542.84. The

---

[5]Tyre v. Aetna Life Ins. Co., 353 P.2d 725 (Cal. 1960).

[6]Guerrero v. Guerrero, 502 P.2d 1077 (Ariz. Ct. App. 1972); Moore v. California-Western States Life Ins. Co., 67 S.W.2d 932 (Tex. Civ. App. 1934).

[7]Guerrero v. Guerrero, 502 P.2d 1077 (Ariz. Ct. App. 1972).

[8]Great Am. Reserve Ins. Co. v. Sanders, 525 S.W.2d 956 (Tex. 1975); Rowlett v. Mitchell, 114 S.W. 845 (Tex. Civ. App. 1908).

[9]Johnson v. Johnson, 47 P.2d 1048 (Wash. 1935).

[10]Union Mut. Life Ins. Co. v. Broderick, 238 P. 1034 (Cal. 1925).

[11]CAL. FAM. CODE § 852 (a) (Deering 1995 & Supp. 1996).

[12]*E.g., In re* Mendenhall's Estate, 6 Cal. Rptr. 45 (Cal. Ct. App. 1960); *In re* Leuthold's Estate, 324 P.2d 1103 (Wash. 1958).

other policy insured the life of the wife and had a cash surrender value of $252.00. The spouses divided the other property between them, but left open for the court's later determination whether the cash surrender value of the policies constituted community property. The trial court and Court of Civil Appeals ruled that the cash value was community property. The Texas Supreme Court affirmed the decisions of those courts, stating the following:

> Article 4619, Vernon's Annotated Civil Statutes, as amended in 1927, defines community property as follows:
>
> "All property acquired by either the husband or wife during marriage, except that which is the separate property of either, shall be deemed the common property of the husband and wife; and all the effects which the husband and wife possess at the time the marriage may be dissolved shall be regarded as common effects or gains, unless the contrary be satisfactorily proved."
>
> The word "property" has been frequently defined and its meaning determined by many decisions of the courts. In the case of *Titus v. Terkelsen,* 302 Mass. 84, 18 N.E.2d 444, 445, the court, in discussing the word "property," said:
>
> "It is a word of comprehensive meaning. . . . In its ordinary legal signification it 'extends to every species of valuable right and interest, and includes real and personal property. . . .' "
>
> . . . It is true that in the early decisions of the courts of this country, including the decisions of the courts of this State, it was held in some of them that policies of life insurance were not property. . . . Many of the modern decisions hold that a life insurance policy is property. In the case of *Grigsby v. Russell,* 222 U.S. 149, . . . Mr. Justice Holmes, speaking for the Supreme Court of the United States, said: "Life insurance has become in our days one of the best recognized forms of investment and self-compelled saving. So far as reasonable safety permits, it is desirable to give life policies the ordinary characteristics of property. . . ."
>
> The word "property" in our bankruptcy laws is construed to include the "cash surrender value" of life insurance policies, and such property rights pass to the creditors of the insured. The courts recognize the right of the insured to pay his creditors the "cash surrender value" of his policy and retain the policy. . . . The courts of this State have held that the "cash surrender value" of a policy is property, and may be considered and treated as community property. . . .

* * * * *

> The trial court and Court of Civil Appeals correctly held that the cash surrender value of the policies was community property, and that respondent was entitled to judgment for one-half thereof.
>
> The rule announced in the case of *Whitesell v. Northwestern Mutual Life Insurance Company, supra* as well as in any other cases holding contrary to the rule announced herein, is expressly overruled.[13]

Exoneration Statutes

Fortunately for insurers, the community property states have statutes that make payment of the death benefit to the named beneficiary, in good faith and without knowledge of an adverse claim, sufficient to discharge the insurer of liability. These are called *exoneration statutes*. They exonerate—that is, excuse—the insurer from liability if a spouse should make a claim to proceeds that the insurer has already paid to a third party. The California exoneration statute reads as follows:

---

[13]Womack v. Womack, 172 S.W.2d 307 (Tex. 1943).

[W]hen the proceeds of, or payments under, a life insurance policy become payable and the insurer makes payment thereof in accordance with the terms of the policy, or in accordance with the terms of any written assignment thereof if the policy has been assigned, such payment shall fully discharge the insurer from all claims under such policy unless, before such payment is made, the insurer has received, at its home office, written notice by or on behalf of some other person that such other person claims to be entitled to such payment or some interest in the policy.[14]

Ordinarily, such a statute will protect the insurer. If any doubt exists as to whom the insurer should make payment, the insurer can obtain the surviving spouse's consent or file an interpleader action. Interpleader actions are discussed in Chapter 16, "Equitable Remedies."

Creditors' Rights

A creditor is a person to whom money is owed by another person, the debtor. Creditors can have rights in life insurance policies in two ways. First, if the creditor is the policyowner, assignee, or beneficiary of the policy, the creditor has rights derived directly from the policy. Second, a creditor with no rights under the policy terms sometimes has rights to the debtor's property, including insurance policy values. State statutes provide that a creditor can obtain a judgment in court against her debtor and seize certain property that belongs to the debtor. Sometimes the creditor can seize the debtor's life insurance policy values, although exemption laws often protect life insurance policy values from creditors' claims.

Creditors' Rights under the Policy

A creditor who has had the foresight to protect himself against possible loss by insuring his debtor's life and naming himself beneficiary is entitled to repayment from the policy proceeds of the debt and of any premiums he paid.[15] Courts often hold that the creditor is entitled to the entire proceeds, even though the amount of the insurance is greater than the amount of the debt, as long as the difference is not so great as to suggest that the creditor secured the insurance for wagering purposes.[16]

A debtor may transfer some of the rights in a policy he owns to a creditor as security for a loan. This is called a *collateral assignment*. The creditor is called a collateral assignee. A collateral assignee usually has a right to share in the insurance proceeds only to the extent of the debt remaining unpaid at the insured debtor's death, plus any outstanding interest and any premiums that the creditor paid. Assignments are discussed in greater detail in Chapter 14, "Assignments and Other Transfers."

In some instances, a debtor who owns a policy insuring his own life names the creditor as beneficiary to secure a loan. This method of securing a loan is not as popular with creditors as is the collateral assignment, because the creditor cannot reach prematurity values of the policy. If the creditor is beneficiary of the debtor's

---

[14]Cal. Ins. Code § 10172 (West 1993).

[15]Sachs v. United States, 412 F.2d 357 (8th Cir. 1969), *cert. denied,* 396 U.S. 906 (1969).

[16]Rittler v. Smith, 16 A. 890 (Md. 1889); Ulrich v. Reinoehl, 22 A. 862 (Pa. 1891); E.W.H., Annotation, *Rights in Respect of Proceeds of Life Insurance under Policy Naming Creditor as Beneficiary,* 115 A.L.R. 741 (1938).

policy, then usually the creditor will be entitled to receive from the proceeds only the amount of the unpaid debt and outstanding interest, plus any premiums that the creditor paid, although in a minority of cases the courts have held that the creditor is entitled to the entire proceeds.

Creditors' Rights to Property of the Debtor

Every state has its own procedures that a creditor can employ to sue a debtor, obtain a judgment, and have property of the debtor applied to satisfy the judgment. Some types of property are specified by state constitution or statute to be exempt from creditors' claims. Life insurance values are often exempt from creditors' claims.

Exemptions from Creditors' Claims

An *exemption* is a right given by law to a debtor to retain certain property free from seizure by his creditors. It is a right created by constitution or statute. It does not exist at common law.

The purpose of exemption laws is to protect an unfortunate debtor and the debtor's family, as well as the public. Granting an insolvent debtor the right to retain a homestead, household goods, wearing apparel, the tools of the debtor's trade, and part of his wages allows him to remain self-supporting. It keeps the debtor and the debtor's family from becoming a burden on the public.

Exemption of life insurance values from creditors' claims protects the debtor's family from destitution. Laws exempting life insurance values from creditors' claims encourage people to provide for their dependents through the purchase of life insurance.

Insurance Exemptions

There must be a positive constitutional or statutory provision for the exemption of insurance moneys from the claims of creditors, or such an exemption will not exist. Most states have laws protecting insurance moneys from seizure. Types of insurance moneys that are protected under various state exemption laws include death benefits, cash values, accrued dividends and interest, health insurance benefits, disability income benefits, and payments under annuity contracts.

Each state's exemption law governs exactly which insurance moneys the state will protect, but these laws differ widely from state to state. Some insurance exemptions derive from statutes that enabled a married woman to apply for and own insurance on her husband's life and, incidentally, included a provision exempting such insurance from the claims of her husband's creditors. Several states have statutes that establish a liberal exemption in favor of life insurance but limit the exemption to the amount of insurance that a stated maximum amount of premiums can purchase annually. Others follow the lead of an early New York statute and establish a broad exemption for life insurance policies insuring the life of the debtor or policies owned by the debtor insuring the life of another. In addition, there are numerous miscellaneous insurance exemption laws in effect.

In 1976, the National Conference of Commissioners on Uniform State Laws drafted a model law, the Uniform Exemptions Act. The purpose of this model law is to encourage the states to adopt uniform exemption statutes. The commission has stated that the present laws are mostly archaic and that some of them are unduly generous while others are exceedingly niggardly.[17] Only Alaska has enacted a statute based on the model law.[18]

Creditors of the Policyowner-Insured

Whether or not a creditor of the policyowner-insured can obtain the policy values depends on a number of factors: the applicable state exemption law, the beneficiary named, the creditor's identity, and whether the creditor is trying to reach cash values or the death benefit.

Cash Values.   The policyowner's creditors ordinarily cannot seize the policy-owner's right to surrender the life insurance policy for cash if the exemption law protects the proceeds. If the cash surrender value could be seized, this would defeat the purpose of the statute, which is to protect the beneficiary.

Although in the majority of cases the cash surrender value of a life insurance policy has been unavailable to the policyowner's creditors, this is not always true. In some states, the courts have held that creditors may reach the cash surrender value of a policy if the statute exempts only the death benefits.[19] Policy loan values that the policyowner has actually received ordinarily are not exempt from the claims of the policyowner's creditors once the policyowner has the money.[20]

If the federal government is the policyowner's creditor because the policyowner has not paid her federal income taxes, a federal tax lien attaches to the loan value of the policy up to the amount of the tax.[21] The federal tax lien applies despite a state exemption statute to the contrary. If the policyowner has not made other arrange-ments to pay the government, the insurer must pay the government the loan value, up to the amount of the unpaid tax, 90 days after the government notifies the insurer that the government is collecting the tax from the loan value (notice of levy). However, the policy will remain in force.

An insurer can make policy loans to the policyowner without regard to possi-ble federal tax liens if the government has not given the insurer actual notice of a federal tax lien at the time the loan is made. The insurer may make automatic pre-mium loans even after the insurer has received notice of a federal tax lien as long as the insurer had no notice of the lien at the time the automatic premium loan agree-ment was made.

Death Benefits.   Exemption laws commonly provide that the death benefits of a life insurance policy owned by the insured that names a spouse or children as beneficiary shall be exempt from the claims of creditors of the policyowner. Some exemption laws provide merely that the policy must be payable to a third person, that is, some-one other than the policyowner or the policyowner's estate.

If the policyowner-insured owes federal income taxes, the state exemption laws regarding creditors' claims to the death benefits apply to the federal government, just

---

[17]Quoted in the Prefatory Note to the Unif. Exemptions Act, 13 U.L.A. 207 (1986).

[18]Alaska Stat. § 9.38.010 to .510 (1994 & Supp. 1995).

[19]Brown v. Gordon, 90 F.2d 583 (2d Cir. 1937); Hilliard v. Wisconsin Life Ins. Co., 117 N.W. 999 (Wis. 1908).

[20]Kuhn v. Wolf, 16 N.E.2d 1017 (Ohio Ct. App. 1938).

[21]Federal Tax Lien Act of 1966, 26 U.S.C.A. §§ 6321, 6332(b) (West 1989 & Supp. 1996).

as those laws apply to any other creditors.[22] The exception to this rule occurs if a federal tax lien has attached to the cash values of the policy before the policyowner-insured's death. In that case, out of the proceeds the beneficiary must pay the federal government the tax up to the amount of the cash values.[23]

If the estate of an insured is named beneficiary, the insurer will pay the death benefits to the executor or administrator of the estate. The executor or administrator has certain duties as a matter of law, and one of these duties is to pay the decedent's debts.[24] In the absence of a statute to the contrary, the executor or administrator can use death benefits paid to the insured's estate to pay the decedent's debts exactly as she would any other moneys or property belonging to the estate.

Bankruptcy of the Policyowner-Insured.   Under the federal Constitution, Congress is authorized to make "uniform laws on the subject of Bankruptcies throughout the United States."[25] Nevertheless, under the federal Bankruptcy Reform Act of 1978, Congress gave a bankrupt debtor a choice between the exemptions granted by state statute or federal exemptions created under the act, unless the state passes a law prohibiting selection of the federal exemptions.

The federal exemptions cover life insurance values. A bankrupt debtor is allowed to keep unmatured life insurance policies that he owns.[26] That is, the bankruptcy trustee cannot surrender the policies for their cash value.[27] Policy loan values and accrued dividends and interest are exempt to the extent of a total of $8,000.[28]

If a bankrupt debtor chooses her state's exemption statute rather than the federal statute, the available exemptions will vary widely from state to state. In determining whether an insurance policy she owns will pass to the trustee in bankruptcy, the court first rules out unmatured policies that have no cash surrender value. In those cases, no property exists to which the trustee can take title. Those policies that do have a cash surrender value will then be viewed in the light of the applicable state statute. Policies exempt from the claims of the policyowner's creditors will not pass to the trustee in bankruptcy.

Payment of Premiums in Fraud of Creditors.   An insolvent policyowner who pays insurance premiums ordinarily will not lose his exemptions from creditors' claims as long as he did not intend to defraud the creditors. However, policyowners cannot use statutes exempting life insurance values as a means of intentionally defrauding creditors.

The creditors must prove the policyowner's intent to defraud in order to defeat the exemption. For example, in one case a creditor established an intent to defraud because an insolvent debtor bought an unreasonably large amount of insurance.[29]

---

[22]Commissioner v. Stern, 357 U.S. 39 (1958).

[23]United States v. Bess, 357 U.S. 51 (1958).

[24]A *decedent* is a dead person. This term is commonly used in legal contexts.

[25]U.S. Const. art. I, 8, cl. 4.

[26]11 U.S.C.A. § 522(d)(7) (West 1993). This rule does not apply to credit life insurance contracts.

[27]A bankruptcy trustee is the representative of the estate in bankruptcy. Among many other duties, the bankruptcy trustee collects property of the estate, sells it to pay creditors, investigates the financial affairs of the debtor, and makes reports to the court.

[28]11 U.S.C.A. § 522(d)(8) (West 1993 & Supp. 1996).

[29]Hise v. Hartford Life Ins. Co., 13 S.W. 367 (Ky. 1890).

Premiums Paid from Wrongfully Taken Funds.   If one person has wrongfully taken the funds of another person to pay life insurance premiums, the courts usually hold that the person whose money was wrongfully taken is entitled to receive at least part of the proceeds.[30] Exemption statutes generally do not apply if a person whose funds were wrongfully taken and used to pay premiums is seeking relief. The courts ordinarily will hold that the proceeds in such a case are "impressed with a constructive trust" in favor of the person whose funds were wrongfully taken. That is, the court will construe, or interpret, the situation as if the person who wrongfully took the funds had held the policy proceeds in trust for the person whose funds were taken. A few courts have reached the same result by stating that the wronged person is entitled to a lien against the proceeds.

The main question in these cases concerns the amount of money the wronged person is entitled to recover out of the policy proceeds. As a general rule, if the policyowner paid all the premiums with wrongfully taken funds, then all the policy proceeds are payable to the person whose funds were taken. However, if the policyowner paid only part of the premiums with wrongfully taken funds, then the person from whom the funds were taken is generally held to have a right to a proportionate share of the proceeds. A minority of courts have held that the wronged person is entitled to recover only the amount of the premiums wrongfully taken.

One case illustrating the majority rule involved the president of a bank who misappropriated the bank's funds and used them to pay three-fourths of the premiums of several policies insuring his life. His wife and children were the named beneficiaries. After his death, the court ruled that three-fourths of the proceeds belonged to the bank and only one-fourth to the insured's wife and children.[31]

An insurer faced with conflicting claimants in a situation where premiums were paid with wrongfully taken funds would most likely file a suit in interpleader. Interpleader is discussed in Chapter 16, "Equitable Remedies."

Creditors of the Beneficiary

Whether creditors of the beneficiary can reach the insurance proceeds depends on a number of factors: the wording of the state exemption statute; whether the proceeds are paid in a lump sum or are left with the insurer for deferred settlement; and whether a clause in the policy protects the proceeds from claims of the beneficiary's creditors.[32]

Some exemption statutes protect the insurance proceeds from claims of the policyowner's creditors but not from claims of the beneficiary's creditors. In other states, the statute exempts the proceeds from the claims of creditors of both the policyowner and the beneficiary.

If the exemption statute does not protect the proceeds from the beneficiary's creditors, the creditors can garnish proceeds that are in the hands of the insurer as soon as the beneficiary has a right to receive them. *Garnishment* is a remedy a court can impose at the request of a creditor to obtain property that belongs to a debtor but is in the hands of a third person. For example, in many states a creditor might be able

---

[30]R.W. Mowson, Annotation, *Right with Respect to Proceeds of Life Insurance of One Whose Funds Have Been Wrongfully Used to Pay Premiums,* 24 A.L.R. 2d 672 (1952).

[31]Vorlander v. Keyes, 1 F.2d 67 (8th Cir. 1924).

[32]L.S. Tellier, Annotation, *Proceeds of Life Insurance Left with Insurer after Maturity of Policy as Subject to Claims of Creditors of Beneficiary,* 164 A.L.R. 914 (1946).

to garnish a portion of the debtor's wages each pay period until the entire debt is paid off. If a statute protects policy proceeds from the beneficiary's creditors, the proceeds cannot be garnished while the insurer holds them. In some states, once the insurer pays the proceeds to the beneficiary, the exemption statutes continue to protect the proceeds; in other states, the proceeds become subject to the claims of the beneficiary's creditors.

The federal exemptions under the Bankruptcy Reform Act of 1978 apply to a life insurance benefit payable to a dependent bankrupt debtor at the death of an insured person on whom the debtor was dependent for support.[33] Thus, a bankrupt dependent spouse could keep insurance proceeds paid at the death of the other spouse to the extent reasonably necessary for the support of the bankrupt spouse and the bankrupt spouse's dependents.

Spendthrift Trusts and Life Insurance Spendthrift Clauses

In some instances, the policyowner can protect the proceeds of a life insurance policy from the creditors of the beneficiary by including a spendthrift clause in the policy. A *spendthrift clause* in a life insurance policy prevents the creditors of a beneficiary from claiming benefits payable to the beneficiary while those benefits are in the insurer's hands. Spendthrift clauses derive from *spendthrift trusts*.

A trust is an arrangement in which a grantor transfers property to a trustee who administers the property for the benefit of the trust beneficiary. In some instances the grantor is also the trustee or the trust beneficiary. However, a trust requires at least two parties: a trustee and a trust beneficiary. Trusts are described in greater detail in Chapter 11, "Settlement Agreements, Trusts, and Wills."

A *spendthrift trust* is a special type of trust. It provides a fund for the benefit of a person *other than the grantor*, secures the fund against the improvidence of the trust beneficiary, and places it beyond the reach of the trust beneficiary's creditors. Most states permit provisions that prohibit creditors from seizing property in a spendthrift trust.

The theory behind the spendthrift trust is that this arrangement does not harm the creditors of the trust beneficiary. Prior to the creation of the trust, they had no rights in the property. If after the creation of the trust they have no rights, they have lost nothing. Thus, a spendthrift provision does not harm the creditors.

This would not be true of creditors of the grantor, who do have rights in the property of the grantor. Therefore, a grantor cannot put property in trust for himself and exempt that property from the claims of his own creditors.

In regard to life insurance proceeds held by an insurer for deferred payment under a settlement agreement, a true spendthrift trust is not possible. This is because a life insurer and an insurance beneficiary have a debtor-creditor relationship rather than a relationship of trustee and trust beneficiary. Nevertheless, in view of the emphasis in the law on protection of life insurance values from the claims of creditors, it was natural that persons responsible for drafting settlement agreements would think of the spendthrift trust as a means of protecting insurance proceeds from the claims of the insurance beneficiary's creditors. However, since the life insurer's relationship with the insurance beneficiary is not one of trustee and trust beneficiary, the protection of insurance proceeds that an insurer holds under a settlement agreement was not

---

[33] 11 U.S.C.A. 522(d)(11)(C) (West 1993).

possible without special statutes. Well over half of the states have now enacted such statutes.

Illustrative of this type of statute is the following provision of the Illinois Insurance Code:

> Trust Settlements. Any domestic life company shall have the power to hold the proceeds of any policy issued by it under a trust or other agreement upon such terms and restrictions as to revocation by the policyholder and control by beneficiaries, and with such exemptions from the claims of creditors of beneficiaries other than the policyholder as shall have been agreed to in writing by such company and the policyholder. Upon maturity of a policy in the event the policyholder has made no such agreement, the company shall have power to hold the proceeds of the policy under an agreement with the beneficiaries. Such company shall not be required to segregate funds so held but may hold them as part of its general company assets. A foreign or alien company, when authorized by its charter or the laws of its domicile, may exercise any such powers in this State.[34]

This statute gives the insurer the power to hold policy proceeds under an agreement that provides for exemptions from the claims of creditors of a beneficiary other than the policyowner. Thus, a policyowner who is the payee under a settlement agreement cannot make an agreement with the insurer that will preclude the policyowner's own creditors from any rights in those funds. This is in accord with the previously mentioned point regarding grantors. Just as a grantor cannot protect herself from the claims of her creditors through a spendthrift clause in a trust document, neither can a policyowner protect herself from the claims of her creditors through a spendthrift clause in an insurance policy or settlement agreement.

Spendthrift clauses included in life insurance policies or settlement agreements appear in many different forms. The clause in the illustrative policy in the Appendix, Figure 2, reads as follows:

> **Surrender of Benefits**
> Unless the right was reserved in the Settlement Option election, no payee is allowed to (*a*) assign or borrow against the proceeds of an Option, (*b*) receive any installment payments in advance, or (*c*) make any changes in the provisions elected. All benefits shall be exempt from the claims of creditors to the maximum extent permitted by law.

Divorce of the Policyowner and Beneficiary

In most states, a divorce between the policyowner and the beneficiary will not affect their respective rights in the life insurance policy in the absence of a policy provision, property settlement agreement, or divorce decree clause to the contrary.[35] A small minority of states have laws that, upon divorce, cause an irrevocable beneficiary designation to become revocable,[36] or cause the beneficiary designation to become void.[37]

---

[34] 215 Ill. Comp. Stat. 5/241 (Michie 1993).

[35] F.G. Madara, Annotation, *Divorce of Insured and Beneficiary as Affecting the Latter's Right in Life Insurance,* 175 A.L.R. 1220 (1948).

[36] Minn. Stat. Ann. § 61A.12(4) (West 1996).

[37] Mich. Comp. Laws Ann. § 552.101(1)(2) (West 1988); Ohio Rev. Code Ann. § 1339.63(B)(1) (Anderson Supp. 1993); Okla. Stat. Ann. tit. 15, § 178(A) (West Supp. 1996).

In many instances, a divorce decree contains a clause providing for the disposition of insurance policies covering the life of one of the spouses.[38] Frequently, the divorce decree requires that the policyowner-spouse maintain the insurance and keep the other spouse or the minor children as beneficiaries. Sometimes, the spouses include these terms in a property settlement agreement, and the court incorporates the settlement agreement into the divorce decree. As part of the court decree, the terms of such a settlement agreement become enforceable by the court.

A number of problems can arise in connection with clauses disposing of life insurance policies in divorce decrees. If, contrary to the requirements of the divorce decree, the policyowner names a second spouse or some other person as beneficiary, both the first spouse (or the children) and the named beneficiary might claim the proceeds. This situation often forces the insurer to interplead, assuming that the insurer learns of the claim of the first spouse before paying benefits. However, if the insurer pays benefits to the named beneficiary in good faith before learning of the first spouse's claim, it probably will not be liable a second time.

Divorce decree clauses disposing of life insurance policies are not always written clearly enough for the insurer to be certain as to which policies the clauses refer. An interpleader action might be necessary in these instances also.

If the policyowner-spouse must maintain the policy for the benefit of the ex-spouse or the children, the policyowner cannot obtain a loan on the policy in order to pay the premiums, according to those courts that have considered the question. One court pointed out that allowing the policyowner to pay the premiums by reducing the value of the insurance would violate the purpose of the divorce decree.[39]

Killing of the Insured by the Beneficiary

If the beneficiary wrongfully kills the insured, the law usually will not permit him to receive the policy proceeds. If the beneficiary applied for the policy with the intention of killing the insured for the insurance money, some courts have declared the policy void.

In the more usual situation, the insured applied for the policy and later the beneficiary (often the spouse of the insured) killed the insured. In this instance, the death benefits will be payable. The legal question then becomes, to whom shall the benefits be paid?

The beneficiary could be entitled to the benefits if the killing was not wrongful. For example, if the evidence clearly established that the beneficiary killed the insured in self-defense, she ordinarily would not be disqualified from receiving the benefits.

If the beneficiary wrongfully killed the insured, and is therefore disqualified from receiving the benefits, usually a secondary beneficiary or the insured's estate will be entitled to the benefits.

The law governing payment of the benefits when the beneficiary kills the insured is described more fully in Chapter 18, "Performance of the Insurance Contract."

---

[38]John J. Michalik, Annotation, *Divorce: Provision in Decree That One Party Obtain or Maintain Life Insurance for Benefit of Other Party or Child,* 59 A.L.R. 3d 9 (1974).
[39]Hart v. Hart, 30 N.W.2d 748 (Iowa 1948).

Summary

Property, in the strict legal sense, means rights of possession, use, control and disposition—that is, ownership rights. However, the term *property* is popularly associated with the things over which a person exercises ownership rights.

There are two main classes of property: real property and personal property. Real property consists of a right over land and anything that is attached to land. A right over anything that is not land or attached to land, such as a chair, a bracelet, or a contract, is personal property. The chair and bracelet are choses in possession. A chose in possession is something tangible of which a person has actual possession. A contract right is a chose in action. A chose in action is a right that can be enforced by a legal action or a suit in equity.

The policyowner and the beneficiary have rights under the life insurance contract terms. Other people sometimes acquire life insurance contract rights by operation of law. Wives or husbands in community property states, creditors of the policyowner or beneficiary, trustees in bankruptcy, and divorced spouses sometimes acquire such rights. The estate of the insured or a secondary beneficiary might acquire such rights if the primary beneficiary wrongfully kills the insured.

In community property states, a husband and wife each has an undivided one-half interest in property acquired during the marriage, except for property either spouse acquired by gift or inheritance or under a will. If a policyowner pays premiums with community property funds, and the spouse is the beneficiary, the proceeds are ordinarily the beneficiary's separate property. If a policyowner makes a third person the beneficiary of such a policy, the policyowner's spouse could have an interest in the proceeds unless the spouse consents to the designation of the third person. Exoneration statutes in the community property states ordinarily will protect an insurer that pays proceeds in good faith to a third person who is named beneficiary if the insurer does not have notice of the spouse's adverse claim.

A creditor has rights under the policy terms if the creditor is a policyowner, assignee, or beneficiary. Creditors have rights to certain property of their debtors. However, state exemption statutes, which vary greatly from state to state, often protect life insurance policy values from creditors. If a policyowner has paid premiums for the purpose of defrauding creditors or with wrongfully taken funds, usually the policy values are not protected.

Divorce between the policyowner and beneficiary ordinarily will not affect their rights in the policy in the absence of a property settlement, divorce decree, or policy provision to the contrary. A small minority of states have laws that cause an irrevocable beneficiary designation to become revocable or cause the beneficiary designation to become void upon divorce.

If the beneficiary wrongfully kills the insured, the law usually will not permit the beneficiary to receive the proceeds. If the beneficiary applied for the policy with the intention of killing the insured, some courts have held the policy void. If the policy was applied for in good faith, usually a secondary beneficiary or the insured's estate will be entitled to the benefits.

ILLUSTRATIVE CASE

This case involved the community property rights of the divorced wife of the beneficiary in the proceeds of a life insurance policy insuring the life of the beneficiary's father.

SHERIDA JEAN COBB DENT, Appellant,

v.

DOUGLAS RAY DENT, Appellee[40]
Court of Appeals of Texas, Fort Worth

Before BURDOCK, JOE SPURLOCK, II and HILL, JJ.
HILL, Justice.

Sherida Dent appeals from her divorce judgment, urging in her sole point of error that the trial court erred in characterizing the proceeds of an insurance policy as the separate property of her husband, Douglas Dent.

We reverse and remand, because we find that the proceeds of the insurance policy are community property.

---

[40]689 S.W.2d 521 (1985).

The parties stipulated that during the marriage Douglas purchased a life insurance policy insuring the life of his father, C.W. Dent. All premiums on the policy were paid with community funds. The father died prior to the divorce hearing. The trial court characterized the proceeds of the policy as Douglas' separate property, presuming a gift of the proceeds to have been intended and completed by the death of the insured.

Ordinarily, the proceeds of life insurance purchased with community funds are community property. *Brown v. Lee,* 371 S.W.2d 694 (Tex. 1963). The proceeds of life insurance policies purchased during the marriage on the life of a third person with one of the spouses named as the beneficiary are community property. Douglas bases his claim to the proceeds as his separate property on the exception to the rule as expressed in *Brown,* to the effect that where the named beneficiary is surviving, a gift of the policy rights to the beneficiary is presumed to have been intended and completed by the death of the insured. *Brown v. Lee,* 371 S.W.2d at 696. Douglas maintains that since he is a surviving beneficiary, the property became his separate property upon the death of his father, the insured.

We do not find the exception to be applicable in this case because the facts of this case do not justify any presumption of a gift by Sherida of her community interest in the proceeds to Douglas. A husband lacks the authority to give his wife's interest to himself.

A close reading of the case of *Brown v. Lee* reveals that the rule relied on by Douglas is the rule which is applicable when the insured and beneficiary are husband and wife and the insured has died, leaving the beneficiary as the survivor. In such a case, the courts presume an intention on the part of the deceased to give the benefit of the insurance proceeds to the surviving spouse, a reasonable presumption with just results under those facts. We believe that in the case of such policies, it is natural to assume that a spouse would leave his or her community interest in the property to the surviving spouse. We see no reason under the facts of this case to presume such an intent.

Douglas also relies on the case of *Alexander v. Alexander,* 410 S.W.2d 275 (Tex. Civ. App. 1966). He cites the case as authority for his position that the named beneficiary of a life policy is entitled to receive the proceeds of the policy regardless of the classification of the funds used to purchase the policy. The case actually is authority for the proposition that the named surviving beneficiary is not entitled, as a matter of law, to the proceeds of the policy. The court in *Alexander* reversed a summary judgment granted by the trial court in favor of the named beneficiary in a suit brought by the deceased's wife to recover the proceeds of two life insurance policies.

We do not take issue with the holding of the court in *Davis v. Tennessee Life Ins. Co.,* 562 S.W.2d 868 (Tex. Civ. App. 1978), another case cited by Douglas. This case appears to be a restatement of a line of authority which authorizes a spouse to make arrangements for family members whom they are under a moral obligation to support. The court in *Davis* held that a wife was not entitled to any portion of a life policy in which the deceased husband had named his mother as the beneficiary. Douglas cites no case which would authorize his providing for himself in this manner.

The case of *Pope Photo Records, Inc. v. Malone,* 539 S.W.2d 224 (Tex. Civ. App., 1976), the final case cited by Douglas, involved a creditor of a husband and wife who sought to collect its debt from the proceeds of the husband's life policy payable to the wife as beneficiary. The creditor asserted that the implied gift to the wife was void under the provisions of TEX. BUS. & COM. CODE ANN. sec. 24.03 (Vernon 1968), which voids gifts as to an existing creditor unless the debtor has enough property in this state at the time of the transfer subject to execution to pay all of the existing debts. The court rejected the creditor's contention, holding that the controlling date of the transfer was the date of beneficiary designation, and there was no evidence that the husband and wife were insolvent on or before the date the wife was designated beneficiary. We do not find this case to be helpful in determining the question in this case as to the characterization of the proceeds of a policy on the life of a third person with one of the spouses as beneficiary.

Douglas cites no case involving such a policy which would hold that the proceeds become the separate property of the beneficiary spouse.

* * * * *

[W]e reverse and remand so that the trial court may make a just and equitable division of the property in accordance with this opinion.

Questions for Review

1. Define the term *property.*
2. What is meant by real property? Personal property?
3. With regard to community property:
   a. What is the community?
   b. Under what conditions is property considered to be separate property? Under what conditions is property considered to be community property?
   c. Under what conditions is the community terminated?

4. What is the function of exoneration statutes?

5. What is meant by the term *exemption statute* with respect to the rights of creditors to their debtors' life insurance values?

6. Tell how federal tax liens can relate to life insurance. How do state exemption statutes affect them?

7. Describe the operation of a spendthrift clause in a life insurance policy or settlement agreement. Tell why such an arrangement is not a true spendthrift trust.

8. As a general rule, if a policyowner paid all premiums on a life insurance policy out of embezzled funds, what are the rights of the person from whom the money was embezzled?

9. If the beneficiary wrongfully kills the policyowner-insured, who will usually be entitled to receive the policy proceeds?

10   BENEFICIARY DESIGNATIONS AND CHANGES

Chapter Outline

The beneficiary is the person the policyowner names (designates) to receive the benefits payable when the insured dies. The right to designate the beneficiary is perhaps the most important right that the policyowner has. The right to change the beneficiary, granted under most policies, is also an important right. In this chapter, the legal aspects of beneficiary designations and changes are discussed.

The Policyowner's Right to Choose the Beneficiary

Generally speaking, a person who applies for insurance on her own life can name anyone as beneficiary. The contract itself grants this right. However, the right can be subject to limitations, as discussed below.

The Right Provided by the Policy

The illustrative policy in the Appendix, Figure 2, provides the following:

> Beneficiary. The beneficiary named in the application will receive the death proceeds unless you name a new beneficiary.

The owner of a life insurance contract has many rights under the contract, but these rights do not include ownership of the death benefit. However, the policyowner does have the right to appoint the person who will own the death benefit. Typically, the policyowner insures his own life and appoints another person beneficiary. In some instances he appoints his estate beneficiary. In cases in which the policyowner insures the life of another person, the policyowner might appoint himself beneficiary, but, as policyowner, he does not own the death benefit.

Limitations on the Right to Choose the Beneficiary

Insurable interest requirements, community property rights, the policyowner's minority, or statutory restrictions on group insurance sometimes limit the policyowner's right to choose any beneficiary she wishes. These limitations are discussed in this subsection.

Insurable Interest.   In cases in which the policyowner has insured the life of another person, the beneficiary ordinarily must have an insurable interest in the life of the insured. Therefore, the policyowner's choice of beneficiaries is restricted to those persons with an insurable interest. This will not be the case if the policyowner insures his own life, because a person has an unlimited insurable interest in his own life and usually can name anyone as beneficiary.

Even if an applicant is applying for insurance on his own life, the insurer will probably inquire into his reasons for naming a beneficiary who appears to have no insurable interest, unless state law does not permit such an inquiry. Insurers follow this practice to avoid any possibility that the applicant is purchasing the insurance for speculative purposes.

Community Property Rights.   A spouse living in a community property state has an undivided one-half interest in property that the couple acquires during the marriage, except property that the other spouse acquires by gift, by inheritance, or under a will. If a spouse in a community property state purchases a life insurance policy during the marriage and pays premiums with community funds, each spouse has rights in the policy. If the policyowner-spouse designates a third person as beneficiary without the consent of the other spouse, the designation of the third person often will be effective as to only half of the proceeds.

Minor Policyowners.   Minors have limited contractual capacity. A minor's contracts ordinarily are voidable by the minor. For this reason, insurers usually will not contract with minors unless a statute makes the insurance contract binding on the minor. Most states have statutes allowing a minor above a certain age to enter into binding contracts for life insurance. These statutes usually limit the classes of people that the minor is permitted to name as beneficiary. The New York statute is illustrative. It reads as follows:

> A minor above the age of fourteen years and six months shall be deemed competent to enter into a contract for, be the owner of, and exercise all rights relating to, a policy of life insurance upon the life of the minor or upon the life of any person in whom the minor has an insurable interest, but the beneficiary of such policy may be only the minor or the parent, spouse, brother, sister, child or grandparent of the minor.[1]

Group Life Insurance Restrictions.   Although a person insured under a group life insurance policy has most of the rights to name or change the beneficiary that the owner of an individual life insurance policy has, there is ordinarily one special restriction on this right. A person insured under a group policy usually cannot name the group policyholder as the beneficiary. Most state statutes regulating group insurance include this restriction, although some states allow the insured to name the group policyholder as beneficiary if the policyholder will use the benefits to fund an employee benefit plan.[2]

Beneficiaries and Their Rights

A beneficiary's rights depend on the type of beneficiary designation that the policyowner has made. The beneficiary designation may be revocable or irrevocable. The beneficiary may be a primary or a contingent beneficiary, a creditor or a donee beneficiary, and an intended or an incidental beneficiary. Each of these classifications and its effect on the beneficiary's rights are discussed in this section.

Revocable and Irrevocable Beneficiaries

A revocable beneficiary designation ordinarily allows the policyowner to change the beneficiary at will, whereas an irrevocable designation prevents such a change unless the beneficiary consents. Because the policyowner can terminate the rights of a revocable beneficiary whenever the policyowner wishes, a revocable beneficiary has a mere expectancy in the death benefit. That is, the revocable beneficiary can expect to receive the death benefit, but he has no guarantee that he will realize this expectation. Furthermore, the policyowner need not obtain the consent of a revocable beneficiary to exercise policy rights. However, at the moment of the insured's death (or the expiration of the time period specified in a survivorship clause) a revocable beneficiary's right to the death benefit becomes completely vested.

An applicant or policyowner can name a beneficiary irrevocably if she wishes. An irrevocable beneficiary has an immediate vested right to the death benefit. The policyowner cannot reduce or destroy this vested right without the beneficiary's consent. For example, the policyowner cannot take out a policy loan or collaterally assign the policy without the irrevocable beneficiary's consent.

However, an irrevocable beneficiary's vested right is subject to termination if the policy is no longer in force at the time of the insured's death. In that case, no one has

---

[1]N.Y. Ins. Law § 3207(a) (McKinney 1985).
[2]Tex. Ins. Code art. 3.50 § 1(6)(d) (Vernon Supp.1996); Haw. Rev. Stat. § 431:10D–202(a) (1988).

a right to a death benefit. In addition, most present-day policies terminate the rights of a beneficiary, whether revocable or irrevocable, if the beneficiary predeceases the insured. Usually, if a beneficiary predeceases the insured, the policyowner will again have a right to name a beneficiary, either revocable or irrevocable.

Primary and Contingent Beneficiaries

The **primary beneficiary** is the person who will receive the death benefit if he is living at the time of the insured's death (or living at the expiration of the time period specified in a survivorship clause).[3] The primary beneficiary is sometimes called the first beneficiary or the direct beneficiary.

A policyowner can designate more than one primary beneficiary. In that case, the primary beneficiaries share the death benefit equally or in other proportions specified by the policyowner.

If no primary beneficiary is living at the insured's death and the policyowner named a contingent beneficiary, the insurer will pay the death benefit to the contingent beneficiary. There can be contingent beneficiaries on more than one level. Also, the policyowner can name more than one contingent beneficiary on each level.

A contingent beneficiary on the first level is called a secondary beneficiary or a first contingent beneficiary. The **secondary beneficiary** will receive the death benefit if no primary beneficiary is living at the insured's death.

A contingent beneficiary on the second level is called a **tertiary beneficiary** or a second contingent beneficiary. The tertiary beneficiary will receive the death benefit if no primary or secondary beneficiary is alive at the death of the insured.

If, at the death of the insured (or at the expiration of the time period specified in a survivorship clause), at least one of the primary beneficiaries is living, the expectancy of all contingent beneficiaries is automatically extinguished. The primary beneficiary will receive the full death benefit. If in such a case the primary beneficiary dies before the insurer has paid her the death benefit, payment will be made to her personal representative—that is, to the primary beneficiary's estate. No contingent beneficiary will have a right to any of the proceeds. On the other hand, if no primary beneficiary is living at the insured's death, but a secondary beneficiary is living, the secondary beneficiary becomes entitled to the death benefit (subject to any survivorship clause), and any tertiary beneficiary's expectancy will be extinguished.

Donee and Creditor Beneficiaries

A **donee** is a person who receives a gift. A **donee beneficiary** is a person whom the policyowner names as beneficiary but who gives no consideration to the policyowner in return. The donee beneficiary is the most common type of beneficiary named in life insurance contracts. For example, if a husband purchases insurance on his life and names his wife beneficiary, the wife is ordinarily a donee beneficiary.

A **creditor beneficiary** is a person whom the policyowner names as beneficiary because the policyowner owes a debt to that person. When the insurer pays the death benefit to the creditor beneficiary, the debt will be extinguished to the extent of the

---

[3]If there is a survivorship clause (time clause) in the policy, the rights of the primary beneficiary will be extinguished if he dies within a specified number of days after the insured's death.
Survivorship clauses are discussed in Chapter 11, "Settlement Agreements, Trusts, and Wills," and in Chapter 18, "Performance of the Insurance Contract."

death benefit. If the death benefit is greater in amount than the debt, the excess ordinarily belongs to the contingent beneficiary, if there is one, and if not, to the policyowner or his estate.

Intended and Incidental Beneficiaries

An **intended beneficiary** is a person whom the parties to a contract intended to benefit from performance of the contract. Donee beneficiaries and creditor beneficiaries are intended beneficiaries. An intended beneficiary acquires rights under the contract and can sue to enforce those rights.

An **incidental beneficiary** is a person who benefits from a contract but who has no rights under it. The parties to the contract did not make the contract for the purpose of benefiting an incidental beneficiary. For example, suppose that Julia Rossi owns a policy insuring her life and that her estate is the beneficiary. Suppose that the death benefit policy is the estate's only asset. Suppose also that Rossi owes Sophia Adamski money and that the debt is unsecured.[4] If Rossi dies, her personal representative has a right to collect the death benefit. The personal representative also has a duty to pay Rossi's debt to Adamski. Adamski will therefore benefit if the insurer pays Rossi's personal representative the death benefit. But Adamski cannot maintain a legal action against the insurer to force the insurer to pay the death benefit to the personal representative. Adamski is an incidental beneficiary. The insurance contract was not intended to benefit her.

Beneficiary Designations

A clear, current beneficiary designation is extremely important to the policyowner, the beneficiary, and the insurer. It is important to the policyowner because he purchased the life insurance primarily to protect the beneficiary. A clear and current beneficiary designation allows the insurer to carry out the policyowner's intent. The insurer can readily ascertain who is the proper beneficiary, pay that person the death benefit without delay, and obtain a valid release. Neither the beneficiary nor the insurer will have to resort to costly and time-consuming court action to determine the proper person to pay. Improper beneficiary designations cause much trouble and expense; however, drafting a beneficiary designation properly is easy, once certain principles are understood.

The policyowner should review the beneficiary designation frequently enough to be certain that it reflects his current circumstances. For example, the instances are numerous in which a long-divorced spouse has collected a death benefit merely because the policyowner neglected to change the beneficiary designation. In the absence of law to the contrary, the insurer is contractually bound to pay the named beneficiary, no matter how unjust this may appear. Some insurers periodically send notices to their policyowners urging them to review their beneficiary designations and make desired changes.

It is desirable for a policyowner to name a contingent beneficiary (or beneficiaries). If a policyowner-insured and the primary beneficiary die at the same time, the

---

[4]An unsecured debt is a debt for which the debtor has not pledged any of her property to the creditor.

policyowner will not have an opportunity to name another primary beneficiary. Even if the primary beneficiary dies long before the insured, the policyowner might forget to name another primary beneficiary.

Most beneficiary designations are simple. The insurance application contains a section in which the names of primary and contingent beneficiaries are to be written. Frequently, the beneficiaries' names are not written on the policy itself, although many insurers do follow this practice.

Often, the insurer will not be called to act on a beneficiary designation for many years. By then, all persons involved in the phrasing of the designation might be dead or unavailable. The designation, therefore, must clearly express the policyowner's wishes.

The designation of the person who is to receive the benefits should name or describe that person in enough detail so that he is readily identifiable. For example, if a policyowner-insured wishes to name her husband as primary beneficiary and her mother as secondary beneficiary, the designation can read as follows: "To William Henry Smith, husband of the insured, if living at the death of the insured; otherwise to Jane Elizabeth Martin, mother of the insured." If the policyowner-insured wishes to name her estate, the designation can read: "To the executors, administrators, or assigns of the insured." In the second instance, the designation does not name the person to whom the insurer will pay the proceeds, since the identity of the executors or administrators cannot be known until after the insured's death. It does describe the person with sufficient clarity so that she is readily identifiable. Payment made to the person so described will discharge the insurer of its obligations under the policy.

Designation of a Spouse or Fiancée

If an applicant designates his or her spouse as beneficiary, the spouse is usually so described, as, for example, "Daniel Allen Janecek, husband of the insured." A wife should be designated by her given names—"Pauline Barbara Jackson, wife of the insured," not "Mrs. James Charles Jackson." This type of designation, if kept current, ordinarily will carry out the wishes of the policyowner, as it indicates with certainty the person to whom the benefits are to be paid.

The courts have held, almost unanimously, that words such as "wife of the insured" are descriptive only. The name itself is controlling. For example, if a policyowner-insured names as beneficiary "Joanne Ellen Panopolos, wife of the insured," when Helena Maria Panopolos is actually his legal wife, the benefits ordinarily will be payable to Joanne Ellen, even though the description, "wife of the insured," is incorrect.

The same will be true of a description such as "fiancée." One case[5] involved the following beneficiary designation: "To Mariam Amelia Tatum, Fiancée, if living, otherwise to William George Scherer, Father." The policyowner-insured was killed while in military service. About five months before his death, his fiancée wrote to him saying that she was going to marry another man. The former fiancée did marry the other man, but the insured did not change the beneficiary designation, although he expressed his intent to do so and sent for a change-of-beneficiary request form. At the insured's death, both the former fiancée and the father claimed the proceeds. The insurer paid the money to the court, asking the court to decide who was rightfully entitled to it. The court said:

---

[5]Scherer v. Wahlstrom, 318 S.W.2d 456 (Tex. Civ. App. 1958).

In Simmons v. Simmons, 272 S.W.2d 913, we held that where a beneficiary is named or can otherwise be definitely identified, her designation as wife is descriptive only. The rule applies in this case to appellee. Her name as beneficiary is followed in the policy by the word "Fiancée," and it may well be that insured would not have named her beneficiary except for his engagement to her, yet the fact remains that from February, when the engagement was broken, until July 13, when he was killed, he did not change the beneficiary nor did he do all he could have reasonably done to change the beneficiary.

The court therefore held that the proceeds were payable to the former fiancée rather than to the insured's father.

If the policyowner makes a beneficiary designation of "wife" without a name, the lawful wife will be entitled to the benefits. A wife in a common-law marriage[6] will be entitled to the benefits just as will any other lawful wife.

However, a designation such as "wife," "husband," or "fiancée," without naming the beneficiary, should be avoided. Such designations can result in ambiguity, and legal disputes can arise if the marital status changes or is questionable.

Designation of Children

A policyowner may designate children as policy beneficiaries either by name or as a class. There are advantages and disadvantages to both of these methods of designation.

If children are designated by name, the identity of the beneficiaries is clear. However, children born after the policyowner makes the designation will not receive a share of the death benefit unless the policyowner remembers to change the designation to include them. The result of such an oversight usually can be avoided by designating children as a class.

Class Beneficiary Designations.   A *class beneficiary designation* is a designation that names several people as a group, without listing them individually. "Children of the insured," "nieces and nephews of the insured," and so forth are class beneficary designations. Most insurers will allow policyowners to make class beneficiary designations, but some will not because of the problems that can arise with this type of designation. One problem involves locating all members of the class after the insured's death. The insured's death can occur many years after the policyowner made the designation, and the members of the class may be widely scattered. Some may have died, in which case their deaths must be verified. The insurer must account for all class members because each, if living, has a claim to a share of the death benefit.

Another problem with designating children as a class is that the courts are not agreed on the exact meaning of the term *children*. Some courts have held that the term *children* includes illegitimate children, but others have held that it does not. The trend is to include illegitimate children. Children born after the policyowner made the designation are usually included, but they have been excluded in some cases. The same is true of a child born after the insured's death.

The courts are generally agreed that adopted children, legitimated children,[7] children who have reached majority, and children of a prior marriage are included in the term *children* unless specifically excluded in the designation. The courts are also

---

[6]A common-law marriage is created by an agreement to marry, followed by cohabitation, but without a wedding ceremony. In most states, valid common-law marriages cannot be contracted.

[7]A legitimated child is a child born out of wedlock whose parents later marry.

generally agreed that the term *children* does not include grandchildren and stepchildren.

The policyowner should make it clear in the designation which children he intends to include and which he intends to exclude. For example, if the policyowner intends to exclude children of a prior marriage, he must clearly spell this out. In one case, the policyowner-insured had designated as beneficiary his second wife or, if she was not living, "their children." The court held that the insured's children by a prior marriage were also included.[8]

Issue and Heirs.   In drafting designations of children as a class, the policyowner should choose the terms carefully and with knowledge of their meaning. Ordinarily, the policyowner should use the term *children*. People sometimes use the terms *issue* or *heirs* when they mean *children.*

The term **issue** includes all lineal descendants, no matter how remote the relationship. That is, it includes children, grandchildren, great-grandchildren, and so on. Issue should be used only if the intent is to include all lineal descendants.

The term *heirs* should be avoided because of the uncertainties associated with its meaning. **Heirs** usually means those persons entitled to inherit the property of a person who has no will. Each state has a statute spelling out who these persons are. These statutes differ from state to state and are subject to change. A typical statute of this type will specify as heirs the spouse and children, if living; the children, if no spouse is living; the parents, if no spouse or child is living; the brothers and sisters, if no spouse, child, or parent is living; and so forth.

A legal maxim, often repeated, is that "a living person has no heirs." This means that it is impossible to know who will be a person's heirs until that person dies. For example, suppose that, on Monday, Florence Green had as heirs apparent[9] her husband, Roger, and her two children, Stephanie and Brian. If on Tuesday, Florence, Roger, Stephanie, and Brian were involved in a fatal automobile accident and Florence were to die an hour after the deaths of her husband and children, her actual heirs might be her parents or, if they were not living, her brothers and sisters, and so on down the line in accordance with the law of her state of residence.

Per Capita and Per Stirpes Designations.   *Per capita* and *per stirpes* are terms that derive from the law of wills and intestate distribution.[10] These terms also have application in life insurance beneficiary designations.

Per capita means "by head" or "by individual." It also means to share equally. Most beneficiary designations are on a per capita basis. For example, if the policyowner names three primary beneficiaries and does not specify how the death benefit should be apportioned, each will receive one-third of the death benefit. If only two survive the insured, those two will each receive one-half. This is a per capita distribution.

Sometimes a policyowner-insured wishes to provide for descendants of a deceased child by making a per stirpes beneficiary designation. **Per stirpes** means "by family branches." A per stirpes beneficiary designation is a method of dividing the

---

[8]Pape v. Pape, 119 N.E. 11 (Ind. Ct. App. 1918).

[9]An heir apparent is someone who will inherit the estate of another person if the heir apparent outlives the other person and the other person makes no will.

[10]*Intestate distribution* means distribution of the property of a person who dies without leaving a valid will.

benefits among the living members of a class of beneficiaries (such as the children of the insured) and the descendants of deceased members of the class. Children of a deceased member share their parent's portion of the benefit equally, as representatives of their deceased parent. Grandchildren of a deceased member share their deceased grandparent's share equally if no child of the deceased member is living, and so forth. A per stirpes designation might read as follows:

> In equal shares to the children of the insured who survive the insured, except that if any of said children shall predecease the insured leaving issue who survive the insured, then the share of such deceased child to his or her issue in equal shares, per stirpes.

For example, suppose a policyowner-insured with three children, Thomas, Janet, and Frederick, made the per stirpes beneficiary designation indicated above. If at the insured's death all three children were living, each would get one-third of the death benefit. Assume, however, that Thomas and Janet survived the insured but that Frederick died before the insured, leaving two children who were living at the insured's death. In this case, Thomas and Janet would each receive one-third of the death benefit, and each of Frederick's two children would receive one-sixth. In other words, each of Frederick's two children would share equally Frederick's third as representatives of their deceased parent.

Suppose, however, that at the insured's death Frederick and Janet were living, but that Thomas had died leaving no descendants. In that case, Frederick and Janet would each receive one-half of the death benefit.

As a final example, suppose Frederick and Janet were living at the insured's death, but Thomas was deceased. Suppose also that Thomas left no living children but did leave three grandchildren who were living at the insured's death. In that case, Frederick and Janet would each receive one-third of the death benefit. Thomas's three grandchildren would each receive one-ninth—that is, one-third of Thomas's one-third.

Note that the per stirpes beneficiary designation quoted above is specific as to who is to receive the benefits. This is desirable because the courts in different jurisdictions have interpreted the per stirpes principle differently where all members of the class most closely related to the insured (the children) have predeceased the insured. The majority view is that the grandchildren of the insured then move up into the place of the children, sharing equally, and that the great-grandchildren receive the share of a deceased grandchild. The minority view is that the grandchildren take their parents' shares by representation.

Irrevocable Designations of Minors.   Usually it is not advisable to designate minors as irrevocable beneficiaries. A policyowner often needs the consent of an irrevocable beneficiary to assign the policy, take out a policy loan, change the beneficiary, or exercise other ownership rights. A minor is not competent to give consent, nor can any other person give consent on behalf of the minor. If the policyowner needs an irrevocable beneficiary's consent, the policyowner would have to wait to exercise ownership rights until a minor irrevocable beneficiary reaches majority and gives the necessary consent.

Guardians.   If life insurance benefits become payable to a beneficiary who is a minor, the insurer usually cannot pay the minor directly, because the minor is not competent to give the insurer a release. A release is the giving up of a right or claim, ordinarily in exchange for consideration. A release that a beneficiary gives to a life insurer in exchange for the death benefit frees the insurer from its obligation under the life insurance contract.

Since a minor beneficiary cannot give the insurer a release, the insurer might hold the benefits at interest until the minor has reached majority, usually age 18. Alternatively, a court can appoint a guardian of the minor's estate. The guardian can receive the benefits on behalf of the minor and give the insurer a release.

Parents sometimes wish to name as beneficiary of a life insurance policy a person they desire to become guardian of their minor children in the event that both parents die while their children are minors. However, naming such a person as beneficiary can cause problems. First, the person named might not be living at the time of the death of the last parent to die. Second, even if the parents name a person guardian in their wills and the person is living when the last parent dies, the court might not appoint the person guardian. Finally, when the death benefit becomes payable the children may have reached majority and be competent to receive the death benefit. If the policyowner wishes his or her children to receive life insurance proceeds, a beneficiary designation such as the following will avoid these problems:

> To Robert Samuel Gold, husband of the insured, if living; otherwise to Jerome David Gold, son of the insured, if he has reached the age of majority. If Jerome David Gold has not reached the age of majority, then to his legally appointed guardian as his custodian.

Alternatively, the parent can establish a trust for the benefit of the children during their minority, in which case the trustee will be the beneficiary.

Designation of the Insured's Personal Representative

A policyowner-insured sometimes desires that the insurer pay life insurance benefits to her personal representative. A *personal representative* is the executor of an estate, if there is a will naming an executor, or the administrator of an estate that has no executor. A personal representative manages the estate of a decedent until the decedent's debts have been paid and the remaining assets in the estate have been distributed. Payment of insurance proceeds to the personal representative of the insured is payment into the insured's estate. Inclusion of insurance proceeds in the estate provides money for the personal representative to use to pay funeral expenses, taxes, and other debts of the insured. A beneficiary designation of a personal representative might read: "To the executors, administrators, or assigns of the insured."

Designation of a Trustee

If the policyowner desires that the insurer pay life insurance proceeds into a trust, she will designate the trustee as beneficiary. A trustee is sometimes a natural person but more often is a corporation, such as a bank and trust company. The designation of a corporate trustee has certain advantages. First, the continued existence and qualification of a corporation is more certain than that of a natural person. Second, when the policyowner names a corporation as trustee, ordinarily the policyowner will prepare the trust agreement with the advice of legal counsel.

Inter Vivos Trusts. An *inter vivos trust* takes effect during the lifetime of the grantor. Ordinarily, if the trustee of an inter vivos trust is the primary beneficiary of life insurance, the policyowner-insured should name her estate contingent beneficiary. This is good practice because the trust sometimes terminates before the insured's death and the usual policy provision makes the benefit payable to the insured's estate if there is no primary or contingent beneficiary *living*. In the case of a terminated trust, this language creates an ambiguity because the trust has simply ceased to exist as a legal relationship, and thus there is no longer a trustee, but the beneficiary has not died.

The wording of a beneficiary designation of a natural person as trustee might read as follows:

> William Kaufmann, as Trustee, or his successor or successors in trust, under trust agreement, between Hannah Appleton and William Kaufmann, dated May 23, 1997, and supplements or amendments thereto, if said agreement shall then be in force and, if not, to the executors, administrators or assigns of the insured.

A designation of a corporate trustee might be worded as follows:

> The Reliable Bank and Trust Company of Chicago, Illinois, an Illinois corporation, or its successors in trust, under trust agreement between John Garcia and the Reliable Bank and Trust Company dated August 14, 1997, and supplements or amendments thereto, if said agreement shall be in force and, if not, to the executors, administrators, or assigns of the insured.

From the insurer's point of view, it is advisable to add a second paragraph to such a designation, absolving the insurer of any responsibility if the trustee does not dispose of the death benefit according to the provisions of the trust, thus:

> In no event shall the Ajax Life Insurance Company be responsible for the application or disposition by the Trustee of the sum payable. The payment to and receipt by the Trustee shall be a full discharge of the liability of the Ajax Life Insurance Company for any amount paid to such Trustee.

Testamentary Trust. A *testator* is a deceased person who died leaving a valid will. A person who makes a will can create a *testamentary trust* in the will. The testamentary trust will take effect at the testator's death. If the trustee of the testamentary trust is named beneficiary of a life insurance policy, it is advisable in this case also to name the executors or administrators as contingent beneficiaries, because the will might be changed or might not be valid. A beneficiary designation of a testamentary trustee might read as follows:

> The trustee named in the last will of the insured; provided, however, that if no will of the insured has been admitted to probate within ninety (90) days after the date of death of the insured, or if the will admitted to probate within such ninety (90) days fails to name a trustee, or if the will admitted to probate within such ninety (90) days names a trustee but no trustee shall have qualified within one (1) year after the date of death of the insured, payment shall be made to the executors, administrators, or assigns of the insured.
>
> The Ajax Life Insurance Company shall not be obliged to inquire into the terms of any trust affecting this policy or its sum payable and shall not be chargeable with knowledge of the terms thereof. Payment to and receipt by the trustee, or payment to and receipt by the insured's executors, administrators, or assigns, as hereinabove provided, shall fully discharge all liability of the company to the extent of such payment.

Designation of a Sole Proprietorship or a Partnership

Business firms of various types are often the beneficiaries of life insurance. A *sole proprietorship* is an unincorporated business owned by one person. The business and the person are legally the same entity. Therefore, if a policyowner-insured designates her sole proprietorship as beneficiary, the insurer will pay the death benefit to the executor or administrator of her estate.

A *partnership* is an association of two or more persons to carry on an unincorporated business. A partnership is not always or for all purposes considered a distinct legal entity. Therefore, ordinarily the partners themselves, as well as the partnership, should be named when a partnership is designated beneficiary. Such a designation might read as follows:

> Forsyte and Company, a partnership composed of Diana Elizabeth Forsyte and Francis Sergio Giannini.

Designation of a Corporation

A *corporation* is a legal entity, authorized by law to carry on a business of a specified nature. A policyowner can and should designate a corporation that is the beneficiary of the life insurance policy by its corporate name. One form of such a designation would read as follows:

> The Rawlings Company of Austin, Texas, a Texas corporation, its successors or assigns.

In this designation the primary beneficiary is the Rawlings Company and the contingent beneficiary is the corporation's successors or assigns. For this reason, when the policyowner makes a designation of this kind, no other contingent beneficiary should be named.

Designation of Multiple Beneficiaries

A policyowner may name more than one person as primary beneficiary, secondary beneficiary, or tertiary beneficiary and can apportion the death benefit in any manner she desires, if the insurer agrees to the arrangement. For example, the law permits a policyowner to designate multiple primary and contingent beneficiaries and to provide that each will get a different portion of the death benefit. If the policyowner makes no provision as to which beneficiary gets which portion of the death benefit, the beneficiaries will share equally.

Where No Beneficiary Is Designated or Is Living

If a policyowner does not designate a beneficiary, or if all primary and contingent beneficiaries die before the insured, the policy usually provides who will be beneficiary. Often, this will be the policyowner or the executor or administrator of the policyowner's estate.

Some policies include a list of classes of persons who will receive the death benefit if no named beneficiary survives. For example, the eligible beneficiaries in such an instance might be, in order of preference, the insured's surviving spouse, child or children, parent or parents, and executors or administrators. This is called a *succession beneficiary designation provision.*

Facility-of-Payment Clauses

Many home service life insurance policies[11] contain a *facility-of-payment clause* permitting the insurer to choose as beneficiary a person appearing to the insurer to be equitably entitled to part or all of the death benefit because that person has incurred expenses of the insured's last illness or burial. The courts have upheld facility-of-payment clauses because they enable the insurer to pay out quickly for these expenses. Because people often purchase home service life insurance policies with expenses of the insured's last illness and burial in mind, this policy provision is reasonable.

Some group life insurance policies also include such a facility-of-payment clause with a limit on the amount that the insurer can pay out under the clause. This limit is sometimes required by statute.

Designation if the Policyowner Insures the Life of Another Person

If a policyowner insures the life of another person, usually the policyowner designates himself as beneficiary. For example, a husband might buy insurance on his wife's life and name himself beneficiary. Or a corporation might buy insurance on a key employee's life and name the corporation as beneficiary.

A person other than the policyowner is sometimes named beneficiary, as where a wife buys insurance on her husband's life and names their children as beneficiaries. Whether the policyowner names herself or another as beneficiary of a policy insuring a life other than her own, the designated beneficiary usually must have an insurable interest in the proposed insured's life at the time of the designation.

Change of Beneficiary

Most modern life insurance contracts define the rights of a policyowner to designate and change the beneficiary in a policy provision similar to the following, which appears in the illustrative policy in the Appendix, Figure 2:

> You may name a new beneficiary by filing a written request with us. The written consent of any irrevocable beneficiary will be required. Your change-of-beneficiary request will not be effective until recorded by us at our Home Office. Once recorded, the change will be effective as of the date you signed the request whether or not you or the Insured is alive when we record the change. However, the change will be subject to any payments made or other action taken by us before your request was recorded in our Home Office.

Without a clause granting the right to change the beneficiary, no such right exists.

Limitations on the Right to Change the Beneficiary

Even though the policy contains a clause reserving the right to change the beneficiary, that right might be limited. For example, divorce decrees or property settlement agreements can limit the right to change the beneficiary, as can community property laws. The right of an incompetent policyowner to make beneficiary changes might also be limited.

---

[11]A home service life insurance policy is a policy serviced by an agent who collects premiums weekly or monthly. These policies are usually for relatively small amounts. Home service life insurance is also called industrial, debit, or district insurance.

Divorce of the Policyowner and Beneficiary.   In the absence of a statute to the contrary, the divorce of the policyowner and the beneficiary does not, in itself, affect the beneficiary designation or the policyowner's right to change the beneficiary designation. However, applicable law is in effect in a few states. For example, under Michigan law divorce automatically terminates a wife's interest as beneficiary unless the divorce decree itself provides differently.[12] Minnesota has a statute permitting the policyowner to change the beneficiary designation after divorce, even if the designation is irrevocable.[13]

Even if no applicable law is in effect, a property settlement agreement or a divorce decree can affect the right to change the beneficiary. Often, such a property settlement agreement or divorce decree will require that the policyowner maintain the policy in force and keep the policyowner's ex-spouse or child as beneficiary.

For example, in one case,[14] the policyowner had taken out policies on his life, naming his wife beneficiary. Two years later, the policyowner and the beneficiary executed a property settlement agreement in which the policyowner promised to name his wife the sole irrevocable beneficiary of the policies. The policyowner delivered the policies to her. The policyowner and the beneficiary subsequently divorced. The divorce decree repeated the requirement that the policyowner name his wife as sole irrevocable beneficiary and required that the policyowner continue to pay the premiums on the policies.

The policyowner then purported to make his estate the beneficiary. Later, he borrowed from one Beulah Wheeler the money to pay the premiums then due. The next year, he and Beulah Wheeler married. The policyowner again purported to change the beneficiary designation, this time naming his second wife, Beulah, as beneficiary. He also wrongfully procured the policies and gave them to Beulah.

When the policyowner died, both the first and second wives claimed the death benefits. The insurer paid the death benefits to the court, asking the court to decide who was rightfully entitled to the money. The court awarded the second wife the amount of the premium that she had loaned the policyowner, but the court held that the first wife had an equitable interest as beneficiary that could not be terminated without her consent. The pertinent part of the decision reads as follows:

> It has been determined that while a named beneficiary of a policy which provides for a change thereof by the [policyowner], secures only a contingent interest therein, a subsequent agreement of the [policyowner] in consideration of a settlement of property rights in contemplation of a divorce by the terms of which he covenants to make her sole, irrevocable beneficiary of the policy, vests her with an equitable interest therein which may not be defeated without her consent.

Sometimes, the policyowner will regain the right to change the beneficiary when the ex-spouse is no longer entitled to the policyowner's support. This could be the case if the ex-spouse remarries. Also, a minor child who reaches majority might no longer be entitled to be maintained as beneficiary. [15]

---

[12]MICH. COMP. LAWS ANN. § 552.101 (West 1988); Starbuck v. City Bank & Trust Co., 181 N.W.2d 904 (Mich. 1970); Minnesota Mut. Life Ins. Co. v. Hendrick, 25 N.W.2d 189 (Mich. 1946).
[13]MINN. STAT. ANN. § 61A.12 (4) (West 1996).
[14]Mutual Life Ins. Co. v. Franck, 50 P.2d 480 (Cal. Ct. App. 1935).
[15]Cooper v. Cooper, 314 P.2d 1 (Cal. 1957).

Community Property Rights.   If a spouse in a community property state is the beneficiary of a policy that the other spouse purchased with community funds, the policyowner-spouse cannot change the beneficiary without the beneficiary-spouse's consent, according to some cases.[16] In other cases, the courts have held that the policyowner-spouse can change the beneficiary designation, but that the spouse who was beneficiary will be entitled to part of the death benefit.[17]

Incompetence.   Generally, a minor who is a policyowner has a right to change a revocable beneficiary designation, but that change is voidable by the minor. Some states statutes limit the competence of a minor policyowner to make a beneficiary change by restricting the classes of persons that the minor can name as beneficiary.

The competence of an adult policyowner to make a valid beneficiary change is sometimes called into question because of mental infirmity due to advanced age, accident, or illness. A mentally incompetent policyowner does not have the power to make an effective change of beneficiary. The test of mental competence to make a beneficiary change is similar to the test of competence to make a will or execute a deed. One court summarized it as follows:

> The test to be applied in determining the mental competency of deceased at the time the change in beneficiary was attempted is: Did he have sufficient mental capacity to understand the extent of his property and how he wanted to dispose of it, and who were dependent upon him.[18]

Ordinarily, the person questioning the mental competence of the policyowner to make a beneficiary change is the one standing to lose because of the change—that is, the previously designated beneficiary. The burden then is on that person to prove that the policyowner did not have the competence to make a valid beneficiary change at the time she attempted to make the change.

The guardian of a mentally incompetent or minor policyowner cannot make a valid change of beneficiary on behalf of the ward, as a general rule. However, occasional cases have held that this can be done if an appropriate court order supports it.

Usually, an insurer that has paid the death benefit to a beneficiary that an incompetent policyowner designated will be protected from having to pay again if the incompetence of the policyowner was unknown to the insurer both at the time the change was made and at the time the insurer paid the death benefit. In the absence of any facts that would suggest incompetence, the law does not require that the insurer inquire into the competence of the policyowner to make a change of beneficiary. One court quoted this rule in a leading case as follows:

> [I]f the insured was insane when a change of beneficiary was made by him, and the insurer without notice of such insanity, acted in good faith upon the paper as genuine, indorsed the policy accordingly, and on his death, still in ignorance of his insanity, paid the money in good faith to the beneficiary as changed, the company would have been protected.[19]

---

[16]Metropolitan Life Ins. Co. v. Skov, 51 F. Supp. 470 (D. Ore. 1943).

[17]McBride v. McBride, 54 P.2d 480 (Cal. Ct. App. 1936).

[18]Harris v. Copeland, 59 N.W.2d 70 (Mich. 1953).

[19]New York Life Ins. Co. v. Federal Nat'l Bank, 151 F.2d 537 (10th Cir. 1945), *cert. denied,* 327 U.S. 778(1946), *reh'g denied,* 327 U.S. 816 (1946).

Methods of Beneficiary Change

Generally, the terms of the policy govern the manner in which the policyowner must make the beneficiary change. If the policy does not require any specific method, any manner in which the policyowner clearly indicates his intent to change the beneficiary will suffice. There are several methods of beneficiary change specified in insurance policies. These are the filing method, the endorsement method, and the endorsement at the insurer's option method. If the policyowner fails to comply with the method of beneficiary change specified in the policy, the change will nevertheless be effective if the policyowner's actions meet the requirements of the substantial compliance rule discussed below. Finally, under some circumstances it is possible to make a beneficiary change by will.

Filing.   The great majority of modern life insurance policies require that the policyowner file a written request with the insurer for a change of beneficiary. This is commonly called the filing, or recording, method of beneficiary change. The insurer retains a record of the new designation in its files and returns a copy to the policyowner. The advantage of this method over the older endorsement method is that the policyowner does not have to submit the policy to the insurer. The illustrative policy in the Appendix, Figure 2, requires filing of the beneficiary change request.

Endorsement.   The endorsement method of beneficiary change was relatively standard at one time but has fallen out of favor with insurers. Under the endorsement method, the policyowner must submit the policy to the insurer. The insurer types (endorses) the new beneficiary designation on the policy to make the designation effective. Those policies requiring that the insurer give consent to the change of beneficiary ordinarily also require endorsement to indicate the insurer's consent. As with endorsement, few insurers now require such consent.

Endorsement at the Insurer's Option.   A third method of beneficiary change some insurers use is endorsement at the insurer's option. This method is a compromise between the filing and endorsement methods. Insurers using the endorsement at the insurer's option method ordinarily allow a policyowner to change a beneficiary designation by filing a written request but reserve the right to require that the policyowner submit the policy for endorsement of the change if the insurer deems it advisable. Usually, the insurer will not require endorsement unless the requested designation suggests a possible problem that a review of the policy could resolve.

The Substantial Compliance Rule.   The courts usually hold that the policyowner cannot change the beneficiary by any method other than the method that the policy requires. However, one well-established exception is known as the *substantial compliance rule.*

Under the ***substantial compliance rule,*** if the policyowner has done everything possible to comply with the beneficiary change procedure set forth in the policy but has failed because of circumstances beyond her control, the courts of most jurisdictions will hold that the change of beneficiary is effective. The substantial compliance rule rests on a common equitable principle that a court of equity does not demand impossible things. Courts have often applied the substantial compliance rule in cases in which the beneficiary deliberately withholds the policy from the policyowner to prevent the insurer from endorsing a new beneficiary designation on it. If the policyowner has executed a request for a change of beneficiary, has sent it to the insurer, and has otherwise done everything in her power to comply with the policy requirements, the change will be effective in most jurisdictions, even though the policyowner cannot send the policy to the insurer for endorsement.

In one case,[20] a husband who owned a policy insuring his life became estranged from his wife, who was the revocable beneficiary. The husband wished to change the beneficiary designation to his sister, but his wife had possession of the policy and would not give it to him so that he could send it to the insurer for the endorsement the policy required. The policy provided that the policyowner could designate a new beneficiary "by filing written notice thereof at the Home Office of the Company accompanied by the Policy for suitable indorsement thereon" and that the change would "take effect when indorsed on the policy by the Company and not before." The husband filed two written notices at the home office of the insurer, each directing the insurer to change the beneficiary from his wife to his sister.

After the husband's death, the court held that the change of beneficiary was effective because the husband did all he could to change the beneficiary, even though he could not submit the policy for endorsement. The court said:

> The insured's intent that the proceeds of the policy in suit should be payable to his sister, and should not be payable to his wife, was clear. In attempting to effect a change of beneficiary in substantial compliance with the terms of the policy, the insured did all that it was practicable for him to do, in view of the fact that he did not have the policy, that his wife had it, and was holding it in order to prevent a change of beneficiary. It is a reasonable inference that a demand upon her for the policy would have been futile, and we do not believe that the insured was required to sue her for its possession. We think that the right of the appellee [the sister] to the proceeds of the policy, under the facts as found by the District Court, was, in equity, superior to the claim of the appellant [the wife]. The appellant was in no position to take advantage of the failure of the insured and the insurer to bring about an indorsement upon the policy of the change of beneficiary.

A court ordinarily requires that the policyowner show a significant degree of compliance if the substantial compliance rule is to apply. Courts generally agree that a policyowner's mere statement of intention to change the beneficiary is not enough to effect the change. Nor is it enough that the policyowner requested a change of beneficiary form, or even completed a written request, if the policyowner did not deliver or mail the request to the insurer. If the policy requires the policyowner to submit the policy to the insurer for endorsement and he neglects to do so, usually the attempted beneficiary change will be ineffective. However, if the policy has been lost, destroyed, stolen, or is being withheld from the policyowner, thus preventing him from submitting it, a court ordinarily will hold that compliance with all the other requirements satisfies the substantial compliance rule.

The facts of substantial compliance cases usually weigh more heavily than the facts of cases in any other area of life insurance law. For example, in one case the Japanese imprisoned the policyowner-insured, a member of the armed forces, in the Philippines during World War II.[21] His captors allowed him to write only to members of his family. He twice sent postcards to his mother in which he stated his intention to change the beneficiary on his life insurance policy to name the mother.

The policy provided the following specific manner for changing a beneficiary designation:

---

[20]Doering v. Buechler, 146 F.2d 784 (8th Cir. 1945).
[21]Finnerty v. Cook, 195 P.2d 973 (1948).

By filing written request therefor at the home office, in such form as the company may require, such change to take effect only when endorsed hereon by the company at its home office during the lifetime of the insured.

However, the policy was in the hands of the policyowner's lawyer in Manila, and therefore the policyowner could neither submit a change form to the insurer nor submit the policy for endorsement. He died while still in prison.

The court held that the policyowner had made an effective change of beneficiary. His intent was clear and under the circumstances he had done all that he possibly could do to change the beneficiary. Hence, the substantial compliance rule applied.

Beneficiary Change by Will.   If a definite procedure for making a beneficiary change is specified in the policy, and this is usually the case today, the general rule is that the policyowner must follow the procedure, or the change will not be effective. In such a case, if the policy does not provide for a change by will, an attempted change by will is ineffective.

However, if a life insurance policy does not require that a policyowner make a beneficiary change in any specific manner, as is true of some policies issued many years ago, a beneficiary change generally can be made by will. In addition, a policyowner usually can make a beneficiary change by will if the method of beneficiary change that the policy requires is not an exclusive method.

Courts of some jurisdictions have held that a policyowner-insured's change of beneficiary by will cannot be valid, since the rights of a beneficiary vest at the moment of the insured's death, and the will is not valid until that time. In one case,[22] in which the policyowner-insured attempted to change the beneficiary in his will, the court said:

> A will does not become operative until death; prior to death it is revocable at the whim of the testator, and the objects of the testator's bounty have no vested rights. In that respect it is very similar to the rights of a beneficiary under a life insurance policy in which the insured reserves the right to change the beneficiary such as we have in the instant case. However, upon death the beneficiary's right becomes vested, and that being the case, no expression in the insured's will purporting to assign his life insurance policy or change the beneficiary can be effective. At death he no longer has a policy to assign. It has passed to his heirs, if no beneficiary was designated; if a beneficiary is named it passes to such beneficiary. He cannot then change the beneficiary because the right of the named beneficiary has vested.

The court therefore held the attempted change by will to be ineffective.

---

[22]Cook v. Cook, 111 P.2d 322 (Cal. 1941).

Summary

Ordinarily, a person who applies for life insurance on his own life can name whomever he wishes as beneficiary. Insurable interest requirements will limit this right if a policyowner insures the life of another person. Community property rights, the policyowner's minority, or group insurance statutory restrictions also can limit the policyowner's right to name the beneficiary.

A policyowner can ordinarily designate a beneficiary revocably or irrevocably. A revocable beneficiary usually has a mere expectancy, but no rights, in the policy; an irrevocable beneficiary has rights in the policy. The policyowner can designate primary and contingent beneficiaries. The primary beneficiary will receive the death benefit if living at the insured's death (or if living at the expiration of the time period specified in a survivorship clause). If the primary beneficiary is not then living, the contingent beneficiary will receive the benefit, if living. A beneficiary is either a donee beneficiary—that is, one who gives no consideration to the policyholder in return for being named beneficiary—or a creditor beneficiary, who gives such consideration. A beneficiary is also either intended or incidental. Only intended beneficiaries have rights under the contract.

A policyowner should draft a beneficiary designation carefully and review it frequently. Policyowners can specifically name or merely describe beneficiaries, depending on the type of designation. Most insurers allow class designations, such as "children of the insured." Class designations will usually include members of the class born after the designation is made. However, the insurer may have difficulty locating all members of the class. Policyowners can name personal representatives, trustees, proprietorships, partnerships, or corporations as beneficiaries.

The policy must grant the policyowner the right to change the beneficiary, or no such right exists. Even if the policy grants such a right, and most modern policies do, divorce decrees or property settlement agreements, community property rights, or the incompetence of the policyowner may limit the policyowner's right to change the beneficiary.

Most modern policies specify the procedure that a policyowner must use to change the beneficiary. Ordinarily, the policyowner must follow the specified procedure or the change will be ineffective. The filing method is most commonly specified today, but some policies require endorsement of the policy, or endorsement at the insurer's option. If, because of circumstances beyond the policyowner's control, she is unable to strictly comply with the change-of-beneficiary procedure that the policy requires, the courts usually hold the change effective if the policyowner's intent was clear and she did everything possible to comply with the required procedure. A policyowner can make a beneficiary change by will in some jurisdictions if the policy does not specify another procedure or if the specified procedure is not exclusive.

ILLUSTRATIVE CASE

The following case is included here to illustrate the mechanics of beneficiary designations and principles of insurable interest.

WESLEY D. CORDER, Plaintiff
v.
PRUDENTIAL INSURANCE COMPANY, Defendant [23]

Matthew J. Jasen, Justice.

This is a motion by plaintiff for summary judgment.[24]

An insurance policy was issued to deceased Anna M. Corder in the amount of $5,000.00 on April 27th, 1960. The beneficiaries listed in said policy were Wesley D. Corder, husband of the insured, if living, otherwise Willa Eakman, mother of the insured. On April 15th, 1963 the named insured died. Subsequently, the plaintiff brought action to collect said proceeds from the insurance company who in turn interpleaded Willa Eakman as Administratrix of the Estate of Anna M. Corder. The administratrix answered the complaint herein and interposed a counterclaim that the proceeds of the insurance policy in question be paid to her. . . . [T]his court on December 30th, 1963 permitted the insurance company to deposit the proceeds of said policy with the Treasurer of the County of Erie, to be disposed of in accordance with the direction of this court. . . . [25]

It is the contention of the plaintiff that he is the named beneficiary and therefore entitled to the proceeds.

The mother-administratrix in opposing this motion proceeds upon two theories. First, by reason of fraud of the plaintiff the proceeds of the policy belong to the estate of the insured, and secondly, that plaintiff was not the husband of the insured and that therefore the insurance contract is void by virtue of the deceased's breach of warranty in representing him as her husband.

---

[23]248 N.Y.S. 2d 265 (N.Y. Sup. Ct. 1964).

[24]Summary judgment is an immediate judgment granted by the court without further proceedings, generally on the basis of documents filed with the court and without the testimony of witnesses.

[25]This means that the named beneficiary sued to collect the proceeds and the insurer filed an interpleader action, asking the court to decide between the named beneficiary and the administratrix of the insured's estate. The administratrix interposed a counteraction but the court permitted the insurer to pay the proceeds into court and have the court decide who was entitled to payment.

As to the contention of fraud, the administratrix fails to set forth any evidentiary facts sufficient to raise a question of fact.

The remaining argument of the administratrix is that inasmuch as the plaintiff was not the husband of the insured he has no insurable interest and therefore no valid right to the benefits under the policy.

It is conceded that the Wesley D. Corder, who brings this action is the Wesley D. Corder named as beneficiary by the deceased in the insurance policy, and that he is the particular person intended by the insured to be the beneficiary of said proceeds.

Where the deceased effects the insurance upon her own life, it is well-established law that she can designate any beneficiary she desires without regard to relationship or consanguinity.

Section 146 of the Insurance Law provides in part that:

1. Any person of lawful age may on his own initiative procure or effect a contract of insurance upon his own person for the benefit of *any person*. . . . (Emphasis supplied.)

Since the undisputed proof shows that the application for the policy was made by the insured deceased, there is no issue of insurable interest on the part of the plaintiff.

The use of the term "husband" in this connection, was merely descriptive of the relationship which the assured claimed existed between her and the beneficiary. Even though the named beneficiary was not actually the insured's husband, it does not alter the basic fact that the plaintiff is the person to whom the deceased had intended that the proceeds of the policy be paid. . . . For the reasons stated, motion for summary judgment granted.

Questions for Review

1. Define the word *beneficiary* as used in the life insurance context.

2. Distinguish between a revocable and an irrevocable beneficiary.

3. Why is a revocable beneficiary said to have a mere expectancy prior to the insured's death? What is the nature of such a beneficiary's right after the insured's death?

4. What are the rights of a contingent beneficiary if:
   a. The primary beneficiary survives the insured?
   b. The primary beneficiary does not survive the insured?

5. Briefly summarize some of the possible problems that can result from:
   a. Designating minor children as irrevocable beneficiaries.

   b. Class beneficiary designations.

6. Explain what is meant by a per stirpes beneficiary designation.

7. Why is it not advisable to designate a guardian by name as a beneficiary under a life insurance policy?

8. What is the general rule concerning an insurer's liability if it pays the proceeds of a life insurance contract to a beneficiary who was designated by a mentally incompetent policyowner?

9. Distinguish between the endorsement and the filing methods of beneficiary change.

10. Briefly summarize the rule of substantial compliance with respect to beneficiary changes.

11   Settlement Agreements, Trusts, and Wills

Chapter Outline

Applicants for life insurance often prefer to have the insurer distribute the policy proceeds to the beneficiary over a period of time rather than in a lump sum. The applicant can accomplish this by choosing a settlement option provided in the policy and entering into a settlement agreement with the insurer, or by arranging for the proceeds to be put into a trust. This chapter contains discussions of settlement agreements and trusts, and of the law of wills as it bears on settlement agreements and trusts. Finally, it contains a discussion of will substitutes, of which the life insurance contract is an example.

Settlement Agreements

One way that a life insurance applicant can provide an income to the beneficiary, rather than payment in a lump sum, is to choose a settlement option, or options. The applicant's wishes will then be set forth in a settlement agreement, which the parties usually will make part of the life insurance contract. The settlement agreement states the person, or persons, to receive the benefit payable and which optional method, or methods, of settlement the applicant elected.

Most modern policies include a settlement options provision. Typically, the applicant can elect one or more settlement options for each beneficiary designated. If no settlement option is in effect at the insured's death, the beneficiary ordinarily can choose a settlement option and enter into a settlement agreement with the insurer. Usually, the beneficiary also can designate contingent payees.

The term **payee,** rather than the term *beneficiary,* ordinarily denotes a person receiving life insurance proceeds under a settlement agreement. Often, a person who is a payee under a settlement agreement will not have been a beneficiary under the policy. For example, a beneficiary entitled to a lump sum settlement might elect to receive the proceeds over a period of time under a settlement agreement and name another person to receive any benefits that remain payable at the beneficiary's death. The person named is a contingent payee, but he would not necessarily have been a contingent beneficiary under the policy.

The illustrative policy in the Appendix, Figure 2, has the following provision:

Election of Options
You may elect to have all or part of the proceeds of this Policy applied under one of the following settlement options. You may cancel or change a previous election, but only if you do so prior to the death of the Insured or the endowment maturity date of the policy, if applicable. If you do not elect a settlement option prior to the Insured's death, the beneficiary may do so provided the election is made within one year after the date of death of the Insured. Any settlement option election will be subject to the limitations and conditions set forth [in the policy].

Settlement Agreement versus Lump Sum Payment

For several reasons, an applicant might enter into a settlement agreement rather than have the benefits paid to the beneficiary in a lump sum. Beneficiaries often have little experience in managing large sums of money. An inexperienced beneficiary might invest the insurance proceeds imprudently or dissipate the proceeds in other ways. Unscrupulous people might take advantage of an inexperienced beneficiary. The policyowner can prevent this by entering into a settlement agreement. Moreover, if the policyowner leaves the proceeds in the insurer's hands for distribution under a settlement agreement, a spendthrift clause generally can be included in the agreement. Such a clause will protect the proceeds from the beneficiary's creditors.

The policyowner or beneficiary also can provide for payment of part of the proceeds to a contingent payee through a settlement agreement. A settlement agreement provides planning flexibility. It also assists in solving the problems that occur when the insured and primary beneficiary die at the same time. This last point is discussed later in this chapter.

Choice by Policyowner or Beneficiary

If the policyowner does not enter into a settlement agreement, many policies provide that the beneficiary can do so after the insured's death. Careful thought should be given to whether the policyowner or beneficiary should choose the settlement option. If the policyowner has much more experience than the beneficiary at managing money, the policyowner probably should make the choice. Moreover, the policyowner usually can make the choice less emotionally. The beneficiary will have to make the choice shortly after the insured's death, a time when rational thought about money matters can be difficult. Finally, the beneficiary might lose the protection from his creditors provided by a spendthrift clause if he, rather than the policyowner, chooses the settlement option.

However, sometimes the choice of settlement option is best left to the beneficiary. A choice the policyowner made years before the death benefit became payable might have become entirely inappropriate. The family configuration could have changed greatly due to births, deaths, marriages, divorces, illnesses, retirements, or the maturing of children. Inflation can cause income amounts chosen years before to be inadequate for the beneficiary's needs. If the policyowner chooses the settlement option, she should review the settlement agreement frequently.

The Four Types of Settlement Options

There are four basic types of settlement options: interest income, income for a fixed period, income of a fixed amount, and income for life. Each of these options has its variations. Often, one settlement agreement contains two or more options in combination.

Interest Income Option.   Under the *interest income option,* the proceeds are left with the insurer. The insurer pays interest of at least a guaranteed rate at intervals agreed on between the insurer and the policyowner (or the beneficiary if the beneficiary chooses the option). If the policy permits, the policyowner can give the primary payee a limited or unlimited right to withdraw part or all of the principal, or no withdrawal rights at all. The policyowner can also give the primary payee the right to change to another settlement option, if the policy permits. Usually, the policyowner or beneficiary names a contingent payee, or payees, to receive any amount remaining unpaid at the death of the primary payee.

The interest income option section of the illustrative policy in the Appendix, Figure 2, reads as follows:

> We will hold the proceeds on deposit and pay or credit interest at the rate of at least 3 percent per annum. Payment of interest will be at such times and for such periods as are agreeable to you and us.

This policy guarantees interest at a rate of at least 3 percent per year. Most insurers pay interest in excess of the guaranteed amount if earned. This is called a dividend, extra interest, or surplus interest. The illustrative policy states the following: "We may pay or credit excess interest of such amount and in such manner as we determine."

Use of the interest income option is sometimes appropriate when the payee will be earning her own income for a period of time, after which she can receive the principal under another option. Use of the interest option might also be indicated if the interest alone is sufficient to provide needed income to the payee. After the payee's death, the principal could be payable to successor payees. For example, a policyowner could have the interest paid to his wife during her lifetime and name his children successor payees. The children are called successor payees, rather than contingent payees, because, in this situation, they are certain to succeed to the principal if they are living at the time of the primary payee's death.

Income for a Fixed Period Option.   Under the *income for a fixed period option,* the insurer agrees to retain the policy proceeds and make regular payments in equal amounts for a period specified by the policyowner or by the beneficiary if the beneficiary chooses the option. The income for a fixed period option clause in the illustrative policy in the Appendix, Figure 2, reads as follows:

> We will pay the proceeds in equal installments over a period of from one to thirty years. The amount of each installment will be based upon the period and the frequency of the installments selected from [the income for a fixed period table]. Higher payments may be made at our discretion.

The income for a fixed period table in the illustrative policy is shown below.

If the primary payee dies before the specified period has elapsed, the contingent payee will receive the remaining money, either in a lump sum or under one of the settlement options, as agreed to between the policyowner or beneficiary and the insurer.

Income for a Fixed Period Table

Monthly Income for a Fixed Period per $1,000 of Proceeds, at 3 Percent Annual Interest, Compounded Annually

Years	Monthly Installment	Years	Monthly Installment	Years	Monthly Installment
1	$84.47	11	$8.86	21	$5.32
2	42.86	12	8.24	22	5.15
3	28.99	13	7.71	23	4.99
4	22.06	14	7.26	24	4.84
5	17.91	15	6.87	25	4.71
6	15.14	16	6.53	26	4.59
7	13.16	17	6.23	27	4.47
8	11.68	18	5.96	28	4.37
9	10.53	19	5.73	29	4.27
10	9.61	20	5.51	30	4.18

Note: Annual, semiannual, or quarterly installments shall be determined by multiplying the monthly installment by 11.839, 5.963, or 2.993, respectively.

Income of a Fixed Amount Option.   Under the *income of a fixed amount option,* the insurer retains the policy proceeds and pays them out at regular intervals in a specified amount until the fund is exhausted. Extra interest payments extend the period but do not change the amount of each payment. A provision from the illustrative policy in the Appendix, Figure 2, follows:

> We will pay the proceeds in equal installments in the amount and at the intervals agreed upon until the proceeds applied under this option, with interest of at least 3 percent per annum, are exhausted. The final installment will be for the then remaining balance only.

If the primary payee dies before the fund is exhausted, the contingent payee will receive the remaining money, either in a lump sum or under one of the settlement options, as agreed to between the policyowner or beneficiary and the insurer.

Income for Life Option.   Under the *income for life option,* the insurer retains the proceeds and pays them out to a named payee in an income of a guaranteed amount for the entire lifetime of that payee. The option can take several forms.

First, the option can take the form of a straight life income. This is the same as a straight life annuity. It will provide the largest periodic payments of any form of income for life option, but nothing further will be payable by the insurer after the payee dies. Because the payee could die soon after the payments begin, many people prefer other forms of the income for life option.

A *life income with period certain* is another form of income for life option. If the primary payee of a life income with period certain dies before the end of a specified period—usually 5, 10, or 20 years—the insurer will continue the payments to a contingent payee until the end of the specified period.

Often, another variation of the income for life option is available. Under this variation, two people receive periodic payments for as long as they both live, with payments continued to the survivor for that person's lifetime as well. This is called a *joint and survivor annuity.* The settlement agreement might provide that the insurer will reduce the amount of each payment at the first death or, alternatively, that the survivor will continue to receive payments in the original amount.

The privilege of having guaranteed payments made for the remainder of the payee's lifetime, no matter how long the payee might live, is unique to life insurance. This privilege creates a security for the payee not otherwise available and makes the income for life option desirable in many situations.

Limitations on Settlement Agreements

Limitations on settlement agreements set forth in the illustrative policy in the Appendix, Figure 2, should be noted at this point. One of these reads as follows:

> The amount applied under any Settlement Option must be at least $2,000 and must be sufficient to provide a periodic installment or interest payment of at least $20.

The insurer has included this limitation because it is inefficient to make payments of small amounts over long periods of time. Moreover, such payments are of little value to the recipient.

The second limitation in the illustrative policy concerns payment under a settlement agreement to a beneficiary who is not a "natural person receiving for his or her own benefit." Such a settlement agreement is available only with the insurer's consent. Beneficiaries in this category are trustees, guardians, executors, partnerships, and corporations.

Some policies provide that the payee can withdraw the proceeds under certain options. However, such policies sometimes prohibit the payee from withdrawing part, rather than all, of the proceeds. The right of withdrawal usually will not apply to the life income option.

Contingent Beneficiaries and Contingent Payees

The rights of a contingent beneficiary under a life insurance policy and those of a contingent payee under a settlement agreement are not the same. If the primary beneficiary is living at the time of the insured's death (or at the expiration of the period specified in a survivorship clause), the contingent beneficiary's expectancy is extinguished. The contingent beneficiary has no right to any of the proceeds.

By contrast, the death of the insured does not extinguish a contingent payee's expectancy. On the contrary, settlement agreements customarily state that the contingent payee will receive amounts unpaid at the primary payee's death.

Let us take two fact situations. Suppose Herbert Stark is a policyowner-insured with a wife and three minor children. He has designated his wife, Noreen, as primary beneficiary of a policy insuring his life and his children as secondary beneficiaries. The insurer is to pay the benefit in a lump sum.

If Herbert dies before Noreen, the proceeds belong to Noreen, and the children's expectancy under the policy is extinguished. Noreen can receive the proceeds in a lump sum, or if the policy so provides, she can select a settlement option. If she selects a settlement option, she can name the children, someone else, or no one as contingent payees. The proceeds are hers, and she is free to name anyone she wishes. Only if she names the children as contingent payees will they acquire the right to receive any guaranteed payments unpaid at her death.

Now suppose Herbert had entered into a settlement agreement instead. If he named Noreen as primary payee and the children as contingent payees, the insurer is obligated to pay to the children any money undistributed at Noreen's death.

A contingent payee has a right to enforce payment from the insurer after the death of the primary payee. This right derives from the policy itself if the policyowner entered into the settlement agreement. If, on the other hand, the beneficiary entered into the settlement agreement, some courts have held that the right derives from the agreement between the insurer and the beneficiary.

Short-Term Survivorship and Settlement Agreements

The use of a settlement agreement can eliminate the problems that can occur when the insured and the primary beneficiary die in a common disaster. A *common disaster* is any single catastrophe—such as an automobile or airplane accident, a fire, a flood, a tornado, a hurricane, or an earthquake—in which two or more people lose their lives. Because an insured and primary beneficiary are often spouses or business partners, or have some other close relationship, it is not unusual for them to be together when a catastrophe strikes. For this reason, it is not unusual for them to lose their lives in a common disaster.

If the insured and the beneficiary die simultaneously in a common disaster, the state's simultaneous death act will provide a reasonably satisfactory solution. A simultaneous death act provides that if the deaths are simultaneous or if it is impossible to determine which person died first, the insured shall be deemed to have outlived the beneficiary unless a clause in the policy provides to the contrary. Thus, a contingent beneficiary will receive the proceeds if one has been named. If the policyowner did not name a contingent beneficiary, the policy usually states who will receive the proceeds.

However, if the beneficiary survives the insured for even a short time, the right to the proceeds will vest in the beneficiary. The proceeds will then pass into the beneficiary's estate on the beneficiary's death. This result might not be in accordance with the intention of the policyowner-insured.

For example, suppose that Alice Bennett was Jim Bennett's second wife, and that Jim Bennett had three grown children of his first marriage and no children of his second marriage. His insurance was payable to "Alice Margaret Bennett, wife of the insured, if living, otherwise to the living children of the insured, equally." He wanted Alice to have the insurance proceeds if she survived him, but if she did not survive him, he wanted his children to have the proceeds.

Now suppose that Jim and Alice Bennett were flying in their small private plane when the engine failed, causing the plane to crash. Assume that Jim Bennett was killed instantly but that Alice lived to talk to the first people on the scene, although she was dead on arrival at the hospital. Assume that she had no will. The proceeds vested in Alice because she was living at Jim Bennett's death. The administrator of Alice's estate will claim the proceeds and will use them to pay Alice's debts. The administrator will distribute the remainder to her relatives under the applicable state law. Jim Bennett's children will not receive the proceeds, even though this was almost certainly his intention.

Survivorship Clauses.   Now suppose that Jim Bennett had made his beneficiary designation as follows:

> Alice Margaret Bennett, wife of the insured, if living on the thirtieth day after the death of the insured; otherwise equally to the children of the insured who are living on the thirtieth day after the death of the insured, if any; otherwise to the executors, administrators, or assigns of the insured.

In this case, Jim Bennett's children would have received the death benefit if any of them were living on the 30th day after his death. If none was living, Jim Bennett's estate would have received the death benefit.

This type of beneficiary designation includes what is called a survivorship clause, a time clause, or a delay clause. The beneficiary designation or the policy itself might contain such a clause. A *survivorship clause* requires that the beneficiary survive the insured for a specified length of time before becoming entitled to the insurance proceeds. This clause takes care of many short-term survivorship problems. But now suppose that Alice survived Jim Bennett by 31 days but then died of her injuries. Again, Alice's creditors or relatives would receive the proceeds, rather than Jim Bennett's children.

Settlement Options.   Choice of a settlement option, rather than a lump sum payment, can solve the short-term survivorship problem. If Jim Bennett named Alice as primary payee, if living, and his children as contingent payees, the children's rights would not have terminated at Jim Bennett's death. Instead, the children would have been entitled to receive any of the policy proceeds remaining after Alice's death. The settlement option would have carried out Jim Bennett's wishes, regardless of the order of his and Alice's deaths or of Alice's outliving the period indicated in a survivorship clause.

A properly drafted life insurance trust could also solve the short-term survivorship problem. Trusts will be discussed in the following section.

Trusts

In certain situations, the use of a trust is preferable to the use of a settlement agreement. This section contains a brief description of the law of trusts and a discussion of the ways that trusts can be used to distribute insurance proceeds.

Trustees, Trust Beneficiaries, and Grantors

A *trust* is a fiduciary relationship in which one person, the *trustee,* holds legal title to property, [1] subject to an obligation to manage the property for the benefit of another person, the *trust beneficiary,* who has equitable title.

A person who owns property creates a trust when she transfers the property to a trustee (or trustees) to manage for the benefit of the trust beneficiary (or beneficiaries). The person who creates the trust is called the *grantor,* settlor, trustor, donor, or creator of the trust. Ordinarily, a trust document, sometimes called a trust agreement, trust instrument, or deed of trust, spells out the rights of all parties to the trust. The grantor controls the terms of the trust document.

The grantor can also be the trustee or the beneficiary. Therefore, three parties are not necessary for a trust to exist. However, there must be at least two parties, because the same party cannot be grantor, trustee, and trust beneficiary. The trustee and the trust beneficiary cannot be identical.

The grantor can create a trust to take effect during the grantor's lifetime. Such a trust is called an *inter vivos trust,* or a living trust. The grantor can also create a trust by a provision in his will. This trust will become effective only at the grantor's death and only if the will is valid. It is called a *testamentary trust.*

Trusts developed early in English law, but English common law did not protect the interests of trust beneficiaries. When the English courts of equity began to develop, trust beneficiaries started to look to those courts for protection of their interests. In the 15th century, the courts of equity began to protect the interests of trust beneficiaries. Toady, trust beneficiaries continue to enforce their interests in equitable actions. For this reason, it is said that trust beneficiaries have "equitable title" in the trust property. The trustee has legal title. Legal title is title enforceable in a legal action. Legal title allows the trustee to manage the trust property but not to benefit from it.

Life Insurance Trusts

Life insurance trusts have one or more life insurance policies or policy proceeds as trust property. Life insurance trusts are a type of inter vivos trust. Life insurance trusts can be revocable or irrevocable. In creating a revocable life insurance trust, the policyowner usually deposits the policy, or policies, with the trustee. The trustee is made beneficiary, but the policyowner retains ownership of the policy and all ownership rights. The policyowner can revoke or change the trust or change the beneficiary. The policyowner has complete control.

A revocable life insurance trust can be funded or unfunded. If the policyowner conveys money or income-producing property sufficient to pay the premiums to the trustee along with the policy, the trust is funded. If only the life insurance policy is conveyed to the trustee, the trust is unfunded unless the policy has a cash value sufficient to pay the premiums. The policyowner will pay the premiums if the trust is unfunded.

In the case of an irrevocable life insurance trust, the policyowner will irrevocably assign ownership of an existing policy to the trustee. The trustee will be made policy beneficiary. Or the trustee will apply for a new policy and, again, the trustee will be the policy beneficiary. As its name implies, an irrevocable trust cannot be revoked by the policyowner. An irrevocable life insurance trust can be funded or unfunded.

---

[1]Also called the trust res, trust corpus, trust principal, or the subject matter of the trust.

An irrevocable life insurance trust can have estate tax advantages over the revocable trust and is often a necessary estate planning device for people with large estates. On the other hand, the policyowner retains control of the policies in a revocable trust.

A type of life insurance trust that is useful in certain situations is the contingent life insurance trust. This trust provides protection for minor children if both of their parents should die.

In setting up a contingent life insurance trust, ordinarily one parent is made primary beneficiary of the other parent's life insurance policy. The children are named secondary beneficiaries, except that the trustee of the contingent trust would be substituted as secondary policy beneficiary for those children who had not yet reached majority at the time of the insured's death. The minor children would be beneficiaries of the trust. The trustee could be substituted as contingent payee if a settlement agreement were in effect.

Responsibilities of the Insurer

The insurer is not a party to a life insurance trust. The insurer has no responsibility for determining whether such a trust is valid, although it should verify the existence of a trust document.

Most insurers allow a policyowner to name a trustee as policy beneficiary if the trust is an inter vivos trust and a trust document is in existence at the time the policyowner makes the beneficiary designation. The insurer will usually request the date of the trust and the names of the parties to the trust to verify that a trust document actually exists. If the insurer did not do this, an applicant for insurance might name a trustee as policy beneficiary but never get around to creating the trust. The insurer has a responsibility to avoid recording a beneficiary designation of a nonexistent beneficiary. Moreover, some states have laws requiring the insurer to verify the existence of the trust.[2]

If the policyowner never created a trust, but named a trustee as policy beneficiary, the insurer would distribute the policy proceeds in accordance with the policy's provision for settlement in the absence of a beneficiary designation. However, the task of establishing that the policyowner never created a trust would delay settlement and might be difficult to accomplish.

Although the insurer will ask for verification that a trust document exists, some insurers prefer not to review the trust document itself. These insurers are concerned that a court might charge them with responsibilities of administering the trust. However, insurance trust documents usually contain a clause relieving the insurer of any such responsibility. In addition, the insurer can require a clause in the beneficiary designation relieving the insurer of such responsibility.

Testamentary Trusts

Life insurance proceeds are sometimes made payable to the executor or administrator of the policyowner-insured's estate with a provision in the policyowner-insured's will that the executor or administrator will hold the proceeds in trust. These arrangements are not, strictly speaking, insurance trusts.

---

[2]N.Y. Est. Powers & Trusts Law § 13–3.3 (McKinney Supp. 1996).

A testamentary trust is more likely to prove invalid than an inter vivos trust, because the validity of the testamentary trust depends on the successful probate of the will. A will might be lost or revoked, or a probate court might declare the will invalid. An insurer that permits an applicant to designate a testamentary trustee as beneficiary must take care to see that the designation provides for these possibilities. A suggested beneficiary designation of a testamentary trustee appears in Chapter 10, "Beneficiary Designations and Changes."

Rules of Law Bearing on Trusts

Two rules of law that lawyers must take into account when drafting trust documents are the rule against perpetuities and the rule against accumulations. These rules are aimed at preventing remoteness of vesting of property interests.

The Rule against Perpetuities.   For the public good, the law tries to keep property in the channels of commerce. To this end, a long-standing rule of law known as the *rule against perpetuities* prevents people from tying up property for too long a time.

The rule against perpetuities developed at common law in England. The common-law rule is in force in a majority of states. In some states, statutes have modified the rule. The rule against perpetuities applies to deeds and wills as well as to trusts. The rule in all its applications is highly complex. The following is a simplified explanation.

The rule against perpetuities safeguards against remote contingent interests in property tying up the property indefinitely. For example, suppose a grantor attempted to put her property in trust. She wanted her children, then her grandchildren, then her great-grandchildren, and on down the line of her descendants—in perpetuity—to receive the income from her property. Complete title to the property would never vest in anyone as long as the grantor had descendants. No one would have the right to sell or otherwise transfer the property, because unborn persons with future rights in the property could not give their consent to the transfer. This arrangement could keep the property out of the channels of commerce forever.

The *rule against perpetuities* prevents this from happening. The rule is often stated as follows: "No interest is good unless it must vest, if at all, not later than 21 years after some life in being at the creation of the interest." Thus, the period begins at the creation of the interest. Any interests, or rights, created by a trust, for example, must vest during a period as measured by the lifetime of a person living at the time the trust is created, plus 21 years. If any possibility exists that an interest the trust attempted to create will not vest within the time the rule against perpetuities prescribes, the interest is void.

The following is an example of a trust that does not violate the rule against perpetuities. Suppose that, in his will, Bruce Sanders created a trust to begin at his death. His granddaughter, Nancy Murphy, is to receive the income from the trust property if she is living at his death. On Nancy Murphy's death, her descendants are to receive the income from the trust property for 21 years. At the end of the 21 years, the trustee is to transfer legal title to the property to Nancy Murphy's descendants, and the trust will end. Nancy Murphy's descendants can then sell or otherwise transfer the property if they desire. The property will again be in the channels of commerce. This trust does not violate the rule against perpetuities because no interest in the trust property will vest after the end of a life in being at the creation of the interest (Nancy Murphy's life) plus 21 years.

If Nancy Murphy is four years old at the time of Bruce Sanders's death, and if she lives to be 96, the property could remain in trust for 92 years (her remaining lifetime) plus 21 years, or a total of 113 years. Thus, the rule against perpetuities does not prevent an interest in property from vesting over 100 years from the creation of the interest if the measuring life lasts long after the interest is created. Because human beings rarely live past 100, however, the time that the property will be kept out of the channels of commerce is definitely limited.

The rule against perpetuities applies to both testamentary and inter vivos trusts. It applies to life insurance trusts just as to other inter vivos trusts. The policyowner who elects to have the insurer pay the policy benefits to a trustee, therefore, must avoid violation of the rule against perpetuities in the trust document.

Although there is little law on the subject, the rule against perpetuities appears not to apply to life insurance settlement agreements as a general rule. This is because the beneficiary's interest in the insurance proceeds vests on the insured's death. The proceeds are a debt that the insurer owes to the beneficiary. For example, in *Holmes v. John Hancock Mutual Life Insurance Co.,*[3] the court said that the New York rule against perpetuities did not apply to a settlement agreement, although an identical provision in a trust document would have violated the New York rule. On the other hand, at least one court has said that the rule against perpetuities does apply to settlement agreements.[4]

Because the law disfavors devices that keep property out of the channels of commerce indefinitely, life insurers usually limit settlement plans to a period that accords with the rule against perpetuities. A settlement agreement naming the policyowner-insured's spouse as primary payee and their children as contingent payees ordinarily fulfills the wishes of the policyowner and runs no risk of violating the rule against perpetuities.

The Rule against Accumulations.   The *rule against accumulations* prohibits one person from directing that property accumulate income for another person too far into the future. For example, suppose an accumulation provision in a trust requires the trustee to add the income of the trust to the trust principal instead of giving the income to the trust beneficiary. At common law, no rule limits the time during which the income can accumulate except that the rule against perpetuities requires ownership of the accumulation to be vested within the period measured by a life in being plus 21 years. A few states have passed statutes, based on the English Thellusson Act of 1800, that specify other periods of time during which income is permitted to accumulate. One of these periods is the minority of an infant living at the time the interest was created. In other words, it is permissible to accumulate interest for a trust beneficiary who is a minor until he reaches the age of majority.

Because this is a simple and practical rule, many life insurers, as a matter of company policy, do not permit interest on proceeds left under the interest option to accumulate except during the minority of a beneficiary. Other insurers permit interest to accumulate for longer periods in special situations.

---

[3]41 N.E.2d 909 (N.Y. 1942).
[4]First Nat'l Bank and Trust Co. v. Purcell, 244 S.W.2d 458 (Ky. 1951).

Settlement Agreements and Trusts Compared

The policyowner who does not wish to place the responsibility of investing and managing life insurance proceeds on her beneficiary can either enter into a settlement agreement or establish a life insurance trust. The functions of settlement agreements and life insurance trusts are similar in many respects. The insurer or trustee holds and invests the proceeds and pays these proceeds to the payee or trust beneficiary according to the policyowner's or grantor's directions. Nevertheless, the policyowner must take the many differences between settlement agreements and trusts into account in choosing which to use. The most significant of these differences are discussed below.

Discretion.   A trustee can exercise a considerable amount of discretion in carrying out the terms of the trust if the grantor directs the trustee to do so. On the other hand, insurers will administer settlement agreements strictly in accordance with the provisions of the policy and settlement agreement. This is one of the most significant considerations in deciding between a trust and a settlement agreement.

If the needs of the beneficiary are difficult to anticipate or if different beneficiaries will have different needs, a life insurance trust might be the preferable way to handle the proceeds. A grantor can give a trustee the power to increase or decrease payments made to various beneficiaries in accordance with their needs as the trustee determines. The life insurer cannot assume any responsibility for exercising discretion in any payments it makes.

Flexibility.   Generally speaking, a trust is more flexible than a settlement agreement. Frequent changes in the amounts the trustee pays to the beneficiary are possible under a trust. However, the policyowner can build some flexibility into a settlement agreement. For example, the policyowner can elect the interest option and give the beneficiary full rights of withdrawal, as well as the right to elect one or more other options if and when that seems desirable. Nevertheless, the policyowner must specify these variations in advance under a settlement agreement, and no one can determine these variations during the payout period solely on the basis of the beneficiary's needs at that time.

Safety of Proceeds.   If safety of the insurance proceeds is of paramount importance, as in the case of a small estate, the policyowner will favor a settlement agreement, rather than a trust. A settlement agreement guarantees the safety of the insurance proceeds and a minimum rate of interest. A trust, on the other hand, offers no guarantees whatsoever, either as to principal or income.

Return on Investments.   The grantor of a trust can free the trustee from many restrictions that the law would otherwise impose on investment of trust funds and provide that the trustee can invest the trust property in stocks and other types of equities. This can considerably enhance the prospects of gain, especially over the long term, although it also enhances the prospects of loss. The investment possibilities open to the insurer are limited and conservative by law.

Life Income.   The insurer will guarantee a life income if the policyowner or beneficiary chooses the life income option. The grantor can specify a life income for the trust beneficiary but cannot guarantee either the amount or the duration of payments.

Expense.   A corporate trustee charges a fee for the administration of a trust, whereas an insurer offers settlement services at no additional cost. Therefore, a trust might not be advisable if the amount of the proceeds is small. Even if the amount of the proceeds is large, a settlement agreement is adequate for the needs of many beneficiaries. However, if the policyowner-insured's estate is large and made up primarily of property other than life insurance proceeds, a trust for the unified administration of all the property might be desirable.

Counseling.   A trustee can act as a personal counselor to the trust beneficiary. The trustee can advise the trust beneficiary as to the management of the beneficiary's property. An insurer will not function as a personal counselor.

Title.   A trustee has legal title to the proceeds, and the trust beneficiary has equitable title. An insurer and a payee under a settlement agreement usually have a debtor-creditor relationship, although in some states, statutes permit a life insurer to act as a trustee with respect to any policy proceeds it retains.[5] However, both the payee and the trust beneficiary can enforce their rights against the insurer or trustee.

Segregation of Funds.   The trustee usually segregates the property of an individual trust from the property of other trusts and ordinarily invests, manages, and accounts for each trust separately, although laws in some states allow the commingling of the funds of small trusts for investment purposes.

The insurance proceeds that a life insurer retains under a settlement agreement are not segregated. They are commingled with the insurer's other funds for investment purposes. The smallest amount of retained proceeds thus shares income and losses with the largest.

Wills

A *will,* like a trust or a settlement agreement, is an instrument for the disposition of property. This section contains a discussion of the law of wills and its relationship to trusts and settlement agreements.

Historically, a will was an instrument that directed the disposition of real property after the death of the owner. A testament directed the disposition of personal property. The document that directed the disposition of both real and personal property was called a last will and testament. The term *will* now applies to a document formerly called a last will and testament. In other words, now a person's will can dispose of both real and personal property.

A deceased person who died leaving a valid will is called a ***testator.*** Such a person is said to die testate. Ordinarily, a testate person's property passes to other persons according to the terms of the will.

For a will to be valid, the testator must execute it in accordance with the probate code of the relevant state. State statutes commonly provide that a will is effective as to any property in the state if the testator executed the will in accordance with (1) the state's probate code, (2) the probate code of the testator's state of

---

[5]*E.g.,* Iowa Code Ann. § 508.32 (West 1988).

residence at the time of his death, or (3) the probate code of the state in which the will was executed.

The probate code of each state prescribes the requirements for making a valid will. These requirements vary somewhat from state to state. They involve the capacity of the testator, techniques for revoking prior wills, the formalities of execution of the will, and so forth. The formalities of execution involve the required number of witnesses to the will and their qualifications, the nature and location of the testator's signature in the will, and many other details. The portion of a state's probate code that prescribes the formalities of execution is generally called the **Statute of Wills.** The state requires these formalities of execution to prevent the probate of fraudulent or coerced wills. To **probate** a will is to prove its validity in court.

A will has several important characteristics. First, it is revocable at the whim of the testator. Second, the testator can change a will whenever she desires. Third, during her life, a testator has control over property she owns that the will mentions. The testator can dispose of such property as she sees fit. Fourth, until it is admitted to probate, a will can be kept secret or highly confidential. This allows the testator to feel free to name whomever she wishes as beneficiary under the will. Finally, a will is not effective until the testator's death, regardless of when the testator executed it.

If a person dies without a valid will, he dies intestate. The word **intestate** also means the person himself. An intestate's property will pass to living persons according to the intestate statute of the relevant state. An intestate statute provides that the intestate's surviving spouse will get most or all of the property if the intestate has no children living at the time of the his death. If children are living, ordinarily the spouse will get one-half or one-third and the children the remainder. If the intestate has no living spouse, the children or other descendants take all of the estate. If no spouse or children survive the intestate, the intestate's parents take all or share with his brothers and sisters. Next in line will be the intestate's nieces and nephews or next of kin. Each state has its own intestate statute, which can vary from this pattern.

Will Substitutes

The law regarding testamentary disposition of property is quite strict. Nevertheless, there are some ways to pass property after one's death without a will. These will substitutes, which include joint tenancy, contracts, and trusts, are discussed in the following subsections.

The use of will substitutes does not preclude the use of a will. Ordinarily, a person should not dispense with a will merely because he is using will substitutes.

Joint Tenancy

One person can pass property at his death to another person without a will if the property is in *joint tenancy.* If two or more persons hold property with equal rights to share in its enjoyment during their lives and rights of survivorship, they are joint tenants. **Rights of survivorship** means that, on the death of one joint tenant, the deceased tenant's share of the property automatically goes to the survivor, or survivors. No will is necessary. Thus, joint tenancy is a valid will substitute.

Contracts

A contract that creates a present interest in the parties will not be void for the lack of a will's formalities, even though an obligation under the contract is due at one party's death. A contract differs from a will in that the beneficiary under a will gives no consideration in exchange for being named beneficiary, whereas with a contract the parties exchange consideration. Therefore, the dangers of fraud or coercion, which make formalities of execution necessary for wills, are not as apt to be present in the case of contracts.

Life Insurance Contracts.   A life insurance contract is unquestionably a valid will substitute. Courts do not consider investment in life insurance an attempted testamentary disposition in violation of a state's Statute of Wills.

A life insurance contract has many of the advantages of a will. For example, the policyowner can keep the beneficiary and the amount of the benefits secret. Secrecy is one of the advantages of a will. Just as a person has control of property he has willed, a policyowner-insured can have control of the insurance contract until her death. The policyowner can ordinarily change the beneficiary, can borrow on or assign the policy, or can surrender the policy and receive the cash value.

An insurance contract has advantages that a will does not have. The life insurance beneficiary can receive the proceeds without a court proceeding. The life insurance proceeds, unlike property passing through the estate under a will, are frequently exempt from the claims of the policyowner-insured's creditors. Property passing through the estate under a will might be subject to estate taxes. On the other hand, life insurance proceeds that do not pass through an estate are not subject to estate taxes if the insured was not the owner of the policy during the three years prior to his death.[6]

Settlement Agreements.   A policyowner-insured's designation of a payee, or payees, in a settlement agreement is a valid will substitute. As in the case of the life insurance contract itself, courts do not consider a settlement agreement elected by the policyowner-insured to be an attempted testamentary disposition in violation of the relevant Statute of Wills. One rationale for this is that the policyowner-insured does not own the proceeds and therefore does not pass them to others at his death. However, if a beneficiary entitled to receive a lump sum instead elects a settlement option and chooses a contingent payee to receive the proceeds at the beneficiary's death, the question of whether this is an attempted testamentary disposition in violation of the relevant Statute of Wills arises.

For example, suppose Howard Yoshida owns a life insurance policy insuring his life for $100,000. His wife, Amy, is the beneficiary. The proceeds are payable to Amy in a lump sum. Following Howard's death, Amy elects to leave the proceeds under the interest option with full right of withdrawal. She elects to have the settlement agreement drawn so that any sum remaining at her death shall be payable equally to her children who are then living.

It is clear that Amy owns the proceeds. She has a complete right to the proceeds just as if the money were on deposit in her bank. She agrees with the insurer that any

---

[6]People with estates large enough to be subject to estate taxes often have the trustee of an irrevocable life insurance trust purchase the insurance on their lives. The trustee will be the owner and beneficiary of the insurance, which will avoid estate taxes.

sums it holds at her death are to be paid to contingent payees. Some litigants have claimed that such an arrangement is an attempted testamentary disposition that violates the Statute of Wills. However, several court decisions have upheld the validity of a settlement agreement entered into by a beneficiary and naming other persons to receive sums remaining at the beneficiary's death.[7]

Trusts

A grantor can create a revocable inter vivos trust under which the trust income is payable to the grantor during the grantor's lifetime and the principal is payable to a trust beneficiary after the grantor's death. Such a trust will not be invalid as an attempted testamentary disposition made without a will, as long as administration is in the hands of the trustee and the trust creates a present interest in the trust beneficiary. Thus, trusts can be valid will substitutes.

Life insurance trusts are also valid will substitutes. Because of the strong public policy favoring life insurance, the courts have upheld these trusts as nontestamentary transactions, even if the policyowner reserves many rights of control over the policy and the trust.

---

[7]Mutual Ben. Life Ins. Co. v. Ellis, 125 F.2d 127 (2d Cir.1942), *cert. den.* 316 U.S. 665 (1942); Wasson v. Pyron, 414 S.W.2d 391 (Ark. 1967); Hall v. Mutual Life Ins. Co., 122 N.Y.S.2d 239 (N.Y. App. Div. 1953), *aff'd,* 119 N.E.2d 598 (N.Y. 1954); Toulouse v. New York Life Ins. Co., 245 P.2d 205 (1952).

Summary

A policyowner can provide for deferred payout of life insurance proceeds to the beneficiary by entering into a settlement agreement or by making the proceeds payable to a trustee. If the proceeds are payable in a lump sum, the beneficiary ordinarily can elect a settlement option. The four types of settlement options are the interest income option, the income for a fixed period option, the income of a fixed amount option, and the income for life option. The income for life option can be in the form of a straight life income, a life income with period certain, or a joint and survivor annuity. Often, a settlement agreement contains a combination of two or more settlement options.

The rights of a contingent beneficiary differ from the rights of a contingent payee. A contingent beneficiary's rights are extinguished if the primary beneficiary is alive at the time of the insured's death or at the expiration of the time period specified in a survivorship clause. A contingent payee's rights are not extinguished in such a case. At the death of the primary payee, a contingent payee will become entitled to any remaining amounts payable.

Sometimes a policyowner prefers to make the policy proceeds payable to a trustee, rather than have them paid out under a settlement agreement. A trust is a fiduciary arrangement in which one person, the trustee, holds property for the benefit of another person, the trust beneficiary. Trusts can be either inter vivos (created during the grantor's lifetime) or testamentary (created by the grantor's will). A life insurance trust is an inter vivos trust that has life insurance policies or proceeds as trust property. Life insurance trusts can be either revocable or irrevocable and either funded or unfunded. Funded life insurance trusts contain money or income-producing property that the trustee uses to pay policy premiums. Two rules of law bearing on all trusts are the rule against perpetuities and the rule against accumulations.

Trusts allow more discretion and flexibility than do settlement agreements. The trustee can act as a counselor to the trust beneficiary. On the other hand, if the policyowner or beneficiary enters into a settlement agreement, the insurer can guarantee safety of the proceeds and a life income, which a trust cannot. A trust presents a possibility of a greater return on investment than a settlement agreement, but also a possibility of a greater loss. A trust usually involves greater expense than a settlement agreement.

Like a trust or settlement agreement, a will provides for the disposition of property. It is an instrument directing disposition of property after the owner's death. A testator must have executed the will in accordance with the probate code of the relevant jurisdiction for the will to be valid. If the will is invalid, the owner's property will pass under the relevant state intestate statute, unless it passes by a valid will substitute.

Joint tenancy, certain trusts, and certain contracts, including life insurance contracts, are valid will substitutes. A settlement agreement that the policyowner enters into is a valid will substitute. However, if the beneficiary enters into a settlement agreement naming a contingent payee to receive the proceeds remaining at the beneficiary's death, the question arises as to whether or not this is an attempted testamentary disposition in violation of the Statute of Wills. Several courts have upheld the validity of this arrangement.

ILLUSTRATIVE CASE

In the following case, the court held that a settlement agreement did not constitute a testamentary disposition in violation of the state's Statute of Wills.

VIRGINIA COOK, Appellant,

v.

METROPOLITAN LIFE INSURANCE COMPANY, Appellee[8]
United States Court of Appeals, Fourth Circuit.
Argued May 9, 1984.
Decided July 12, 1984.

PER CURIAM:[9]

In this action based on diversity jurisdiction, plaintiff Virginia Cook appeals the decision of the district court granting summary judgment to Metropolitan Life Insurance Company. Finding that the contract between the insured and the insurer clearly provided for interest payments during the lifetime of the primary beneficiary and that the agreement did not violate West Virginia law, we affirm the decision of the district court.

In 1936 Metropolitan Life Insurance Company issued to Howard Cook four life insurance policies, each with a face value of $5,000. In his application for these policies Cook named his wife Virginia as primary beneficiary and his daughter as contingent beneficiary. He answered "yes" to the question whether he reserved the right to change the beneficiary at any time without the consent of the designated beneficiary. The policies, which were virtually identical, provided for the insured to choose the method of payment to take effect after his death or upon surrender of the policy. Of the four options available, (1) interest payments, (2) installment payment, (3) life income or (4) annuity, Howard Cook selected the first option for payments to his wife. In 1937 an "election of mode of settlement"

containing the following provision was mailed by the insured to the home office of Metropolitan Life:

> In accordance with and subject to the provisions of the above numbered policies, I HEREBY DIRECT that the amount payable under the said policies, upon my death, shall be returned by the Company in accordance with the provisions of Option One of the MODES OF SETTLEMENT and interest thereon shall be paid to Virginia R. Cook, my wife, the beneficiary of record, during her lifetime. Upon the death of my said wife, the interest then accrued on the amount retained by the Company under Option One shall be paid at once in one sum to Janice Cook, my daughter, and the amount retained shall be further retained by the Company and paid out to my said daughter in accordance with the provisions of Option Two of the MODES OF SETTLEMENT. . . . (Emphasis added)

The policy contained the following description of Option One:

> OPTION 1. (INTEREST PAYMENTS)—By the payment of interest either annually, semi-annually, quarterly or monthly, at the rate of three per centum per annum on the amount retained by the Company, the first interest payment being payable at the end of one year, six months, three months or one month respectively, according to the mode of interest payment elected, and by the payment upon the death of the payee, or at the end of a certain number of years, as specified in said written election, of the amount retained by the Company, together with any accrued interest, to such payee, or to the person designated in said election; or, if there be no person so designated, to the executors or administrators of such payee.

---

[8]742 F.2d 110 (1984).

[9]*Per curiam* means "by the court" and is used to distinguish an opinion of the whole court from an opinion written by any one judge.

The statement mailed to the insurer, which was recorded by Metropolitan Life, also specified that Howard Cook's wife should "not have the right, at anytime, to withdraw the amount retained by the Company under Option One." The insured reserved the right to cancel, through written notice to the insurer, the directions given.

After Howard Cook's death in 1982, his widow surrendered the policies and Metropolitan Life issued her a supplementary contract for interest payments at the rate of 7% per annum. (The insurer is paying 7% rather than 3% because it agreed to increase the rate if a higher interest rate was declared under the interest payments option). Preferring to receive a lump sum payment of the face amounts of the four policies plus all accumulated interest, plaintiff filed suit.

Plaintiff raises several arguments. The first, that there were certain conditions precedent to election of a mode of settlement that were not met, is refuted by the language of the policy. Plaintiff relies on the following provision:

Upon written election made to and accepted by the Company, in accordance with the provisions hereinafter contained, the whole or any part of the amount payable according to the terms of this policy will, (1) upon receipt of due proof of death of the insured, or (2) upon surrender of this Policy for its Cash Surrender Value after it has been in force for at least five years, be retained by the Company and paid out in accordance with one of the following options:

As noted by the district court, this provision controls the defendant's method of payment after a valid election is made. It does not, however, provide conditions prece-dent to the insured's right to make an election. The insured exercised his right of election and the written election was accepted by Metropolitan Life. The contract in effect at the time of the insured's death provided for the payment of interest only to Virginia Cook and, upon her death, for installment payments of the proceeds to the Cooks' daughter. The rights of the beneficiaries vested under the contract at the insured's death and under the contract Virginia Cook had only the right to receive interest payments.

Plaintiff also argues that the insured's written election of mode of settlement violates West Virginia law . . . because it constitutes a testamentary disposition without conforming to the Statute of Wills. . . . Although a life insurance policy resembles a will in that it may become operative at death, a life insurance policy is fundamentally different because it is a contractual agreement between insurer and insured and, as such, need not conform to the Statute of Wills.

* * * * *

Under the terms of the contract, the primary beneficiary is to receive interest payments until her death at which time her daughter is to receive the accrued interest in one payment and thereafter to receive monthly installment payments. The intentions of the parties to the contract were clearly expressed in the contract itself and there is no reason to thwart these intentions.

Accordingly, the decision of the district court is AFFIRMED.

Questions for Review

1. Distinguish between beneficiaries and payees of death benefits under life insurance policies.
2. Contrast the position of a contingent beneficiary when the primary beneficiary survives the insured with that of a contingent payee when the primary payee survives the insured.
3. What is the problem when the insured and the beneficiary die under conditions where it is not possible to prove who died first? How do the state simultaneous death acts handle this problem?
4. What is the potential problem if the primary beneficiary dies shortly after the death of the insured? Suppose that the policy names a contingent beneficiary. Tell why this may not solve the problem of short-term survivorship. How does a survivorship clause attempt to solve the problem? What are the weaknesses of this proposed solution?
5. Contrast the relative advantages and disadvantages of using a settlement agreement, as opposed to a trust, to distribute the death benefit to the beneficiary.
6. Distinguish between an inter vivos and a testamentary trust.
7. Describe the rule against perpetuities. Describe the rule against accumulations.
8. (*a*) How does a person die intestate? (*b*) How does this affect the distribution of the property of the deceased?
9. What is meant by an attempted (unsuccessful) testamentary disposition of property?
10. There are several ways to pass property to another after one's death without a will. Describe these will substitutes.

12 PREMIUMS AND DIVIDENDS

The operation of an insurer turns on the regular collection of premiums, their investment, and the payment of claims. A premium is the agreed price paid to the insurer for assuming and carrying the risk. The purpose of this chapter is to discuss legal problems that can occur in connection with premium payments and premium abatements (dividends).

The Initial Premium

The initial premium and the application constitute the consideration that the life insurance applicant gives in exchange for the insurer's promises. This consideration is necessary to put the policy in force. Most insurance policies expressly declare that they are not effective unless the initial premium is paid and the insurer delivers the policy during the lifetime and continued insurability of the proposed insured. Thus, the promises of the life insurer become binding when delivery of the policy and payment of the initial premium have occurred.[1]

Conversely, no premium is due unless the insurer assumes the risk. If the insurer declines the risk, the insurer must return the initial premium to the applicant. A great deal of life insurance law centers on the initial premium because of the essential role it plays in the formation of the life insurance contract.

Presumption of Payment of the Initial Premium

Most policies provide that the insurance will not become effective until the initial premium is paid. Nevertheless, if the insured dies soon after the policy was delivered and the beneficiary has possession of the policy, even though the initial premium was not paid a court might hold that the policy is in force.

Many policies, particularly older ones, contain a clause referring to the "initial premium, receipt of which is hereby acknowledged," or similar language. The majority of courts have held that if an insurer has unconditionally delivered a policy containing such a clause, the policy is in force.[2] The legislatures of some states have enacted this rule into statutory law. For example, the California Insurance Code contains the following language:

---

[1]If a premium receipt has been issued to the applicant, promises that the insurer made in the premium receipt itself will become binding before the policy is delivered.

[2]Jack W. Shaw, Jr., Annotation, *Conclusiveness of Recitation, in Delivered Insurance Policy, that Initial Premium Has Been Paid,* 44 A.L.R. 3d 1361 (1972).

An acknowledgment in a policy of the receipt of premium is conclusive evidence of its payment, so far as to make the policy binding.[3]

Note that this statute says that the acknowledgment is conclusive evidence of receipt of the premium *so far as to make the policy binding.* If the initial premium has not been paid, and the insurer can prove this, the insurer can recover the premium under both statutory and case law. In the usual case in which this issue arises, the insured has died and the insurer deducts the initial premium from the death benefit before paying the death benefit to the beneficiary.

In a minority of states, policy language acknowledging receipt of the initial premium will raise a rebuttable presumption that the policy is in force. A ***rebuttable presumption*** is a presumption that a party can overturn by showing the court proof to the contrary.

If the policy does not acknowledge receipt of the initial premium, the beneficiary's possession of the policy after the insured's death ordinarily creates a rebuttable presumption that the policy is in force. For example, in *Woloshin v. Guardian Life Insurance Co. of America,*[4] the policy was in the possession of the insured at the time of his death, which occurred one month after the insurer issued the policy. The insurer refused to pay the death benefit, contending that the initial premium had never been paid. The question was whether the beneficiary's possession of the policy after the insured's death creates a presumption that the insurer delivered the policy with intent to be bound. The court said:

> The evidence does not support the contention of defendant [the insurer] that the policy was delivered to Woloshin for inspection merely and that the delivery, therefore, was not absolute. The agent mailed the policy to him with a bill for the premium. No interim receipt[5] was taken pending payment. Delivery of the policy was made on the credit of the assured and resulted in a contract between the parties conditioned only by its terms. But assuming that the question of conditional delivery were in issue, that question, clearly, was for the jury. "The beneficiary's lawful possession of a life insurance policy after the death of the insured, and especially when, as here, there is no allegation of fraud, accident, artifice, or mistake, to impeach this possession, prima facie sustains the burden of proof resting on the plaintiff, by raising a strong presumption that the policy was not only manually delivered but was also *legally* delivered to the insured, and puts the defendant in a position where, to avoid an adverse verdict, it must offer evidence of the conditional delivery alleged, sufficiently convincing to countervail the strong presumption of legal delivery arising from the lawful possession of the policy by the beneficiary."

If, however, the applicant is put on notice by language in the application that the agent has no authority to extend credit, the insurer often will not be bound in a similar situation.

Waiver of Timely Payment of the Initial Premium

An insurer is sometimes said to have waived timely payment of the initial premium in situations as described above in Woloshin. As another example, in *Henderson v. Capital Life & Health Insurance Co.,*[6] a mother applied for a policy insuring the life of a minor child. The policy was delivered while the mother was away from home.

---

[3]*Cal. Ins. Code* § 484 (West 1993). Conclusive evidence of payment means that the law will not permit such evidence to be challenged by the insurer.

[4]22 A.2d 54 (Pa. Super. Ct. 1941).

[5]A receipt showing that the policy was held for inspection only.

[6]18 S.E.2d 605 (S.C. 1942).

The father of the child testified that the agent left the policy and said that he would collect the initial premium on his next visit. The agent assured the father that the policy was then in force. Before the agent's next visit, the child died.

On learning of the child's death, the agent went to the client's house and picked up the policy, saying he would do everything he could to obtain the death benefit for the beneficiary. However, the death benefit was not paid, and the agent refused to return the policy. In the lawsuit that followed, the lower court held that the insurer had waived timely payment of the premium. On appeal, the Supreme Court of South Carolina agreed, stating:

> Under the well-settled rule, the company may waive the time and method of the payment of premium. . . . It has been repeatedly held in this State that the manner and method of the payment of the initial premium may be waived and that credit may be extended for the initial premium.

Renewal Premiums

All premiums paid after the initial premium are ***renewal premiums.*** The majority of courts consider payment of the renewal premium a condition precedent to continued coverage under a life or health insurance policy.[7]

Ordinarily, the policyowner does not promise to pay the renewal premium. Therefore, the renewal premium is not a debt that the policyowner owes, and the insurer cannot sue the policyowner to recover the renewal premium if the policyowner refuses to pay it. Nonpayment of the renewal premium by the end of the grace period will simply cause the policy to lapse. Thus, a minority of courts have held that nonpayment of the renewal premium constitutes a condition subsequent, cutting off the rights of the policyowner.[8]

Whole life insurance renewal premiums are usually paid once a year during the lifetime of the insured. Alternatively, these premiums can be paid over shorter time periods. For example, a policyowner might wish to pay for the entire contract in annual installments over 5, 10, or 20 years. Sometimes, a policyowner pays for the entire contract with a single premium.

Courts in some early cases took the view that a whole life insurance policy annual renewal premium paid for two things. First, it paid for the cost of insurance for the year in question; second, it paid for the right to renew the insurance for another year.[9] However, by the weight of authority today the annual whole life renewal premium is part-payment of the whole contract, not simply payment for the year in question. This view squares with single premium and 5-, 10-, or 20-pay whole life insurance.

An actuary-lawyer turned judge wrote a U.S. Supreme Court opinion discussing whole life insurance renewal premiums. Justice Joseph P. Bradley had served as consulting mathematician for a leading life insurer before becoming a member of the U.S. Supreme Court. With this background, he was well equipped to write the

---

[7]Pierce v. Massachusetts Acci. Co., 22 N.E.2d 78 (Mass. 1939); Browne v. John Hancock Mut. Life Ins. Co., 180 A. 746 (Pa. Super. Ct. 1935). See the discussion of conditions precedent and conditions subsequent in Chapter 6, "Formation of the Life Insurance Contract."

[8]Thomas v. Northwestern Mut. Life Ins. Co., 75 P. 665 (Cal. 1904); Masonic Relief Ass'n v. Hicks, 171 S.E. 215 (Ga. Ct. App. 1933).

[9]*E.g.,* Worthington v. Charter Oak Life Ins. Co., 41 Conn. 372 (1874).

opinion in *New York Life Insurance Co. v. Statham*.[10] This opinion reads in part as follows:

> We agree with the court below [the court from which the appeal was taken], that the contract is not an assurance for a single year, with a privilege of renewal from year to year by paying the annual premium, but that it is an entire contract of assurance for life, subject to discontinuance and forfeiture for nonpayment of any of the stipulated premiums. Such is the form of the contract, and such is its character. It has been contended that the payment of each premium is the consideration for insurance during the next following year, as in fire policies. But the position is untenable. It often happens that the assured pays the entire premium in advance, or in five, ten, or twenty annual installments. Such installments are clearly not intended as the consideration for the respective years in which they are paid; for, after they are all paid, the policy stands good for the balance of the life insured, without any further payment. Each installment is, in fact, part consideration of the entire insurance for life. It is the same thing, where the annual premiums are spread over the whole life. The value of assurance for one year of a man's life when he is young, strong and healthy, is manifestly not the same when he is old and decrepit. There is no proper relation between the annual premium and the risk of assurance for the year in which it is paid. This idea of assurance from year to year is the suggestion of ingenious counsel. The annual premiums are an annuity, the present value of which is calculated to correspond with the present value of the amount assured, a reasonable percentage being added to the premiums to cover expenses and contingencies. The whole premiums are balanced against the whole insurance.

This case represents the prevailing view of the courts today.

Time of Payment of the Renewal Premium

Renewal premiums must be paid on or before a date specified in the policy unless the insurer gives an extension of time. In this respect, it is said that "time is of the essence," which means that if June 20 is the specified date, and the insurer has not given an extension, payment on June 21 is too late. However, payment can be made at any time prior to midnight on the specified date. If a premium is due on a nonbusiness day, payment on the following business day usually will be sufficient.

Renewal Premium Due Date

Because life insurance policies usually stipulate that the insurance will not become effective unless the initial premium is paid and the policy delivered during the continued good health of the proposed insured, a number of days sometimes will elapse between the policy date and the date on which the insurance becomes effective. The *policy date* is a date written on the policy and is usually either the date of the application or the date that the insurer issued the policy. The date on which the insurance becomes effective is called the effective date. For example, the insurer might date and issue the policy November 15 but deliver it and receive the initial premium on December 5. The question then arises, from which date should the insurer compute the renewal premium due date, the policy date or the effective date?

Policies usually specify that the renewal premium due date is calculated from the policy date. Thus, if the policy date is April 23, 1997, and the premium is paid

---

[10]93 U.S. 24 (1876).

annually, the typical policy would specify that the first renewal premium due date would be April 23, 1998. According to the majority of courts, if the policy specifies a renewal premium due date, as is nearly always the case, that date will govern, even though the policyowner receives insurance for a period slightly shorter than the period stated in the policy. These courts take the position that the terms of the policy are not ambiguous, and therefore the policy is enforceable as written. This reasoning is followed in *D. & P. Terminal, Inc. v. Western Life Insurance Co.*[11] That decision reads in part as follows:

> The only question is the date premiums were to be paid to avoid a lapse in coverage. These dates were specifically decided and clearly set out in the insurance contract. We cannot write another contract for the parties . . . expressing dates contrary to those established by the parties. When the intention of the parties is clear and unambiguous, as it is here, the Court may not assume an ambiguity. It is the duty of the Court to give effect to this intention. . . . According to the contract, the premiums were due November 5, February 5, May 5, and August 5. Failure to pay on these dates, plus any grace period, would cause a lapse in coverage.

Backdated Policies

Where the policy is backdated at the applicant's request so that the premium amount will be smaller, the renewal premium due date ordinarily runs from the policy date, regardless of when the insurer delivered the policy. This is true even though backdating results in payment for a period of time when there was no coverage. However, some states have laws limiting the length of time a policy can be backdated. The most typical limit is six months.

Grace Period

The insurance laws of most states require that life insurance policies that an insurer issues or delivers in the state must include a grace period of a month or 31 days within which the renewal premium can be paid without lapse of the policy. The grace period runs from the due date of the renewal premium in default. Payment can be made at any time prior to midnight of the last day of grace or on the following business day if the last day of grace falls on a nonbusiness day.

The initial premium does not have a grace period because the contract ordinarily is ineffective, for lack of consideration, until the initial premium has been paid.

Extension of Time for Payment of the Renewal Premium

Because prompt payment of the renewal premium is for the insurer's benefit, the insurer can waive prompt payment and grant extensions of time for payment. Such extensions are not unusual. A grace period does not follow the extension period. For example, if the renewal premium is due on June 10, the grace period ends on July 11, and the insurer grants a two-week extension of time (until July 25) in which to pay the premium, no grace period will follow the extension. Moreover, usually the insurance is not in force if the insured dies before the premium has been paid during the extension period, unless it is in force under a nonforfeiture option.

---

[11]368 F.2d 743 (8th Cir. 1966).

Renewal Premiums Paid in Advance

Although most policyowners pay their renewal premiums as they fall due, some policyowners are concerned that they might not be able to meet future payments. Persons whose incomes are irregular, for example, sometimes wish to pay premiums in advance. Or an older person might wish to make a gift to a grandchild of a policy on the grandchild's life and pay premiums in advance, so that no more premiums need be paid until the child is grown.

To accommodate such needs, most insurers allow premiums to be paid in advance for a specified period of time. As a general rule, insurers accept premiums paid in advance on a discounted basis for not longer than 20 years. The insurer will give the payor a receipt that specifies the circumstances under which the money so paid can be withdrawn and the disposition of any premiums that remain unearned at the death of the insured.

Generally speaking, a life insurer has the authority to accept advance payment of premiums because this activity is reasonably related to the insurer's business. However, when such sums are subject to withdrawal at the request of the payor, the insurer is providing a service that resembles that provided by banks. An insurer does not have the legal authority to operate a banking business. To distinguish the advance premiums from a bank deposit, insurers limit the payor's right to withdraw the unapplied portion of the fund. Sometimes, the payor is limited as to the date on which she can make a withdrawal. In other instances, the payor can withdraw only the entire unapplied amount. In still others, the request to withdraw is subject to deferral at the insurer's option.

The insurer will refund advance premiums that are unearned at the insured's death according to the terms of the receipt that the insurer originally gave the payor. Ordinarily, the receipt will provide that these funds will be paid to the beneficiary, to the payor, or to the payor's estate.

Method of Payment of the Premium

The insurer can make whatever terms it wishes with respect to the method by which an initial or renewal premium must be paid. It has the right to demand payment in cash. Alternatively, it can accept another method of payment such as a personal check, a promissory note, a bank draft, or a money order. The insurer can also extend credit for a premium payment. Acceptance of these other methods of payment can create legal problems, which are discussed in this section. Legal problems associated with premium payment by policy loan or by application of policy dividends are also discussed.

Payment by Personal Check

It is customary today to pay a premium by personal check. When the insurer has received the check, the premium has been paid, even though some time will elapse before the insurer receives the actual cash. However, ordinarily, the courts assume that insurers condition payment of a premium by check on the bank's honoring the check when it is properly presented. That is, usually there is an implied condition that the check must be honored.

If a check is dishonored, the insurer can either lapse the policy for nonpayment of the premium or attempt to collect on the dishonored check. If it elects to lapse the policy, it should act promptly, return the check, request the return of the premium receipt, and declare the policy forfeited.

If the insured dies while the insurer is attempting to collect on the dishonored check, the court might hold that the insurer waived its right to lapse the policy and that it must pay the benefits. *Sjoberg v. State Automobile Insurance Association* illustrates the effect of electing to rely on a dishonored check.[12] This was a suit brought on a $5,000 insurance policy after the insured died in an automobile accident. The insurer contended that the policy had lapsed prior to the date of death because of nonpayment of the renewal premium. The facts showed that the death occurred on August 5 and that the quarterly renewal premium, due July 1, was paid by personal check on July 8, well within the grace period. However, the bank returned the check to the insurer with the notation "insufficient funds." The insurer did not return the check, rescind the receipt, and declare the policy forfeited, as it had the right to do. Instead, it requested the local agency to contact the insured and secure a "bankable check or other remittance." This had not been accomplished at the date of the insured's death.

The court noted the general rule that, if there is no agreement to the contrary, an insurer conditions payment by check on the bank's honoring the check. However, the court said that in this case the insurer's failure to declare a forfeiture after the bank dishonored the check indicated its intention to keep the policy in force. The court said:

> On the occasion in question [the insurer] gave the insured a full receipt of the premium upon receiving his check. There was some delay in the presentation of the check for payment but when it was returned dishonored defendant [the insurer] did not repudiate the transaction but wrote his agents to contact insured to get "bankable check or other remittance." The agent notified the insured thereof. Neither the letter nor the conversation between defendant's agent and the insured referred to a forfeiture of the policy. Instead the whole tenor of both was to effect the collection of the check. Such negotiations indicate an intention to keep the policy in force. . . . They indicate defendant's election to rely upon the check rather than upon forfeiture and reinstatement. . . . The District court held that the defendant waived its right to forfeit the policy and elected to keep the policy in force. We agree with this holding of the court.

An insurer must promptly present a check in payment of premium to the bank for collection. Retention of the check for an unreasonably long time might cause the insurer to be estopped from declaring a forfeiture of the policy if the insured dies and the bank dishonors the check after the last day of grace.

According to a majority of courts, if the insurer accepts a postdated check, the check is payment of the premium as of the date of the receipt given for it, provided that the bank honors the check on the date it bears.[13]

A minority of courts take the view that acceptance of a postdated check is equal to an extension of credit by the insurer. Thus, these courts hold that if the insured dies after the insurer received the check, and the bank dishonors the check after the

---

[12]48 N.W.2d 452 (N.D. 1951).

[13]W.E. Shipley, Annotation, *Receipt of Check for Insurance Premium as Preventing Forfeiture for Nonpayment,* 50 A.L.R. 2d 630 (1956).

insured's death, the benefits will be payable because the insurer extended credit to the policyowner by accepting the check.[14]

Payment by Promissory Note

An insurer can waive the requirement that a premium be paid by cash or check and can accept a ***promissory note*** instead. A promissory note is a written promise to pay a stated sum of money.

In legal effect, the unconditional acceptance of a promissory note for an insurance premium constitutes payment of the premium.[15] If the policyowner defaults on payment of the note, the insurer's remedy is to sue for payment of the note. The insurer cannot declare the policy lapsed for nonpayment of the premium.

However, insurers usually do not accept a promissory note unconditionally. An insurer usually accepts a promissory note on the express condition that it will not operate as payment of the premium if the promisor does not pay the note when due. The policy, the note, or both, ordinarily will contain a provision that the policyowner will forfeit the policy if the note is not paid when due.

Payment by Credit

Insurers almost never extend credit for payment of the premium. If the agent extends credit on behalf of the insurer, the agent must have authority from the insurer to do so. An attempted credit extension will not bind the insurer if the agent exceeded his authority to extend credit.[16]

However, the insurer's agent can pay the premium and extend credit to the policyowner on the agent's own behalf. If the insured dies before the policyowner repays the agent, the policy benefits will nevertheless be payable.

Payment by Automatic Premium Loan

The automatic premium loan provision will be in effect only if the policyowner elects it. If the policyowner elects the ***automatic premium loan provision,*** the insurer can establish a policy loan to pay a premium that remains unpaid at the end of the grace period. Most life insurance policies with cash values include an automatic premium loan provision. Such a provision appears in the illustrative policy in the Appendix, Figure 2.

An insurer will make an automatic premium loan only if necessary to prevent lapse and only if the policy has a loan value. Customarily, the insurer will notify the policyowner if the insurer has made such a loan.

The automatic premium loan has both advantages and disadvantages for the policyowner. Among the advantages are that the automatic premium loan prevents an inadvertent lapse of the policy. Furthermore, the automatic premium loan maintains accidental death and disability benefits in force. These benefits would not remain in force if the policy lapsed and continued under a nonforfeiture option. The automatic premium loan prevents the necessity of reinstatement of the policy and protects

---

[14]John Hancock Mut. Life Ins. Co. v. Mann, 86 F.2d 783 (7th Cir. 1936).

[15]Raney v. Piedmont S. Life Ins. Co., 387 F.2d 75 (8th Cir. 1967); Narver v. California State Life Ins. Co., 294 P. 393 (Cal. 1930).

[16]Hill v. Philadelphia Life Ins. Co., 35 F.2d 132 (4th Cir. 1929).

against the danger that the policyowner will not be able to reinstate the policy because the insured has become uninsurable. Reinstatement is discussed in Chapter 15, "Lapse and Reinstatement."

One of the disadvantages of the automatic premium loan is that, if used indiscriminately, it can give the policyowner a false sense of security. Often, the establishment of the first loan is the beginning of a process that ultimately results in lapse. The continued use of the automatic premium loan drains away cash values so that, at the time of lapse, little, if any, value remains to be applied under the nonforfeiture options. In addition, if the insured dies while the policy is in force, the death benefit will be smaller if policy values were used to pay premiums.

According to the majority of courts, the payment of a premium by an automatic premium loan enhances the cash value of the policy, just as payment of the premium by the policyowner would have done.[17] That is, the cash value will decrease by the amount of the loan but will increase due to payment of the premium. A minority of courts have held that payment of a premium by automatic premium loan does not enhance the policy's cash value.[18]

The insurer is under no duty to notify the policyowner that the loan value is insufficient to pay the premium due[19] unless there is a statute requiring such notice.[20] Likewise, the insurer does not have to notify the policyowner of the length of time that the policy will be kept in force by the available loan value.[21]

Payment by Dividends

The general rule is that an insurer cannot declare a life insurance policy forfeited for nonpayment of a premium if it has in its possession dividends belonging to the policyowner sufficient to pay the premium, and the policyowner has not elected to have the dividends applied in some other manner.[22] Ordinarily, the policyowner elects a dividend option when she fills out the application. If the policyowner chooses an option other than the payment of premiums, the insurer will have neither the duty nor the right to apply the dividends to pay the premium.

If the dividends are not sufficient to pay the whole premium, the insurer is not obligated to make a partial payment unless it has agreed to do so, according to the majority rule. However, the insurer has a duty to notify the policyowner of the additional amount needed to pay the premium.[23] The policyowner would not know the additional amount to pay if such a notice is not sent, because she cannot know the dividend amount unless the insurer tells her. If the insurer does not notify the policyowner of the additional amount, the insurer cannot lapse the policy for nonpayment of the premium.

---

[17]Sovereign Camp, W.O.W. v. Harris, 114 S.W.2d 449 (Ark. 1938); Balyeat v. American Nat'l Ins. Co., 265 N.W. 774 (Mich. 1936).

[18]de Almada v. Sovereign Camp, W.O.W., 67 P.2d 474 (Ariz. 1937).

[19]General Am. Life Ins. Co. v. Butts, 18 S.E.2d 542 (Ga. 1942).

[20]Lester v. Aetna Life Ins. Co., 433 F.2d 884 (5th Cir. 1970), *cert. denied,* 402 U.S. 909 (1971).

[21]General Am. Life Ins. Co. v. Butts, 18 S.E.2d 542 (Ga. 1942).

[22]The dividends referred to in this subsection are policyowners' dividends, not stockholders' dividends. For an explanation of the difference between these two types of dividends, see the section below entitled "Dividends."

[23]Mau v. Union Labor Life Ins. Co., 106 A.2d 748 (N.J. Super. Ct. 1954).

Persons Making Payment of the Premium

From the insurer's standpoint, ordinarily it is irrelevant who pays the premium. The insurer will accept the premium from whoever tenders it.

Payment of the premium, by itself, usually does not give the payor any right to insurance proceeds. Thus, a person with no interest in the policy who voluntarily paid the premium would ordinarily have no right to any of the proceeds.

Usually, the policyowner pays the premium or authorizes someone else to do so. The beneficiary, an assignee, a trustee, an agent or broker, or some other person sometimes pays the premium. The legal questions that can arise when someone other than the policyowner pays the premium are discussed in this section.

Payment by Order on a Bank or Employer

Sometimes, the policyowner authorizes his bank or employer to pay the premium. Preauthorized check plans, electronic fund transfers, and payroll deduction plans help the policyowner keep the policy in force.

Preauthorized Check Plans.   Under a *preauthorized check plan,* the policyowner pays premiums by authorizing the insurer to draw checks to the insurer's own order on the policyowner's bank account.[24] Usually, this is done monthly. The policyowner, in addition to authorizing the insurer to draw checks, also authorizes the bank to accept and process the checks.

A separate agreement between the insurer and the bank provides that the insurer will indemnify the bank for any liability the bank might incur by participating in the plan. Some bankers opposed preauthorized check plans in the past on the ground that, because the policyowner is not notified each time the insurer draws a check, overdrafts could occur. The indemnity agreements between the insurer and the bank help to counter such objections.

Preauthorized check plans help policyowners who are already paying many bills monthly by also putting insurance premium payments on a monthly basis. In addition, such plans free the policyowner from having to remember to pay the premium, thus helping to prevent inadvertent lapse of the policy.

Generally speaking, if the check clears through regular banking channels, the premium is paid just as effectively as if the policyowner had drawn it personally. If the check does not clear, the insurer ordinarily will take the same action it would take when the bank returns any other check. However, the insurer must promptly draw and present the check. If the insurer fails to do so, it cannot claim nonpayment of the premium.[25]

Preauthorized Electronic Fund Transfers.   Banks have computers programmed to transfer funds from one account to another electronically. Thus, the bank can transfer funds from the policyowner's account to the account of the insurer without a check being written. This is a *preauthorized electronic fund transfer.*

---

[24]Allan E. Korpela, Annotation, *Construction and Effect of Arrangement under Which Insurance Premiums Are Paid Automatically via Insurer's Draft on Insured's Bank Account,* 45 A.L.R. 3d 1349 (1972).
[25]Pacific Mut. Life Ins. Co. v. Watson, 137 So. 414 (Ala. 1931).

In 1978, Congress passed the Electronic Fund Transfer Act.[26] Among other things, the act requires that a policyowner-depositor having his bank electronically transfer funds to an insurer sign an authorization permitting the transfers. State laws also govern electronic fund transfers.

Payroll Deduction Plans.   Under a payroll deduction plan, a policyowner authorizes her employer to withhold the premium from her salary and forward it directly to the insurer.[27] This is usually done monthly.

The federal government also has a payroll deduction plan for members of the military service. The government makes deductions monthly and will continue to make deductions until the policyowner authorizes their discontinuance.

Payment by the Beneficiary

Sometimes, the beneficiary pays the premiums. Assume, for example, that Arnold Wallace owns a policy on his life and has named his wife, Margaret, as revocable beneficiary. Arnold takes no interest in his family or the policy. Margaret pays the premiums as they fall due. Several years later, Arnold and Margaret divorce, and Arnold remarries. He then wishes to change the beneficiary designation to his new wife, Paulette. The general rule is that payment of the premiums by the beneficiary will not prevent the policyowner from changing the beneficiary designation in accordance with the policy provisions. Of course, if Arnold had named Margaret irrevocable beneficiary, he could not have changed the beneficiary designation without her consent, under the laws of most states.

Thus, a revocable beneficiary might pay the premiums of a life insurance policy for many years without the payments enlarging her mere expectancy. However, if the policyowner promised the proceeds to a revocable beneficiary who paid the premiums, the courts frequently award the beneficiary the amount of the premiums she paid.[28] A person who pays premiums under the mistaken impression that he is beneficiary might also be entitled to recover the amount of the premiums he paid.[29]

A life insurance beneficiary who is the trustee of a funded life insurance trust has a duty to pay insurance premiums under the terms of the trust. Failure to pay the premiums is a breach of the trustee's fiduciary duty. The trust beneficiary can maintain a suit against the trustee for such a breach.

Payment by an Assignee

Under a typical collateral assignment, the assignee is under no duty to pay the premium. However, if the collateral assignee does pay the premium, the assignee has a right to recover the premium paid, in addition to any unpaid debt for which the policyowner made the assignment and interest on the debt.

[26]15 U.S.C.A. § 1693 *et. seq.* (West 1982 & Supp.1996).

[27]Steven M. Cassidy & Robert A. Marshall, *Payroll Deduction Plans—What Are They?,* J. Aᴍ. Sᴏᴄ'ʏ CLU & CʜFC, Jan. 1991, at 38.

[28]New York Life Ins. Co. v. Walls, 124 F. Supp. 38 (N.D. W. Va. 1954); Perry v. Perry, 484 S.W.2d 257 (Mo. 1972); Walsh v. John Hancock Mut. Life Ins. Co., 293 A.2d 71 (Pa. Super. Ct. 1972); Leal v. Leal, 401 S.W.2d 293 (Tex. Civ. App. 1966); Annotation, *Right of Named Beneficiary, upon Change of Beneficiary, to Recover Premiums Paid on Life Insurance Policy,* 92 A.L.R. 3d 1330 (1979).

[29]Fendler v. Roy, 58 S.W.2d 459 (Mo. 1932); Metropolitan Life Ins. Co. v. Tesauro, 120 A. 918 (N.J. Ch. 1923).

An absolute assignee is in the same position with respect to paying the premium as was the original policyowner. That is, an absolute assignee ordinarily has no duty to pay the premium, but someone must make the premium payments or the policy will lapse.

Payment by Agent or Broker

If the insurer's agent (or a broker) extends credit to the policyowner and pays the premium, the policy will be in force, even if the policyowner fails to repay the agent.[30] The agent's recourse would be to sue the policyowner on the debt.

Persons Receiving Payment of the Premium

Most life insurance policies today provide that renewal premiums shall be paid to the insurer at its home office or to an authorized agent in exchange for an official receipt signed by the corporate secretary and countersigned by the agent. Payment to the home office results in few problems. Payment to an agent usually does not present any problem if the agent promptly remits the payment to the home office.[31]

Payment made to an agent that the insurer has authorized to receive payment is payment to the insurer. If the agent fails to remit the money to the insurer, the insurer can sue the agent to collect it, but as far as the policyowner is concerned, the premium has been paid.

If the agent was not actually authorized to collect the premium but promptly remits it to the insurer, no problem arises. However, if an agent without express authority collects the premium but fails to remit it, a question might arise as to whether the agent had apparent authority. If the policyowner can establish the agent's apparent authority to collect premiums, the legal effect is that the insurer was paid when the agent received the payment.

The policyowner's payment to her own agent is not payment to the insurer where the agent fails to remit the payment to the insurer. Payment to a broker will be payment to the insurer if the broker is the insurer's agent for collection of premiums. If the broker is the policyowner's agent to remit premiums, payment to the broker is not payment to the insurer. The actions of the parties usually will govern whether the broker is the agent of the policyowner or of the insurer when collecting premiums.

Premium Notices

A life insurer ordinarily has no legal duty to send a notice that premium payment is due unless a statute or a policy provision requires such notice. Nevertheless, insurers routinely send premium notices because premium notices are an effective means of keeping life insurance contracts in force.

If an insurer has consistently sent premium notices over an extended period of time, even though not required to do so, a majority of courts will estop the insurer

---

[30]Markel v. Travelers Ins. Co., 510 F.2d 1202 (10th Cir. 1975).

[31]Elizabeth T. Tsai, Annotation, *Person to Whom Renewal Premium May Be Paid or Tendered so as to Bind Insurer,* 42 A.L.R. 3d 751 (1972).

from lapsing the policy if it discontinues the practice without warning and the premium is not paid when due. For example, suppose that an insurer has sent a policyowner premium notices 30 days before the premium was due each year for 10 years. If the insurer fails to send a premium notice in the eleventh year and the insured dies 10 days after the expiration of the grace period, a court most likely would estop the insurer from lapsing the policy. The insurer then would have to pay the death benefit. However, if the insurer had informed the policyowner beforehand of its intention to stop sending premium notices, the court would not estop the insurer from lapsing the policy.

The insurer also has a duty to send a premium notice if the policyowner cannot know the amount due without one. For example, where dividends are to be applied to reduce the premium, the insurer knows the amount of the dividends but the policyowner does not. The insurer must send the policyowner a premium notice stating the amount remaining to be paid on the premium after dividends are applied, or the insurer cannot lapse the policy for nonpayment of the premium when due.

Some states have statutes requiring that the insurer send a premium notice to the policyowner. These states limit the right of an insurer to lapse the policy for nonpayment of the premium if the insurer has not sent the notice.[32] The New York statute reads in part as follows:

> **Notice of premium due under life . . . insurance policy;** . . . No policy of life insurance . . . delivered or issued for delivery in this state . . . shall terminate or lapse by reason of default in payment of any premium . . . in less than one year after such default, unless a notice shall have been duly mailed at least fifteen and not more than forty-five days prior to the day when such payment becomes due.[33]

Excuses for Nonpayment of the Premium

There is almost no excuse for nonpayment of a premium relating to circumstances involving only the policyowner. Thus, courts generally hold that the policyowner's illness, accident, poverty, illiteracy, incapacity, or disappearance do not excuse his failure to pay the premium. Nearly all of the valid excuses relate to some agreement or act of the insurer, or to conditions of war that made timely payment impossible.

This is a sound proposition of law, because payment of the premium is a condition precedent to the insurer's duty to perform its promises. Nonpayment of the premium is therefore a defense that the insurer has for its nonperformance. Nevertheless, many circumstances arise in which the insurer has made some agreement or done some act that results in the insurer's inability to declare the policy lapsed for nonpayment of the premium.

Agreement by the Insurer

In certain situations the insurer might agree not to lapse the policy for nonpayment of the premium. For example, if the insurer has agreed to apply the net cash value to pay the premium, it cannot declare the policy lapsed if the policy has a sufficient net cash value to pay the premium then due. Or, if the policy contains a waiver-of-premium clause or rider, the insurer cannot declare the policy lapsed for nonpayment

---

[32]*E.g.,* 215 Ill. Comp. Stat. 5/234 (Michie 1993).
[33]N.Y. Ins. Law § 3211 (McKinney 1985 & Supp. 1996).

of the premium if the insured is disabled and hence has a right to have the premium payment waived.

Insurers often expressly waive timely payment. An offer to extend the time for the payment of an overdue premium is an express waiver of timely payment. Such an offer, called a *late remittance offer,* appears in the Appendix, Figure 12. Note that the waiver of timely payment offer is made on strict conditions: the insured must be alive, the offer is for a limited period, and the protection is not in force from the end of the grace period until the overdue premium is paid.

Implied Waiver of Timely Payment

If the insurer has repeatedly accepted late payment, a court will usually hold that the insurer has waived timely payment by implication. For example, in *Gleed v. Lincoln National Life Insurance Co.,*[34] the insurer had habitually accepted premiums beyond the grace period. The insured died while the premium was in default. The insurer was estopped to declare a forfeiture of the policy. The court said:

> On the issue of waiver and estoppel the evidence is that for a period of six years all premiums had been paid by Mrs. Boggs to Hansen [the insurer's agent], either in cash or by her personal check, and that no one of these payments was exchanged for the company's receipt signed by the president or secretary as required in the policy. It is also in evidence that each and all of these payments were made in this manner while the insured was in default, and in many cases after the period of grace had expired. During this period of six years, eighteen separate premiums became due. Fourteen of these were accepted by appellant [the insurer] after the period of grace had expired. In only one instance—September, 1940—the appellant demanded and received an application for reinstatement.

* * * * *

> [W]e conclude that the course of conduct in relation to the payments of premiums running over a period of six years was such that the respondents [the beneficiaries] were entitled to assume that the terms of the policy need not be adhered to strictly, and that the appellant was estopped from insisting upon a strict compliance with those terms until it had given the respondents reasonable notice of its change in policy.

The insurer can protect itself from such implied waivers by expressly providing in a notice of default, such as that in the Appendix, Figure 12, that a late premium will be effective only if paid during the lifetime of the insured. This is illustrated by *Hutchinson v. Equitable Life Assurance Society of the United States,*[35] in which the court stated the following:

> The plaintiff [the beneficiary] contends that Florida applies a blend of waiver and estoppel to an insurer who follows a course of dealing with the payment of premiums so as to induce the insured to believe that a delay in his premium payment will not give rise to a forfeiture. Plaintiff then concludes that this principle applies to the instant case.
>
> The fallacy of plaintiff's argument is that the default notices expressly stated that there would be no reinstatement if the insured died prior to receipt of the defaulted premium; thus there was no course of conduct by the insurer which in any way could have led the insured to believe that a default payment would be accepted after his death or that the policy had not lapsed. Accordingly there can be no waiver or estoppel.

---

[34]150 P.2d 484 (Cal. Ct. App. 1944).
[35]335 F.2d 592 (5th Cir.1964).

Insurer's Refusal of Tender

A tender of payment that the insurer refused to accept is generally an excuse for nonpayment. ***Tender*** here means an unconditional and timely offer to pay the full sum due in a medium of payment (cash, check, and so forth) acceptable to the insurer. If the insurer refuses a tender, it cannot declare the policy forfeited because of nonpayment of premium. A tender preserves the policyowner's rights as much as payment.[36] For example, in *Harms v. John Hancock Mutual Life Insurance Co.*[37] the beneficiary tendered the premium payment to the insurer's collecting agent two days before the grace period expired. The collecting agent refused the money, saying he would collect it 20 days later. The insured died 13 days after the grace period had expired. The death benefits were payable, because the tender acted to prevent the policy from lapsing. The court discussed the case as follows:

> The insurance in this case was solicited by an agent of the defendant insurer named Balistreiri who collected the first two premiums and called at plaintiff's house on June 20, 1945 to collect the last quarterly premium. This was two days before the expiration of the grace period. Defendant's agent informed Mrs. Hatch that he had come to collect her son's insurance. She told him that the son was sick and would not have a paycheck until July 5th and that she would have to pay the premium herself although she wished that the youngster would pay for his own insurance. She extracted three ten dollar bills from her pocketbook and told the agent that he might as well take it. The agent declined and said that he would hold the matter open until the 10th of July so that the boy would have a chance to pay it. As he left plaintiff said, "Well, Mr. Balistreiri, it's right here," and the agent said, "It's all right, Mrs. Hatch. I will hold it open until the 10th of July."
>
> The jury found that plaintiff Josephine Hatch offered to pay and that the agent put off the matter as above indicated.
>
> It is contended by appellant [the insurer] that the agent having no authority to issue policies could not grant an extension of time for the payment of a premium. This contention misses the point and the case is governed adversely to appellant by *Baumann v. Metropolitan Life Ins. Co.,* 144 Wis. 206, 128 N.W. 864. The point is that the amount of the premium was offered to a collecting agent of the company who declined to take the money and under those circumstances it must be held that plaintiff was "deterred from making such payment by conduct or statements on the part of such agent which induced in her an honest belief that a failure to then make the payment or tender would not then be relied upon by the company to work a failure or forfeiture of the policy."

Even though a tender acts as payment to prevent lapse of the policy, the insurer will still be entitled to recover the amount of the premium. If the insured has died the insurer will have a right to deduct this amount plus interest from the death benefit.

An insurer's wrongful cancellation of a policy is tantamount to a declaration that it will refuse a tender of premium. Such an act by the insurer will excuse the tender itself.[38] For example, *Western & Southern Life Insurance Co. v. Giltnane*[39] involved a weekly premium policy with a four-week grace period. The policyowner-insured had regularly paid the premiums on the policy until she applied for additional insurance

---

[36]Beatty v. Mutual Reserve Fund Life Ass'n, 75 F. 65 (C.C.A.Cal. 1896), *aff'd,* 93 F. 747 (C.C.A.Cal. 1899); Kincaid v. New York Life Ins. Co., 66 F.2d 268 (5th Cir. 1933).

[37]34 N.W.2d 687 (Wis. 1948).

[38]P.M. Dwyer, Annotation, *Wrongful Termination of Policy by Insurer, or False Information to Insured in That Regard, as Excusing Further Tender and Payment of Premiums or Assessments,* 122 A.L.R. 385 (1939), *supp. by* K.A. Drechler, Annotation, 160 A.L.R. 629 (1946).

[39]163 S.W. 192 (Ky. 1914).

and was found at that time to be an uninsurable risk. The insurer then wrongfully canceled the original policy and refused to receive any more premiums. Seven months later, the insured died. The court held that the benefits were payable, saying:

> When the insurance company notified the insured that it would not receive from her any further premiums, this dispensed with the necessity of making a tender of the premiums thereafter. It would be a rather curious rule, to say the least of it, that would allow an insurance company to defeat the payment of a policy upon the ground that the premiums had not been regularly paid, when it declined to receive them, insisting that it had canceled the policy.

Failure of the Insurer's Agent to Collect the Premium

If the insurer has designated an agent to collect the premium, the failure of the agent to do so might excuse the nonpayment. For example, in *Standard Life Insurance Co. v. Grigsby,*[40] the insurer had instructed the beneficiary to pay the collecting agent at the agent's office. The beneficiary did this until the November premium was due. In November, and again in December, the beneficiary tried repeatedly to locate the collecting agent so as to pay the premium on time. When the beneficiary did locate the agent, the agent told her that the insurer had canceled the policy for failure to pay the premium due in November. The beneficiary then tendered the November and December premiums, but the insurer refused these payments. The insured died a few months later. The court held that the insurer had wrongfully canceled the policy and that the nonpayment was excused. The benefits were therefore payable.

Failure to Send a Premium Notice

As pointed out above, the insurer's failure to send a premium notice might serve as an excuse for nonpayment of the premium. Although the general rule is that the insurer has no duty to send such a notice, a statute or the insurance contract sometimes imposes such a duty. In addition, the insurer has a duty to send a premium notice if the policyowner has no other way to know how much to pay. Finally, a court will ordinarily estop an insurer from lapsing the policy if the insurer has consistently sent premium notices, then discontinues the practice without warning, and the premium is not paid when due.

Failure of the Post Office to Deliver a Premium

If the insurer regularly accepts premiums by mail, and the policyowner mails a premium in what ordinarily would be sufficient time to reach the insurer before the end of the grace period, the insurer cannot lapse the policy because the mail was delayed and the premium arrived late.[41] Even if the premium is lost in the mail, the courts will not allow the insurer to lapse the policy if the policyowner or

---

[40]140 N.E. 457 (Ind. Ct. App. 1923).

[41]Mutual Reserve Fund Life Ass'n v. Tuchfeld, 159 F. 833 (C.C.A. Tenn. 1908); Travelers Ins. Co. v. Brown, 35 So. 463 (Ala. 1903); Minnick v. State Farm Mut. Auto Ins. Co., 174 A.2d 706 (Del. Super. Ct. 1961); Hartford Life & Annuity Ins. Co. v. Eastman, 74 N.W. 394 (Neb. 1898); Kenyon v. Knights Templar & M. Mut. Aid Ass'n, 25 N.E. 299 (N.Y. 1890); Coile v. Order of United Commercial Travelers of Am., 76 S.E. 622 (N.C. 1912).

beneficiary can establish that the premium was mailed on time.[42] This will not be true, however, if the insurer has not sanctioned use of the mail to transmit premiums.[43]

Failure to Pay Premiums Due to War

When communications between the policyowner and the insurer are cut off because their respective countries are at war, payment of the premium is, of course, impossible. The legal effect of nonpayment of premiums during war has been decided differently in different states. After the Civil War, the courts of some states held that war merely suspends the contract. After the war, back premiums can be paid and the contract revived. The courts of other states held that the contract terminates according to its terms if premiums are not paid, regardless of the reason for nonpayment.

The U.S. Supreme Court in *New York Life Insurance Co. v. Statham*[44] held that the contract terminates but that the policyowner is entitled to the equitable value of the policy arising from the premiums already paid. The equitable value as defined in *Statham* is approximately the reserve value. The Court in Statham construed federal common law, which was abolished after the *Erie Railroad Co. v. Tompkins*[45] decision. *Statham,* therefore, does not have the weight at the present time that it had prior to the *Erie* decision.

After World War I, the Treaty of Versailles provided that if the war prevented the payment of premiums, contracts that had lapsed could be surrendered for cash as of the date of lapse or restored within three months following the date of the treaty on payment of arrearages of premiums, plus interest. Of the numerous treaties signed at the close of World War II, none repeated the provisions of the Treaty of Versailles. Generally speaking, after World War II, American insurers took the position that, because many of their contracts contained automatic nonforfeiture provisions, an equitable course of action was simply to carry out the contracts according to their terms.

Return of Premiums

Ordinarily, if an insurer has assumed the risk, it has a right to keep the whole premium paid. However, exceptions to this general rule exist and will be discussed in this section.

Another general rule is that, if the insurer has not assumed the risk, it has not earned and must return the premium. Exceptions to this rule will also be discussed in this section.

---

[42]G.J.C., Annotation, *Delay of Remittance in Mail as Affecting Forfeiture or Loss of Rights Through Nonpayment,* 1 A.L.R. 677 (1919).

[43]Rice v. Grand Lodge of A.O.U.W., 72 N.W. 770 (Iowa 1897); Beeman v. Supreme Lodge, Shield of Honor, 64 A. 792 (Pa. 1906).

[44]93 U.S. 24 (1876).

[45]304 U.S. 64 (1933), *cert. denied* 305 U.S. 637 (1938). This case is discussed in Chapter 1, "Insurance and the Law."

Risk Assumed

There are several exceptions to the general rule that when the insurer has assumed the risk, it can keep the premium. For example, in the absence of a statute to the contrary, ordinarily a minor-policyowner who disaffirms the insurance contract is entitled to a return of the premiums she paid. However, in some jurisdictions the insurer will have a right to deduct the cost of the coverage that the minor received.

The insurer must return premiums that are paid under a mistake of fact. For example, if the premium payor believes the insured to be alive when the insured is actually dead, the insurer must return premiums paid after the insured's death. This sometimes happens in cases in which the insured has disappeared.

The insurer must return premiums paid in advance if the insured dies before the insurer has earned the premiums. For example, suppose a grandmother were to purchase a life insurance policy on the life of her one-year-old grandchild and were to pay 20 annual premiums in advance at the time she bought the policy. If the child died at age 16, the insurer must return the four unearned annual premiums according to the terms of the premium receipt.

Often the policy itself contains provisions that require return of premiums under certain circumstances. The illustrative policy in the Appendix, Figure 2, contains several such provisions. One of these is in the free look clause. This clause states that the policyowner has a right to return the policy at any time within a specified number of days after receiving it and that "any premium paid will be refunded to the owner."

Another policy clause providing for return of premiums is the suicide clause. This clause provides that, if the insured dies by suicide within the suicide period, the insurer's "liability will be limited to the amount of the premiums paid, less any indebtedness."

If the insurer wishes to rescind the contract for misrepresentation in the application, ordinarily the insurer must return the premiums paid. Failure to promptly tender back the premiums to the policyowner after discovery of the misrepresentation could jeopardize the insurer's right to rescind the policy.

Some persons have a right to have the amount of the premium payments they have made refunded to them out of the proceeds. For example, if a named revocable beneficiary who has been promised the proceeds pays the premiums, and later the policyowner names someone else beneficiary, the courts frequently award the original beneficiary the amount he paid. A collateral assignee can also recover from the policy proceeds the amount of the premiums she has paid.

Risk Not Assumed

If the insurer has not assumed the risk, it ordinarily must return the premium. For example, if an insurer receives an application and the initial premium but finds the applicant uninsurable, it must return the premium when it rejects the application. The insurer has not assumed the risk and has no right to the premium. The same is true if the insurer issues a policy that differs from that applied for and the applicant rejects the policy as issued. Again, the insurer has not assumed the risk and must return the initial premium.

According to the majority of courts, the insurer must return premiums paid on policies that are void *ab initio,* that is, void from the beginning, because of a lack of insurable interest, unless there was fraud by the applicant. The insurer must also return the premium, according to the majority of courts, if the policy is void *ab initio* because it was issued without the insured's knowledge or consent. For example, in *Magers v. Western & Southern Life Insurance Co.,*[46] the applicant took out policies on the lives of her two brothers, who did not know about the policies. The policies were void from the beginning because the brothers did not consent to them. The court allowed the applicant to recover the premiums she paid.

Dividends

It is unfortunate that the term *dividends* is used for both stockholders' dividends and policyowners' dividends, because this usage can result in confusion. Corporations pay **stockholders' dividends** to the owners of corporate stock. Such dividends are usually paid out of the corporation's accumulated earnings by resolution of the corporation's board of directors. Insurers pay **policyowners' dividends** to the owners of participating insurance policies. Whenever the term *dividends* is used in this book, it will refer to policyowners' dividends, unless otherwise indicated.

Usually, mutual insurers issue participating policies, whereas stock insurers issue nonparticipating policies.[47] However, this is not always true. Some mutual insurers issue both participating and nonparticipating policies. Some stock insurers issue participating policies or both participating and nonparticipating policies.

Nonparticipating policies are issued at a fixed premium. The policyowner has no right to a refund of part of the premium. The premium of a nonparticipating policy must be calculated with great care, because the insurer has no margin of safety.

Participating policies are issued at a premium high enough to cover all likely future experience. The insurer expects to be able to operate on a smaller premium. The difference is a margin of safety. The insurer refunds any excess premium if the experience of that class of policy warrants such a refund. This refund is the dividend. The dividend is a premium abatement. The policyowner does not pay income tax on this dividend because it is not income. The policyowner is simply receiving back part of the premium he paid.[48] By contrast, stockholders' dividends are taxable income to the stockholder receiving them.

Right to Dividends

The insurer does not have to pay a dividend unless it has sufficient earned surplus. Moreover, the insurer has a right to keep surplus for contingencies, as it deems necessary, as long as it acts in good faith.[49]

The insurer must treat policyowners equitably in distributing dividends. The insurer can divide policies into classes based on the type of policy or other criteria, but it must treat policyowners in any one class alike.

---

[46]344 S.W.2d 312 (Mo. Ct. App. 1961).

[47]Both mutual and stock insurers are corporations. The difference between them lies in their ownership. Mutual insurers are owned by their policyowners, who are both owners and customers, whereas stock insurers are owned by their shareholders.

[48]Interest on dividends is taxed as income to the policyowner, however. 26 C.F.R. § 1.61–7(d) (1996).

[49]Royal Highlanders v. Wiseman, 299 N.W. 459 (Neb. 1941).

The policyowner can assign dividends to another person. In addition, creditors of the policyowner can seize the dividends unless a state statute exempts them from seizure.

The right to elect the way in which the insurer will apply dividends is one of the valuable rights that a policyowner has under a participating life insurance policy. Carrying out the policyowner's wishes as to dividends is an important responsibility of the insurer.

Dividend Options

Most states have statutes regulating the distribution of dividends. Typically, such statutes specify the rights of the owners of participating policies to participate in the insurer's surplus, and the methods of surplus distribution. For example, the Illinois statute,[50] requires that a participating policy include "[a] provision that the policy shall participate annually in the surplus of the company beginning not later than the end of the third policy year. . . . " This statute also provides that

> the insured under any annual dividend policy shall have the right each year to have the dividend arising from such participation either paid in cash, or applied in reduction of premiums, or applied to the purchase of paid-up additional insurance, or be left to accumulate to the credit of the policy, with interest at such rate as may be determined from time to time by the company.

As in Illinois, the statutes in many other states require annual participation in the earned surplus of the insurer. Some states, notably Illinois and New York, specify the optional methods that a policy must provide for the application of dividends. However, this does not prevent the insurer from offering additional options.

Most participating life insurance contracts provide four dividend options. The policyowner can elect to have the dividend applied in one of the following ways:

1. Paid to the policyowner in cash.
2. Applied to reduce premium.
3. Applied to purchase paid-up additions to the policy.
4. Accumulated with interest.

One-Year Term Insurance Dividend Option.   Many insurers provide a special option in some policies that permits the policyowner to use the dividend to purchase term insurance for one year. This is often called the fifth dividend option. This option permits the policyowner to have the dividend (or part of it) used to purchase one-year term insurance that will be payable in addition to the face amount of the policy. This insurance is, of course, payable only if the insured dies during the one-year term. However, the policyowner can buy new term insurance with each year's dividends.

The amount of additional insurance permitted under this option is sometimes limited to the amount of the cash surrender value of the policy. Excess dividends not needed to purchase this amount of term insurance will be applied under another option. If the one-year term insurance dividend option is elected, the policyowner usually can take out a maximum policy loan and the beneficiary will still receive the full face amount of the policy. Typically, the one-year term insurance that the

---

[50]215 Ill. Comp. Stat. 5/224 (1)(e) (Michie 1996).

policyowner can purchase under this option will replace a maximum policy loan until the insured is quite old.

Other Dividend Privileges.   It is fairly standard practice to include a policy provision permitting the application of accumulated dividends to pay up the policy or to mature it as an endowment if the policyowner wishes.

Automatic Dividend Option

State laws regulating dividends often provide that, if the insurer offers dividend options, the insurer shall specify which option will take effect if the insured does not elect an option. A review of the participating policies of various insurers indicates that most insurers choose the paid-up additions option as the automatic dividend option.

A few states specify which option shall take effect automatically if the policyowner makes no election. Unfortunately, these states do not all specify the same option. For example, one state provides that dividends shall be paid in cash;[51] others require that the paid-up additions option be put into effect.[52] Some insurers deal with these differing state requirements by providing in their policies that, if the policyowner does not elect an option, the insurer will apply the dividend either to purchase a paid-up addition or as the laws of the state in which the policy is delivered may require.

---

[51]IND. CODE ANN. § 27–1–12–5(a)(6) (West 1993).

[52]N.Y. INS. LAW § 4231(b)(4) (McKinney 1985); OHIO REV. CODE ANN. § 3915.05(F) (Anderson 1989).

Summary

The initial premium, along with the application, is the consideration that puts the life insurance contract in force. Nevertheless, if the insured dies soon after the policy was delivered and the beneficiary has possession of the policy, even though the initial premium was not paid a court might hold that the policy was in force. In such a case, if the insurer unconditionally delivered a policy containing a clause acknowledging receipt of the premium, the majority view is that the policy is in force. If the policy does not contain such a clause, the majority view is that a rebuttable presumption arises that the policy is in force.

Courts usually consider payment of a renewal premium to be a condition precedent to continued coverage under an insurance policy. However, the policyowner does not owe the insurer the renewal premium. Failure to pay a renewal premium will simply cause the policy to lapse. A renewal premium must be paid before the end of the grace period or the policy will lapse unless the insurer waives timely payment expressly or by implication. If the policy specifies a date for payment of the renewal premium, as is nearly always the case, usually that date will govern. Renewal premium due dates of backdated policies ordinarily run from the policy date.

The insurer has a right to be paid in cash but can accept checks, promissory notes, or other methods of payment. Payment by personal check is, by implication, conditioned on the check's being honored. Acceptance of a promissory note, on the other hand, constitutes premium payment regardless of whether or not the promisor pays the promissory note, unless, as is usually the case, there is an express condition that the note must be paid when due. Renewal premiums also can be paid by automatic premium loans or by accumulated policyowner dividends.

Persons other than the policyowner often pay the renewal premiums. Sometimes, the policyowner's bank or employer pays premiums out of the policyowner's funds. The beneficiary sometimes pays renewal premiums out of the beneficiary's own funds. In such a case, the policyowner will still be able to change a revocable beneficiary designation, but the beneficiary is sometimes entitled to recover the premiums he paid. A collateral assignee usually has no duty to pay the premiums, but if the assignee does pay, she can recover the premiums paid.

The insurer's home office or authorized agent can receive the premium. If an agent without express authority collects the premium but fails to remit it to the insurer, the insurer will be bound if the agent had apparent authority to collect the premium.

The insurer has no duty to send notices of premium due unless there is a statute or policy provision to the contrary. However, if an insurer has sent premium notices, it cannot stop the practice without warning and lapse the policy of a policyowner who was relying on receiving the notice.

There is almost no valid excuse for nonpayment of the premium that is not based on some act or omission of the insurer. However, often the insurer has made an agreement or done something that will excuse nonpayment. The insurer's waiver of payment or of timely payment, refusal of tender, wrongful cancellation of the policy, or failure to collect the premium ordinarily excuses nonpay-

ment. If the insurer has sanctioned use of the mail for remitting premiums, and the policyowner mails the premium in what ordinarily would be sufficient time to reach the insurer, the insurer cannot lapse the policy because the premium was delayed or lost in the mail.

The policyowner usually will not have a right to return of premiums once the insurer has assumed the risk. However, exceptions occur if a minor-policyowner disaffirms a policy, premiums were paid under a mistake of fact or in advance, or if the policy provides for a return of premiums under certain circumstances, such as the return of the policy during the free look period or suicide of the insured during the suicide exclusion period.

Policyowner dividends, paid to the owners of participating insurance policies, are a refund of excess premium. The policyowner owns the dividends and has a right to elect the way in which the insurer will pay dividends. The usual options are cash payment, premium reduction, purchase of paid-up additions, or accumulation with interest. Some insurers permit the purchase of one-year term insurance with the dividends.

ILLUSTRATIVE CASE

In this case, the court held that the insurer had conditioned payment of a premium by check on the bank's honoring the check when the insurer properly presented it for payment.

TRUDY C. NOBLE, Administratrix
v.
JOHN HANCOCK MUTUAL LIFE INSURANCE COMPANY[53]
Appeals Court of Massachusetts, Middlesex

Before HALE, C.J., and GRANT and ARMSTRONG, JJ.
HALE, Chief Justice.

This is an appeal by the plaintiff from a judgment of the Superior Court which dismissed her claim for the proceeds of a life insurance policy. The judge made findings of fact which we summarize below.

The plaintiff was the named beneficiary of a life insurance policy issued by the defendant to Nelson Noble, the plaintiff's husband. The policy provided for payment of $26,000 to the beneficiary if the insured should die while the policy was in full force. Quarterly premiums of $209.66 were due on (or within a thirty-one day grace period following) the twenty-third of March, June, September and December of each year, and had been paid through December 23, 1969. A notice of the premium

due on March 23, 1970, was mailed to Nelson Noble at his home address. The defendant did not receive a payment of that premium by March 23 or within the grace period. On May 15, at which time Noble was confined to a hospital, Richard Klein, the defendant's district manager, had a telephone conversation with the plaintiff in which he explained to her that the premium on her husband's life insurance policy was overdue. He advised her to send him a check to cover the premium and she did so on May 17.

On or about May 28, while Nelson Noble was still hospitalized, the plaintiff received a notice from the defendant indicating that the next quarterly payment of $209.66 was due on June 23. The plaintiff became confused, thinking that the premium referred to in this notice was the one she had paid. She called the defendant's office and tried to contact Klein. She was informed that Klein was not in the office. She then talked with "one of

[53]386 N.E.2d 735 (Mass. App. Ct. 1979).

the girls in the office'' (whose identity and position are not apparent in the record) and explained the problem. The woman advised the plaintiff to stop payment on the original check and to send a new check and the premium notice that she had received. On May 28 the plaintiff stopped payment on the original check. Neither the plaintiff nor Nelson Noble (who had been released from the hospital around June 20) made a subsequent payment on the policy. Nelson Noble died on July 22, 1970.

1. The plaintiff argues that the defendant's receipt of the check mailed in accordance with Klein's instructions constituted an unconditional acceptance of the check as payment of the premium. We disagree. Absent an agreement to the contrary, a waiver or an estoppel, the receipt of a check constitutes only an acceptance conditional upon the check's being honored when properly presented. Merely giving the insurer possession of the check is not a payment of the premium. The payment would have become absolute if the check had been honored by the drawee on presentation, but the plaintiff prevented this occurrence by her stop payment order. Therefore, at the time of Nelson Noble's death, the March 23 premium payment was unpaid, the policy, by its terms, had lapsed, and the plaintiff was not entitled to any proceeds.

2. The plaintiff contends that she should nonetheless prevail because the defendant is estopped from asserting the lapse of the policy prior to the death of Nelson Noble because her failure to pay the premium due on March 23 resulted from her reliance on the suggestion of the defendant's agent that she stop payment on her original check.

"The basis of an estoppel is a representation . . . intended to induce a course of action on the part of the person to whom the representation is made, and where, as a consequence, there is detriment to the person relying on the representation and taking the action." *Capozzi's Case,* 4 Mass. App. 342, 347, 347 N.E.2d 685, 689 (1976), quoting *De Sisto's Case,* 351 Mass. 348, 351-352, 220 N.E.2d 923 (1966). The plaintiff's claim of an estoppel fails because the actions she took did not amount to reasonable reliance on the instructions of the defendant's agent. The woman in the defendant's office recommended a stop of the first check only in conjunction with the tender of another check. The record shows that plaintiff stopped payment on her original check as suggested but disregarded the essential second step of the instruction by failing to send another check. This selective compliance with the advice of the defendant cannot be said to be sufficient reliance to form the basis of an estoppel.

Judgment affirmed.

Questions for Review

1. Contrast the legal significance of the initial premium with that of the renewal premiums for a life insurance policy.

2. According to the majority of courts, is the payment of a renewal premium a condition precedent to continued coverage, or is nonpayment a condition subsequent cutting off the rights of the policyowner?

3. What alternatives does an insurer have when it learns that the bank has dishonored a premium check? What are the possible legal effects if the insurer attempts to collect on the dishonored check?

4. Suppose that an insurer has unconditionally accepted a promissory note in payment of a premium and that the policyowner fails to pay the note when due. What remedy does the insurer have? Do insurers usually accept promissory notes unconditionally? Why or why not?

5. Briefly summarize the preauthorized check plan for paying life insurance premiums. What are the principal arguments for and against the preauthorized check plan?

6. What are the principal advantages of the automatic premium loan? What are the disadvantages?

7. Under what circumstances is a life insurance company required to send premium notices?

8. Discuss briefly the insurer's duty with respect to the application of dividend accumulations when a premium remains unpaid at the end of the grace period.

9. Describe three situations in which the policyowner will be excused for nonpayment of a premium.

10. List four dividend options.

13   POLICY LOANS AND NONFORFEITURE BENEFITS

Chapter Outline

The level premium, legal reserve system of life insurance results in cash values that policyowners can use to obtain policy loans and nonforfeiture benefits. The legal aspects of policy loans and nonforfeiture benefits are described in this chapter.

Cash Values

If a life insurance policy has a cash value, the insurer will provide policy loans and nonforfeiture benefits. Whole life and endowment[1] insurance policies have cash values, whereas most term insurance policies do not. Under most term insurance policies, the policyowner merely pays for pure life insurance for a limited period of time.

The earliest life insurance policies were term policies. Life insurance for extended periods or for the whole of life did not become practical until development of the level premium, legal reserve system. Under this system, the insurer charges the same amount of premium each year during an extended period, often the insured's lifetime. The premium in the early years exceeds the amount needed for the policy's share of current-year claims. These excess funds become a part of the insurer's invested assets. The insurer establishes reserve liabilities equivalent to the excess funds to provide for the time in later years when the level premium is less than the policy's share of the current-year claims.

This system results in a policy cash value that the policyowner can receive if he chooses to take out a cash policy loan. The policyowner can also use the cash value to pay the premium. If the policyowner chooses to surrender the policy, he can receive the cash surrender value. The cash surrender value is the ***net cash value***—that is, the cash value minus any unpaid policy loans and unpaid loan interest, plus any dividends, any interest on dividends, and the net value of any paid-up additions (other than paid-up term insurance additions).[2] If the policyowner allows the policy to lapse but does not choose to surrender the policy, he can use the cash surrender value to purchase extended term insurance or paid-up reduced insurance.

Policy Loans

The owner of a life insurance policy with cash values can obtain money using the policy as security. This can be done in two ways. First, the policyowner can pledge the policy to a bank or other lending institution as security for a loan. Alternatively, the policyowner can receive an advance of the net cash value from the insurer under the loan provision of the policy.

Insurers provided the first policy loans voluntarily. No laws at that time required policy loans. The automatic premium loan, or a practice similar to it, was in use as early as 1845[3] and was well established by the 1890s. Thus, the earliest policy loans were provided to keep policies in force. This, of course, benefited policyowners, beneficiaries, and insurers. Later, insurers expanded the policy loan privilege to permit policyowners to receive cash from the insurer.

---

[1]Endowment insurance is a form of life insurance in which the face amount is payable to the policyowner at the end of a specified period, or to the beneficiary if the insured dies before that; for example, an endowment payable at the insured's age 65.

[2]*Paid-up additions* means additional life insurance purchased with policy dividends.

[3]Daniel J. Reidy, *The Policy Loan Provision,* in THE LIFE INSURANCE POLICY CONTRACT 189 (Harry Krueger & Leland T. Waggoner eds. 1953).

Policy Loans Contrasted with True Loans

The term *policy loan* is a misnomer. A policy loan is not truly a loan. A true **loan** is the transfer of money by one person, the creditor, to another person, the debtor, on agreement that the debtor will return to the creditor an equivalent sum at a later date, usually plus interest. A policy loan differs from a true loan in that the policyowner does not agree to repay the money that the insurer transferred to her. Rather, a **policy loan** is an advance of money that the insurer eventually must pay out under the policy. Thus, a policy loan does not create a creditor-debtor relationship between the insurer and the policyowner.

In one of the leading court decisions involving policy loans, Justice Oliver Wendell Holmes said:

> The so-called liability of the policyholder never exists as a personal liability, it is never a debt, but is merely a deduction in account from the sum the plaintiffs [the insurer] ultimately must pay.[4]

The illustrative policy in the Appendix, Figure 2, states that "This Policy is the sole security for any loan." Because the insurer has the right to deduct any unpaid policy loan and unpaid loan interest from the cash value to arrive at the cash surrender value, the insurer is 100 percent secured against loss if the policyowner does not repay the loan and surrenders the policy or allows it to lapse. Moreover, because the insurer can deduct the loan value and interest from the death benefit after the insured's death, the insurer is also 100 percent secured if the policyowner has not repaid the loan and interest at the time of the insured's death. For these reasons, insurers do not require repayment of the loan or interest. The foregoing is consistent with the view that a policy loan is not truly a loan, but rather an advance of money that the insurer ultimately must pay.

Although the term *policy loan* is a misnomer, it is commonly used in the life insurance industry. The term is therefore used in this book.

Premium Loans and Cash Loans

There are two types of policy loans: premium loans and cash loans. **Premium loans** are advances of policy cash values that the insurer makes to the policyowner for the purpose of paying the premium. Automatic premium loans are advances that the insurer makes under a policy clause providing that, if the policyowner fails to pay a premium by the end of the grace period, the insurer will automatically advance the amount of the premium if the policy has a sufficient net cash value. The illustrative policy in the Appendix, Figure 2, provides the following:

> **Automatic Premium Loan**
> This provision will be in effect only if you have requested it in the application or in a written request at a time when no premium is unpaid beyond its grace period. You may cancel the effect of this provision in the same manner.
> If this provision is in effect, any premium which remains unpaid at the end of a grace period will be paid by automatic loan. We may change the frequency of premium payment so that the interval between premium due dates is three, six, or twelve months after the first premium has been paid by automatic loan. If the loan value of this Policy is not sufficient to pay the premium due, the Nonforfeiture Benefit Options will apply.
> Any automatic loan will be subject to the Policy Loan provisions.

---

[4]Board of Assessors v. New York Life Ins. Co., 216 U.S. 517 (1910).

Automatic premium loan provisions usually are not required by law. However, most insurers include such a provision in their policies because it helps to prevent lapse of the policy.

Cash loans, or request loans as they are sometimes called, are advances of cash that the insurer makes to the policyowner for her to use for whatever purpose she wishes. Usually, when people speak of a policy loan they mean a cash loan. Nevertheless, premium loans are also policy loans. Premium loans and cash loans are advanced from the same cash values, have the same interest rates, and are both made on the sole security of the policy. Note that the illustrative policy quoted above states that an automatic premium loan "will be subject to the Policy Loan provisions." A policy provision permitting a policy loan under cash value policies is required in well over one-half of the states. Therefore, most cash value policies contain a policy loan provision.

Amount of the Policy Loan

The illustrative policy in the Appendix, Figure 2, provides the following:

> You may obtain a loan from us whenever this Policy has a loan value. The loan value is the amount which, with interest at the loan interest rate stated [in the policy] computed to the next premium due date, or to the next Policy anniversary if no further premiums are payable, will equal the cash surrender value [the net cash value] on such date or anniversary. Any premium due and unpaid at the time the loan is made will be deducted from the loan proceeds.

Thus, the amount that the policyowner can obtain from the insurer as a policy loan changes over time. For example, at the end of policy year three, the illustrative policy has a cash or loan value of $1,626.00. At the end of year five, this value is $3,888.00.

Interest on Policy Loans

The policyowner who takes out a policy loan does not promise to repay either the principal or the interest on the loan. The illustrative policy provides the following:

> We will charge daily interest on policy loans at the rate stated [in the policy]. Interest is payable on each policy anniversary. Any interest not paid when due is added to the loan.

However, if the interest accumulates so that the total of principal and interest is greater than the cash surrender value, the policy will expire. The illustrative policy contains the following clause:

> Whenever the indebtedness on this Policy is more than the Policy's guaranteed cash surrender value, this Policy terminates. We will mail a notice to your last known address, and to that of any assignee whose interest we have recorded, at least 31 days before such termination.

In other words, interest is payable, but the policyowner does not have to pay it. If the total of the unpaid loan and accrued interest exceeds the cash surrender value at any time, the policy simply expires.

The insurer must charge interest on a policy loan. The most important reason for this is that the insurer bases policy values on the assumption that it will be able to invest at a projected rate of interest the portion of the premiums not used for expenses and to pay claims. If the cash value were advanced to the policyowner interest free, the intricate structure of the level premium would be adversely affected.

Nevertheless, the interest rate for a policy loan is not ordinarily the same as the rate assumed in calculating the policy values. Usually, the policy loan interest rate is higher, because the insurer wishes to discourage policy loans and because processing policy loans, many of which are for small amounts, is expensive.

All states have laws specifically regulating life insurance policy loan interest rates. Before 1981, the most common allowable maximum interest rate was 8 percent. Then, in the early 1980s, the great majority of states enacted a variable policy loan interest rate statute based on the NAIC Model Policy Loan Interest Rate Bill.

This rush to allow variable policy loan interest rates resulted from the high interest rates that policyowners could obtain on other investments in the early 1980s. Many policyowners took out policy loans at the rate established in their policies (as low as 4 percent in older policies) and invested the money in money market funds, certificates of deposit, and other investments yielding up to several times as much as the interest on the policy loans. This created a serious cash outflow problem for insurers and drained insurance policy values.

Variable policy loan interest rate statutes will help to prevent similar problems in the future, although they do not affect the policy loan interest rate provided by a policy already in force when the relevant statute was enacted. Policies issued after the effective dates of these statutes can include a provision that the policy loan interest rate will fluctuate with an indicator of other interest rates. Laws patterned on the NAIC Model Policy Loan Interest Rate Bill mandate the use of Moody's Monthly Corporate Bond Yield Average.[5] The model bill further provides that "The maximum rate for each policy must be determined at regular intervals at least once every 12 months, but not more frequently than once in any three-month period."[6]

A variable policy loan interest rate benefits policyowners, beneficiaries, and insurers. Policyowners benefit because insurers can set the policy loan interest rate close to the interest rate that the insurer can earn on its new investments. The insurer does not have to set the policy loan interest rate higher to protect itself from fluctuations in the interest rates in the general economy. Beneficiaries benefit from variable policy loan interest rates because variable rates discourage policyowners from draining their policies of value, which frequently results in policy lapse or a lower death benefit. Insurers benefit because the variable rate protects them from sudden large cash outflows resulting from demands for policy loans in times when interest rates on new investments are higher than policy loan interest rates.

Endorsement

The life insurance policy is the sole security for a policy loan. At one time, many insurers required that the policyowner deliver the policy to the insurer for endorsement of the loan agreement on it. Such endorsement is for the benefit of the insurer; therefore, the insurer can waive the endorsement. Today, most insurers do not require endorsement, because endorsing the policy each time the insurer grants a loan is expensive and inconvenient. However, some insurers reserve the right to require endorsement at the insurer's option.

---

[5]MODEL POLICY LOAN INTEREST RATE BILL § 2A (Nat'l Ass'n Ins. Comm'rs 1981).
[6]*Id.,* § 3D.

Deferment

The illustrative policy in the Appendix, Figure 2, provides that the insurer can postpone, or defer, a policy loan for up to six months. This provision reads as follows:

> We have the right to postpone your loan for up to six months unless the loan is to be used to pay premiums on any policies you have with us.

Three-fourths of the states require that a life insurer include in its cash value policies a clause reserving the right to defer a policy loan; several other states specifically permit the insurer to include such a clause. The policy loan deferment provision is intended to protect life insurers in case unusual economic conditions cause large numbers of policyowners to seek policy loans. Such a situation could jeopardize the insurers' financial stability.

Ordinarily, the insurer does not utilize the policy loan deferment provision. Insurers usually process policy loans immediately. Even in times when policyowners are seeking policy loans in large numbers, such as in the early 1980s, insurers have resisted deferring loans.

Note that the deferment provision does not apply to premium loans. Insurers do not defer premium loans even for payment of premiums on other policies that the insurer has issued. The reason for this is that a premium loan does not require the insurer to pay out cash.

Extended Term and Reduced Paid-Up Policies

If a policy loan is outstanding at the time that the policyowner exercises one of the nonforfeiture benefit options, the loan and any unpaid interest will be deducted in computing the available cash surrender value. The illustrative policy provides the following:

> The term "cash surrender value" as used in this Policy means the cash value shown in the Table of Guaranteed Values . . . , less any existing indebtedness. . . .
>
> You may apply the cash surrender value to purchase a fully paid whole life policy for a reduced amount of insurance. . . .
>
> The amount of. . . . [extended] term insurance will be the Sum Insured less any indebtedness. . . . The term period will begin on the due date of the first unpaid premium and will be such as the cash surrender value will provide as a single net premium at the insured's then attained age.

Note that the insurer deducts the amount of the unpaid policy loan, plus unpaid loan interest, twice in the case of extended term insurance. First, the insurer deducts it from the table of guaranteed values to arrive at the cash surrender value. Next, the insurer deducts it from the face amount of the policy to arrive at the amount of extended term insurance available. This procedure is discussed below in the section entitled "Nonforfeiture Benefits."

If the policyowner uses the cash surrender value to purchase extended term insurance, the policy loan provision will not apply to the extended term insurance. The illustrative policy prohibits such loans as follows: "You cannot obtain a loan if this Policy is in force as Extended Term Insurance." Some policies, such as the illustrative policy, provide no cash values for extended term insurance. As to policies that do provide a cash value for extended term insurance, this cash value steadily decreases, and eventually no cash value would remain to be security for a loan.

If the policy is in force under the reduced paid-up insurance option, the policyowner can obtain a loan of the policy's net cash value. However, according to the majority of courts, if the accumulating interest causes the amount of the loan plus the interest to exceed the policy's cash value, and the policyowner does not repay the loan or interest, the policy will expire and no death benefit will be payable.[7]

The Beneficiary's Rights

A revocable beneficiary has a mere expectancy, rather than rights, under a life insurance policy. An insurer therefore does not require a revocable beneficiary's consent to a policy loan. Nor is the consent of an irrevocable beneficiary needed if the policy clearly states that the policyowner has a right to obtain a policy loan without such consent. If the policy does not so state, the policyowner must obtain an irrevocable beneficiary's consent.

According to the majority of courts, a beneficiary has no right to recover from a policyowner-insured's estate the amount of a policy loan that the insurer deducts from the proceeds.[8] The beneficiary is entitled only to the net proceeds, because that is the intention of the parties to the contract. The illustrative policy states that "[a]ny indebtedness will be deducted from any proceeds paid under this Policy."

Repayment of Policy Loans

A policyowner ordinarily can repay a policy loan or interest before the insured's death if the policyowner so desires. The illustrative policy in the Appendix, Figure 2, states the following:

> If this Policy is in force and not on Extended Term Insurance, your loan can be repaid in full or in part at any time before the Insured's death. However, any loan repayment must be at least $20 unless the balance due is less than $20, in which case the loan repayment must be for the full amount of the loan.

Note that the policy says that the policyowner can repay the loan, not that she must repay it. Moreover, in two situations, the policyowner ordinarily cannot repay the loan: where the insured has died or where the extended term insurance nonforfeiture benefit is in effect. However, some insurers do permit repayment after the insured's death so that the insurer can distribute the total proceeds under a settlement agreement according to the policyowner's plan.

If the policyowner does not repay the loan, the insurer will obtain payment from one of two sources of money: the policy's cash value or the death benefit.

Nonforfeiture Benefits

Nonforfeiture laws require that insurers include nonforfeiture benefits in their cash value life insurance policies. Nonforfeiture laws and nonforfeiture benefits are discussed in this section.

---

[7]Jones v. Mutual Life Ins. Co., 113 So. 314 (Ala. 1927).

[8]E. LeFevre, Annotation, *Right of Beneficiary as against Estate of Insured Who Borrowed on the Policy,* 31 A.L.R. 2d 979 (1953).

Nonforfeiture Laws

In 1943, the National Association of Insurance Commissioners adopted the Standard Nonforfeiture Law for Life Insurance. The NAIC has amended this model law a number of times since its adoption. Nearly all states have statutes based on the current version of this model law. In addition, the NAIC has adopted two model nonforfeiture regulations. One is the NAIC Model Rule (Regulation) Permitting Smoker/Nonsmoker Mortality Tables for Use in Determining Minimum Reserve Liabilities and Nonforfeiture Benefits. The other is the NAIC Procedure for Permitting Same Minimum Nonforfeiture Standards for Men and Women Insured under 1980 CSO and 1980 CET Mortality Tables. As their titles indicate, state regulations based on the first of these model regulations govern nonforfeiture values provided by policies with separate premium rates for smokers and nonsmokers, and statutes based on the second of these model regulations govern policies with the same nonforfeiture values for men and women. Nearly three-fourths of the states have adopted each of these model regulations.

Statutes patterned on the Standard Nonforfeiture Law for Life Insurance require that, in the case of surrender of a whole life or endowment insurance contract that has been in effect for a minimum period specified in the law, usually three years, the insurer must provide a cash surrender value. In addition, if the policy lapses the insurer must offer either extended term insurance in the net face amount or paid-up insurance in a reduced amount, or a choice between them. Either the extended term insurance nonforfeiture benefit or the reduced paid-up insurance nonforfeiture benefit must become operative automatically if the policy lapses and the policyowner does not elect a nonforfeiture benefit. Extended term insurance is the automatic nonforfeiture benefit that most policies provide. The insurer must include in the policy a table of nonforfeiture benefits and a statement of the methods used in calculating the benefits. Examples of these appear on pages 523 and 529.

Insurers compute the nonforfeiture benefits in a policy using a method prescribed by law. The computation is based on current mortality tables, a rate of interest permitted by law, and an initial expense allowance. The nonforfeiture benefits in an older policy may be based on mortality tables that are now outmoded. Other laws governing the computation of nonforfeiture benefits may also have changed since the insurer issued the policy. However, the policy is lawful as written because new laws ordinarily cannot require changes in contracts already in effect.

The Cash Surrender Benefit

One of the nonforfeiture benefits that life insurance policies with cash values provide is the ***cash surrender benefit.*** This benefit gives the policyowner the option of surrendering the policy to the insurer in return for the policy's cash surrender value. The ***cash surrender value*** is the amount of cash available to the policyowner on surrender of the policy before the policy matures. This value is determined by statute and by the terms of the policy. The illustrative policy in the Appendix, Figure 2, defines the cash surrender value as follows:

> The term "cash surrender value" as used in this Policy means the cash value shown in the Table of Guaranteed Values . . . , less any existing indebtedness. . . . The table assumes that premiums have been paid to the end of the policy year indicated and that there is no indebtedness. We will determine the cash value at any time within a policy year, with allowance for the time elapsed in such year and for the period premiums have been paid.

The policy defines the term *indebtedness* to mean "unpaid policy loans and unpaid loan interest."

The Table of Guaranteed Values has been calculated for $100,000 of whole life insurance on a 34-year-old male insured, rated standard. The cash values for the first five years are as follows:

End of Policy Year	Cash or Loan Value
1	$ 0.00
2	541.00
3	1,626.00
4	2,742.00
5	3,888.00

The illustrative policy states that these values have been calculated on the basis of the 1980 Commissioners Standard Ordinary Mortality Table. The policy further states that the cash values equal or exceed those the laws of the state governing the policy require and that the insurer has filed a detailed statement of method of computation with the state insurance department.

The illustrative policy is a nonparticipating policy. Thus, its cash surrender value is the cash value on the surrender date, less any unpaid policy loans and unpaid loan interest. In the case of a participating policy, the cash surrender value is the cash value on the surrender date, plus any dividends, interest on dividends, and the net value of any paid-up additions credited to the policy, less any unpaid policy loans and unpaid loan interest. With both nonparticipating and participating policies, the cash surrender value is the net cash value.

The illustrative policy requires that the policyowner surrender the policy to the insurer if the policyowner wishes to receive the cash surrender value. According to most courts, the policyowner must comply with this policy requirement to be entitled to receive the cash surrender value from the insurer.[9]

As with the payment of cash loans, the insurer ordinarily has the right to defer payment of the cash surrender value for up to six months from the date the policyowner surrenders the policy. Laws in nearly all of the states require a policy provision conferring this right.[10] This right to defer payment of the cash surrender value is intended to protect the insurer from a drain on its cash and other current assets should severe adverse economic conditions cause large numbers of policyowners to surrender their policies.

The Extended Term Insurance Benefit

The **extended term insurance benefit** provides insurance in the face amount of the policy, less any unpaid policy loan and policy loan interest, extended for such period as the cash surrender value will purchase.

The illustrative policy in the Appendix, Figure 2, provides the following:

---

[9]*E.g.,* Interstate Life & Acci. Co. v. Jackson, 30 S.E.2d 208 (Ga. Ct. App. 1944); Board of Trustees of Unitarian Church v. Nationwide Life Ins. Co., 211 A.2d 204 (N.J. Super. Ct. App. Div. 1965).

[10]*E.g.,* 215 Ill. Comp. Stat. 5/229.2 (Michie 1993).

Extended Term Insurance. If the Premium Class shown [in the policy] is "Standard," you may continue the Policy as paid-up term insurance. The amount of such term insurance will be the Sum Insured less any indebtedness. The term period will begin on the due date of the first unpaid premium and will be such as the cash surrender value will provide as a net single premium at the Insured's then attained age. At the end of the term period all insurance under this Policy will terminate.

Most policies include a chart showing the period for which the insurer will extend the insurance for each of the first 20 years. Such a chart appears in the illustrative policy in the Appendix, Figure 2. (However, these periods would change if there were an outstanding policy loan.) On request, the insurer will compute the period for other years.

A legal question that sometimes arises concerns the date on which the extended term insurance begins. The courts ordinarily hold that this date is the due date of the premium in default, not some later date such as the end of the grace period.[11] This date is sometimes expressed in the policy. The illustrative policy states that "The term period will begin on the due date of the first unpaid premium."

Another legal question that occasionally arises with extended term insurance concerns the deduction of any unpaid policy loan and unpaid loan interest from both the cash value and the face amount of the policy to determine the amount of extended term insurance and the length of time it will be in effect. This common practice of insurers is sometimes misunderstood by persons unfamiliar with insurance, who feel that it unfairly penalizes the policyowner. Actually, the procedure is fair, and the courts generally support it for two reasons.[12] First, the insurer must deduct the unpaid policy loan and unpaid loan interest from the cash value because the loan amount has already been advanced to the policyowner. Second, deduction of the unpaid loan and interest amount from the face value of the policy to determine the amount of extended term insurance is balanced by the longer term for which the insurer provides the lower amount of insurance. Moreover, deduction of the unpaid loan and interest amount from the face value is justified because otherwise the policyowner who lapses his policy with an outstanding loan against it would have a larger amount of insurance than he would have if he continued to pay the premiums.

For example, suppose a policyowner with a $50,000 policy takes out a $5,000 policy loan. Only $45,000 would be payable at the insured's death, as long as the loan remained unpaid and the policy remained on a premium-paying basis (ignoring loan interest for purposes of this example). If the policyowner allowed the policy to lapse and chose the extended term insurance nonforfeiture benefit, the insurer will deduct the $5,000 loan from the $50,000 face amount of the policy to determine the amount of extended term insurance that would be payable. If the insurer did not do this, the beneficiary would be entitled to $50,000 after the policy lapsed, whereas she would have been entitled to only $45,000 while the policy was still on a premium-paying basis. However, if the cash surrender value is used to purchase $45,000 of extended term insurance, rather than $50,000 of extended term insurance, the extended term insurance will be in effect for a longer period of time.

[11]Coons v. Home Life Ins. Co., 13 N.E.2d 482 (Ill. 1938); Life & Cas. Ins. Co. v. Wheeler, 96 S.W.2d 753 (Ky. 1936); Dressel v. Mutual Ben. Life Ins. Co., 154 S.W.2d 360 (Mo. Ct. App. 1941); Hutchinson v. National Life Ins. Co., 195 S.W. 66 (Mo. Ct. App. 1917).

[12]Williams v. Union Central Life Ins. Co., 291 U.S. 170 (1934); Miner v. Standard Life and Acci. Ins. Co., 451 F.2d 1273 (10th Cir. 1971); Mayers v. Massachusetts Mut. Life Ins. Co., 11 F. Supp. 80 (E.D.N.Y. 1935), *aff'd*, 77 F.2d 1007 (2d Cir. 1935), *cert. denied* 296 U.S. 594 (1935).

The Reduced Paid-Up Insurance Benefit

Reduced paid-up insurance is ordinarily available as one of the nonforfeiture options. The *reduced paid-up insurance benefit* provides paid-up insurance of the kind and for the duration that the policy provided immediately prior to lapse, in whatever amount the cash surrender value will purchase. That is, if the original policy was a whole life policy, the reduced paid-up policy will be a whole life policy. If the original policy was an endowment at age 65, the reduced paid-up policy will be an endowment at age 65, and so forth.

The illustrative policy in the Appendix, Figure 2, is a whole life policy. It provides the following reduced paid-up insurance nonforfeiture option:

> Paid-Up Insurance. You may apply the cash surrender value to purchase a fully paid whole life policy for a reduced amount of insurance. The amount of such insurance will be that amount which the cash surrender value will buy when applied as a net single premium at the Insured's then attained age as of the due date of the first unpaid premium. Reduced Paid-Up Insurance has cash and loan values.

The Automatic Nonforfeiture Benefit

If the policyowner fails to elect a nonforfeiture option, the policy must by law provide an automatic nonforfeiture benefit.[13] The illustrative policy in the Appendix, Figure 2, provides the following:

> You may elect a Nonforfeiture Benefit Option within 60 days of the due date of the first unpaid premium. Your written election should be sent to us at our Home Office. If no election is made during this period, we will
>
> 1. If the Premium Class . . . is other than "Rated," automatically continue this Policy as Extended Term Insurance . . . or
> 2. If the Premium Class . . . is "Rated," automatically continue this Policy as Paid-Up Insurance.

This is a typical automatic nonforfeiture benefit provision. Note that a standard policy provides extended term insurance. A rated, or substandard, policy provides reduced paid-up insurance.

Incomplete Nonforfeiture Benefit Transactions

If the insured dies before a nonforfeiture benefit transaction is complete, a question that can arise is whether the nonforfeiture benefit or the death benefit is payable.[14] These two sums can be significantly different, and they might be payable to different persons. Therefore, a court action sometimes ensues where there is doubt concerning the completion of the nonforfeiture benefit transaction. Most of the cases in this area involve the cash surrender benefit option, although in some cases, the policyowner was attempting to exercise the extended term insurance benefit option or the reduced paid-up insurance benefit option.

---

[13]*E.g.,* 215 Ill. Comp. Stat. 5/229.2 (Michie 1993); Tex. Ins. Code Ann. art. 3.44a § 2(3) (Vernon 1981).

[14]J. F. Ghent, Annotation, *Insured's Exercise of Election under Life Insurance Policy as Affected by His Death before Complete Consumation of Option,* 15 A.L.R. 3d 1317 (1967).

The general rule in these cases is that the right to exercise a nonforfeiture benefit option is a continuing, irrevocable offer from the insurer to the policyowner.[15] When the policyowner accepts the insurer's offer according to its terms (exercises the option), the acceptance is binding on both parties, even if the insured dies before the insurer has completed its part of the transaction.[16] Thus, if a policyowner notified the insurer of her decision to take the cash surrender value and surrendered the policy, but the insured died before the insurer paid the cash surrender value, the majority of courts would hold that the insurer did not owe the death benefit to the beneficiary. Rather, the insurer would pay the cash surrender value to the policyowner, or to the policyowner's estate if the policyowner was also the insured.

In one case, the court described a nonforfeiture benefit option as an offer that the policyowner (who was also the insured) bought and paid for as follows:

> The privilege to exercise the option of surrendering the policies for their cash value was one bought and paid for by the insured; such option is an offer contained in the policy contract and is from the company to the insured and it is his right to accept the offer, within a specified time, and his acceptance completes the contract; the company has no right to accept or reject; its obligation to pay is absolute.[17]

As with other offers, a policyowner must accept a nonforfeiture benefit option according to its terms. Thus, the policyowner must comply with the requirements for acceptance of a nonforfeiture benefit option as set forth in the policy.

For example, in one case,[18] a policyowner had a right to apply for the cash surrender value within one month of default in payment of the premium. This nonforfeiture benefit option required surrender of the policy. The premium due date was July 31. The policyowner did not pay the premium. On August 4 and again on September 1, the policyowner requested the cash surrender value. However, he did not surrender the policy, so he did not accept the cash surrender benefit option according to its terms. The policyowner had therefore made a counteroffer to the insurer. The insurer did not accept the counteroffer. The insured died on September 2. The insurer was therefore liable for the face amount of the policy under the automatic nonforfeiture benefit, which provided for extended term insurance.

Additional Benefits

Life insurance policies frequently provide additional benefits, such as an accidental death benefit, disability benefits, or guaranteed insurability benefits. These benefits are not always available after the policy lapses and is continued as extended term or reduced paid-up insurance. A clause in the policy that excludes additional benefits after such a nonforfeiture benefit takes effect is valid. For example, the accidental death benefit rider shown in the Appendix, Figure 5, states that "This Rider shall terminate upon . . . [t]he date the Policy is continued under a nonforfeiture benefit option."

If no policy provision expressly excludes additional benefits after continuation of the policy as extended term or reduced paid-up insurance, the courts look to other

---

[15]Pacific States Life Ins. Co. v. Bryce, 67 F.2d 710 (10th Cir. 1933); Green v. American Nat'l Ins. Co., 452 S.W.2d 1 (Tex. Civ. App. 1970).

[16]Lipman v. Equitable Life Assur. Soc'y, 58 F.2d 15 (4th Cir. 1932).

[17]Pack v. Progressive Life Ins. Co., 187 S.W.2d 501 (Mo. Ct. App. 1945).

[18]Conservative Life Ins. Co. v. Bollinger, 200 N.E. 149 (Ohio Ct. App. 1935).

policy language to determine the intent of the parties. In some cases, courts have held the additional benefits payable, and in others, not payable.

The Beneficiary's Rights

Ordinarily, the policyowner has the right to exercise the nonforfeiture benefit options, including a surrender of the policy for its cash surrender value, without the consent of a revocable beneficiary. An irrevocable beneficiary's consent usually will be necessary if the policyowner wishes to surrender the policy for its cash surrender value unless the policy specifically states otherwise.[19] Life insurance policies ordinarily do not require an irrevocable beneficiary's consent to the exercise of the extended term or reduced paid-up insurance nonforfeiture benefit options. However, an irrevocable beneficiary has the right to remain beneficiary of the extended term or reduced paid-up insurance.[20]

---

[19]Morse v. Commissioner, 100 F.2d 593 (7th Cir. 1938).
[20]O'Brien v. New England Mut. Life Ins. Co., 17 A.2d 555 (N.J. Sup. Ct. 1941).

Summary

Under the level premium, legal reserve system, a cash value builds up in whole life and endowment insurance policies. If the policyowner wishes to receive the cash value, or a part of it, but wishes to keep the policy in force, the insurer will advance the cash value to the policyowner. Such an advance is called a cash loan or request loan. The policyowner can also have the insurer apply the cash value to reduce or pay a premium. This is called a premium loan. Cash loans and premium loans are the two types of policy loans.

The term *policy loan* is a misnomer. A policy loan is actually an advance of money that the insurer eventually must pay out under the policy. A policy loan does not create a debtor-creditor relationship between the policyowner and the insurer, because the policyowner does not have to repay the loan or loan interest. However, the policyowner can repay the loan and interest before the insured's death if she desires, unless the extended term insurance nonforfeiture benefit is in effect.

The insurer must charge interest on a loan because it bases policy values on the assumption that it can invest unused premiums. Most states now allow variable policy loan interest rates to protect policyowners, beneficiaries, and insurers from the results of fluctuating interest rates in the general economy. The insurer can defer making a cash loan to a policyowner for up to six months. If the loan and interest accumulate so that together they are greater than the cash surrender value, the policy will expire.

Rather than taking out a policy loan, the policyowner can, if he wishes, surrender the policy and receive the cash surrender value (the net cash value). As with the cash loan, the insurer has the right to defer payment for up to six months, although insurers rarely exercise this right.

If the policy lapses, the policyowner can use the cash surrender value to purchase extended term insurance or reduced paid-up insurance. Under the extended term insurance option, the insurer extends insurance for the face amount of the policy, minus any unpaid policy loans and unpaid interest, for the period that the cash surrender value will provide. This period ordinarily begins on the due date of the premium in default, not at the end of the grace period. The insurer deducts any unpaid policy loan and interest from both the cash value and the face amount in computing the amount and duration of the extended term insurance. The reduced paid-up insurance option provides paid-up insurance of the kind and for the duration that the policy provided immediately prior to lapse, in whatever amount the cash surrender value will purchase.

An automatic nonforfeiture benefit provision is required by law. If the policy lapses and the policyowner fails to elect a nonforfeiture benefit, the automatic nonforfeiture benefit specified in the policy will apply. For policies rated standard, the typical automatic nonforfeiture option is extended term insurance.

Occasionally, an insured person dies after the policy-owner has attempted to exercise a nonforfeiture benefit option, but before the transaction is complete. In these cases, the majority of courts have held that the option is a continuing, irrevocable offer from the insurer to the policyowner that, if accepted according to its terms, results in a contract binding on both parties.

ILLUSTRATIVE CASE

> In the following case, the insured owned two policies on his life and had outstanding policy loans on both. The policy beneficiaries sued the insured's estate for reimbursement of the amounts of the loans. The insurer had deducted the outstanding policy loan amounts from the policy proceeds. The trial court ruled in favor of the beneficiaries. The state supreme court reversed the trial court's ruling.

In re SCHWARTZ' ESTATE[21]
Pennsylvania Supreme Court, Eastern District

ALLEN M. STEARNE, Justice.

The question involved is whether a "policy loan" upon a life insurance policy is a debt of such a nature as enables the designated beneficiary, upon the insured's death, to require the loan to be repaid from the insured's general estate, thus enabling the beneficiary to receive the full insurance proceeds. The court below ruled that it was such a debt and directed its repayment. This appeal followed.

George J. Schwartz, the decedent, was insured by two policies of life insurance, each in the amount of $5,000. In one policy decedent named two of his daughters beneficiaries, and in the other he designated his first wife. Neither policy reserved the right to change beneficiaries. But each policy *obligated* the company to make "loans" to the insured to the limit of its cash surrender value. "Loans" were granted in the aggregate amount of $3,466.80.

By his will the testator-insured directed his executors "to pay my funeral expenses and all my just debts as soon after my decease as may conveniently be done." It was upon the theory that the "policy loans" created a debtor-creditor relationship between the insured and insurer, that the learned court below decreed that the beneficiaries were entitled to reimbursement from the general estate in order that they should receive the full face amounts of the policies.

In support of its ruling the court below relied upon our decision in Wilson's Estate, 363 Pa. 546, 70 A. 2d 354, wherein we decided that in an assessment of transfer inheritance tax, credit must be allowed for an indebtedness of the decedent-insured where a loan was made to him *by a bank,* and his life insurance policy, payable to designated beneficiaries, was pledged as collateral security. We said, at page 551 of 363 Pa., at page 356 of 70 A. 2d: "Decedent (settlor) merely assigned the insurance policies *as collateral* for his loan. As with any other collateral, when a loan is repaid the collateral is returned to the owner. Had the creditor bank used decedent-settlor's insurance collateral to liquidate its loan, the designated insurance beneficiaries could have enforced their claim against the estate of the decedent under their right of *subrogation,*[22] to the same extent as if they had been the original creditor."

In the case now before us, contradistinguished from the facts in Wilson's Estate, *supra,* the "debt" was owed to the *insurance company* and not to a third person with the insurance policy assigned as collateral. This raises the narrow but important question whether any sound difference exists between the fundamental natures of these transactions. More accurately: does such an insurance "loan" from the insuring company *upon the policy itself* create a debtor-creditor relationship?

The learned court below, and counsel at argument stated that they have been unable to find any reported case in this jurisdiction which has decided this question. Our own research has disclosed none. But courts in at least six other jurisdictions have considered the problem. They unanimously agree that a "loan" granted pursuant to a policy right does not create a debtor-creditor

---

[21]87 A.2d 270 (1952).

[22]Subrogation is the right given to a creditor to be substituted for another and to succeed to the other's rights. In this situation, the court says, the beneficiaries had the right to be substituted for the original creditor, that is, the creditor bank, and thus be repaid out of the estate of the decedent.

relationship. The nature of such a "policy loan" has recently been discussed in Fidelity Union Trust Co. v. Phillips, 5 N.J. Super. 529, 68 A. 2d 574. It is said, at page 575 of 68 A. 2d: "A clear distinction is drawn between a loan made by an insurance company to an insured against a life policy, and a collateral loan made by a third party secured by an assignment or pledge of the policy on the life of the borrower. The former 'is not a loan in the strict technical sense, for there is no obligation of repayment on the insured, but rather an advancement on the cash value of the policy, the repayment of which will reinstate the depleted insurance without the issuance of a new policy and the submission of evidence of insurability. A "loan" by the insurer in such circumstances does not give rise to the relationship of debtor and creditor.' David v. Metropolitan Life Insurance Co., 135 N.J.L. 106, 50 A. 2d 651, 653 (Sup. Ct. 1947), affirmed 136 N.J.L. 195, 54 A. 2d 731 (E. & A., 1947). Mr. Justice Holmes declared in Board of Assessors v. New York Life Insurance Co., 216 U.S. 517, 30 S. Ct. 385, 386, 54 L. Ed. 597, 1910, 'This is called a loan. It is represented by what is called a note, which contains a promise to pay the money. But as the plaintiff (insurance company) never advances more than it already is absolutely bound for under the policy, it has no interest in creating a personal liability, and therefore the contract on the face of the note goes on to provide that if the note is not paid when due, it shall be extinguished automatically by the counter credit for what we have called the reserve value of the policy. In short, the claim of the policy holder on the one side and of the company on the other are brought into an account current by the very act that creates the latter. The so-called liability of the policyholder never exists as a personal liability, it never is a debt, but is merely a deduction in account from the sum that the plaintiffs ultimately must pay.' Therefore, when an insurance company advances to an insured a sum of money against his policy, and upon the death of the insured retains the amount required to satisfy the 'loan' or advance, the beneficiary named in the policy is not entitled to recover from the estate of the insured the amount by which the insurance had been depleted by borrowings by the insured upon the policy."

* * * * *

Substantially the same rule was adopted by this Court in Black's Estate, 341 Pa. 264, 19 A. 2d 130. The insurance policy there included a provision almost identical with that now under consideration, except that payment by insurer was more accurately termed an "advance" rather than a "loan." Decedent had bequeathed his business to his son subject to payment of all his personal and business debts. A dispute arose between the son and the widow, as residuary legatee, as to whether certain items were debts or obligations payable out of the business.

Concerning a cash advance to decedent from his insurance company, we said in 341 Pa. at page 270, 19 A. 2d at page 133: "The auditor and court below held that the advance was not such a debt as was required to be paid out of the business of decedent. With that conclusion we are in accord, for the association could not make any claim against the estate of decedent. It could not have proceeded against the decedent at the date of his death. Consequently there was no indebtedness, as clearly appears from a perusal of the agreement. The policy holder had the right to repay the advance made but he could not be compelled to do so."

While counsel for appellees point to factual distinctions between that case and the present one, such distinctions have no bearing on the legal principle here involved.

Legal digests and text writers appear to be equally unanimous. "Although a policy loan is termed a 'loan,' it differs from an ordinary commercial loan, and, in fact, is not a 'loan' in the ordinary sense of the word. It is merely a deduction from the sum insurer ultimately must pay, and is more accurately described as an advance": 44 C.J.S. Insurance, § 337, p. 1291. Accord: 29 Am. Jur. Insurance, § 463; Goldin on Insurance in Pennsylvania (2d ed.) page 631; 2 Couch on Insurance, § 335; Cooley's Briefs on Insurance (2d ed.) page 157.

Appellees argue that the insured's will and his testamentary scheme, considered in the light of his family circumstances, reveal that he intended his insurance beneficiaries to receive the full face amount of the policies. But the insured's *testamentary intent* is not the controlling consideration. We are obliged first to determine his *contractual* intent at the time he entered into the contracts of insurance wherein the rights of the insurance beneficiaries were created. We cannot interpret the meaning of contracts entered into on June 11, 1913, by speculating on testamentary intent adopted by insured in his testamentary scheme of April 2, 1949, nearly thirty-six years thereafter. The terms of the insurance contracts are clear and unambiguous; they give the insured an absolute right to demand at any time an advancement of any sum of money up to the reserve value of the policies. Under no discernible doctrine could it be held that the insured was incurring a *personal liability* by exercising this contract right. The insured could, of course, have directed by his will that the "policy loans" be paid out of his general assets so that the beneficiaries would receive the face amounts of the policies. As he chose not to do this we have no power to do it for him. We cannot construe a direction to pay "debts" as applicable to an advancement of money which did not create a personal liability. As an insurance policy loan does not create a debtor-creditor relationship, the beneficiaries of these policies so encumbered are entitled only to the *net* proceeds.

Decree reversed at appellees' cost.

Questions for Review

1. Explain what is meant by the statement "The term *policy loan* is a misnomer."
2. Describe the two types of policy loans that usually are available.
3. Most of the states now have variable policy loan interest rate laws. Describe the typical provisions of these laws.
4. Under what two situations will an insurer ordinarily prohibit the repayment of a policy loan?
5. Why do insurers charge interest on policy loans?
6. What is the purpose of the provision reserving to the insurer the right to defer granting a cash policy loan?
7. Summarize the statutory requirements concerning policy provisions for nonforfeiture benefits.
8. Outline briefly the limitations of the nonforfeiture benefits as compared to the benefits provided by a policy in force on a premium-paying basis.
9. Under the extended term insurance nonforfeiture benefit option:
   a. How does the insurer determine the amount of term insurance?
   b. How does the insurer determine the length of the term insurance period?
10. Under the reduced paid-up insurance nonforfeiture benefit option:
    a. What kind of insurance does the insurer provide?
    b. How does the insurer determine the amount of insurance?
11. Suppose that the policyowner surrendered the policy and requested the cash surrender value, but the insured died before the insurer could pay the requested amount. If the policyowner and the beneficiary both made claim for payment, what would you expect the court decision to be? Why?

14 ASSIGNMENTS AND OTHER TRANSFERS

Chapter Outline

One of the most important aspects of property ownership is the owner's legal power to transfer his rights in the property to another person. The owner ordinarily can transfer some or all of his rights, conditionally or unconditionally.

An *assignment* is a property owner's transfer of some or all of his ownership rights in the property to another person. A property owner who transfers his ownership rights is called an assignor; the person to whom ownership rights are transferred is called an assignee. The word *assignment* ordinarily refers to the transfer of choses in action, although it can denote the transfer of other ownership rights. *Assignment* also means a written document used to effect a transfer of rights in certain kinds of property, usually choses in action.

As a general rule, a policyowner will assign his rights in an insurance policy for one of three purposes: to make a gift of the policy, to sell the policy, or to pledge the policy as security for a loan. If the policyowner wishes to give the policy away or to sell it, he ordinarily will make an absolute assignment. If the policyowner wishes to pledge the policy as security for a loan, he ordinarily will make a collateral assignment.

A policyowner might also transfer ownership rights in a life insurance policy in some way other than an assignment, such as by intestate succession, by will, by property settlement or divorce decree, by a sale of assets, or by equitable assignment.

The purpose of this chapter is to describe the various types of assignments, the requirements for assignment, and the rights and duties of the assignor, assignee, beneficiary, and insurer. This chapter will also briefly explain the other ways to transfer rights in life insurance policies.

Absolute Assignments

An *absolute assignment* of a life insurance policy is the policyowner's irrevocable transfer of all of her rights in the policy. Ordinarily, a policyowner makes an absolute assignment in order to give the policy away or to sell it.

Gifts

If a policyowner absolutely assigns the policy to a person who exchanges nothing in return for it, the assignment is a gift. A *gift* is a voluntary transfer of property to another person, made without receiving consideration in return.

A gift requires contractual capacity on the part of the donor (the assignor in the case of a gift by assignment), voluntary intent to make a gift, delivery of the property to the donee (the assignee), and acceptance by the donee.[1] A valid gift is a transfer in the present. A mere promise to make a gift in the future is unenforceable.

Absolute assignments without consideration—that is, gifts—are usually made to family members. For example, a grandmother might purchase a life insurance policy on a grandchild's life and absolutely assign the policy to the grandchild when the grandchild reaches the age of majority. Or a person might absolutely assign a policy insuring her own life to another family member to avoid estate taxes.

---

[1]E. Le Fevre, Annotation, *Gift of Life Insurance Policy,* 33 A.L.R. 2d 273 (1954).

Sales

An absolute assignment made in return for consideration is a sale. Policyowners sometimes absolutely assign life insurance policies purchased for business purposes in return for consideration. For example, if a corporation owns a policy insuring the life of a key employee, the corporation might sell the policy to the key employee if she terminates employment. The corporation would absolutely assign the policy to the employee in return for consideration from her.

The Beneficiary's Rights on Absolute Assignment

As a general rule, an absolute assignment cannot destroy an irrevocable beneficiary's rights under an insurance policy without the beneficiary's consent. If the beneficiary designation is revocable, the courts have taken two views. According to one view, an absolute assignment destroys the interest of a revocable beneficiary.[2] The other view is that the absolute assignment, by itself, does not result in a change of beneficiary.[3] Of course, the assignee, as the new owner, can change the beneficiary if she desires. This appears to be the better view.

Collateral Assignments

At one time, borrowers customarily secured a loan by designating the lender as irrevocable beneficiary of the borrower's life insurance policy. This type of protection for lenders is uncommon today. Modern life insurance policies often include a significant cash value that can protect the lender during the insured's lifetime. A collateral assignment can give the assignee a right to the cash surrender value on default of the loan, as well a right to repayment of the loan and loan interest from the death benefit. Thus, lenders prefer the protection of a collateral assignment to the protection afforded by being named irrevocable beneficiary.

A *collateral assignment* is a policyowner's temporary transfer of some policy rights to a bank or other lender to provide security for a loan. The rights in the policy that the policyowner transfers are intended to revert to the policyowner when she has repaid the loan and loan interest.

The policyowner has the primary obligation to repay the loan and loan interest. The policy used as collateral is merely a secondary source of repayment if the policyowner defaults on the loan or dies while the loan is outstanding and the loan and loan interest are not repaid from funds in her estate. That is, the policyowner and the lender contemplate that the policyowner will repay a loan made to her and that she will not use the policy values for this purpose.

Collateral Assignment Forms

For many years, the form widely used for collateral assignments was the Assignment of Life Insurance as Collateral approved by the Bank Management Commission of the American Bankers Association. The American Bankers Association and the Association of Life Insurance Counsel jointly developed this form.

---

[2]Penn Mut. Life Ins. Co. v. Forbes, 200 Ill. App. 441 (1916).
[3]Continental Assur. Co. v. Conroy, 209 F.2d 539 (3d Cir. 1954); Rountree v. Frazee, 209 So.2d 424 (Ala. 1968).

The American Bankers Association no longer approves this collateral assignment form because variations in state laws make it unsuitable for use in some states. The American Bankers Association now recommends that lenders obtain the proper form from the insurance department of the state in which the policyowner will make the assignment.

Nevertheless, collateral assignment forms today incorporate many of the features of the original American Bankers Association form, and the original form is still in use in some states. A copy of the original form appears in the Appendix, Figure 13.

Under the American Bankers Association collateral assignment form, the policyowner transfers five rights to the lender. First, the policyowner transfers the sole right to collect the net proceeds of the policy at the death of the insured. However, the lender promises that it will pay to the beneficiary named by the policyholder the excess of the proceeds over the amount of remaining debt. Second, the policyowner transfers to the lender the sole right to surrender the policy and receive the cash surrender value. Third, the policyowner transfers the sole right to obtain a policy loan. The lender agrees not to exercise the right to surrender the policy or to take out a policy loan unless the policyowner defaults on the loan that the lender made, or fails to pay a premium and the lender has mailed notice of default to the policyowner. Fourth, the policyowner transfers to the lender the sole right to receive dividends. Finally, the policyowner transfers to the lender the sole right to exercise the nonforfeiture benefit options.

The policyowner keeps other rights. These include the right to collect disability benefits, to designate and change the beneficiary, and to elect an optional mode of settlement. The lender agrees, on request, to forward the policy to the insurer for endorsement of beneficiary changes or settlement agreements that the policyowner makes.

The lender under the American Bankers Association collateral assignment form is under no obligation to pay the premiums. However, if the lender does pay the premiums, it will add the amount of the premiums it paid to the debt that the policyowner owes.

The Beneficiary's Rights on Collateral Assignment

The American Bankers Association collateral assignment form has a blank for the signature of the beneficiary. The beneficiary's consent to the terms of the assignment prevents conflicts between the beneficiary and the lender over the death benefits. It also eliminates the need for the beneficiary's consent when the lender wishes to exercise prematurity rights.

If the beneficiary consents to the collateral assignment, he cannot later object to repayment of the loan and loan interest from the policy proceeds. For this reason, modern collateral assignment forms require the beneficiary's signature.

Unless the policy provides otherwise, if an irrevocable beneficiary does not consent to the assignment, her rights are usually superior to the collateral assignee's. Therefore, in this situation, the collateral assignee will not be able to recover the amount of the debt from the cash surrender value or from the death benefit. In other words, an irrevocable beneficiary has a vested interest in the policy that the collateral assignment cannot take away without her consent.

As to a revocable beneficiary who does not consent to a collateral assignment, ordinarily the assignee's rights to the policy proceeds are superior to the beneficiary's rights.[4] The court in one case stated the reasons for this rule as follows:

> From an every day, practical standpoint it is desirable to hold that an assignee of a policy containing a clause permitting a change of beneficiary and an assignment of the policy secures a right in the proceeds of the policy superior to the rights of the named beneficiary. If an assignee, in the absence of the consent of the beneficiary, does not obtain such right it will be practically impossible for an insured to borrow on a policy in time of need of financial aid in those cases where compliance with the form prescribed in the policy cannot be followed. No bank or individual would be likely to lend on the security of a policy where the right to enforce the reduction of the security to cash would only mature in case the insured outlived the beneficiary, and where the continued life of the policy depends upon the payment of the annual premium. As stated in the case of *Matter of Whiting, D.C.,* 3 F.2d 440, 441: "To hold that the beneficiary of such policy has a vested interest would be tantamount to destroying the 'changed beneficiary' provisions of the policy itself."[5]

If the assignment clearly indicates that the collateral assignee's interest in the policy is limited to the amount of the debt (that is, the amount unpaid on the loan, plus unpaid loan interest and any premiums that the assignee paid), the beneficiary will be entitled to receive any amount remaining after repayment of the debt to the collateral assignee from the death benefit. Even if the assignment does not indicate that the collateral assignee's interest is limited, the beneficiary ordinarily will receive the excess amount, particularly if the policyowner and assignee had no relationship other than debtor and creditor.

Absolute Assignments Intended to Secure Loans

Although policyowners use absolute assignments primarily for the gift or sale of a policy, they sometimes use an absolute assignment to secure a loan. In such an instance, if the policyowner, or the beneficiary after the insured's death, can prove that the purpose of the assignment was to serve as security for a loan and not as a permanent transfer of all rights to the assignee, the general rule is that the court will treat such an assignment as if it were a collateral assignment.

Illustrative of this rule is the case of *Albrent v. Spencer,*[6] which the Wisconsin Supreme Court decided in 1957. There, the policyowner made an absolute assignment of policies on his life as collateral security for the payment of a note on which approximately $140,000 was due. After the insured's death, the assignee collected the entire proceeds of the policies, satisfied the indebtedness, and retained the difference, allegedly amounting to approximately $90,000. The court summarized the question in the case as follows:

> We consider that the case presents the issue of whether it is against public policy for a creditor of the insured to avail himself of an absolute assignment of a previously pledged life insurance policy issued upon the life of the debtor, which assignment is intended to end the creditor-debtor relationship. . . .
>
> It offends one's sense of justice that a creditor should realize more out of the proceeds of the policy than the principal and interest due on the loan for which the policy was pledged plus any expenditure of the creditor for premiums necessary to protect his

---

[4]McAllen State Bank v. Texas Bank & Trust Co., 433 S.W.2d 167 (Tex. 1968).
[5]Davis v. Modern Industrial Bank, 18 N.E.2d 639 (N.Y. 1939).
[6]81 N.W.2d 555 (Wis. 1957).

security. To uphold the result reached below in the instant case would be to encourage creditors to bring pressure upon necessitous debtors to convert the rights of the creditor from that of the pledgee to that of owner in order that he might gamble upon the life of the insured in the hope of realizing the difference between the amount due on the loan and the face of the policy. In the instant case it is alleged that such difference amounted to the huge sum of approximately $90,000. . . .

[A]ny purported absolute assignment by a debtor to a creditor of a policy, which had previously been pledged as security to the creditor is only valid between the immediate parties to the extent of enabling the creditor to realize the cash surrender value of the policy. If the creditor after receiving such absolute assignment and the creditor-debtor relationship is terminated, continues to hold the policy for the purpose of gambling upon the life of the insured, he becomes a constructive trustee[7] for the benefit of the estate of the deceased of any proceeds received upon the death of the insured, to the extent that such proceeds exceed the amount that would have been due such assignee if the creditor-debtor relationship had not been extinguished.

The Insurer's Role in Assignments

The insurer has a crucial role in the assignment process. Insurers draft many policies with assignment clauses that govern the method by which the policyowner must make an assignment in order to bind the insurer, or that prohibit assignment altogether. Even if no clause appears in the policy, the policyowner or the assignee must notify the insurer of the assignment, or the insurer will not be liable if it does not act in accordance with the assignment. Moreover, the insurer is not responsible for inquiring into the validity of the assignment unless it has knowledge of circumstances that make that validity questionable.

On the other hand, the insurer has certain duties toward the assignee. First, if the insurer has notice of the assignment, the insurer must not disregard the assignment if it appears valid, unless the policy prohibits assignment. Second, the insurer is bound by law in some states to give the assignee notice of a premium due.

Absolute Assignment Clauses

Some insurers provide an *ownership clause* that the policyowner must comply with if the insurer is to be bound by the absolute assignment of the policy. The illustrative policy in the Appendix, Figure 2, has such a clause. It reads in part as follows:

> You may name a new owner or contingent owner at any time while the Insured is living by filing a written request with us. Your written request will not be effective until it is recorded in our Home Office. Once recorded, the change will be effective as of the date you signed the request whether or not you or the Insured is alive when we record the change. However, the change will be subject to any payments made or other action taken by us before your request was recorded in our Home Office.

Other insurers require the use of an absolute assignment form that the policyowner must complete and return to the insurer. Still others require endorsement on the policy itself to effect an absolute assignment of the policy.

---

[7]A constructive trustee is the trustee of a trust that a court creates because the trustee holds legal title to property by wrongful means.

Collateral Assignment Clauses

Many life insurance policies contain a collateral assignment clause. The following clause from the illustrative policy in the Appendix, Figure 2, is an example:

> You may assign this Policy as collateral for a loan without the consent of any revocable beneficiary. We are not bound by any assignment unless it is in writing and recorded at our Home Office. We are not responsible for the validity of any assignment. The rights of an assignee will at all times be subject to any indebtedness to us at the time the assignment is recorded by us, and, if applicable, to loans granted at anytime by us under the automatic premium loan provision of the Policy.

Note that this clause makes five important points. First, the consent of a revocable beneficiary is not necessary for a collateral assignment.

Second, the insurer requires notice of the assignment and states its intention that the assignment will not be binding on it in the absence of such notice.

Third, the insurer states its intention not to be responsible for the validity of a collateral assignment. This part of the absolute assignment clause is discussed in the subsection below entitled "Clauses Regarding Validity of the Assignment."

Fourth, the insurer makes clear that an assignee's rights are subject to any unpaid policy loans and unpaid policy loan interest. In other words, the insurer can deduct the amount of such loans and interest from the cash value or death benefit before paying the assignee.

Fifth, the insurer establishes its right to make automatic premium loans at any time, because it has a contractual duty to do this if the automatic premium loan provision is in effect.

Clauses Prohibiting Assignment

Life insurance policies providing a small amount of insurance, such as home service policies, sometimes contain clauses that prohibit assignment of the policy. If there is no statute or regulation that prevents the insurer from prohibiting such assignments, the clause is enforceable. The result in such a case will be that the insurer will have no duty to pay the assignee if the policyowner makes an assignment.

Clauses Requiring Consent of the Insurer

If the life insurance policy requires the consent of the insurer to an assignment, the insurer must give its consent or the assignee will have no rights against the insurer.[8] If the policy does not expressly require the insurer's consent, such consent is not necessary. The illustrative policy in the Appendix, Figure 2, does not require the insurer's consent to an assignment, but many life insurance policies do require such consent.

Clauses Requiring Notice to the Insurer

Policies often require that the policyowner or assignee give notice of an assignment to the insurer. As noted above, the illustrative policy in the Appendix, Figure 2, requires that the policyowner send the insurer a written request that will effect an

---

[8]Thomas v. Metropolitan Life Ins. Co., 87 S.E. 303 (Ga. 1915); Resnek v. Mutual Life Ins. Co., 190 N.E. 603 (Mass. 1934); Hutsell v. Citizens' Nat'l Bank, 64 S.W. 2d 188 (Tenn. 1933).

absolute assignment when the insurer records it. The policy further provides that a collateral assignment will not bind the insurer unless the assignment is in writing and recorded at the insurer's home office.

Such a notice requirement is for the protection of the insurer. The insurer can therefore waive the notice requirement, as a general rule. The insurer could, for example, waive a requirement of written notice and accept oral notice instead.

If the insurer has notice of an assignment, it should not pay out policy proceeds without regard to the rights of the assignee.[9] If the insurer does so, a court might compel it to pay again to the assignee.

If no policy provision requires notice to the insurer of an assignment, the policyowner can assign the policy without such notice. However, the assignee would be wise to inform the insurer of the assignee's rights in the policy. An insurer is not liable to an assignee if it pays the death benefit to a named beneficiary in ignorance of the assignee's rights.[10]

Clauses Regarding Validity of the Assignment

The assignment provision in most life insurance policies expressly states that the insurer assumes no responsibility for the validity of the assignment of the policy. The validity of an assignment is governed by factors over which the insurer has no control and of which it often has no knowledge. Some of these factors are the mental competence of the assignor, the law of the state in which the policyowner makes the assignment, and compliance with any formal requirements for assignment, such as delivery of a written assignment or of the policy.

The court that decided *New York Life Insurance Co. v. Federal National Bank of Shawnee, Oklahoma*[11] stated the law regarding the insurer's responsibility for the validity of assignments. In that case, the policyowner-insured and the beneficiary joined in an assignment of the life insurance policy. The insurer advanced the full policy loan value to the assignee and, after the insured's death, paid the assignee the death benefit. The bank, acting as the beneficiary's guardian, sued the insurer to recover the death benefit for the beneficiary. The beneficiary's guardian alleged that the policyowner was mentally incompetent at the time the assignment was made. The court held that the insurer had no duty to inquire into the mental competence of the policyowner. If an insurer in good faith makes payment to an assignee of record, a court cannot require it to pay a second time. Pertinent excerpts from this decision are as follows:

> No case has been cited, and our search has failed to reveal one, which has compelled an insurance company to pay a policy a second time when in good faith it has paid the amount of the policy to a new beneficiary or to an assignee, on the ground that the assignment or the change in beneficiary was void because of lack of mental capacity of the insured at the time the change was made, and that is so even though the original beneficiary did not join in the application for change of beneficiary or in the application for the assignment of the policy. The cases upon which the appellee relies to sustain its contention in this respect are not in point.

---

[9]Morticians' Acceptance Co. v. Metropolitan Life Ins. Co., 53 N.E.2d 30 (Ill. App. Ct. 1944), *aff'd,* 58 N.E.2d 854 (Ill. 1945).

[10]Kot v. Chrysler Corp., 292 N.W. 531 (Mich. 1940).

[11]151 F.2d 537 (10th Cir. 1945), *cert. denied,* 327 U.S. 778 (1946), *reh'g denied,* 327 U.S. 816 (1946).

There is yet another reason why the Bank [the beneficiary's guardian] may not prevail. That part of the policy which gave the insured the right to assign contains this provision: "The company assumes no responsibility for the validity of any assignment." This provision was a part of the contract made at a time when the parties were competent to contract, and must be given effect. There is no ambiguity or uncertainty as to the meaning of this provision. It can only mean that the Company shall not become liable by virtue of the assignment which for any reason was invalid. There was a good reason for the inclusion of such a provision. The Company had a large number of policy-holders. Many requests for the assignment of policies would be received. The Company no doubt realized that fraud, duress or undue influence might be practiced in many instances which would go to the validity of the assignment, or that assignments might be invalid for many other reasons, including impaired mental capacity or even lack of mental capacity to make the assignment. If the Company was to be charged with liability if an assignment was invalid for any of these reasons, it would of necessity be compelled to deny the right to assign, or in each instance would be compelled to carefully investigate the application before it was granted. This would place an impossible burden upon the Company. It was for these reasons that the Company in substance said to the insured: "We will give you the right to assign, but we shall not be liable if for any reason the assignment is invalid."

Clearly, the court in this case upheld the right of the insurer to pay an assignee in good faith. However, the court added an important comment as follows:

This provision would not, of course, protect the Company in case of an irregular assignment because that would put it upon notice, or in cases in which it had knowledge of the mental condition of the insured, or in cases in which it had knowledge of facts which should put it upon inquiry. But this is not such a case.

Thus, if the insurer knows that the assignor is mentally incompetent, it cannot disregard that knowledge. Nor can it disregard irregularities on the face of a written assignment. The insurer must investigate any facts known to it that would arouse suspicion in the mind of a reasonable person.

Reassignment after Repayment of the Debt

Once the policyowner has repaid the debt that she owed to the collateral assignee, she is entitled to the return of the rights assigned. The assignee ordinarily will reassign those rights to the policyowner.

Just as insurers do not assume responsibility for the validity of an assignment, neither do they assume responsibility for the validity of a reassignment. However, the insurer must have evidence of a reassignment before it will allow the owner of a policy that was collaterally assigned to exercise the rights the policyowner had transferred to the assignee. Such a reassignment might be a formal statement of the rights reassigned—signed and witnessed—or a simple statement on the letterhead of the assignee that the policyowner has paid the debt and that therefore the assignee has reassigned all policy rights to the policyowner. If the insurer has doubts about the adequacy of the reassignment, it should seek the advice of its legal counsel.

Notice to the Collateral Assignee of Premium Due

The collateral assignee sometimes chooses to pay the premium to keep the policy in force. The insurer must accept the premium payment from the collateral assignee.

Under the laws of a minority of states, the insurer is under a duty to notify a collateral assignee of a premium due. For example, the California Insurance Code contains the following:

When a policy of life insurance is . . . assigned in writing as security for an indebtedness, the insurer shall, in any case in which it has received written notice of the name and address of the assignee, mail to such assignee a written notice, postage prepaid and addressed to the assignee's address filed with the insurer, not less than 10 days prior to the final lapse of the policy, each time the insured has failed or refused to transmit a premium payment to the insurer before the commencement of the policy's grace period or before such notice is mailed. The insurer shall give such notice to the assignee in the proper case while such assignment remains in effect, unless the assignee has notified the insurer in writing that such notice is waived.[12]

Requirements for Assignment

A number of formal requirements are necessary to create a valid assignment that will bind the assignor, the beneficiary, and the insurer. The most important of these are compliance with the policy terms, legal capacity of the assignor (and of the beneficiary if his consent is necessary), and notice to the insurer. Some states also require a written assignment and delivery of the assignment, or of the policy. A minority of states require that an absolute assignee have an insurable interest in the life insured.

Compliance with the Policy Terms

Ordinarily, the parties to the assignment must comply with the conditions for assignment stated in the policy, or the assignee cannot enforce the assignment against the insurer. Thus, as noted above, the policyowner must comply with requirements that the insurer give consent to the assignment or that the policyowner or assignee give written notice of the assignment to the insurer, or else the assignment will not bind the insurer.

Legal Capacity of the Assignor

The assignor must have the required legal capacity to make an assignment. If the assignor is a minor, the assignment will be voidable by the minor unless a statute says otherwise. If the assignor lacks the mental capacity to make an assignment, the assignment will not be valid. In the absence of circumstances leading the insurer to believe that the assignor does not have the requisite capacity, the insurer has no duty to ascertain the capacity of the assignor.

Written Assignment

An assignment does not have to be in writing, unless a statute or policy provision requires it. Nevertheless, it is customary and desirable to have a written assignment.

The written assignment does not have to be in any particular form to be legally effective. However, it must identify the policy and indicate the assignor's intention to transfer it to the assignee. A collateral assignment should precisely spell out the rights assigned and the duties of the parties. The assignor must, of course, sign the assignment. The assignment must contain the signature of any irrevocable beneficiary.

---

[12]Cal. Ins. Code § 10173.2 (West 1993). See also 215 Ill. Comp. Stat. 5/234 (Michie 1993); N.Y. Ins. Law § 211(e) (McKinney 1985).

Delivery of the Assignment or Policy

If there is no written assignment, delivery of the policy will usually be necessary. If there is a written assignment, delivery of the assignment alone will be adequate.

Constructive, rather than actual, delivery will suffice. **Constructive delivery** occurs when the assignor releases the policy or assignment with intent to be bound by it, as, for example, when the assignor puts it in the mail for delivery to the assignee. Delivery to the assignee's agent, rather than to the assignee personally, will also constitute constructive delivery. Note that an assignor's constructive delivery to an assignee is much the same as an insurer's constructive delivery of a policy to an applicant.

Insurable Interest of the Assignee

The question of when the assignee must have an insurable interest in the life insured occurs only if a policy has been absolutely assigned. A court will not hold a collateral assignment to be invalid for lack of insurable interest on the part of the collateral assignee.

Absolute Assignments of Policies Purchased in Good Faith.   Absolute assignments of policies purchased in good faith and without intent to evade the law against wagering in human life are valid in a majority of jurisdictions, even though the assignee has no insurable interest in the insured's life.[13] That is, if the proper insurable interest exists when the policy is purchased, and it is not purchased for the purpose of later assigning it to a person who could not have purchased it originally, the policy-owner can absolutely assign the policy to whomever he wishes. It does not matter that the absolute assignee has no insurable interest. This majority view is well stated by the Missouri Supreme Court in *Butterworth v. Mississippi Valley Trust Co.*[14] There the court said:

> There is some difference of opinion. But the prevailing view, and the greater weight of authority and the better and more soundly reasoned conclusions of the courts was tersely expressed by Mr. Justice Holmes in *Grigsby v. Russell,* 222 U.S. 149, 32 S.Ct. 58, 59, 56 L.Ed. 133, wherein, in ruling this precise question, he said, in part: "And cases in which a person having an interest lends himself to one without any, as a cloak to what is, in its inception, a wager, have no similarity to those where an honest contract is sold in good faith." The principle of the good faith of the assignment transaction runs like a scarlet thread through the better reasoned cases. The decided trend of adjudications unquestionably is to establish the rule that an insurable interest in the insured by the assignee of a policy of life insurance is not essential to the validity of the assignment if the party to whom it was issued in good faith had an insurable interest, and if the assignment was in good faith and not made to cover up a gambling transaction. We unequivocally approve that rule.
>
> Without the power of assignment life insurance contracts would lose much of their value. In a commercial age and with a commercial people, and in recognition of commercial practices, the courts are not unaware of the frequent necessity for the transfer by assignment of such contracts in the usual course of every day business. To limit the assignment of such contracts otherwise valid to those having an insurable interest, and to

---

[13]C.T. Drechsler, Annotation, *Validity of Assignment of Life Insurance Policy to One Who Has No Insurable Interest in Insured,* 30 A.L.R. 2d 1310 (1953).

[14]240 S.W.2d 676 (Mo. 1951).

thus ignore the bona fides of assignments of convenience or necessity, would not only impair the value of such contracts as a plan of estate building and economic protection but would work unconscionable injury to policyholders who are no longer financially able to or who no longer desire to continue such contracts.

The courts in a very few states have taken the view that an absolute assignee must have an insurable interest in the insured's life even if the assignment was made in good faith. They have based their decisions mainly on the rationale that an absolute assignment to an assignee without insurable interest would tend to encourage the murder of the insured as much as would the issuance of a policy to an applicant without an insurable interest.

Absolute Assignments of Policies Purchased in Bad Faith.   If the policyowner takes out the policy with the intent to assign it absolutely to a person with no insurable interest, the assignment ordinarily will be void, although the contract of insurance itself will be valid. The law strictly prohibits trafficking in human lives.

Successive Assigneees

Occasionally, a policyowner assigns the same rights in the same policy to two different assignees. In such a situation, the insurer might face conflicting assignees. Ordinarily, the insurer will pay the proceeds into court by interpleader and let the court decide which assignee is entitled to the proceeds. Interpleader is discussed in Chapter 16, "Equitable Remedies."

For example, suppose that Peter Pohlmann assigns the $50,000 Life insurance policy he took out on his own life to Amy Atwood as security for a $50,000 loan. Pohlmann delivers a written assignment to Atwood but keeps the policy. Shortly after this, Pohlmann delivers a written assignment of the same policy to Brian Bouchard as security for another $50,000 loan. Two weeks later and before Pohlmann has made payments on either loan, Pohlmann is killed in an airplane accident. Which assignee will be entitled to the policy proceeds, Atwood or Bouchard?

First, suppose that Bouchard notified the insurer of his assignment immediately, and Atwood failed to notify it at all. Suppose Atwood was in Europe at the time of Pohlmann's death and did not hear of it until her return. Meanwhile, the insurer, in good faith, paid the death benefit to Bouchard. The insurer would not have to pay Atwood, because it paid Bouchard in good faith and in ignorance of the assignment to Atwood.

The American Rule.   Now, suppose that Bouchard notified the insurer of his assignment immediately and Atwood notified the insurer of her assignment a week later. If Pohlmann was accidentally killed a few days after the insurer received notice of the assignment to Atwood, who would receive the death benefit, Atwood or Bouchard?

In about one-half of the states, Atwood would be entitled to the money, under what is called the American rule. This rule states that the right of the first assignee is superior to that of a subsequent assignee. Here, Atwood was the first assignee. The order in which the assignees gave the insurer notice of their assignments is irrelevant under the American rule.

The English Rule.   About one-half of the states follow the English rule. Under the English rule, the first assignee to give notice of his or her assignment to the insurer would be entitled to the death benefit, regardless of the order in which the policyowner made the assignments. Since Bouchard gave notice of his assignment one week before Atwood gave notice of hers, Bouchard would be entitled to the death benefit in those states that follow the English rule.[15]

As a final example, suppose that the policy had a face value of $175,000, and Pohlmann had made successive assignments to Atwood and to Bouchard to secure a $50,000 loan that each of them had made. Here, the insurer can pay Atwood $50,000, pay Bouchard $50,000, and pay the remaining $75,000 of the death benefit to the named beneficiary.

Assignments by the Beneficiary

The beneficiary, like the policyowner, usually can transfer her rights in the life insurance policy. Before the insured's death, the beneficiary can transfer whatever rights she possesses.[16] An irrevocable beneficiary can transfer her rights. Ordinarily, such rights are vested, but they are subject to divestment if the beneficiary predeceases the insured or the policy expires. Even a revocable beneficiary can transfer his expectancy.

When the insured dies (or at the end of the period specified in a survivorship clause), the rights of the beneficiary (whether revocable or irrevocable) to the policy proceeds become vested. The beneficiary's rights are then no different from rights to any other sum of money. Rights of this kind are usually assignable.

A policy provision prohibiting assignment is ordinarily ineffective to prevent the beneficiary from making an assignment of the benefits after the insured's death. The court in one case expressed this rule as follows:

> The general rule, supported by a great wealth of authority, is that general stipulations in policies, prohibiting assignment thereof except with the insurers' consent, or upon giving some notice, or like conditions, have universally been held to apply only to assignments before loss, and, accordingly, not to prevent an assignment after loss.[17]

However, spendthrift clauses in settlement agreements can impose restrictions on the beneficiary's ability to assign the proceeds.[18]

Other Transfers

Transfer of the policyowner's rights in a life insurance policy is sometimes made in some way other than by an assignment of the policy. Such a transfer can be made by intestate succession, by will, by property settlement agreement or divorce decree, or by sale of the assets of a business. In addition, actions that would not amount to a legal assignment of the policy sometimes result in an equitable assignment—that is,

---

[15]W.S.R., Annotation, *Priority as between Different Assignees of the Same Chose in Action as Affected by Notice to Debtor,* 31 A.L.R. 876 (1924), *supp. by* R.P.D., Annotation, 110 A.L.R. 774 (1937).

[16]Sloan v. Breeden, 124 N.E. 31 (Mass. 1919).

[17]Lain v. Metropolitan Life Ins. Co., 58 N.E. 2d 587 (Ill. 1944).

[18]Chelsea-Wheeler Coal Co. v. Marvin, 35 A.2d 874 (N.J. 1944); Michaelson v. Sokolove, 182 A. 458 (Md. 1936).

an assignment that is enforceable in a suit in equity. Transfers other than by assignment are discussed in this section.

Intestate Succession

A person who dies without a valid will dies intestate. The property of such a person, who is called an intestate, will pass to other persons according to the intestate statute of the relevant state. If the intestate owned a life insurance policy insuring the life of another, a person or persons described in the intestate statute will succeed to the intestate's interests in the policy.

For example, suppose that Susan Chung dies intestate, without debts, and that she owned a life insurance policy insuring her husband's life. Suppose that Chung had no children. If the intestate statute of her state of residence provides that an intestate's surviving spouse will succeed to all of the intestate's property if the intestate has no children, her husband will become the policyowner.

Wills

A person who owns a life insurance policy on the life of another person has valuable property that he can transfer under the terms of his will. The will need not specifically mention the policy. For example, suppose that Frank Rycek owned a policy insuring the life of his brother Paul. If Frank died with a valid will directing that all of his property pass to his sister, his sister would become the policy's new owner.

Property Settlement Agreements and Divorce Decrees

A property settlement agreement or divorce decree can operate to modify the policyowner's rights in the policy. For example, such an agreement or decree might require a policyowner to keep a life insurance policy in force for the benefit of an ex-spouse or children. Or the policyowner might agree in a property settlement to transfer ownership of a policy to a spouse, or the court might order the policyowner to do so.

Sale of Assets

A sale of all the assets of a business will result in the transfer of a life insurance policy that the business owns. For example, in *Brand v. Erisman,*[19] a partnership had purchased policies on the lives of the partners. When the partners later sold all the assets of the partnership, including all "contracts . . . rights or choses in action," they transferred the insurance policies to the purchaser along with the other assets of the business.

Equitable Assignments

An assignment that is not enforceable in a legal action because it does not meet the requirements of a legal assignment might be enforceable in an equitable action if fairness so requires. For example, in *Sundstrom v. Sundstrom*[20] the Supreme Court of Washington held that a policyowner had equitably assigned a policy insuring his life to his wife, even though the policyowner had not fulfilled the legal requirements for an assignment.

---

[19]172 F.2d 28 (D.C. Cir. 1948).
[20]129 P.2d 783 (Wash. 1942).

The policyowner had named his mother as the original beneficiary. His wife had worked and supported the policyowner, who had arthritis and was able to work only sporadically. Together, they had paid back to the policyowner's parents the money his parents had charged him for furnishing care prior to his marriage. When the policyowner and his wife had reduced that indebtedness to a relatively small sum, the policyowner changed the beneficiary to his wife and gave her the policy, telling her that it was hers. Seven years later, the wife was seriously injured in an automobile accident. After a few weeks, her husband closed out their joint bank account and went back to his parents, taking with him the life insurance policy. The wife sued for divorce, and the policyowner changed the beneficiary back to his mother. Before the divorce decree became final, the policyowner died. The wife and the policyowner's mother both claimed the death benefit. The insurer paid the death benefit into the court by interpleader and was dismissed from the lawsuit. On this set of facts, the court held that there was an equitable assignment in favor of the wife, reasoning as follows:

> We are convinced that this evidence, if believed by the trial court, fully warranted it in finding that the insured had made an equitable assignment of the policy to respondent [the wife] in 1932. It is apparent that he was at the time a hopeless cripple. For four years, his wife had faithfully worked to help support him, and had given him every attention possible. More than that, her earnings had been the principal means by which his personal, premarital debt to his parents had been reduced from five hundred eighty dollars to seventy dollars. Presumably he not only felt a deep affection for her, but also was sincerely grateful for all that she had done. In addition, he had agreed to transfer the policy to her as soon as *they* got "the folks" paid up. The language employed by him when he delivered the policy to her indicated that it was his intention then and there to invest her with full ownership of the proceeds thereof.
>
> It is true that no formal written assignment of the policy was executed, as required by the provision of the policy hereinabove quoted. But that provision, as we have seen, is designed solely for the protection of the insurance company, and its rights are in no way involved here. Although the transaction between the insured and the respondent with reference to the transfer of the policy was simple and informal, it was only natural for a husband and wife to deal with each other in that way at a time when the relationship between them was one of affection and when there was no occasion for either of them to suspect the other of possible future double-dealing. Nor would it be expected that a wife, even if she were aware of the express requirements of the policy and were familiar with legal phraseology, would insist, under the circumstances then existing, that the terms of the transaction be reduced to writing. The evidence amply justifies the conclusion that it was the insured's intention on October 28, 1932, to transfer to respondent a present interest in the ultimate proceeds of the policy, that he delivered the policy to respondent for that purpose, and that by the form of expression which he then used he made an absolute appropriation of such proceeds to her, relinquishing further control or power of revocation with reference thereto. That being the case, the trial court had sufficient grounds for holding that the insured effected an equitable assignment of the insurance policy to the respondent.

Summary

Transfer of a chose in action, such as an insurance policy, ordinarily is called an assignment. A policyowner can make a gift or a sale of her life insurance policy by absolute assignment, whereas a pledge of the policy as security for a loan is usually by collateral assignment.

An absolute assignment is the irrevocable transfer of all of the policyowner's rights. An absolute assignment cannot destroy an irrevocable beneficiary's rights without the beneficiary's consent. An absolute assignment destroys the interest of a revocable beneficiary, according to one view. According to another view, an absolute assignment, by itself, does not affect the interest of a revocable beneficiary.

A collateral assignment is the temporary transfer of some of the policyowner's rights, made as security for a loan. When the policyowner repays the loan, the lender ordinarily reassigns those rights to the policyowner. Modern collateral assignment forms usually contain a line for the beneficiary's signature. If an irrevocable beneficiary does not consent to a collateral assignment, the beneficiary's rights usually are superior to the assignee's. According to the majority rule, a collateral assignee's rights are superior to a revocable beneficiary's rights. Ordinarily, courts treat an absolute assignment intended to secure a loan as a collateral assignment.

The insurer has a crucial role in the assignment process. Insurers draft many policies with assignment clauses governing the method of assignment or requiring the insurer's consent. The policyowner must comply with these clauses, or the assignment will not bind the insurer. Moreover, the policyowner or assignee must notify the insurer of the assignment. The insurer will not be liable to the assignee if, in ignorance of the assignee's rights, it pays policy proceeds to other persons who appear entitled to them. However, if the insurer has notice of an assignment, and the policy does not prohibit assignment, the insurer cannot pay proceeds without regard to the assignee's rights.

The insurer does not take responsibility for the validity of an assignment. It has no control of and, ordinarily, no knowledge of the factors that govern such validity. However, if it does know that the assignment might not be valid, it cannot disregard that knowledge.

For a valid assignment to be binding on all parties, certain formal requirements must be met. These include compliance with the policy terms, legal capacity of the assignor, and notice to the insurer. Some states require a written assignment and delivery of the assignment or of the policy to the assignee. The assignee of a collateral assignment need not have an insurable interest in the insured's life. According to the majority rule, an absolute assignee does not need an insurable interest if the policy was purchased in good faith and not with intent to evade the law against wagering in human life.

The rights of successive assignees depend on the order of the assignments in jurisdictions following the American rule. The first assignee's rights are superior to the rights of a later assignee. Under the English rule, the rights of the first assignee to give notice to the insurer are superior, regardless of the order of the assignments.

The beneficiary, like the policyowner, can transfer her rights in the policy before the insured's death. After the insured's death, ordinarily a policy provision prohibiting assignment will not prevent the beneficiary from transferring her right to the proceeds, although a spendthrift clause in a settlement agreement might do so.

A policyowner can transfer his rights in a life insurance policy in ways other than by a specific assignment of the policy. Intestate succession, wills, property settlement agreements, divorce decrees, sales of assets, or equitable assignments often effect such transfers.

ILLUSTRATIVE CASE

This case involves a collateral assignment of a life insurance policy to a bank. The court discusses the rights of the assignee, assignor, and insurer.

JEFFERSON TRUST & SAVINGS BANK OF PEORIA,
Plaintiff-Appellee
v.
THE LINCOLN NATIONAL LIFE INSURANCE CO.,
Defendant-Appellant[21]
Appellate Court of Illinois, Third District

STENGEL, Justice.

The assignee of a life insurance policy, Jefferson Trust & Savings Bank of Peoria (plaintiff), brought suit against defendant [The Lincoln] National Life Insurance Company to recover the cash surrender value of the policy.

Both parties filed motions for summary judgment. The circuit court entered summary judgment in favor of plaintiff and defendant appeals.

The policy contained an "automatic Premium Loan Privilege" which provided that any premium not paid before the expiration of the grace period was to be treated as paid and charged automatically as a loan against the policy with interest from the due date of the premium.

---

[21]325 N.E.2d 384 (1975).

Insured assigned the policy to plaintiff bank as collateral security for a loan, and the assignment was filed with the defendant [the insurer] as required by the policy. Both before and after the assignment, defendant made numerous loans under the automatic premium loan privilege. When plaintiff later surrendered the policy to obtain the cash surrender value, defendant set off all outstanding loans plus interest, and tendered $3,009.46. Plaintiff refused the tender, filed this action, and was awarded judgment for $7,768.50, from which judgment defendant appeals.

The amount in dispute represents loans against the policy made by defendant after the assignment. Plaintiff contends that the automatic loan privilege was revoked by the terms of the assignment and that notice of the assignment was sufficient to accomplish revocation. Defendant denies that notice of the assignment was written notice of revocation as required under the terms of the policy.

Paragraph 13 of the policy provides:

> The Automatic Premium Loan Privilege will be granted either at the request of the Insured in the application for this policy or upon subsequent written request received by the Company at its Home Office prior to the expiration of the grace period allowed for payment of any premium. *This Privilege may be revoked at any time upon written notice to the Company at its Home Office* (emphasis added).
>
> If the request has been made for the Automatic Premium Loan Privilege and such request remains unrevoked, any premium not paid before the expiration of the grace period shall be treated as paid and charged automatically as a loan against this policy with interest from the due date of the premium.

The assignment did not contain specific words of revocation of the loan privilege. Plaintiff contends, however, that specific words of revocation are unnecessary, and that the assignment given to defendant contained provisions so inconsistent with the automatic loan privilege that the privilege was revoked. Under the terms of the assignment, plaintiff acquired the sole right to obtain loans on the policy and had no obligation to pay premiums or interest on policy loans. Plaintiff argues that these two provisions of the assignment were patently inconsistent with the continuation of the automatic premium loan privilege which would permit the previous policyholder to impair the cash value of the policy by refusing to make payment of premiums.

Is such an inconsistency sufficient to revoke the automatic loan privilege? We think not.

In *Hoffman ex rel. Keithley v. New York Life Ins. Co.,* 230 Ill. App. 533 (2d dist., 1923), the insured executed two notes in lieu of premium payments which were liens against the policy, and then assigned the policy as security for a debt. The insured subsequently executed renewal notes against the policy. The assignee paid two annual premiums, and then applied for the cash surrender value of the policy. The assignee denied the right of the insur-

ance company to deduct the outstanding loans from the cash value because he had no notice of the loans. The court held that the assignee stood in the shoes of his assignor, that it was his duty to ascertain the rights of the insured under the policy, and that the loans should be deducted from the cash surrender value.

Courts in other jurisdictions have similarly held that the cash surrender value due the assignee was subject to a setoff for premium loans made subsequent to the assignment, and have held that where the assignee has the policy with full opportunity to examine its provisions, the assignee is subject to the rights and conditions of that policy. In both of these cases the insurance companies had notice of the assignment.

The parties here agree that the original insurance policy was a valid binding contract and that as assignee of the policy, plaintiff took the policy subject to the same terms and conditions as the insured. The rule in Illinois is well established that an insurance policy is not a negotiable instrument and that an assignee takes subject to the conditions expressed in the policy and is in no better position than his assignor. We believe it is clear that, in the absence of a revocation, assignment of the policy in the case before us would not preclude defendant from setting off subsequent premium loans in computing the cash surrender value due plaintiff.

In support of its contention that the loan provision was revoked, plaintiff urges application of the rule that permits revocation of an offer by an act which is inconsistent with the continuation of the offer and which is brought to the attention of the non-revoking party. This rule can have no application in the case before us where a contract is already in existence and binding upon the parties in all of its provisions. Plaintiff also points to a comparable rule applicable to termination of a principal-agent relationship, citing *Van Houton v. Trust Co. of Chicago,* 413 Ill. 310, 109 N.E. 2d 187 (1952), where the court held that express notice by the agent to the principal that the agency is terminated is not essential. The court there stated the rule to be "... that *unless the parties have manifested otherwise* to each other, a principal or agent has notice that authority to do an act has terminated, or is suspended, if he knows, or has reason to know, should know, or has been given notification of the occurrence of an event from which the inference reasonably would be drawn." [Emphasis added.] This rule cannot support plaintiff's theory because here the contractual requirement of written notice is such a manifestation as would remove this case from the rule by the terms of the rule itself.

We must reject plaintiff's contention that the rules of law set forth in the cases involving revocation of offers and termination of agencies have any bearing on the case before us. Here the assignee stands in the position of its assignor and is subject to the automatic premium loan provision until it acts to revoke in writing, and such revocation is not effected by implication or mere constructive notice from the assignor by reason of the instrument of assignment.

If the premium loan provision had been revoked, either expressly or constructively, the insured's failure to pay premiums could have resulted in a forfeiture of the policy with an even greater impairment of the cash surrender value than would result from loans made under the automatic premium loan privilege. We conclude that the terms of the assignment permitted insured to impair the cash surrender value in any event and that plaintiff may actually be in a better position now than if revocation had occurred.

We hold that plaintiff, as assignee of a life insurance contract, took subject to the terms and conditions of the contract, including the provision that the automatic premium loan privilege could be revoked only upon written notice of revocation to defendant. The notice of assignment of the policy by the insured was not sufficient written notice to revoke the privilege. All outstanding premium loans plus interest must be set off against the cash surrender value of the policy.

The order of the circuit court granting summary judgment to plaintiff on the issue of liability is reversed, and defendant's motion for summary judgment is granted, and the cause is remanded for determination of damages consistent with this opinion.

Judgment reversed and remanded.

STOUDER, P. J., and BARRY, J., concur.

Questions for Review

1. What is an assignment?
2. How does an absolute assignment differ from a collateral assignment?
3. What are the requisites for a valid assignment?
4. Is notice to the insurer essential for the validity of an assignment? Is such notice essential for any other purpose?
5. Under what circumstances does an absolute assignment constitute the making of a gift? A sale?
6. Why do most policies state that the insurer assumes no responsibility for the validity or effect of an assignment?
7. Contrast the rights of the beneficiary with those of a collateral assignee:
   a. When the beneficiary designation is revocable.
   b. When the beneficiary designation is irrevocable.
   c. When the beneficiary has joined in making the assignment.
   d. When the beneficiary has not joined in making the assignment.
8. What rights does a policyowner transfer to the assignee under the American Bankers Association collateral assignment form? What rights does a policyowner reserve under the American Bankers Association collateral assignment form?
9. How have the courts generally interpreted the rights of the assignee and beneficiary when a policy is assigned absolutely for collateral purposes?
10. Describe the American and English rules regarding the rights of successive assignees.
11. What is meant by an equitable assignment?

15   LAPSE AND REINSTATEMENT

If a life insurance premium is not paid by the end of the grace period, the policy lapses. Thereafter, the policy is effective only as its nonforfeiture section, if any, provides. However, most life insurance contracts contain a reinstatement provision that enables the policyowner to return a lapsed policy to a premium-paying status. Reinstatement of a lapsed policy restores the benefits and privileges that the policyowner previously enjoyed.

The reinstatement provision gives the policyowner a right that can be valuable. If the policy has been in effect for several years, it might include privileges that the insurer does not offer in its new policies. For example, the policy might contain settlement options that the insurer no longer offers or that provide for more favorable interest or mortality assumptions than those in the insurer's new policies. Policy loan interest rates in a reinstated policy might be lower than rates in new policies. Prematurity rights attain significant value sooner in a reinstated policy than in one newly issued. Premium payments might be lower for the old policy than for a new policy. In addition, the procedure for reinstatement is ordinarily simpler than that involved in applying for a new policy.

Nevertheless, sometimes the owner of a lapsed policy should apply for a new one rather than reinstate the original policy. The policyowner might prefer to have a universal or variable life insurance policy rather than reinstate a regular whole life insurance policy. Furthermore, to reinstate a policy the policyowner must pay all the back premiums with interest. Thus, if several years have passed since the policy lapsed, the policyowner might have to pay a large sum to reinstate it.

Because the insured must be currently insurable if the insurer is to reinstate the policy, insurability will not be a factor in deciding whether to reinstate the original policy or obtain a new one. If the insured is currently insurable, either alternative is available.

The purposes of this chapter are to describe lapse and reinstatement and to discuss the legal problems related to reinstatement.

Lapse and Expiration

The word *lapse* has been defined as a "default in premiums before a policy has a nonforfeiture value."[1] After the policy has developed a nonforfeiture value, it is said to lapse "except as to the nonforfeiture benefits."

A policy *expires* when it ceases to provide coverage. A policy will expire on the termination of the nonforfeiture benefit that the policyowner chose, or on the termination of the automatic nonforfeiture benefit if the policyowner did not choose a nonforfeiture benefit. For example, if a policyowner had chosen the extended term insurance nonforfeiture benefit and the policy lapsed for nonpayment of the premium due on October 2, 1997, the end of the grace period, the policy might expire 10 years and 143 days later, on January 22, 2008, when the extended term insurance ran out. If the policyowner had chosen the reduced paid-up insurance nonforfeiture benefit, the policy might remain in effect until the insured's death, in which case the insurer would perform the contract by paying the death benefit that the reduced paid-up insurance provided, but the policy would not be said to expire. Performance is discussed in Chapter 18, "Performance of the Insurance Contract."

As another example, the policyowner might decide to surrender the policy for its the cash surrender value. Once the policyowner has surrendered the policy for its cash surrender value, the policy expires.

Reinstatement Laws

Most states have laws requiring that life insurance policies issued or delivered in the state include a reinstatement provision. For example, the New York statute requires that life insurance policies contain the following:

> [A provision] that the policy shall be reinstated at any time within three years from the date of default, unless the cash surrender value has been exhausted or the period of extended insurance has expired, if the policyholder makes application, provides evidence of insurability, including good health, satisfactory to the insurer, pays all overdue premiums with interest at a rate not exceeding six per centum per annum compounded annually, and pays or reinstates any other policy indebtedness with interest at a rate not exceeding the applicable policy loan rate or rates determined in accordance with the

---

[1]Lewis E. Davids, Dictionary of Insurance, 263 (7th ed.1990).

policy's provisions. This provision shall be required only if the policy provides for termination or lapse in the event of a default in making a regularly scheduled premium payment.[2]

As a general rule, insurers are more liberal than the reinstatement statutes require. Reinstatement is usually to the insurer's advantage because reinstatement keeps the policy in force. Thus, insurers customarily include reinstatement provisions in their policies, whether or not a statute requires it. Although insurers often have a right under state law to deny reinstatement after extended term insurance has expired, they ordinarily do not take advantage of this right.

Nevertheless, life insurance policies usually forbid reinstatement if the policyowner has surrendered the policy for cash. The surrender of a policy is a deliberate act by the policyowner, and insurers therefore consider that cash surrender terminates the contractual relationship. Insurers discourage cash surrender by prohibiting reinstatement after cash surrender.

Reinstatement Provisions

Even if no statute or policy provision gives the policyowner the right to reinstate, the insurer and policyowner could agree to reinstate the policy. However, a policy provision is desirable because it guarantees the right to reinstate, clarifies the terms of reinstatement, and helps to assure that the insurer will treat all policyowners uniformly.

The reinstatement provision in a life insurance policy usually provides that, if the policy lapses for nonpayment of premium, it can be reinstated at any time within three years from the date of lapse. In some policies the period is five years. The policyowner must furnish evidence of the insured's insurability, including good health, that is satisfactory to the insurer. All unpaid back premiums must be paid with interest. If there was an unpaid policy loan on the date of lapse, either the loan must be repaid with interest or the insurer can reinstate the loan with interest.

The reinstatement provision in the illustrative policy in the Appendix, Figure 2, reads as follows:

If this Policy lapses due to an unpaid premium, it may be reinstated subject to the following conditions:

1. The Insured must be alive and still insurable by our standards; and
2. Any indebtedness which existed at the time of termination must either be paid or reinstated with interest compounded annually at the loan interest rate shown on page three; and
3. Each unpaid premium must be paid, with interest of 6% per annum compounded annually, from its due date to the reinstatement date; and
4. The request for reinstatement must be made by you in writing and submitted to our Home Office within 5 years after the date the Policy lapses; and
5. If you are not the Insured, the request for reinstatement must also be signed by the Insured if age 15 or older, last birthday, on the reinstatement date.

A Policy which has been surrendered for its cash value may not be reinstated.

[2]N.Y. Ins. Law § 3203a (10) (McKinney 1985).

This provision is typical in most respects. It prohibits reinstatement if the policy has been surrendered for its cash surrender value. However, expiration of the policy after it has been in effect as extended term insurance will not prevent the policy-owner from reinstating the policy. The policyowner may reinstate the policy within five years of lapse. This provision is more liberal than the provision that the typical reinstatement statute requires.

Insurability for Reinstatement

The illustrative policy states that "[t]he insured must be alive and still insurable by our standards" for the insurer to reinstate the policy. This requirement that the insured be insurable at the time of reinstatement prevents antiselection. Antiselection means the tendency of persons who are poorer risks to seek insurance to a greater extent than do persons who are better risks.

Arguably, reinstating a lapsed policy after the insured has become uninsurable would place the insurer in no worse position than if the insured had become uninsurable while the policy continued on a premium-paying basis. This would be true if all lapsed policies were reinstated. As a matter of fact, they are not, and it is those insureds who have become uninsurable who are most interested in reinstatement. Those who are still insurable are less apt to apply for reinstatement. Life insurance involves the application of the law of large numbers to a group of insureds whose risks of death are reasonably comparable. Therefore, the mortality experience of the insurer would be adversely affected if insurers permitted reinstatement without the insurability requirement.

As a general rule, *insurability* has the same meaning as used in connection with reinstatement that it has in connection with an original application, except as to the insured's age. The insurer is free to consider such factors as habits, occupation, and finances, as well as good health, just as if the insurer were considering an application for a new policy of life insurance.

Thus, the great majority of courts have held that *insurability* is a broader term than *good health* and includes the other factors just mentioned. This point of view is expressed in *Kallman v. Equitable Life Assurance Society.*[3] In that case, the policy-owner-insured met the requirements of insurability as to his health, but the insurer refused to reinstate his policy because of his financial situation and the large amount of insurance on his life that he was already carrying. The insurer's refusal to reinstate was challenged in a court action filed shortly after the insured had committed suicide. The court upheld the insurer's decision, saying:

> The distinction between "good health" and "insurability" might be illustrated in the case of a criminal condemned to death. On the eve of his execution he might be found to be in perfect physical condition, but it could not be reasonably contended that his situation did not affect his insurability. There are numerous circumstances which affect insurability. In Ginsberg v. Eastern Life Insurance Co. of New York . . . the court said that it is common knowledge that an insurance company will not reinstate a policy where it is known that the insured is financially insolvent and the circumstances show probability of suicide. . . .
>
> We are of the opinion that the language of the statute and of the policy "evidence of insurability satisfactory to the company" does not limit the inquiry upon an application for reinstatement to the good health or good physical condition of the insured. . . . Here,

---

[3]288 N.Y.S. 1032 (N.Y. App. Div. 1936), *aff'd,* 5 N.E.2d 375 (N.Y. 1936).

the insured's pecuniary circumstances coupled with his heavy over insurance, entirely out of line with his incoming financial condition, had a definite bearing upon his longevity and created a moral hazard which directly affected his insurability.

A few cases support the position that the term *insurability* means the same as *good health* in connection with reinstatement.[4] However, this is decidedly a minority view.

The illustrative policy reinstatement provision requires that the insured be "still insurable by [the insurer's] standards." Reinstatement provisions often require that the policyowner furnish evidence of insurability "satisfactory to the insurer." There have been several interpretations of the meaning of the phrase "satisfactory to the insurer." Some courts have held that the judgment and conscience of the insurer's officers are controlling,[5] whereas other courts compel reinstatement if the insured reasonably meets the insurer's insurability standards.[6]

The majority rule is that the courts will consider the practices of other insurers and determine whether the insurer's decision is reasonable on that basis. The California Supreme Court in *Kennedy v. Occidental Life Insurance Co.*[7] summarized this position as follows:

> The overwhelming weight of authority is to the effect that an agreement to reinstate an insurance policy upon "satisfactory evidence" of insurability does not give the insurer the power to act arbitrarily or capriciously, but that evidence which would be satisfactory to a reasonable insurer is all that is required.

Payment of Unpaid Premiums, with Interest

When the policyowner reinstates the policy, the insurer has the right under statute and case law to require the payment of all unpaid premiums, with interest. This puts the insurer in the position in which it would have been if the policy had never lapsed and the insurer had had the premiums to invest. The illustrative policy requires that "[e]ach unpaid premium must be paid, with interest of 6 percent per annum compounded annually, from its due date to the reinstatement date."

The amount of interest that the insurer can charge to reinstate is spelled out in the statutes of many states. The most common rate is 6 percent, although a few states allow 8 percent.

Death during Review of the Reinstatement Application

The conditions in the reinstatement provision of an insurance policy are conditions precedent, and therefore they must be met before the reinstatement will become effective. If the insured dies after the reinstatement application has been submitted but before the conditions have been met, the beneficiary can receive only the nonforfeiture benefits, if any, under the lapsed policy. In other words, merely completing an application for reinstatement is not enough to effect reinstatement if all the conditions are not met.

---

[4]Missouri State Life Ins. Co. v. Hearne, 226 S.W. 789 (Tex. Civ. App. 1920); Smith v. Bankers Nat'l Life Ins. Co., 265 N.W. 546 (Neb. 1936).

[5]Conway v. Minnesota Mut. Life Ins. Co., 112 P. 1106 (Wash. 1911).

[6]Lane v. New York Life Ins. Co., 145 S.E. 196 (S.C. 1928).

[7]117 P.2d 3 (Cal. 1941).

For example, suppose Therese Bixby is the owner of a policy insuring her life. The policy has a reinstatement provision identical to that in the illustrative policy in the Appendix, Figure 2. Bixby's policy lapses and the extended term insurance becomes effective. Three years later, after the extended term insurance has expired, Bixby applies to have the policy reinstated and submits evidence of insurability. Two days after submitting the reinstatement application, Bixby dies in a fire without having submitted the unpaid premiums. The beneficiary will not be entitled to the death benefit because Bixby failed to meet all the conditions for reinstatement.

Now suppose that Bixby submitted the unpaid premiums with the reinstatement application. She dies before the insurer has had an opportunity to review the application and evidence of insurability. If the evidence of insurability clearly indicates that Bixby was insurable at the time of application, what is the insurer's liability?

The majority view is that if the policyowner has a contractual right to reinstate the policy and has performed the conditions precedent before the insured's death, the reinstatement will be effective, even though the insurer has not yet approved the reinstatement at the time of death.[8] Illustrative of this view is *Bowie v. Bankers Life Co.,*[9] a federal case construing Colorado law in which the policyowner-insured had applied for reinstatement, furnishing evidence of insurability satisfactory to a reasonable insurer and otherwise meeting all requirements specified in the policy. Before the insurer had approved the reinstatement application, the insured was drowned when his automobile plunged over a bridge. The court held the reinstatement effective, saying:

> Where a policy contains a provision of this kind, where proof of insurability which is not open to valid objection as to form or substance is submitted within the authorized time, where payment of all premiums presently in arrears plus interest thereon is tendered, where the insured thus fully complies with the conditions of his contract, and where his death is wholly accidental and in no way involved in his proof of insurability, the policy is reinstated and the restoration relates back to the time of the submission of the application and the tender of the premiums.

On the other hand, a minority of courts take the position that the insurer must have a reasonable time in which to approve or disapprove the application for reinstatement. If the insured should die during that time, the policy is not reinstated.[10]

However, the insurer must act promptly on an application for reinstatement. As a general rule, the courts hold that an unreasonable delay in acting on the reinstatement application constitutes an implied waiver of the insurer's right, if any, to decline to reinstate the policy. Illustrative of this point of view is *Waldner v. Metropolitan Life Insurance Co.,*[11] in which the Kansas Supreme Court said:

> The defendant [the insurer] could not indefinitely hold the application for reinstatement without disapproving it, retain the money of the insured until long after her death, and thereafter escape liability on the ground the insured had not provided satisfactory proof of insurability.

---

[8]A.M.S., Annotation, *Death of Insured or Other Loss Pending Application Not Effectively Granted, for Reinstatement of Life or Accident Insurance, after Lapse,* 105 A.L.R. 478 (1938), *supp.* by A. M. Swarthout, Annotation, 164 A.L.R. 1057 (1946).

[9]105 F.2d 806 (10th Cir. 1939), *aff'd on rehearing,* 121 F.2d 779 (10th Cir. 1941).

[10]Exchange Trust Co. v. Capitol Life Ins. Co., 49 F.2d 133 (10th Cir. 1931); Rocky Mt. Sav. & Trust Co. v. Aetna Life Ins. Co., 154 S.E. 743 (N.C. 1930); Gressler v. New York Life Ins. Co., 163 P.2d 324 (Utah 1945).

[11]87 P.2d 515 (Kan. 1939).

Continuation of the Original Contract

By the great weight of authority, the reinstatement of a policy under the terms of a reinstatement provision is a continuation of the original contract and not the creation of a new contract.[12] A few courts have held that the reinstated contract is a new contract rather than a continuation of the original contract.[13] Such a holding is particularly likely if the policyowner does not have a contractual right to reinstate the policy,[14] or if the policyowner requests that the policy terms be changed.[15]

Whether the reinstated contract is continuing or new can be an important question. First, the application of the incontestability and suicide provisions might differ if the contract is new rather than continuing. Second, the insurer might have a right to add conditions to a new contract but not to one that is continuing. Finally, laws governing a new contract might be different from those governing a continuing contract.

Contestability of the Reinstated Policy

The law in the great majority of jurisdictions is that the contestable period of a reinstated policy runs anew for the same period after reinstatement but that the new contestable period applies only to statements made in the application for reinstatement.[16] The court in *Sellwood v. Equitable Life Insurance Co. of Iowa*[17] explained the majority rule as follows:

> The authorities reason that, since it is fundamental that fraud vitiates everything into which it enters . . . it cannot be supposed that the parties intended that an insured should have what Judge Learned Hand . . . characterized as "a license forever to cheat the insurer"; and that the reasons for the public policy that, absent fraud, statements by an insured in an application for insurance should be deemed to be representations and not warranties and that a limit should be set on the time within which the insurer should have the right to contest the policy for false statements of the insured in an application, apply to an application for reinstatement the same as to one for the original issuance of the policy itself. This view has been adopted by many authorities, regardless of whether the reinstatement be regarded as the continuation of the original contract of insurance or the making of a new one. . . . We adopt the rule that, upon reinstatement of a lapsed life insurance policy, the incontestable clause runs anew as to misrepresentations in the application for reinstatement. This rule is not only supported by the weight of authority, but also is a just and fair one.

States that have resolved by statutory enactment the question of the contestability of a reinstated policy have adopted this majority rule. For instance, the West Virginia Insurance Code contains the following:

---

[12]Trapp v. Metropolitan Life Ins. Co., 70 F.2d 976 (8th Cir. 1934), *aff'd*, 72 F.2d 374 (8th Cir. 1934), *cert. denied*, 293 U.S. 596 (1934); Prudential Ins. Co. v. Mason, 16 N.E.2d 69 (Mass. 1938).

[13]MacDonald v. Metropolitan Life Ins. Co., 155 A. 491 (Pa. 1931).

[14]Johnson v. Life Ins. Co. of Virginia, 169 So. 159 (La. Ct. App. 1936).

[15]Franklin Life Ins. Co. v. Parish, 109 F.2d 276 (5th Cir. 1940).

[16]P. G. Guthrie, Annotation, *Insurance: Incontestable Clause as Affected by Reinstatement of Policy,* 23 A.L.R. 3d 743 (1969).

[17]42 N.W.2d 346 (Minn. 1950).

The reinstatement of any policy of life insurance or annuity contract hereafter delivered or issued for delivery in this State may be contested on account of fraud or misrepresentation of facts material to the reinstatement only for the same period following reinstatement and with the same conditions and exceptions as the policy provides with respect to contestability after original issuance.[18]

A minority of cases hold that the reinstatement itself is a separate agreement that, because it contains no incontestable provision, can be contested for fraud at any time.

A further point arises in connection with the contestability of a reinstated policy. This has to do with attachment of a copy of the reinstatement application to the policy. As a general rule, when a request for reinstatement reaches the insurer, the policy is in the hands of the policyowner. For that reason, the courts generally have held that a copy of the reinstatement application need not be attached to the policy for the insurer to avail itself of a defense based on misrepresentation in the application. However, some of the states have enacted statutes requiring the insurer to furnish a copy of the reinstatement application to the policyowner or beneficiary on request.[19]

Reinstatement and the Suicide Clause

If the policy contains a suicide clause, usually the suicide period will not run anew from the date of reinstatement.[20] Most courts reach this conclusion on the theory that reinstatement does not create a new contract but rather revives the original contract and continues it in force as from its original date.

Even in a jurisdiction where the courts hold that reinstatement gives rise to a new contract, the language of the policy might be such that the suicide clause will not run anew upon reinstatement. This was the holding in *Tatum v. Guardian Life Insurance Co.*[21] Renowned judge Learned Hand wrote the *Tatum* opinion. The opinion contains an excellent discussion of the suicide and incontestable clauses, as they relate to reinstatement, as follows:

> Were we free to decide the point as res nova,[22] we should say that the reinstatement of a lapsed policy is not a new contract at all, when the insured can revive it merely by satisfying the company of his insurability and by paying the arrears. Those are the conditions upon what by the lapse has become a conditional obligation; but which is still an obligation from which the insurer cannot withdraw at will, being bound to approve if he is in fact satisfied. . . . But although we are . . . to consider the policy as though it has been issued anew on February 14, 1933, it by no means follows that in construing it we must read it as though it spoke throughout from that date. By its very terms the policy is "reinstated"; the parties have thus chosen a word which presupposes, not a new contract, but the revival of an old one. The insured must pay not a single premium, but all arrears; and hereafter only at the old rate, however many years have passed. All benefits—e.g., the surrender and loan value, term and paid-up insurance—go again into force as of the original date; they do not begin anew. Moreover, in the case at bar the defence of suicide

---

[18]W.Va. Code § 33–13–26 (1996).

[19]Fla. Stat. Ann. § 627.408(2) (West 1996); S.D. Codified Laws Ann. § 58–11–41 (1996).

[20]Ferdinand S. Tinio, Annotation, *Time When Period Provided for in Suicide Clause of Life or Accident Policy Begins to Run,* 37 A.L.R. 3d 933, § 8 (1971).

[21]75 F.2d 476 (2d Cir. 1935).

[22]*Res nova* means "a new matter."

was limited to one year from "the date hereof"; that is, the date upon the policy. . . . Perhaps too the contrast between that phrase in the policy at bar and "the date of issue" in the incontestability clause, may be taken as some indication of a change of intent. Judged textually therefore, there is very good reason for holding that the clause speaks from the original date. It is of course true that our interpretation exposes the insurer to a risk which it would otherwise escape. An insured who had let a policy lapse might at any time within three years conceive the notion of getting it reinstated and then killing himself. Nevertheless we are disposed to hold that even on the theory of a new contract, which we should not ourselves have adopted, the reinstated policy is to be referred pro tanto[23] to the date of the original; at least that insurer who prepared the instrument must bear the doubts, so far as there are any. In the only decisions in which the point has arisen this has been the result. . . . Though the new contract be a reissue of the policy as of the date of the renewal, it would force beyond all reason the meaning of the incontestability clause to say that it barred a fraud which did not even exist when the policy became incontestable. The clause is one of limitation, not a license forever to cheat the insurer; unless construed in that preposterous way it must be an exception to the general principle that the policy as reinstated speaks from its old date. It may be the only exception; at least the suicide clause is not one.

Thus, Judge Hand ruled in this case that the suicide clause ran from the original policy date and not from the date of reinstatement, even though the law of the jurisdiction was that a reinstated policy was a new contract.

Addition of New Contract Terms

The courts have held that an insurer cannot impose new contract terms at the time of reinstatement if the policyowner has a contractual right to reinstate the policy.[24] For example, some insurers have attempted to add a war hazard exclusion clause at the time of reinstatement. Assume that, at the time an insurer was issuing policies without war hazard exclusion clauses, it issued to Oliver Ewing, age 21, a whole life policy with a reinstatement clause. Three years later, the policy lapsed for nonpayment of the premium. Two years after lapse, Ewing applies for reinstatement, submitting satisfactory evidence of insurability and the unpaid premiums plus interest. At this time, the insurer is issuing all of its new policies with a war hazard exclusion clause if the applicant is between the ages of 18 and 45. Can the insurer include a war hazard exclusion clause in Ewing's reinstated policy, as it is currently doing in all new policies issued to applicants in Ewing's age group? The cases indicate that it cannot.

In *Schiel v. New York Life Insurance Co.,*[25] a federal court, construing Arizona law, held that an insurer could not add an aviation hazard exclusion clause on reinstatement of a policy insuring the life of a prospective military pilot. There, the court said:

> The Company made no claim that Schiel had become uninsurable for ordinary life purposes in the amount originally written; in fact it conceded by its conduct that he was insurable for those purposes and in that amount. It declined, however, to reinstate the

---

[23]*Pro tanto* means "to a certain extent."
[24]Hogan v. John Hancock Mut. Life Ins. Co., 195 F.2d 834 (3d Cir. 1952).
[25]178 F.2d 729 (9th Cir. 1949), *cert. denied,* 339 U.S. 931 (1950).

ordinary life policy except upon a condition importing a concept of insurability at variance with the policy as written. This we think it might not do.

An understanding of the view taken may require some further analysis of the terms of the original policy. The clause relating to occupation has been quoted earlier. It provides that the policy is free of conditions as to residence, travel, occupation, and military and naval service. . . . [T]he insurer had contracted that the policy was free of conditions pertaining to any legitimate occupation, whether in connection with the armed services or otherwise. The condition imposed on reinstatement of the ordinary life coverage for all practical purposes nullified the occupation clause. Under guise of reinstatement the insurer undertook to rewrite the contract in such fashion as to repudiate a risk assumed at the outset. If it could do that it could with equal facility have excluded altogether the risks of military service or travel, whereas the insured's liberty of action in all those matters was a measure of his insurability fixed and determined by the original contract. Without further laboring the point, we add only that the word "reinstate," as used in the policy, is entitled to be given its ordinary meaning, which is to restore to a former state or position.

This case states the general rule that the insurer cannot add new conditions to a life insurance policy when reinstating it. *Occidental Life Insurance Co. v. Fried,*[26] a federal court case construing Connecticut law, summarizes the rule as follows:

An application for reinstatement, however, if accepted by the insurer, does not alter the terms and conditions of the basic contract of insurance; they customarily are already embodied in the policy itself, including any endorsements or documents attached. Upon reinstatement, the terms and conditions of the original policy do not change; premium rates, cash surrender value, loan value, beneficiary designation, an insured's indebtedness under the policy—in short, all basic obligations and rights—remain the same. The reinstatement provision is merely another contingent contractual feature of the policy pursuant to which the insured, having permitted his policy to lapse, is entitled, upon compliance with the conditions prescribed therein, including production of satisfactory evidence of insurability, to reinstatement of the original contract.

Law Governing the Reinstated Policy

The determination of which law governs the reinstated contract might depend on whether the contract is continuing or new. For example, laws mandating contract terms enacted between the original effective date and the reinstatement date will ordinarily be applicable if the contract is new, but not if it is continuing. In *Johnson v. Life Insurance Co. of Virginia,*[27] a statute requiring that, after lapse, an amount equal to the reserve be applied to purchase extended term insurance was enacted after the original policy date but before reinstatement. The reinstated policy lapsed. The court held that the reinstated contract was new because the policyowner had no contractual right of reinstatement. Therefore, the contract was subject to the statute. Thus, the beneficiary was entitled to the face amount as extended term insurance.

In addition, a question has sometimes arisen as to which state's laws govern the reinstated policy. For example, if the policyowner were living in state A when the policy was issued, but living in state B when it was reinstated, state A's laws might govern if the policy were continuing, whereas state B's laws might govern if it were new.

---

[26]245 F. Supp. 211 (D. Conn. 1965).
[27]169 So. 159 (La. Ct. App. 1936).

Summary

If a life insurance premium is not paid by the end of the grace period, the policy lapses except as to any nonforfeiture benefits. However, most life insurance policies contain a reinstatement provision that is required by state statutes. Because reinstatement is usually to the insurer's advantage, reinstatement provisions tend to be more favorable to the policyowner than state reinstatement statutes require.

Reinstatement provisions ordinarily give the policyowner the right to reinstate a lapsed policy at any time within three (or five) years from the date of lapse if the policyowner complies with certain conditions precedent. The conditions precedent usually are as follows: The policyowner must submit to the insurer a reinstatement application, evidence of the insured's insurability, and all unpaid premiums with interest. Any unpaid policy loans must be repaid with interest or be reinstated.

Insurability in connection with reinstatement usually has the same meaning that it has in connection with the original application, except for age. Ordinarily, the courts have held that *insurability* is a broader term than merely *good health* and includes such factors as habits, occupation, and finances. Insurability "satisfactory to the insurer," according to the majority view, means insurability satisfactory to a reasonable insurer.

According to the majority view, if the insured dies after all the conditions precedent in the reinstatement provision have been complied with but before the insurer has reviewed and approved the reinstatement application, the reinstatement will nevertheless be effective. The minority view is that the insurer must be permitted a reasonable time in which to accept or reject the reinstatement application. However, the insurer must act promptly or it might be held to have waived its right, if any, to reject the reinstatement application.

A reinstated life insurance policy is generally contestable for misstatements in the reinstatement application only, for the same length of time after reinstatement as the length of the original contestable period. However, the suicide period ordinarily does not run anew after reinstatement.

A reinstated policy, by the great weight of authority, is a continuing, rather than a new, contract. Therefore, the insurer usually cannot add new conditions to a reinstated life insurance policy.

ILLUSTRATIVE CASE

In this case, a beneficiary sued a life insurer for an amount allegedly due under a life insurance policy that allowed reinstatement. The court discussed whether a reinstatement creates a new contract or revives the old contract.

DOROTHY M. FEDER, Plaintiff

v.

BANKERS NATIONAL LIFE INSURANCE COMPANY, Defendant[28]
Superior Court of New Jersey, Law Division

STAMLER, J. S. C.

Plaintiff Dorothy M. Feder sues for the proceeds of a life insurance policy issued by defendant Bankers National Life Insurance Co. upon the life of her deceased husband David Feder. The policy issued and was dated June 4, 1962 for the face amount of $50,000. The annual premiums were $854.40 and the insured elected to pay the premiums on a monthly basis of $77 each. The initial June and July 4 premiums were paid by the insured but the premium due August 4 was not paid. Under the standard nonforfeiture provisions of the policy the insured was entitled to a grace period for payment of the overdue premium of 31 days, during which time the policy would remain in force. Paragraph 2 of the policy relating to the grace period provides:

> In the payment of any annual premium or installment thereof under this policy, except the first, a grace of 31 days will be allowed, during which time the policy will remain in force.

On September 5 the grace period expired. On September 1, 1962 the insured executed a written application for reinstatement of the policy which was submitted to the

---

[28]233 A.2d 395 (N.J. Super. Ct. Law Div. 1967), *aff'd,* 242 A.2d 632 (N.J. Super. Ct. App. Div. 1968), *cert. denied,* 244 A.2d 296 (N.J. 1968).

company, together with two monthly premium payments on September 24, representing the monthly payments due in August and September. Following investigation the company approved of reinstatement of the policy on September 24, 1962. The subsequent premium for October was not paid, and again pursuant to the grace period provisions of the contract, the insured was permitted 31 days to make payment of that premium. The insured died on November 10, 1962.

The foregoing represents agreed facts. Only two factual determinations were required to be submitted to the jury.

Plaintiff contended that on November 7, 1962 (three days before death) the insured paid in cash $77 (the monthly premium charge) to defendant through its agent, and that acceptance of the premium constituted a waiver by defendant. Defendant denied that any such payment was made, and the jury agreed. There is therefore no substance to this contention of plaintiff.

Plaintiff then takes the position that the premium payment made on September 24 created a new premium period and that subsequent premiums were not due on the fourth of each month. She argues that the payment made on that date was for the period September 24 to October 24 and therefore the grace period would have terminated on November 24. Accordingly, it is urged that the assured's death on November 10 occurred within the grace period. Relying for the most part on cases treating with accident and health policies, plaintiff states that the company cannot claim a premium for any period of time in which no coverage is afforded. These contentions implicitly contain the acknowledged rule that no contractual obligation is supportable without underlying consideration.

The question then is: Does the acceptance on September 24 of the reinstatement application and premium create a new and different contract or is it the revival of the old?

Plaintiff contends that it is a new contract, with September 24 as its premium date. Defendant asserts that it is a reinstatement of the old contract, the premium date of which is fixed at September 4.

The authorities support defendant's view. The following relevant language is found in 3A Appleman, Insurance Law and Practice, § 1971, p. 700 (1967):

> It has been held that a reinstatement can only be brought about by a valid contract between the parties. To this end, there must be a meeting of minds of the parties, application and acceptance, valid consideration, and full knowledge of the circumstances under which the application is made and the money paid. Under this rule, the parties have the right to fix the terms of such reinstatement.
>
> The foregoing rule concerns the contract governing the reinstatement, which contract has its inception when the insured applies for reinstatement and its termination upon the

acceptance by the insurer of that application. The question logically arises, then, as to whether the new policy is itself a different contract, a continuation of the intermediate contract, or a revival of the old.

On this point, no case seems to hold that the intermediate contract, that is, the contract inducing the reinstatement, continues. There is a division of authority, however, upon the question as to whether the old contract is thereby automatically revived. A few courts have held that a new contract of insurance is thereby created, containing new warranties, new conditions, and the like, just as if no prior policy had ever existed. This is definitely a minority holding. The overwhelming majority of courts hold that the old contract is thereby reinstated and revived, and the new policy is merely a continuation of the old coverage.

As noted, most of the cases cited by plaintiff deal with reinstatement of accident or health policies. It is clear that life insurance policies must fall into a different category. A reinstated life policy continues at the same premium rate, instead of increasing to the age at which insurance is reinstated; the incontestability clauses and suicide provisions run from the earlier date; the cash surrender and loan value are reached at an earlier date; paid-up extended term options are sooner reached. There can be no doubt about the essential and important equities and reservations of right in a life policy over and beyond those of a reinstated accident and health policy. *Cf. Kampf v. Franklin Life Ins. Co.,* 33 N.J. 36, 161 A.2d 717 (1960), where the court stressed the importance of the "birth" date of a life policy and the advantages of an earlier "birth" date.

In *Acacia Mutual Life Ass'n v. Kaul,* 114 N.J.Eq. 491, 169 A. 36 (Ch.1933), the court said:

> The reinstatement of the policy was not the issuance of a new policy nor the reissuance of the original policy. It was the waiver of the lapse of the original policy, and the reinstatement of that policy in full force and effect according to its terms, all its terms. One of those terms is the incontestability clause. No contest can be made therefore on the original policy itself . . . (at p. 492, 169 A. at p. 36)

This language was directed to the insurer's claim, in its action for rescission of the policy, of fraudulent misrepresentations inducing the original insurance [*sic*] of the policy. (Rescission was granted in the case of the reinstatement contract and judgment rendered for the insurer.) The above quotation is set forth for its reference to "all the terms" of an insurance contract being given full effect upon reinstatement.

The case of *New York Life Ins. Co. v. Weiss,* 133 N.J.Eq. 375, 32 A.2d 341 (E. & A. 1943), cited in the briefs of both parties, was a suit by the insurer to cancel and rescind a life insurance policy for fraudulent representations. Insofar as it is relevant at all, it stands only for the proposition that reinstatement is a contract separate and distinct from the original contract of insurance.

A foreign decision very similar to, if not indistinguishable from, the present case is *Travelers Protective Ass'n of America v. Ziegler,* 250 S.W. 1115 (Tex. Civ. App.1923). The insured in that case paid his last premium on January 15, 1921, covering the six months ending on June 30, 1921. The "dues" for the next six-month period should have been paid on or before June 30 to avoid the lapse which occurred by virtue of the Association's by-laws. The insured died on July 2, 1921.

It [was] the contention of appellee that, as deceased was reinstated on *January 15, 1921,* and on that date paid the semi annual dues of $5.50, he had fully paid up to *July 15,* and consequently was not in arrears for the dues when he was killed on July 2. (at p. 1116)

In answer the court said:

Under that contention deceased suffered no penalty whatever for becoming delinquent, but could by becoming delinquent at the end of each successive 6 months gain nearly a month free from dues and return to the fold. (at p. 1117)

It must therefore be concluded that notwithstanding the reinstatement, the original premium dates and policy dates remained and that the grace period had expired five days before death.

* * * * *

The ineluctable conclusion is that on all contentions plaintiff has failed to demonstrate her right to recover on the lapsed policy.

A judgment of no cause for action will be entered against plaintiff.

Questions for Review

1. Distinguish between lapse and expiration.
2. List the requirements for reinstatement found in the typical reinstatement provision of a life insurance policy.
3. Distinguish between *insurability* and *good health.*
4. What is meant by *antiselection*? How is the insurability requirement for reinstatement related to antiselection?
5. What is the majority view concerning the meaning of the phrase *satisfactory to the insurer* in connection with the evidence of insurability required for reinstatement?
6. Ordinarily, reinstatement results in a continuation of the original contract. Under what conditions have courts held that reinstatement creates a new contract?
7. What is the law in the majority of states regarding the application of the incontestable clause to a reinstated policy?
8. What is the general rule as to the application of the suicide clause to a reinstated policy?
9. On what grounds have the courts generally held that the insurer must not put new contract terms into a reinstated policy?

16   EQUITABLE REMEDIES

Chapter Outline

The same legal and equitable remedies that are available to any contracting party ordinarily are available to the parties to a life insurance contract. However, certain equitable remedies are especially important to insurers because of the types of disputes that develop over life insurance contracts. For example, the equitable remedy of *interpleader* is often vital in dealing with disputes between two or more claimants to the policy benefits. Insurers sometimes seek the remedy of *rescission* if an application for insurance contains a material misrepresentation. The remedy of *reformation* could be necessary if a mistake were made in drafting the policy. Finally, if a dispute has arisen between an insurer and a claimant, one of the parties might seek a *declaratory judgment* to determine the parties' rights and duties.

These remedies originated in the English courts of equity and usually are subject to equitable principles. Equitable principles will therefore be examined in this chapter, so that the reader can gain a better understanding of the equitable remedies. The remedies themselves will also be examined in detail.

Equitable Principles

The courts of equity developed in England because of the rigidity of the common-law courts. Thus, equity courts have always been more flexible in their approach to dispensing justice than have law courts. Equity courts developed their own rules that a person requesting equitable relief had to follow. Today, courts of law and courts of equity have merged in most jurisdictions in the United States, and parties often seek both legal and equitable relief from the same judge in the same court action. Nevertheless, many equitable principles still prevail, the most important of which are discussed below.

No Adequate Remedy at Law

The function of equity is to supplement, not to replace, the law. Therefore, to maintain a suit in equity the plaintiff must not have an adequate remedy in an action at law. In most situations, the legal remedy, which is usually damages (money), is sufficient to do justice to the plaintiff. But in some situations, damages will not suffice.

For example, suppose Bruce McDonald's neighbor has built a stone fence that juts onto McDonald's property. Suppose also that the neighbor refuses to remove the fence. McDonald does not want damages. He wants the fence removed.

Or suppose McDonald's neighbor holds excessively loud parties night after night, and the parties are interfering with McDonald's sleep and damaging his health. Again, damages will not suffice. McDonald wants the noise to stop.

Finally, suppose the Jordan Life Insurance Company has discovered a material misrepresentation in an application for a life insurance policy it issued 18 months ago. Suppose also that Jordan Life tenders back the premiums the policyowner paid and tells the policyowner that it wishes to rescind the policy, but the policyowner will not accept the premiums or agree to the rescission. Damages will not suffice here, either. Jordan Life wants to have the contract rescinded—that is, decreed void by the court.

In each of these situations, McDonald or Jordan Life could seek an equitable remedy, because the legal remedy of damages will not provide relief. In the first case, the court could command the neighbor to remove the fence. This command is called a ***mandatory injunction***—a command that a person do something. In the second case, the court could command the neighbor to stop holding the loud parties. This command is called a ***prohibitory injunction***—a command that a person stop doing something. In either case, the court could enforce its command. If the neighbor did not obey, she could be fined or jailed for contempt of court.

As to Jordan Life's suit for rescission of the life insurance contract, the court could restore Jordan Life to the position it had before it entered into the contract. That is, the court could decree the contract void, on the condition that Jordan Life return all premiums paid on the contract.

Clean Hands

One important maxim of equity is that "a person who comes into equity must come with clean hands." This means that the court will deny relief to the plaintiff in a suit in equity if she has acted unfairly or dishonestly as to the matter at issue. The equity court was originally called "the court of the King's conscience." A court of conscience will not spend its time and the public's money helping a person who has acted inequitably.

Laches

Another maxim of equity is that "Equity aids the vigilant." This means that the plaintiff in equity must not unreasonably delay in enforcing his rights, if such delay will harm the defendant. If the plaintiff has unreasonably delayed, and the delay has harmed the defendant, the plaintiff will be guilty of *laches.* A court will deny equitable relief to a plaintiff who is guilty of laches.

For example, suppose Bruce McDonald had known that the stone fence encroached on his property as his neighbor was building the fence. Suppose McDonald did not complain to the neighbor until the fence was complete. The equity court likely would hold McDonald guilty of laches and deny him equitable relief.

Equity and the Jury

Ordinarily, in a lawsuit, the jury decides questions of fact and the judge decides questions of law. If a case involves a dispute as to what actions were taken, what events occurred, or what circumstances existed (the facts), the jury will hear the evidence and decide what is true. This is called a finding of fact. However, the judge makes the ruling on the legal effect of the facts so decided.

In a suit in equity, there ordinarily is no jury. The judge, therefore, has the power to decide every question, whether of fact or of law, that comes before the court. The constitutionally guaranteed right to a jury trial does not apply to suits in equity.[1] If it seems advisable, the judge in a suit in equity sometimes submits a question of fact to a jury for decision, but as a general rule the finding of the jury will be advisory only.

A 1949 case brought in the U.S. District Court for the District of Maryland illustrates this aspect of equity.[2] In that case, an insurance company brought suit to have the court decree two policies of life insurance void on the ground that the insured had misrepresented material facts in the applications. The defendants requested a jury trial, but the court held that the issues were equitable, rather than legal, and that the defendants had no right to a jury trial. The opinion reads in part as follows:

> It is very well known that the Federal rules of civil procedure while generally merging law and equity cases for procedural matters, were not intended to destroy the distinction

[1] In some states, there are statutes providing for the trial of fact issues by a jury in certain equitable actions.

[2] Connecticut Gen. Life Ins. Co. v. Candimat Co., 83 F. Supp. 1 (D. Md. 1949).

between law and equity with respect to the matter of jury trials. In a typical case for equitable relief, such as the instant case, there was no right to a jury trial. On the contrary it is well established both by federal and Maryland law and judicial decisions that in equity cases, where there is no adequate remedy at law, there is no right to a jury trial at common law or by statute.

Interpleader

If two or more persons claim money or other property that is in the possession of a third person who does not claim to be the owner, the third person can give the property to the court and ask the court to decide who is entitled to it. This is the equitable remedy of *interpleader.* Interpleader is important to insurers, because they often face conflicting claimants to insurance proceeds. When a life insurance policy has been in force for many years—with beneficiary changes, assignments and reassignments, and other policy transactions occurring—conflicting claims may arise among successive beneficiaries, beneficiaries and assignees, beneficiaries and persons claiming community property rights, and so forth.

An insurer facing conflicting claims for policy proceeds would be in a difficult position without the equitable remedy of interpleader. The insurer's payment to one claimant, if that claimant is not the one entitled to the proceeds, usually means that the insurer will have to pay the same claim twice. Ordinarily, only a court can decide, with safety to the insurer, who among the conflicting claimants is entitled to the proceeds.

Without interpleader, the insurer also would be exposed to the danger that each claimant would sue it in a separate legal action. This is called a multiplicity of lawsuits. Each claimant conceivably could win his lawsuit and thus subject the insurer to multiple liability. Interpleader prevents this possibility, because once the conflicting claimants are joined in an interpleader suit, the court will prevent them from beginning or continuing another legal action to recover the proceeds. The court commands the claimants not to begin or to cease such actions. In other words, it tells them not to do, or to stop doing, something. Thus, interpleader includes a prohibitory injunction.

One court gave the following concise description of the reasons that the interpleader remedy was developed:

> The fundamental basis for interpleader is to permit the holder of a fund who admits he is not the owner of it to put the fund in the hands of the court, so that claimants with substantial contentions may fight out their claims to it and so that the holder will be shielded from the danger of deciding at its peril who is rightfully entitled to the fund, as well as from the burden of defending and danger of losing separate lawsuits brought by each claimant.[3]

Another reason for development of the interpleader remedy is that it conserves judicial resources. Adjudication of the rights of all claimants in one suit, rather than in two or more suits, prevents duplication of effort by the courts.

Because court action means delay in performing a service that an insurer usually performs promptly, the insurer often encourages conflicting claimants to settle the matter among themselves. However, if they are unwilling to do so, the insurer usually must seek interpleader to protect itself.

---

[3]United Benefit Life Ins. Co. v. Katz, 155 F. Supp. 391 (E.D. Pa. 1957).

Statutory Interpleader

Federal and state interpleader statutes and court rules have liberalized many of the equitable rules of interpleader. The federal Interpleader Act[4] and federal Rule of Civil Procedure 22 govern interpleader in the federal courts. Under the federal Interpleader Act, diversity of citizenship between the insurer and one of the claimants is necessary. Also, $500 or more must be in controversy.

No Adequate Remedy at Law

As with other types of equity suits, in cases involving conflicting claimants to insurance proceeds, the court will allow interpleader only if no adequate remedy at law is available. In almost all cases in which a life insurer seeks interpleader, no adequate remedy at law is available, certainly so if the insurer has a reasonable doubt as to which of two or more conflicting claimants is entitled to insurance proceeds.

If no reasonable doubt exists as to which of the claimants is entitled to the proceeds, some courts deny interpleader because the insurer has an adequate remedy at law.[5] According to these courts, an insurer should pay the claimant entitled to the proceeds and defend itself if the claimant who is not entitled files an action at law. However, usually a reasonable doubt will exist as to who is entitled to the funds; hence, no adequate remedy at law will be available.

Moreover, other courts have held that a stakeholder need not make a judgment as to whether or not a reasonable doubt exists as to which claimant is entitled to the proceeds. One court said:

> The jurisdiction of a federal court to entertain a bill of interpleader is not dependent upon the merits of the claims of the defendants. . . . It is our opinion that a stakeholder, acting in good faith, may maintain a suit in interpleader for the purpose of ridding himself of the vexation and expense of resisting adverse claims, even though he believes that only one of them is meritorious. As the Supreme Court said in *Myers v. Bethlehem Corporation,* 303 U.S. 41, 51 ". . . Lawsuits also often prove to have been groundless; but no way has been discovered of relieving a defendant from the necessity of a trial to establish the fact."[6]

Interpleader Instituted by Plaintiff or Defendant

An insurer can interplead in one of two ways. First, it can file a bill of interpleader as a plaintiff. The bill of interpleader permits the insurer to pay the proceeds into the court and requires the conflicting claimants to bring their claims before the court—that is, to interplead their claims. The court usually will dismiss the insurer from the suit at this point. The insurer is then discharged of all liability. The court will go on to decide which claimant is entitled to the money.

Second, if one of the claimants sues the insurer before the insurer has filed a bill of interpleader, the insurer usually can defend itself by filing a cross bill of interpleader. The court will then bring the other claimant, or claimants, into the suit and dismiss the insurer from it.

---

[4]28 U.S.C.A. §§ 1335, 1397 & 2361 (West 1993 & 1994).

[5]Great Am. Reserve Ins. Co. v. Sanders, 525 S.W.2d 956 (Tex. 1975); Kurz v. New York Life Ins. Co., 168 So.2d 564 (Fla. Dist. Ct. App. 1964), *motion denied,* 174 So.2d 537 (Fla. 1965).

[6]Hunter v. Federal Life Ins. Co., 111 F.2d 551 (8th Cir. 1940).

Disinterested Stakeholder

Ordinarily, to institute an interpleader suit or defend with a cross bill of interpleader, the person holding the money or other property, called the stakeholder, must claim no interest in the property held. He must be a disinterested stakeholder. An insurer holding life insurance policy proceeds is usually a disinterested stakeholder. The insurer itself makes no claim to the proceeds.

Sometimes the insurer does have an interest in the proceeds. In such a case, the insurer can file a bill in the nature of interpleader. The insurer is not then required, as in strict interpleader, to be a disinterested stakeholder.

For example, sometimes an insurer disputes the amount claimed. In one case, the insured changed the beneficiary from his first wife to his second wife and then took out a policy loan. After his death, the first wife claimed that the insurer had no right to change the beneficiary or to grant the loan. When the insurer tendered the policy proceeds to the court, minus the amount of the loan, a controversy arose as to the amount of the insurer's liability. The court held that the insurer was not a disinterested stakeholder and therefore denied the insurer's bill of interpleader.[7] In such a case, a bill in the nature of interpleader would be appropriate.

Claimants Claiming the Same Property

In an interpleader suit, the claimants must be claiming the same property. Again, this is usually the case if an insurer is the stakeholder. The conflicting claimants will be claiming the same policy proceeds.

Conflicting Claimants in Different States

A problem arises when conflicting claimants to the same life insurance proceeds reside in different states. Suppose, for example, that an insurer domiciled in Illinois is licensed to do business in Texas and Florida. The insurer can be sued in both Texas and Florida, because it does business in those states. Now suppose that there are two conflicting claimants to the same life insurance proceeds—one living in Texas and the other living in Florida. The insurer is in danger of being sued in both of those states. The insurer needs a court that can serve process on both claimants in an interpleader suit. Neither the Texas state courts nor the Florida state courts will do. The Texas state courts have no jurisdiction over the Florida resident, and the Florida state courts have no jurisdiction over the Texas resident.

A federal interpleader action is the answer to this problem. The federal interpleader statute confers the power of nationwide service of process on a federal district court in any district where a claimant lives "or may be found."[8] The insurer could therefore institute an interpleader suit in a federal district court in either Texas or Florida. The district court can enter an order restraining the claimants from beginning or continuing a court action elsewhere. The insurer can pay the policy proceeds into the district court and be dismissed from the suit, leaving the conflicting claimants to litigate their rights there.

---

[7]Williams v. Penn Mut. Life Ins. Co., 133 So. 649 (Miss. 1931), *aff'd,* 140 So. 875 (Miss. 1932).
[8]28 U.S.C.A. § 2361 (West 1994).

Rescission

The equitable remedy of *rescission* is also important to insurers. A rescinded contract is void from the beginning.

Rescission can be accomplished in three ways: (1) by an agreement of the parties; (2) by one of the parties declaring rescission of the contract if a legally sufficient ground exists, accompanied by tender of the consideration (in most states this method is ineffective for life insurers because of the incontestable clause, as explained below); or (3) by a decree of rescission issued by a court.

If the application for insurance includes a material misrepresentation, and the insurer discovers the misrepresentation while the insured is alive[9] and within the contestable period, the insurer ordinarily will pursue a rescission of the contract. The insurer usually will first attempt to effect a rescission by agreement with the policyowner. The insurer will tender the premiums back to the policyowner and tell him it wishes to rescind. If the policyowner agrees and accepts the premiums, the rescission will be effective.

If the policyowner will not agree to the rescission, the insurer usually will sue in equity for rescission. In most states, merely declaring a rescission of the contract will not suffice in the case of a life insurance contract because of the incontestable clause. The incontestable clause ordinarily states that the insurer will not contest the validity of the policy, except for nonpayment of premiums, after it has been in force during the insured's lifetime for two years from the policy date. If the insured died more than two years after the policy date, the insurer would lose its misrepresentation defense and could not contest the validity of the policy. Unless the insurer had another defense, it would have to pay the proceeds. Therefore, the insurer will ordinarily sue for rescission in equity if it learns of misrepresentation during the contestable period. If the court grants the rescission, all that the insurer will have to pay is the amount of the premiums paid.

Grounds for Rescission

There are a number of grounds on which one party will have a right to rescind a contract. Mutual mistake as to a material fact is one ground. Misrepresentation of a material fact is another. The mutual mistake or the misrepresentation must have occurred either before or at the time that the parties entered into the contract. The mutual mistake or the misrepresentation cannot have occurred after the contract is in force.

A mutual mistake as to a material fact occurs if both parties are mistaken as to the same material fact. For example, suppose Maurice Renaud paid the Marvel Insurance Company $150,000 for a straight life annuity contract under which Marvel agreed to make monthly payments to Maurice's mother, Jeanne Renaud, for the rest of Jeanne's life. Both Maurice and Marvel believed at the time they entered into the contract that Jeanne, who was 55 years old, was in good health and had a normal life expectancy. In fact, Jeanne had been killed in an airplane accident two days earlier. Since both parties were mistaken as to a material fact—Jeanne's being alive—Maurice will be able to rescind the contract and get back the $150,000 he paid Marvel.

---

[9]A suit for rescission after the insured's death can be maintained where the words *during the lifetime of the insured* are omitted from the incontestable clause. This will be discussed in a later subsection entitled "Rescission and the Incontestable Clause."

The ground for rescission of most importance to insurers is misrepresentation of a material fact. An insurer must select the lives it will insure on the basis of correct information so that the rate of mortality actually experienced approximates that which the insurer predicted using its mortality tables. Misrepresentations of material facts in life insurance applications interfere with the insurer's proper selection of lives to be insured and result in loss to the insurer. Misrepresentations of material facts in applications also interfere with the insurer's ability to set adequate premiums.

Materiality

Rescission of a contract is an appropriate remedy if there was a mutual mistake or a misrepresentation by one party, but usually only if the mistake or misrepresentation is based on a *material fact.* The test of materiality is whether, if a party had known the fact, she would have entered into the contract. If the party would not have entered into the contract knowing the fact, the fact is material.

Misrepresentation of a fact that is not material usually will not be a ground for rescission, although some states will allow rescission for misrepresentation of a fact that is not material if the misrepresentation was intentional, as is discussed below. Many misrepresentations in insurance applications are of facts that are not material. For example, suppose a life insurance applicant discloses a visit to his physician and states as the reason for the visit "ankle sprain." Even if the condition was not techni-cally a sprain, the misrepresentation ordinarily would not be material because it would not have affected the insurer's decision. The New York Insurance Code states the test of materiality as follows:

> No misrepresentation shall be deemed material unless knowledge by the insurer of the facts misrepresented would have led to a refusal by the insurer to make such contract.[10]

Intentional Misrepresentation

Some states have statutes allowing an insurer to rescind a life insurance contract if the applicant intentionally misrepresented a fact, whether or not the fact was mate-rial. The Illinois statute is typical and reads as follows:

> No . . . misrepresentation . . . shall defeat or avoid the policy unless it shall have been made with actual intent to deceive *or* materially affects either the acceptance of the risk or the hazard assumed by the company. [Emphasis added.][11]

Under this type of statute, either intentional misrepresentation or misrepresenta-tion of a material fact will give the insurer a ground on which to rescind the policy.

Fraud

Intentional misrepresentation of a material fact constitutes *fraud.* In every state, fraud is a ground for rescission of a contract. For example, suppose Raymond Han-sen submits an application for life insurance on his own life. The application he completes contains the following question: "Have you ever had, or been told by a

---

[10]N.Y. Ins. Law § 3105(b) (McKinney 1985).
[11]215 Ill. Comp. Stat. 5/154 (Michie Supp. 1996). See also La. Rev. Stat. Ann. § 22:619 (West 1995); Tenn. Code Ann. § 56–7–103 (1994); Wash. Rev. Code Ann. § 48.18.090 (West 1984).

physician that you had, a heart disorder or disease?'' Hansen answers "no," although he knows the answer is false because he had been hospitalized with a severe heart attack six months earlier. Four months after the effective date of the policy, the insurer learns of Hansen's heart attack. In this case, the insurer has a ground for rescission because of Hansen's fraud and will be able to maintain a suit for rescission, because the policy is still within the contestable period.

In some states, misrepresentation statutes prohibit an insurer from using a misrepresentation in the application as a ground for rescission of the policy unless the misrepresentation was fraudulent. A misrepresentation that is material but not intentional will not suffice as a ground for rescission. For example, Ohio requires the following:

> No answer to any interrogatory made by an applicant in his application for a policy shall bar the right to recover upon any policy issued thereon, or be used in evidence at any trial to recover upon such policy, unless it is clearly proved that such answer is willfully false, that it was fraudulently made, that it is material, and that it induced the company to issue the policy, that but for such answer the policy would not have been issued, and that the agent or company had no knowledge of the falsity or fraud of such answer.[12]

In a situation in which an insurer claims the applicant made a fraudulent misrepresentation, it must prove that the applicant acted with intent to deceive. However, the courts will infer an intent to deceive if the facts clearly indicate that there could be no other explanation.

For example, in one Pennsylvania case, the applicant had had at least 13 consultations with four different physicians in a city 100 miles from her home within the two years before the date of application. Yet she stated in her application that she had had no consultations with any physician within the past seven years. The court said:

> The consultations were clearly of such important character and of such recent occurrence as could not be forgotten, and the insured must have been fully cognizant that she hid them from the insurer by her false answer. In this connection, we said in *Evans v. Penn Mutual Life Ins. Co.,* 322 Pa. 547, 553, 186 A. 133, 138: "The circumstances preceding and attending the making of the statements may be such that the insured must be said to have been aware of their falsity at the time or that an inference of fraud is otherwise irresistible, as for instance where an unreported illness or disability of insured was so serious and so recent that he could not have forgotten it."[13]

Misrepresentation Related to the Cause of Loss

A few states take the position that material misrepresentation cannot be used as a basis for rescission of the policy unless the misrepresentation is related to the actual cause of loss. For example, in Missouri, the misrepresentation statute reads as follows:

> No misrepresentation made in obtaining or securing a policy of insurance on the life or lives of any person or persons, citizens of this state, shall be deemed material, or render the policy void, unless the matter misrepresented shall have actually contributed to the contingency or event on which the policy is to become due and payable, and whether it so contributed in any case shall be a question for the jury.[14]

---

[12]Ohio Rev. Code Ann. § 3911.06 (Page 1989).
[13]Bailey v. Pacific Mut. Life Ins. Co., 6 A.2d 770 (Pa. 1939).
[14]Mo. Ann. Stat. § 376.580 (Vernon 1991).

Under a statute of this kind, for example, the court would not permit the insurer to defend a claim denial on the basis of material misrepresentation in the application if the misrepresented facts related to a malignancy and the insured died of a heart attack. Only if the insured died of the malignancy could the insurer defend the claim denial.

Rescission and the Incontestable Clause

The illustrative policy in the Appendix, Figure 2, contains the following language:

> We will not contest the validity of this Policy, except for nonpayment of premiums, after it has been in force during the Insured's lifetime for two years from the Policy Date.

This language stops the running of the incontestable clause at the insured's death. Therefore, if the insured dies prior to the expiration of the contestable period and the incontestable clause includes the phrase *during the lifetime of the insured,* or words to that effect, the insurer ordinarily can use evidence of material misrepresentation in defense of a lawsuit by the beneficiary.

In such circumstances, because the insurer has an adequate remedy at law, the equitable remedy of rescission is not available. For example, assume that Chester Horner, an insured, dies of leukemia three months after issuance of his life insurance policy. Suppose the policy had an incontestable clause containing the phrase *during the lifetime of the insured.* The insurer's investigation reveals that Horner's illness was diagnosed two years prior to his death and that Horner knew of the diagnosis. Nevertheless, his answers to the application questions gave no hint of ill health of any kind, even though two of the questions, if honestly answered, would have elicited information about the leukemia. This, of course, is intentional misrepresentation of a material fact, or fraud. The insurer will deny the claim for the death benefit in accordance with its usual procedures. If the beneficiary sues, the insurer will show the court that the insured misrepresented information material to the appraisal of the risk at the time of application. This ordinarily will constitute an effective defense for the insurer. Consequently, the insurer has an adequate remedy at law, and equitable rescission is not available to it.

However, in most jurisdictions the situation described above would change if the wording of the incontestable clause did not include the phrase *during the lifetime of the insured.* Without this phrase, the incontestable clause continues to run after the insured's death, and the beneficiary could wait until after two years from the policy date to sue. At that time, the policy would be incontestable for any misrepresentations in the application. Therefore, if the phrase *during the lifetime of the insured* is *not* included, the insurer has no adequate remedy at law and can sue for rescission of the contract after the insured's death. However, the insurer would have to bring its suit for rescission during the contestable period.

Reformation

Reformation is an equitable remedy that provides for the revision or interpretation of a written contract to express the original intent of the parties when the contract, as written, fails to do so. The purpose of reformation is not to make a new contract but to change the wording of the existing contract to reflect the original agreement of the parties.

Insurers prepare life insurance policies with the utmost care and use computers to assure a high degree of accuracy. However, mistakes sometimes occur, and a mistake in a life insurance policy is often serious. Perhaps 20-year endowment values were inadvertently included in a 20-pay life policy. Possibly a word processor moved a decimal point one place to the right. Perhaps figures have been reversed. In any case, the insurer must inform the policyowner of the error as soon as the insurer discovers it. The insurer must explain the nature of the error to the policyowner and request permission to correct it.

Assume, however, that the policyowner does not grant permission to correct the error. The policy states the face value as $100,000 instead of $10,000, and the policyowner declares her firm intention to enforce it according to its written terms. At this point, the insurer's lawyer considers the equitable remedy of reformation.

Grounds for Reformation

The general rules that apply to the reformation of other written contracts usually apply to insurance contracts also.[15] The three grounds for reformation of contracts are mutual mistake, unilateral mistake, and misrepresentation.

Mutual mistake occurs if the writing does not conform to the original agreement and both parties are unaware of the discrepancy. For example, suppose someone purchases an annuity contract providing $20,000 per year but by mistake the contract reads $20,000 per month. Neither party is aware of the error. Later, the insurer discovers the error and seeks to correct it. The annuitant refuses and demands $20,000 per month. The equity court will reform the contract to reflect the parties' original intent if the insurer can provide clear and convincing proof of the terms of the original agreement.[16]

In a case of unilateral mistake—that is, where one party knows of the mistake and the other does not—the court can reform the contract, according to the modern trend. A denial of relief would enable the party who knows of the mistake to benefit at the expense of the mistaken party. Reformation acts to conform the writing to the original agreement. Neither party suffers a hardship because each is getting what he originally bargained for.

A case in which the court discussed reformation for mistake is *Flax v. Prudential Life Insurance Co.*[17] There, the policyowner had converted his policy to paid-up whole life insurance in the amount of $2,755. Due to a mistake that the law continues to call a *scrivener's error*—that is, an error by the person who wrote the contract— the cash value stated in the written contract was $5,495.26. The policyowner attempted to recover this cash value from the insurer, but the insurer counterclaimed for reformation of the contract. The court granted the reformation, saying:

> The defendant [the insurer] had no knowledge of the existence of the mistake until during the month of June 1954, at which time, in the course of processing an application by the plaintiff for a loan on the policy, it discovered it. The defendant immediately notified the plaintiff of the mistake and requested him to join in the reformation of the policy to rectify it, which he has refused to do.

---

[15]Irwin J. Schiffres, Annotation, *Reformation of Insurance Policy to Correctly Identify Risks and Causes of Loss,* 32 A.L.R. 3d 661 (1970).

[16]Travelers Ins. Co. v. Bailey, 197 A.2d 813 (Vt. 1964).

[17]148 F. Supp. 720 (S.D. Cal. 1957).

[W]hen, either through mutual mistake or unilateral mistake by one party which is known to the other, the policy does not express the intention of the parties, reformation may be had either when an action is instituted by the insured to enforce its provisions or in a direct action brought by the insurer to make the policy speak verity.

From time immemorial, it has been the function of equity as administered in the federal courts to remedy what is known as "scrivener's mistakes"—mistakes performed by the person who drafted the instrument in such a manner that it did not express what was *actually* agreed. In an early case, the Supreme Court of the United States stated the principle and the reasons for it in this manner:

> There are certain principles of equity, applicable to this question, which, as general principles, we hold to be incontrovertible. The first is, that where an instrument is drawn and executed, which professes or is intended to carry into execution an agreement, whether in writing or by parol, previously entered into, but which, *by mistake of the draftsman, either as to fact or law, does not fulfil, or which violates, the manifest intention of the parties to the agreement, equity will correct the mistake, so as to produce conformity of the instrument to the agreement.* The reason is obvious: the execution of agreements, fairly and legally entered into, is one of the peculiar branches of equity jurisdiction; and if the instrument which is intended to execute the agreement be, from any cause, insufficient for that purpose, *the agreement remains as much unexecuted, as if one of the parties had refused, altogether, to comply with his engagement;* and a court of equity will, in the exercise of its acknowledged jurisdiction, afford relief in the one case, as well as in the other, *by compelling the delinquent party fully to perform his agreement, according to the terms of it, and to the manifest intention of the parties.* . . . [Emphasis added.]

. . . To summarize: The plaintiff either did or did not know of the mistake. *If he did,* it appearing that the mistake *was not known* to the insurer, we have the type of unilateral mistake for which relief by way of reformation is granted. *If he did not* know the mistake, we have a case of mutual mistake for which reformation also lies. Indeed, relief may be granted by disregarding the printed words which the scrivener erroneously failed to delete.

. . . So, if plaintiff's present demands were allowed, he would receive something which he did not bargain or pay for,—something for nothing. The language of the Persian poet applies:

"Sue for a Debt he never did contract,
And cannot answer—
Oh, the sorry trade."[18]

It would be neither good morals nor good law to sanction the application of such a policy to business relations.

On the other hand, a ruling for the defendant avoids a palpable injustice and still allows the plaintiff the full benefit of the contract *he and the company intended* to make.

Judgment will, therefore, be for the defendant.

Thus, the court held that the insurer could pay the amount that the policy should have stated.

Misrepresentation, either innocent or intentional, can also be a ground for reformation. In this case, the court will reform the contract to reflect the expressed intent of the parties, without regard to whether the misrepresenting party actually intended the contract to differ from that expressed intent. In misrepresentation cases, the party seeking reformation knows what he has agreed to but is deluded as to the content of the contract he signed.

---

[18]Omar Khayyám, *Rubáiyát of Omar Khayyám of Naishápúr* (Edward FitzGerald, trans.) in IMMORTAL POEMS OF THE ENGLISH LANGUAGE 360 (Oscar Williams ed. 1961).

For example, suppose Robert Feldman agrees to buy 100 acres of farmland. However, the contract Feldman signs, which the other party prepared, obligates Feldman to buy 200 acres. Feldman can sue for reformation of the written contract to make it reflect his agreement. Note that Feldman does not wish to rescind the contract. He wants to purchase the 100 acres. He merely wants the contract to reflect his agreement.

If an insurer, through misrepresentation of the contents of a policy, leads the applicant to believe that the policy provides coverage not actually stated in the policy, the courts have reformed the policy to conform to the applicant's and the insurer's original agreement.[19]

Burden of Proof

The courts strongly presume that a written contract correctly expresses the intention of the parties. For this reason, the courts will grant reformation only if the plaintiff can produce clear and convincing proof of the terms of the original agreement. Clear and convincing proof is stronger proof than that usually required in civil (noncriminal) court actions. The usual level of proof required in civil actions is a preponderance of the evidence or, simply, more convincing proof than the other side presents. Clear and convincing proof, on the other hand, is proof that will produce a firm belief in the trier of fact's mind of the truth of the allegations that the plaintiff seeks to establish. Thus, the plaintiff's burden of proof in a suit for reformation is more difficult to sustain than that in most civil actions.

Declaratory Judgment

Declaratory judgment suits have their roots in equity, although today the right to a declaratory judgment is granted by federal or state statute. Congress enacted the federal Declaratory Judgment Act[20] in 1934. Most states have declaratory judgment acts patterned on the Uniform Declaratory Judgments Act.[21]

In a ***declaratory judgment,*** as the name implies, the court declares the rights and duties of the parties involved in the suit. A declaratory judgment differs markedly from other suits in equity or actions at law in that it does not require either of the parties to take any action or to pay money to the other.

As to life and health insurance contracts, the declaratory judgment has many applications. Questions involving contract interpretation, claims, and the legality of insurance regulations are among those that can be resolved by a declaratory judgment.

Contract Interpretation

A court can resolve questions involving the interpretation of an insurance contract by a declaratory judgment. *Liner v. Penn Mutual Life Insurance Co.*[22] illustrates this point. In the *Liner* case, the court interpreted two life insurance policies, one naming as beneficiary the insured's son, and the other his daughter. The policyowner-insured

---

[19]Layh v. Jonas, 535 P.2d 661 (Idaho 1975).

[20]28 U.S.C.A. §§ 2201, 2202 (West 1994).

[21]The Uniform Declaratory Judgments Act is a model law approved in 1922 by the National Conference of Commissioners on Uniform State Laws and by the American Bar Association.

[22]145 N.Y.S.2d 560 (N.Y. App. Div. 1955).

had intended these policies to provide for the educational expenses of his son and daughter. Both policies provided that, on the death of the insured, the insurer was to hold the proceeds under the interest option with interest payable to the insured's widow, as trustee, during the minority of each beneficiary. Each policy gave the widow the right to withdraw $500 per year in a lump sum until the insurer received an affidavit from a college stating that the beneficiary of the policy was enrolled there. After the insurer's receipt of the affidavit, $1,250 per year could be withdrawn.

Both policies contained accidental death coverage, and because the insured's death was accidental, this additional benefit was payable. The question before the court was whether the amounts that could be withdrawn would be doubled, since the total amount payable was doubled. The beneficiaries asked for declaratory judgments to that effect, but the insurer contended that the accidental death benefit merely doubled the sum payable and had no effect on the withdrawal privileges. The trial court held in favor of the contention of the insurer, and the beneficiaries appealed.

The appellate court reversed the trial court's judgment, ruled for the beneficiaries, and discussed the question in this way:

> The purpose of the insured throughout these transactions was to protect his children during approximately the first twenty years of their lives and to insure that they would receive a college education. The period during which he desired to assist them was substantially certain and known to him; it would not vary according as he might or might not die an accidental death. Regardless of the manner in which he might die, he wished to assist his children through college so that they could take care of themselves. That would require twenty years, not forty. Yet the insurance company interprets the withdrawal privileges so that the duration of the protection period varies according to the way in which the insured met his death. We think the desired protection period would be the same in either case.

* * * * *

> We conclude that the withdrawal privileges . . . should be doubled. Nothing else would satisfy the purpose of the insured to provide for his children during a fixed period of their lives which would not vary according to the manner of his death, and nothing else would satisfy his direction set forth in the supplemental contract that the extra $5,000 be distributed "in addition to and together with" the basic death benefit.
>
> The judgments should be reversed and judgments granted to the plaintiffs declaring that $1,000 may be withdrawn each year until receipt of the affidavit mentioned in the change of beneficiary and $2,500 per year thereafter.

Claim Questions

Life insurers have found the declaratory judgment helpful in a number of claims situations. Sometimes information needed to settle the claim has not been made available to the insurer but is in the hands of the beneficiary, her attorney, or others. The declaratory judgment provides the insurer with a method for bringing the matter into court for resolution.

For example, if a policyowner presents a claim for disability benefits, and the insurer denies liability on the ground that the insured is not disabled according to the policy terms, an action for a declaratory judgment is one of the most effective ways of clarifying the rights and duties of the parties.

Another claims situation in which a suit for declaratory judgment can sometimes assist the insurer is denial of the accidental death benefit. It is often said that, if an insurer denies the accidental death benefit, payment of the face amount "finances a lawsuit." If a good possibility exists that the beneficiary will file a lawsuit against the insurer, an immediate suit by the insurer for a declaratory judgment offers one way to ascertain the facts while evidence is fresh and witnesses are still available.

This same advantage is occasionally present if an insurer denies a claim for the face amount itself. Even though the insurer is convinced of the soundness of its decision, it nevertheless remains vulnerable to a suit by the beneficiary until the expiration of the relevant statute of limitations or the period of time for suit specified in the policy. During that time, witnesses might die or become widely scattered, and ascertaining the facts becomes progressively more difficult.

In addition, some states have statutory penalties imposed for wrongful and vexatious delay in settling life insurance claims. A court decision unfavorable to the insurer, made after the expiration of the period specified in these statutes, means the insurer will have to pay a statutory penalty as well as the policy proceeds. In certain instances, a declaratory judgment action filed shortly after the loss has occurred might enable the insurer to avoid the penalty.

Insurance Regulations

In a situation in which an insurer questions the legality of an insurance regulation adopted by an insurance commissioner, the insurer might sue the insurance commissioner in an action for declaratory judgment. Without a declaratory judgment, the insurer is left with the choice of either complying with a regulation it believes is illegal or refusing to comply. Refusing to comply could result in fines or other penalties if the insurer was wrong about the regulation's legality.

For example, in *Telles v. Commissioner of Insurance,*[23] two insurers and other plaintiffs sued the Massachusetts Insurance Commissioner to obtain a ruling as to whether the commissioner could lawfully issue regulations prohibiting life insurers from using gender-based mortality tables to classify proposed insureds and determine insurance rates. The lower court ruled that the commissioner did have such authority. On appeal, the Supreme Judicial Court of Massachusetts vacated[24] the ruling of the lower court, stating that the commissioner lacked either express or implied authority to issue the regulations. The insurers were then able to resume their use of gender-based mortality tables without concern about violating the law.

In a concurring opinion in the *Telles* case, one of the justices noted:

> If the commissioner thought that the use of gender-based mortality tables violated [the Equal Rights Amendment of the Massachusetts Constitution] he should have sought a declaratory judgment. . . . [The Massachusetts Insurance Code] expressly authorizes gender-based discrimination in the determination of insurance premiums. In the face of such express authorization, the commissioner was without the power to prohibit the practice, even if he believed the Constitution itself forbids it. The commissioner must seek a judicial declaration on the constitutionality of the various statutes.

Thus, suits for declaratory judgment are useful to insurance commissioners as well as to insurers.

---

[23]574 N.E.2d 359 (Mass. 1991).

[24]***Vacated*** here means "annulled."

Summary

Four remedies that developed in equity are of special importance to insurers. These are interpleader, rescission, reformation, and the declaratory judgment.

In most instances, the general principles of equity govern these remedies. One of these principles requires that the plaintiff in equity have no adequate remedy at law. The usual remedy at law is damages. People seeking relief in equity ordinarily want some other type of relief, such as a mandatory or prohibitory injunction, which is not available at law.

A second principle of equity is that a person seeking an equitable remedy must come into equity with clean hands; that is, the person must have acted fairly and honestly as to the matter at issue. A third principle is that the plaintiff must not delay seeking relief in equity, if such delay would harm the defendant. If the plaintiff so delays, he will be guilty of laches and the equity court will deny him relief.

Interpleader is an equitable remedy that allows an insurer, faced with conflicting claimants to policy proceeds, to pay the proceeds to a court and be dismissed from the case. The court will order the claimants to litigate the matter among themselves. Without interpleader, the insurer would be in danger of paying more than once and of having to defend a multiplicity of lawsuits.

The equitable remedy of rescission allows an insurer to have the life insurance contract decreed void within the contestable period if the policy application contains a misrepresentation. The misrepresentation usually must be of a fact that is material to the risk. A material fact is a fact that, if known to the insurer, would have kept it from entering into the contract. In some states, a misrepresentation that is intentional but not material is a ground for rescission. In all states an intentional material misrepresentation (fraud) is a ground for rescission of a contract.

Reformation is the equitable remedy whereby a court revises or interprets a written contract to conform the contract to the original agreement of the parties. The grounds for reformation are mutual mistake, unilateral mistake, and misrepresentation. A court will grant reformation only if the plaintiff can produce clear and convincing proof of the terms of the original agreement.

Declaratory judgment suits have origins in equity, although today federal or state statutes grant the right to institute a declaratory judgment suit. A declaratory judgment is a judgment that declares the rights and duties of the parties without requiring either party to take any action or pay any money to the other.

ILLUSTRATIVE CASE

Many cases involving the life insurance contract demonstrate the usefulness of the equitable remedy of interpleader. The following is one such case.

GREAT AMERICAN RESERVE INSURANCE COMPANY, Petitioner
v.
VIOLET SANDERS, Respondent[25]
Supreme Court of Texas

POPE, Justice.

Great American Reserve Insurance Company filed an interpleader suit in district court naming as defendants the insured's ex-wife, Violet Sanders, and surviving widow, Jessie Sanders. The petition also named Hill Metropolitan Funeral Directors, Inc. because of an assignment to it by Violet Sanders for part of the insurance proceeds to cover the insured's funeral expenses. The trial court awarded the $5,000 insurance proceeds to Violet Sanders, less

$1,208.60 awarded to the funeral home by virtue of its assigned interest, and less $500 attorney fees to the insurer-stakeholder, Great American Reserve Insurance Company. The court of civil appeals reversed and remanded. We reverse the judgment of the court of civil appeals and affirm that of the trial court.

This case presents us with two separate questions. First, whether there was a bona fide claim made by each of the rival claimants such as will allow the insurer-stakeholder to resort to the equitable remedy of interpleader. Second, whether Article 3.62, Vernon's Tex. Ins. Code Ann., imposes an absolute duty upon an insurer to either pay a claimant or interplead rival claim-

---

[25]525 S.W.2d 956 (1975).

ants within 30 days of the time demand is made for the proceeds.

The case was submitted to the trial court upon an agreed statement of facts. Nathaniel and Violet Sanders were married in 1960. They obtained a divorce on July 30, 1969, and Violet was awarded custody of their five minor children. The court ordered Nathaniel Sanders to pay $35.00 per week for child support.

Nathaniel Sanders married Jessie Mae Sanders in February, 1971. They separated in early summer of 1971, though no divorce action was brought by either party. Subsequent to this separation, in September, 1971, Violet Sanders threatened to bring contempt proceedings against Nathaniel because of his failure to make child support payments. Nathaniel proposed instead that he take out a $5000 life insurance policy, with Violet as beneficiary, and also that he begin making regular support payments. Nathaniel secured a certificate of insurance from Great American Reserve Insurance Company through a group plan available to employees of the City of Dallas. Violet was named as beneficiary and was given possession of the certificate.

Nathaniel's failure to make regular support payments continued and on February 14, 1973, a Dallas County Domestic Relations Court entered a commitment for contempt against him because of his delinquent child support payments amounting to $2478.00. The commitment was suspended, however, as long as Nathaniel made the $35.00 per week payments.

Nathaniel Sanders died on April 3, 1973. Violet Sanders assigned $1213.60 to Hill Metropolitan Funeral Directors, Inc. from the insurance proceeds. On May 9, 1973, both Violet and Jessie Mae filed proof of death with the insurer, and claimed the proceeds of the policy. Great American Reserve filed its petition in interpleader on June 15, 1973, wherein it admitted liability under the policy, and deposited the $5000.00 proceeds in the registry of the court. Great American alleged that it had honest doubts as to who was entitled to the proceeds, and asked $500 for attorney fees.

The trial court granted an agreed partial summary judgment in favor of the funeral home for $1208.60, by virtue of its assigned interest in that amount by Violet Sanders. Great American was awarded $500 out of the fund for attorney fees, and the trial court determined that Violet Sanders was entitled to the balance.

Violet appealed the trial court's award of $500 to the insurer for attorney fees, and also appealed the trial court's refusal to award her attorney fees and a 12% penalty provided for in Article 3.62, Tex.Ins.Code Ann. The court of civil appeals held that Great American had a duty to make an investigation within thirty days after the claim for proceeds was made, in order to determine who was entitled to the proceeds. According to that court, this investigation would have revealed the indisputable merit of

Violet's claim and shown that Jessie's claim was entirely spurious. The court also held that Article 3.62 required the insurer to either pay a claimant within 30 days of demand for the proceeds, or to file its petition in intervention within this same period. We think that the court of civil appeals has placed a burden on the insurer not contemplated by Article 3.62.

Great American was entitled to maintain an interpleader suit if there existed a reasonable doubt, either of fact or law, as to which of the rival claimants was entitled to the proceeds of the policy. If the insurer's doubt is a reasonable one, and for that reason it in good faith declines to pay the named beneficiary, but admits liability and deposits the funds into court, it is liable only for the face amount of the policy.

We must examine the nature of the conflicting claims in order to determine whether or not Great American was faced with a reasonable doubt as to which claim was superior. Violet Sanders was the named beneficiary, and had possession of the certificate of insurance. According to Article 3.48, Tex.Ins.Code Ann., an insurer may pay the named beneficiary of a policy without concern for further liability unless it receives notice of an adverse, and bona fide, claim to the proceeds.

Great American in this case was faced with an adverse claim, filed on the same day as Violet's claim, by Jessie Mae Sanders. An investigation of this claim would reveal that Jessie Mae was Nathaniel's wife at the time he took out the certificate of insurance, at all times when premiums were paid, and at the time of his death.

These facts raise the possibility that Jessie Mae was entitled to the proceeds, or some part thereof, on the ground that Nathaniel's act of naming his ex-wife beneficiary of a policy purchased with funds of the community of Nathaniel and Jessie Mae, was constructive fraud upon Jessie Mae. It was held in *Givens v. Girard Life Ins. Co.*, 480 S.W.2d 421, 426 (Tex.Civ. App.–1972, writ ref'd n. r. e.) that the widow "establishes constructive fraud prima facie by proof that life insurance was purchased with community funds for the benefit of an unrelated person, and the beneficiary then has the burden to justify such use of community funds."

The beneficiary may rebut the prima facie case by showing special circumstances which justify the purchase of the life insurance. Obviously, the fact that the unrelated person is named as beneficiary and has possession of the policy does not rebut the prima facie case. The fact that the policy was to secure delinquent support payments for the benefit of the insured's minor children may be sufficient justification for the purchase of the policy, but this is not a determination which the insurance company should have to make.

The question of whether use of community funds is constructive fraud upon the wife is a difficult one. It is stated in Johanson, *Revocable Trusts and Community Property: The Substantive Problems,* 47 Tex.L.Rev. 537, 568 (1969):

> As a group the cases do not give clear guidelines. At best, they point up the factors that bear on the decision whether a transfer is likely to be held in constructive fraud of the wife's rights. Among the factors that have been emphasized are the relationship of the transferee to the transferor or his wife; whether there are special circumstances that tend to justify the transfer; the value of the assets transferred in relation to the total value of the community estate; and whether the wife has adequately been provided for out of the remaining community property and the separate property of the husband.

To require the insurance company in this case to discover every fact that may be a circumstance justifying use of the community funds, decide which facts are true and which are false, and apply the law of constructive fraud to those facts would defeat the very purpose of interpleader. An insurance company should not be compelled to act as judge and jury. Since we hold that interpleader was prop-

erly available to Great American, we also uphold the trial court's award to it of $500 attorney fees.

The court of civil appeals held that Great American was not in good faith in failing to interplead within 30 days under Article 3.62. That statute assesses a 12% penalty and reasonable attorney fees against the insurance company in favor of the rightful claimant where the company has failed to pay the claimant within 30 days. Several cases have held that where circumstances exist which make interpleader a proper remedy, as in this case, failure to pay the money into the court within 30 days after demand does not make the insurer liable for the penalty and attorney fees. In this case, the interpleader suit was filed thirty-seven days after the demands for the proceeds were received. We are not deciding whether in another case a period of delay before interpleading the competing claimants might be so unreasonable as to justify imposition of the statutory penalty.

We reverse the judgment of the court of civil appeals and affirm that of the trial court.

Questions for Review

1. What conditions are prerequisite to the plaintiff who seeks relief in equity?
2. Distinguish between the two types of injunctions.
3. Discuss equity and the jury.
4. Give an illustrative situation that might lead an insurer to seek each of the following remedies in equity: interpleader, rescission, reformation, and declaratory judgment.
5. What is a disinterested stakeholder?
6. What are the grounds upon which rescission can be sought?
7. What is the significance of the legal concept of materiality in relation to rescission?
8. Define *fraud* in relation to the rescission of a contract.
9. Discuss the proof that the court requires the plaintiff to produce in a reformation suit. Why is this level of proof required?
10. Describe the nature of the judgment in a suit for declaratory judgment.

17 POLICY CONTESTS AND THE INCONTESTABLE CLAUSE

Chapter Outline

A *contest* of a life insurance policy is a court action to determine the validity of the policy. For example, if the application for a life insurance policy contains a material misrepresentation, the insurer might bring suit to rescind the policy on the ground that the policy is invalid. Such action would constitute a policy contest. Or, if a beneficiary sues the insurer for the death benefit and the application contains a material misrepresentation, the insurer might defend itself on the ground that the policy is invalid. This action also would be a policy contest.

Contracts are invalid if there are certain defects in their formation. According to a basic rule of general contract law, a party who discovers that the other party made a material misrepresentation at the time of the contract's formation can, at any time, rescind the contract or defend himself on the ground that the policy is invalid.

However, life insurance policies have a unique clause—the incontestable clause—that abrogates this basic rule after a specified period of time, usually two years. In other words, because of the incontestable clause, ordinarily a life insurer can rescind the policy or defend against payment of the death benefit, on the ground that the policy is invalid, only during the first two years following the policy's date of issue. The purpose of this chapter is to discuss policy contests and the incontestable clause.

Valid, Void, and Voidable Contracts

As explained in Chapter 2, "Contracts," contracts are valid, void, or voidable. A *valid contract* is enforceable in either a lawsuit or a suit in equity, depending on the remedy sought. Certain requirements relating to offer, acceptance, consideration, competency of the parties, and legality of purpose must be met if an agreement is to be a valid informal contract.

To say a contract is void is actually a contradiction in terms, since the word *contract* means an agreement enforceable by court action. If the agreement is not enforceable by court action, it is not a contract. However, the terms *void contract,* or *contract void ab initio* (contract void from the beginning) are commonly used and will be used in this book.

A life insurance contract will be void ab initio if, for example, the required insurable interest is not present. Insurable interest is of such fundamental importance that its absence will make an attempted life insurance contract void—that is, no contract at all.

A *voidable contract* is enforceable until a party who has the right to do so takes some action to disaffirm the contract. An informal contract is ordinarily voidable if there are certain defects in its formation. A party's lack of contractual capacity, a mutual mistake of the parties, or a party's material misrepresentation are some of the formation defects that make a contract voidable by one or more of the parties.

Material Misrepresentation

This chapter deals primarily with life insurance policy contests based on material misrepresentation.[1] If one party has misrepresented a material fact that induces the other party to enter into a contract he would not have entered into if he had known the truth, the other party can maintain a suit for rescission or defend an action for performance of the contract.

An insurer most commonly discovers a material misrepresentation in an application for a life insurance contract during its investigation of an early death claim. An

---

[1]Material misrepresentation is discussed in detail in the section entitled "Rescission" in Chapter 16, "Equitable Remedies."

early death claim is a claim for death benefits filed shortly after the policy became effective. An early death claim arouses the insurer's suspicions that there may have been a material misrepresentation. Material misrepresentations are not significant with respect to claims under older policies because of the incontestable clause, as discussed below. If the insurer discovers material misrepresentation while investigating an early death claim, it can deny the claim on that basis. Because the insurer would not have entered into the contract as applied for if it had known the truth, it is entitled to deny the claim and refund the premiums paid.

Sometimes the insurer discovers a material misrepresentation in a life insurance application while the insured is still living. Perhaps the insurer is investigating a disability claim that the insured has filed or reviewing a second application for insurance on the insured's life. During such claim or application reviews, the insurer sometimes discovers information revealing that a living insured has misrepresented her health history. If the insurer discovers information of this kind during the policy's contestable period, it usually takes prompt action to rescind the policy. Ordinarily, the insurer, after verifying its information completely enough to support a suit for rescission, notifies the policyowner that it has elected to rescind the policy and is returning the premiums paid. If the policyowner refuses the refund of premiums, the insurer must initiate a suit to have the court rescind the policy.

For two reasons a life insurer will take prompt action to rescind the policy if it discovers material misrepresentation in the policy application while the insured is still living. First, if it does not take prompt action, the court might find that the insurer was guilty of laches, that is, of an unreasonable delay that harmed the policyowner. If the insurer acts promptly to rescind the policy, the policyowner might be able to obtain other insurance, perhaps at substandard rates. However, if the insurer delays, the insured could become uninsurable. Second, the insurer will take prompt action to rescind the policy because the policy will have an incontestable clause as required by law. An incontestable clause establishes a deadline—in most states, two years from the date of issue of the policy—beyond which the insurer cannot contest the policy's validity on the ground of material misrepresentation.

Breach of Conditions

A material misrepresentation in the application is the most common reason insurers seek to rescind life insurance contracts. The breach of a condition precedent to the effectiveness of the contract can also give the insurer a ground for rescission. However, according to the majority view, such conditions precedent are incontestable after the contestable period has expired.

For example, most life insurance policies state that a proposed insured must be in good health when the policy is delivered. This requirement is a condition precedent to the effectiveness of the contract. Suppose that Laurence Wiseman, a proposed insured, was in good health at the time he filled out and signed the application for life insurance. Wiseman answered all questions on the application truthfully. The application indicated Wiseman had had no significant health problems. However, two weeks after submitting the application, and before the insurer mailed the policy, Wiseman unexpectedly suffered a massive heart attack. Shortly thereafter, the soliciting agent went to Wiseman's office to deliver the policy and left it with Wiseman's secretary, who did not mention the reason for Wiseman's absence. The policy had a two-year incontestable clause. Two years and three months after the policy was delivered, Wiseman had another heart attack from which he died.

While processing the claim for the death benefit, the insurer learned of the first heart attack. The insurer cannot contest the validity of the policy on the ground that a condition precedent to the policy's effectiveness was not met. The incontestable clause prevents such a contest after the contestable period has expired. However, if the insurer had learned of Wiseman's heart condition during the contestable period, it could have contested the policy.

Conditions precedent differ from exceptions to coverage and limitations of the risk. Conditions precedent relate to the effectiveness—that is, the validity—of the policy, whereas exceptions and limitations spell out the risk the insurer is assuming under the policy. Examples of exceptions and limitations are the suicide clause, the war hazard exclusion clause, the aviation hazard exclusion clause, and the misstatement of age clause.

Unfortunately, some courts have not distinguished between conditions precedent to effectiveness of the policy on the one hand and exceptions to coverage and limitations of the risk under the policy on the other. As explained in the section below entitled "Conflict with Other Policy Provisions," this lack of understanding has resulted in a conflicting body of law.

Contest of the Policy

The majority rule is that the word *contest,* as applied to the incontestable clause, means a court action challenging the validity of the policy.[2] A contest can arise from the insurer's defense of an action at law brought by the beneficiary. An insurer can also initiate a contest as a suit in equity against the policyowner to rescind the policy.

To contest the policy, the insurer must file an answer in defense or bring suit within the contestable period. Even if the court does not render judgment until after the contestable period has expired, the insurer will have contested the policy within the contestable period.

Generally speaking, action taken by the insurer outside of court is not a contest. Denial of liability, repudiation of the policy, or tender of premiums do not constitute a contest. Nevertheless, if an insurer tenders the premiums to the policyowner, and the policyowner agrees to rescind, accepts the premiums, gives a release, and surrenders the policy, this will protect the insurer from liability.[3]

A suit to have the court reform the contract so that it will conform to the original agreement of the parties is not a contest of the policy. Thus, the incontestable clause does not prevent the insurer from seeking reformation after the contestable period has expired.[4]

---

[2]*E.g.,* American Life Ins. Co. v. Stewart, 300 U.S. 203 (1937); Densby v. Acacia Mut. Life Ass'n, 78 F.2d 203 (D. C. Cir. 1935); Fields v. Universal Life & Acci. Ins. Co., 424 S.W.2d 704 (Tex. Civ. App. 1968).

[3] Eichwedel v. Metropolitan Life Ins. Co., 270 S.W. 415 (Mo. Ct. App. 1925); Telford v. Metropolitan Life Ins. Co., 228 N.Y.S. 54 (N.Y. App. Div. 1928), *aff'd,* 166 N.E. 311 (1928).

[4]C. T. Drechsler, Annotation, *Incontestable Clause as Applicable to Suit to Reform Insurance Policy,* 7 A.L.R. 2d 504 (1949); Schaefer v. California-Western States Life Ins. Co., 69 Cal. Rptr. 183 (Cal. Ct. App. 1968); Johnson v. Consolidated Am. Life Ins. Co., 244 So. 2d 400 (Miss. 1971).

Development of the Incontestable Clause

An incontestable clause ordinarily provides that, after the policy has been in force for two years from the issue date and during the lifetime of the insured, the validity of the policy will be incontestable. For example, the clause in the illustrative policy in the Appendix, Figure 2, reads as follows:

> We will not contest the validity of this Policy, except for nonpayment of premiums, after it has been in force during the Insured's lifetime for two years from the [date of issue]. This provision does not apply to any rider providing accidental death or disability benefits.

Incontestability means that the insurer cannot challenge the validity of the policy—that is, maintain a suit in equity to rescind the policy or defend a lawsuit for policy benefits—on the basis of a material misrepresentation in the application or breach of a condition precedent to effectiveness of the policy.[5]

The incontestable clause is unique to life insurance. In fact, it directly opposes the basic rule of contract law that "fraud vitiates a contract"—that is, fraud invalidates a contract, making it unenforceable against the defrauded party. As regards a life insurance contract, this rule must be revised to read, "Fraud vitiates a contract, unless it is a life insurance contract with an incontestable clause and the contestable period has expired."

What is so unusual about a life insurance contract that insurers should be required by law to include in it a provision contrary to a basic rule of contract law? To answer this question, knowledge of the history of insurance generally, and the history of warranties and representations specifically, is necessary.

Warranties

A *warranty* is a statement guaranteed to be true in all respects. In the early days of insurance, statements an insurance applicant made were considered to be warranties. If a statement were untrue in any respect the contract could be rescinded, even though the applicant did not know the statement was untrue and even though the statement was not material.

The warranty doctrine was first applied in marine insurance, where it did not result in hardship to the insured because, ordinarily, no extensive period of time elapsed between the making of the contract and any dispute that arose about its validity. However, application of the doctrine of warranties to life insurance did create hardships.

Often, life insurance premiums had been paid over a long period and the misstatements concerned were trivial, yet the insurer would disaffirm the contract after the insured died. The beneficiary was left without policy benefits unless she sued the insurer and won. The beneficiary's lawsuit was made difficult because she had to defend against an alleged misstatement made many years earlier in the application and about which she might know little or nothing. Ordinarily, the person who had made the statement, the insured, was dead. Thus, the beneficiary was seriously handicapped in a dispute about the truth of statements in the application.

---

[5]See the discussion of breaches of conditions precedent above.

During the latter half of the 18th and early part of the 19th centuries, the courts of England and the United States enforced warranties in insurance contracts with technical exactness. If warranted facts were not true exactly as stated, the insurer could avoid the contract at any time. Insurers found that by the latter half of the 19th century, their readiness to litigate with respect to every deviation from the absolute truth in the application was creating distrust in the public. Insurers had gained a reputation, as one commentator put it, of being "the great repudiators."

An English company, London Indisputable Life, was the first insurer to attempt to counteract the distrust that strict enforcement of the warranty doctrine had created. In 1848, it included a provision in its charter relinquishing the right to contest a policy for any reason whatsoever. In 1864, in the United States, the Manhattan Life Insurance Company introduced the first policy clause providing for incontestability.

By the time of the Armstrong Investigation (a study of life insurance companies authorized by the New York state legislature in 1905), a majority of life insurers in the United States were voluntarily including an incontestable clause in their policies. The Standard Policy Provisions Law, enacted in New York following the Armstrong Investigation, mandated that life insurance policies include an incontestable clause. Later, the Committee of Fifteen, appointed in the wake of the Armstrong Investigation, recommended model state legislation that mandated an incontestable clause. A majority of the states subsequently enacted laws patterned on this model legislation.

Representations

A *representation,* as contrasted with a warranty, is an applicant's statement of facts on which the insurer bases its decision to issue, or not to issue, the policy applied for. Unlike a warranty, a representation need not be true in all respects, but need only be true as to facts material to the risk. If the applicant's statements are representations, the insurer ordinarily cannot rescind the contract or defend a suit for benefits on the ground of misrepresentation of a fact unless that fact is material to the risk. If the applicant's statements were warranties, the insurer could so defend or rescind, whether or not the misrepresented fact is material to the risk.

Modern state insurance codes commonly require that life insurance policies contain a provision declaring that, in the absence of fraud, all statements in the application shall be deemed representations and not warranties. The illustrative policy in the Appendix, Figure 2, states: "All statements made by or for the insured will be considered representations and not warranties." Thus, the doctrine of warranties, as applied to life insurance, is primarily of historical interest.

Conflict with Other Policy Provisions

The rule in the majority of states is that the incontestable clause relates only to contests of the validity of the policy. Moreover, lawyers and students of life insurance contracts generally agree that life insurers originally included the incontestable clause as a waiver of their right to contest the policy for misstatements by the applicant. Nevertheless, the way in which insurers have typically worded the clause has cast doubt on this assumption. Incontestable clauses usually read as follows: "This policy shall be incontestable after it has been in force during the lifetime of the insured, for a period of two years from the issue date, *except for nonpayment of premiums.*" [Emphasis added.]

A logical question concerning such a clause is this: Why does the incontestable clause say it is not applicable to the nonpayment of premiums if the purpose of the clause is to prevent a contest in the event of a misstatement in the application? Sometimes, an incontestable clause states that it does not apply to the war hazard exclusion clause or some similar clause, and in that instance the same question arises.

If these exceptions or limitations had never been included in the incontestable clause, there would probably have been little question as to its legal effect. The word *contest* would have been accepted as meaning a court challenge to the validity of the contract, based on rules applicable to contracts generally. The incontestable clause would have been accepted for what it was undoubtedly intended to be—a pledge of good faith in the form of a waiver, after a specified period of time, of any right that the insurer might otherwise have had to challenge the validity of the contract.

When a life insurer denies a claim on the basis that premiums were not paid by the end of the grace period or that the insured was killed as the result of military service, it is denying the claim on a different basis than when it asserts it has no liability because the contract is invalid by reason of material misrepresentation. If the insurer contends it has no liability because renewal premiums were not paid or because the insured died as a result of military service, it is assuming that the contract is valid and alleging either the policyowner's failure to fulfill the contract's conditions or a violation of the contract's terms. The insurer is not contending that the policy is not valid. A policy provision stating that the contract will be incontestable except for nonpayment of premiums or death as a result of military activities creates doubt as to the meaning the insurer intended to give to the word *contest.*

Moreover, if an insurer states that the incontestable clause does not apply to the nonpayment of premiums but does not mention the war hazard exclusion clause, does this mean it cannot defend a claim based on the death of a soldier in war under the war hazard exclusion clause if the contestable period has expired? A maxim of contract interpretation, *expressio unius est exclusio alterius,* has led some courts to rule that it does.

Expressio unius est exclusio alterius means "the expression of one thing implies the exclusion of another." In other words, the expression in a contract of one or more things in a class implies the exclusion of all unexpressed things in the same class. Nonpayment of premiums, the war hazard exclusion clause, the suicide clause, and similar clauses comprise the class in this instance. According to the courts in some jurisdictions, if the policy were to state that the incontestable clause is not applicable to nonpayment of premiums and to the suicide clause, but were not to mention the war hazard exclusion clause or aviation hazard exclusion clause, the latter two clauses would not be effective after the contestable period because they were not specifically excluded from the operation of the incontestable clause.[6]

The Majority View

Probably the best statement of the majority view concerning the impact of the incontestable clause on other policy provisions is found in *Metropolitan Life Insurance Co. v. Conway.*[7] Judge Benjamin Cardozo, who later became a justice of the U.S. Su-

---

[6]*E.g.,* Mutual Reserve Fund Life Ass'n v. Austin, 142 F. 398 (C.C.A. Mass. 1905); Fore v. New York Life Ins. Co., 22 S.W.2d 401 (Ark. 1929); Goodwin v. Provident Saving Life Assur. Soc'y, 66 N.W. 157 (Iowa 1896); Bernier v. Pacific Mut. Life Ins. Co., 139 So. 629 (La. 1932).
[7]169 N.E. 642 (1930).

preme Court, wrote this opinion in 1930. The suit was between an insurer and the Superintendent of Insurance of New York. The superintendent had refused to approve an aviation hazard rider that limited the insurer's liability to the amount of the reserve if the insured's death occurred at any time due to certain aviation activities. The superintendent took the position that the provisions of the rider were inconsistent with the incontestable clause required by New York law.

The insurer's position was that it was free to specify risks that it was unwilling to assume throughout the life of the contract, even though the policy became incontestable after two years. Thus, the insurer argued that under a policy with an aviation hazard exclusion, the insurer, in paying only the amount of the reserve if death occurred due to aviation activities, was carrying out the terms of the policy and not contesting its validity. The lower appellate court decided in favor of the insurer. The Court of Appeals of New York upheld the lower appellate court's decision as follows:

> We agree with the Appellate Division in its holding that rider and statute in this instance are consistent and harmonious. The provision that a policy shall be incontestable after it has been in force during the lifetime of the insured for a period of two years is not a mandate as to coverage, a definition of the hazards to be borne by the insurer. It means only this, that within the limits of the coverage the policy shall stand, unaffected by any defense that it was invalid in its inception, or thereafter became invalid by reason of a condition broken. Like questions have arisen in other jurisdictions and in other courts of this state. There has been general concurrence with reference to the answer.

The Minority View

Although *Conway* represents the majority view, a minority view also exists. Two years after *Conway* was decided, the Louisiana Supreme Court heard the same question concerning an aviation hazard exclusion clause in *Bernier v. Pacific Mutual Life Insurance Co.*[8] The Louisiana court in *Bernier* took the minority view, stating:

> The provision in a life insurance policy, making the contract incontestable after a stated period, means something more than that the insurer cannot then contest the validity of the policy on the ground of breach of a condition; it means that the company cannot then contest its obligation to pay, on due proof of the death of the insured, the amount stated on the face of the policy, except for a cause of defense that is plainly excepted from the provision making the policy incontestable.

Thus, the *Bernier* court in effect held that the incontestable clause was a mandate to coverage and that an insurer could not "contest its obligation to pay" except for a reason plainly reserved in the wording of the incontestable clause itself. A few other courts have taken a similar view, although not always for the same reasons.

The Model Statute

Because of this divergence of opinion in the courts, in 1947 the Life Insurance Association of America and the American Life Convention appointed a committee to draft a recommended statutory provision. This committee drafted a statutory provision adopting the majority position of *Conway*. It reads as follows:

> A clause in any policy of life insurance providing that such policy shall be incontestable after a specified period shall preclude only a contest of the validity of the policy, and shall

---

[8]139 So. 629 (La. 1932).

not preclude the assertion at any time of defenses based upon provisions in the policy which exclude or restrict coverage, whether or not such restrictions or exclusions are excepted in such clause.

One-half of the states have enacted laws patterned on this model statute.

The Misstatement of Age Clause

Because the age of the insured has such an important relationship to the risk of death, life insurers commonly used misstatement of age clauses before the introduction of the incontestable clause. In cases in which the insured's age was misstated in the application, a misstatement of age clause allows the insurer to pay death benefits according to the amount of insurance the premiums would have purchased at the insured's correct age. However, with the growing use of the incontestable clause the question arose as to whether an adjustment for misstatement of age could be made after the expiration of the contestable period. In other words, was an adjustment for misstatement of age also a contest of the policy that would be barred by the incontestable clause after the expiration of the contestable period?

In some of the earlier policies, misstatement of age appeared in the incontestable clause as an exception. Under these policies, the incontestable clause did not prevent an adjustment for misstatement of age because misstatement of age was specified as an exception in the incontestable clause itself.

If misstatement of age is not excepted in the incontestable clause, the majority of courts have reached the conclusion that the two clauses do not conflict. For instance, in one 1939 case,[9] the court said:

> The suit is based on a life insurance policy issued to Oliver P. Langan, a citizen of Missouri, with his wife (plaintiff) as beneficiary. The policy is for the face amount of $10,000, annual premium $434, age of insured stated as 53 and contract commencing January 13, 1927. The policy provides that after one year from its date it shall be incontestable except for nonpayment of premiums, and also contains the following: "If the age of the Insured has been understated, the amount payable hereunder shall be such as the premium paid would have purchased at the correct age; if the age of the Insured has been overstated the company will return the excess premium, or premiums, paid."
>
> In his application, the insured stated that he was born on July 14, 1873, and that his age at nearest birthday was 53 years.
>
> . . . The beneficiary (plaintiff) furnished sworn proof of death to the defendant, in which she stated that insured was born on July 14, 1871, and that she derived this information from the family Bible. A statement furnished by the undertaker also stated that insured was born on July 14, 1871.
>
> . . . [Plaintiff] contended that the defendant could not legally avoid paying the face amount of the policy for two reasons: (1) Because of the provision in the policy for incontestability; (2) because the age adjustment clause in the policy comes within the prohibition of our statute dealing with misrepresentations, which reads as follows: "No misrepresentation made in obtaining or securing a policy of insurance on the life or lives of any person or persons, citizens of this state, shall be deemed material, or render the policy void, unless the matter misrepresented shall have actually contributed to the contingency or event on which the policy is to become due and payable, and whether it so contributed in any case shall be a question for the jury."
>
> . . . [The insurer] contends: (1) The incontestability provision is not applicable because defendant is not contesting the provisions of the policy, but is only seeking to

---

[9]Langan v. United States Life Ins. Co., 130 S.W.2d 479 (Mo. 1939).

confine its liability within the express terms of the policy; (2) that the misrepresentation statute does not apply because it refers only to misrepresentations made to obtain a policy and not to terms agreed upon and expressly written in the policy itself.

. . . [W]e conclude that the weight of authority is that an incontestable clause does not prevent the enforcement of an age adjustment clause contained in the same policy.

Contests Not Barred by the Incontestable Clause

The general rule is that after the expiration of the contestable period, all contests relating to the validity of the policy are barred. Like most rules, this rule has its exceptions. These exceptions—fraudulent impersonation, lack of an insurable interest, and procurement of the policy with an intent to murder the insured—are discussed in this section.

Fraudulent Impersonation

The majority rule is that if application is made to insure the life of one person, but another person, fraudulently impersonating the proposed insured, signs the application or takes the medical examination, the incontestable clause will not bar the insurer from contesting the policy at any time. For example, in *Obartuch v. Security Mutual Life Insurance Co.,*[10] a suit was filed for death benefits on the life of Frank Obartuch. The insurer admitted that the contestable period had elapsed but denied liability on the ground that Obartuch either did not sign or did not knowingly sign the application. Moreover, the insurer alleged that a person unknown to it was fraudulently substituted for Obartuch at the medical examination. The court's conclusions of law were as follows:

1. That it is contrary to public policy for any person to obtain life insurance by substituting an individual other than the named insured for medical examination, and a policy secured by such substitution is void.

2. That the incontestable clause in the policies in suit does not preclude the defense that the person examined by the defendant's medical examiner was not Frank Obartuch, but someone else who impersonated said Frank Obartuch.

3. That said policies did not constitute a valid contract with Frank Obartuch and, if valid at all, were contracts upon the life of the person examined by the defendant's medical examiner.

4. That there was never any valid contract of life insurance upon the life of Frank Obartuch because he never knowingly signed any application therefor or authorized any other person to sign an application for him.

Quoting from another case, *Maslin v. Columbian National Life Insurance Co.,*[11] the court pointed out:

There cannot be the slightest doubt that the person whom an insurance company intends to make a contract with and intends to insure is the person who presents himself for physical examination.

* * * * *

---

[10]114 F.2d 873 (7th Cir. 1940), *cert denied,* 312 U.S. 696 (1941), *reh'g denied,* 312 U.S. 716 (1941).

[11]3 F. Supp. 368 (S.D.N.Y. 1932).

The defendant's only contract was with the man who made the application and took the examination.

In the *Ludwinska* case,[12] a similar situation is considered. The person named as the insured was an imbecile and the application for insurance was made by her sister who also impersonated the named insured at the medical examination. The court held that if anyone was insured it was the sister and not the one named in the policy.

Lack of an Insurable Interest

The incontestable clause does not bar a policy contest based on lack of an insurable interest, according to the majority view.[13] A well-established rule is that a person cannot enter into a valid and enforceable contract insuring the life of another person if the beneficiary has no insurable interest in the life of the insured. Such a contract is void from the beginning because it is against public policy. Therefore, if no contract came into existence in the first place, the incontestable clause never existed either.

Policy Procured with Intent to Murder the Insured

If the applicant procured the policy with the intent to murder the insured, the incontestable clause will not bar a contest of the policy.[14] The policy is void from the beginning, and the incontestable clause is not operative.

For example, in *Henderson v. Life Insurance Co. of Virginia*,[15] the insured, a 15-year-old boy, was induced by his foster father, James Thomas, the applicant and beneficiary, to sign an application indicating consent to the insurance on his life, or the application was in fact signed by someone else. Thomas falsely represented that he was the insured's natural father. Thus, Thomas took out eight policies on the insured's life with six different insurers. Thomas later murdered the insured, was caught, convicted, and sentenced to life imprisonment.

The insured's administrator sued for the benefits on behalf of the insured's estate because Thomas, the named beneficiary, was disqualified from receiving the benefits. The question before the court was whether the insurer could contest the validity of the contracts even though each contestable period had elapsed. The court said:

> [T]he incontestable clause does not constitute a bar to the defense that the insurance was procured with the express purpose of murdering the insured and thus derive the benefits thereunder, or the defense that a contract was wagering. Both of these circumstances make the contract void as against public policy, and no rights in favor of any one can accrue thereunder. As one court pointedly said, the incontestable clause is no more a part of the contract than any of its other provisions, and, when the contract falls, it brings with it all of its constituent parts.

Thus, the court held that no benefits were payable to anyone.

---

[12]Ludwinska v. John Hancock Mut. Life Ins. Co., 178 A. 28 (Pa. 1935).

[13] *E.g.,* Aetna Life Ins. Co. v. Hooker, 62 F.2d 805 (6th Cir. 1933), *cert. denied,* 289 U.S. 748 (1933); Carter v. Continental Life Ins. Co., 115 F.2d 947 (D.C. Cir. 1940); Home Life Ins. Co. v. Masterson, 21 S.W.2d 414 (Ark. 1929); Charbonnier v. Chicago Nat'l Life Ins. Co., 266 Ill. App. 412 (1932); Wharton v. Home Sec. Life Ins. Co., 173 S.E. 338 (N.C. 1934); Clement v. New York Life Ins. Co., 46 S.W. 561 (Tenn. 1898); *but see,* New England Mut. Life Ins. Co. v. Caruso, 73 N.Y.2d 74 (1989).

[14]Goldstein v. New York Life Ins. Co., 231 N.Y.S. 161 (N.Y. Sup. Ct. 1928), *modified,* 234 N.Y.S. 250 (N.Y. App. Div. 1929); Columbian Mut. Life Ins. Co. v. Martin, 136 S.W.2d 52 (Tenn. 1940).

[15]179 S.E. 680 (S.C. 1935).

Contestability of Disability Benefit and Accidental Death Benefit Provisions

When insurers first introduced the incontestable clause, they offered only life insurance itself in a life insurance policy. Therefore, the early legislation requiring incontestable clauses related only to life insurance.

In the years that followed, life insurers began offering disability benefits, either as clauses in the life insurance policy or as riders to it. Since that time, the courts have decided many cases concerning the contestability of both disability benefit provisions and accidental death benefit provisions.

Many courts have recognized that life insurance and disability insurance are essentially different and that the differences provide sound reasons for holding that the statutory incontestable requirements do not apply to disability benefit provisions. Disability insurance claims, unlike life insurance claims, often arise before the contract has been in force for a long period of time. Witnesses, including the insured, are usually readily available. Moreover, when disability benefit provisions are held to be contestable, the person penalized is usually the contracting party, unlike life insurance where the person penalized is usually a beneficiary who is not the contracting party. Granting the contracting party immunity from the consequences of his own misrepresentation or fraud is difficult to justify.

In 1922, the National Convention of Insurance Commissioners recommended that the states amend their statutes requiring incontestable clauses to permit life insurers to exclude disability and accidental death benefit provisions from the operation of the incontestable clause. A large majority of the states have since incorporated an amendment of this kind into their statutes. The incontestable clause in the illustrative policy in the Appendix, Figure 2, states: "This provision does not apply to any rider providing accidental death or disability benefits."

In the case of *Equitable Life Assurance Society v. Deem,*[16] the court upheld the insurer's right to exclude disability and accidental death benefit provisions from the operation of the incontestable clause. The court said:

> The policy as a whole includes three separate kinds of insurance, which constitute in reality three major promises of insurance protection, life, accident and disability. It seems entirely clear that the insurer intended to avail itself of the statutory authority to make the incontestable clause inapplicable to the latter two of these risks, and thus excepted from the clause those provisions of the policy relating to them.
>
> * * * * *
>
> While ambiguities which fairly exist in insurance policies must be resolved in favor of the insured, it is not permissible for courts by a strained and over-refined construction of ordinary words to create an ambiguity which would not otherwise exist. . . . And while the incontestable clause is a valuable feature of life insurance and is to be liberally construed to effectuate its beneficent purpose, there is no reason to deny to the insurer the option given by statute to except from its operation the additional features of disability and double indemnity benefits, where its purpose to do so has been definitely expressed. "To make a contract incontestable after the lapse of a brief time is to confer upon its holder extraordinary privileges. We must be on our guard against turning them into weapons of oppression."

Thus, if the incontestable clause contains an appropriate exception, the majority of the courts have upheld the insurer's right to contest the validity of the disability or

---

[16]91 F.2d 569 (4th Cir. 1937), *cert. denied,* 302 U.S. 744 (1937).

accidental death benefit provisions after the expiration of the contestable period. However, some courts have denied insurers this right. Numerous cases have arisen on this question, and the decisions are conflicting.

If the incontestable clause does not specifically except disability and accidental death benefit provisions, the majority of courts hold these provisions subject to the incontestable clause. After the expiration of the contestable period, the insurer generally cannot contest the validity of such a policy with respect to any of its provisions.

The Phrase *During the Lifetime of the Insured*

Most life insurance policies today include the phrase *during the lifetime of the insured,* or similar wording, in the incontestable clause. The illustrative policy in the Appendix, Figure 2, states: "We will not contest the validity of this Policy, except for non-payment of premiums, after it has been in force *during the Insured's lifetime* for two years from the [date of issue]." [Emphasis added.]

Insurers have not always included the phrase *during the lifetime of the insured* in the incontestable clause. Insurers originally assumed that the death of the insured stopped the running of the contestable period. In other words, insurers assumed that if the insured died during the contestable period, the policy would never become incontestable and the insurer could contest the policy at any time.

However, in 1918, in *Monahan v. Metropolitan Life Insurance Co.,*[17] the plaintiff beneficiary challenged this assumption. The facts of *Monahan* were these: The insured died during the contestable period. The insurer denied the beneficiary's claim for the death benefit on the basis of breach of the warranties in the application. Thereupon, the beneficiary waited until the expiration of the contestable period before bringing suit.

The policy's incontestable clause read: "After two years this policy shall be non-contestable, except for nonpayment of premiums." The Illinois Supreme Court interpreted this clause literally. Because the contestable period had expired at the time the lawsuit was filed, the court said the insurer was precluded from defending on the basis of breach of warranties in the application. In short, the court held that the insured's death did not automatically stop the running of the contestable period.

The Statutory Remedy

Following the *Monahan* decision, an insurer's only remedy in similar situations would have been to bring suit for rescission during the contestable period. In many instances, this would have been inconvenient. In other instances—for example, if the insured died near the end of the contestable period—it would have been impossible.

For these reasons, shortly after the *Monahan* decision, Illinois and New York amended their statutes to permit the inclusion of the phrase *during the lifetime of the insured* in incontestable clauses. Soon thereafter, the National Convention of Insurance Commissioners recommended legislation permitting the inclusion of the phrase *during the lifetime of the insured* in incontestable clauses.

Today, courts generally agree that a life insurance policy that has an incontestable clause containing this phrase never becomes incontestable if the insured dies before the expiration of the contestable period. In other words, when the insured's

---

[17]119 N.E. 68 (Ill. 1918).

death occurs before the end of the contestable period, the policy has not been in force for "two years during the lifetime of the insured." Therefore, even if the beneficiary sues more than two years after the policy's date of issue, the insurer can contest the validity of the policy.

Omission of the Phrase During the Lifetime of the Insured

If the incontestable clause contains the phrase *during the lifetime of the insured* and the insured dies during the contestable period, the insurer can defend a lawsuit on the ground of material misrepresentation or breach of a condition precedent even if the beneficiary brings the lawsuit more than two years after the policy's date of issue. Therefore, the insurer has an adequate remedy at law. Because the insurer has an adequate remedy at law, it cannot bring suit in equity for rescission of the contract.

However, some insurers feel that it would be to their advantage to have the facts decided in an equity court where a judge ordinarily decides the facts, rather than in a court of law where a jury will probably decide them. For this reason, these insurers might omit the words *during the lifetime of the insured* from the incontestable clause. If these words do not appear in the incontestable clause, and the insured dies during the contestable period, the insurer will ordinarily lose the right to contest the validity of the policy after the contestable period expires. Thus, the insurer does not have an adequate remedy at law and is entitled to bring an action in equity to have the policy rescinded. These insurers feel that the added burden of instituting a suit in equity is offset by the advantage of having a judge, rather than a jury, decide the facts.

Massachusetts Mutual Life Insurance Co. v. Goodelman,[18] decided by the U.S. District Court for the Eastern District of New York in 1958, illustrates the availability of the equitable remedy of rescission if the incontestable clause does not contain the phrase *during the lifetime of the insured.*

This case concerned a policy issued to Leon Goodelman on February 27, 1956, insuring his life in the amount of $100,000. The insured died on December 22, 1957, only slightly more than two months before the expiration of the contestable period. Within the contestable period, the insurer elected to rescind the policy and tendered the premiums paid on it. The insurer based its decision to rescind on material misrepresentation, because the insured did not disclose on the application that he was suffering from diabetes and arteriosclerosis. The beneficiary would not agree to rescind.

On February 20, 1958, seven days before the expiration of the contestable period, the insurer instituted a suit in equity for rescission of the contract. It took this action because the incontestable clause did not contain the phrase *during the lifetime of the insured.* After the expiration of the contestable period, the beneficiary sued the insurer for the proceeds of the policy (the "second action" mentioned in the quotation below) and filed a motion that the court dismiss the insurer's suit in equity for rescission on the ground that the insurer had an adequate remedy at law. The court denied the beneficiary's motion to dismiss as follows:

> The grounds urged by defendant [the beneficiary] for dismissal of the instant action for rescission is that the sole issue between the parties is basically legal in nature; that the plaintiff [the insurer] has a complete and adequate remedy at law in that it can assert its claims of fraud and misrepresentation in the aforesaid second action and thus assure the present defendant of her right to a trial by jury of that action.

---

[18]160 F. Supp. 510 (E.D.N.Y. 1958).

The principal issue on this motion is whether the Mutual Company had the right to resort to a court of equity with its claims for rescission or should have delayed action until the beneficiary sued on the policy and then interposed its defenses in such action. Mutual contends that if it had delayed bringing its action beyond the two year period from date of issue of the policy, it would have lost its right to defend by the operation of the incontestability clause in the contract. It reads as follows:

Incontestability. This policy . . . shall be incontestable after it has been in force for a period of two years from its date of issue.

It is crystal clear from a mere reading of the provision that if Mutual had any remedy pertaining to the policy, such remedy must be asserted within the two year period, in this case prior to February 27, 1958. It could not be availed of beyond that time.

. . . Mutual was not precipitate in instituting its action for rescission. It delayed doing so until its claim was about to be outlawed by the incontestability clause. In fact, barely one week remained for it to take action or forfeit its right to do so. In a similar rescission case, American Life Insurance Co. v. Stewart, 300 U.S. 203, 57 S.Ct. 377, 379, 81 L.Ed. 605, the plaintiff's right to resort to equity by way of claim for rescission was upheld. Mr. Justice Cardozo writing for the Court, said:

If the policy is to become incontestable soon after the death of the insured, the insurer becomes helpless if he must wait for a move by some one else, who may prefer to remain motionless till the time for contest has gone by. . . . Accordingly an insurer, who might otherwise be condemned to loss through the mere inaction of an adversary, may assume the offensive by going into equity and there praying cancellation.

The court thus held that the insurer did not have a remedy at law and could bring its action in equity. If the incontestable clause had included the words *during the lifetime of the insured,* the insurer would have had a remedy at law and could not have maintained a suit in the equity court.

Date from Which the Contestable Period Runs

Most individual life insurance policies contain two dates, the date of issue and the policy date. Often these dates are the same. For example, a policy might say that the date of issue is August 8, 1997, and that the policy date is also August 8, 1997. However, in some policies, particularly backdated policies, the policy date and the date of issue are not the same.

Most individual life insurance policies provide that the incontestable and suicide periods begin on the date of issue. The policy date is used to calculate the renewal premium due date. However, if the policy does not specify the date from which the contestable period begins to run, and the date of issue and policy date are not the same, an ambiguity could arise as to which date should govern. As in other instances in which there is an ambiguity, courts ordinarily construe the terms of the policy most favorably toward the policyowner and the beneficiary, in this case to give incontestability at the earliest possible time.

Summary

A contest of a life insurance policy is a court action to determine the validity of the policy. In a policy contest, the insurer either brings a suit in equity to rescind the contract or defends its denial of benefits in a lawsuit that the beneficiary brings, on the ground that the policy is not valid. The insurer can contest the policy's validity if there has been either a material misrepresentation in the application or a breach of a condition precedent to effectiveness of the policy and the incontestable clause does not preclude the contest.

The incontestable clause of a life insurance policy states that the validity of the policy cannot be contested once the contestable period has passed. The incontestable clause relates to contests of the validity of the policy and not to denial of benefits under policy exceptions and limitations, according to the majority view. Such exceptions and limitations are ordinarily effective after the contestable period has passed.

The incontestable clause does not bar certain policy contests. Even after the contestable period has expired, according to the majority view, fraudulent impersonation, lack of an insurable interest, and procurement of the policy with intent to murder the insured, are grounds for a contest of the policy.

A life insurance policy often specifically excludes disability and accidental death benefits from the operation of the incontestable clause. Statutes in a large majority of states permit such an exclusion. If the policy does not contain such an exclusion, the majority view is that the policy will become incontestable as to the disability and accidental death benefits when the contestable period has expired.

Most incontestable clauses today include the phrase *during the lifetime of the insured.* This phrase stops the running of the contestable period if the insured dies before the policy has become incontestable. In other words, the policy will never become incontestable if the insured dies during the contestable period and the incontestable clause contains this phrase. The insurer will be able to defend a lawsuit on the ground that the policy is invalid whenever the beneficiary brings suit. The insurer therefore has an adequate remedy at law and cannot sue in equity for rescission. Some insurers feel that it is to their advantage to sue in equity because a judge, rather than a jury, ordinarily decides the facts in an equity suit. For this reason, some insurers do not include the phrase *during the lifetime of the insured* in the incontestable clause so as to preserve their right to sue for rescission in equity if the insured dies within the contestable period.

ILLUSTRATIVE CASE

In the following case, the court discusses the phrase *during the lifetime of the insured* in the incontestable clause.

EDWARD B. CROW, Plaintiff-Appellant, v. CAPITOL BANKERS LIFE
INSURANCE COMPANY and JEAN COOLEY, individually and as agent for
Capitol Bankers Life Insurance Company, Defendants-Appellees.
Supreme Court of New Mexico[19]

FROST, Justice.

In applying for a life insurance policy from Capitol Bankers Life Insurance Company (Capitol), Edward and Kathy Crow made misrepresentations about Kathy's health history. As required by New Mexico law, the policy contained an incontestability clause, stating that, after two years from the date the policy was issued, the coverage could not be challenged. Kathy died of ovarian cancer less than two years after the policy was issued. Upon learning of the misrepresentations, Capitol denied payment of death benefits to Edward. Edward filed suit claiming that the incontestability clause prevented Capitol from challenging the policy.

We conclude that the incontestability clause should not be enforced because the language of the insurance contract required that the insured be alive for the entire two-

year period. We also conclude that, because there is strong evidence in the record of fraud and misrepresentation on the part of the Crows, Capitol properly refused to award the death benefits to Edward.

I.   Facts

Kathy Crow, a registered nurse, was diagnosed with ovarian cancer in October 1985. From the date of the diagnosis through the time of her death in 1990, she was under almost continuous care for cancer. She first met with Dr. George Ritcher, a specialist in gynecologic oncology, on October 2, 1985. Upon discovery of the cancer, she soon thereafter underwent a hysterectomy and an oophorectomy. Kathy then began a series of chemotherapy treatments that ended in July 1986.

A month after concluding the chemotherapy, on August 6, 1986, Dr. Richter [*sic*] performed a "second look" operation. Biopsies taken from various locations in her

---

[19]891 P.2d 1206 (1995).

abdominal cavity revealed the continued presence of cancer. Dr. Richter [*sic*] suggested at trial that historically a large percentage of patients who have a positive second look will succumb to the disease. Kathy then underwent another year of chemotherapy which ended in August 1987. During the same year Kathy also had minor surgery to remove a kidney stone.

About the same time her chemotherapy treatments ended, in August 1987, Kathy married Edward Crow. The couple purchased a home the following month. In the mortgage paperwork they indicated they would like to be contacted by a life insurance agent. Shortly thereafter, Jean Cooley, an agent for Capitol, contacted the Crows offering to sell them a policy. They told Cooley to call back after the first of the year in 1988.

In December 1987 Kathy complained of lower abdominal pain. New tests revealed evidence of a possible recurrence of cancer including a suspicious soft tissue mass in her pelvis.

Cooley called in mid-January 1988 and scheduled an appointment for February 25, 1988, to sell life insurance to the Crows. She came to their house on the appointed day and personally prepared two life insurance applications, one for Kathy and one for Edward.

Kathy's "HEALTH STATEMENT," as completed by Cooley, was in "PART C" of the application. Question 2(f) asked, "To the best of your knowledge and belief has the proposed insured within the last 10 years been treated for or had any known indication of . . . [a] stone or other disorder of kidney, bladder, prostate, or reproductive organs?" Cooley marked "Yes" to this question with the explanation that Kathy had suffered from a kidney infection and had a kidney stone removed. No problem with Kathy's reproductive organs was noted.

Most significantly, question 2(j) asked about any treatments or indications of "[c]ancer, cyst, or any tumor disorder of skin or lymph glands?" To this, Cooley marked Kathy's response: "No." Question 9(a) asked, "Has the Proposed Insured ever had any disorder of menstruation, pregnancy, or of the reproductive organs or breasts?" and Kathy's answer was "No." Cooley submitted the completed application documents to Capitol.

On March 23, 1988, Capitol issued the Crow's life insurance contract. Under the terms of the contract, this was the "Issue Date." Cooley delivered the documents to the Crows the same day. As required by New Mexico law, NMSA 1978, Section 59A–20–5 (Repl. Pamp. 1992), the portion of the contract insuring Edward's life contained an incontestability clause. This clause provided that, "during the lifetime of the Insured," Capitol could not contest statements made in the application after two years from the issue date. Appended to Edward's insurance policy was the "OTHER INSURED RIDER" (Rider), which was a policy insuring Kathy's life. The Rider also contained an incontestability clause. It differed from the one in Edward's policy in that it lacked any reference to "the lifetime of the Insured." Husband and wife were each covered for $77,900.00.

On March 25, 1988, two days after Cooley delivered the insurance policies, Kathy was informed by Dr. Richter [*sic*] that her cancer had recurred. Biopsies taken March 31, 1988, confirmed this diagnosis. Dr. Ritcher met with both Kathy and Edward on April 15, 1988, to discuss the alternatives for treatment. Five days later Kathy called Dr. Ritcher to tell him she wanted to continue aggressively fighting the disease with chemotherapy.

Apparently she continued with the chemotherapy until she went to Corpus Christi, Texas almost two years later in February 1990, to be with her family. She died on February 26, 1990. Her death certificate listed the immediate cause of death as "Aspiration Pneumonia" with "Papillary Adeno Carcinoma" as the significant condition that contributed to her death.

In March 1990 Edward called Cooley and told her Kathy had died. Cooley was "flabbergasted" when she learned that cancer was the cause of death and that Kathy "had it before." When Cooley asked Edward why the disease was not disclosed on the insurance application, he answered, "We thought she was all right."

Within a day or two Edward again called Cooley to ask if Capitol would pay the claim since the death certificate listed the immediate cause of death as aspiration pneumonia rather than cancer. Cooley replied that she did not know and indicated that her authority was limited to sending in the claim. She asked Edward again why he and Kathy had not disclosed the cancer. This time he asserted that Cooley had never asked them about it.

On March 6, 1990, Capitol opened its "Death Claim Checklist." Capitol mailed to Edward the "PROOFS OF DEATH—BENEFICIARY'S STATEMENT," which he completed and returned to the insurance company on March 14, 1990. Edward listed the "Cause of Death" as "Aspiration Pneumonia." In response to the question, "When did deceased first complain of or give other indications of his/her last illness?" he answered "1–27–89" though Kathy's cancer was diagnosed in 1985. When asked, "When did deceased first consult a physician for his/her last illness?" he responded "2–2–90" though she had been treated by Dr. Richter [*sic*] as early as 1985. One question asked for the names of all physicians who attended Kathy during the final three years of her last illness, as well as the dates of attendance, and the condition treated. Edward listed a physician from the hospital in Corpus Christi where Kathy died as treating her from "2–2–90" to "2–26–90" for "Pneumonia Aspiration." With remarkable understatement, Edward also listed Dr. Richter [*sic*], with no dates of attendance, as treating her for an "OBGYN Condition."

On April 23, 1990, Capitol wrote to Edward notifying him that, because Kathy's statements on Part C of the application constituted "a material misrepresentation of her health history," payment of the death benefits was being denied. Thus, despite the language of the incontestability clause, Capitol contested the policy after it had been in force for more than two years.

Edward filed a civil complaint on February 21, 1991, against Capitol and Cooley claiming breach of insurance contract, breach of covenant of good faith and fair dealing,[20] and violation of the New Mexico Insurance Practices Act. Edward included an allegation that, because Capitol denied the benefits more than two years after the issue date, it was forbidden by the incontestability clause from challenging any statements made in the original application.

Capitol and Cooley responded with the affirmative defense of fraud and misrepresentation on the part of the Crows. Capitol also claimed that because Kathy died within two years of the Issue Date, the incontestability provision contained in her Rider became inapplicable, and the validity of the policy could therefore be challenged.

After a trial on the merits, a jury determined that Capitol did not breach the terms of the life insurance contract. The jury also found that Kathy made false statements to Cooley. The court awarded judgment for Capitol and Cooley.

On appeal, Edward asserts that the trial court erred by not enforcing, as a matter of law, the incontestability clause. We believe the trial court acted properly. The dispositive issues in this case are whether the incontestability clause was unenforceable and whether Kathy's misrepresentations on the insurance application released Capitol from its obligations under the contract. No other matters need be addressed.

II.   The Incontestability Clause

New Mexico law requires that each life insurance policy contain "a provision that the policy . . . shall be incontestable, except for nonpayment of premiums, after it has been in force during the lifetime of the insured for a period of two (2) years from its date of issue." Accordingly, Edward's policy contained a clause that "[w]ith respect to the initial Specified Amount, we will not contest this policy after it has been in force during the lifetime of the Insured for the contestable period shown on the Schedule Page." The Schedule Page stated, "THE CONTESTABLE PERIOD IS 2 YEARS." The Rider that insured Kathy's life also provided that, "[a]fter two years from its Issue Date, this Rider shall be incontestable as to statements made in the application."

---
[20]The covenant of good faith and fair dealing is discussed in Chapter 18, "Performance of the Insurance Contract."

We base our decision in this case on a single narrow issue: whether this particular clause requires that the insured be alive for the entire two-year contestable period. We conclude, under traditional theories of contract interpretation, that the policy issued by Capitol required Kathy to be alive for two years from the issue date for the incontestability clause to be enforceable. We reach this conclusion even though Kathy's Rider lacked the "during the lifetime of the insured" language.

Edward wishes us to address whether Capitol properly contested the policy within the period specified by the clause. Because the incontestability clause in this case was voided by Kathy's death, we need not address this matter. For the same reason we need not address Capitol's allegation that, the incontestability clause notwithstanding, when fraud is alleged, the validity of an insurance policy can be contested at any time.

III.   Standard of Review

Though certain elements of construction are unique to insurance contracts, generally they are construed by the same principles governing the interpretation of all contracts. Incontestability clauses are no exception to this generality.

The clauses in question will be interpreted by their own terms and conditions. To the extent that the insurance company in drafting the insurance form is responsible for the language of the policy, any ambiguity will be resolved in favor of the beneficiary. However, to the extent the wording of the incontestability clause is prescribed by statute, and not controlled by the insurance company, the language will not be strictly construed against the insurer. Rather, the language will be interpreted so as to fulfill the statutory intent behind the required language.

IV.   Incontestability Clause Is Voided
by the Death of the Insured

The phrase, "during the lifetime of the Insured" in the incontestability clause of Edward's policy has consistently been interpreted by other jurisdictions to mean that the insured must remain alive for the entire two-year period before the policy becomes incontestable.

Since this phrase is derived from the statute, we will, under the standard of review just discussed, not construe it strictly against Capitol. The two-year limitation was not intended by the legislature to be an absolute bar to contestability. The "during the lifetime of the insured" language of Section 59A–20–5, was meant specifically to condition contestability on the survival of the insured for two years after policy was issued.

Edward asserts that the Rider should be read separately from his own life insurance policy. He emphasizes that the Rider's incontestability clause flatly requires the expiration of two years before the policy becomes incontestable. Unlike his policy, it makes no requirement that the policy be in force for two years "during the lifetime of the Insured." Thus he claims, under the clear and unambiguous language of the Rider, Kathy's death would not preclude the clause from being enforced.

It is a basic tenet of contract construction that a "memorandum may consist of several writings." Restatement (Second) of Contracts § 132 (1979). If two or more writings are part of a single transaction and concern the same subject matter, then they are a single contract. Whether multiple documents consist of a single contract is determined by considering the intentions of the parties and the surrounding circumstances. Edward's insurance contract and the Rider are to be read as a single contract as long as the circumstances establish that they relate to the same transaction.

The language of the policy shows that the two writings were intended by the parties to be a single contract. The "SCHEDULE PAGE," which is the first sheet after the cover page, contains the statement that "THE CHARGE FOR ANY ADDITIONAL BENEFITS WHICH ARE PROVIDED BY RIDER IS SHOWN BELOW," suggesting that, while the Rider may have certain additional provisions, it actually incorporates the terms of Edward's policy. The Rider, contained entirely on the tenth sheet of the policy, begins with the statement, "Based on the application for this rider and the payment of the premium, *this rider is made part of this policy.*" (Emphasis added.) The last paragraph of the Rider, entitled "RIDER PART OF POLICY" provides:

> This rider is attached to and made a part of this policy as of the Issue Date of this rider in return for the application and payment of premiums. The Issue Date of this rider is the Issue Date of the policy to which it is attached, unless a different date is shown below.

The same paragraph also states that "[a]ll the provisions of the policy apply to this rider, except those that are inconsistent with this rider." Under the contract doctrine discussed herein, any inconsistency between the two incontestability clauses in question is immaterial. The policy and the Rider are unquestionably to be construed as parts of a single transaction within a single memorandum.

Another basic principle of contract construction is that "[a] writing is interpreted as a whole, and all writings that are part of the same transaction are interpreted together." Restatement (Second) of Contracts § 202(2) (1979). Edward urges that, because the Rider lacks the "lifetime of the insured" language, we should isolate its incontestability clause from the rest of the contract. This approach would violate the principle that no part of the contract can be isolated and interpreted distinctly from the rest of the contract. Moreover, the entire contract is to be considered in the interpretation of any individual part. Each word, phrase, and section of a contract should be analyzed in its context within the contract as a whole so as to realize the intentions of the parties.

Our conclusion that the Rider's incontestability clause cannot rationally be isolated and distinguished from the clause in Edward's policy is supported by several arguments. First, the "during the lifetime of the insured" language is required by New Mexico statute. Under traditional contract theory, state laws are incorporated into and form a part of every contract whether or not they are specifically mentioned in the instrument. Edward does not claim there is a fault in the language of the statute. The language of Section 59A–20–5, is thus a part of the entire contract and cannot be isolated from any individual section. Though not specifically mentioned, the "during the lifetime of the insured" language of the statute was implicitly incorporated into the incontestability clause of the Rider.

A second important reason for refusing to distinguish the Rider's incontestability clause is that the interpretation urged by Edward violates public policy. A contract is unenforceable if it violates public policy, especially public policies that engender the writing of statutes. The incontestability clause promotes two important public policies. First, it protects the insurance company by giving it an adequate window of time in which to investigate an application for life insurance so as to discover any material misrepresentations on the part of the applicant. Second, it protects the insured from having to defend against a possibly specious challenge long after acquisition of the policy. Thus, by requiring prompt investigation of statements made in an insurance application, the clause furthers the public policy of denying protection to those who make fraudulent claims. The "during the lifetime" wording is part of that public policy. If the insured dies of a serious illness a short time after obtaining a life insurance policy, the insurance company should be permitted to investigate in contemplation of a challenge. It would be against public policy for the Rider in the instant case to prevent Capitol from investigating the fact that Kathy died of cancer a short time after representing to the insurance company that she had no such disease. The public policy behind the "during the lifetime" language of Edward's policy is equally a part of the Rider though not expressly articulated.

Finally, no rational reason has been offered for making the incontestability clause of the Rider different from that of Edward's policy. It is possible to imagine some provisions of an insurance contract that would be different for husband and wife such as the premium cost or the amount of benefits received. However, there is no logical reason why the incontestability clause should apply differently to two parties who are covered by the same contract. Furthermore, there is no logical reason why one clause should incorporate relevant state law and public policy, and the other should not. The law will always seek to effectuate a reasonable over an unreasonable interpretation of a contract.

Thus, Kathy's death within the contestable period fixed the rights of the parties; the incontestability clause became a nullity even though the contestable period had expired. The policy could thus be contested by Capitol.

V.   Misrepresentations Bar Recovery

Since, by the terms of the insurance contract, the incontestability clause became unenforceable upon Kathy's death, Capitol was not bound by that time constraint in contesting the policy. A question in an insurance application propounded for the purpose of determining the existence of a significant bodily disorder allows the insurer to evaluate whether the disorder makes the insured an unacceptable risk. A material misrepresentation in answering such a question will render the policy void.

A misrepresentation on an insurance application is material if the insurer would not have entered into the contract but for the misrepresentation. By concealing the true nature of her health, Kathy induced Capitol to enter a contract it otherwise would have rejected. Capitol relied upon the misrepresentation and, as a result, was deprived of the opportunity to estimate its risk under the contract.

Capitol bears the burden of proving that the Crows' fraudulent misrepresentations are sufficient to avoid its liability on the contract. The insurer can prove misrepresentation in several ways. For example, misrepresentation is indicated when the insurer relies upon statements that were certainly known by the insured to be untrue, or when these statements "are of such a character as clearly to prove a conscious misrepresentation." *See* 7 George J. Couch, *Couch Cyclopedia of Insurance Law 2d* § 37:106. Kathy's claim on the application that she had never been treated for "[c]ancer, cyst, or any tumor disorder of skin or lymph glands," was of such a character.

Also, misrepresentation is suggested by the brevity of time between the applicant's representation about her health and the occurrence of the disease. Though entirely dependent upon the specific facts of each case, this brevity of time can indicate to the company that the insured knew she was afflicted with the disease at the time she applied for insurance. In this case, two days after the issue date of the insurance policy, Kathy was told her cancer had reappeared. This circumstance implies misrepresentation on the part of the Crows.

Evidence of misrepresentation can also be found if the insured does not disclose that she knows she suffers from a serious disease which is statistically likely to shorten her life. Kathy suffered from a form of cancer that Dr. Richter [*sic*] described as "the worst disease we deal with," because it is difficult to detect early and almost impossible to completely eradicate. Kathy's physicians recounted several discussions in which they informed Kathy of the nature of her disease. As a registered nurse she was at least as competent as most people to understand its consequences. There can be little doubt that both she and Edward were aware that ovarian cancer was likely to shorten her life.

In the Crows' policy, Capitol explicitly noted that "[i]n issuing this policy, we have relied on statements made in the application." Kathy made statements about her health in the application, the statements were incorporated into the policy, and in reliance upon the truth of those statements Capitol issued the policy. Because a jury found that the representations were false and were material to the risk being assumed by the insurance company, the policy was properly voided.

VI.   Conclusion

For the foregoing reasons we find that Kathy's death rendered the incontestability clause of her life insurance policy unenforceable, and that because of Kathy's misrepresentations about her health on the application form, Capitol properly refused to pay death benefits to Edward, her beneficiary. We therefore affirm the judgment of the trial court.

IT IS SO ORDERED.

FRANCHINI and MINZNER, JJ.,concur.

Questions for Review

1. Discuss valid, void, and voidable contracts.
2. Define the term *policy contest.*
3. How does the breach of a condition precedent to effectiveness of the policy relate to policy contests?
4. Discuss the history of the incontestable clause.
5. Define the term *warranty.*
6. Define the term *representation.*
7. Explain the effect an incontestable clause ordinarily would have if

   a. Death was the result of suicide within two years after the policy issue date.
   b. The policy application contained a misstatement of age.
8. Under what circumstances does an incontestable clause not bar policy contests?
9. Does an incontestable clause apply to disability and accidental death benefit provisions? Explain.
10. Discuss the effect of the phrase *during the lifetime of the insured* in an incontestable clause.

18 PERFORMANCE OF THE INSURANCE CONTRACT

Chapter Outline

Contract performance occurs when the acts required by the contract are completed. A life insurance contract is performed when all the promises it contains have been carried out. Ordinarily, this happens when the insured has died and the insurer pays the death benefit to the beneficiary.

A life insurance contract requires that proof of loss be submitted after the insured's death. The illustrative policy in the Appendix, Figure 2, provides the following:

> If the Insured dies while this policy is in force, we will pay the sum insured to the Beneficiary, when we receive at our Home Office due proof of the Insured's death, subject to the provisions of this Policy.

Thus, the insurer's claim examiner will check to make certain that the policy was in force at the insured's death. Due proof of the insured's death is usually made by means of a certified death certificate that the beneficiary submits to the insurer. Because death benefits are often necessary for the support of an insured's survivors, life insurers consider the prompt payment of such benefits an essential part of their contractual responsibilities. In the great majority of cases, no problems arise and the insurer pays the death benefit promptly.

However, in some instances the insurer encounters legal problems in performing the contract. The primary purpose of this chapter is to explore significant legal problems related to life insurance contract performance; however, the sections containing discussions of releases, compromise settlements, unfair claims settlement practices laws, the reasonable expectations doctrine, and claims litigation also pertain to health insurance.

Establishing the Proper Payee

Ordinarily, the beneficiary designation in a life insurance policy has been properly drafted, and there is no question as to whom the death benefits are payable. However, in a small minority of cases a problem does arise in establishing the proper payee. The problems involved in these cases will be discussed in this section.

No Named Beneficiary

Under most ordinary life insurance contracts, if no beneficiary is alive at the death of the insured, the policy provides that the death benefits will be paid to the policyowner or to the policyowner's estate. Some policies, notably group life insurance policies covering federal government employees or persons in the armed services, provide a listing of contingent beneficiaries, in order of preference, if no beneficiary is named. Under this government insurance, these contingent beneficiaries are the insured's widow or widower, children and descendants of deceased children (by representation), parents or parent, estate, or next of kin.[1]

Executor or Administrator Beneficiaries

A policyowner-insured sometimes names the executor or administrator of his estate as primary beneficiary. At other times, the executor or administrator will be the proper payee under the policy terms because all named beneficiaries have predeceased the insured.

---

[1]5 U.S.C.A. § 8705 (West 1996).

When an executor or administrator is the claimant, the insurer will require evidence of her appointment by the court. Ordinarily, the insurer requests a certified copy of the letters of administration appointing an administrator or letters testamentary appointing an executor.

Trustee Beneficiaries

When a trustee is named beneficiary, the insurer will need evidence of the trustee's appointment and power to act before paying the trustee. The insurer will require a certified copy of the trust agreement in some situations. Sometimes, the original trustee named in the trust has died, resigned, or been removed. In any of these situations, the insurer must be certain that the person claiming to be the successor trustee has been duly appointed. If the trustee of a testamentary trust is the policy beneficiary, the probate court must determine the validity of the will creating the trust before the insurer can pay the trustee.

Assignee Beneficiaries

Policyowners often make collateral assignments of life insurance policies when the policyowners borrow money.[2] Assignment of the policy to the lender secures the loan made to the policyowner. Usually these assignments are made pursuant to the terms of an assignment form that gives the assignee—usually a bank or other lending institution—the right to receive from the insurer as much of the net proceeds of the policy as the assignee proves, by affidavit filed with the insurer, to be due under the assignment. The form provides that the remainder of the proceeds, if any, is to be paid in accordance with the beneficiary designation, settlement agreement, or other assignment of record.

In the absence of a settlement agreement spendthrift clause to the contrary, a beneficiary with vested rights in a life insurance policy usually can assign his right to the death benefit to another person. The death benefit is then payable to the person receiving the right—the assignee.

Incompetent Beneficiaries

Generally speaking, a minor or mentally incompetent person cannot give the insurer a binding release for payment of the death benefit. For this reason, payment of the death benefit to an incompetent beneficiary requires careful handling and, often, the involvement of the insurer's lawyers.

In the absence of a statute to the contrary, a minor can disaffirm a release during his minority or within a reasonable time after he reaches majority. For this reason, whenever a minor is the beneficiary, the insurer must carefully examine the relevant state laws to determine what benefits, if any, it can safely pay directly to the minor, and what benefits it must pay to a guardian of the minor's estate, if one has been appointed, or hold at interest for the minor until his majority.

In some states, a minor over a certain age, usually 15 or 16, can make specified contracts for life, accident, or health insurance and can give a binding release for benefits payable to the minor under such a contract. The Alabama statute provides the following:

---

[2]Collateral assignments are discussed in Chapter 14, "Assignments and Other Transfers."

(*b*) Any minor of the age of 15 years or more, as determined by the nearest birthday, may, notwithstanding his minority, contract for annuities or for insurance upon his own life, body, [or] health . . . or on the person of another in whom the minor has an insurable interest. Such a minor shall, notwithstanding such minority, be deemed competent to exercise all rights and powers with respect to, or under . . . [such contracts]. . . . (*c*) Any annuity contract or policy of life or disability insurance procured by or for a minor under subsection (*b*) of this section, shall be made payable either to the minor or his estate or to a person having an insurable interest in the life of the minor.[3]

Thus, for example, if a 15-year-old minor in Alabama contracted for life insurance on the life of her mother and named herself beneficiary, the minor could give a binding release for the death benefit.

In many instances, the minor is not the policyowner, and a statute such as the one quoted above does not apply. For example, a policyowner might name his minor child the beneficiary of a policy insuring the policyowner's life. Some states have a statute allowing an insurer to make limited payments to a parent or to another person caring for the minor in such an instance. A few states have a statute allowing an insurer to pay out limited amounts directly to a minor who has reached a specified age. The Montana statute reads as follows:

Any minor domiciled in this state who has attained the age of 16 years shall be deemed competent to receive and to give full acquittance and discharge for a payment or payments in aggregate amount not exceeding $3,000 in any one year made by a life insurer under the maturity, death, or settlement agreement provisions in effect or elected by such minor under a life insurance policy or annuity contract, provided such policy, contract, or agreement shall provide for the payment or payments to such minor and if prior to such payment the insurer has not received written notice of the appointment of a duly qualified guardian of the property of the minor.[4]

In the absence of a statute permitting payment to a minor without a guardian, only a court-appointed guardian of the minor's estate is competent to give a binding release for benefits due the minor beneficiary. Therefore, when the guardian of a minor's estate files a claim for insurance proceeds, the insurer will require a certified copy of the court order of appointment.

Ordinarily, a parent will not be able to give an insurer a binding release for a death benefit due his minor child unless a court appoints the parent as the guardian of his minor child's estate. The parent's status as parent, by itself, usually does not make the parent legally competent to give a binding release without such court appointment. Similarly, court appointment as guardian of the minor's person of someone who is not the minor's parent does not make the appointee competent to give the insurer a binding release for a death benefit due the minor, unless that person has been appointed as guardian of the minor's estate also.

If no guardian of the minor's estate is appointed and no statute permits the insurer to pay the proceeds without such a guardian, the insurer ordinarily must hold the proceeds at interest until the minor beneficiary reaches the age of majority. The beneficiary herself can then give a binding release.

As with minor beneficiaries, mentally incompetent beneficiaries cannot give the insurer a binding release. If the court has appointed a guardian of the incompetent beneficiary's estate, the payment can be made to such a guardian. If the beneficiary is

---

[3]Ala. Code § 27–14–5 (1986).
[4]Mont. Code Ann. § 33–15–502(1) (1995).

institutionalized, small amounts of insurance proceeds sometimes can be paid to a trust account that the institution maintains for the beneficiary.

When the Beneficiary Kills the Insured

Because the law protects human life and prohibits anything that encourages murder, it does not allow people to profit from their own wrongdoing. Therefore, a beneficiary who intentionally and wrongfully kills the insured is usually disqualified by law from receiving the death benefit.

Killings That Are Not Wrongful.   Unless a state statute provides to the contrary, if a beneficiary kills the insured, the killing must be wrongful to disqualify the beneficiary from receiving the death benefit. For example, a killing in lawful self-defense is not wrongful; therefore, a beneficiary who kills the insured in lawful self-defense ordinarily will not be disqualified from receiving the death benefit.[5] Such a killing is justifiable homicide. The same result will occur if the beneficiary kills the insured in the lawful defense of another person. Moreover, a beneficiary who accidentally kills the insured ordinarily will not be disqualified from receiving the death benefit.[6] A beneficiary who was insane at the time he killed the insured usually will not be disqualified unless the policy specifically provides otherwise.[7] Finally, a beneficiary who was very young when she killed the insured might not be disqualified from receiving the death benefit.

Lesser Degrees of Wrongful Killing.   Not all wrongful killing is murder. A wrongful killing can be classified as first-degree murder, second-degree murder, voluntary manslaughter, involuntary manslaughter, reckless homicide, and so forth. Each state has its own classifications of wrongful killing.

The laws of the states regarding disqualification of beneficiaries who kill the insured differ considerably. In one state, a statute provided that a beneficiary would be disqualified from receiving the death benefit only if he was convicted of murdering the insured. A beneficiary in that state was convicted of voluntary manslaughter of the insured, not of murder. The court held that the beneficiary was entitled to the policy proceeds.[8] In another state, a beneficiary was disqualified from receiving policy proceeds when her culpable negligence resulted in the insured's death.[9] Culpable negligence is a lesser degree of wrongful killing than voluntary manslaughter. The insurer must carefully examine the law of the relevant state in regard to beneficiaries who kill the insured to determine if the beneficiary is disqualified. To protect itself, the insurer often must file a bill of interpleader and pay the proceeds to the court.

Acquitted Beneficiary.   Sometimes, the beneficiary is acquitted of the murder of the insured after being tried in a criminal proceeding. Such acquittal does not necessarily mean that the beneficiary is entitled to receive the policy proceeds. A suit to enforce payment of life insurance proceeds is a civil action, and the degree of proof required in a civil action is not the same as that required in a criminal case. In civil

---

[5]Provident Life & Acci. Ins. Co. v. Carter, 345 So. 2d 1245 (La. Ct. App. 1977).

[6] Franklin Life Ins. Co. v. Strickland, 376 F. Supp. 280 (N.D. Miss. 1974).

[7]Holdom v. Grand Lodge of Ancient Order of United Workmen, 43 N.E. 772 (Ill. 1895); Simon v. Dibble, 380 S.W.2d 898 (Tex. Civ. App. 1964).

[8]Rose v. Rose, 444 P.2d 762 (N.M. 1968).

[9]Quick v. United Benefit Life Ins. Co., 213 S.E.2d 563 (N.C. 1975).

actions, facts usually must be proved by a preponderance of the evidence, whereas in criminal cases the defendant's guilt must be proved beyond a reasonable doubt. Thus, a person could be acquitted of a charge of murdering the insured yet be disqualified to receive the death benefit in a civil action. For example, suppose that Jeffrey Brown, the insured, is killed by Barbara Brown, his wife and primary beneficiary. If she is acquitted of the charge of murder in a criminal proceeding by reason of temporary insanity, she still could be judged disqualified to receive the life insurance benefits in a civil action.[10]

Policies Procured in Good Faith.   In instances in which the insured has procured the policy, or in which the beneficiary has procured the policy in good faith and without intent to murder the insured, the benefit will be payable to someone, even though the beneficiary is disqualified because he killed the insured. The question then arises as to whom the benefits should be paid. The insurer must consult state law on this point also. Some states have statutes providing that the contingent beneficiary will receive the proceeds.[11] Other states have statutes providing that the proceeds shall be paid as if the beneficiary who killed the insured had predeceased the insured.[12] Still others provide that the benefits are payable to the insured's estate.[13]

Policies Procured with Intent to Murder.   In the rare instance in which the insurer proves that the beneficiary purchased an insurance policy with the intent to murder the insured, the insurer does not have to pay the proceeds to anyone, according to the majority view. In such an instance, the policy is void. For example, in *Ellis v. John Hancock Mutual Life Insurance Co.*[14] the bigamous wife of the insured, intending to kill the insured, procured the policy, naming herself as primary beneficiary and her two daughters by a previous marriage as contingent beneficiaries. The wife then conspired and contracted with two other people to murder the insured. The court stated, "It is well settled in Arkansas that when the beneficiary in a life insurance policy wrongfully kills the insured, public policy prohibits a recovery by the beneficiary." The court went on to say, "The general rule of law is that a life insurance policy is void from its inception and the insurer is relieved of all liability upon the subsequent homicide of the insured where it is proved that a beneficiary procured the policy possessing a then present intention to murder the insured." The court therefore held that no benefits were payable to anyone because the policy was void.

Common Disasters

If the insured and the primary beneficiary are killed in a *common disaster,* the insurer must determine who died first. If both were killed at the same instant, or if they died in such a way that it cannot be determined who died first, the state's simultaneous death act will apply.

---

[10]In *United States v. Kwasniewski*, 91 F. Supp. 847 (E.D. Mich. 1950), a contingent payee was disqualified from receiving the remaining proceeds, although he was acquitted of the murder of the primary payee by reason of insanity. See also California-Western States Life Ins. Co. v. Sanford, 515 F. Supp. 524 (E.D. La. 1981).

[11]*E.g.,* OR. REV. STAT. § 112.515 (1990).

[12]*E.g.,* R.I. GEN. LAWS § 33–1.1–11 (1995).

[13]*E.g.,* OKLA. STAT. ANN. tit. 84 § 231 (West Supp. 1996).

[14]586 F. Supp. 649 (E.D. Ark. 1984).

A ***simultaneous death act*** provides that, unless there is a clause in the policy to the contrary, if an insured and beneficiary die simultaneously, or if it is impossible to tell who died first, it will be deemed that the beneficiary died first. State simultaneous death acts are patterned on the Uniform Simultaneous Death Act drafted by the National Conference of Commissioners on Uniform State Laws.

Although the simultaneous death acts of the states vary somewhat, Illinois's act is typical. It reads as follows:

> No sufficient evidence of survivorship. If the title to property or its devolution depends upon priority of death and there is no sufficient evidence that the persons have died otherwise than simultaneously and there is no other provision in the will, trust agreement, deed, contract of insurance or other governing instrument for distribution of the property different from the provisions of this Section:
>
> * * * * *
>
> (*d*) If the insured and the beneficiary of a policy of life or accident insurance have so died, the proceeds of the policy shall be distributed as if the insured had survived the beneficiary.[15]

If the beneficiary survives the insured for even a short time, the state's simultaneous death act will not apply. If the policy or the beneficiary designation has a survivorship clause, that clause might determine who is to receive the proceeds. A survivorship clause provides that the beneficiary must survive the insured by a specified number of days, or the benefits will be paid as if the beneficiary had died before the insured. The survivorship clause in the illustrative policy in the Appendix, Figure 2, reads:

> If any beneficiary dies simultaneously with the Insured or during the 14 days immediately following the date of death of the Insured, the proceeds of the Policy shall, unless otherwise provided in the application or in a written request, be paid to the same payee or payees and in the same manner as if the deceased beneficiary had died before the Insured. Any reference in this Policy to a beneficiary living or surviving shall mean living on the 15th day immediately following the date of death of the Insured.

If the policyowner has entered into a settlement agreement naming a contingent payee, the contingent payee will receive the remaining proceeds when the primary payee dies. This will be true whether the primary payee and the insured die simultaneously, or whether the primary payee survives the insured. A settlement agreement is often a good way to solve the problems connected with short-term survivorship. See the discussion on this subject in Chapter 11, "Settlement Agreements, Trusts, and Wills."

Conflicting Claimants

Sometimes, the insurer faces two or more claimants to the death benefit. For example, a policyowner-insured might have entered into a property settlement agreement as part of a divorce decree in which he agreed to maintain his former spouse or minor children as beneficiaries. If the policyowner-insured then named a second spouse as beneficiary, two or more parties might claim the death benefit. Or, as another example, a policyowner-insured might have partially completed a beneficiary change at the time of her death. If the intended beneficiary claims that the insured substantially

---

[15]775 Ill. Comp. Stat. 5/3–1 (Michie 1993).

complied with the policy provisions regarding beneficiary change, but the original beneficiary denies this claim, the insurer will again face conflicting claimants.

The insurer ordinarily will encourage conflicting claimants to settle their differences among themselves. If the conflicting claimants agree on a division of the benefits, and each gives the insurer a release from all claims to the benefits, the insurer can pay the claimants according to their agreement. If the claimants will not agree, and if any question exists as to which person is entitled to the proceeds, the insurer usually will pay the proceeds to the court in an interpleader action. Interpleader is discussed in Chapter 16, "Equitable Remedies."

Unclaimed Benefits

Sometimes, the life insurer cannot find the proper payee of a death benefit. In this situation, the insurer does not become the owner of the unclaimed benefit. Rather, the benefit becomes subject to a state unclaimed property statute. Usually, the unclaimed property statute of the state of the beneficiary's last known address governs. If there is no last known address of the beneficiary, the law presumes that the beneficiary's last known address is the same as the insured's. If no address of the insured or the beneficiary is known, the statute of the insurer's state of domicile will govern.[16]

Nearly all states have unclaimed property statutes, most of which are patterned on the Uniform Disposition of Unclaimed Property Act, a model law drafted by the National Conference of Commissioners on Uniform State Laws. An unclaimed property statute also applies to other types of unclaimed property, for example, to unclaimed bank deposits. These statutes are sometimes called escheat statutes, but this is a loose use of the term *escheat*. **Escheat** means reversion of ownership of property to a state in the absence of persons legally entitled to take claim to the property. Under most unclaimed property statutes, the state merely holds and uses the property but does not own it.

Ordinarily, the state law provides that the insurer will hold the unclaimed death benefit for five years, after which time it will be considered abandoned. The insurer must then report the death benefit to the state. State officials will advertise the death benefit's existence in a newspaper and send a notice to the beneficiary's last known address, if any. If no one claims the death benefit, the insurer must pay it to the state.

The state has full use of the funds, but under most unclaimed property statutes the beneficiary can claim the funds from the state at any time. In a few states, however, the state becomes the owner of the property after holding it for a specified number of years. In such a case, the property truly does escheat to the state.

Suicide of the Insured

Suicide is the intentional killing of oneself. The effect of an insured's suicide on the performance of the life insurance contract is discussed in this section.

The Suicide Exclusion Clause

Most modern life insurance policies contain a clause stating that death benefits will not be payable if the insured dies by suicide within a certain period, usually one or

---

[16]Texas v. New Jersey, 379 U.S. 674 (1965), *supp. by* Texas v. New Jersey, 380 U.S. 518 (1965).

two years from the policy date of issue. The insurer will return only the amount of the premiums paid, less the amount of any unpaid policy loans and loan interest. The illustrative policy in the Appendix, Figure 2, has the following provision:

> If the Insured dies by suicide, while sane or insane, within two years from the [date of issue], our liability will be limited to the amount of the premiums paid, less any indebtedness.

The suicide exclusion clause represents a compromise between two competing interests. On the one hand, the best interests of the policyowners as a group must be considered. If the insurer made no effort to prevent a person who was contemplating suicide from securing life insurance benefits for her dependents, the other policyowners would have to share the resulting higher costs of life insurance.

On the other hand, the economic loss to the insured's dependents is just as great when the insured commits suicide as when she dies in some other manner. The purpose of life insurance is to protect against economic loss resulting from an insured's death.

A policy provision such as the one quoted above furnishes sufficient protection against those who might be tempted to have their dependents profit from their contemplated suicides. Few people will apply for life insurance with the intention of waiting two years before committing suicide. The provision also protects the beneficiary of an insured who commits suicide two or more years after the policy is issued.

Suicide Exclusion Statutes.   Some states have statutes defining the period during which the risk of suicide can be excluded from a life insurance contract. The Tennessee statute quoted below is typical:

> [T]he following causes of death may be excepted by a provision in the policy:
>   (A) Suicide committed, while sane or insane, within two (2) years from the date of issue of the policy.[17]

A few states specify a one-year period. One state, Missouri, provides that suicide shall not be a defense to the payment of the death benefit unless the insurer can prove that the insured contemplated suicide at the time of application.[18] Because proving an intent of this kind would be impossible in most suicide situations, the practical effect of the Missouri statute is to nullify the suicide provision of life insurance policies issued in Missouri.

Suicide While Sane or Insane.   Suicide exclusion clauses in most modern life insurance policies except the risk of death by suicide *while sane or insane*. If a suicide exclusion clause does not include the phrase *while sane or insane*, most courts interpret the clause to refer only to the insured's suicide while he is sane.[19] If the suicide exclusion clause does contain the phrase *while sane or insane*, self-destruction by an insane insured ordinarily will not be covered during the exclusion period.[20] However, even where the phrase is included, courts in a minority of jurisdictions hold that an insane insured must have had an intention to kill himself and a consciousness of the physical nature and consequences of his act. In other words, if the insured was unable

---

[17]TENN. CODE ANN. § 56–7–2308 (5)(A) (1994).

[18] MO. ANN. STAT. § 376.620 (Vernon 1991).

[19]Cole v. Combined Ins. Co., 480 A.2d 178 (N.H. 1984).

[20]Aetna Life Ins. Co. v. McLaughlin, 380 S.W.2d 101 (Tex. 1964).

to resist his insane impulses, or was so insane as to not understand what he was doing, the suicide exclusion will not apply in these jurisdictions.[21]

The Burden of Proof

The majority of modern suicide cases concern the factual question of whether the insured's death was, or was not, suicide. The law maintains a presumption against suicide. In many states, this is a strong presumption. The rationale for the presumption against suicide is that human beings generally possess a love of life, an instinct to preserve life, and a fear of death. Therefore, if an insurer believes that an insured committed suicide and denies a claim for the death benefit on that ground, and the beneficiary sues, the insurer must plead suicide as an affirmative defense and will have the burden of proving that the insured's death was caused by suicide.

For example, in *Still v. Metropolitan Life Insurance Co.*,[22] the insured died as a result of three bullet wounds in the chest. Powder burns were found on his shirt and skin, indicating that the gun had been fired at close range. The insured was found sitting in his automobile in a parking lot. The appellate court said:

> There was evidence that the decedent was having financial difficulty; that he had recently been involved in an automobile accident in which a person had been killed and a claim was pending against him on account of it; and that he was depressed. It was also shown that the decedent purchased a gun two days before his death; and that this was the gun found just below his hands in his automobile. One of the bullets passed through the body into the seat. There were no signs of violence. A physician, who was also the coroner that investigated the death, testified that the decedent could have fired into his body three times before losing consciousness.
>
> On the other hand, there was evidence that the decedent was not depressed; that just before his death he appeared as normal as always; that he had a cast on his right arm as a result of the automobile accident; and that although it would not be impossible, it would be difficult to fire a pistol with that hand. There was some testimony that the decedent sometimes carried money in a long type billfold chained to his belt or in his coat pocket, and that this was not found among his personal effects; that decedent could have been shot and robbed.
>
> In a case such as this, until the evidence preponderates against death by homicide, the jury is obliged to presume that homicide was the case, i.e., there is a presumption against suicide which remains until so dispelled. . . .
>
> The jury decided the presumption had been overcome and that the decedent had committed suicide. There is ample evidence to support their conclusion and it will not be disturbed.

Because the death was caused by suicide and the policy's suicide exclusion period had not expired, the death benefit was not payable. The insurer was liable only for the amount of the premiums paid.

The *Still* decision is unusual because the presumption against suicide is often impossible for the insurer to overcome. The large majority of jury verdicts in suicide cases are in the beneficiary's favor. However, statistical studies have shown that the insurer has a better chance of winning at appeal than at trial.[23]

---

[21]Vicars v. Aetna Life Ins. Co., 164 S.W. 106 (Ky. 1914).

[22]165 S.E. 2d 896 (Ga. Ct. App. 1968).

[23]Paul J. Harriton, *The Presumption Against Suicide—Is It Presumptuous?*, AM. COUNCIL OF LIFE INS., LEGAL SEC. PROCEEDINGS, Nov. 1983, at 279.

Suicide and the Accidental Death Benefit

Suicide by a sane person is not an accidental death. The insured who commits suicide can foresee the death and could have prevented it. Generally, in a suit for an accidental death benefit the beneficiary has the burden of proving that the death was by accident or by accidental means. However, where suicide is an issue, the majority of courts have placed the burden on the insurer of proving that the insured committed suicide, and hence that the death was not accidental or by accidental means. A minority of courts have held that the beneficiary's burden of proving death by accident includes proving that the death was not by suicide.

Policies without a Suicide Exclusion Clause

Some policies do not exclude deaths caused by suicide from coverage. In the absence of a suicide exclusion clause, the death benefit ordinarily will be payable if the insured dies as a result of suicide, with two exceptions.

First, if the insured purchased the policy in contemplation of suicide, the death benefit will not be payable because such a purchase is a fraud on the insurer.[24] Second, if the insured was sane at the time of the suicide, and the insured's estate is the beneficiary, the death benefit might not be payable.[25]

Disappearance of the Insured

Insured persons sometimes disappear. The beneficiary who believes that the absent insured is dead then faces the problem of proving the death. The legal problems created by the insured's disappearance are discussed in this section.

Mysterious Disappearance

Sometimes, the disappearance of an insured person has no explanation. This is called a mysterious disappearance. Most states have laws providing that a person who has mysteriously disappeared will be presumed dead if certain criteria have been met. Ordinarily, there are four criteria. First, the person must have been continuously absent from her home for a specified period of time, usually seven years. Second, the absence must have been unexplained. Third, persons most likely to have heard from the missing person must have heard nothing. Fourth, the beneficiary must have been unable to locate the missing person by diligent search and inquiry.

The presumption of death is rebuttable, meaning that a party who wishes to refute the presumption of death can present evidence that the missing person is alive. If evidence is presented to show that the missing person is alive, the jury will decide the question of survival. If such evidence is not offered, the presumption of death will stand and the court will declare the missing person dead. The beneficiary of the policy then has proof of the insured's death, and the insurer must pay the death benefit.

---

[24]Parker v. Des Moines Life Ass'n, 78 N.W. 826 (Iowa 1899); Metropolitan Life Ins. Co. v. Hedgepath, 185 S.W. 2d 906 (Tenn. 1945).

[25]Robert E. Keaton & Alan I. Widiss, Insurance Law: A Guide to Fundamental Principles, Legal Doctrines, and Commercial Practices, § 5.3(3) (1988).

The Uniform Absence as Evidence of Death and Absentee's Property Act abolishes the presumption of death. This model act provides that the jury will decide issues of whether and when death occurred in each case. Two states have laws patterned on this model act.

Explainable Disappearance

Some disappearances are explainable. There are two types of explanation for the disappearance of an insured. First, there might be reason to believe that the insured purposely disappeared. Second, the missing insured might have been exposed to a specific peril, such as an airplane crash.

Purposeful Disappearance.   An insured person may have had any of several reasons to purposely disappear. The insured might have been in financial or marital difficulty, or could be a fugitive from the law. Sometimes, the insured has told others that he planned to disappear. The insurer can use such circumstances in an attempt to rebut the presumption that the insured is dead.

Specific Peril.   If the missing insured was exposed to a specific peril, such as an airplane crash, a boating accident, or a fire, the beneficiary will often be able to prove the death by circumstantial evidence without waiting for the presumption of death to arise. For example, suppose a small boat containing the insured and several other persons capsized in a violent storm at sea and the bodies of all on board were recovered, except the body of the insured. The beneficiary would probably be able to establish the insured's death by circumstantial evidence without waiting several years for the presumption of death to arise.

Expiration of the Policy

Many life insurance policies on the lives of persons missing for extended periods expire for nonpayment of premiums before the presumption of death arises. The beneficiary then faces the problem of proving that the insured actually met death prior to the date the policy expired. If the beneficiary fails to prove that the insured died before the policy expired, no benefits are payable.

If an insured has disappeared, the beneficiary should keep the policy in force until a court establishes the insured's death. If the beneficiary can then prove that the insured died on a date prior to the end of the period during which premiums were paid, the beneficiary can recover from the insurer the amount of the overpayment of premiums, as well as the death benefit.

Reappearance

Sometimes, an insured reappears after having been declared dead by a court and after the death benefit has been paid to the beneficiary. Generally, the insurer then has the right to recover the money because it was paid under a mistake of fact.

However, if the insurer paid less than the full amount of the benefit in a compromise settlement of a doubtful claim (also called an accord and satisfaction), it usually cannot recover the benefit, unless it and the beneficiary have agreed that it can do so if the insured reappears. Compromise settlements are discussed in a following section.

War and Aviation Hazard Exclusion Clauses

War and aviation hazard exclusion clauses are discussed in detail in Chapter 8, "Added Benefits and Limitations." War hazard exclusion clauses are either status clauses or result clauses. If a policy contains a status clause, the insurer usually must determine whether the insured died while in the military service in time of war. If the policy contains a result clause, the insurer ordinarily must determine if the insured died as a result of military activities.

The aviation hazard exclusion usually limits the benefit payable if death occurs as a result of certain specified aviation activities. The increasing safety of aviation has resulted in a liberalization of aviation restrictions. Today, the restrictions ordinarily do not apply if the insured is a fare-paying passenger on a scheduled air carrier.

Computation of the Amount Payable to the Beneficiary

The amount payable to the beneficiary of a life insurance policy is ordinarily computed by adding:

1. The face amount of the policy, or the reduced amount if the policy is effective under the reduced paid-up nonforfeiture option, as adjusted for any misstatement of age. The face amount of a universal life policy or a variable life policy usually changes over time. Thus, the face amount at the date of the insured's death governs.
2. Any paid-up additions.
3. Any accidental death benefit payable.
4. Any premiums paid in advance if the premium receipt states that they are payable to the beneficiary.
5. Refund of any part of a premium paid for a period of time beyond the month in which the insured's death occurred, if the law so requires or the policy so provides.
6. Any interest required by state law, or payable under the insurer's own rules.

From this total the insurer will subtract:

1. Any unpaid policy loans and loan interest.
2. Any premium payable but unpaid at the date of the insured's death.
3. Any amount already paid out under an accelerated benefits provision.

The remainder is the amount payable.

If death was the result of suicide during the suicide exclusion period, the liability of the insurer under most policies is limited to the amount of premiums paid, without interest. If death was the result of war or aviation activities, and death from these causes was a risk not assumed under the contract, the liability is ordinarily the amount of premiums paid or the amount of the reserve, whichever is larger.

Releases

A release is the giving up of a right or claim, usually in exchange for consideration. Thus, if a creditor has a right to receive a sum of money from a debtor, the creditor ordinarily will release that right in exchange for the money due. The creditor must deliver the written release to the debtor for the release to be effective.

Usually, the recipient of the release must give consideration to the giver of the release, or the release will not be valid. The payment of one debt is not consideration for the release of another debt. This rule becomes important to life insurers when the insurer denies a claim for an accidental death benefit. If the beneficiary gives the insurer a release of the beneficiary's claim to the accidental death benefit, the insurer's payment to the beneficiary of the death benefit (one debt) is not consideration for the beneficiary's release of the accidental death benefit (another debt). The attempted release of the beneficiary's claim to the accidental death benefit would be invalid for lack of consideration. However, the insurer's payment of a sum in addition to the death benefit, not necessarily amounting to the entire accidental death benefit, would be consideration for the release, as discussed below in "Compromise Settlements."

Compromise Settlements

A *compromise settlement* or *accord and satisfaction* is an agreement between two or more persons to settle a matter in dispute between them and the performance of the promises made in that agreement. *Compromise settlement* is the term most frequently used in insurance contract performance contexts. However, *accord and satisfaction* is a more accurate term because accord and satisfaction applies only to contract disputes, whereas *compromise settlement* applies to other disputes as well as to contract disputes.

If the existence or amount of a debt is in dispute, the debt can be discharged by a compromise settlement. For example, suppose a beneficiary claimed that the insured had died in an accident, whereas the insurer claimed that disease was the cause of death. The parties would be disputing the existence of the debt for the accidental death benefit. Suppose also that under the policy, the amount of the accidental death benefit was $100,000. If the beneficiary agreed with the insurer to accept $50,000 in discharge of the disputed debt, and the insurer paid the beneficiary $50,000, they would have entered into a compromise settlement.

Unfair Claims Settlement Practices Laws

The NAIC added a section dealing with unfair claims settlement practices to the Unfair Trade Practices Model Act in 1971 and, in 1990, deleted it from that model act and made it part of a new model act, the Unfair Claims Settlement Practices Act. All but a very few states have laws patterned on the Unfair Claims Settlement Practices Act.

The Unfair Claims Settlement Practices Act mandates that insurers promptly investigate claims and promptly settle any claim on which liability has become reasonably clear. Among other prohibitions, the model act forbids misrepresentations as to coverage and delays in communications regarding claims.

The NAIC has also adopted the Unfair Life, Accident and Health Claims Settlement Practices Model Regulation to implement the model act. About one-half of the states have regulations patterned on the model regulation or have related laws.

Regulations patterned on the model regulation require that an insurer provide claim forms within 15 days after receiving notice of a claim. Upon receipt of proof of loss, the insurer must begin any necessary investigation of the claim within 15 days. The insurer must affirm or deny liability on claims within a reasonable time and tender payment for amounts not in dispute within 30 days of affirmation. With each claim payment the insurer must provide an explanation of benefits. This must include a reasonable explanation of the computation of benefits and, for a health insurance claim, the name of the provider (that is, the doctor, hospital, or other provider of health care services) or services covered and the dates of service. The insurer must respond within 15 days to a written communication relating to a pending claim. If the insurer determines that it must deny a claim, it must send written notice of denial to the claimant within 15 days of the determination. These and many other details of claims settlement practices are set forth in the model regulation.

The Unfair Claims Settlement Practices Act provides that the insurance commissioner can punish an insurer for unfair claims settlement practices. Punishment can be in the form of a fine or suspension or revocation of the offending insurer's license, or a combination of these.

The Reasonable Expectations Doctrine

A doctrine permitting the courts to honor the reasonable expectations of policyowners and beneficiaries has been emerging since the 1960s. The ***reasonable expectations doctrine*** can be stated as follows: The courts will honor the reasonable expectations of policyowners and beneficiaries, even if the strict terms of the policy do not support those expectations.

The implementation of the reasonable expectations doctrine has resulted in what one author termed "judge-made insurance."[26] The claimant's expectation of coverage, the insurer's part in creating that expectation, and the unfairness of a policy provision are factors that can influence the court to grant coverage where the policy does not provide it.

For example, in one case[27] an airplane passenger purchased a round-trip ticket from Los Angeles to Dayton, Ohio. Before leaving Los Angeles, he also purchased from a vending machine an accidental death policy covering the round-trip and mailed the policy to his wife, the named beneficiary. The policy stated that it covered "travel on . . . scheduled air carriers."

As part of his return trip, the insured planned a flight from Terre Haute, Indiana, to Chicago, Illinois. The flight from Terre Haute to Chicago was canceled, and the insured was forced to take an unscheduled air carrier rather than the scheduled carrier he had planned to take. He was killed when the unscheduled carrier crashed.

The court held that the $62,500 in benefits was payable to the beneficiary because "[i]n this type of standardized contract, sold by a vending machine, the insured may *reasonably expect* coverage for the whole trip which he inserted in the policy,

---

[26]Kenneth S. Abraham, *Judge-Made Law and Judge-Made Insurance: Honoring the Reasonable Expectations of the Insured,* 67 Va. L. Rev. 1151 (1981) [hereinafter Abraham].

[27]Steven v. Fidelity and Cas. Co., 377 P.2d 284 (Cal. 1962).

including reasonable substituted transportation necessitated by emergency." [Emphasis added.]

Note that the terms of the contract were not ambiguous. As was stated in Chapter 2, "Contracts," under traditional contract rules the courts do not impose their interpretation if the terms of the contract are clear and unambiguous. Thus, the reasonable expectations doctrine is a departure from traditional contract rules.

A number of legal scholars have criticized this departure. They argue that it results in two conflicting bodies of contract law, one with a rationale that courts should not interpret clear and unambiguous contract language and the other with a rationale that the courts should honor the reasonable expectations of the policyowner despite clear and unambiguous policy language to the contrary. Second, they argue that the court considers only the reasonable expectations of the policyowner and not the reasonable expectations of the insurer. This creates uncertainty for the insurer that must result in higher premium charges. Finally, they argue, some informed policyowners will have coverage provided them that they did not expect merely because an average policyowner would have expected it.[28]

Examples of reasonable expectations cases include those involving temporary insurance under a conditional premium receipt in which the courts have held that the applicant could reasonably expect immediate coverage on payment of the initial premium,[29] cases in which the policy contained coverage restrictions that made the policy of little value to the policyowner,[30] and cases in which there were inconspicuous exclusions.[31]

Claims Litigation

A denial of a life or health insurance claim can result in a lawsuit between a policyowner or beneficiary and the insurer. If an insurer's claim examiners thoroughly investigate each claim, act with reasonable dispatch, give equal consideration to the claimant's rights and the rights of the insurer, reach a proper claims decision, and communicate that decision with a clear explanation to the claimant, the insurer can avoid much claims litigation.

Claims litigation results in a number of additional expenses for an insurer. First, there is the expense resulting from the time the insurer's employees (including attorneys the insurer employs as in-house counsel) and agents spend assisting in the defense of the suit. Although insurers usually hire outside attorneys who work in law firms to present the defense of the suit in court, the insurers often must call on their employees and agents to help the outside attorneys.

Second, the costs of litigation itself can be substantial. These costs include not only the outside attorney's fees but also costs for investigation, transcripts, expert witness fees, travel, and a number of other expenses necessary for the proper defense of the lawsuit. A trial will ordinarily cost at least several thousand dollars. Lengthy, complex trials can cost much more.

---

[28]Abraham, *supra* note 26; Scott B. Krider, Note, *The Reconstruction of Insurance Contracts Under the Doctrine of Reasonable Expectations,* 18 J. MARSHALL L. REV. 155 (1984).

[29]Damm v. National Ins. Co. of Am., 200 N.W. 2d 616 (N.D. 1972).

[30]Kievit v. Loyal Protective Life Ins. Co., 170 A. 2d 22 (N.J. 1961).

[31]Karol v. New Hampshire Ins. Co., 414 A. 2d 939 (N.H. 1980).

Third, if the insurer loses the lawsuit, it might have to pay extra-contract damages to the plaintiff, as well as contract damages. The various types of damages are discussed below.

Compensatory Damages

The court awards ***compensatory damages*** to the plaintiff to compensate for a wrong done to him. Compensatory damages fall into several categories. First, if an insurer loses a lawsuit, it will have to pay contract damages. ***Contract damages*** are the amount the court holds that the insurer owes under the terms of the insurance contract. In other words, contract damages are the amount of the policy proceeds.

Second, an insurer that loses a lawsuit might have to pay extra-contract compensatory damages. ***Extra-contract damages*** are awards of money in addition to the amount payable under the contract.[32] For example, an insurer might have to pay the plaintiff's attorney's fees as extra-contract compensatory damages. These, like the insurer's own attorney's fees, can be substantial. Also, the plaintiff's court costs might be assessed as extra-contract compensatory damages against an insurer that loses a lawsuit.

A prevailing plaintiff might also recover other extra-contract compensatory damages from the insurer. For example, the court might award damages for the plaintiff's emotional distress and anxiety caused by the insurer's wrongful denial of a claim.

Punitive Damages

Punitive damages punish a defendant found to have acted in a malicious, fraudulent, or oppressive manner toward the plaintiff. Punitive damages, also called *exemplary damages*, are intended to make an example of the defendant and thus dissuade others from similar behavior.

Historically, courts have awarded punitive damages in tort lawsuits but not in contract lawsuits. A tort is a wrongful act causing harm. Where the wrongful act was intentional and outrageous, most courts have allowed the jury to award punitive damages. For example, assault is a tort for which punitive damages have been awarded.[33]

Punitive damages have not been recoverable in contract lawsuits unless the conduct constituting the breach of contract was also a tort.[34] The primary purpose of contract remedies has been to compensate the plaintiff rather than to punish or make an example of the defendant.

In 1957, the California appellate courts began developing the tort of breach of the covenant of good faith and fair dealing, which covenant they said was implied in insurance contracts.[35] Breach of the implied covenant of good faith and fair dealing is both a breach of contract and a tort. If such a breach occurs, punitive damages can be awarded in California if the insurer's conduct is found to be malicious, fraudulent, or oppressive.

---

[32]Extra-contract damages include punitive damages as well as extra-contract compensatory damages.

[33]Maxa v. Neidlein, 163 A. 202 (Md. 1932).

[34]Boise Dodge, Inc. v. Clark, 453 P.2d 551 (Idaho 1969).

[35]Gruenberg v. Aetna Ins. Co., 510 P.2d 1032 (Cal. 1973); Silberg v. California Life Ins. Co., 521 P.2d 1103 (Cal. 1974).

A breach of the implied covenant of good faith and fair dealing is sometimes called *bad faith*. To characterize a breach of the implied covenant of good faith and fair dealing as bad faith is misleading. Bad faith in this context does not mean "positive misconduct of a malicious or immoral nature."[36] Rather, it means that the insurer denied a claim without a reasonable basis. If an insurer is found guilty of bad faith in California, the court can award extra-contract compensatory damages to the plaintiff.

In California, if an insurer has denied a claim without a reasonable basis, and the court determines that the insurer also acted with malice, oppression, or fraud, punitive damages can be assessed against the insurer. *Malice* means conduct intended to cause injury or despicable conduct carried on with a willful and conscious disregard of the rights of others. *Oppression* means despicable conduct that subjects a person to cruel and unjust hardship in conscious disregard of that person's rights. *Fraud* means intentional misrepresentation, deceit, or concealment of a material fact known to a person with the intention of thereby causing injury to another.[37]

For example, in the landmark California case of *Fletcher v. Western National Life Insurance Co.*,[38] the plaintiff was an impoverished laborer with eight children and a fourth-grade education who had purchased a disability income policy from the defendant in 1963. He sustained back and leg injuries in 1965 while lifting a 361-pound bale of rubber. Numerous doctors examined him and agreed that this accident had disabled him. The insurer paid the plaintiff the $150 per month benefit for over a year but then seized upon a statement in one of the medical reports to demand that the plaintiff return this money. This statement was that the "plaintiff's disability was contributed to by a preexistent congenital defect in the lumbosacral spine and a preexisting osteoarthritis condition." The insurer did not investigate to determine if the plaintiff knew of a preexisting defect but accused him of misrepresentation in his policy application.

The plaintiff filed suit, after which the insurer made disability income payments only at long intervals and only after repeated demands by the plaintiff's attorney. The lack of regular payments caused great hardship for the plaintiff and his family.

The plaintiff asked the court for a declaration that he was entitled to the policy benefits so long as he was disabled, for compensatory and punitive damages for intentional infliction of emotional distress, and for compensatory and punitive damages for fraud in inducing him to buy the policy.

The court held that the insurer had acted in an outrageous manner and that its actions caused the plaintiff to be frightened, worried, and upset. The plaintiff therefore was entitled to damages for emotional distress.

The court also held that the plaintiff could recover in tort for breach of the implied covenant of good faith and fair dealing. The court said:

> An insurer owes to its insured an implied-in-law duty of good faith and fair dealing that it will do nothing to deprive the insured of the benefits of the policy. . . . The violation of that duty sounds in tort notwithstanding that it may also constitute a breach of contract. . . . [P]unitive damages may be recovered upon a proper showing of malice, fraud or oppression even though the conduct constituting the tort also involves a breach of contract.

---

[36]Neal v. Farmers Ins. Exchange, 582 P.2d 980 (Cal. 1978).
[37]Cal. Civ. Code Ann. § 3294 (West Supp. 1996).
[38]89 Cal. Rptr. 78 (Cal. Ct. App. 1970).

The court therefore affirmed the trial court's awards of $60,000 in compensatory damages and $180,000 in punitive damages against the insurer, as well as $10,000 in punitive damages against the insurer's claims manager.

Although California is the forerunner in this area, it is by no means the only state in which punitive damages are a concern to insurers. To date, over one-half of the states have adopted the concept of the implied covenant of good faith and fair dealing, or some other theory of liability, and have allowed punitive damages against life and health insurers.[39] Some punitive damages awards against life and health insurers have been in the millions of dollars.[40]

A few states have expressly rejected or limited the California approach.[41] Courts of other states have not yet taken a position. Insurers must be wary even of those states that have not taken a position, or have rejected or limited punitive damages, because such a state could unexpectedly adopt a different position. For example, for many years the Alabama courts had held that, in the absence of fraud, an insurer would be liable only for breach of contract if it improperly denied a claim. Then, in 1981, the Alabama Supreme Court authorized recovery for a separate tort of bad faith arising out of a claim denial.[42] Alabama has since gained a reputation for large punitive damages awards. Two important U.S. Supreme Court cases challenging the constitutionality of punitive damages began in the Alabama courts.

The Constitutionality of Punitive Damages.   In recent years, the U.S. Supreme Court has heard several cases challenging the constitutionality of punitive damages. The most successful basis of such challenges is the Due Process Clause of the Fourteenth Amendment of the U.S. Constitution. The Due Process Clause forbids any state to "deprive any person of life, liberty or property without due process of law." This prohibition means, in part, that a state must use fair procedures when it deprives a person (including a corporation) of property, as when a court deprives an insurer of its property (money) by requiring payment of punitive damages to a plaintiff. The most important recent cases dealing with the constitutionality of punitive damages are *Pacific Mutual Life Insurance Co. v. Haslip*[43] and *BMW of North America, Inc. v. Gore*.[44]

In *Pacific Mutual Life Insurance Co. v. Haslip*, the Court held that the punitive damages award by an Alabama court against the Pacific Mutual Life Insurance Co. was not so inherently unfair as to violate the Due Process Clause of the Fourteenth Amendment. Alabama had used the traditional common-law approach, under which (1) the jury initially determines whether punitive damages will be awarded and, if so, the amount of the award; (2) the trial judge instructs the jury to consider the gravity of the wrong committed by the defendant and the need to deter similar conduct; and (3) the trial judge and the appellate courts review the jury's determination to ensure that it is reasonable. The U.S. Supreme Court did note its "concern about punitive

---

[39]A. S. Klein, Annotation, *Insurer's Liability for Consequential or Punitive Damages for Wrongful Delay or Refusal to Make Payments Due under Contracts,* 47 A.L.R. 3d 314 (1973).

[40]Sparks v. Republic Nat'l Life Ins. Co., 647 P.2d 1127 (Ariz. 1982), *cert. denied,* 459 U.S. 1070 (1982). In the *Sparks* case, the Arizona Supreme Court awarded the plaintiffs $1,551,000 in compensatory damages, $80,000 in attorney's fees, and $3,000,000 in punitive damages.

[41]*E.g.*, Kewin v. Massachusetts Mut. Life Ins. Co., 295 N.W.2d 50 (Mich. 1980); Spencer v. Aetna Life & Cas. Ins. Co., 611 P.2d 149 (Kan. 1980).

[42]Gulf Atlantic Life Ins. Co. v. Barnes, 405 So. 2d 916 (Ala. 1981).

[43]499 U.S. 1 (1991)

[44]116 S. Ct. 1589 (1996).

damages that 'run wild.' " The Court also said that "unlimited jury discretion—or unlimited judicial discretion for that matter—in the fixing of punitive damages may invite extreme results that jar one's Constitutional sensibilities." But, the Court continued:

> As long as the discretion is exercised with reasonable constraints, due process is satisfied. . . . The Alabama Supreme Court's post-verdict review ensures that punitive damages awards are not grossly out of proportion to the severity of the offense and have some understandable relationship to compensatory damages. . . . We are aware that the punitive damages award in this case is more than 4 times the amount of compensatory damages, is more than 200 times the out-of-pocket expenses of respondent Haslip. . . . While the monetary comparisons are wide and, indeed, may be close to the line, the award here did not lack objective criteria.

In a vigorous dissent to *Haslip*, Supreme Court Justice O'Connor argued that Alabama's procedural scheme for imposing punitive damages was unconstitutionally vague because it gave the jury no usable standards and too much discretion. Thus, she argued, the punitive damages award against Pacific Mutual was fundamentally unfair.

The *Haslip* decision disappointed many people in the insurance industry as well as in other businesses subject to punitive damages awards. However, in 1996, the U.S. Supreme Court decided *BMW of North America v. Gore*, in which the Alabama courts had assessed compensatory damages of $4,000 and punitive damages of $2 million against an automobile manufacturer for failing to disclose that an automobile it sold had been repainted. The U.S. Supreme Court reversed the judgment, holding that the $2 million punitive damages award was "grossly excessive." The Court stated:

> Elementary notions of fairness enshrined in our constitutional jurisprudence dictate that a person receive fair notice not only of the conduct that will subject him to punishment but also of the severity of the penalty that a State may impose.

Nevertheless, the Court also stated that it was "not prepared to draw a bright line marking the limits of a constitutionally acceptable punitive damages award." Therefore, the insurance industry, as well as other industries, is urging Congress to enact laws setting clear standards for punitive damages awards.

State Statutes Limiting Punitive Damages.   In recent years there have been a number of state laws enacted limiting punitive damages awards. Generally speaking, these limits fall into three categories: caps on punitive damages award amounts; provisions for payment of part or all of punitive damages awards to state agencies rather than to plaintiffs; and mandatory separation of proceedings to determine liability from proceedings to determine punitive damages.

For example, Florida caps punitive damages at three times the amount of compensatory damages,[45] whereas North Dakota caps punitive damages at the greater of two times the amount of compensatory damages, or $250,000.[46] Georgia allocates 75 percent of punitive damages awards, less a proportionate part of litigation costs, to the state treasury.[47] Illinois permits the court to apportion punitive damages awards

---

[45]Fla. Stat. §§ 768.73 (1)(a) and (b) (West Supp. 1996).

[46]N.D. Cent. Code § 32–03.2–11(4) (1996).

[47]Ga. Code Ann. § 51–12–5.1 (e)(2) (Michie Supp. 1996).

among the plaintiff, the plaintiff's attorney, and the Illinois Department of Rehabilitation Services.[48] In California, a trial in which punitive damages are requested must be bifurcated—that is, separated—into liability and damages phases, at the application of the defendant.[49] In Kansas, the trier of fact determines the defendant's liability for punitive damages, but the judge determines the amount of such damages.[50]

ERISA Preemption.   In 1987, the U.S. Supreme Court decided, in *Pilot Life Insurance Co. v. Dedeaux,*[51] that the federal Employee Retirement Income Security Act[52] preempted state common-law tort actions against employers' group health insurers. That is, the insured must pursue his remedies under ERISA, which does not provide for punitive damages, jury trials, or damages for emotional distress. The impact of this ruling is enormous, because large numbers of people are covered under employer group life and health insurance policies governed by ERISA.

---

[48]735 ILL. COMP. STAT. § 5/2–1207 (Michie 1993).

[49]CAL. CIVIL CODE ANN. § 3295 (d) (West Supp. 1996).

[50]KAN. STAT. ANN. § 60–3701 (a)–(b) (1994).

[51] 481 U.S. 41 (1987).

[52]Pub. L. No. 93–406, 88 Stat. 829 (codified as amended in scattered sections of 5, 18, 26, 29, 31 and 42 U.S.C.).

Summary

A life insurance contract is performed when all the promises it contains are carried out. Ordinarily, contract performance is a routine matter that involves obtaining from the beneficiary a completed claim form and proof of the insured's death, computing the amount due, and paying out that amount. However, occasionally problems arise in adjusting the claim.

The insurer sometimes must investigate to determine the proper payee. If no beneficiary has been named, the policy usually will provide that the proceeds are payable to the policyowner or, if the policyowner is the insured, the policyowner's estate. If the policyowner's estate is the beneficiary, the benefits will be paid to the executor or administrator of the estate, and the insurer will require evidence of the executor's or administrator's appointment by the court. Likewise, if a trustee is named beneficiary, the insurer will require evidence of the trustee's appointment in the deed of trust. If the policy was collaterally assigned, the insurer will require an affidavit from the assignee stating the amount of proceeds due the assignee.

Incompetent beneficiaries cannot give the insurer a binding release for payment of the proceeds. In the case of minor incompetents, a court-appointed guardian of the minor's estate can receive the proceeds and give a binding release, or the insurer can hold the proceeds at interest until the minor reaches majority. In some states, statutes allow small amounts to be paid directly to a minor. The guardian of the estate of a mentally incompetent person can receive proceeds on behalf of the incompetent and give a binding release.

A beneficiary who wrongfully kills the insured will usually be disqualified from receiving the death benefit. Each state has its own law governing such disqualification. Acquittal of the beneficiary in a criminal trial does not necessarily mean that the beneficiary will qualify to receive the death benefit, because the standard for proving guilt in a criminal trial differs from the standard for proving liability in a civil trial. If the policyowner procured the policy in good faith and without intent to murder the insured, the death benefit will be payable to someone, usually the contingent beneficiary or the insured's estate. If the policyowner procured the policy with intent to murder the insured, no proceeds are payable to anyone, according to the majority view.

If the insured and beneficiary die simultaneously in a common disaster, under the state simultaneous death act it will be presumed that the beneficiary died first. If the beneficiary survives the insured for a short time (several hours, for example), the act will not apply. However, if the policy or the beneficiary designation contains a survivorship clause, the beneficiary must survive the insured for the period of time specified in the clause to receive the benefits.

If conflicting claimants to the death benefit cannot resolve their differences, the insurer will ordinarily file a bill of interpleader and deposit the benefit with the court.

An unclaimed death benefit will be turned over to the state after a certain period of time, usually five years, has elapsed.

No death benefit will be payable if the policy contains a suicide exclusion clause and the insured commits suicide during the exclusion period (usually within one or two years after the policy date of issue). The burden of proving suicide falls on the insurer. If the suicide exclusion clause includes the words *while sane or insane*, the policy ordinarily will not cover self-destruction by an insane insured during the suicide exclusion period. If the insured died by suicide, the accidental death benefit usually will not be payable, because a suicide is not an accidental death.

If an insured mysteriously disappears, in most states a presumption of death will arise after seven years if the insured was continuously absent from his home without explanation, if the persons most likely to hear from the insured have heard nothing, and if the insured cannot be located by diligent search and inquiry. If the missing insured was exposed to a specific peril, the beneficiary will often be able to prove the death by circumstantial evidence without waiting for the presumption of death to arise.

Claim examiners must take the requirements of the Unfair Claims Settlement Practices Act into account when evaluating claims. An increasing number of courts also honor the reasonable expectations of the policyowner or beneficiary.

If the insurer denies a claim, the claimant sometimes sues the insurer. Claims litigation can be expensive for insurers, because the courts sometimes assess legal fees, court costs, damages to compensate the plaintiff for emotional distress, and punitive damages against insurers, in addition to contract damages. Proper claims handling is therefore important, because it helps to protect insurers from liability and assures that claimants receive fair treatment.

ILLUSTRATIVE CASE

In this case, the insured husband of the beneficiary had disappeared without explanation. The court held that the beneficiary's efforts to locate him were sufficiently diligent to establish the fact of his probable death.

MARY BORZAGE

v.

METROPOLITAN LIFE INSURANCE COMPANY[53]
Circuit Court of Connecticut,
Appellate Division

KOSICKI, Judge.

The plaintiff is the beneficiary on three insurance policies on the life of her husband, Max Borzage. In her substituted complaint, on which the case was tried before a jury, the only allegations seriously disputed concerned the unexplained disappearance and absence of Max Borzage as giving rise to a presumption that he had died on December 24, 1959, seven years after his unexplained disappearance.

After the plaintiff rested, the defendant moved for a directed verdict, which motion the court denied. The defendant offered no evidence through its own witnesses, and the case was submitted to the jury, which returned a verdict for the plaintiff to recover $6700. . . . The defendant has based its appeal on the insufficiency, as a matter

of law, of the plaintiff's offering of the evidentiary prerequisite that the insured's absence be unexplained. . . .

From an examination of the transcript of evidence, it appears that the jury were entitled to find the following facts. Max Borzage was married to the plaintiff in 1927, and the family lived in Hazelton, Pennsylvania, from 1929 until after the time of his disappearance. He was a bricklayer and stonemason by trade. In late 1941 or 1942, at the beginning of World War II, Borzage left Hazelton to work at the Pentagon and was employed there; later he engaged in his own business in Washington, D.C. During a period of ten years, until Christmas in 1952, his visits to his home, wife and children were of decreasing frequency. After Christmas in 1952, he left home and was never heard from again by his wife, his father, his brother, or two of his adult sons. The wife continued to make payments of premiums on all three insurance policies on the life of Max Borzage, and it is conceded that the policies are not in default.

---

[53]270 A.2d 688 (1970).

No proof of death could be furnished, and the plaintiff relies solely on the common-law rule giving rise to a presumption of death from an unexplained absence of seven years. To establish a presumption of death under the common law, arising out of a disappearance and unexplained absence of seven years, the plaintiff must allege and prove an unexplained absence, a diligent search for the insured, and circumstances justifying the conclusion that death is the probable reason for the absence.

The presumption of death arising from an unexplained absence of seven years is not a presumption of law but a rule of reasoning. "It is an inference from the fact of the absence of seven years or more taken in connection with all the circumstances showing that, although diligent investigation has been made by the person seeking to prove the fact of death, the fact of the absence remains 'unexplained.' The inference must reasonably follow from the fact of absence and the circumstances of diligent investigation that death is the probable reason for the absence. The burden of proving that the absence is 'unexplained' for this period is upon the person seeking to prove the fact of death, and unless diligent efforts have been made to find the absent one his absence cannot be held to be 'unexplained.' " Potter v. Prudential Ins. Co., 108 Conn. 271, 276, 277, 142 A. 891, 894.

There was evidence which, if believed by the jury, would be sufficient to establish the following facts. After the unexplained disappearance of Max Borzage in 1952, the plaintiff engaged an attorney and paid her to go to Washington to find her husband. The attorney's inquiries and search proved unavailing. The plaintiff also kept in contact with the family of Max Borzage, who attempted to find him in 1956 and thereafter.

From this evidence the jury could infer that, considering the plaintiff's financial circumstances and the burdens of raising her family and supporting herself and her family, her efforts were diligent and there was little else she could do to establish the fact of probable death. Moreover, it appears from the trial transcript that the defendant conceded that a diligent search had been made by the plaintiff.

It appears from the record that, at the request of the defendant, the plaintiff, on January 9, 1967, filled out and signed a "disappearance questionnaire." Apparently, no independent investigation was attempted by the defendant, and the plaintiff testified that she had never heard from the defendant. At the time of trial in May, 1969, Max Borzage had not been heard from or located, and nothing had been discoverable concerning his continued existence, for sixteen and one-half years. At that time, if living, he would have been sixty-seven years of age. The physical mortality of man is an uncontestable fact. If the defendant did not pursue search or inquiry, the jury might reasonably have concluded that it had good reason not to do so; and, if so, it was equally proper for the wife not to extend her search for her missing husband.

The defendant, apparently in reliance upon its policies, stressed the necessity of proof of death by production of a death certificate. In its defense, it emphasized certain hypotheses, such as Borzage's lack of moral stability, nonsupport of his family, and previous convictions, as casting doubt on the inference to be drawn from his disappearance and long-continued unexplained absence. The answer, if any is needed, to the defendant's claim of insufficient proof of diligent inquiry by the plaintiff to justify the jury's verdict may be found in Kaminskas v. John Hancock Mutual Life Ins. Co., 129 Conn. 394, 395, 28 A.2d 847, 848, where the court said: "The plaintiff's failure to pursue inquiries more diligently during this period was a circumstance for the consideration of the trial court; but we cannot say that, as matter of law, it was sufficient to invalidate the inference that his continued absence was probably due to death, which must be drawn from a consideration of all the relevant circumstances, including a diligent search. . . ."

The presumption of death is that the absent person's life ceased or that his death occurred at the expiration of the seven-year period. "Fortifying logical deductions of fatality is that diligence of search failed to uncover any clue to his whereabouts. The time element is also important as affording an inference of death shortly before discovery of his disappearance. The inference or presumption of continued existence of any particular fact, including that of life, steadily diminishes in force with a lapse of time. The probabilities of non-existence drawn from the circumstances increases as the factual presumption decreases." Pacific Mutual Life Ins. Co. v. Meade, 281 Ky. 36, 43, 134 S.W.2d 960, 964.

We have consulted the court's memorandum of decision, which is a part of the record, denying the defendant's motion to set aside the verdict. This we are empowered to do in order to determine the basis of the judgment. The court agrees with the defendant's claim that Max Borzage's disappearance, in its initial phase, may have been explainable; but his long-continued absence did not adequately present a situation where the issues of fact, as a matter of law, had to be withdrawn from the jury. The court's instructions to the jury were not attacked as being erroneous, and the verdict cannot be disturbed.

There is no error.

In this opinion DEARINGTON and KINMONTH, JJ., concurred.

Questions for Review

1. Describe the problem insurers face on the death of the insured if a minor is named as beneficiary. Describe the way in which some states have alleviated this problem.

2. If no beneficiary survives the insured, what usually happens to the policy benefits?

3. What problems do insurers face when the beneficiary kills the insured? How are these problems usually handled?

4. What is the problem that the state simultaneous death acts are designed to solve?

5. Explain how the suicide of the insured affects the performance of the life insurance contract
   a. If there is a suicide clause in the policy.
   b. If there is no suicide clause.
   c. If there is an accidental death benefit provision.

6. What conditions must be met for an insured who has disappeared to be presumed to be legally dead? After an insured has been presumed to be legally dead what are the insurer's rights
   a. If the insurer has paid the full death benefit and the insured reappears?
   b. If, as a compromise, the insurer has paid less than the full death benefit?

7. Indicate the different items that the insurer might have to take into account in calculating the total amount to be paid to a beneficiary.

8. Describe the doctrine of reasonable expectations.

9. What are contract damages? What are punitive damages? What are the purposes of punitive damages?

19   GROUP INSURANCE

Chapter Outline

A book about life and health insurance law would not be complete without a chapter about group insurance law. Group insurance covers a large percentage of the population in the United States. Group life insurance in force in the United States at the end of 1995 amounted to $4,777.9 billion, or 38 percent of the total life insurance in force. Group life insurance in force has grown spectacularly since its beginnings in 1911 and continues to grow, having almost doubled since 1985.[1] Group health insurance now provides the great majority of health benefits paid by health insurers in the United States.[2]

Many of the rules of law that apply to individual life or health insurance also apply to group insurance. Many other rules of law are unique to group insurance. The most important of the rules unique to group insurance will be discussed in this chapter. This chapter does not purport to be a comprehensive explanation of group insurance law. Such an explanation would require a space many times that allotted here.

History of Group Life Insurance Law

Modern group insurance began with the efforts of those in charge of Montgomery Ward and Company to replace the failing Montgomery Ward employees' mutual benefit association with an insured plan covering all Montgomery Ward employees. Such employees' mutual benefit associations provided a small death benefit and temporary disability benefits through dues and assessments of their members.

The officers of Montgomery Ward developed a plan and began negotiations with several insurers in 1910. In 1912, the Equitable Life Assurance Society of the United States (Equitable) issued a group life insurance policy that covered all Montgomery Ward employees.

The Montgomery Ward policy established a pattern for employer-employee group life insurance policies. For a premium paid by the employer, it insured the lives of the 2,912 employees of Montgomery Ward for the benefit of beneficiaries the employees selected. The policy insured the lives of all employees, regardless of insurability. The employer was not a beneficiary. Although there have been variations from this scheme, as with contributory policies for which the employee pays part of the premium, it is essentially the scheme followed today.

By 1915, several other major life insurers had begun to issue group life insurance policies. However, there was widespread criticism of such insurance. Many insurance executives felt it was unsound to issue life insurance without individual underwriting. Some felt that charging lower premiums for group life insurance was unfairly discriminatory.

Such criticisms were quieted somewhat in 1917 when the National Association of Insurance Commissioners developed a standard definition of group life insurance

---

[1] American Council of Life Insurance, Life Insurance Fact Book 5 & 17 (1996).

[2] Health Insurance Association of America, Source Book of Health Insurance Data 15 (1996).

and standard policy provisions for group life insurance policies. The NAIC incorporated these provisions into a model bill that it amended over the years. In 1956, the NAIC adopted a new model bill that has also undergone various amendments, the most recent being in 1988. The 1956 bill, as amended, is referred to in this book as the current model act or the model act.[3] Most of the states have enacted statutes based on some version of these group life insurance model bills.

Because revisions to the model bills have been made many times, the provisions of a state's group life insurance law depend on which version of the model bill the state followed, at least in those 38 states that have patterned their laws on the model bills. Some states have not based their group life insurance laws on the model bills, and several have no statutory definition of group life insurance, although all have some statutory requirements relating to group life insurance. Thus, group life insurance statutes vary considerably among the states.

The states with laws based on the NAIC model bills have statutes defining group life insurance and statutes mandating standard provisions that must be included in group life insurance policies. The next two sections deal with these definitions of group life insurance and with mandated standard group life insurance policy provisions.

Group Life Insurance Definitions

The 1917 model bill defined group life insurance as "that form of life insurance covering not less than 50 employees, with or without medical examination," under a policy issued to the employer. The policy could be *noncontributory*—that is, with premiums paid by the employer—or *contributory*—that is, with premiums paid jointly by the employer and the employees. Under noncontributory policies, all the eligible employees had to be insured or "all of any class or classes thereof determined by conditions pertaining to their employment." Under contributory policies, at least 75 percent of employees eligible had to be insured. The amount of life insurance available to each employee was to be based on a plan prohibiting individual selection. That is, the employee's position within the group could be used as a basis for the amount of life insurance, but two similarly situated employees could not be insured for different amounts. Finally, the employer could not be the beneficiary of an employee's life insurance.

This definition has been revised over the years. In 1946, for example, the definition was revised to reduce the number of required lives from 50 to 25. The 1954 model bill reduced the number to 10. The current model bill, now called a model act, states no minimum number of required lives for employer-employee groups.

The 1946 revision of the model bill recognized a number of types of groups in addition to employer-employee groups. It also recognized the right of an insurer to require evidence of individual insurability.

The current NAIC Group Life Insurance Model Act recognizes the following as eligible groups: (1) employees of an employer; (2) debtors of a creditor or creditors; (3) members of a labor union or similar employee organization; (4) employees of two or more employers, or members of one or more labor unions or similar employee

---

[3]In 1980, the word *bill* was changed to *act*. The meaning of the terms *model bill* and *model act* is, for practical purposes, the same. A bill introduced into a legislature becomes an act if passed.

organizations, or employees of one or more employers and members of one or more labor unions (trusteed groups); (5) members of an association or associations; (6) members of a credit union or credit unions; and (7) groups deemed to be valid at the discretion of the commissioner of insurance (discretionary groups).

Employer-Employee Groups

Employer-employee groups were the first type of group insured and the only type allowed under the 1917 model bill. The employer-employee group is still by far the most important type of group. In the United States, 88.7 percent of the total amount of group life insurance in force has been issued to employer-employee groups.[4]

Under the current model act, the insurer can issue the policy to either the employer or the trustees of a fund established by the employer. The model act permits the policy to define the term *employees* as including employees of subsidiary corporations. *Employees* can also be defined as the employees, individual proprietors, and partners of affiliated businesses if the employer and affiliated business are under common control. Retired and former employees can be included in the group, as can directors of a corporate employer.

Earlier model bills required that the policy insure a minimum number of employees when issued. The current model act contains no such requirement. The current model act also contains no requirement that the policyholder pay part of the premium, nor any requirement that at least 75 percent of eligible employees be covered under contributory policies. These requirements were found in earlier model bills and appear in the group life insurance laws of some states. However, the current model act has retained the requirement, contained in earlier model bills, that noncontributory policies cover 100 percent of eligible employees, except those employees who reject such coverage in writing. Finally, an insurer can exclude or limit coverage on any person as to whom evidence of insurability is not satisfactory.

Creditor Groups

Under the current model act, a policy insuring the lives of debtors can be issued to the creditor, its parent holding company, or a trustee or an agent designated by two or more creditors. The creditor, the debtors, or both can pay the premium. With the exception of insurance on open-end credit, the amount of insurance on the life of a debtor cannot exceed the amount of the debt. The insurer can exclude debtors on whom evidence of insurability is not satisfactory.

Death benefits under a creditor group life insurance policy are paid to the creditor. The benefit payment reduces or extinguishes the debtor's obligation to the creditor. Any excess is paid to a beneficiary the insured debtor has designated.

Certain requirements that appeared in earlier model bills have been eliminated in the current model act but still appear in the creditor group life insurance laws of some states. Notably, these requirements are that (1) a debt payable in a lump sum be payable within 18 months; (2) there be a ceiling on the amount of life insurance; (3) the group have at least 100 new entrants during the first policy year; and (4) a contributory group cover at least 75 percent of eligible debtors.

---

[4]American Council of Life Insurance, Life Insurance Fact Book 29 (1996).

Labor Union Groups

In labor union groups, the labor union or other employee organization is the policy-holder. Union members, or classes of union members, are insured for the benefit of persons other than the union, its officials, its representatives, or its agents. Under the current model act, the premium can be paid from union funds or from members' contributions, or both. Under noncontributory policies, all eligible members must be covered.

Earlier model bills required that the labor union group have at least 25 members when the policy is issued and that contributory plans cover at least 75 percent of eligible members. These requirements appear in the labor union group life insurance laws of some states.

Trusteed Groups

An insurer can issue a group life insurance policy to a trust established by two or more employers, by one or more labor unions, or by one or more employers and one or more labor unions. The employees or union members are insured for the benefit of persons other than an employer or union.

In noncontributory groups, the policy must cover all eligible members who do not reject such coverage in writing. Insureds can contribute funds to pay part or all of the premium under the current model act. This was not true under earlier model bills. In addition, requirements as to minimum group size found in earlier model bills are not found in the current model act.

Association Groups

The current model act has added, as an eligible group, the members of an association, or of one or more associations under a trust. The association must have been organized and maintained for at least two years for purposes other than that of obtaining insurance. It must have at least 100 members when the insurance goes into force.

Credit Union Groups

The current model act has also added, as an eligible group, the members of a credit union or of one or more credit unions under a trust. The credit union groups insure their members for the benefit of persons other than the credit union. In other words, this type of group insurance is not creditor insurance. Its purpose is to protect the credit union members and the beneficiaries they designate, not to protect the credit union.

Discretionary Groups

The current model act allows for groups that do not fall into any of the categories described above, as long as the group meets the requirements specified in the act. These requirements are that the group policy be in the best interests of the public, result in economies of acquisition or administration, and provide benefits reasonable in relation to the premiums charged.

The model act attempts to deal with the problems group insurers experience when they issue a group master policy in one state and a second state attempts to regulate the policy as to persons living in the second state (often called extraterritorial jurisdiction). Some states will not allow group insurers to cover their residents under a group master policy issued in another state unless the group is a type that the first state recognizes. The model act provides that if the commissioner of insurance of any state that has adopted the model act finds that the group qualifies as a discretionary group, coverage under the group policy can be offered in all other states that have adopted the model act. This reciprocal provision reads in part as follows:

> No [discretionary] group life insurance coverage may be offered in this state by an insurer under a policy issued in another state unless this state or another state having requirements substantially similar to [the discretionary group requirements of the model act] has made a determination that the requirements have been met.

Group Life Insurance Standard Provisions

The standard provisions sections of the current model act specify certain provisions that must be included, in substance, in a group life insurance policy. These provisions can be made more favorable to the insureds, or more favorable to the policyholder and equally favorable to the insureds. There are 12 standard provisions and a supplementary bill relating to conversion privileges. Unlike the group life insurance definitions sections, the group life insurance standard provisions sections of the current model act are substantially similar to those in earlier model bills. Differences will be pointed out in the following subsections.

Grace Period Provision

A group life insurance policy must contain a provision granting a grace period of at least 31 days for the payment of any premium due except the first. The grace period provision requirement is the same as that for individual life insurance policies, with the notable exception that under a group policy the insurer can maintain a suit against the policyholder to recover any premium not paid during the grace period.

The group life insurance policy will be in force during the grace period unless the policyholder gives the insurer written notice of discontinuance in advance of the date of discontinuance and in accordance with the terms of the policy. Thus, if a policyholder does not give written notice of discontinuance and does not pay the premium, the policy will still be in force during the whole grace period, after which time it will lapse. Or the policy might be in force for none or part of the grace period if the policyholder gives the discontinuance notice.

The model act states: "The policy may provide that the policyholder shall be liable to the insurer for the payment of a pro rata premium for the time the policy was in force during such a grace period." The reason such a clause is permitted is that the insurer must pay claims for deaths of insured persons occurring during the time the policy was in force during the grace period. If the policyholder does not pay the insurer the pro rata premium for the grace period, the insurer can sue and recover it. Such an unpaid premium can amount to many thousands of dollars in the case of a large group. Ordinarily, under an individual life insurance policy, the insurer cannot maintain a suit to recover a premium not paid during the grace period, although, if the insured dies during the grace period, the insurer can recover the unpaid premium out of the death benefit.

Incontestable Clause

A group master policy provides two kinds of contestable periods, one applying to the group master policy itself and the other applying to evidence of insurability submitted by insureds. First, the model act provides that the validity of the group master policy will be incontestable except for nonpayment of premiums after it has been in force for two years. However, contests of the validity of a group master policy are relatively rare. Such contests usually involve misrepresentation of the employer-employee relationship. The cases are in conflict as to whether the incontestable clause precludes a group insurer from defending a lawsuit for death benefits on the ground that the policyholder and the insured did not have an employer-employee relationship. For example, in *John Hancock Mutual Life Insurance Co. v. Dorman*[5] the court held that the incontestable clause in a group life policy prevented the insurer from defending a suit for the death benefit on the ground that a director of the policyholder-corporation was not covered because the director was not an employee. The insurer argued that the policy was invalid as to the director, but the court ruled that after the contestable period had expired, the insurer could not show that the director lacked the attribute of being an employee.

On the other hand, in *Fisher v. Prudential Insurance Co.*[6] the court held that the insurer could defend a claim for benefits on the ground that the insured had never been an employee of the policyholder, even though the contestable period had expired. The plaintiff argued that the insurer could no longer contest the validity of the policy, but the court said that the incontestable clause was never intended to enlarge the coverage of the policy or to force an insurer to insure lives it never intended to cover.

This last case represents the better view in the author's opinion. Moreover, the current model act provides that no incontestable provision "shall preclude the assertion at any time of defenses based upon provisions in the policy which relate to eligibility for coverage."

The second type of contestable period relates to evidence of insurability submitted by an insured. Ordinarily, insureds do not submit evidence of insurability in order to be covered by a group life insurance policy. However, if an employee under a contributory plan applies for coverage after the enrollment deadline, he usually will have to submit evidence of insurability. In addition, an employee usually will have to submit evidence of insurability if she is a member of a class eligible for amounts of life insurance in excess of the insurer's guaranteed issue limit, or if the group is small, as, for example, a group with two or three people.

The *evidence of insurability,* often called a *health certificate,* is an application form with questions pertaining to the proposed insured's health. As with individual insurance, the insurer will approve or reject this evidence of insurability at its home office. Also, as with individual insurance, there is a specified contestable period after which the validity of the insured's coverage will be incontestable as to misstatements in the evidence of insurability.

The model act requires group life policies to contain a clause such as the following:

> [N]o statement made by any person insured under the policy relating to his insurability shall be used in contesting the validity of the insurance with respect to which the state-

---

[5]108 F.2d 220 (9th Cir. 1939).
[6]218 A.2d 62 (N.H. 1966).

ment was made after the insurance has been in force prior to the contest for a period of two years during such person's lifetime, nor unless it is contained in a written instrument signed by him.

Application Provision

The application provision is closely related to the incontestable clause. The application provision required by the model act has three parts.

First, the group life insurance policy must provide that the insurer will attach a copy of the policyholder's application, if any, to the master policy when it is issued. This corresponds to some degree to the entire contract provision in individual life insurance policies.

Second, the group life insurance policy must provide that all statements made by the policyholder, or by the persons insured, shall be deemed representations and not warranties. The legal effect of making all statements representations and not warranties is the same in group insurance as in individual insurance. That is, misstatements must be material to the risk if the insurer is to contest the validity of the policy or the individual coverage based on the misstatements, unless a statute provides otherwise.

Third, the group life insurance policy must provide that no statement made by an insured shall be used in a contest of the policy unless a copy of the instrument containing the statement is furnished to the insured or, in the event of the insured's death or incapacity, to his beneficiary or personal representative.

Because group policies often insure large numbers of persons, it would be virtually impossible, in many cases, to require that the instrument containing the insured's statement (usually an evidence of insurability) be attached to and made part of the policy, as with individual life insurance. Thus, the model act requires only that a copy of the instrument be furnished to the insured or, in the event of the insured's death or incapacity, to his beneficiary or personal representative.

Evidence of Insurability Provision

The model act requires that group life insurance policies have "[a] provision setting forth the conditions, if any, under which the insurer reserves the right to require a person eligible for insurance to furnish evidence of individual insurability satisfactory to the insurer as a condition to part or all of his coverage."

When a person eligible to be insured under a contributory plan chooses not to be insured, then later changes her mind and applies for the insurance, there is a possibility that a change in her health induced her change of mind. Insurers therefore require evidence of insurability in such a situation and in some other situations. The situations in which the insurer will require evidence of insurability must be spelled out in the group policy, according to the model act.

Misstatement of Age Provision

The model act requires that group life insurance policies contain "[a] provision specifying an equitable adjustment of premiums or of benefits or of both to be made in the event the age of a person insured has been misstated, such provision to contain a clear statement of the method of adjustment to be made."

Settlement Provision

The model act requires that a group life insurance policy include a provision that the death benefit shall be payable to the person the insured has designated as beneficiary, "except that where the policy contains conditions pertaining to family status the beneficiary may be the family member specified by the policy terms."

The insured under a group life policy ordinarily has the right to name the beneficiary. Except for creditor plans, in many states the policyholder cannot be named beneficiary, but otherwise the insured is unrestricted in his choice of beneficiary. In other respects, the general rules applicable to individual life insurance beneficiary designations also apply to beneficiary designations under group life insurance. Usually, the beneficiary designation is revocable, and the insured can change the beneficiary whenever he wishes by complying with the policy procedures for beneficiary change.

In the event the insured does not designate a beneficiary, the group policy itself can provide for one, as can an individual life insurance policy. In some group policies, this will be the insured's estate. Or the group policy can provide for a succession beneficiary designation, making proceeds payable to the first living relative of the insured listed, as described in a list such as spouse, children, parents, and brothers and sisters. The objective of a succession beneficiary provision is to avoid the necessity of having a court appoint a personal representative of the insured. Such an appointment would be necessary if the death benefit were payable to the insured's estate.

Under the model act, the policy can also reserve to the insurer the right to pay up to $2,000 "to any person appearing to the insurer to be equitably entitled thereto by reason of having incurred funeral or other expenses incident to the last illness or death of the person insured." This is a facility-of-payment clause. If it is included in the policy, the insurer can, at its option, pay small amounts to anyone who has assumed the expenses of the insured's last illness or burial.

The model act does not require settlement options in group policies. Nevertheless, group life insurance policies usually provide one or two settlement options, although it is not customary to permit elaborate settlement arrangements. Usually, either the fixed period installment option or the fixed amount installment option is available—sometimes both. A life income option is sometimes provided or might be available by special agreement with the insurer, even when it is not expressly provided in the group master policy itself.

The settlement provision required by the model act is not applicable to creditor insurance, nor are the conversion provisions or the provision for continuation of coverage during disability, all of which are discussed below. These provisions are not appropriate to creditor insurance.

Certificate Provision

Under the model act, the group life insurance master policy must also provide that the insurer will issue certificates to the policyholder for delivery to each of the insured persons. The certificate must specify the insurance protection provided for the insured, the beneficiary the insured has chosen, and the rights of the insured to convert to individual insurance if his group insurance terminates. The model act also requires a provision regarding continuation of insurance in the event of the insured's total disability. This provision must be described in the certificate.

A creditor group life insurance certificate is required only to describe the insurance coverage and to specify that the death benefit shall first be applied to reduce or extinguish the indebtedness and the excess, if any, paid to the beneficiary that the insured has named. The creditor must deliver a certificate of insurance to each debtor.

Ordinarily, certificates are included in booklets describing the group insurance policy. If the group life insurance policy is part of an employee welfare benefit plan sponsored by an employer or union, the booklet will usually include the summary plan description required by the Employee Retirement Income Security Act. A summary plan description is a written summary of the provisions of the plan.

Conversion Privileges

The model act requires that an employee be allowed to convert his group coverage, without providing evidence of insurability, to an individual policy on termination of employment or termination of the group master policy. Conversion is an important aspect of group insurance and will be described in some detail in this section.

Conversion at Termination of Employment.   Laws patterned on the model act require a standard provision that gives the insured a right to convert his group life insurance coverage to an individual life insurance policy when his personal coverage under the group policy terminates because of termination of his employment or termination of his membership in a class eligible for group life insurance.

Employment can terminate because the insured resigned, was discharged, or was laid off. If an employee terminates employment for any reason, he must have the right to obtain an individual life insurance policy from the group insurer without providing evidence of insurability. However, the insurer is not required to issue an individual policy unless the person whose group insurance terminated applies for the individual policy and pays the first premium within the conversion period. The conversion period begins on termination of employment and lasts at least 31 days. Earlier model bills required that the person converting have the right to choose any form of individual life insurance policy, except term insurance, that the insurer currently issues to applicants of the person's age and for the amount applied for. The current model act allows the insurer to offer term insurance also as a conversion option if it wishes to do so. As a result of the *Norris* decision discussed in Chapter 6, "Formation of the Life Insurance Contract," many insurers have a special unisex policy used only for conversions.

The model act provides that the conversion amount shall be no more than the amount the person was entitled to under the group policy. Under the model act, from this amount the insurer can subtract "the amount of any life insurance for which such person becomes eligible under the same or any other group policy within 31 days after such termination." The individual policy does not have to include disability benefits or other supplementary coverages. The premium for the individual policy must be at the customary rate for the kind of policy, for the amount of coverage, for the class of risk in which the insured is placed at the time of conversion, and for her attained age on the date that the individual policy becomes effective.

To illustrate, suppose Donna McCracken lives in a state with a group conversion statute based on the current model act. She is insured for $50,000 under her employer's group life insurance policy. She quits her job, goes to work for another company within 31 days after her resignation, and becomes eligible for $20,000 of group life insurance under her new employer's group life insurance policy. In addition to her new group life coverage of $20,000, McCracken will have the right to purchase up to $30,000 of individual life insurance from her former employer's insurer without providing evidence of insurability.

Conversion at Policy Termination. Under laws patterned on the model act, in the event the group policy terminates, or is amended to terminate the insurance of a class of employees, an employee whose coverage ceases can convert to an individual life insurance policy without providing evidence of insurability. However, such an employee must have been insured under the group policy for at least five years.

The individual policy can provide the smaller of $10,000 or the amount of insurance the employee had under the group policy, minus the amount of group insurance for which he becomes eligible within 31 days of termination.

Other features of this conversion privilege are the same as those on conversion at termination of employment. However, some employees will be ineligible for conversion at group policy termination because of the five-year rule. Also, conversion at termination of the group policy is apt to provide less insurance than conversion at termination of employment.

To illustrate, suppose Elwin Van Eck lives in a state with a group conversion statute based on the current model act. He is insured for $50,000 under his employer's group life insurance policy when it terminates. Van Eck has been insured under this group policy for more than five years. Another insurer issues a group life insurance policy to Van Eck's employer before 31 days have elapsed. Under the new policy, Van Eck has $20,000 of life insurance. Van Eck has a right to purchase an individual life insurance policy in the smaller of two amounts—$10,000, or the former coverage minus the present coverage. The former coverage, $50,000, minus the present coverage, $20,000, is $30,000. Thus, Van Eck can purchase up to $10,000 of individual life insurance without providing evidence of insurability. Contrast Van Eck's conversion rights with those of McCracken in the example above.

Extension of Death Benefit Provision. The model act requires a provision for a death benefit in the highest amount for which an individual life insurance policy would have been issued if the employee dies during the conversion period and before an individual policy becomes effective. It does not matter that the employee did not apply for an individual policy. The death benefit will be payable whether or not the employee applied. Ordinarily, the practical effect of this clause is to extend the group policy coverage during the 31-day conversion period.

Supplementary Bill Relating to Conversion. A supplementary bill prepared by the NAIC relates to the conversion privilege. It does not require a policy provision and thus is not a part of the group life insurance standard provisions section of the model act but is in a separate section of its own. The supplementary bill extends, to a maximum of 60 days, the period during which the employee can apply for an individual policy, unless the policyholder or insurer has notified the employee of her conversion rights at least 15 days before the end of the 31-day conversion period. This extended period for conversion will expire 15 days after such notice has been given. However, the supplementary bill does not require that the extension of coverage, described in the subsection above, be provided beyond the end of the conversion period. Many states have enacted the supplementary bill.

Continuation of Coverage during Disability

The current model act includes a requirement for continuation of an insured's group life insurance coverage during the insured's total disability. This requirement did not appear in earlier model bills.

The provision for continuation of group life insurance during total disability applies only where active employment is a condition of insurance. Thus, it applies to employer-employee groups. The insured can continue coverage during his total disability by paying to the policyholder the portion of the premium he would have paid if he had not been disabled. The continuation is to be for six months unless the insurer approves continuation under another policy provision or the policy terminates earlier.

Nonforfeiture Provisions

Although most group life insurance is yearly renewable term insurance without cash values, some group life insurance does build cash values. If the group life insurance is on a plan other than term, the model act requires that the policy contain nonforfeiture provisions equitable to both the insureds and the policyholder. However, these group policy nonforfeiture provisions need not be the same as the nonforfeiture provisions that must be included in individual life insurance policies.

Dependent Group Life Insurance

The earlier model bills did not provide for life insurance covering the lives of the insured's dependents. The current model act contains a section entitled "Dependent Group Life Insurance." This section provides that a group life insurance policy (except for a creditor policy) can insure the employees or members against loss due to the death of a spouse or dependent child. The policyholder, the employee or member, or both, can pay the premium for this dependent life insurance. Noncontributory plans with dependent coverage must cover spouses and all dependent children. However, the insurer can exclude or limit the coverage of a spouse or dependent child whose evidence of insurability is unsatisfactory.

The amounts of life insurance for a covered spouse or dependent child cannot exceed 50 percent of the amount of the employee's or member's life insurance. The certificate must contain a statement describing the dependent insurance.

An employee can convert her group dependent life insurance to individual insurance along with the insurance on her own life. The employee can convert dependent life insurance at the time of termination of her employment or at termination of the group policy.

The model act further requires that a conversion privilege shall be available to dependents themselves under two circumstances. First, at the death of the insured employee or member, a surviving dependent can convert to an individual life insurance policy without providing evidence of insurability. Second, if the dependent's group life insurance coverage terminates because he ceases to be a qualified family member, he can convert to an individual policy. Divorce of a dependent spouse or maturity of a dependent child are the usual reasons that a dependent ceases to be a qualified family member.

In many respects, the model act reflects the current practice of insurers regarding dependent life insurance, although the model act tends to be more liberal as to benefits and conversion by dependents. Group life insurance covering the lives of spouses and dependent children is authorized by statute in many states and is issued in other states by permission of the insurance commissioner.

The Actively-at-Work Requirement

Group insurance policies covering employees commonly contain an actively-at-work requirement. An employee must be actively at work on the date she becomes eligible for group insurance coverage, or she will not be covered until she returns to work. For example, a noncontributory group policy might provide that a new employee will become eligible for group insurance coverage when she has been employed for 30 days. If an employee is absent from work on the date she becomes eligible for group insurance coverage, she will not be covered until the first day she returns to work.[7]

The actively-at-work requirement prevents persons who are too ill to work from being insured under the group policy. Ordinarily, those who are actively at work are reasonably able-bodied. Thus, the actively-at-work requirement is an important underwriting tool.

Actively-at-work requirements are stated in many different ways in group insurance policies. The courts generally have upheld them as valid and unambiguous.

McLean v. Metropolitan Life Insurance Co.[8] illustrates the operation of the actively-at-work clause. In that case, the employee, a factory worker, began work on June 18, 1951, and worked until September 1, 1951, when he went on disability leave. He never returned to work. On September 16, 1951, he became eligible for group insurance coverage and would have been covered if he had been actively at work. He died on February 5, 1952. The court held that he was not covered under the policy, saying:

> The Court finds nothing ambiguous about the term "actively at work," and, from the facts stipulated, John H. McLean was not "actively at work" at any time after September 1, 1951. In fact he was totally disabled, unable to work, and did not appear at his place of employment after September 1, 1951.
>
> Furthermore, the fact that he was totally disabled by reason of an accidental injury incurred in the course of his employment and could not be actively at work in no way met the requirements of the group policy.
>
> The Court finds that the terms of the group policy are clear and that the insurance never became effective in the case of John H. McLean. Judgment is therefore rendered for the defendant with costs.
>
> . . . John H. McLean became eligible for insurance ninety days after June 18, 1951, or September 16, 1951. His insurance became effective on that date provided he was "actively at work" on that date. If he was not "actively at work" on that date, then his insurance became effective on the next following day on which he was "actively at work."

---

[7]If the group policy is contributory—that is, requires that employees pay part or all of the premium—the eligible employee usually will not be covered unless she also makes written application for coverage.

[8]153 N.E.2d 349 (Ohio Ct. Com. Pleas 1957).

Actively at Work Full-Time

Some group insurers phrase the actively-at-work clause to require that the employee be actively at work full-time. Some courts have held that the term *full-time* is ambiguous. However, if the term is defined in hours, such as "full-time means 30 or more work hours per week," the courts are less likely to hold it ambiguous.[9]

Increase in the Amount of Life Insurance

If the amount of group life insurance covering an employee increases, usually the increase will not become effective unless the employee is actively at work. The increase will become effective if and when an absent employee returns to active work.

For example, in *Smillie v. Travelers Insurance Co.*,[10] the group life insurance policy provided for an increase in the amount of life insurance for insured employees who were actively at work on June 1, 1977. One insured employee, Charles M. Smillie II, was confined to the hospital from May 20, 1977, until his death on June 4, 1977. The court held that the increase in coverage was not effective for Smillie. The beneficiary received the amount of insurance in effect before the increase.

Termination of Group Insurance

Group life insurance policies cover the members of employee groups, union groups, association groups, or other groups. A group policy will insure a person only if she is a member of the group. As a general rule, a person's group insurance terminates when she ceases to be a member of the group.

Although various provisions in employer-employee group policies can extend coverage under some circumstances, such policies typically provide that an employee's group coverage ceases when her employment ceases. A termination provision might read as follows:

> The insurance of an insured employee shall automatically terminate on the earliest of the following dates:
>
> *a.* The date of termination of such employee's active status in any of the eligible classes of employment;
>
> *b.* The date of termination of this policy; and,
>
> *c.* If this is a contributory plan, the date of expiration of the last period for which the participant has made a contribution.

For purposes of this discussion, the relevant subsection of this provision is subsection *a.* Thus, if the death of an insured employee occurs prior to the date his employment terminates, he will have been insured, and the death benefit will be payable. If the death occurs after that date, the person will not have been insured on the date of death (except for coverage provided during the conversion period or during disability).

---

[9]Daniel E. Feld, Annotation, *Group Insurance: Construction of Provision Limiting Coverage to Full-Time Employees,* 57 A.L.R.3d 801 (1974).

[10]302 N.W.2d 258 (Mich. Ct. App. 1980).

Questions sometimes arise as to what constitutes termination of employment. If an employee resigns,[11] retires,[12] or is discharged by the employer,[13] ordinarily the employment is held to have terminated. If the employee does not express an intention to resign, this intention can sometimes be inferred from other circumstances. Thus, in a case in which an employee did not formally resign but told his wife he was quitting and applied for unemployment compensation, the court held that he had terminated employment.[14]

As a general rule, the courts will not hold a mere absence from work,[15] or a leave of absence,[16] to be termination of employment. The courts are divided as to whether layoffs or strikes constitute a termination of employment. As to strikes, the majority view is that the striking employee has, in effect, quit his employment on joining the strike and that therefore his employment terminated.

The sale of a division of a policyholder-company can give rise to a question as to whether the employees working in the division terminated employment. In *Pan American Life Insurance Co. v. Garrett,*[17] an electric company sold its transportation division to another company. The employees continued working in their jobs, but for the buyer-company. The court held that the employees had terminated employment with the seller-company and were no longer insured under the group insurance policy covering its employees.

Group Insurance Policy Premiums and Dividends

The policyholder typically remits the group insurance policy premiums to the insurer. As with individual insurance, the premium is payable prior to the period of coverage. Group premiums might be paid from the funds of the policyholder, from the funds of the insured persons if the state law permits, or from the funds of both. If the entire premium is paid from the policyholders' funds, the plan is called noncontributory. If the insured persons contribute part or all of the premium, the plan is called contributory. Usually, under group insurance contributory plans, the employee must sign an application and authorize deduction of the premium contribution from his salary. Under noncontributory plans, each eligible employee is ordinarily required to complete an enrollment card, even though the plan will cover all eligible employees. The enrollment card serves as a record of coverage and as a beneficiary designation form.

---

[11]Wyatt v. Security Benefit Life Ins. Co., 283 P.2d 243 (Kan. 1955); Murphy v. Chrysler Corp., 11 N.W.2d 261 (Mich. 1943); Metropolitan Life Ins. Co. v. Cole, 178 S.E. 43 (Va. 1935); C.T. Drechsler, Annotation, *Termination of Coverage under Group Policy with Regard to Termination of Employment,* 68 A.L.R.2d 8 (1959).

[12]Young v. Minton, 176 S.E. 662 (Ga. Ct. App. 1934); Lynch v. Central States Life Ins. Co., 281 Ill. App. 511 (1935).

[13]Kowalski v. Aetna Life Ins. Co., 165 N.E. 476 (Mass. 1929); Szymanski v. John Hancock Mut. Life Ins. Co., 8 N.W.2d 146 (Mich. 1943); Lineberger v. Security Life & Trust Co., 95 S.E.2d 501 (N.C. 1956).

[14]Gilby v. Travelers Ins. Co., 248 F.2d 794 (8th Cir.1957).

[15]Shea v. Aetna Life Ins. Co., 198 N.E. 909 (Mass. 1935); Smith v. Aetna Life Ins. Co., 152 S.E. 688 (N.C. 1930); Thompson v. Pacific Mills, 139 S.E. 619 (S.C. 1927).

[16]Peyton v. Metropolitan Life Ins. Co., 148 So. 721 (La. Ct. App. 1933); MacDonald v. Pennsylvania Mut. Life Ins. Co., 186 A. 234 (Pa. Super. Ct. 1936).

[17]199 S.W.2d 819 (Tex. Civ. App. 1946).

Dividends

As with individual insurance policies, group insurance policies can provide for a return of part of the premium. Such a return of premium usually is called a *dividend* if the insurer is a mutual company and a *premium refund* or retroactive rate credit if the insurer is a stock company.

The insured persons ordinarily are not entitled to receive any dividends or premium refunds that become payable under a group insurance policy. The policyholder is entitled to receive the dividend or premium refund. Under some state laws, however, if the dividend or premium refund exceeds the premiums that the policyholder has paid, the excess must be used for the benefit of the insureds.

Creditor Group Insurance Rates

Creditor group insurance differs markedly from other types of group insurance. With creditor group insurance, the creditor is the beneficiary. In other types of group insurance, the employer, union, association, or other policyholder is often prohibited by statute from being designated beneficiary.

In some instances, the creditor is the insurer's agent and receives a commission on the sale of the policy. The creditor might not pay any portion of the premiums, but the creditor sometimes receives dividends or premium refunds. Finally, the creditor makes the decision as to which policy will be purchased.

Under these circumstances, an insurer that offers group insurance to a creditor at a *higher* premium rate often will be at a competitive advantage. The creditor receives a higher commission if the premium rate is higher. The debtors, who have no choice as to which policy is purchased, ordinarily must pay the higher premiums.

Because of this reverse competition in the creditor group insurance field, creditor group insurance statutes and regulations establish maximum rates insurers can charge. Most states have laws patterned on the NAIC Consumer Credit Insurance Model Act and Model Regulation, which require that creditor group insurance benefits equal a reasonable percentage of premium and that schedules of premium rates be filed with the insurance commissioner. Some states have established a scale of creditor group insurance premium rates that insurers cannot exceed without permission from the insurance commissioner.

Conflict of Laws

A group insurance policy often is issued by an insurer domiciled in one state to a policyholder domiciled in another state, with insureds and beneficiaries residing in yet other states. Therefore, questions can arise as to which state's law must be applied. Courts use conflict of laws rules to determine the answers.

Generally, the law of the place of contracting determines the validity and effect of a contract. The place of contracting is the place where the last act necessary to put the contract into force was performed. The last act is ordinarily delivery of the group master policy. Thus, the law of the policyholder's state of domicile usually will govern. However, a growing number of courts follow the center of gravity or grouping of contacts rule under which the court will apply the law of the state that has the greatest interest in the outcome of the case.

Thus, sometimes the law of the state where the group policy was delivered will govern the performance of the contract, and sometimes the law of the state where the certificate was delivered will govern. Which law applies will depend on the conflict of laws rules of the state in which the case is tried. This can be a critical difference. The outcome of the case can depend on which state's law governs.

In *Poffenbarger v. New York Life Insurance Co.*[18] the court was faced with the question of whether to apply the law of the District of Columbia, where the group policy was delivered, or the law of West Virginia, where the certificate was delivered. The court said:

> Defendant contends [that] . . . this case should be governed by District of Columbia law inasmuch as it was there that the group policy was delivered to the Trustees. It is well established in West Virginia that the *lex loci contractus* [the law of the place where the contract is made] governs the nature, construction and validity of contracts. However, beyond that general principle, neither statute nor decisional law is available to indicate West Virginia's choice of the law to be applied in this troublesome area of group insurance contracts and the delivery of certificates thereunder. In the absence of state decisional law, it is the responsibility of the federal court to determine what the highest state court would find the law to be on this point if the same case were before it. . . . [I]t is not unreasonable to assume that our West Virginia court in a case such as this might choose to apply the relatively new "grouping of contacts" theory of the conflict of laws. This theory would permit the forum [court] to apply the law of the jurisdiction most intimately concerned with the outcome of the particular litigation. In the present case the State of West Virginia would appear to have a legitimate concern in the outcome of the litigation. This manifest interest of a state in the area of insurance on its residents was recognized in another context by the Supreme Court in *McGee v. International Life Ins.* Co., 355 U.S. 220, 78 S.Ct. 199, 2 L.Ed.2d 223 (1957). It occurs to me that a West Virginia Court would and should recognize as significant the fact that the certificate was delivered in this state to the insured who was a resident of the state at the time, and that the plaintiff-beneficiary, as a West Virginia resident, is properly and logically entitled to litigate her claim in this forum. Additionally, it is noted that West Virginia legislation relative to group life insurance demonstrates a valid concern in regard to the issuance and delivery of such certificates in this state.
>
> The totality of these contacts and circumstances alone might well persuade the West Virginia Court to apply West Virginia law. . . . Certainly such a conclusion would not offend the basic principles of justice.

Federal Taxation of Group Life Insurance

This book does not purport to explain the taxation of life and health insurance. Nevertheless, the federal tax law has had such an impact on the development of group life insurance that this topic must be mentioned.

The Internal Revenue Code provides that the cost of group term life insurance paid by the employer is tax-exempt to the insured employee up to $50,000 of coverage.[19] Moreover, the amount of premium paid by the employer is tax-deductible to the employer as a business expense. This provision of the Internal Revenue Code has been in effect for more than three decades. It has had the effect of encouraging employers to purchase group term life insurance and has resulted in a valuable benefit for employees.

However, if an employer were to purchase permanent, rather than term, life insurance, the amount of the premiums that the employer paid would not be tax-exempt

---

[18]277 F. Supp. 726 (S.D. W. Va. 1967).
[19]26 U.S.C.A. § 79 (West Supp. 1996).

to the employees. It would be subject to taxation as additional compensation. There-fore, the great majority of group life insurance is term insurance. The employer itself can deduct premiums it paid for group permanent life insurance, just as with group term life insurance.

ERISA and Group Insurance

The Employee Retirement Income Security Act of 1974[20] has a substantial impact on group insurance plans. ERISA is applicable to group life and health insurance plans covering employees, except governmental and church plans, plans maintained for the purpose of complying with workers' compensation laws, and certain plans covering nonresident aliens. Under ERISA, group life and health insurance plans covering employees (as well as many other types of nonpension plans providing benefits for employees) are called employee welfare benefit plans. An employer is not required to establish an employee welfare benefit plan. However, if an employer establishes an employee welfare benefit plan, the plan will be subject to the numer-ous requirements stated in ERISA. These requirements are complex and apply dif-ferently to different types of plans. This section will briefly describe the most important of these requirements.

An employee welfare benefit plan must be established pursuant to a written in-strument. This instrument must describe how the plan is to be financed and how benefits are to be received. The plan instrument usually names one or more fiduciar-ies who will administer the plan. Ordinarily, the employer, someone working for the employer, or a trustee will be named plan administrator. A plan administrator must act solely for the benefit of the plan participants and beneficiaries.

Reporting and disclosure are important responsibilities of a plan administrator. The plan administrator must provide a summary plan description to all participants. The summary plan description must be filed on request with the federal Department of Labor when the plan is initiated. The summary plan description must describe the plan in a manner that the average plan participant can understand. An annual report must be filed with the Internal Revenue Service.

ERISA requires that a reasonable claims procedure be set forth in the summary plan description. In the case of an insured employee welfare benefit plan, the in-surer's claims procedures will suffice. A fiduciary who will review claim denials must be indicated in the plan. This can be the plan administrator, an insurer, or an-other person or organization.

FEGLI and SGLI

The Federal Employees' Group Life Insurance Act of 1954[21] established a plan of group life insurance for nearly all the civilian employees of the federal government. The Federal Employees' Group Life Insurance Plan (FEGLI) is the largest group life insurance plan in the world.

The Federal Employees' Group Life Insurance Act authorized the Civil Service Commission to purchase "from one or more life insurance companies a policy or

---

[20]Public L. No. 93–406, 88 Stat. 829 (codified as amended in scattered sections of 5, 18, 26, 29, 31 and 42 U.S.C.).
[21]5 U.S.C.A. §§ 8701–8716 (West 1996).

policies" of group insurance to provide the benefits the act outlined. The insurer or insurers from whom the insurance was to be purchased were required to (1) be licensed in 48 states and the District of Columbia and (2) have group life insurance in force in an amount equal to at least 1 percent of the total amount of employee group life insurance in the United States in all life insurers.

When the act became effective in 1954, eight insurers met these requirements. However, for ease of administration the Civil Service Commission elected to purchase only one policy from the Metropolitan Life Insurance Company. The policy became effective on August 29, 1954. The other qualifying insurers participated as reinsurers. The law also provides for reinsurance by smaller life insurers. In recent years, about 50 life insurers have participated as reinsurers. The number changes each year.

Because of the reinsuring arrangements, the conversion privilege available to the insured employees differs somewhat from that provided under the usual employees' group life insurance policy. For example, if a group life insurance policy issued by the Argus Life Insurance Company insures the employees of the A.B.C. Manufacturing Company, a terminating employee is entitled to have an individual life insurance policy issued to him by the Argus Life Insurance Company without evidence of insurability. However, under FEGLI the converting insured can purchase an individual policy from any participating insurer that has applied for authority to issue individual life insurance contracts and that has met the requirements set forth by the federal Office of Personnel Management.

The Office of Personnel Management, not the insurer, is responsible for furnishing each insured employee with a certificate that states the benefits to which that employee is entitled, the beneficiary of those benefits, and the persons to whom claims are to be submitted. The certificate must include a summary of all the provisions of the policy that affect the insured.

The law creating the Servicemen's Group Life Insurance Plan (SGLI) was enacted in 1965.[22] SGLI is supervised by the Veterans Administration. SGLI is structured in a manner similar to FEGLI. That is, a primary insurer issues the group policy and other insurers provide reinsurance for the primary insurer. SGLI is available to members of the uniformed services on active duty or in training and to certain members of the Ready Reserve and Retired Reserve.

The interpretation of the Federal Employees' Group Life Insurance Act is generally a matter for the federal courts. One court explained this as follows:

> The construction of the federal statute is, in the first instance, a federal question. There is no well developed body of state law on the issue here presented, nor is there any overwhelming state interest that would suggest here that Congress intended that the courts look to the various states for the procedural rules to be applied in naming beneficiaries in federal insurance policies. In the interest of uniformity it is much better that the federal courts here develop a separate body of law rather than look to state law—and fifty different interpretations.[23]

However, courts sometimes answer questions involving the determination of family relationships in accordance with state law. The case of *Metropolitan Life Insurance Co. v. Thompson*[24] summarizes this rule. The court discussed the application of state law, rather than federal law, to questions of family relationships as follows:

---

[22]38 U.S.C.A. §§ 1965–1979 (West 1991 & Supp. 1996).

[23]Sears v. Austin, 292 F. 2d 690 (9th Cir. 1961), *cert. denied,* 368 U.S. 929 (1961).

[24]368 F.2d 791 (3rd Cir. 1966), *cert. denied,* Thompson v. Thompson, 388 U.S. 419 (1967).

[T]here being no federal law of domestic relations, whether a particular claimant falls within the federally-defined classification [of beneficiaries] must often be resolved with reference to state law.

Group Health Insurance

Group health insurance is an extremely important type of coverage. In 1994, over 82 million persons in the United States were insured under group health insurance contracts.[25] Nevertheless, until 1983 the NAIC had not developed a model act for states to follow when drafting laws governing group health insurance contracts. To date, only one-fifth of the states have laws patterned on the model act. As a result, in most states group health insurance contracts are not subject to as much detailed regulation as group life insurance contracts. However, many states have a statutory definition of groups eligible for group health insurance, and some states specify required policy provisions.

Group health insurance is patterned in many respects on group life insurance. For example, both group life and group health insurance are issued as master policies with certificates distributed to the insured persons. The actively-at-work and termination provisions in a group health insurance contract operate similarly to those in a group life insurance contract. Conflict of laws rules apply to group health insurance just as they apply to group life insurance. Group health insurance premium and dividend payments are similar to those for group life insurance.

In other respects, group health insurance resembles individual health insurance. This will be explained in Chapter 20, "Health Insurance." Some unique aspects of group health insurance also will be discussed in that chapter.

Wholesale and Franchise Insurance

Wholesale life insurance and franchise health insurance are hybrids between individual and group insurance. Wholesale or franchise insurance covers a group of people, but an individual insurance policy, rather than a group certificate, is issued to each insured in the group. There is usually an agreement with an employer or association that the insurer may sell the wholesale or franchise policies to employees or members. An employer will ordinarily deduct the premiums from employees' wages and remit the premiums to the insurer. An association will usually collect the premiums from the members and remit them to the insurer.

The NAIC has drafted a model act defining franchise insurance that has been enacted by well over half the states. Several other states have statutes or regulations governing franchise insurance that are not based on the model act.

Franchise insurance is defined in the model act to be individual accident and health insurance issued to five or more employees of one employer or ten or more members of a trade or professional association or union. Members of other associations, formed for purposes other than obtaining insurance, and with a two-year active existence and a constitution or bylaws, can also be issued franchise insurance.

---

[25]HEALTH INSURANCE ASSOCIATION OF AMERICA, SOURCE BOOK OF HEALTH INSURANCE DATA 15 (1996).

Summary

Group life insurance has grown spectacularly since its beginnings in 1911 and now amounts to 38 percent of all life insurance in force in the United States. Group health insurance provides the great majority of health benefits paid by health insurers.

Group life insurance covers employer-employee groups, creditor groups, labor union groups, trusteed groups, association groups, credit union groups, and other groups at the discretion of the insurance commissioner. Not all of these are permissible groups in all states, but the types of groups that state statutes permit has continued to expand.

Most states have statutes specifying certain provisions that must be included in group life insurance policies. These are the grace period provision, incontestable clause, application provision, evidence of insurability provision, certificate provision, and conversion provisions, among others. Some of these provisions are similar in purpose to those found in individual life insurance policies, but others, such as the certificate and conversion provisions, are unique to group insurance.

The most common type of group insurance contract is the employer-employee contract. These contracts usually have an actively-at-work provision, which requires that an eligible employee be actively at work on the date her insurance becomes effective. If the employee is not actively at work, her insurance will become effective on the first day she returns to work, assuming that she has applied for the coverage if the plan is contributory. The actively-at-work requirement is an important underwriting tool that assures that those in the group are reasonably able-bodied. The courts generally uphold actively-at-work clauses.

Group life insurance usually terminates when the insured ceases to be a member of the group, although policy provisions often extend the insurance for a period of time after termination of group membership. An employee ceases to be a member of the employee group on termination of employment. If an employee resigns, retires, or is discharged, his employment has terminated. Absence from work is not termination, as a general rule. The courts are divided as to whether a striking employee has terminated employment.

Tax laws that exempt the cost of group term life insurance, up to $50,000 face amount, from income taxation to an employee if the employer pays the premium have spurred the growth of this coverage. Group permanent life insurance is not similarly tax-exempt; for this reason, most group life insurance is term insurance. In either case, the employer can deduct the premium it paid as a business expense.

ILLUSTRATIVE CASE

This case concerns the actively-at-work clause in a group life insurance policy.

SMITH

v.

FOUNDERS LIFE ASSURANCE COMPANY OF FLORIDA [26]
Court of Appeals of Georgia

BANKE, Chief Judge.

Daisy Smith sued Founders Life Assurance Company to recover $22,000 in death benefits allegedly owed her pursuant to a group insurance policy covering the employees of the Macon-Bibb County Water and Sewerage Authority, which had employed her deceased husband, George Edward Smith, prior to his death. . . . Concluding as a matter of law that Mr. Smith was not covered under the terms of the policy, the trial court granted the insurance company's motion for summary judgment and denied Mrs. Smith's motion for summary judgment. Mrs. Smith appeals.

After working for the Macon-Bibb County Water and Sewerage Authority for many years, Mr. Smith was forced to cease working on March 24, 1983, due to the illness which ultimately resulted in his death. At the time of his death, which occurred on June 6, 1983, he was considered by the Authority to be a full-time employee on sick leave.

Prior to June 1, 1983, the Authority's employees, including Mr. Smith, had been covered by a policy of group insurance issued by Prudential Insurance Company. The

---

[26] 333 S.E.2d 5 (Ga. Ct. App. 1985).

Prudential policy expired on that date and was replaced by a policy issued by the appellee, Founders Life Assurance Company. Founders Life denied Mrs. Smith's claim for death benefits on the ground that Mr. Smith had not been "actively employed" or "actively working" between the effective date of the policy and the date of his death. Thereafter, Mrs. Smith submitted a claim for death benefits to Prudential Insurance Company, which paid her the full amount of such benefits due under the terms of its policy.

The Founders policy specifies that "each employee actively employed 30 or more hours per week . . . on the date of issue hereof is eligible for insurance from the date of issue. . . ." However, the policy further provides as follows: "EFFECTIVE DATES OF INSURANCE. Each eligible employee shall become insured automatically on the date he becomes eligible for insurance *except that an employee who is not actively at work . . . on such date shall not become insured until the next following day on which he is actively at work. . . .*" (Emphasis supplied.) The term "actively at work" is defined elsewhere in the policy to mean "the actual expenditure of time and energy in the service of the employer. . . ."

Although Mr. Smith was undoubtedly "actively employed" by the Authority at the time of his death and was thus an "eligible" employee under the terms of the policy, it is undisputed that he had not been "actively at work" at any time between the date of his death and the policy's issue date. Therefore, under the unambiguous provisions of the policy governing the "effective dates of insurance," the coverage never took effect as to him. It necessarily follows that the trial court was correct in granting Founders Life's motion for summary judgment and in denying the appellant's motion for summary judgment. We reject the appellant's contention that a fact issue exists as to whether the coverage became effective by estoppel, there being no suggestion in the record that Founders Life ever collected any premium payments from Mr. Smith, through the agency of his employer or otherwise. This fact distinguishes the present case from such cases as *Cason v. Aetna Life Ins. Co.,* 91 Ga. App. 323, 332, 85 S.E.2d 568 (1954), and *American Home Mut. Life Ins. Co. v. Harvey,* 99 Ga. App. 582(1)(b), 109 S.E.2d 322 (1959).

Judgment affirmed.

McMURRAY, P.J., and BENHAM, J., concur.

Questions for Review

1. What were the grounds of criticism against the early group life insurance plans?
2. Briefly summarize the 1917 standard group life insurance definition.
3. List four groups that the current NAIC Group Life Insurance Model Act recognizes as eligible groups for group life insurance.
4. Briefly discuss each of the following required provisions for group life insurance policies under the model act:
   a. The grace period provision.
   b. The misstatement of age provision.
   c. The incontestable clause.
5. Briefly summarize the conversion rights that a group life insurance policy must grant
   a. If an employee's group coverage terminates because employment terminates.
   b. If an employee's group coverage terminates because of termination of the group policy.
6. Contrast the position of an employer group policyholder with that of a creditor group policyholder.
7. Describe the purpose of the actively-at-work provision.
8. Under which of the following situations could a question arise as to the termination of an employee's insurance under his employer's group life insurance plan?
   a. The employee resigns.
   b. The employee is discharged.
   c. The employee goes on strike.
9. What is the purpose of the Federal Employees' Group Life Insurance Act of 1954?
10. How has the federal income tax law spurred the growth of group life insurance?

20　HEALTH INSURANCE

Chapter Outline

There are several kinds of health insurance. One kind provides for reimbursement of medical, hospital, or surgical expenses when an insured person is sick or injured. Another kind provides for replacement of lost income when an insured person is unable to work due to disability. Still others provide for vision or dental care expenses or accidental death and dismemberment benefits. A relatively new type of health insurance provides for the expenses of long-term care in a nursing home or for other custodial care.

Health insurance is provided under both individual and group contracts. In the United States, group health insurance covers many more people than does individual health insurance. Nevertheless, individual health insurance has been more heavily regulated than group health insurance, due in part to the absence, until 1983, of a National Association of Insurance Commissioners model group health insurance law.

The law of health insurance has much in common with the law of life insurance. For example, most of the principles of contract and agency law that apply to life insurance also apply to health insurance. Many of the rules of law relating to accidental injury under the accidental death benefit provisions of life insurance policies also apply to accidental injury under health insurance policies. The same laws that govern disability benefits in life insurance policies usually govern disability benefits in health insurance policies as well. The purpose of this chapter is to briefly describe the laws unique to health insurance.

The Uniform Individual Accident and Sickness Policy Provision Law

In 1950, the NAIC adopted the Uniform Individual Accident and Sickness Policy Provision Law, which, with few variations, all states except Utah have enacted.[1] The term *accident and sickness insurance* is an older term for what now is called health insurance. The term *health insurance* will be used in this book except when referring to the uniform law.

The uniform law defines accident and sickness insurance as "insurance against loss resulting from sickness or from bodily injury or death by accident, or both." The uniform law applies to health insurance policies insuring one person or insuring a person and certain of his family members and dependents. It does not apply to workers' compensation insurance, liability insurance, reinsurance, blanket insurance, or group insurance. Moreover, the uniform law does not apply to annuity contracts, life or endowment insurance policies, or any accidental death, dismemberment, or disability coverages in such policies.

Restatement of the Uniform Law in Simplified Language

In 1979, the NAIC adopted the Restatement of the NAIC Uniform Individual Accident and Sickness Policy Provision Law in Simplified Language. The Restatement is intended to be a guideline for those drafting individual health insurance policies that must be written in simplified language. Because many states now have laws requiring simplified language in individual health insurance policies, the Restatement was a needed modernization of the uniform law. The Restatement was not intended to change the meaning of the uniform law but rather merely to restate its required provisions and some of its optional provisions in simplified language. The following sections quote the uniform law in the simplified language of the Restatement.

---

[1]Wisconsin enacted the Uniform Accident and Sickness Policy Provision Law but repealed it in 1975 and replaced it with other legislation that contains some of the provisions of the uniform law.

Persons Covered

The individual health insurance policy must insure one person, or more than one person if an adult member of a family applies for the policy and the additional persons are certain family members or dependents. The additional persons who can be insured under the policy are the applicant's spouse, dependent children or any of the applicant's children under a specified age not exceeding 19 years, and any other dependents of the applicant.

Ordinarily, individual health insurance policies provide that children of the insured are eligible for coverage until they are 19, or until 23 if they are full-time students. A number of states have enacted laws requiring that a mentally or physically handicapped child who is incapable of self-support be permitted to remain insured past the limiting age.

All states have statutes requiring the inclusion of newborn children under their parents' health insurance policies. The NAIC has endorsed a Model Newborn Children Bill requiring that both individual and group health policies providing coverage for family members cover newborn children from the moment of birth. Over four-fifths of the states have enacted this bill into law; other states have related statutes regarding newborns. If payment of an additional premium is required to provide coverage for the newborn child, these laws typically permit the insurer to require that the policyowner give the insurer notice of the birth of the child and submit the additional premium within 31 days of the birth. If these requirements are not met, the insurance coverage for the newborn will not continue beyond the 31-day period.

Required Provisions

Laws patterned on the Uniform Individual Accident and Sickness Policy Provision Law require that insurers include certain provisions in all individual health insurance policies. These required provisions are an entire contract provision, a provision for a time limit on certain defenses (similar in some respects to an incontestable clause in a life insurance policy), a grace period provision, a reinstatement provision, several claims provisions, a provision limiting the time in which legal actions can be brought, and a change of beneficiary provision.

Entire Contract Provision.   Each individual health insurance policy must provide that the "policy [with the application and attached papers] is the entire contract between the Insured and the Company." An individual health insurance policy also must state that no change in the policy is valid unless an executive officer of the insurer approves the change and endorses it on the policy. Finally, there must be a statement that no agent has the authority to change the policy or waive any of its conditions. Thus, the entire contract provision in an individual health insurance policy is similar to that in an individual life insurance policy.

Time Limit on Certain Defenses Provision.   The first section of the time limit on certain defenses provision has the same general purpose as an incontestable clause in a life insurance policy. As with the incontestable clause, the basic purpose of the first section of the time limit on certain defenses provision is to limit the period in which an insurer can rescind the policy or defend a claim denial based on a material misrepresentation in the application. The first part of the time limit on certain defenses provision, as it appears in the uniform law, reads as follows:

After three years from the issue date only fraudulent misstatements in the application shall be used to void the policy or deny any claim for loss incurred or disability that starts after the three year period.

Thus, after an individual health insurance policy has been in effect for the required period it will be incontestable, except for fraudulent misstatements in the application. About three-fourths of the states have statutes requiring a period of not more than two years during which the policy will be contestable. This is more favorable to insureds than the three-year period suggested by the uniform law.

Note that fraud is specifically excluded from the operation of the health policy's time limit on certain defenses provision. Fraud is the intentional misrepresentation of a material fact that is communicated to another who is injured as a result of reasonably relying on the misrepresentation. Fraud is not ordinarily excluded in a life insurance policy incontestable clause. The life insurance policy will be incontestable even if the misrepresentation was fraudulent. This difference reflects the wider variety of claims problems encountered in health insurance than in life insurance. In addition, a health insurance applicant usually is alive and can be questioned about a misstatement the insurer believes might be fraudulent, whereas a life insurance applicant is often dead at the time the insurer becomes aware of such a misstatement. Health insurance fraud is discussed in the section entitled "Management of Health Care Costs."

The time limit on certain defenses clause can have optional wording in those individual health insurance policies that provide the insured the right to continue the policy in force until age 50 or after or, in the case of a policy issued after age 44, for at least five years from its date of issue. Under laws patterned on the uniform law, such long-term individual health insurance policies can contain a provision stating that "[a]fter this policy has been in force for three years during the Insured's lifetime (excluding any period during which the Insured is disabled), the Company cannot contest the statements in the application." Note that this provision does not except fraud and that it contains the phrase *during the lifetime of the insured,* or words to that effect. It is therefore much the same as the typical life insurance policy incontestable clause.

The time limit on certain defenses provision also contains a second section that deals with preexisting diseases or conditions. In the uniform law, it reads: "No claim for loss incurred or disability that starts after 3 years from the issue date will be reduced or denied because a sickness or physical condition not excluded by name or specific description before the date of loss had existed before the effective date of coverage."

The important topic of preexisting conditions is discussed in a section below.

Grace Period Provision.   The uniform law requires that an individual health insurance policy include a grace period provision. Unlike the grace period for life insurance policies, which is usually 31 days, the grace period for individual health insurance policies can be as short as 7 days for weekly premium policies or 10 days for monthly premium policies. However, the grace period must be at least 31 days if premiums are payable on any basis except weekly or monthly. As with life insurance, the coverage provided under an individual health insurance policy remains in force during the grace period.

If an individual health insurance policy is renewable at the insurer's option (optionally renewable policies), the grace period provision must include a statement that, if the insurer gives timely notice of its intention not to renew the policy beyond the period for which a premium has been paid, there will be no grace period. Thus, if the insurer has notified the insured of its intention not to renew the policy beyond a specified date, there will be no grace period for the premium that would otherwise have become due on that date. Such a provision, as it appears in the uniform law, reads as follows:

> Grace Period: This policy has a 31-day grace period. This means that if a renewal premium is not paid on or before the date it is due, it may be paid during the following 31 days. The grace period will not apply if, at least 30 days before the premium due date, the Company has delivered or mailed to the Insured's last address shown in the Company's records written notice of the Company's intent not to renew this policy. During the grace period, the policy will stay in force.

The insurer can reserve the right to deduct any unpaid premium from the settlement of a claim that arises during the grace period. This right is not a required part of the grace period provision but can be provided in a separate optional provision.

Reinstatement Provision.   Laws patterned on the uniform law require a reinstatement provision in individual health insurance policies that differs considerably from the reinstatement provision in life insurance policies. If the insurer does not require a reinstatement application for an individual health insurance policy, the policy must provide that the insurer's acceptance of a premium after lapse will automatically reinstate the policy. If the insurer requires an application for reinstatement and issues a conditional premium receipt to the applicant, the reinstatement will be effective as of the date the insurer approves the reinstatement. If the insurer fails to act on the reinstatement application within 45 days of the date of the conditional receipt, the policy will be reinstated automatically.

A reinstated individual health insurance policy covers only those losses resulting from accidents that occur after the effective date of reinstatement or from sicknesses that begin more than 10 days after the reinstatement. Thus, there is a 10-day waiting period for sickness coverage after reinstatement, but not for coverage of accidents.

After reinstatement, the rights and duties of the insured and insurer are subject to any provisions added in connection with the reinstatement. Thus, the insurer can reinstate an individual health insurance policy subject to restrictive conditions that were not part of the policy prior to lapse. In other words, the reinstatement of a lapsed health insurance policy does not necessarily mean the policy is fully restored to its former status. In this way, a reinstated individual health insurance policy differs from a reinstated life insurance policy, to which the insurer usually cannot add new conditions.

Claims Provisions.   Laws patterned on the uniform law require that individual health insurance policies include several provisions relating to health insurance claims. First, there is a notice of claim provision. The insurer must be given notice of a claim within 20 days after the occurrence or commencement of any loss covered by the policy, or as soon thereafter as is reasonably possible. Some claims, such as an accidental death claim, for example, will be based on the occurrence of a loss. Others, such as a disability income claim or a claim for hospital benefits, will be based on a loss that commences on a certain date and might continue for some time. Therefore, notice must be given to the insurer within 20 days after the occurrence of a loss in the one instance or the commencement of a loss in the other instance.

If it is not reasonably possible for an insured to give notice of a claim to the insurer within 20 days, later notice will suffice. For example, suppose an insured was struck by a fast-moving truck and was in a coma for an extended period of time. It might not be reasonably possible for the insured to provide notice of the claim to the insurer within the 20-day period. However, another person can give notice of the claim to the insurer on the insured's behalf.

If the policy provides disability income coverage for a period of at least two years, the insurer can include a provision requiring notice of continuance of disability.

Second, an individual health insurance policy must provide that the insurer will furnish claim forms within 15 days of the date it receives notice of a claim. If the insurer does not furnish claim forms within 15 days, the policy must provide that the claimant will be considered to have fulfilled the proof of loss requirements if she merely files written proof of the occurrence on which the claim is based and of the character and extent of the loss.

Third, the policy must provide that the claimant must furnish written proof of loss to the insurer within 90 days of the date of loss except in the case of a claim for disability income payments. In the case of a claim for disability income payments, the claimant must furnish proof of loss within 90 days after the end of the period for which payment is due. The policy must also provide that if it is impossible for the insured to comply with these requirements, it will be sufficient if he furnishes such proof as soon as possible, but no later than one year from the date proof of loss would otherwise have been required.

Note the difference between the requirements for notice of claim and those for proof of loss. Notice of claim must be given within 20 days, but 90 days are allowed to present proof of loss, because proof of loss might require a doctor's statement, or a death certificate in the case of an accidental death benefit.

Fourth, an individual health insurance policy must specify that the insurer will pay a claim immediately on receipt of proof of loss unless periodic payments are involved. The insurer must make periodic payments, such as disability income payments, at least monthly.

Fifth, the policy must provide that all benefits are payable to the insured if she is alive. Accidental death benefits must be payable to a named beneficiary or to the insured's estate if no beneficiary is named. Other accrued benefits that are unpaid at the insured's death are payable either to the insured's estate or a named beneficiary, at the insured's option.

Finally, the policy must include a provision that the insurer at its own expense shall have the right to have the insured physically examined during the time a claim is pending. The insurer also has the right to require an autopsy in case of the insured's death, unless forbidden by law.

Legal Actions Provision.   An individual health insurance policy must provide that a claimant cannot bring an action at law or in equity against the insurer until 60 days after written proof of loss has been furnished to the insurer in accordance with the policy terms. Nor can the claimant bring such an action after three years from the time the claimant furnished written proof of loss. In other words, the provision must state that if the claimant decides to sue the insurer, he cannot bring the suit earlier than 60 days, or later than three years, after he has submitted proof of loss.

Beneficiary Change Provision.   If an individual health insurance policy provides an accidental death benefit, laws patterned on the uniform law also require a change of beneficiary provision. This provision must state that, unless the policyowner has designated an irrevocable beneficiary, the policyowner has reserved the right to change the beneficiary. The provision must also state that the consent of a revocable beneficiary will not be required for the policyowner to surrender, assign, or otherwise deal with the policy.

Optional Provisions

Laws patterned on the uniform law require that certain optional provisions in an individual health insurance policy be as favorable to the insured as the optional provisions in the uniform law. These optional provisions include payment of claims provisions, a misstatement of age provision (essentially the same as that in a life insurance policy), overinsurance provisions, an illegal occupation provision, and a provision excluding from coverage any loss resulting from the use of intoxicants and narcotics.

Payment of Claims Provisions.   In addition to the required payment of claims provisions, the insurer can, at its option, include certain other provisions relating to claims payment. One of these concerns benefits payable to the insured's estate or to a minor or other incompetent person. Such a provision can read:

> If benefits are payable to the Insured's estate or a beneficiary who cannot execute a valid release, the Company can pay benefits up to $1,000 to someone related to the Insured or beneficiary by blood or marriage whom the Company considers to be entitled to the benefits. The Company will be discharged to the extent of any such payment made in good faith.

If the individual health insurance policy provides payment for hospital, medical, surgical, or nursing services, it can contain a provision that the insurer may, at its option, pay the benefits directly to the hospital, physician, or other provider of care. However, if the insured directs otherwise in writing by the time proofs of loss are filed, the insurer must follow the insured's direction.

Change of Occupation Provision.   An insurer can include in an individual health insurance policy a provision relating to a change by the insured to an occupation either more or less hazardous than his occupation at the time of application. If, on the one hand, the insured becomes ill or has an accident at a time when he is engaged in a more hazardous occupation, the insurer will adjust the benefit to the amount the premium paid would have purchased at the more hazardous occupation. That is, the insurer will adjust the benefit downward but will not adjust the premium amount.

If, on the other hand, the insured changes to a less hazardous occupation, the insurer will not adjust the benefit upward but must reduce the premium rate accordingly. The insurer must also return any excess unearned premium.

Overinsurance Provisions.   Insurers wish to discourage overinsurance. *Overinsurance* occurs when a person is insured in an amount that is excessive in relation to the loss insured against. For example, if disability income insurance covers a person in excess of her disposable income, the person is overinsured. It would be profitable for the person to be disabled. The person might be tempted to submit claims for a borderline, or even nonexistent, disability. Even if the disability income insurance equaled or was slightly less than the person's disposable income, she might prefer to receive the disability income rather than work. This would also be overinsurance. Just as with disability income insurance, a person can be overinsured for medical, surgical, or hospital expenses.

Overinsurance is a serious problem that the health insurance industry and the insurance regulators have not yet solved. Compensation for actual losses, not windfall profits, is a desirable objective. Overinsurance of some people creates higher premiums for all.

The optional overinsurance provisions in the uniform law will not solve the problem of overinsurance, but they do help to mitigate it. The optional overinsurance provisions deal with situations in which an insurer has issued more than one health insurance policy covering the same loss or in which two or more insurers have each issued policies covering the same loss. Another overinsurance provision in the uniform law deals with disability income benefits that are too high in relation to the insured's earnings.

Generally speaking, overinsurance provisions allow an insurer to treat excess insurance it has issued as void or to make a proportional reduction in its benefit payment if another insurer has issued a policy covering the same loss. The insurer must return the premiums paid for the excess insurance.

For example, suppose an insured had two or more health insurance policies issued by one insurer covering the same loss. The uniform law provides that an individual health insurance policy can include a provision that insurance issued by the insurer covering a particular loss in excess of a stated amount shall be void. Alternatively, there can be a provision that the insured can elect among the policies he has with the insurer. Such a provision might read:

> Other Insurance in This Insurer: If the Insured has more than one policy of hospital expense insurance, only one policy chosen by the Insured will be effective. The Company will refund all premiums paid for all the other policies.

Two optional provisions concern insurance with other insurers, one to be included in policies covering losses on an expense-incurred basis and the other to be included in policies covering losses on a non-expense-incurred basis. An example of a policy that pays benefits on an expense-incurred basis is one that pays 80 percent of incurred expenses for a semiprivate hospital room. An example of a policy that pays on a non-expense-incurred basis is one that pays $150 per day while the insured is hospitalized, regardless of the expenses incurred.

These optional overinsurance provisions limit the insurer's liability to a specified portion of the total loss suffered by the insured where she has other valid coverage. The overinsurance provision can be drafted to include in the definition of *other valid coverage* that provided by group health insurance, Blue Cross/Blue Shield plans, and so forth.

The last optional overinsurance provision deals with the relation of the insured's earnings to her disability income benefits. If the policy includes this provision and the total amount of benefits payable under all valid disability income coverages on the insured exceeds a specified percentage of his earnings, the insurer will adjust the disability income benefit payable downward. That is, the amount payable by an insurer with a relation-of-earnings-to-insurance provision in its policy is limited to a proportionate part of the benefits that would otherwise be payable. However, the benefits payable under all disability income coverages cannot be reduced below $300 a month unless the total coverage is less.

Illegal Occupation Provision.   Another optional provision the insurer is permitted to include in an individual health insurance policy is the illegal occupation provision. This provision can read: "The Company will not be liable for any loss which results from the Insured committing or attempting to commit a felony or from the Insured engaging in an illegal occupation."

Insurers include illegal occupation provisions in health insurance policies because an insured's commission of or attempt to commit a felony or engagement in an illegal occupation increases his risk of injury or sickness. Assume, for example, that a person insured under an individual health insurance policy providing hospital benefits is injured as a result of a gunshot wound received during his commission of a burglary. If his policy contains an illegal occupation provision, any resulting hospital expenses will not be payable.

Intoxicants and Narcotics Provision.   The purpose of the intoxicants and narcotics provision is similar to that of the illegal occupation provision. An insurer is permitted to include an intoxicants and narcotics provision in a health insurance policy because, if an insured is drunk or under the influence of a narcotic, the risk that she will suffer injury or sickness is increased. This provision can read: "The Company will not be liable for any loss resulting from the Insured being drunk or under the influence of any narcotic unless taken on the advice of a physician."

Definition of Terms

A health insurance policy usually defines a number of terms. Among these are *injury, sickness, preexisting condition, hospital,* and *physician.*

Injury and Sickness

Health insurance policies generally insure against loss resulting from injury or sickness. Therefore, these terms are often defined in the policy.

Nearly one-half of the states have adopted the NAIC Model Regulation to Implement the Individual Accident and Sickness Minimum Standards Act (NAIC Accident and Sickness Minimum Standards Regulation). This model regulation requires a definition of *injury* no more restrictive than the following:

> Injury or injuries, for which benefits are provided, means accidental bodily injury sustained by the insured person which are the direct cause, independent of disease or bodily infirmity or any other cause and occur while the insurance is in force. . . . [I]njuries shall not include injuries for which benefits are provided under workmen's compensation, employer's liability or similar law, motor vehicle no-fault plan, unless prohibited by law, or injuries occurring while the insured person is engaged in any activity pertaining to any trade, business, employment, or occupation for wage or profit.

Under the model regulation, the definition of *sickness* cannot be more restrictive than the following:

> Sickness means sickness or disease of an insured person which first manifests itself after the effective date of insurance and while the insurance is in force. There will be a probationary period which will not exceed thirty (30) days from the effective date of the coverage of the insured person. Sickness shall not include sickness or disease for which benefits are provided under any workman's compensation, occupational disease, employer's liability or similar law.

Note that the injury must be sustained, or the sickness or disease must first manifest itself, after the effective date of the coverage and while the policy is in force.

Preexisting Conditions

A *preexisting condition* is a physical or mental condition of the insured that manifested itself prior to the effective date of the insured's health insurance policy. Thus, for example, if the insured receives medical treatment after the effective date of the policy for injuries suffered in an accident that occurred before the effective date, the claim will be properly denied. However, if an illness existed without apparent symptoms at the time the policy became effective, the illness will be covered because it had not manifested itself prior to the effective date. The word *manifest* means "to show plainly."

Older policies did not use the term *first manifest* but rather covered losses for sickness *commencing* after the effective date of the policy. Sicknesses sometimes have their origins in conditions that existed prior to the policy's effective date but of which there were no apparent symptoms. This language in the older policies, applied to such conditions, caused misunderstandings and disputes between insureds and insurers. Many states therefore require that health insurance policies contain the words *first manifest* in the definition of the term *sickness*. If the policy contains the *first manifest* language, it will exclude only preexisting conditions that exhibited apparent symptoms prior to the effective date.

The NAIC Individual Accident and Sickness Insurance Minimum Benefits Standards Model Regulation contains the following definition of the term *preexisting condition*:

> "Preexisting condition" shall not be defined to be more restrictive than the following: Preexisting condition means the existence of symptoms which would cause an ordinarily prudent person to seek diagnosis, care or treatment within a five (5) year period preceding the effective date of the coverage of the insured person or a condition for which medical advice or treatment was recommended by a physician or received from a physician within a five (5) year period preceding the effective date of the coverage of the insured person.

This further limits the definition of *preexisting condition* in those states that have adopted the model regulation. Nearly one-half of the states have done so.

As previously noted, the Uniform Individual Accident and Sickness Policy Provision Law requires a time limit on certain defenses provision that precludes denial or reduction of a claim arising three years after the policy issue date, if the denial is based on a condition that the policy does not specifically exclude by name. Therefore, if an applicant has had treatment for a lower back injury and states this on the health insurance application, the underwriter could decide to accept the application but issue the policy with an amendment rider excluding benefits for medical treatment or hospitalization resulting from disease or injury to the lower back. Under a policy with such an amendment rider, the claim examiner can properly deny a claim for benefits for such treatment at any time.

Hospital

The insurer's intent under hospital policies is to provide benefits if the insured is confined in a hospital but not if he needs only custodial care. For this reason, many policies define the term *hospital*. Such definitions must be carefully drafted, or they will fail to accomplish their purpose.

For example, in *Travelers Insurance Co. v. Page*[2] the health policy insuring the plaintiff's dependent child included the following definition of *hospital*:

> The term *hospital* as used herein means an institution which meets all of the following tests: (*a*) It is engaged primarily in providing medical care and treatment of sick and injured persons on an in-patient basis at the patient's expense and maintains diagnostic and therapeutic facilities for surgical and medical diagnosis and treatment of such persons by or under the supervision of a staff of duly qualified physicians; (*b*) It continuously provides twenty-four hour a day nursing service by or under the supervision of registered graduate nurses and is operated continuously with organized facilities for operative surgery; and (*c*) It is not, other than incidentally, a place of rest, a place for the aged, a place for drug addicts, a place for alcoholics or a nursing home.

The insured child was confined in a psychiatric nursing home that contained facilities for suturing and other minor surgery. The nursing home did not have facilities for major surgery. The plaintiff admitted that if any of the patients had required even a tonsillectomy, the nursing home would have transferred the patient to a general hospital. The insurer therefore contended that the institution was not a hospital, as the term was defined in the policy. However, the court determined that the policy definition of *hospital* did not mention major surgery and that to impose a requirement that the facility must be equipped to do major surgery would be going beyond the terms of the policy. The court said:

> We must, therefore, in construing the term most favorably to the insured, construe it to mean that the facilities for any "operative" surgery continuously maintained as provided in the policy is a sufficient compliance therewith. To say that operative surgery means that an institution to be a hospital under the policy must have facilities for both minor and major surgery would be equivalent to saying that it must have facilities for all surgery. The policy does not require this. If the policy had even gone so far as to specify major surgery, we could not require that the hospital have facilities for all major surgery; neither can we require that it have facilities for all types of operative surgery. The policy did not require it and neither can we.

The NAIC Accident and Sickness Minimum Standards Model Regulation requires that an individual health insurance policy define the term *hospital* no more restrictively than the following:

> A Hospital is an institution operated pursuant to law and is primarily and continuously engaged in providing or operating, either on its premises or in facilities available to the hospital on a prearranged basis and under the supervision of a staff of duly licensed physicians, medical, diagnostic and major surgical facilities for the medical care and treatment of sick or injured persons on an in-patient basis for which a charge is made and provides 24 hour nursing service by or under the supervision of registered graduate professional nurses.

The definition can exclude convalescent homes, rest homes, and nursing facilities; facilities primarily affording custodial, educational, or rehabilitative care; facilities for the aged, drug addicts, or alcoholics; and military hospitals.

Physician

Health insurance policies frequently define the term *physician* in order to limit payments under the policy to expenses for treatment given by a qualified practitioner.

---

[2]169 S.E.2d 682 (Ga. Ct. App. 1969).

However, some states regulate this definition by statute to prevent insurers from defining the term *physician* narrowly. For example, Illinois requires that if benefits for the expenses of any medical treatment are payable, they must be payable on an equal basis for the services of any person licensed to give the treatment.[3] The following illustrative definition should meet the requirements of such statutes:

> *Physician* means a licensed practitioner of the healing arts performing services within the scope of his license as provided by the laws of the jurisdiction in which such practitioner resides.

Benefit Provisions

Health insurance policies provide a wide array of coverages. Hospital, medical, and surgical expense coverages and disability income coverages are the most important. Major medical policies provide an important type of coverage. Major medical policies are intended to cover the major expenses that result from long periods of hospital confinement or expensive surgical procedures.

Medicare supplement policies provide health insurance coverage for those expenses that Medicare does not cover. The regulation of Medicare supplement policies will be discussed in a following section.

Health insurance policies can also provide accidental death and dismemberment benefits. Some limited health insurance policies provide benefits only if the insured is injured as the result of an accident or only if he contracts a specified disease, such as cancer. Some policies limit coverage to travel accidents. Vision and dental care expense policies are becoming more common, usually as group insurance. Long-term care insurance provides benefits when the insured is confined to a nursing home or needs other custodial care. Disability income policies provide income when the insured is disabled and unable to work.

Mandated Benefits

The states have enacted laws mandating that various types of benefits be included in health insurance policies. Among such laws have been those mandating coverage for newborn and handicapped children of the insured, as discussed above. Other laws mandate coverage for alcoholism and drug addiction treatment, maternity expenses, outpatient treatment, home health care, treatment of mental illness, hospice care, health examinations, mammography, or in vitro fertilization. Moreover, the states have enacted various laws requiring that treatment by chiropractors, podiatrists, optometrists, psychologists, nurse-midwives, or other specified health care professionals be covered in health policies.

State-mandated benefit statutes usually apply to both individual and group health insurance policies. These statutes have been voluminous, diverse, and sometimes conflicting, creating serious compliance problems for insurers, especially in regard to group health insurance.[4]

---

[3] 215 ILL. COMP. STAT. 5/370(b) (Michie Supp. 1996).

[4] R. YOUNGER, MANDATED INSURANCE COVERAGE—THE ACHILLES HEEL OF STATE REGULATION? (1982).

The federal government recently mandated that insurers provide benefits for 48-hour hospital stays for mothers and infants after normal births and 96-hour stays following a cesarean section.[5] Another recent federal mandate requires that health care plans of employers with 50 or more employees have annual and lifetime benefit caps for mental health care equal to such benefit caps for treatment of physical illnesses.[6]

In addition to these specifically mandated benefits, many states have adopted minimum standards for individual hospital, medical, surgical, major medical, and disability income policies. In 1976, the NAIC adopted the Model Individual Accident and Sickness Insurance Minimum Standards Act and a model regulation to implement the act. The NAIC Model Minimum Standards Regulation requires, for example, that a basic hospital expense-incurred policy provide at least 80 percent of a semiprivate room rate or, alternatively, at least $30 per day for 31 days. Such a policy must provide 80 percent of miscellaneous hospital expenses up to $1,000 (or, alternatively, 10 times the room and board charge) with a $100 deductible. The insurance commissioner can raise these amounts as appropriate.

One-half of the states have enacted laws or adopted regulations requiring minimum standards in individual health insurance policies. In some states, these statutes and regulations do not follow the NAIC models. This lack of uniformity has been a source of concern to the health insurance industry because of the expense of conforming to different standards in different states.

Exclusions and Limitations

Most individual health insurance policies list conditions for which the insurer will not pay benefits. Generally, these conditions are listed in a section of the policy entitled "Exclusions and Limitations." These exclusions and limitations differ from one type of health insurance policy to another. For example, disability income policies typically include only a few exclusions or limitations. Usually, benefits under a disability income policy are not payable in the event that the disability results from war, an attempt to commit suicide, or self-inflicted injury.

Medical, hospital, and surgical expense policies often contain more exclusions. Thus, such a policy might exclude losses incurred as a result of the following:

1. Injury or sickness for which the insured is entitled to benefits under Medicare, or any workers' compensation law, occupational diseases law, or any similar law.
2. Care or treatment received while confined in facilities provided by the Veterans Administration unless the insured has a legal obligation to pay for the treatment or services provided.
3. Sickness contracted or injury sustained as a result of war, declared or undeclared, or any act or hazard of war.
4. Injury or sickness of the insured while in the army, navy, air force, or other armed service of any country. (The insurer will return the pro rata unearned premium for any period of such service to the insured on request.)

---

[5]Pub. L. No. 104–204, 110 Stat. 2874, § 2704 (1996).
[6]Pub. L. No. 104–204, 110 Stat. 2874, § 712 (1996).

5. Pregnancy, childbirth, abortion, miscarriage, or any complications thereof.

6. Any attempt at suicide, whether sane or insane, or any intentionally self-inflicted injury.

7. Dental treatment of the teeth or gums unless required because of injury to natural teeth.

State legislatures and insurance departments have reduced the number of allowable exclusions in recent years. For example, the insurer cannot exclude coverage for treatment of tuberculosis in some states. In some states, the insurer cannot exclude coverage for treatment of alcoholism. State laws often require coverage for treatment of mental illness.

Cancellation and Renewal Provisions

Individual health insurance policies often include restrictions on renewability. Some policies include an optional cancellation provision that allows the insurer to cancel the policy at any time. The insurer has only to give the policyowner the required notice and refund the premium paid for coverage beyond the cancellation date. However, the number of these freely cancellable policies has diminished greatly because insurance departments discourage insurers from issuing them.

A second type of individual health insurance policy is optionally renewable. Under an optionally renewable policy, the insurer cannot cancel the policy whenever it decides to do so, but it can refuse to renew the policy. The insurer must give the policyowner notice of its intention not to renew. Many states limit the insurer's right to refuse renewal. Some states do not permit the insurer to refuse renewal except on a policy anniversary. Thus, if the insurer issued the health insurance policy on March 1, 1997, the insurer could not refuse to renew it until March 1, 1998, even though the premiums were payable monthly or quarterly. This guarantees at least one year's coverage. Other states forbid the insurer to refuse renewal except under certain specified conditions.

Some individual health insurance policies can be continued at the option of the policyowner. In this category are noncancellable, or noncancellable and guaranteed renewable, policies. The NAIC recommends that the states require insurers to use these terms as follows:

The terms "non-cancellable" or "non-cancellable and guaranteed renewable" may be used only in a policy which the insured has the right to continue in force by the timely payment of premiums set forth in the policy (1) until at least age 50, or (2) in the case of a policy issued after age 44, for at least five years from its date of issue, during which period the insurer has no right to make unilaterally any change in any provision of the policy while the policy is in force.[7]

About one-third of the states require this terminology.

Finally, some individual health insurance policies are guaranteed renewable. Guaranteed renewable policies—in those states that require the NAIC-recommended terminology—are the same as noncancellable or noncancellable and guaranteed renewable policies, except that under a guaranteed renewable policy the insurer is permitted to make changes in premium rates by classes.

---

[7]NONCANCELLABLE AND GUARANTEED RENEWABLE TERMINOLOGY DEFINED (Nat'l Ass'n of Ins. Comm'rs 1960).

A number of states require that renewability provisions appear on the face page of an individual health insurance policy. Renewability provisions are important. The policyowner should not have to search the policy to ascertain them.

Caswell v. Reserve National Insurance Co.[8] illustrates the importance of complying with a state statute requiring renewability provisions to appear on the policy's face page. *Caswell* involved a policy that was nonrenewable at the insurer's option. The insurer had paid the insured benefits for expenses resulting from a heart attack, after which the insurer offered to renew the policy only on the condition that a rider excluding payment of future benefits for heart and circulatory system diseases be attached to the policy. The insurer maintained that, because it had the right to refuse renewal outright, it had the right to insert a new exclusion in the policy and refuse renewal unless the insured accepted the exclusion. The policyowner tendered the renewal premium and insisted on renewal of the policy as it was originally written. The insurer refused. The policyowner, who had sustained further medical expenses, sued, claiming that the benefits would have been payable under the terms of the policy as originally written.

The policyowner contended that the policy was in violation of a Louisiana statute requiring renewability provisions to appear on the face page of the policy. This statute read:

> In any case where the policy is subject to cancellation or renewal at the option of the insurer, there shall be prominently printed on the first page of such policy a statement so informing the policyholder.

The insurer contended that the renewability provision appeared on the first page of the policy proper and that the outside, or cover, page should not be considered part of the policy. The court, however, noted that the cover page included a few items of policy information and held that the renewability provision did not appear on the face page of the policy as required, saying:

> Therefore, we hold that as a matter of law the requirements of the statute were not complied with in that the page on which the caveat was inserted was not the first page of the policy as was required.

The court therefore held that the insurer could not require the policyowner to accept a new exclusion as a condition of renewal and that the benefits were payable as the policyowner contended.

Medicare and Medicare Supplement Policies

Medicare is a government program that provides hospital, medical, and surgical benefits for most persons age 65 and over and for certain disabled persons who are younger. The Medicare program is made up of two parts: a basic plan covering hospital room and board and related expenses (Part A Medicare) and a supplementary medical plan providing for the cost of physicians' services (Part B Medicare).

Medicare covers, with various limitations, the costs of the following: inpatient hospital care, posthospital extended care in a skilled nursing facility, home health care, hospice care, physicians' services, some prescription drugs, x-rays and other diagnostic tests, blood, ambulance services, splints, casts, rental of hospital beds,

---

[8]272 So. 2d 37 (La. Ct. App. 1973).

prosthetic devices, braces, artificial body parts, and physical therapy, among other benefits.

Although Medicare provides substantial benefits, insureds often need to purchase additional health insurance called Medicare supplement or Medigap health insurance policies. Provided by private insurers, Medicare supplement policies are designed to bridge the significant gaps that often exist between the cost of medical treatment and the amount of the benefits that Medicare will pay.

Both federal and state laws regulate Medicare supplement insurance. A federal law known as the Baucus Amendment[9] encourages the states to adopt the Medicare supplement insurance standards contained in the NAIC Medicare Supplement Insurance Minimum Standards Model Act and Regulation. The NAIC adopted the model act and regulation to assist states in complying with the Baucus Amendment. Most states have enacted the model act and all states have adopted the model regulation.

The model act and regulation require specific definitions of certain Medicare supplement policy terms, such as the terms *accident, Medicare benefit period, convalescent nursing home, hospital, physician,* and *sickness*. The model act and regulation prohibit certain policy provisions. For example, Medicare supplement policies cannot contain benefits that duplicate benefits provided by Medicare. An outline of policy coverage must be given to applicants for Medicare supplement policies. The model regulation also governs the replacement of Medicare supplement policies.

The federal Omnibus Budget Reconciliation Act of 1990 (OBRA)[10] required the NAIC to revise the Medicare Supplement Insurance Minimum Standards Model Act and Regulation and the states to revise their regulation of Medicare supplement insurance accordingly. Under OBRA, insurers can market only 10 standard Medicare supplement policies, although a 1995 amendment to OBRA also allows managed care Medicare supplement policies, called Medicare select policies. The Medicare Supplement Insurance Regulation, as revised by the NAIC, spells out the benefits required in these 10 standard policies. A core set of basic benefits must be included in all Medicare supplement insurance policies.

Federal law also mandates an open enrollment period for Medicare supplement insurance policies. The open enrollment period applies to "an application for a policy or certificate that is submitted prior to or during the six month period beginning with the first day of the first month in which an individual is both 65 years of age or older and is enrolled for benefits under Medicare Part B." During the open enrollment period, a person cannot be denied a Medicare supplement insurance policy that is available for sale or be charged a higher premium because of health problems. Insurers can limit benefits for preexisting conditions for only six months after the Medicare supplement policy becomes effective.

Under OBRA, insurers have to maintain loss ratios of at least 65 percent on individual Medicare supplement policies and 75 percent on group Medicare supplement policies. That is, a policy form must be expected to return as aggregate benefits to those insured at least 65 percent of the aggregate amount of premiums the insurer earns on individual policies and 75 percent of the aggregate amount of premiums the insurer earns on group policies. If the expected loss ratio for a policy form is not maintained, the insurer must make a refund or give a credit against premiums due.

---

[9]42 U.S.C.A. § 1395ss (West 1992 & Supp.1996).
[10]Pub. L. No.101–508.

Long-Term Care Policies

Medicare does not pay for most long-term nursing home or other custodial care, nor do Medicare supplement policies. In recent years, the public has become increasingly aware of this gap in coverage and concerned about the exhaustion of savings and other resources that can result from long-term custodial care. Because the elderly population is growing at a rate three times faster than that of the general population, the market for long-term care policies is substantial.

In 1987, the NAIC adopted the Long-Term Care Insurance Model Act and in 1988 the Long-Term Care Insurance Model Regulation. Nearly all of the states have laws patterned on the model act, the model regulation, or both.

The purpose of the Long-Term Care Insurance Model Act and the model regulation is to promote the availability of long-term care insurance products, protect applicants for long-term care insurance from deceptive sales or enrollment practices, establish standards for long-term care insurance, facilitate public understanding of the product, and facilitate flexibility and innovation in the development of long-term care insurance.

The model act and regulation apply to both group and individual insurance policies providing at least 12 months of coverage in a setting other than an acute care unit of a hospital. Excluded from the definition of long-term care insurance are Medicare supplement insurance policies, hospital expense and indemnity policies, medical-surgical expense coverage, disability income coverage, accident-only policies, specified-disease-only policies, limited health benefit policies, and life insurance policy clauses providing lump sum accelerated death benefits, if such accelerated benefits are not conditioned on the receipt of long-term care.

Under laws patterned on the model act, an insurer can issue group long-term care policies to employers, labor organizations, or a combination of these under a trust; to professional, trade, occupational, or other associations; and to other groups in the discretion of the insurance commissioner.

Long-term care insurance policies cannot "be cancelled, nonrenewed, or otherwise terminated on grounds of the age or the deterioration of the mental or physical health of the insured" under the model act. Such policies cannot "provide coverage for skilled nursing care only or provide significantly more for skilled care in a facility than coverage for lower levels of care." The model act requires this latter provision because the majority of persons needing long-term care require primarily intermediate or custodial care, not skilled nursing care. This is the essence of long-term care insurance.

According to the model act, long-term care policies, other than group policies, cannot use a definition of the term *preexisting condition* that is more restrictive than the following:

> Preexisting condition means a condition for which medical advice or treatment was recommended by, or received from a provider of health care services, within six months preceding the effective date of coverage of an insured person.

Long-term care policies, again excepting group policies, cannot "exclude coverage for a loss or confinement which is the result of a preexisting condition unless such loss or confinement begins within six months following the effective date of coverage of an insured person." The insurance commissioner can extend the six-month limitation periods in both of the above provisions.

The Long-Term Care Insurance Model Regulation contains detailed requirements as to long-term care insurance application and policy contents, policy replacement, agent licensing, loss ratios, filing, and marketing.

By the end of 1994, over 3.8 million long-term care policies had been purchased from 121 insurers.[11] Individual long-term care policies predominated when long-term care insurance first became available, but group policies have grown rapidly in number.[12]

Group Health Insurance

Group health insurance policies cover the same losses that individual health insurance policies cover, that is, medical, hospital, and surgical expenses; loss of income due to disability; loss due to accidental death or dismemberment; dental and vision care expenses; long-term care expenses; and so forth. A group health insurance policy can cover dependents of the insured, as can an individual health insurance policy.

In many respects, the rules of law that govern individual health insurance policies also govern group health insurance policies. For example, health coverages mandated by state laws usually apply to both individual and group health insurance policies. However, some laws, such as those discussed below, are unique to group health insurance.

The Group Health Insurance Model Acts

In 1983, the NAIC adopted the Group Health Insurance Definition and Group Health Insurance Standard Provisions Model Act (the Group Health Insurance Model Act). The permissible groups under this model act are the same as those in the current Group Life Insurance Model Act. That is, under the Group Health Insurance Model Act, an insurer can issue group health insurance to an employer, a creditor, a labor union, a trust established by employers and unions, an association, a credit union, or other group which in the insurance commissioner's opinion is in the public interest. The Group Health Insurance Model Act provides for dependent group health insurance.

A number of the group health insurance policy provisions required by the Group Health Insurance Model Act are similar to the provisions required by the Group Life Insurance Model Act. However, a number of provisions in each model act are not found in the other, because the provision is appropriate to one type of insurance but not to the other. For example, the Group Health Insurance Model Act requires "[a] provision that the insurer shall have the right and opportunity to examine the person of the individual for whom claim is made when and so often as it may reasonably require during the pendency of claim under the policy." The Group Health Insurance Model Act also requires provisions relating to disability claims and to preexisting conditions. About one-fifth of the states have group health insurance laws patterned on this model act. Most other states have some laws governing group health insurance.

---

[11]HEALTH INSURANCE ASSOCIATION OF AMERICA, SOURCE BOOK OF HEALTH INSURANCE DATA 19 (1996).

[12]*More Employers Planning to Offer LTC Insurance,* NAT'L UNDERWRITER, LIFE & HEALTH/FIN. SERVICES EDITION, Nov. 9, 1992, at 24; Bertram N. Pike, *Group LTC: Is It Right for You?,* RESOURCE, Apr. 1992, at 14.

In 1976, the NAIC adopted the Group Health Insurance Mandatory Conversion Privilege Model Act. About one-third of the states have laws based on this model act. Another third have laws governing conversions by group health insureds to individual health insurance policies that are not patterned on the model act.

Laws patterned on the Group Health Insurance Mandatory Conversion Privilege Model Act require that group health insurance policies providing hospital, surgical, or major medical benefits on an expense-incurred basis (excluding specific-disease-only or accidental-injury-only policies) provide that a person who has been insured under the group policy for at least three months, and whose coverage has been terminated, shall be entitled to purchase an individual health insurance policy from the insurer without providing evidence of insurability. However, if the person's coverage was terminated because he failed to pay a required contribution to the premium, he will not be entitled to convert to an individual health insurance policy. Neither will he be entitled to convert if the group health insurance policy was terminated but replaced by a similar policy within 31 days, or if he is eligible for Medicare or other specified health coverages. He must make application for the converted policy and pay the initial premium within 31 days after termination of the group coverage.

The effective date of the individual health insurance policy must be the day following the termination of the group coverage. The individual policy must cover dependents who were covered under the group health insurance policy. The individual policy cannot exclude a preexisting condition not excluded by the group policy. However, the insurer is not required to issue an individual policy that offers benefits in excess of those provided under the group policy.

Coordination of Benefits Provisions

Overinsurance is a difficult problem in individual health insurance, and an even more difficult problem in group insurance. Overinsurance under individual health insurance policies can be controlled to a certain extent through underwriting requirements. If issuance of an individual health policy would result in the applicant's being overinsured, the insurer can disapprove the application entirely or offer the applicant a reduced amount of insurance. With group insurance, however, it is not practical to underwrite each insured person. Moreover, coverage under a group plan often results automatically from a person's employment. The same accident possibly could entitle the insured person to benefits from her employer's group health insurer, her spouse's employer's group health insurer, a workers' compensation insurer, an automobile liability insurance carrier, and an individual health insurer.

Insurers attempt to control overinsurance in group health insurance by including a coordination of benefits provision in their group health insurance policies. A coordination of benefits provision specifies that the insurer will not pay benefits for amounts reimbursed by other group insurers. If the insured has group health insurance under more than one master policy, the coordination of benefits provision limits total benefits to 100 percent of expenses covered and designates the order in which the group insurers are to pay benefits.

In 1985, the NAIC adopted completely revised Group Coordination of Benefits Regulations and Guidelines, taking into account such modern realities as two-worker families, dependent children of divorced insureds, and covered retirees who found full-time employment elsewhere and thus have double group health insurance coverage. An efficient, fair coordination of benefits system requires that all group policies reflect the same coordination of benefits rules. To make certain that all group policies do reflect the same rules, most of the states have adopted the Group Coordination of Benefits Model Regulation.

Continuation of Group Health Coverage

In 1986, Congress enacted the Consolidated Omnibus Budget Reconciliation Act (COBRA),[13] which requires that employers sponsoring group health plans offer continuation of coverage under the plan to employees and their spouses and dependent children who have lost coverage because of the occurrence of certain qualifying events. COBRA applies to both self-funded and insured health plans. Employers with fewer than 20 employees, the federal government, and churches are exempt from COBRA.

Under COBRA, employees and their spouses and dependent children have a right to continue group health coverage for 18 months if they lose coverage due to a reduction in the employee's work hours or to termination of employment for reasons other than the employee's gross misconduct. Special rules for disabled persons may extend this period to 29 months. Spouses and dependent children have a right to continue coverage for three years if they lose coverage because of the death of the employee, the divorce or legal separation of the employee and spouse, the employee's entitlement to Medicare, or a child's ceasing to qualify as a dependent. Bankruptcy of the employer that results in loss of coverage can also trigger the right to continuation coverage.

When an employer's group health plan becomes subject to COBRA, the employer must notify covered employees and their dependents of their rights. The employee or a family member must notify the plan administrator of a divorce, legal separation, or a child's ceasing to qualify as a dependent. The employer must notify the plan administrator of the employee's death, reduction in hours, termination of employment, or Medicare entitlement. The plan administrator must then notify the person losing coverage of his right to continue coverage.

If an eligible person chooses to continue coverage, he must pay for it unless the employer elects to pay for part or all of it. The coverage must be identical to the coverage the plan provides to similarly situated employees or family members. The person cannot be required to provide evidence of insurability in order to continue group health coverage.

Continuation coverage terminates if the employer no longer provides health coverage for any of its employees, if the premium is not paid on time, or if the covered person either becomes covered under another group health plan or becomes entitled to Medicare. However, if the person becomes covered under another group plan that excludes or limits benefits for any preexisting condition of the person, COBRA continuation coverage will not terminate. If continuation coverage rights terminate solely because of expiration of the time period, the covered person can convert to a conversion health plan maintained by the employer.

In 1996, Congress passed the Health Insurance Portability and Accountability Act.[14] This federal law allows an employee who moves from a job at which she was covered by an employer group health plan for at least 12 months to a job with another employer that has a group health plan, to receive immediate coverage under the new employer's health plan, including coverage for preexisting illnesses. If an em-

---

[13]Pub. L. No. 99–272, tit. X, 100 Stat. 82, 222 (1986).
[14]Pub. L. No. 104–191, 110 Stat. 1936 (1996).

ployee has been covered by a group health plan for at least 18 months and moves to a job without a group health plan, he will be guaranteed the right to purchase an individual health insurance policy with no waiting period for preexisting conditions.

Management of Health Care Costs

Rapidly rising health care costs in the 1980s and early 1990s spurred the development of numerous cost containment measures. Employers (which pay for a large percentage of the health care in the United States through employee welfare benefit plans), health insurers, and the federal and state governments have searched for ways to contain health care costs while assuring quality health care. Their creativity has resulted in a profusion of health care cost containment measures that are continuing to evolve. These measures, which are discussed below, include minimum premium plans; employer self-funded plans, with or without administrative services only contracts or insurer-provided stop-loss agreements; health maintenance organizations; point-of-service plans; preferred provider arrangements; utilization review; case management; and health care fraud prevention and detection.

Traditional fee-for-service indemnity health insurance policies have always included features aimed at controlling health care costs. Some of these features are described in the "Exclusions and Limitations" and the "Coordination of Benefits" sections. Other cost-controlling features include deductible and coinsurance amounts that the insured person must pay; limitation of benefit payments to health care providers' reasonable and customary charges; and exclusion of payment for most cosmetic surgery. Nevertheless, the rise in health care costs has resulted in a rapid expansion of the cost containment measures noted above.

Minimum Premium and Self-Funded Plans

Minimum premium plans were developed in the 1960s. Under a ***minimum premium plan,*** an employer purchases a group health insurance policy from an insurer, but claims are paid up to the annual expected claims liability with the employer's own funds. The insurer pays additional claims, if any, from its funds. The premium for a minimum premium policy is lower than it would be if the insurer paid all the claims from its own funds. Because the premium is lower, the premium tax is also lower than under traditional group health insurance policies.

The minimum premium plan was the forerunner of the self-funded plan, also called the self-insured plan. Under a fully ***self-funded plan,*** an employer pays for all claims out of its own funds. Because the employer pays no premiums, it avoids paying premium tax. In addition, a self-funded health plan does not have to include certain benefits that state laws mandate be included in health insurance policies. These benefits are discussed in the "Mandated Benefits" section.

Employers that adopt self-funded health plans often contract with insurers or with independent third-party administrators to administer the plan. Under an ***administrative services only contract,*** an insurer assumes no risk, pays no premium taxes, and retains no reserves. Rather, the insurer makes its expertise in benefit design, actuarial science, and claims handling available to the self-funded employer.

An employer with a self-funded plan also might enter into a stop-loss contract with an insurer. Under a typical ***stop-loss contract,*** an insurer provides a self-funded employer with protection against catastrophic occurrences. In the event that claims under the employer's self-funded health plan exceed a specified percentage over the expected level of claims, the insurer will reimburse the employer for such excess payments. The insurer does not owe or pay benefits directly to employees covered under the self-funded plan.

Managed Care

A growing number of people in the United States receive health care from some type of managed care organization. ***Managed care organizations*** include health maintenance organizations and preferred provider arrangements. Many employers offer employees a choice between coverage under a traditional fee-for-service indemnity group health insurance policy and one or more managed care plans. In addition, an ever-growing number of Medicare and Medicaid recipients are enrolled in managed care plans. Self-employed people and others who provide their own insurance often choose managed care plans because they are usually more affordable than traditional insurance.

Health insurers have been heavily involved in developing managed care. Large insurers own or have merged with managed care organizations. In addition, health insurers often employ managed care tools, including utilization review to make certain that people insured under traditional health insurance policies do not overutilize health care services, and case management to tailor benefits to the needs of insureds with severe health problems.

Health Maintenance Organizations.   Health maintenance organizations (HMOs) had their beginning over 50 years ago in California. HMOs now serve millions of subscribers nationwide. Federal law requires employers with more than 25 employees to offer an HMO as an alternative to group health insurance under conditions spelled out in the law.[15]

A ***health maintenance organization*** is a prepaid health care delivery system under which subscribers pay an enrollment fee in exchange for medical care. HMO subscribers are usually restricted to obtaining health care from HMO physicians. A subscriber who obtains health care from a non-HMO physician generally will have to pay for those services herself. Ordinarily, a subscriber selects from the HMO's roster a primary care physician who coordinates her health care. If this physician deems it medically necessary, he refers the subscriber to specialists. HMOs provide physical examinations and other preventive care that usually is not paid for by traditional health insurance. HMO subscribers pay smaller deductibles and coinsurance amounts than they would if they were covered under a traditional health insurance policy.

HMOs are usually organized in one of three forms: the staff model, the independent practice model, or the group model. A staff model HMO hires salaried physicians and often owns its own hospital and other health care facilities. An independent practice model HMO contracts with a physician association to provide medical care to HMO subscribers. The association, in turn, contracts with private physicians who agree to provide prepaid health care to HMO subscribers while continuing to provide health care to their non-HMO patients. A group model HMO provides prepaid health care through contracts with individual medical provider groups. The lines between the independent practice model and the group model are often blurred.

---

[15]HMO Act of 1973, Pub. L. No. 93–222, as amended.

In 1973, the NAIC adopted the Health Maintenance Organization Model Act. In an introductory comment to the model act, the NAIC noted:

> An HMO, by its very nature, may provide incentives toward lessening costs in delivering health care. It has a limited membership prepaying fixed sums of money. The providers are obligated to deliver a specified set of health care services. The fixed amount of income provides incentive to control expenses and costs. The HMO provides a mechanism to analyze costs, expenses and utilizations of services, and affords a means to implement measures to enhance efficiency.

The Health Maintenance Organization Model Act or related legislation has been enacted in all states. The purpose of the model act is to authorize the establishment and operation of HMOs, provide a legal framework for them, and provide for their regulation. Under state laws patterned on the model act, an HMO must have a certificate of authority from the state. HMOs must issue contracts to subscribers that meet the standards laid out in the model act. State laws patterned on the model act also require HMOs to have quality assurance programs, grievance procedures, and protections against insolvency. Other features of the model act relate to HMO investments, insurance department examinations of HMOs, and HMO producers.

Preferred Provider Arrangements.   A *preferred provider organization* (PPO) is an arrangement in which an insurer, employer, or other organization enters into contracts with physicians, hospitals, and other health care providers to provide health care services to a defined group of patients on a predetermined, discounted, fee-for-service basis. Covered persons or their employers pay a premium to the organization. The organization reimburses the providers directly for their services. A *preferred provider network* consists of a group of physicians or hospitals, or both, that offer a system of health care through contracts with insurers or self-funded employers. Preferred provider arrangements have many configurations.

The covered persons in a preferred provider arrangement are not obligated to use the preferred providers' services, but they are strongly encouraged to do so through financial incentives such as lower deductibles, higher benefit levels, and reduced co-insurance payments. Many health insurers offer preferred provider benefit plans to group policyholders as an alternative to traditional fee-for-service indemnity group health insurance.

The lines between HMOs and preferred provider arrangements sometimes are indistinct. For example, some HMOs have a point-of-service option. Subscribers to an HMO with a *point-of-service option* can use health care providers outside the HMO's provider network and the HMO will pay part of the charges, although a subscriber typically will have to pay 20 to 30 percent herself. An HMO with a point-of-service option is essentially the same as a PPO. Another type of managed care organization, the *exclusive provider organization* (EPO), is essentially the same as an HMO. A subscriber to an exclusive provider organization chooses a primary care physician from the EPO's roster. The primary care physician coordinates the subscriber's health care. The subscriber pays for health care he receives outside the EPO's network of health care providers.

Over one-half of the states have statutes or regulations governing some aspect of preferred provider arrangements, but only a few of these laws are patterned on the Preferred Provider Arrangements Model Act adopted by the NAIC in 1987.

Utilization Review.   Utilization review is an important managed care cost-cutting tool. *Utilization review* is the process of examining the health care given by physicians, hospitals, and other health care providers to detect and eliminate unnecessary or inappropriate care. Utilization review includes precertification of elective hospitalizations, mandatory second opinions on contemplated surgery, and prospective and concurrent review of a patient's length of stay in a hospital. Various organizations provide utilization review services to those who require them, but many managed care organizations have their own utilization review personnel.

Utilization review has sometimes caused strains between managed care organizations and physicians or patients and occasionally lawsuits have resulted. Denial of benefits for procedures that the managed care organization considers to be experimental, and hence not medically necessary, has been one reason for litigation.[16]

Case Management.   *Case management,* also called large case management, catastrophic case management, or individual case management, involves tailoring benefits to individual situations when the patient's illness or injury is severe. The types of cases for which case managers are most effective include high-risk pregnancies, preterm births, traumatic brain injuries, cancer, congenital defects, AIDS, and stroke.[17]

Unlike utilization review personnel who examine the medical necessity of the treatment provided, case managers look for alternatives for the patient. The case manager's goal is to help the patient get the most appropriate treatment. For example, under case management an insurer might agree with its insured and his physician to pay for home care, even though home care is not payable under the health insurance policy terms. This could be advantageous to all concerned, as the insured could return home rather than stay in the hospital, and the insurer would lower its costs. Case management is also an important adjunct of long-term disability claims services, offering rehabilitation services that might enable the insured to return to work. Case management is an extremely cost-effective aspect of managed care. A Health Insurance Association of America survey showed that insurers can realize a return of $30 for every dollar spent on case management.[18]

Most case managers are registered nurses. A few are social workers, mental health professionals, or physical or occupational therapists. Case managers are employed by insurers, hospitals, rehabilitation facilities, or independent case management companies. Case managers can take an examination to receive a Certified Case Manager designation.[19]

Detection and Prevention of Health Care Fraud

Fraudulent misrepresentations in life insurance applications have been discussed in earlier chapters. However, health care fraud is a much greater problem than life insurance fraud. In the United States, fraud committed against insurers (including casualty insurers) cost the public an estimated $79.9 billion dollars in 1994, a 17 percent increase from the prior year. Approximately 66 percent of insurance fraud is directed against health insurers.[20]

[16]Erik Larson, *The Soul of an HMO,* TIME, Jan. 22, 1996, at 44.

[17]*Case Management Saves, NWNL Finds,* RESOURCE, Aug. 1992, at 36.

[18]Matthew P. Schwartz, *Case Management Programs Show Solid Returns,* NAT'L UNDERWRITER, LIFE & HEALTH/FIN. SERVICES EDITION, Jan. 8, 1996, at 5.

[19]Matthew P. Schwartz, *Case Managers Tackle First Certification Exam,* NAT'L UNDERWRITER, LIFE & HEALTH/FIN. SERVICES EDITION, June 7, 1993, at 39.

[20]Steven Brostoff, *Growing Public Tolerance Increases Fraud Claims,* NAT'L UNDERWRITER, LIFE & HEALTH/FIN. SERVICES EDITION, June 3, 1996, at 31.

People engaged in health care fraud are always looking for new opportunities to defraud insurers, employers, and the federal and state governments. Methods in use include overbilling; billing for unnecessary health care services, or for services not rendered or supplies not used; falsifying medical records; and paying kickbacks.[21] Some health care fraud rings fake automobile accident injuries.[22] Others set up sham diagnostic laboratories, offer free or low-cost diagnostic tests, require health insurance information from the people tested, and then bill their insurers for tests that have not been made, sometimes for thousands of dollars. Sham diagnostic laboratories operate out of mobile units or store fronts and continually change their names, locations, and tax identification numbers so that they will not be apprehended.[23]

Physician ownership of diagnostic facilities such as laboratories and radiation centers has proved a major complication in the fight against health care fraud. One study showed that physician-owned facilities in Florida made twice as many tests per patient as facilities not owned by physicians.[24] Unfortunately, insurers do not always know about physician ownership, nor can they easily analyze the owner-physicians' referral patterns.

   Some physicians offer to waive the patient's portion of a bill for health care services so that the patient won't disclose fraud against the insurer. Some bill for services not provided or double bill for the same service.[25] Some ambulance services, nursing homes, clinics, and home health care organizations also have been involved in health care fraud schemes.[26] Although only a small percentage of health care providers engage in health care fraud, the impact of their fraudulent practices on health care costs is large.[27]

Because the time required to conduct fraud investigations is incompatible with legal requirements to pay claims promptly, insurers' efforts to combat health care fraud have been hampered.[28] In addition, antitrust and privacy laws limit the amount of information insurers are permitted to share, further hampering their efforts to detect and prevent health care fraud. Moreover, federal laws prohibiting mail fraud have proved inadequate to protect insurers against health care fraud.[29] Although combating health care fraud is a daunting task, Congress, state legislatures, law enforce-

---

[21]Brae Canlen, *Rx for Fraud,* CAL. LAWYER, Oct. 1996, at 18; Robert G. Knowles, *Deterrence Measures Urged for Health Care Fraud,* NAT'L UNDERWRITER, LIFE & HEALTH/FIN. SERVICES EDITION, Jan. 9, 1995, at 17; Matthew P. Schwartz, *Senate Report Details Rampant Health Care Fraud,* NAT'L UNDERWRITER, LIFE & HEALTH/FIN. SERVICES EDITION, Aug. 1, 1994, at 46.

[22]Mary Jane Fisher, *FBI Chief; Criminal Element Infiltrating Healthcare,* NAT'L UNDERWRITER, LIFE & HEALTH/FIN. SERVICES EDITION, Apr. 3, 1995, at 53.

[23]Brae Canlen, *Rx for Fraud,* CAL. LAWYER, Oct. 1996, at 18; Jennifer Landes, *Insurers Win RICO Suit against Russian Emigres,* NAT'L UNDERWRITER, LIFE & HEALTH/FIN. SERVICES EDITION, Mar. 5, 1990, at 53; David C. Jones, *Illinois Blues Helping FBI in "Lab Scam" Probe,* NAT'L UNDERWRITER, LIFE & HEALTH/FIN. SERVICES EDITION, Jan. 7, 1991, at 32; Harry S. Miller, *Rolling Lab Operations Costing Insurers Billions,* NAT'L UNDERWRITER, LIFE & HEALTH/FIN. SERVICES EDITION, Mar. 4, 1991, at 55.

[24]Steven Brostoff, *GAO: Health Care Fraud Runs up $70 Billion Tab,* NAT'L UNDERWRITER, LIFE & HEALTH/FIN. SERVICES EDITION, May 18, 1992, at 1.

[25]Robert G. Knowles, *Deterrence Measures Urged for Health Care Fraud,* NAT'L UNDERWRITER, LIFE & HEALTH/FIN. SERVICES EDITION, Jan. 9, 1995, at 17.

[26]*Supra,* note 22.

[27]Jim Connaly, *Rising Health Costs Blamed on Several Factors,* NAT'L UNDERWRITER, LIFE & HEALTH/FIN. SERVICES EDITION, Nov. 7, 1988, at 3.

[28]*Id.*

[29]Matthew P. Schwartz, *Senate Report Details Rampant Health Care Fraud,* NAT'L UNDERWRITER, LIFE & HEALTH/FIN. SERVICES EDITION, Aug. 1, 1994, at 46.

ment agencies, insurance commissioners, and insurers are combining their efforts in the fight.

The Federal Health Insurance Portability and Accountability Act.   One stated purpose of the Health Insurance Portability and Accountability Act of 1996[30] is "to combat waste, fraud and abuse in health insurance and health care delivery." This act bolsters the federal government's investigation and auditing powers and increases the likelihood that health care providers and others who commit health care fraud will be caught and punished. Under the act, people who make intentional misrepresentations on health insurance claim forms could be guilty of a federal crime punishable by up to five years in prison.

State Insurance Fraud Prevention Laws.   In response to the need for better state laws aimed at insurance fraud prevention, in 1995 the NAIC adopted the Insurance Fraud Prevention Model Act, which combined and expanded three insurance fraud prevention model laws adopted in the 1980s. Over two-thirds of the states revised their insurance fraud protection laws in the 1990s, but as of this writing none were patterned on the new model law.

Law Enforcement Involvement.   The Federal Bureau of Investigation increased its health care fraud task forces threefold between 1992 and 1996.[31] Health care fraud squads have been established in seven of the FBI's largest field offices.[32] The new federal Health Insurance Portability and Accountability Act will accelerate these increases. In addition, the act requires coordination of federal, state, and local law enforcement agencies to combat all forms of health care fraud. Such increased law enforcement involvement and coordination is essential in combating health care fraud.

Insurers' Fraud Control Units.   Most insurers now have fraud control units. Insurers' fraud control units have been cost-effective, saving nine dollars for every dollar spent to operate them.[33] Fraud control units require the participation of the insurers' claim examiners, in-house counsel, medical department personnel, utilization review personnel, and case managers.

Education About Insurance Fraud.   Insurance-industry-sponsored efforts to educate the public about insurance fraud are an important tool in the effort to decrease fraud. Many people think of insurance fraud as a "victimless" crime, but in 1994 the average family paid $966 in higher insurance costs because of insurance fraud.[34] The insurance industry is trying to educate the public to understand that the true victims of insurance fraud are American families.[35]

---

[30]Pub. L. 104–191, 110 Stat. 1936 (1996).

[31]Brae Canlen, *Rx for Fraud,* CAL. LAWYER, Oct. 1996, at 18.

[32]*Supra,* note 22.

[33]*Id.*

[34]Editorial comment, *Fight against Fraud Picks up,* NAT'L UNDERWRITER, LIFE & HEALTH/FIN. SERVICES EDITION, June 10, 1996, at 46.

[35]PR Newswire, *Wisconsin State Attorney General and U.S. Attorney's Office Join Blue Cross on the Internet in Fighting Insurance Fraud,* June 10, 1996; Walter Bussewitz, *A National Assault on Health Care Fraud,* NAT'L UNDERWRITER, LIFE & HEALTH/FIN. SERVICES EDITION, Apr. 4, 1988, at 31; Walter Bussewitz, *Active Year for Health Fraud Association,* NAT'L UNDERWRITER, LIFE & HEALTH/FIN. SERVICES EDITION, Feb. 6, 1989, at 13; *supra,* note 25.

Insurer's employees also need to be informed about insurance fraud if they are to combat it effectively. One of the purposes of the National Health Care Anti-Fraud Association, founded by health insurers and located in Washington, DC, is the education of insurers' employees about health care fraud.[36]

---

[36]Walter Bussewitz, *Active Year for Health Fraud Association,* NAT'L UNDERWRITER, LIFE & HEALTH/FIN. SERVICES EDITION, Feb. 6, 1989, at 13.

Summary

Health insurance covers losses that the insured suffers as a result of illness or accident. Some health insurance policies cover hospital, medical, and surgical expenses. Some replace lost income if the insured is disabled and unable to work. Others provide accidental death or dismemberment benefits, travel accident insurance, vision or dental care benefits, or long-term care benefits. Group health insurance policies cover more people than individual health insurance policies, but individual health insurance policies are more heavily regulated.

Individual health insurance policies must conform to the provisions of state laws that in nearly all states are patterned on the NAIC Uniform Individual Accident and Sickness Policy Provision Law. The uniform law provides that an individual health insurance policy is a policy covering one person, or covering an applicant and certain of her family members and dependents.

The individual health insurance policy provisions required by the uniform law include an entire contract provision, a provision for a time limit on certain defenses, a grace period provision, a reinstatement provision, several claims provisions, a provision limiting the time in which the claimant can bring legal actions, and a change of beneficiary provision. Most of these provisions differ somewhat from life insurance policy provisions.

The time limit on certain defenses provision found in individual health insurance policies is similar to the incontestable clause in a life insurance policy, except that the provision in a health insurance policy excludes fraud. In addition, the health insurance policy provision deals with preexisting conditions. Under an individual health insurance policy, a preexisting condition cannot be the basis for reduction or denial of a claim after the policy has been in force for three years unless the policy excludes the condition by name.

Unlike the grace period in life insurance policies, which is usually 31 days, the grace period in an individual health insurance policy can be as short as 7 days in weekly premium policies or 10 days in monthly premium policies. The reinstatement provision in an individual health insurance policy differs from that in an individual life insurance policy in that the health insurer can add new restrictive conditions to the reinstated policy.

A health insurer can include certain optional provisions in an individual health insurance policy. Some of these optional provisions are the change of occupation provision, the misstatement of age provision, the overinsurance provisions, the illegal occupation provision, and the intoxicants and narcotics provision.

Probably the most important of these optional provisions are the overinsurance provisions. Overinsurance occurs when an insured has more than one source of coverage and stands to make a profit if he becomes ill or has an accident. Overinsurance is a serious problem that the insurance industry has not yet solved.

The definitions of terms in health insurance policies are of crucial importance. Health insurance policies often define the terms *injury, sickness, hospital,* and *physician.* Some states have regulations governing the way in which health insurance policies define these terms. The terms *injury* or *sickness* are usually defined to include only injuries that occurred or sicknesses that first manifest themselves after the effective date of the policy.

Many states have laws mandating that specified benefits be included in both individual and group health insurance policies. These benefits include coverage of newborn and handicapped children of the insured, and payment for alcoholism and drug addiction treatment, maternity expenses, outpatient treatment, home health care, and treatment of mental illness. In addition, many states have laws mandating that insurers honor claims for covered treatment provided by chiropractors, podiatrists, optometrists, psychologists, or other health professionals.

Individual health insurance policies have four basic types of provisions governing the insured's right to continue the policy. Some policies contain clauses making the policy freely cancellable by the insurer at any time. Insurance departments discourage the use of these clauses. Other individual health insurance policies have clauses that allow the insurer to refuse to renew the policy. Still other policies are noncancellable or guaranteed renewable. The insurer can change the premium rate of a policy that is guaranteed renewable but not of a policy that is noncancellable. Some states have laws mandating that cancellation and renewal provisions appear on the face page of the policy.

Medicare supplement policies provide coverage for hospital and medical expenses that Medicare does not cover. Such policies must conform to the standards contained in the NAIC Medicare Supplement Insurance Minimum Standards Model Act and Regulation. Medicare does not cover long-term care in a nursing home or other custodial care. Long-term care insurance policies can fill this gap in coverage. Nearly all of the states have laws patterned on the NAIC Long-Term Care Insurance Model Act, the Long-Term Care Insurance Model Regulation, or both.

Group health insurance policies cover the same losses that individual health insurance policies cover, and many rules of individual health insurance apply to group poli-cies as well. Overinsurance is a problem for group health insurers, just as it is for individual health insurers. Coordination of benefits clauses in group health insurance policies help to reduce overinsurance.

COBRA requires continuation of health insurance benefits under many employers' group health plans if employees, their spouses, or dependent children lose coverage because of the occurrence of certain qualifying events. The person continuing coverage must pay for the coverage, which ordinarily will last 18 months or three years, depending on the reason for loss of coverage.

Rapidly rising health care costs have spurred the development of numerous cost containment measures, including minimum premium plans, employer self-funded plans, administrative services only agreements, stop-loss contracts, health maintenance organizations, preferred provider arrangements, utilization review, case management, and health care fraud detection and prevention.

ILLUSTRATIVE CASE

In the following case, the court discusses preexisting condition exclusions in health insurance policies.

MUTUAL HOSPITAL INSURANCE, INC.,
Appellant (Defendant Below),
v.
MORRIS L. KLAPPER and MARIETTA KLAPPER,
Appellees (Plaintiff Below)[37]
Court of Appeals of Indiana,
Second District.

BUCHANAN, Presiding Judge.

CASE SUMMARY—This is an appeal from a summary judgment[38] entered in favor of plaintiffs-appellees, Morris L. and Marietta Klapper (Klapper), based on their claim for Blue Cross benefits for a "preexisting condition" excluded by a health insurance policy issued by defendant-appellant, Mutual Hospital Insurance, Inc. (Blue Cross). We reverse.

FACTS—The facts most favorable to Klapper (appellee) and in support of the judgment are:

On December 15, 1969, a family health insurance policy issued by Blue Cross to Klapper became effective. It contained the following provision:

"ARTICLE XII—BLUE CROSS BENEFITS

* * * * *

E. Pre-Existing Conditions.
    For any illness, injury or *condition which existed* prior to the effective date of the membership of the patient, Blue Cross will pay for hospital service only after a lapse of two hundred and seventy (270) consecutive days from the effective date of such membership." (Emphasis supplied.)
    (Hereinafter referred to as the "exclusionary clause.")

On January 13, 1970, as the result of a routine eye examination, Klapper's four-year-old daughter (Laurel) was discovered to have contracted an eye condition known as bilateral optic atrophy. The eye doctor estimated that the medical origin of this disease was some time between November of 1967 and July of 1969. How-

---

[37]288 N.E.2d 279 (1972).

[38]If no issue of fact exists, the trial judge will grant a party's motion for a summary judgment and decide the issues of law. In this case, the appeals court ruled that the trial court erred in granting a summary judgment to the insureds because an issue of fact did exist.

ever, neither the parents nor Laurel were aware of this disease or condition prior to January 13, 1970. There had been no previous symptomatic manifestations of the disease nor were there any complaints of eye discomfort by Laurel.

Laurel underwent surgery for this condition, being hospitalized from January 21, 1970 through February 11, 1970. Blue Cross denied payment of medical and surgical bills amounting to $892.05 on the ground that the disease "existed" prior to the effective date of the policy (December 15, 1969) and was therefore excluded by the exclusionary clause.

After Klapper filed suit to enforce the denied claim, both parties filed Motions for Summary Judgment agreeing that only a question of law existed. Klapper's Motion was granted and Blue Cross appeals.

ISSUES

ISSUE ONE—Does an illness "exist" within the meaning of a health insurance policy clause excluding pre-existing conditions, at such time as it becomes known to the insured or is capable of being diagnosed by a physician, or does an illness "exist" at the inception of its medical origin, regardless of when it becomes known to the insured or capable of diagnosis?

ISSUE TWO—Was a material issue of fact before the trial court as to whether Laurel's eye condition was capable of being diagnosed by a physician?

As to ISSUE ONE, Blue Cross contends that the word "existed" contained in the exclusionary clause must be given its usual and ordinary meaning. If a disease is capable of being diagnosed, even though it has not yet manifested itself in the form of symptoms, it is in existence for purposes of health insurance coverage.

Klapper's position is that an illness is in existence when it first manifests itself or becomes known to the victim, and as the eye condition was not diagnosed until January 13, 1970, after the effective date of the insurance policy, his claim is valid.

As to ISSUE TWO, the parties make no argument. We deem it necessary to raise ISSUE TWO because on the basis of the record there was no consideration by the trial court or the parties of the material issue of fact as to whether Laurel's condition was capable of being diagnosed by a physician prior to the effective date of the policy (December 15, 1969).

DECISION

ISSUE ONE—An illness "exists" within the meaning of a health insurance policy excluding pre-existing conditions at such time as the illness becomes known to the insured or is capable of being diagnosed by a physician.

The medical origin of an illness does not determine its existence.

With no pertinent Indiana authority to guide us, we seek succor from other jurisdictions. While there appear to be some cases to the contrary, most states adhere to the rule found in Southards v. Central Plains Insurance Co., (1968) 201 Kan. 499, 441 P.2d 808:

> " 'It is generally recognized that provisions in a health or hospital insurance policy requiring that the illness or disease from which the assured suffers originate a specified time after the date of the policy to be within the policy coverage are strictly construed against the insurer, and *the illness, disease, or disability will ordinarily be deemed to have its inception when it first becomes manifest or active or when there is a distinct symptom or condition from which one learned in medicine can with reasonable accuracy diagnose the disease.*' " (Emphasis supplied.)

Similarly, in Royal Family Ins. Co. v. Grimes, (1964) 42 Ala. App. 481, 168 So.2d 262, it was held that:

> "It is a well established rule of law that the 'word "originates," as appears in the exclusionary provision of the policy, refers ordinarily to the time the sickness or disease is manifested, *although the medical cause existed prior to this time.*' " (Emphasis supplied.)

The mere presence of latent germs or seeds of illness in the body prior to the issuance of a policy of health insurance does not alone preclude recovery. There must be something beyond the mere medical origin of the illness. Dowdall v. Commercial Travelers Mutual Acc. Ass'n, *supra*; Wilkins v. Grays Harbor Community Hospital, *supra*; Royal Family Ins. Co. v. Grimes, *supra*.

From these cases we deduce the desirable rule for adoption in Indiana to be that for a disease or illness or condition to "exist" in a health insurance policy sense it must have become manifest or active or there must be some distinct symptom or condition from which a physician can make an accurate diagnosis of the disease.

Most cases have adopted the majority rule apparently on the basis that while insurance companies need protection from unscrupulous applicants who would fraudulently attempt to gain coverage for an illness of which they are already aware, such protection need not go so far as to consider a disease to exist at the time of its medical inception. Furthermore, to consider a disease to exist at a time when the victim is blissfully unaware of the medical "seeds" visited upon his body, is to set a trap for the unwary purchaser of health insurance policies.

The majority rule recognizing a disease only to be in existence when it first manifests itself or is known to the victim or is capable of being diagnosed by a physician serves the dual purpose of protecting insurers from fraudulent applicants seeking coverage for known diseases while protecting innocent premium-paying insureds from being deprived of benefits for pre-existing conditions of which they have no knowledge. . . .

ISSUE TWO—It is our opinion that Summary Judgment was improper because there was a material issue of fact as to whether Laurel's eye condition was capable of being diagnosed by a physician prior to the effective date of the policy.

In ruling on a motion for summary judgment, the trial court may not determine questions of fact; rather, the trial court's inquiry is limited to a sole determination of whether or not a factual controversy exists. The mere fact that both parties have filed motions for summary judgment does not alone establish the absence of a material issue of fact. . . . Moreover, the burden of proof is on the party seeking summary judgment to establish the nonexistence of a material issue of fact.

When a trial court is considering a motion for summary judgment, the contents of the pleadings, depositions, answers to interrogatories, admissions and affidavits must be liberally construed in favor of the party against whom the motion for summary judgment is directed. . . . As a consequence, any doubt as to the existence of a material issue of fact should be resolved in favor of the party against whom the motion for summary judgment is directed. . . .

A review of the Affidavits in support of and in opposition to Klapper's Motion for Summary Judgment discloses only these assertions concerning Laurel's condition: that Laurel had not complained of any eye trouble or that she had any previous diseases of the eye prior to the effective date of the policy; that there were no symptomatic conditions which would have prompted Klapper to take Laurel to an eye doctor for an eye examination; and that this disease was discovered only upon a routine eye examination a few weeks after the effective date of the policy.

The Affidavits further indicate that the eye doctor and the physician who performed the surgery informed the Klappers that Laurel's condition probably had its medical onset at some time between November of 1967 and July of 1969. However, this appears to be nothing more than an estimate by the physician of the date of the *medical origin* of this disease. If the physician was correct that Laurel's condition merely had its medical origin prior to the effective date of the policy, then the disease was not in existence pursuant to the majority rule adopted herein.

However, the majority rule states an alternative element in determining the existence of a disease, *i.e.,* whether or not the disease was *capable* of being diagnosed by a physician prior to the policy's effective date. There is no statement in the Affidavits or elsewhere in the record to indicate that this factual question was before the trial court.

Klapper, in seeking Summary Judgment, had the burden of proving the nonexistence of all material issues of fact as a prerequisite to Summary Judgment. . . . This he failed to do. The cases espousing the rule of liability as to when a disease comes into existence also hold that if an insurer seeks to avoid liability on the ground that the disease complained of falls within an exclusionary clause, the burden is on the insurer to establish the facts which bring the case within the specified exception.

We interpret these cases as meaning that this principle comes into operation subsequent to a determination as to the propriety of Summary Judgment, *i.e.,* as a defense at trial after a finding by the trial court that a material issue of fact exists in this respect. This case should, therefore, be reversed and remanded to the trial court to determine if a material issue of fact exists as to whether Laurel's eye condition was capable of being diagnosed by a physician prior to the effective date of the policy.

Summary Judgment is therefore reversed and remanded to the trial court for further proceedings not inconsistent with this opinion.

SULLIVAN and WHITE, JJ., concur.

Questions for Review

1. List five provisions that the NAIC Uniform Individual Accident and Sickness Policy Provision Law requires to be included in an individual health insurance policy.

2. Briefly summarize the entire contract policy provision in an individual health insurance policy.

3. List two ways in which the grace period provision in individual health insurance policies can differ from the grace period provision in individual life insurance policies.

4. If an individual health insurance policy is reinstated effective as of September 5, and the insured becomes ill on September 10, will benefits be payable for loss incurred as the result of such illness? Why or why not?

5. What is the purpose of the time limit on certain defenses provision?

6. List four optional provisions that can be included in an individual health insurance contract.

7. For what reasons do insurers endeavor to discourage overinsurance?

8. List and briefly summarize two policy provisions that an insurer can include in an individual health insurance policy for the purpose of reducing the benefits payable if the insured has two or more policies providing the same type of benefits.

9. Define and differentiate between a cancellable health insurance policy and an optionally renewable health insurance policy. What is the difference between a noncancellable health insurance policy and a guaranteed renewable health insurance policy?

10. What is a preexisting condition? Under what circumstances does the NAIC Uniform Individual Accident and Sickness Policy Provision Law require that preexisting conditions be covered?

11. Under what circumstances will an employee, the employee's spouse, or dependent children have a right to continuation of group health coverage under COBRA? Who pays for such continuation coverage?

12. Describe the following:
    a. Employer self-funded plans.
    b. Health maintenance organizations.
    c. Preferred provider arrangements.
    d. Utilization review.
    e. Case management.

13. Name two ways in which insurers are fighting health care fraud.

21 ANNUITY CONTRACTS

An ***annuity contract*** is an agreement that one person or organization will make periodic payments to another at regular intervals for a specified period of time, such as for a specified number of years or for the life of the recipient. The recipient is called the ***annuitant***. The term ***annuity*** means both the periodic payments and the annuity contract itself.[1]

A natural person may sell an annuity contract to another person. Such annuity contracts are called ***private annuities***. However, this book deals only with annuity contracts that life insurers issue.

Insurers' sales of annuity contracts have increased significantly in recent years, due in large part to the aging of the population. The median age of the typical life insurance buyer is 32, whereas the median age of the typical annuity buyer is 48.[2] People become increasingly concerned about saving for retirement as they grow older. Individual deferred annuities are good vehicles for retirement saving. Individual deferred variable annuities have the additional advantage that they can help protect the contract holder from the ravages of inflation.

The growth of the small group annuity market has been spurred by the increase in the number of employers installing 401(k) plans. Group annuities are often used to fund 401(k) plans.[3] A ***401(k) plan*** is a profit-sharing or stock bonus plan under which an employee can choose to receive an amount in the form of currently taxable compensation—that is, cash that will be currently taxed as income—or defer receipt of this amount so that it will be taxed at a future time. Section 401(k) of the federal Internal Revenue Code permits this tax deferral. Another name for a 401(k) plan is a cash or deferred arrangement (CODA).

Banks and financial planners, as well as traditional insurance sales forces, sell annuity contracts. Bank sales of annuity contracts increased after the U.S. Supreme Court decided *Nationsbank of North Carolina v. Variable Annuity Life Insurance Co.*[4] in 1995 and *Barnett Bank v. Nelson*[5] in 1996. In *Nationsbank,* the Supreme Court held that national banks may serve as agents in the sale of both variable and fixed annuity contracts. In *Barnett Bank,* the Court held that a federal statute permitting national banks to sell insurance in small towns preempted a Florida statute prohibiting banks from selling most types of insurance.

In this chapter, the rights of annuitants and beneficiaries and the various types of annuity contracts will be described. State and federal statutes, regulations, and case law governing annuity contracts also will be discussed.

The Contract Holder, Annuitant, and Beneficiary

Ordinarily, a person enters into an individual annuity contract so that she can receive guaranteed payments commencing at a specified date, such as the date of her retirement, and continuing for her lifetime. Such a person is both the annuity contract

---

[1]This is the usual definition of the term *annuity*. However, a statute may define the term somewhat differently, depending on the context.

[2]Linda Koko, *Put Accent on Retirement Savings in Annuities,* Nat'l Underwriter, Life & Health/Fin. Services Edition, Jan. 30, 1995, at 7; *An Older Market,* Fin. Services Wk., July 22, 1991, at 1.

[3]Cynthia Crosson, *Companies Thrive in Small Group Annuity Market,* Nat'l Underwriter, Life & Health/Fin. Services Edition, Nov. 9, 1992, at 7.

[4]115 S. Ct. 810.

[5]116 S. Ct. 1103.

holder and the annuitant, as is the case with most annuity contracts. However, when an annuity contract holder enters into an annuity contract to benefit another person, the other person is the annuitant. The insurer makes the periodic payments to the annuitant, regardless of who the contract holder may be.

Contractual Capacity

The parties to an annuity contract, like the parties to any other contract, must have contractual capacity. With annuity contracts, the question of contractual capacity usually involves the mental capacity of the contract holder. However, in the great majority of the cases in which the mental capacity of the contract holder has been an issue, the courts have held that the contract holder did have the requisite mental capacity. In one case, the court stated that age, infirmity, illiteracy, or inexperience in business do not make a person incompetent to enter into an annuity contract.[6]

The Insurer-Annuitant Relationship

The insurer and annuitant usually have a debtor-creditor relationship, not a trustee-trust beneficiary relationship. The relationship between insurer and annuitant corresponds to the debtor-creditor relationship between an insurer and the beneficiary of a matured life insurance policy.[7]

An annuity contract, like a life insurance policy, is a chose in action. The annuitant usually can maintain a lawsuit against the insurer to enforce annuity payments.

An annuitant ordinarily can assign his rights under the annuity contract.[8] Thus, an annuitant can give or sell to another person the right to receive the periodic payments.

The Beneficiary

The beneficiary of an annuity contract is the person who will receive the annuity contract value if the annuitant dies during the accumulation period of a deferred annuity. Deferred annuities are described in the section below. If the annuitant dies during the income period and payments are to be continued after his death during a period certain, the beneficiary will receive these payments. As is the case with a life insurance contract, the contract holder of an individual annuity can change the beneficiary if this right is reserved in the contract.

Types of Annuity Contracts

Annuity contracts can differ from one another in many ways. This section explores some of these important differences.

Immediate and Deferred Annuity Contracts

Under an ***immediate annuity contract,*** the insurer begins making the periodic payments to the annuitant one period after the contract holder pays the insurer the pur-

---

[6]Stockett v. Penn Mut. Life Ins. Co., 106 A. 2d 741 (R.I. 1954).

[7]Hughes v. Sun Life Assur. Co., 159 F.2d 110 (7th Cir. 1947); Chatham Co. Hosp. Auth. v. John Hancock Mut. Life Ins. Co., 325 F. Supp. 614 (S.D. Ga. 1971).

[8]3A C.J.S. *Annuities* § 17 (1973).

chase price for the annuity contract. The first of the periodic payments might fall due 1 month, 3 months, 6 months, or 12 months after payment of the purchase price, as requested by the contract holder.

Deferred annuity contracts are usually purchased to supplement retirement income. Under some deferred annuity contracts, the insurer begins making periodic payments a specified number of years after the contract holder pays a single premium or commences paying installment premiums. Under other deferred annuity contracts, the insurer begins making periodic payments when the annuitant reaches a specified age—age 65, for example.

The period during which premium payments are being made and accumulated at interest under a deferred annuity contract is called the **accumulation period.** The period during which the insurer is making payments to the annuitant is called the **income period** or the *payout period.*

Single Premium and Installment Premium Annuity Contracts

Under a **single premium annuity contract,** the contract holder pays one premium. Under an **installment premium annuity contract,** the contract holder pays a series of premiums. Most installment premium annuity contracts allow the contract holder to pay whenever and in whatever amount she wishes, within specified limits. These annuity contracts are called **flexible premium contracts**. Some installment premium annuity contracts specify the amount and time of the premium payments. These annuity contracts are called **scheduled premium contracts**.

Straight Life, Joint and Survivor, and Life with Period Certain Annuity Contracts

An annuity contract under which the insurer makes periodic payments only during the annuitant's lifetime is a **straight life annuity contract.** A **joint and survivor annuity contract** provides periodic payments during two annuitants' lifetimes and continues the payments, in whole or in part, after one annuitant's death to the surviving annuitant for the surviving annuitant's lifetime. Joint annuitants are usually spouses.

An **annuity for life with period certain** is an annuity payable for at least a specified number of years and thereafter for as long as the annuitant lives. If the annuitant dies before the specified number of years have elapsed, the insurer makes the remaining payments to a named beneficiary. For example, a person might purchase an annuity for life with a period certain of 10 years. If the annuitant died two years after the income period had begun, the insurer would make the periodic payments to the named beneficiary for eight years. On the other hand, if the annuitant died 12 years after the income period had begun, the named beneficiary would receive nothing.

An **income for life with refund annuity** is similar to an annuity for life with period certain, except that an income for life with refund annuity guarantees that the insurer will pay out at least the purchase price of the annuity. If the annuitant does not live long enough to collect the purchase price as periodic payments, the insurer will pay the remainder of the purchase price to a named beneficiary.

Fixed and Variable Annuity Contracts

During the accumulation period of a **deferred fixed annuity contract,** the premiums, minus service charges, are accumulated at rates of interest set by the insurer. The insurer determines the amount of each periodic payment that the insurer will make to the annuitant at the time these periodic payments begin. Thus, the insurer guarantees the amount of each payment. The annuitant might receive more than the guaranteed amount through dividends, but will never receive less than the guaranteed amount.

The value of the accumulated premiums paid for a ***variable annuity*** depends on the investment results of a separate account. A ***separate account*** is a pool of investments that an insurer establishes and maintains, without consideration of the investment results of the insurer's other assets. The insurer does not guarantee the amount of each periodic payment that it will make to the annuitant. Rather, the amount of the payment depends on the amount in the separate account.

Some annuity contracts are a combination of fixed and variable. That is, the insurer puts part of the premium in a fixed annuity and part in a variable annuity.

Individual and Group Annuity Contracts

An ***individual annuity contract*** is a contract between an individual purchaser and an insurer in which the insurer agrees to make periodic payments to the purchaser, or to another person, in exchange for a premium or premiums. A ***group annuity contract*** provides periodic payments, usually at retirement, to each person in a group of covered persons. The insurer ordinarily issues a group annuity master contract to an employer to fund a pension or profit-sharing plan for a group of employees. The insurer issues a certificate to each member of the group as evidence of coverage.

Qualified and Nonqualified Annuity Contracts

A ***qualified annuity contract*** is an annuity contract used to fund or distribute, or both fund and distribute, a tax-qualified pension or profit-sharing plan.

Federal tax laws permit an employer to deduct contributions to a tax-qualified plan. Investment earnings on tax-qualified plan assets are not currently taxable. To be tax-qualified, a pension or profit-sharing plan must satisfy complex requirements spelled out in the Employee Retirement Income Security Act and the Internal Revenue Code.

Nonqualified annuity contracts are those that are not purchased for tax-qualified plan purposes. A nonqualified annuity contract is purchased with after-tax dollars, but the investment earnings, called the inside buildup, are not currently taxable if the purchaser is a natural person, or a trust (or other entity) that is an agent for a natural person.[9] Any ownership of an annuity by other than a natural person must be carefully planned to avoid adverse tax consequences because the Internal Revenue Service (IRS) has not as yet issued regulations that would answer certain questions such ownership raises.[10]

Other Features of Annuity Contracts

Features of annuity contracts not previously discussed include guaranteed and current interest rates, charges, death benefits, surrender benefits, and waiver of premium benefits. These features are discussed in this section.

---

[9]I.R.C. § 1572(u).

[10]Norse N. Blazzard & Judith A. Hasenauer, *Using Trusts with Annuities Spurs Questions,* NAT'L UNDERWRITER, LIFE & HEALTH/FIN. SERVICES EDITION, July 15, 1996, at 14; Darlene Chandler, J.D., *Annuity Sales and the "Nonnatural Person" Rule,* NAT'L UNDERWRITER, LIFE & HEALTH/FIN. SERVICES EDITION, July 12, 1993, at 20.

Guaranteed and Current Interest Rates

The interest rate the insurer uses to determine annuity contract values during the accumulation period of a deferred fixed annuity can never be lower than the guaranteed interest rate. The interest rate will usually be a higher rate called the current interest rate. The insurer sets the current interest rate for its annuities and changes that rate from time to time. The method used to set the current interest rate differs from insurer to insurer.

Charges

Insurers may make several types of annuity contract charges. Different insurers sometimes call these charges by different names.

Annuity contract charges fall into four categories: percentage of premium charges, contract fees, transaction fees, and surrender charges. An annuity contract may contain only one or a combination of these charges.

A *percentage of premium charge* is a specified percentage of the premium that the insurer deducts from each premium paid. The insurer may lower the percentage after total premiums paid have reached a certain amount or after the deferred annuity contract has been in force for a specified period.

A *contract fee* is a flat dollar amount that the insurer charges either annually or once at the time the annuity contract is issued. A *transaction fee* is a flat dollar amount that the insurer charges per premium payment.

Finally, the insurer might make a *surrender charge* when an annuity contract holder surrenders his annuity contract. The surrender charge is often a percentage of the premiums paid or of the contract value. Under the terms of some annuity contracts, the insurer reduces or eliminates the surrender charge after the contract has been in force for a specified period.

Death Benefits

Most individual deferred annuity contracts provide that if the annuitant dies before periodic payments begin, the insurer will pay the value of the annuity contract to a named beneficiary as a death benefit. Some fixed annuity contracts provide that the amount paid to the beneficiary will equal the total premiums paid if that amount is greater than the contract value.

Surrender Benefits

An annuity contract terminates if the contract holder surrenders it. Under the terms of most individual deferred annuity contracts, the contract holder is permitted to surrender the contract before the insurer begins making the periodic payments, that is, during the accumulation period. The surrender benefit the contract holder receives at the time the contract is surrendered is equal to the contract value, minus any surrender charge. Many annuity contracts also allow withdrawal of a portion of the contract value, under specified conditions and sometimes with a surrender charge.

Waiver of Premium Benefits

Some insurers allow waiver of premium benefits, similar to life insurance waiver of premium benefits, to be added to their annuity contracts. Thus, if the annuity contract has a waiver of premium benefit and the annuity contract holder becomes totally disabled, the payment of annuity premiums will be waived. The insurer makes an additional charge for the waiver of premium benefit.

Adequacy of Consideration

People buy annuity contracts providing lifetime payments to protect themselves against the risk of outliving their assets. When an insurer issues an annuity contract providing payments for the life of the annuitant, it is assuming the risk that the annuitant might live beyond his life expectancy. In fact, an insurer often pays an annuitant who lives into his 80s or 90s a good deal more in benefit payments than the annuitant paid to the insurer in premiums. This "overpayment" is balanced by the insurer's smaller payouts to annuitants who do not reach their life expectancies.

Sometimes the heirs or the personal representative of an annuitant who did not reach his life expectancy files a suit claiming that the consideration the insurer paid was inadequate and asking the court to rescind the annuity contract so that the insurer will have to return the premiums it received. In the absence of fraud or misrepresentation by the insurer, the courts ordinarily do not grant rescission in such cases.

For example, in one case an insurer issued an annuity contract covering an annuitant with seriously impaired health. The insurer was unaware of the annuitant's health impairment. The annuitant died before attaining the life expectancy on which her premiums were based. The court held that the consideration given by the insurer was adequate and that the annuity contract was valid. Thus, the insurer did not have to return the premiums.[11]

Another court stated the following:

> If insurance companies never profited from an annuity contract, how could it [*sic*] afford to pay those whose lives exceeded the averages upon which their rates were based? The mere fact that an annuitant dies before reaching her expectancy can no more void the annuity than the opposite situation where the annuitant lives beyond the expectancy. Both are within the contemplation of the parties.[12]

Moreover, courts have held that an insurer has no duty to inquire into the health of a proposed annuitant, unless it has knowledge that the annuitant's health is impaired.[13]

Apportionment of Annuities

Annuities are sums payable at specified times. Because nothing is due until the date of payment arrives, the majority of courts that have considered the question of apportionment of annuities have ruled that a pro rata payment will not be due when the annuitant dies, unless a statute or the annuity contract states otherwise.[14]

[11]Rishel v. Pacific Mut. Life Ins. Co., 78 F.2d 881 (10th Cir. 1935).

[12]Moses v. Manufacturers Life Ins. Co., 298 F. Supp. 321 (D.S.C. 1968), *aff'd*, 407 F.2d 1142 (4th Cir. 1969), *cert. denied*, 396 U.S. 827 (1969). See also, Fox v. Northwestern Mut. Life Ins. Co., 136 F. Supp. 766 (D. Idaho 1956); Aldrich v. Travelers Ins. Co., 56 N.E. 2d 888 (Mass. 1944).

[13]Rishel v. Pacific Mut. Life Ins. Co., 78 F.2d 881 (10th Cir. 1935); Woodworth v. Prudential Ins. Co., 15 N.Y.S. 2d 541 (N.Y. App. Div. 1939), *aff'd*, 26 N.E. 2d 820 (N.Y. 1940).

[14]Baird v. Mutual Life Ins. Co., 20 N. E. 2d 141 (Ill. App. Ct. 1939).

For example, suppose that in 1978 James Fong bought an immediate straight life annuity contract without a period certain. The insurer has made annual payments to Fong on each December 31, the due date, since the annuity contract was purchased. Fong received a payment on December 31, 1996, and died on September 20, 1997. The insurer does not owe a pro rata payment for the period from January 1, 1997, to September 20, 1997, because nothing is owed until the due date and the insurer is discharged from further obligation when the annuitant dies.

State Laws Governing Annuity Contracts

The National Association of Insurance Commissioners has adopted a number of model laws that pertain to annuity contracts. Insurance department regulations patterned on the NAIC Replacement of Life Insurance and Annuities Model Regulation govern the replacement of annuity contracts, as well as of life insurance policies. As with life and health insurance policies, annuity contracts must be written in readable language in those states with statutes or regulations patterned on the Life and Health Insurance Policy Language Simplification Model Act. Regulations patterned on the NAIC Model Rules Governing the Advertising of Life Insurance also govern annuity contract advertising. These three model laws are discussed in other chapters of this book and will not be reexamined here.[15] In addition, the NAIC Model Variable Contract Law applies to variable annuity contracts as well as to variable life insurance policies. This model law is discussed below.

The NAIC has also adopted several model laws pertaining only to annuity contracts. Three model laws on which a substantial number of states have patterned their laws are the Standard Nonforfeiture Law for Individual Deferred Annuities; the NAIC Model Rule (Regulation) for Recognizing a New Annuity Mortality Table for Use in Determining Reserve Liabilities for Annuities; and the Model Variable Annuity Regulation. These three model laws are discussed below.

The Standard Nonforfeiture Law for Individual Deferred Annuities

The Standard Nonforfeiture Law for Individual Deferred Annuities applies only to individual deferred fixed annuity contracts during the accumulation period. It does not apply to variable annuities or immediate annuities, or to deferred annuities after the insurer has begun making the periodic payments. All but four states have statutes patterned on this model law. These statutes require that individual deferred fixed annuity contracts contain certain nonforfeiture provisions.

Nonforfeiture Provisions. An individual deferred fixed annuity contract must contain a provision stating that, if premium payments are stopped, the insurer will grant a paid-up annuity benefit. If the annuity contract provides for a lump sum settlement, the contract must also provide that, on surrender of the contract during the accumulation period, the insurer will pay a cash surrender benefit in lieu of a paid-up annuity benefit.

---

[15]The chapters in which these three model laws are discussed are Chapter 4, "Agency in Life and Health Insurance"; Chapter 7, "Structure of the Life Insurance Policy"; and Chapter 22, "Life and Health Insurance Advertising."

Deferral of Payment Provision.   State laws patterned on the Standard Nonforfeiture Law for Individual Deferred Annuities require that the insurer reserve the right to defer payment of the annuity cash surrender benefit. This requirement corresponds to the requirement that a life insurer reserve the right to defer payment of life insurance cash surrender values and policy loans. The right to defer payment protects the insurer from a drain on its cash and other current assets should adverse economic conditions cause large numbers of life insurance policyholders and annuity contract holders to surrender their contracts or to request loans. The insurer must reserve the right to defer payment for six months after the contract holder has surrendered the annuity contract and requested the cash surrender value.

Disclosure Provisions.   Laws patterned on the Standard Nonforfeiture Law for Individual Deferred Annuities also require annuity contracts to contain a statement of the mortality table and interest rates used in calculating any minimum paid-up annuity, cash surrender benefit, or death benefit that is guaranteed under the annuity contract. The contract also must provide enough information for the contract holder to determine the amount of such benefits.

The annuity contract must contain a statement that any paid-up annuity, cash surrender benefit, or death benefit available under the contract is not less than the minimum benefit required by law. The model law spells out the manner of calculating such minimum benefits.

Laws patterned on the model law also require that the annuity contract contain an explanation of the way in which the amount of benefits would be altered by (1) any additional amounts the insurer credits to the contract, (2) any indebtedness to the insurer, or (3) any withdrawals from or partial surrenders of the contract.

Finally, an annuity contract that does not provide a cash surrender or death benefit at least equal to the minimum nonforfeiture amount spelled out in the law must prominently state that such benefits are not provided.

The New Annuity Mortality Table Model Rule

Mortality tables become outdated as the life expectancies of the population change. In 1984, the NAIC adopted the NAIC Model Rule (Regulation) for Recognizing a New Mortality Table for Use in Determining Reserve Liabilities for Annuities (the New Annuity Mortality Table Model Rule). The purpose of this model rule is to recognize certain new mortality tables for use in determining the minimum standard of valuation for annuity contracts. The mortality tables recognized are the 1983 Table "a," which is used for individual annuity contracts, and the 1983 GAM Table, which is used for group annuity contracts. A large majority of states have regulations patterned on this model rule.

The Model Variable Contract Law

In 1970 the NAIC adopted the Model Variable Contract Law. This model law applies to both variable life insurance policies and variable annuity contracts. Over two-thirds of the states have statutes patterned on this model law, and nearly all the rest have related laws.

State statutes patterned on the model law permit life insurers incorporated in the state to establish one or more separate accounts. All income, gains, or losses from assets in the separate account must be credited to or charged against the separate account, without regard to the insurer's other income, gains, or losses. With some exceptions, the assets of a separate account cannot be sold, exchanged, or transferred to another of the insurer's accounts. Amounts in a separate account can be invested without regard to restrictions that the law otherwise imposes on insurers' investments.

Under laws patterned on the model law, a state's commissioner of insurance has sole authority to regulate the issuance and sale of variable life insurance policies and variable annuity contracts. Insurers incorporated in other states are permitted to sell variable life insurance policies and variable annuity contracts in the state if the commissioner is satisfied that the insurer's "condition or method of operation in connection with the issuance of such contracts will not render its operation hazardous to the public or its policyholders" in the state.

The Model Variable Annuity Regulation

The NAIC Model Variable Annuity Regulation has been adopted by about half of the states. A third of the states have related regulations.

Separate Accounts.   Regulations patterned on the model regulation deal with the separate accounts of insurers incorporated in the state, among other things. The model regulation states in part:

> Amounts allocated to any separate account and accumulations thereon may be invested and reinvested without regard to any requirements or limitations prescribed by the laws of this state governing the investments of life insurance companies, and . . . [t]he investments in such separate account or accounts shall not be taken into account in applying the investment limitations otherwise applicable to the investments of the company.

Insurers are ordinarily required by law to invest most of their assets in low-risk investment vehicles such as high-grade bonds and first mortgages. However, the separate accounts that insurers are permitted to use for variable annuity contracts can contain higher-risk investments such as common stocks. Over the long term, common stocks often outperform lower-risk investments, thus helping to protect the annuitant against inflation.

Regulations patterned on the model regulation require that an insurer diversify the assets in a separate account. That is, an insurer must limit the amount of money invested in the stocks or bonds issued by any one entity.

As the term *separate account* implies, the assets in a separate account are kept apart from the insurer's other assets, which are in the insurer's general account or in other separate accounts. The model regulation provides that assets in a "separate account equal to the reserves and other contract liabilities with respect to such account shall not be chargeable with liabilities arising out of any other business the [insurer] may conduct."

Benefit Illustrations.   Regulations patterned on the Model Variable Annuity Regulation prohibit illustrations of variable annuity benefits that are based on "projections of past investment experience into the future or attempted predictions of future investment experience." However, such regulations do permit the use of hypothetical assumed rates of return to illustrate possible levels of benefits.

Disclosure Provisions.   A variable annuity contract must "contain a statement of the essential features of the procedures to be followed by the insurance company in determining the dollar amount of . . . variable benefits." A variable annuity contract must also "state that such dollar amount will vary to reflect investment experience."

Grace Period Provision.   A variable annuity contract must provide "a grace period of 30 days or of one month, within which any stipulated premium falling due after the first may be made, during which grace period the contract shall continue in force."

Reinstatement Provision.   Regulations patterned on the model regulation also require that variable annuity contracts have a reinstatement clause providing that at any time within a specified number of years from the date of the purchaser's failure to make premium payments to the insurer during the annuitant's lifetime, the contract may be reinstated. The contract holder must pay the overdue premiums and all indebtedness to the insurer in order for the insurer to reinstate the annuity contract. The insurer will not reinstate the annuity contract if the insurer has paid the cash surrender value to the contract holder. Thus, reinstatement of a variable annuity contract is similar to reinstatement of a life insurance contract, except that the contract holder does not have to provide evidence of insurability to reinstate a variable annuity contract.

Nonforfeiture Benefits.   Deferred variable annuity contracts must provide nonforfeiture benefits during the accumulation period. These nonforfeiture benefits are similar to those required in a fixed deferred annuity contract. Upon a contract holder's failure to pay premiums on the variable annuity, the insurer must grant a paid-up annuity benefit. Variable annuity contracts providing a lump sum settlement must provide a cash surrender benefit in lieu of a paid-up annuity if the contract holder surrenders the annuity contract during the accumulation period. The model regulation spells out the way in which the insurer must calculate the minimum nonforfeiture amounts.

Investment Reports.   Regulations patterned on the Model Variable Annuity Regulation require that the insurer mail an annual report on the investments in the separate account to each variable annuity contract holder. In the case of a variable annuity still in the accumulation period, the report must show the value of the contract holder's account.

Agent Qualifications.   The Model Variable Annuity Regulation spells out required qualifications for agents who sell variable annuities. In states with regulations patterned on the model, an agent who wishes to sell variable annuities must file with the insurance commissioner evidence that he holds the required federal and state licenses. Federal law requires that agents selling variable annuities be licensed as registered representatives with the National Association of Securities Dealers (NASD). State laws require that agents selling annuities also have an insurance license. In some states, a person must have a special license to sell variable annuities.

Regulations patterned on the model regulation also require that an agent selling variable annuities immediately report to the insurance commissioner any suspension or revocation of her agent's license in another state and any disciplinary action imposed upon her by any federal or state agency with jurisdiction over securities or variable annuity contracts. She must also report any judgment or injunction against her for fraud, deceit, or misrepresentation, or violation of any insurance or securities law.

SEC Regulation

In 1956, in *SEC v. Variable Annuity Life Insurance Co.,* the Securities and Exchange Commission (SEC) brought suit against two variable annuity companies, contending that their variable annuities must be registered with the SEC. The SEC argued that a variable annuity closely resembles a security and therefore is subject to SEC regulation. The U.S. Supreme Court upheld the SEC's position, conceding that the variable annuity contracts contained some insurance features, but pointing out that all the investment risk was borne by the annuitant.[16]

As a result of the *Variable Annuity Life Insurance Co.* decision, variable annuity contracts are regulated by the SEC. Thus, a variable annuity contract must be registered as a security under the Securities Act of 1933. Insurers that issue variable annuities must comply with the statutory and regulatory law applicable to securities.

Supreme Court Justice Douglas, speaking for the majority of the Court in *Variable Annuity Life Insurance Co.,* said:

> While all the States regulate "annuities" under their "insurance" laws, traditionally and customarily they have been fixed annuities, offering the annuitant specified and definite amounts beginning with a certain year of his or her life. The standards for investment of funds underlying these annuities have been conservative. The variable annuity introduced two new features. First, premiums collected are invested to a greater degree in common stocks and other equities. Second, benefit payments vary with the success of the investment policy. The first variable annuity . . . came into existence as a result of a search for a device that would avoid paying annuitants in depreciated dollars. The theory was that returns from investments in common stocks would over the long run tend to compensate for the mounting inflation. The holder of a variable annuity cannot look forward to a fixed monthly or yearly amount in his advancing years. It may be greater or less, depending on the wisdom of the investment policy. . . .
>
> The difficulty is that, absent some guarantee of fixed income, the variable annuity places all the investment risks on the annuitant, none on the company. The holder gets only a pro rata share of what the portfolio of equity interests reflects—which may be a lot, a little, or nothing. We realize that life insurance is an evolving institution. Common knowledge tells us that the forms have greatly changed even in a generation. And we would not undertake to freeze the concepts of "insurance" or "annuity" into the mold they fitted when these Federal Acts were passed. But we conclude that the concept of "insurance" involves some investment risk-taking on the part of the company. The risk of mortality, assumed here, gives these variable annuities an aspect of insurance. Yet it is apparent, not real; superficial, not substantial. In hard reality the issuer of a variable annuity that has no element of a fixed return assumes no true risk in the insurance sense. It is no answer to say that the risk of declining returns in times of depression is the reciprocal of the fixed-dollar annuitant's risk of loss of purchasing power when prices are high and gain of purchasing power when they are low. We deal with a more conventional concept of risk-bearing when we speak of "insurance." For in common understanding "insurance" involves a guarantee that at least some fraction of the benefits will be payable in fixed amounts.

Justice Brennan, concurring in the opinion, added:

> Of course, some urge that even the traditional annuity has few "insurance" features and is basically a form of investment. But the point is that, even though these contracts contain, for what they are worth, features of traditional annuity contracts, administering them

---

[16]359 U.S. 65 (1959).

also involves a very substantial and in fact predominant element of the business of an investment company, and that in a way totally foreign to the business of a traditional life insurance and annuity company, as traditionally regulated by state law. This is what leads to the conclusion that it is not within the intent of the 1933 and 1940 statutes to exempt them.

In 1963, the U.S. Court of Appeals for the Third Circuit decided *Prudential Insurance Co. v. SEC.*[17] In that case, the insurer contended that it was not subject to regulation under the Investment Company Act of 1940. The court agreed that the insurer itself was not an investment company and therefore was not subject to the act, but the court held that the insurer's separate account, resulting from its sale of variable annuity contracts to the public, was an investment company subject to the act.

In 1967, eight years after *Variable Annuity Life Insurance Co.* was decided, the U.S. Supreme Court decided *SEC v. United Benefit Life Insurance Co.,*[18] which involved an annuity contract with guarantees during the income period but with a variable accumulation period. In *United Benefit Life Insurance Co.,* the Court again held that the annuity contract was subject to the operation of the Securities Act of 1933 and the Investment Company Act of 1940.

In June 1986, the SEC promulgated Rule 151.[19] Rule 151 states that an annuity contract, to be exempt from the Securities Act of 1933, must not be marketed primarily as an investment. Moreover, the annuity contract must include guarantees of principal and interest sufficient for the insurer, rather than the contract holder, to be deemed to have assumed the investment risk.

The insurer shall be deemed to assume the investment risk if (1) the value of the contract does not vary according to the investment experience of a separate account; (2) the insurer guarantees principal and interest; (3) the insurer credits a specified rate of interest; and (4) the insurer guarantees that the rate of any interest to be credited in excess of the specified rate will not be modified more frequently than once a year.

In December 1986, six months after Rule 151 was promulgated, the U.S. Court of Appeals for the 7th Circuit decided *Otto v. Variable Annuity Life Insurance Co.*[20] The annuity at issue in *Otto* was a fixed annuity under which the insurer retained complete discretion to modify any excess interest. Because the insurer failed to meet the SEC's one-year guarantee requirement as to excess interest, as spelled out in Rule 151, the court held that the annuity was not excluded from SEC regulation.

The *Otto* decision was the first time that a fixed annuity was held to be subject to federal securities laws. The insurer, in its petition for a writ of certiorari[21] to the U.S. Supreme Court, pointed out that "a substantial portion of the insurance industry has been thrown into jeopardy and confusion by the [*Otto*] decision."

In the *Otto* case, the U.S. Supreme Court refused to review the decision of the federal court of appeals and denied the writ of certiorari. As a result, the federal court of appeals decision is binding authority in the 7th Circuit, which includes Illinois, Indiana, and Wisconsin, and is persuasive authority in other federal circuits. Because of the *Otto* decision, issuers of fixed annuities should follow the one-year rule as to excess interest if they wish to avoid SEC regulation.

---

[17]326 F.2d 383 (3d Cir. 1964), *cert. denied,* 377 U.S. 953 (1964).
[18]387 U.S. 202 (1967).
[19]17 C.F.R. § 230.151 (1996).
[20]814 F.2d 1127 (7th Cir. 1986), *cert. denied,* 486 U.S. 1026 (1988).
[21]A **writ of certiorari** is one way in which a party can obtain appellate review of a case.

Annuity Taxation

Although, as has been stated in earlier chapters, this book generally does not deal with tax law, some understanding of annuity taxation is important to an understanding of annuity contracts. Taxation of nonqualified annuity contracts will therefore be discussed briefly in this section.[22]

A nonqualified deferred annuity owned by a natural person offers tax-deferred growth. There is no annual limit on the amount of money a person can put into a nonqualified annuity, which is not the case with 401(k) and other qualified plans. The annuity contract holder pays the premiums with after-tax dollars, but the investment gain on those premiums is not currently taxable to the contract holder as long as the insurer holds the money. Such tax deferral allows the fund to grow significantly faster than if the investment gain were taxed as income each year. In addition, the contract holder may have retired and may be in a lower tax bracket when he receives annuity payments and pays taxes on the investment gain.

Amounts Not Received as Annuities

Sometimes a contract holder receives part or all of the value of a deferred annuity during the accumulation period. These payments are "amounts not received as annuities" under the Internal Revenue Code and are taxed differently than amounts received as annuities during the income period.

Payouts to the contract holder during the accumulation period allocable to premium payments made before August 14, 1982, are not includable in income, except to the extent that they exceed the contract holder's pre–August 14, 1982, premium payments. That is, the contract holder can withdraw the money that she put in before August 14, 1982, without paying tax. However, any investment gain that is withdrawn will be taxed.

Payouts of premium payments made after August 13, 1982, operate in just the opposite way. For premiums paid after August 13, 1982, a payout during the accumulation period will be considered to consist of the investment gain first and then of the premium payments. If the contract holder is under age 59½ and is not totally disabled, a 10 percent penalty tax is also assessed on a payout of post–August 13, 1982, premiums to the contract holder. Moreover, policy loans from post–August 13, 1982, annuity contracts are considered payouts. Thus, to encourage personal savings for retirement, Congress has made taxation of payouts during the accumulation period less favorable to the contract holder than it was before August 14, 1982. On the other hand, the nonqualified annuity contract holder does not have to begin withdrawals at age 70½, as is the case with 401(k) and other qualified plans.

Amounts Received as Annuities

During the income period of an annuity, a portion of the insurer's periodic payments is taxable to the annuitant. The Internal Revenue Service treats part of each payment as a tax-free return of premium paid, and it treats the remainder as investment gain taxable as ordinary income. When the annuity is payable for the annuitant's life, the excludable amount—that is, the amount not taxed—is determined by an exclusion

---

[22]See generally, I.R.C. § 72 (1996), which governs annuity taxation.

ratio. The exclusion ratio is determined by dividing the contract holder's investment in the contract by the total expected payments from the insurer. The total expected payments from the insurer, called the *expected return,* is calculated using IRS actuarial tables. Because the total expected payments from the insurer under a variable annuity are unknown, the total expected payments are assumed to be equal to the investment in the contract.[23]

If the income period began before January 1, 1987, the excludable amount will not change even if the annuitant outlives his life expectancy. Thus, under such an annuity contract it is possible for an annuitant to recover tax-free more than the amount paid for the annuity. However, for annuity contracts with income periods beginning after January 1, 1987, payments the insurer makes after the annuitant reaches his life expectancy are fully taxable.[24]

Death Benefits

With some exceptions, if an annuity death benefit is paid in a lump sum, the investment gain will be taxed as ordinary income to the beneficiary. If, within 60 days after the annuitant's death, the beneficiary elects to receive periodic payments instead of a lump sum, the periodic payments will be taxed using an exclusion ratio.[25]

Structured Settlements

Structured settlements have increased greatly in number since their beginning in the 1970s, due in part to favorable changes in federal tax laws. A *structured settlement* is an agreement to pay specified sums of money over time, ordinarily to a person claiming tort damages because of personal injury or the wrongful death of a close family member, or to an employee claiming workers' compensation benefits. For example, a workers' compensation carrier might agree to pay $1,000 per month until age 65 to a worker who has been injured on the job. Structured settlements are entered into in situations other than personal injury, wrongful death, and workers' compensation, but these three are the most common.[26] A structured settlement usually results in the purchase from a life insurer of an annuity contract tailored to fit the annuitant's needs.

Structured settlements have several advantages to the recipient over lump sum settlements. First, one study showed that the great majority of recipients of lump sums will dissipate the money within a few years.[27] A structured settlement, on the other hand, can assure that the recipient has income for as long as she needs it. Second, a structured settlement frees the recipient from the burden of managing the funds, as well as from the danger of mismanaging them. Third, a structured settle-

---

[23]Treas. Reg. § 1.72-2(b)(3).

[24]I.R.C. § 72 (b)(2) (1996).

[25]I.R.C. § 72 (h) (1996).

[26]W. Christian Shumate, *New Markets Emerging for SS Annuities,* NAT'L UNDERWRITER, LIFE & HEALTH/FIN. SERVICES EDITION, July 17, 1995, at 21; Cynthia Crosson, *Structured Settlement Cos. Target New Markets,* NAT'L UNDERWRITER, LIFE & HEALTH/FIN. SERVICES EDITION, Nov. 15, 1993, at 10.

[27]Don McNay, *Protect Settlement Pie from Quickly Withering; Personal Injury Settlements,* BEST'S REVIEW, LIFE-HEALTH INS. EDITION, Mar. 1995, at 78.

ment, as its name suggests, is tailored to each situation. For example, a structured settlement can provide extra funds during the college years of a child whose father was killed as the result of the defendant's negligence, in addition to providing funds for the child's regular expenses. The possible disadvantage of a structured settlement to the recipient is that once an annuity is purchased, the recipient has no right to accelerate, defer, increase, or decrease the periodic payments, to cash in the annuity contract for its present value, or to control the investments from which the periodic payments are made.

A structured settlement also has advantages for the person who committed the tort (the defendant-tortfeasor) and his casualty insurer, for the employer self-funded for workers' compensation, for the workers' compensation insurer, and for the court. In cases involving either tort injuries or workers' compensation claims, a structured settlement usually costs less than a lump sum settlement because of the favorable tax treatment described below. In addition, a life annuity contract purchased to fund the structured settlement will require a lower premium if the annuitant has a shorter-than-average life expectancy. The life insurer can determine this by a review of the proposed annuitant's medical files. Because of their lower costs and other advantages, structured settlements help parties settle cases more quickly, thus saving on litigation costs if the case is being litigated. Finally, the defendant-tortfeasor or his casualty insurer can assign their liability to make the structured settlement periodic payments, as explained below.

A majority of the states have adopted some type of structured settlement legislation. Judges usually support structured settlements because a structured settlement prevents a disabled plaintiff from squandering a lump sum and, without other means of support, becoming a ward of the state. Moreover, because structured settlements help parties settle cases more quickly, they help clear court calendars.

Taxation of Structured Settlements

With minor exceptions, for federal income tax purposes a person's gross income does not include the amount of any damages received to compensate her for physical injury or physical sickness, whether as the result of a court judgment or of a settlement agreement between the parties, or under a workers' compensation act.[28] Thus, if a person receives a lump sum settlement on account of physical injury or physical sickness, she will not have to include the amount of the lump sum in her gross income for federal income tax purposes. However, investment earnings on the lump sum will be subject to federal income tax. If, instead, the person agrees to a structured settlement, neither the money used to fund the structured settlement nor the investment earnings on that money will be subject to federal income tax, provided that certain conditions are met. These conditions are (1) the defendant-tortfeasor, his casualty insurer, or an assignee (or, in the case of a workers' compensation claim, the employer or the workers' compensation insurer) must purchase the annuity contract and the annuitant must at no time have actual or constructive receipt[29] of the funds used to purchase the annuity contract; and (2) the annuitant cannot have the right to increase or decrease the periodic payments, or to borrow against or otherwise encumber the periodic payments. Because of this favorable tax treatment, less money usu-

---

[28]I.R.C. § 104 (1996).

[29]A person is in constructive receipt of funds if those funds are unqualifiedly available to her, even though she has not actually received the funds.

ally will be needed to settle the case if the parties enter into a structured settlement than if the money were paid in a lump sum.

In nearly all situations, part of the money is paid in a lump sum and part is paid under a structured settlement agreement. For example, suppose that Gina Kolatch, age 13, is rollerblading down the sidewalk when Alfred Ormsby loses control of his motorcycle, jumps the curb, and runs into Kolatch, partially disabling her. Kolatch's guardian *ad litem*[30] sues Ormsby on Kolatch's behalf asking the court for damages to compensate her for her injuries. Ormsby's casualty insurer and Kolatch agree to a lump sum payment and a structured settlement. Ormsby's casualty insurer pays Kolatch $50,000 in a lump sum. The casualty insurer also purchases an annuity contract from the Upright Life Insurance Company. The annuity contract provides that Upright will make payments of $25,000 to Kolatch on her 18th, 19th, 20th, and 21st birthdays, so that she will have money to attend college. The annuity contract further provides that Kolatch will receive a monthly income for the rest of her life, beginning at age 22. The monthly payment during the first year will be in the amount of $1,250, compounding at 3 percent each year thereafter. Kolatch will not have to pay federal income tax on the lump sum or on the periodic payments made by Upright. However, any investment earnings on the $50,000 lump sum will be taxable.

As another example, suppose that Myrna Jacobs and her young son, David, are the dependent surviving spouse and child of Michael Jacobs, who died from injuries he received in the crash of a commercial airliner. Myrna and David institute a wrongful death action against the airline. In a **wrongful death action,** the plaintiff sues for damages to compensate him for loss suffered because of the death of a close family member caused by the defendant's willful or negligent act.

The airline's casualty insurer pays Myrna $100,000 in a lump sum and purchases a life annuity contract with period certain. The annuity contract will pay Myrna or her estate $5,000 per month for 30 years, and for the remainder of her life if she lives longer than 30 years. In addition, it will pay David $50,000 on each birthday from his 18th through his 24th. This will enable him to obtain a college education and pursue postgraduate studies. Myrna and David will not have to pay federal income tax on any of this money because the money was received on account of physical injuries, those of Michael Jacobs. However, any investment earnings received on the $100,000 lump sum payment will be subject to federal income tax.

Qualified Assignments of Liability

A defendant-tortfeasor or his casualty insurer often wish to assign their liability for the plaintiff's physical injury or physical sickness. They can assign such liability by means of a *qualified assignment.* A **qualified assignment** under federal law means any assignment of a liability to make periodic payments as tort damages on account of physical injury or physical sickness, whether the liability arises by lawsuit or agreement.[31] Often the assignee is a subsidiary corporation of the life insurance company that issues the annuity. The assignee must assume the liability from the defendant-tortfeasor or her casualty insurer. This will be done by contract. The defendant-tortfeasor or her casualty insurer usually pays the assignee the amount necessary to fund the periodic payments. The assignee then ordinarily purchases an annuity (al-

---

[30]A guardian *ad litem* is a court-appointed guardian who acts in litigation on behalf of someone under a disability, such as a minor or a mentally defective person.

[31]I.R.C. § 130 (1996).

though an assignee could fund the periodic payments with U.S. securities if lifetime benefits are not going to be paid). The assignee owns the annuity contract. The periodic payments under the annuity contract must be fixed and determinable as to amount and time of payment. The recipient must not be able to accelerate, defer, increase, or decrease the periodic payments. The assignee's obligation must not be greater than the obligation of the assignor—that is, of the defendant-tortfeasor or his casualty insurer. The periodic payments must be excludable from the annuitant's gross income as described above. Finally, the annuity must be purchased within 60 days before or 60 days after the assignment is made.

To illustrate a typical qualified assignment, suppose that Gerald Munson is badly injured when a defective elevator falls in a clothing store where he is a customer. He sues the owner of the building, the manufacturer of the elevator, and the company that maintains the elevator. The defendants' casualty insurers enter into a structured settlement agreement with Munson whereby Munson will receive $3,000 per month for life. The casualty insurers then make a qualified assignment of their liability to an assignee. The casualty insurers pay the assignee an amount equal to the single premium necessary to purchase the annuity contract. Within 60 days, the assignee purchases from its parent corporation (the life insurer) the single premium annuity contract under the terms of which Munson will receive $3,000 a month for life. The assignee owns the annuity contract. Munson has no control over the annuity contract and cannot accelerate, defer, increase, or decrease the periodic payments. The defendants and their casualty insurers have no more liability for Munson's injuries. Financially stable entities, the assignee and the life insurer, guarantee Munson's $3,000 a month for life.

In the past, qualified assignments were available only to defendants who committed a tort causing physical injury or physical sickness and to their casualty insurers. Qualified assignments were not available to employers that were self-funded for worker's compensation or to worker's compensation insurers. However, in 1997, Congress extended to them the right to make qualified assignments of their liability for injuries to employees if the claim was filed after August 5, 1997. Even if the employer or worker's compensation carrier cannot make a qualified assignment of liability because the claim was filed before that date, they can enter into a structured settlement agreement with the injured employee.

Summary

An annuity contract is an agreement that one person or organization, such as an insurer, will make periodic payments to another for a specified period of time, such as for a number of years or for the life of the recipient. The recipient is the annuitant. The person who enters into the annuity contract is the contract holder. The insurer and annuitant have a debtor-creditor relationship.

There are many types of annuity contracts. Under an immediate annuity contract, the insurer begins making periodic payments to the annuitant one period after the premium has been paid, whereas under a deferred annuity contract the insurer begins making periodic payments a specified number of years after premium payments commence, or when the annuitant reaches a specified age. Under a single premium annuity contract, the contract holder pays one premium; whereas under an installment premium annuity contract the contract holder pays a series of premiums. Under a straight life annuity contract, the insurer makes periodic payments for as long as the annuitant lives. An annuity contract for a period certain provides payments for a specified period of time, whether or not the annuitant lives. Under a fixed annuity contract, the insurer sets the rates at which the premiums will be accumulated and guarantees the amount of each periodic payment. The value of accumulated premiums and the amount of each periodic payment under a variable annuity depend on the amount in a pool of investments called a separate account. Qualified annuity contracts are used to fund tax-qualified plans.

Other features of annuity contracts are guaranteed and current interest rates, charges, death benefits, surrender benefits, and waiver of premium benefits.

State statutes and regulations governing the replacement, readability, and advertising of life insurance contracts also govern annuity contracts. Some state laws apply to annuity contracts only and govern nonforfeiture, disclosure, and other required provisions as well as variable annuity separate accounts, investment reports, and agent qualifications.

In the absence of fraud or misrepresentation, the courts usually will not rescind an annuity contract for inadequacy of consideration merely because the annuitant did not reach her life expectancy. Moreover, an insurer ordinarily has no duty to inquire into the health of a proposed annuitant.

The courts have held that variable annuities are subject to SEC regulation and must be registered as securities under the Securities Act of 1933. Also, separate accounts generally fall within the scope of the Investment Company Act of 1940. Fixed annuities may be subject to SEC regulation if they do not meet certain SEC guidelines.

Annuity contracts offer tax-deferred growth. Payouts to the contract holder during the accumulation period are taxed differently than payouts during the income period.

A structured settlement is an agreement to pay specified sums of money over time, ordinarily to a person claiming damages because of personal injury or wrongful death, or to an employee claiming workers' compensation benefits. Unlike a lump sum settlement, a structured settlement can provide income for as long as the recipient needs it. Moreover, under a structured settlement the recipient is freed from the burden of managing the funds, the structured settlement can be tailored to the situation, and the structured settlement provides a larger amount of tax-free income than is provided by a lump sum settlement. The periodic payments are usually provided to the recipient through an annuity contract purchased from a life insurer. Under federal law, tortfeasors and their casualty insurers can make qualified assignments of their liability to make periodic payments.

ILLUSTRATIVE CASE

In the following case, the administrator of the estate of a deceased annuity contract holder filed a bill in equity. The administrator argued that the contract holder had been incompetent to contract because of physical infirmity and that the insurer had not given adequate consideration for the contract. The administrator therefore asked the court to rescind the contract.

STOCKETT

v.

PENN MUT. LIFE INS. CO. [32]

Supreme Court of Rhode Island

July 16, 1954

CAPOTOSTO, Justice.

This bill in equity was brought by the administrator d.b.n.[33] of the estate of Susan Butler to rescind an annuity contract. The respondent's substantial demurrer[34] was sustained in the superior court on certain grounds. From a

---

[32]106 A. 2d 741 (1954).

[33]D.b.n. is an abbreviation for *de bonis non administratis,* which means "of the goods not administered." An administrator of the goods not administered is the administrator of an estate who succeeds another administrator who has left the estate partially unsettled.

[34]A *demurrer* is a method of raising an objection to a pleading.

decree denying and dismissing the bill, complainant has duly prosecuted his appeal to this court.

The bill alleged that on September 11, 1935 Susan Butler paid $4,000 to the respondent, hereinafter sometimes called the company, for a nonrefunding annuity policy under which she was to receive $28.16 a month for life. Up to the time of her death on June 26, 1937 she had received the total sum of $591.36 from the company. In 1941 an administrator d.b.n. of her estate was appointed, and on March 17 of that year he made demand upon the company for the payment to him with interest of the difference between the $4,000 paid by his intestate and the $591.36 received by her in her lifetime. He repeated such demand in October 1944. The present bill of complaint was filed September 25, 1945. We note here that about two months later the original administrator d.b.n. died and another administrator was appointed to act in his place and stead.

The grounds for rescission alleged in the bill in substance are that when the policy was issued in 1935 Susan Butler was sixty-six years old and illiterate; that her right leg had been amputated to the thigh because of diabetes; that all of those conditions were known to the company at the time it wrote the policy on the reserve basis of the combined annuity tables for 'good' lives; that due to her inexperience in business matters she was 'incompetent to comprehend the nature of the proposed contract'; that the typewritten application and an amendment thereto, both of which she signed by mark, were prepared by the company; that at that time, considering her poor physical condition, she did not have the normal life expectancy of an ordinary person of her age; that there was 'an inequality of the contracting parties, by reason of the inexperience and lack of information of the Applicant as compared with the business experience and information of Respondent Company'; and that in the circumstances the company 'was in a position with reference to said Susan Butler of trust and confidence.'

The bill further alleged that 'An unconscionable advantage was obtained over said applicant'; that the policy being without refund at death showed a grossly inadequate consideration; that respondent's course of action constituted 'imposition or overreaching' in procuring the application; that no valid contract ever came into existence; and that if the purported contract was allowed to stand respondent would be 'unjustly enriched' and the estate of Susan Butler would be 'unjustly deprived' of funds to which it is entitled.

The grounds of demurrer were, first, that it did not appear in the bill that at the time of application for the policy Susan Butler was incompetent or misled by the respondent; second, that the bill did not show that there was an inadequate consideration for the contract, as it was based on a regular annuity schedule; third, that complainant was guilty of laches; and fourth, that the bill did not allege sufficient facts to constitute a cause of action. The demurrer was sustained on the first, second and fourth grounds.

The question presently before us is whether the facts alleged in the bill set forth a cause of action for relief in equity. While a demurrer admits facts well pleaded, it does not admit conclusions without adequate allegations of particular facts in support thereof. It is of no avail merely to aver in general terms, as complainant does in the present bill, that his intestate was incompetent because of physical infirmity; that the consideration for the contract was inadequate; that a fiduciary relationship existed between the deceased and the company; and that the contract was procured through misrepresentation, con-

cealment of material information, undue influence, overreaching and other unconscionable conduct. A bill of complaint is to be considered as a whole and given a reasonable interpretation. In the absence of statute, it will generally be construed against the pleader when its statements are ambiguous, equivocal or uncertain.

A careful examination of the present bill shows that it abounds in conclusions with reference to various grounds for relief in equity, but it is greatly deficient in specific allegations of fact in support of such grounds. Apparently it was intentionally framed in general terms and from a retrospective point of view in an attempt to obtain the relief prayed for by Susan Butler's estate. What actually happened between the parties when she applied for the policy is left almost entirely to conjecture and speculation. For example, even though complainant's intestate may have been advanced in years, infirm, illiterate and inexperienced in business matters, such conditions in themselves do not amount to legal incompetency as alleged, unless it further appears by specific allegations of facts that when the contract was consummated she did not possess sufficient mentality to understand the nature and effect of the transaction, that is, that her mental power for intelligent action had been impaired.

No averments to that effect appear in the present bill. What we have just said respecting the insufficiency of necessary and material allegations as to incompetency applies with equal force to complainant's claim that the intestate was deceived, misled or overreached by fraudulent conduct on the part of the company. The manner in which such unconscionable means as misrepresentation, undue influence or concealment of material facts were exerted upon her are not disclosed. The bare statement that the company stood in a fiduciary relationship to Susan Butler was clearly unwarranted under the allegations of the bill which show only a buyer and seller relation between the parties. Ordinarily an insurance company stands in no fiduciary relationship to a legally competent applicant for an annuity or other insurance contract.

The same deficiency of specific allegations of facts that we have already pointed out in connection with the grounds for relief heretofore mentioned appears in complainant's claim that as a result of inadequate consideration the company will be unjustly enriched if the contract is allowed to stand. That claim is made to rest on the erroneous premise that a nonrefunding annuity contract is based on the life expectancy of the particular individual annuitant, whereas in fact the basis for such a contract is the average life expectancy of a specified group within which the individual may reasonably be included, as plainly appears from one of the few specific allegations in the present bill. In the circumstances therein alleged we find no merit in complainant's contention that because the insured did not live longer the company was injustly enriched to the detriment of her estate. We are of the opinion that on the allegations in the present bill there was no error in sustaining respondent's demurrer.

The complainant's appeal is denied and dismissed, the decree appealed from is affirmed, and the cause is remanded to the superior court for further proceedings.

Questions for Review

1. Define the term *annuitant*.
2. Describe the difference between an immediate annuity contract and a deferred annuity contract.
3. What is an annuity contract accumulation period?
4. Describe a separate account. How does a separate account relate to the insurer's other assets?
5. What nonforfeiture benefits must deferred annuities provide?
6. Will the courts ordinarily rescind an annuity contract for inadequacy of consideration because the annuitant did not reach his life expectancy? Under what circumstances might they do so?
7. Discuss SEC regulation of variable annuities and fixed annuities.
8. Do annuity contracts offer tax-deferred growth?
9. Define the term *structured settlement*. What advantages does a structured settlement offer over a lump sum settlement?

22 LIFE AND HEALTH INSURANCE ADVERTISING

Chapter Outline

The creation of life and health insurance and annuity contract advertisements that are effective marketing tools and that comply with the law is no easy task.[1] Nevertheless, careful compliance with advertising laws is vital, because advertising is highly visible and sanctions for noncompliance can be severe. An understanding of life and health insurance and annuity contract advertising law is therefore necessary for persons engaged in the creation of insurance advertisements, the sale of insurance products, or regulatory compliance. Such understanding can also help claim examiners, because advertising material sometimes must be taken into account in examining a claim.

An *insurance advertisement* is, for purposes of this discussion, any written or spoken material designed to promote public interest in life or health insurance or

---

[1]James W. Kerley, *Use Marketing Materials to Reinforce Compliance,* NATIONAL UNDERWRITER, LIFE & HEALTH/FIN. SERVICES EDITION, Feb. 20, 1995, at 21.

annuity contracts or to induce the purchase of such contracts. Life and health insurance and annuity contract advertising is done through prepared sales presentations, promotional literature, direct mail, telephone, newspapers, magazines, radio, television, and the Internet.

The law governing insurance advertisements includes law governing advertisements generally, as well as law governing insurance advertisements specifically. Each state has its own advertising laws. However, insurance advertisements often cross state lines. Interstate advertising can create an especially complex situation, because the laws of two or more states are involved. Federal laws can also apply to some insurance advertising. This chapter contains a description of the statutes, regulations, and case law governing life and health insurance and annuity contract advertising.

Promotional Literature Presented by Agents

Agents use various types of promotional literature during the solicitation of insurance sales. Insurers usually intend for these materials to be estimates or illustrations and not part of the insurance contract. The majority rule is that written statements regarding surplus earnings, dividends, accumulations, and so forth that are not attached to the policy, or referred to in the policy, are not part of the contract.[2] If the insurer has clearly indicated that such statements are intended only for purposes of illustration, the court is even more likely to hold that they are not part of the contract.

However, if the written estimate or illustration is attached to the policy or if the policy refers to it, the courts sometimes hold that it is part of the contract. For example, in one case a sheet of paper with illustrations showing the amount of surplus earnings that would be apportioned to a life insurance policy at the end of 20 years was pasted to the policy. It followed a statement on the first page of the policy that "the Benefits, Statements and Values on the succeeding pages of this Policy are made a part hereof." The court held that the amount of surplus earnings specified in the illustration sheet was a guaranteed amount rather than an estimate. That amount was therefore declared to be payable to the policyowner.[3]

Although an estimate or illustration is not ordinarily part of an insurance or annuity contract, the insurer must make such a statement in good faith. A person who has been induced to enter into an insurance or annuity contract by intentionally false statements is not without remedy. He will have grounds to sue the insurer for fraud, rescission, or reformation of the contract.[4] Moreover, the courts often honor the reasonable expectations of applicants, policyowners, and beneficiaries even though those expectations are at variance with the terms of the contract. The reasonable expectations doctrine is discussed in Chapter 18, "Performance of the Insurance Contract."

In the 1980s and early 1990s many soliciting agents presented "vanishing premium" illustrations to clients. These illustrations demonstrated how life insurance premiums would "vanish" after several years, assuming that the high interest rates on insurers' quality bond investments continued. High interest rates on such bond investments resulted in high policyowner dividends that could be used to pay renewal

[2]D. E. Ytreberg, Annotation, *Insurer's Statements as to Amount of Dividends, Accumulations, Surplus, or the Like as Binding on Insurer or Merely Illustrative,* 17 A.L.R. 3d 777 (1968).
[3]Legare v. West Coast Life Ins. Co., 5 P.2d 682 (Cal. Ct. App. 1931).
[4]Standard Acci. Ins. Co. v. Harrison-Wright Co., 178 S.E. 235 (N.C. 1935).

premiums. Eventually the dividends would pay the entire renewal premiums and the premiums would vanish, according to the illustrations. When bond interest declined, premiums often did not vanish. Even though many soliciting agents had pointed out that premiums were not guaranteed to vanish, some policyowners felt they had been misled.[5] A rash of lawsuits, including class action lawsuits, followed, attended by publicity unfavorable to insurers.[6]

Other market conduct that has resulted in unfavorable publicity involves sales presentations and promotional literature that represented whole life insurance policies as retirement or college expense saving plans, without identifying the product as life insurance. Insurance departments have levied large fines on insurers that did this type of advertising.[7]

In response to market conduct concerns, the NAIC in 1995 adopted the Life Insurance Illustrations Model Regulation. This model regulation states:

> The purpose of this regulation is to provide rules for life insurance policy illustrations that will protect consumers and foster consumer education. The regulation provides illustration formats, prescribes standards to be followed when illustrations are used, and specifies the disclosures that are required in connection with illustrations. The goals of this regulation are to ensure that illustrations do not mislead purchasers of life insurance and to make illustrations more understandable.

In states that have regulations patterned on the model, an insurer or its soliciting agents are not permitted to "use the term 'vanish' or 'vanishing premium' or a similar term that implies the policy becomes paid up, to describe a plan for using non-guaranteed elements to pay a portion of future premium." Applicants for life insurance must sign a statement indicating that they understand that non-guaranteed elements in an illustration are subject to change and that the agent has said they are not guaranteed. When using an illustration in the sale of a life insurance policy, an insurer is not permitted to "represent the policy as anything other than a life insurance policy." Furthermore, life insurance policy illustrations must conform to the detailed standards set forth in the regulation. When this book went to press, the states were beginning to adopt regulations based on the Life Insurance Illustrations Model Regulation.

Group Insurance Advertising

Although waiver and estoppel ordinarily are not available to broaden coverage under an individual life or health insurance policy,[8] the courts have treated group insurance differently, because the insured person usually has no opportunity to read the group

---

[5] Michael Pinkans, *Days of Vanishing Premium Are Over,* Nat'l Underwriter, Life & Health/Fin. Services Edition, Sept. 9, 1996, at 8.

[6] Editorial Comment, *Marketing Gone Awry,* Nat'l Underwriter, Life & Health/Fin. Services Edition, Oct. 25, 1993, at 14.

[7] Cynthia Crossen & Laura Tuma, *Met Settles with Texas, California,* Nat'l Underwriter, Life & Health/Fin. Services Edition, July 18, 1994, at 1; Carole King, *Hancock Fined $1 Million by New York,* Nat'l Underwriter, Life & Health/Fin. Services Edition, Jan. 8, 1996, at 1.

[8] W. C. Crais III, Annotation, *Comment Note: Doctrine of Estoppel or Waiver as Available to Bring within Coverage of Insurance Policy Risks Not Covered by Its Terms or Expressly Excluded Therefrom,* 1 A.L.R. 3d 1139 (1965).

master policy.[9] Group insureds depend on promotional and explanatory literature and their group certificates for an understanding of their insurance coverage. When the literature and group certificates contain terms more favorable to the insured than the terms of the master policy, the courts often hold that the insurer either has waived the terms in the master policy or is estopped to deny the more favorable statements in the literature or certificates. For example, in one case a group life insurance master policy required yearly proof of disability for an insured to qualify for waiver of premium. The insurer's promotional literature stated that the insured merely needed to submit proof of disability "from time to time." The insured submitted no proof of disability before his death, but the plaintiff beneficiary was able to prove that the insured had been disabled from the termination of his employment until his death. The court held that the insurer had waived the more rigorous requirement of the master policy and allowed the plaintiff-beneficiary to recover the death benefit.[10]

These cases governing group insurance advertising might no longer apply to employer-employee group insurance policies because these policies are now governed by the federal Employee Retirement Income Security Act.

Direct Response Insurance Advertising

Many insurers sell, or solicit an inquiry about, an insurance policy without the use of a soliciting agent. This type of solicitation is called *direct response insurance solicitation.* Other terms for this type of solicitation are *mail order, direct mail,* and *mass merchandising,* but *direct response* is the most accurate term.

Insurers solicit direct response insurance by direct mail or mass media advertisements. Mass media include newspapers, magazines, radio, and television. Insurers use the direct response method primarily to sell life and health insurance policies that are supplemental to the basic policies sold through the regular agency marketing method.

Many legal questions result from direct response solicitation. This section will deal with the most important of these questions.

Direct Response Advertisements Binding the Insurer

Often with direct response solicitation, the applicant simply clips the application form from a newspaper, magazine, or direct mail brochure and applies directly to the insurer. The applicant has no opportunity to discuss the terms of the contract with an agent of the insurer but must rely solely on the advertisement for an understanding of the contract. Courts in some jurisdictions have held that the direct response advertisement is therefore binding on the insurer.

In one case, an insurer had inserted an advertising brochure with an application form into local newspapers.[11] The brochure advertised a family hospital benefit policy. The plaintiff had sent in the application and received a policy. His wife became hospitalized, but the insurer denied hospital benefits because the wife's illness began before the effective date of the policy. The plaintiff filed a declaratory judgment

---

[9]Job A. Sandoval, Annotation, *Group Insurance: Waiver or Estoppel on Basis of Statements in Promotional or Explanatory Literature Issued to Insureds,* 36 A.L.R. 3d 541 (1971).

[10]Lewis v. Continental Life & Acci. Co., 461 P.2d 243 (Idaho 1969).

[11]Craver v. Union Fidelity Ins. Co., 307 N.E.2d 265 (Ohio Ct. App. 1973).

action asking the court to determine whether the policy covered his wife's hospitalization for the preexisting illness.

The policy did contain an exclusion for preexisting illness. The brochure mentioned this exclusion but in such a way that the court felt the average reader would not have understood it. The court looked to the dominant theme of the advertisement, which was immediate, unqualified coverage. The court made this statement:

> [W]here the dominant theme of such advertising, constantly and prominently repeated, is that the insured is immediately covered upon payment of his initial premium "without any qualification whatsoever" and is intended to be so understood by the person who reads it, the fact that one or more caveats may be found inserted within the copy which would or could be read by a sophisticated or suspicious reader to limit or qualify the extent or immediacy of coverage does not necessarily alter or erase the dominant theme of the solicitation, or the overall meaning, intent, and effect of the language therein to the average reader.

The court therefore held that the hospital benefits were payable. The opinion contains the following statement about direct response advertising:

> It seems clear to this court that where a health and accident insurer engages in a plan of solicitation by means of advertising in public newspapers of general circulation, without the intervention of agents, and without physical examinations or medical statements as a condition of the issuance of insurance or of coverage, but where the policy is put into effect by application of the insured on a form attached to the advertising solicitation and the payment of a premium, and where it is obvious the solicitation is intended to and does in fact induce the reader to apply for and secure the policy of insurance, the insurance company is bound by any representations, promises, warranties or undertakings contained in such solicitation.

In another case, an insurer ran a direct response advertisement for travel accident insurance in an automobile club publication.[12] The question before the court in that case was whether the direct response advertisement with its application form constituted a complete offer by the insurer. If so, the mailing of the application with a premium check was an acceptance that completed the contract of insurance.

> The advertisement read: "ENROLL NOW . . . and take along this '365' Travel Accident Insurance wherever you may go. . . . Your club membership automatically qualifies you to enroll." In much smaller type on the application form was printed: "I . . . understand that protection becomes effective the date my certificate of insurance is issued."

The plaintiff's wife applied for travel accident insurance on June 2, 1976, by mailing in a premium check and the completed application. The wife died as the result of an automobile accident on June 3. On June 4, the insurer received the application and premium check and mailed a certificate of insurance to the applicant. When the plaintiff claimed the death benefit, the insurer denied liability on the ground that the insurance was not in effect at the time of death.

The court held that the death benefit was payable, because the advertisement was a complete offer and the mailing of the application and the premium check was an acceptance of that offer. The contract of insurance was created at the time of acceptance, which was one day before the applicant's death. According to the court, the reasonable expectations of the applicant governed and the applicant could reasonably

---

[12]Riordan v. Automobile Club, 422 N.Y.S.2d 811 (N.Y. Sup. Ct. 1979).

expect that she was covered because of statements in the advertisement. Quoting from a similar case from another jurisdiction, the court pointed out:

> [W]hen the potential insurance purchaser cannot consult with an agent to ascertain the parameters of the proposed policy, the concept of an informed meeting of the minds is a myth unless the insurance company clearly and explicitly explains the policy in its literature. To effectuate this goal, the reasonable expectations which such literature raises or does not rebut must govern the interpretations of such policies.[13]

The model Unfair Claims Settlement Practices Act, adopted by the National Association of Insurance Commissioners in 1971, contains a section aimed at direct response advertising. This section prohibits "[a]ttempting to settle or settling claims for less than the amount to [*sic*] that a reasonable person would believe the insured or beneficiary was entitled by reference to written or printed advertising material accompanying or made part of an application." The great majority of states have enacted statutes patterned on the Unfair Claims Settlement Practices Act.

Interstate Direct Response Advertising

Insurers often do interstate direct response advertising. Earlier in this century, an insurer licensed to do business in one state might send direct response advertising material into other states in which it was not licensed and sell policies in those states. During the 1960s, states began passing unauthorized insurers acts. It is unlawful for an insurer to transact direct response insurance business in a state having such an act unless the insurer is appropriately licensed. Many of these laws are based on model acts drafted by the NAIC. These model acts are the Nonadmitted Insurance Model Act, the Unauthorized Insurers Process Act, and the Unauthorized Insurers False Advertising Process Act. Because of these laws, the problem of unlicensed insurers selling insurance by direct response advertising greatly diminished by the 1970s.[14]

Today, the insurer must be licensed and the policy form approved in every state in which the advertisement appears, unless the advertisement says that the policy will not be sold in the state. The advertisement itself must comply with the laws of all states in which the policy will be sold. The insurer must comply with countersignature laws in some states.[15] Thus, interstate marketing of direct response insurance involves a number of legal hurdles for insurers.

The lack of uniformity among the states' policy provisions laws and advertising laws makes it necessary that an insurer's employees in charge of compliance perform a careful review of policy forms and advertising. An insurer must take care that direct mail advertising is not sent into a state in which the insurer is not licensed to do business. Dissemination of mass media advertisements into states in which the insurer is not licensed can be difficult to control because newspapers and magazines often circulate in many states. Radio and television broadcasts may also cross state lines. An insurer usually puts disclaimers in its mass media advertising if that advertising will be distributed or broadcast in states where the insurer is not licensed. These disclaimers say that the policy will not be sold in those states. This will ordinarily protect the insurer against insurance department action.

---

[13]Fritz v. Old Am. Ins. Co., 354 F. Supp. 514 (S.D. Tex. 1973).

[14]Beavan & Braybrooks, *The Sale of Insurance through the Mail,* CLU Journal 18, Apr. 1982.

[15]Countersignature laws are discussed in Chapter 4, "Agency in Life and Health Insurance."

Internet Advertising

The Internet is a network of computers that is rapidly expanding all over the world. A person who owns a personal computer and a modem[16] can gain access to the Internet through companies that provide a connection service. Once connected to the Internet, the person can receive e-mail messages from other Internet users and send e-mail messages to them. In addition, the person can establish a *home page* (also called a *Web page* or *Web site*) that contains information accessible to other Internet users.

Insurers and insurance agents have established home pages containing insurance advertising and consumer information. For example, one insurer uses its home page to provide consumers with information about saving for retirement or for college expenses, developing an estate plan, and starting a business.[17] One agent described his home page as a "24-hour-a-day, 7-day-a-week advertisement."[18] Some agents' home pages include a form that Internet users can fill out to receive price quotations on insurance and annuities.[19] Usually, the agent will send the price quotation by e-mail.

In a few states with electronic signature statutes that allow an applicant to sign an application electronically, an entire insurance transaction could take place on the Internet. In these states, an applicant could apply for insurance on the Internet, sign the application electronically, pay the initial premium by encrypted credit card number,[20] and receive an electronically transferred policy that could be printed on her printer.[21]

Internet advertisements and sales are subject to the same laws as are other forms of insurance marketing, but insurance commissioners are concerned about the difficulty of overseeing Internet marketing. In March 1996, the NAIC established an Internet Marketing Working Group. According to the chairperson of the Working Group, "unlike direct mail and telephone marketing programs, the distinction between advertisement and solicitation on the Internet is more easily blurred and needs clarification."[22]

Regulation by Federal Agencies

The McCarran-Ferguson Act provides that the Federal Trade Commission Act is applicable to the business of insurance only "to the extent that such business is not regulated by State Law." Since the enactment of the McCarran-Ferguson Act in 1945, the Federal Trade Commission (FTC) has attempted to assert jurisdiction over insurance advertising, particularly interstate direct response advertising. In response to these efforts, states have enacted statutes or adopted regulations governing insurance advertising. Within the boundaries of states that have their own laws governing advertising, the FTC is barred from enforcing the Federal Trade Commission Act proscription of false, deceptive, or misleading advertising.

---

[16]A modem is a device used to connect a personal computer to a telephone line.

[17]Amy S. Friedman, *Cos. Explore Internet's Sales Potential,* NAT'L UNDERWRITER, LIFE & HEALTH/FIN. SERVICES EDITION, Oct. 23, 1995, at 7.

[18]Amy S. Friedman, *Agents' Net Home Pages Begin to Generate Leads,* NAT'L UNDERWRITER, LIFE & HEALTH/FIN. SERVICES EDITION, Jan. 22, 1996, at 7.

[19]*Id.*

[20]An encrypted number is indecipherable to all but the intended recipient.

[21]L. H. Otis, *Internet Usage Challenges Insurance Regulators,* NAT'L UNDERWRITER, LIFE & HEALTH/FIN. SERVICES EDITION, June 10, 1996, at 30.

[22]L. David Blair, *We'll Study Gray Areas of Selling Ins. on the Net,* NAT'L UNDERWRITER, LIFE & HEALTH/FIN. SERVICES EDITION, Sept. 9, 1996, at 10.

The U.S. Postal Service (USPS) has the power to deny use of the mails to carry material that is contrary to the public interest. Thus, the USPS has occasionally been involved in regulation of direct response advertising in situations in which fraudulent or misleading advertisements have been sent through the mail. In addition, the mail fraud statute[23] provides that the use of the mails to perpetrate frauds and swindles can result in fines and imprisonment for the guilty persons.

The Federal Communications Commission (FCC) indirectly controls advertising on radio and television. The FCC has the power to revoke or refuse to renew a broadcaster's license if the broadcaster operates its station in a manner that is not in the public interest. Broadcasters therefore review advertisements carefully before broadcasting them. If a broadcaster thinks the FCC might find that an advertisement is objectionable and contrary to the public interest, it ordinarily will refuse to air the advertisement.

The Internal Revenue Service is concerned with advertising of deferred annuity contracts. A deferred annuity contract provides that the purchaser pay premiums to the insurer but that the insurer will begin making annuity payments at a later date. The IRS opposes advertisements stating that deferred annuity contracts are tax shelters. A tax shelter typically allows some part of the taxpayer's income to escape taxation entirely, but the purchase of a deferred annuity does not ultimately avoid tax. Such annuities are legitimate tax-deferral devices, but the IRS has also opposed overemphasis on the tax-deferral aspect of deferred annuities. In addition, the IRS is concerned with advertisements for deferred annuities that disparage the taxing authorities. Statements such as "Don't let Uncle Sam take away your interest" are unacceptable to the IRS.

Finally, the IRS frowns on undue emphasis in advertisements on the savings and investment aspects of deferred annuity contracts. The IRS has taken the position that the retirement income and lifetime payout guarantees of deferred annuity contracts are the proper features to emphasize in advertisements.

The Securities and Exchange Commission is also concerned about annuity contract advertising. In 1979, the SEC stated in a release that it "remained very concerned with the proliferation of contracts which, while styled annuities, are clearly different in their essential terms from traditional annuities and are marketed in a manner involving the offer and sale of securities." The release further stated that in order to avoid the application of the federal securities laws, sellers of such contracts must bear significant mortality and investment risks. The contracts must also be advertised in such a way that they do not relegate the annuity features to fine print while emphasizing features calculated to appeal to investors who desire to "maximize tax-deferred capital accumulation rather than to acquire conventional annuity plans." In 1986, the SEC promulgated Rule 151, which states that an annuity contract must not be marketed primarily as an investment if it is to be exempt from the Securities Act of 1933.

State Laws Governing Insurance Advertising

Insurance advertising is governed by the state advertising laws that govern all types of advertising. It is also governed by laws that specifically apply to insurance advertising.

---

[23]18 U.S.C.A. § 1341-46 (West Supp. 1996).

State Laws Governing All Advertising

Most states have laws that declare the dissemination of deceptive advertising of any sort a misdemeanor. This prohibition includes insurance advertising. Most of these laws are based on the Printer's Ink Model Statute, which was developed in 1911.

State court cases and statutes also prohibit the use of a person's name or likeness for advertising purposes without that person's permission. Such a use is one form of the tort of invasion of privacy. The person whose name or likeness is so used has grounds to sue the advertiser for damages. Invasion of privacy is discussed in Chapter 23, "Privacy and Insurance."

State Laws Governing Insurance Advertising Only

All states have laws specifically governing insurance advertising. Most are patterned on model laws drafted by the NAIC. These include the model Unfair Trade Practices Act, the model Rules Governing Advertisements of Accident and Sickness Insurance, and the model Rules Governing the Advertising of Life Insurance. This section will address these model laws and the state statutes and regulations patterned on them.

The Model Unfair Trade Practices Act

The McCarran-Ferguson Act provides that the Federal Trade Commission Act will apply to the interstate business of insurance to the extent that state law does not regulate this area. The enactment of the McCarran-Ferguson Act spurred the passage of uniform state laws governing insurance advertising. Prior to the enactment of the McCarran-Ferguson Act, the states had made only unrelated, sporadic attempts to regulate insurance advertising. Soon after Congress passed the McCarran-Ferguson Act, the NAIC, in cooperation with the insurance industry, drafted the model Unfair Trade Practices Act. The great majority of states now have laws based on this model act and the other states have related legislation or regulations.

The model Unfair Trade Practices Act declares that its purpose is "to regulate trade practices in the business of insurance in accordance with the intent of Congress as expressed in the [McCarran-Ferguson Act]." It aims to fulfill this purpose by defining and prohibiting unfair trade practices. Among the prohibited unfair trade practices is false advertising.

The model Unfair Trade Practices Act contains a general prohibition against any form of insurance advertising that is "untrue, deceptive or misleading." In addition, the model act lists specific types of false advertising that are unfair trade practices. Among these are (1) a misrepresentation of the "benefits, advantages, conditions or terms of any policy"; (2) a misrepresentation as to "the dividends or share of the surplus to be received on any policy" or "previously paid on any policy"; (3) a misrepresentation either of an insurer's financial condition or "as to the legal reserve system upon which any life insurer operates"; (4) the use of a name or title of an insurance policy that misrepresents the policy's true nature; and (5) a misrepresentation of an insurance policy "as being shares of stock."

Statutes patterned on the model Unfair Trade Practices Act provide that the insurance commissioner shall have power to investigate an insurer to determine if it "has been or is engaged in any unfair trade practice." The commissioner can summon the insurer to a hearing if she has reason to believe that the insurer has engaged in such an act or practice. If, after the hearing, the commissioner determines that the insurer has committed an unfair trade practice, she must issue an order to the insurer to cease and desist the practice. The commissioner can at her discretion fine the insurer $1,000 for each violation up to an aggregate of $100,000. If the insurer acted flagrantly in conscious disregard of the Unfair Trade Practices Act, the penalty can be $25,000 for each violation up to an aggregate of $250,000. The commissioner can also suspend or revoke the insurer's license to do business in that state if the insurer knew, or reasonably should have known, it was violating the act. Thus, the penalties for false advertising can be severe.

The Model Rules Governing Advertisements of Accident and Sickness Insurance

In 1956, the NAIC, in cooperation with the insurance industry and the FTC, developed a comprehensive code of model rules designed to govern accident and health insurance advertising. The model rules were intended to supplement a state's Unfair Trade Practices Act. The NAIC recommended that each state insurance department adopt the model Rules Governing Advertisements of Accident and Sickness Insurance. Only four states—Alaska, Hawaii, Minnesota, and Montana—have not adopted rules governing accident and health insurance advertising.

Interpretive guidelines were added to the model rules to aid insurance commissioners in administering the rules and to help insurers develop advertising in compliance with the rules. Although the drafters did not intend for their interpretive guidelines to be a part of the rules, some states have adopted the interpretive guidelines along with the rules. In those states, the interpretive guidelines are a part of the state regulation of advertising and have the force of law.

Most states have adopted the model rules with variations. Therefore, insurers must check their insurance advertisements to be certain they comply with the regulations of any state in which they will be disseminated.

Preamble. The model rules begin with a preamble that reads in part:

> Although modern insurance advertising patterns much of its design after advertising for other goods and services, the uniqueness of insurance as a product must always be kept in mind in developing advertising of accident and sickness insurance. By the time an insured discovers that a particular insurance product is unsuitable for his needs, it may be too late for him to return to the marketplace to find a more satisfactory product. Hence, the insurance-buying public should be afforded a means by which it can determine, in advance of purchase, the desirability of the competing insurance products proposed to be sold. This can be accomplished by advertising which accurately describes the advantages and disadvantages of the insurance product without either exaggerating the benefits or minimizing the limitations. Properly designed advertising can provide such description and disclosure without sacrificing the sales appeal which is essential to its usefulness to the insurance-buying public and the insurance business. The purpose of the new Rules Governing Advertisements of Accident and Sickness Insurance is to establish minimum criteria to assure such a proper and accurate description and disclosure.

Purpose. The purpose of the model rules is to "assure the clear and truthful disclosure of the benefits, limitations, and exclusions of policies sold as accident and sickness insurance. This is intended to be accomplished by the establishment of guidelines and permissible and impermissible standards of conduct in the advertising of accident and sickness insurance." Interpretive Guideline 1 notes that "Disclosure is one of the principal objectives of these rules."

Applicability.   The model rules are applicable to any accident or sickness insurance advertisement (except Medicare supplement insurance advertisements) when the advertisement is intended for "presentation, distribution or dissemination" in the state. The term *accident or sickness insurance advertisement* is broadly defined as follows:

> An advertisement for the purpose of these rules shall include: (1) printed and published material, audio visual material, and descriptive literature of an insurer used in direct mail, newspapers, magazines, radio scripts, TV scripts, billboards, and similar displays; and (2) descriptive literature and sales aids of all kinds issued by an insurer, agent, producer, broker or solicitor for presentation to members of the insurance-buying public, including but not limited to circulars, leaflets, booklets, depictions, illustrations, form letters and lead-generating devices of all kinds . . . ; and (3) prepared sales talks, presentations, and material for use by agents, brokers, producers and solicitors whether prepared by the insurer or by the agent, broker, producer or solicitor.

The model rules also mandate that:

> Every insurer shall establish and at all times maintain a system of control over the content, form, and method of dissemination of all advertisements of its policies. All such advertisements, regardless of by whom written, created, designed or presented, shall be the responsibility of the insurer whose policies are so advertised.

This provision puts the burden of compliance with accident and sickness insurance advertising law squarely on the insurer.

Definitions.   The model rules contain various relevant definitions such as the definition of *accident or sickness insurance advertisement* noted above. *Policy* for the purpose of the model rules is defined as any accident or sickness "policy, plan, certificate, contract, agreement, statement of coverage, rider or endorsement." However, the model rules will not apply to advertisements of disability, waiver of premium, or double indemnity benefits included in life insurance or annuity contracts.

The model rules' definitions section makes distinctions among *exceptions, reductions,* and *limitations.* For the purpose of the model rules, an **exception** is any provision in a policy whereby the insurer entirely eliminates coverage for a specified hazard. Thus, an exception is a statement of a risk that the insurer does not assume under the policy. For example, the exceptions listed in one health insurance policy include the following, under the title "Non-covered Services":

- Cosmetic or reconstructive surgery.
- Routine eye examinations, eye refractions performed in conjunction with those routine eye examinations, and eye exercising.
- The fitting and cost of hearing aids.
- Routine physical examinations, routine laboratory tests including Pap smears, and preventive inoculations.
- Expenses covered by workers' compensation and occupational disease law.

A **reduction** is any provision that reduces the amount of a benefit. If there is a reduction, the insurer assumes a risk of loss for a specified hazard, but payment on the occurrence of such loss is limited to some amount or period less than would be otherwise payable had such reduction not been included. For example, the reductions listed in one health insurance policy include:

- In vitro fertilization, gamete intra-fallopian transfers, zygote intra-fallopian transfers, and artificial insemination are paid up to a lifetime benefit maximum of $25,000.
- One physician-recommended and medically directed weight reduction program per lifetime if the patient meets the standard criteria for morbid or exogenous obesity as determined by [the utilization review organization]. Benefits are paid at 50 percent of the reasonable and customary rate up to a lifetime maximum of $2,500.

A *limitation* is any provision that restricts coverage but that is not an exception or reduction. A definition of the term *hospital* in a policy is an example of a limitation.

An important revision to the model rules, made in 1974, was the distinction among three types of advertisements: institutional advertisements, invitations to inquire, and invitations to contract. According to the model rules, an *institutional advertisement* has as its sole purpose the promotion of the insurer or of the reader's, viewer's, or listener's interest in the concept of accident and sickness insurance. Some requirements that apply to invitations to inquire or invitations to contract do not apply to institutional advertisements. Institutional advertisements are the least stringently regulated of the three types of advertisements.

The objective of an *invitation to inquire* is to create a desire to inquire further about accident and sickness insurance. An invitation to inquire is limited to a brief description of coverage and must not refer to cost. An invitation to inquire is regulated more strictly than an institutional advertisement but not as strictly as an invitation to contract.

An *invitation to contract* includes terms and cost of the insurance advertised. Terms and cost are the elements necessary to enable a prospective purchaser to decide whether to purchase the insurance. Because a decision to purchase the insurance can be made on the basis of the advertisement alone, invitations to contract are regulated more strictly than are invitations to inquire or institutional advertisements.

Method of Disclosure of Required Information.   Regulations patterned on the model rules permit insurers to use either of two methods to disclose information required to be included in insurance advertisements. Required information, such as exceptions, reductions, or limitations can be set out conspicuously and in close conjunction with the statements to which such information relates. Alternatively, such information may be put under appropriate and prominent captions, such as "Exceptions," "Exclusions," or "Conditions Not Covered." The interpretive guidelines prohibit the use of captions such as "Extent of Coverage" or "Only These Exclusions." The interpretive guidelines state that these captions do not provide adequate notice of the significance of the material.

Form and Content of Advertisements.   Regulations patterned on the model rules require that the form and content of an advertisement of an accident or sickness insurance policy shall be sufficiently complete and clear to avoid either deception or the capacity or tendency to mislead or deceive. The state commissioner of insurance has the authority to determine whether the advertisement is misleading. In making such a determination, the commissioner must examine the overall impression that the advertisement may be reasonably expected to create on a person of average education or intelligence, within the segment of the public to which the advertisement is directed. Advertisements appearing in publications of general circulation are held to different standards than are advertisements appearing in scholarly, technical, or business publications, because the readers of the latter presumably will have a higher level of education.

The model rules state:

> Advertisements shall be truthful and not misleading in fact or in implication. Words or phrases, the meaning of which is clear only by implication or by familiarity with insurance terminology, shall not be used.

If the advertisement contains insurance terms, it must define those terms.

Advertisements of Benefits Payable, Losses Covered, or Premiums Payable. Regulations patterned on the model rules provide that advertisements cannot mislead readers regarding benefits, losses, coverage, or premiums by omitting information or by using ambiguous words or illustrations. The interpretive guidelines of the model rules include 37 illustrations of what must, or must not, appear in accident or sickness insurance advertisements. The following are examples:

1. An advertisement which describes any benefits that vary by age must disclose that fact.
2. An advertisement which states or implies immediate coverage of a policy is unacceptable unless suitable administrative procedures exist so that the policy is issued within fifteen working days after the application is received by the insurer.
3. An advertisement which uses the word "plan" without identifying it as an accident and sickness insurance policy is not permissible.
4. An advertisement which fails to disclose that the definition of "hospital" does not include a nursing home, convalescent home or extended care facility, as the case may be, is unacceptable.

These examples illustrate that a careful study of advertising regulations and interpretive guidelines is necessary for persons who develop accident and health insurance advertising.

Regulations patterned on the model rules prohibit the use of certain words or phrases in a manner that exaggerates any benefits beyond the terms of the policy. Note that these words or phrases are not forbidden as long as they do not exaggerate the benefits. The interpretive guidelines list terms that the advertiser must use with caution to avoid exaggerating benefits. Some of these terms are *pays full coverage,* *replaces income,* and *emergency paycheck.*

Descriptions of policy exceptions, reductions, or limitations, so as to imply that these are benefits, are prohibited. The negative features of exceptions, reductions, or limitations must be fairly described. For example, a waiting period must not be described as a "benefit builder."

The use of words or phrases such as *tax free, extra cash,* or *extra income* in advertisements for hospital benefit policies is also prohibited. Such words or phrases are forbidden because they have the "effect of misleading the public into believing the policy advertised will, in some way, enable them to make a profit from being hospitalized." The interpretive guidelines give additional examples of prohibited words and phrases. The interpretive guidelines state that "[*i*]llustrations which depict paper currency or checks showing an amount payable are deceptive and misleading and are not permissible."

Advertisements of hospital benefits are prohibited if they state that the amount of the benefit is payable on a monthly or weekly basis when, in fact, it is payable on a daily pro rata basis relating to the number of days of confinement. Regulations patterned on the model rules also mandate that "[w]hen the [hospital] policy contains a limit on the number of days of coverage provided, such limit must appear in the advertisement."

Regulations patterned on the model rules govern advertisements of health insurance policies covering specified diseases, such as cancer, or limited types of accidents, such as travel accidents. Advertisements that imply coverage beyond the terms of a specified disease are prohibited. For example, an advertisement for a cancer-only policy cannot be written to imply coverage for other diseases. Synonymous terms for the same disease cannot be used to imply broader coverage than the policy provides. Moreover, advertisements for specified disease policies or for limited accident policies must be conspicuously labeled as such in prominent type. Such a label might read "THIS IS A CANCER ONLY POLICY" or "THIS IS AN AUTOMOBILE ACCIDENT ONLY POLICY."

Direct response advertisements must not imply that the product advertised is "low cost" because no agent commissions are payable. According to the model rules, the reason for this prohibition is that the cost of advertising and servicing such policies is a substantial cost of direct response marketing.

Advertisements that are invitations to contract must disclose exceptions, reductions, and limitations affecting the basic provisions of the policy. A waiting, elimination, probationary, or similar time period between the effective date of the policy and the effective date of coverage must be disclosed. Finally, the use of words such as *just, only,* or *merely* to describe exceptions, reductions, or limitations so as to make these clauses seem unimportant is forbidden.

Advertisements that are invitations to contract must disclose the inclusion of a preexisting condition provision "in negative terms." In other words, the advertisement must not make the preexisting condition provision appear to be a benefit rather than an exclusion. Moreover, the advertisement must define the term *preexisting condition.* The advertisement cannot imply that the applicant's physical condition or medical history will not affect the issuance of the policy or the payment of a claim. Finally, advertisements with application forms must contain a question worded substantially as follows:

Do you understand that this policy will not pay benefits during the first _____ year(s) after the issue date for a disease or physical condition which you now have or have had in the past? _____ YES

Disclosure of Renewability, Cancellability, and Termination Provisions.   Regulations patterned on the model rules require that invitations to contract disclose provisions relating to renewability, cancellability, termination, or modification of benefits. Such disclosure must be made "in a manner which shall not minimize or render obscure the qualifying conditions." The interpretive guidelines provide the following examples: "This policy can be cancelled by the company at any time" or "Renewable at the option of the insurer."

Testimonials and Endorsements.   Third-party testimonials or endorsements must be genuine and represent the current opinion of the endorser. If the person making the testimonial has an interest in the insurer, the advertisement must disclose this relationship. Stockholders, directors, officers, or employees of the insurer fall under this rule. In addition, if the insurer has paid for the testimonial, the advertisement must disclose this fact. When a testimonial refers to benefits paid, the insurer must retain specific claims data for four years or until the report has been filed at the state insurance department's next examination of the insurer. This procedure gives the insurance department the means to verify the authenticity of testimonials used in advertising.

Use of Statistics.   Regulations patterned on the model rules require that statistics used in advertisements be relevant and accurate. An advertisement cannot imply that statistics used are derived from the advertised policy unless they really are. The advertisement must cite the source of any statistics used.

The use of words such as *liberal* or *generous* relating to claim settlements are prohibited. Moreover, the model rules state that "[a]n unusual amount paid for a unique claim for the policy advertised is misleading and shall not be used."

Disparaging Statements.   Statements that disparage other insurers in an insurance advertisement are forbidden. Unfair or incomplete comparisons of policies or benefits of other insurers are also forbidden.

Jurisdictional Licensing and Status.   Regulations patterned on the model rules prohibit an insurer from implying that it is licensed in jurisdictions where it is not, if the advertisement appears in those jurisdictions. Also forbidden is any implication that state or federal governments endorse a particular insurer or its policies. For this reason, words such as *official,* when used to describe applications or policies, are not permissible, because these words tend to mislead.

Identity of the Insurer and Policy.   The advertisement must clearly disclose the insurer's identity. An advertisement that is an invitation to contract must identify the form number of the advertised policy.

Special Offers.   Advertising that implies that purchasers will receive a lower group insurance rate when such a rate is not applied is prohibited. Nor can insurers advertise limited offers that imply that the purchaser will receive a special rate if he purchases during the period of the offer when actually the rate would remain the same if the purchaser applied later. The model rules also prohibit overemphasis on any reduced initial premium rate. Finally, the model rules prohibit the use of "safe driver's awards" or similar special awards in advertisements for accident or sickness insurance.

Statements about an Insurer.   Regulations patterned on the model rules prohibit misleading statements about an insurer's assets, corporate structure, financial standing, age, or relative position in the insurance business. For example, an insurer that has been operating for only a relatively short time may not advertise that it is old. A recommendation by a commercial rating system must not be included in an advertisement unless the advertisement clearly indicates the purpose and scope of the recommendation. For example, it is permissible for an advertisement to state that "The Careful Insurance Company is rated A++ (superior) by A. M. Best Company, independent insurance analysts, on the basis of operating performance and financial strength."

Enforcement Procedures.   Regulations patterned on the model rules mandate that each insurer maintain a file of all its advertisements. A note must be attached to each advertisement in the file indicating the manner and extent of the advertisement's distribution and the form number of any policy advertised. The insurer must keep the advertisements on file for four years or until the next examination report on the insurer is filed, whichever period is longer.

Those insurers that must file an annual statement with the state must also file a certificate of compliance with the state's advertising laws. An officer of the insurer must execute the certificate of compliance. In the certificate, the officer must state that, to the best of her knowledge, information, and belief, the insurer's advertisements disseminated during the past year complied with the advertising laws of the state.

The Model Rules Governing Life Insurance and Annuity Contract Advertising

The NAIC adopted the model Rules Governing the Advertising of Life Insurance in 1975. These model rules govern the advertising of annuity contracts, as well as the advertising of life insurance policies. Over one-third of the states have adopted regulations patterned on these model rules. Ten states have other regulations governing advertisements of life insurance or annuity contracts. The rest have not adopted life insurance or annuity contract advertisement regulations. Thus, the regulation of life insurance and annuity contract advertising is less uniform than that of health insurance advertising.

Life insurance and annuity contract advertising have presented fewer types of problems than has health insurance advertising. Therefore, the regulation of life insurance and annuity contract advertising is less complex. Unlike the model Rules Governing Advertisements of Accident and Sickness Insurance, the model Rules Governing the Advertising of Life Insurance include no interpretive guidelines.

The model Rules Governing the Advertising of Life Insurance are partially patterned on the model Rules Governing Advertisements of Accident and Sickness Insurance. Many sections are substantially the same. For this reason, only the sections unique to the model life insurance advertisement rules will be discussed here.

Definitions.   The model life insurance and annuity advertisement rules do not define the terms *exception, reduction,* and *limitation* or the terms *institutional advertisement, invitation to inquire,* and *invitation to contract.* In a major departure from the model accident and sickness insurance advertisement rules, the model life insurance advertisement rules do not distinguish among institutional advertisements, invitations to inquire, and invitations to contract.

Form and Content of Advertisements.   Unique to the model life insurance and annuity contract advertisement rules is a section dealing with the use of terms such as *investment, profit,* and *savings* in connection with life insurance policies or annuity contracts. Such terms must not be used in a misleading way.

Disclosure Requirements.   If a life insurance advertisement uses a term such as *no medical examination required* when policy issuance is not guaranteed on application, the term must be accompanied by an equally prominent statement that policy issuance could depend on answers to health questions. Advertisements of life insurance policies must clearly indicate that the policy advertised is a life insurance policy if the name of the policy does not include the words *life insurance.*

Advertisements of life insurance policies with level premiums, but with benefits that increase or decrease with the age of the insured, must disclose the changing benefit feature. An advertisement for a policy with nonlevel premiums must prominently describe the premium changes.

In 1988, the NAIC revised the model life insurance and annuity contract advertisement rules to cover the advertising of contracts with "nonguaranteed policy elements." A nonguaranteed policy element is a dividend, premium, cash value, or death benefit of which the amount or payment is not guaranteed by the life insurance or annuity contract. An advertisement must not state or imply a guarantee as to payment or amount of a nonguaranteed policy element. If the advertisement illustrates a nonguaranteed policy element, the illustration must be based on the insurer's current scale and must say that the illustration is not a guarantee of amounts payable in the future.

The section of the model rules that regulates advertisements of deferred annuities and deposit funds deals primarily with disclosure of interest rates. This section also requires that if a deferred annuity or deposit fund does not provide a cash surrender value prior to commencement of benefit payments, the advertisement must disclose that fact.

Servicemarks

Servicemarks are an important part of an insurer's advertising. A servicemark is similar to a trademark, except that a servicemark pertains to services, whereas a trademark pertains to goods. A *servicemark* can be a word, letter, phrase, number, design, or a combination of these that a service company, such as an insurer, uses to identify its services.

An insurer usually has a number of servicemarks. The name and logo of the insurer and the names and logos of its affiliated companies are servicemarks. Policy forms are often given names and logos that are also servicemarks. For example, one insurer calls its travel accident policy "Wings and Wheels." Such a name is a servicemark that the insurer uses in its advertising to identify its travel accident policy.

Servicemarks are valuable property. Rights in a servicemark are acquired through use. The law protects an insurer's servicemarks if they are sufficiently identified with the insurer.

If an insurer intends to adopt a servicemark, such as a name for a new policy form, the insurer's lawyers ordinarily will search certain records to see if the servicemark chosen is available or is already in use. An insurer must not use a servicemark belonging to another insurer. Such use would constitute an infringement of the other insurer's right to the servicemark and could result in a lawsuit.

If the servicemark chosen is available, the insurer may begin to use it at once. After a period of use, the insurer's lawyers will file an application to register the servicemark with the appropriate government agency. This procedure helps to establish the insurer's claim to the servicemark.

Symbols similar to those used to identify trademarks will be used to identify servicemarks that are in use. Before the registration of the servicemark is complete, the symbol ᔆᴹ will signify the insurer's claim to the servicemark. After the servicemark is registered, the letter *R* in a circle (®) will be used.

Summary

Individual life and health insurance and annuity contract advertisements ordinarily are not considered part of the contract, especially if they are not referred to in the policy or attached to it. Nevertheless, the courts often honor the reasonable expectations of applicants, policyowners, and beneficiaries. If group insurance advertising varies from the contract, the courts can estop the insurer from denying terms more favorable to the insured that appear in the advertising or can hold that the insurer waived the less favorable contract terms. The courts also have held that direct response advertisements are binding on the insurer because the applicant has no opportunity to gain an understanding of the insurance by conferring with an agent.

In response to market conduct concerns, in 1995 the NAIC adopted the Life Insurance Illustrations Model Regulation. The purpose of regulations patterned on this model is to provide rules for life insurance policy illustrations that will protect consumers, foster consumer education, ensure that illustrations do not mislead purchasers of life insurance, and make illustrations more understandable.

Direct response insurance is frequently sold through a multistate distribution program. A direct response insurer must be licensed, and the policy approved, in every state in which the advertisement appears, unless the advertisement says that the policy will not be sold in that state. The advertisement itself must comply with the laws of those states in which the insurer will sell the policy. The lack of uniformity among state laws governing policy provisions and advertising can make this a difficult task.

Insurers and insurance agents have established home pages so that they can advertise on the Internet. Internet advertisements and sales are subject to the same laws as are other forms of insurance marketing, but insurance commissioners are concerned about the difficulty of overseeing Internet marketing. The NAIC therefore has established an Internet Marketing Working Group.

The laws governing life and health insurance and annuity contract advertisements include laws governing advertisements generally, as well as laws specifically governing insurance advertisments. Insurance advertisement regulation is performed primarily by the states, although the federal government is sometimes involved through the Federal Trade Commission, the U.S. Postal Service, the Federal Communications Commission, the Internal Revenue Service, or the Securities and Exchange Commission.

Most states have passed statutes patterned on the NAIC model Unfair Trade Practices Act. Statutes patterned on this model act include a section prohibiting false insurance advertising. Supplementing these statutes are regulations governing the advertising of life and health insurance. Many of these regulations are based on the NAIC model Rules Governing Advertisements of Accident and Sickness Insurance and Rules Governing the Advertising of Life Insurance. These model rules spell out in detail the required structure for life and health insurance and annuity contract advertisements. The aim of the rules is to ensure that advertisements do not mislead prospective purchasers of insurance.

Servicemarks are an important part of an insurer's advertising. Servicemarks include the insurer's name and logo and the names and logos of policy forms. Rights in a servicemark are acquired through use. The insurer usually will protect its right to exclusive use of the servicemark by registering the servicemark with the appropriate government agency.

ILLUSTRATIVE CASE

> This case concerns an accident policy covering students. The pamphlet advertising the policy did not contain an exclusion found in the policy. The court therefore held that the language of the pamphlet controlled the students' coverage.

EUGENE E. LAWRENCE et al., Appellants

v.

PROVIDENTIAL LIFE INSURANCE COMPANY, Appellee [24]
Supreme Court of Arkansas

ROBINSON, Justice.

The question on appeal is whether, under the terms of a policy of accident insurance, the assured is entitled to recovery for medical expenses he sustained by reason of an injury to his son, who was insured under the policy. The specific issue is whether the nature of the injury and resulting expenses were excluded under the provisions of the policy.

---

[24]385 S.W.2d 936 (Ark. 1965).

The appellee, Providential Life Insurance Company writes a type of accident insurance called "The Providential School Plan". Among other things, this insurance provides indemnity to the extent of $5,000 for medical expenses for "teachers, students, and non-teaching personnel". Parents of students were solicited to purchase the policy to protect themselves against medical expenses they might incur by reason of injury to their children. The solicitation of parents was made by the insurance company distributing to the school children, to take home, a pamphlet advertising the policy. The pamphlet explained the benefits provided by the policy, those things not covered by the policy and the amount of premium. The pamphlet also contained a pocket on one side where currency or a check could be inserted by the parents in payment of the premium in the event they decided to take the insurance. The pamphlet could then be sent to the insurance company and it became the application of the sender asking that the applicant's child or children be included in a master policy to be issued to the school attended by the children. In this instance the policy was issued to the Brookland Public School District, Brookland, Arkansas.

The printed matter in the application appears to be complete in giving full information about what is not covered by the policy. At least the application shows on its face what the applicant understood was not covered by the policy. The application states:

> THIS INSURANCE DOES NOT COVER . . . Dental expenses of any kind except those resulting from accidental injury to whole, sound natural teeth, eyeglasses, contact lenses or prescriptions therefor; intentionally self-inflicted injuries, injury for which benefits are payable under any Workmen's Compensation Act or Law; an act of war whether such war be declared or undeclared; any form of sickness, disease or infection except pyogenic infections incurred through an accidental cut or wound; services rendered by members of the insured's immediate family or as a part of the school duties by a physician retained by the school system. Expense for physiotherapy, diathermy, heat treatment in any form, antibiotic therapy, manipulation or massage will be payable only when such treatment is performed in hospital to a resident bed patient.

The policy as issued, in addition to the foregoing exclusions named in the application, excluded from coverage, among other things, fighting and "any aggravation of a pre-existing condition". Neither of these exclusions were mentioned in the application made on a printed form prepared by the insurance company. Thus, it will be seen that the exclusion provision of the policy is broader than the exclusion provision of the application.

The policy, when issued, was sent to the Brookland School. A copy was not sent to the applicant, the parent. It is not shown that the insurance company had any reason to believe that the parents of the children named in the policy would ever see the policy.

Appellant, Eugene E. Lawrence, father of David Lawrence, sent in an application in the aforesaid manner naming his children, including David, to be insured. David is afflicted with hemophilia. Some time after the delivery of the policy, David received a cut to the inside of a lip while fighting with another boy. Due to the fact that he was afflicted with hemophilia, the cut did not stop bleeding for a long time. It was necessary to send him to a hospital in Memphis. The hospital and doctor bills finally amounted to $2,454.15. A claim was made against the insurance company; payment was refused on the ground that the policy did not cover an injury due to fighting and that it did not cover an aggravation of a pre-existing condition of hemophilia.

The cause was submitted to the court sitting as a jury on a stipulation of facts. The court rendered a judgment in favor of the insurance company. The assured has appealed.

If the exclusions named in the policy are controlling, the assured cannot recover. On the other hand, if the statement in the application setting out the things not covered by the policy is to prevail, injuries due to fighting or an aggravation of a pre-existing condition are not excluded. One of the contentions of the insurance company is that the exclusions listed in the pamphlet should not prevail because there is a notation thereon that the pamphlet is not a policy. Of course the pamphlet is not a policy, but it did become an application.

At this point it might be well to mention that the policy provides that any form of disease or sickness is not covered by the policy. Although hemophilia may be designated as a disease, the assured is not precluded from recovering on that ground because this court has held many times that the aggravation of a pre-existing dormant condition is not a valid defense in a suit on an accident policy.

We now reach the question of which should prevail—those things listed in the application as not being covered by the insurance or those things listed in the policy as not covered. In the case of *Woodmen of the World Life Ins. Society v. Counts,* 221 Ark. 143, 252 S.W.2d 390, Counts applied for a policy providing double indemnity for accidental death. The policy, as issued, did not contain the double indemnity feature. The insured was accidentally killed. This court held that the insurance company was liable for double indemnity; that it was the duty of the insurance company to write the type of insurance named in the application, or to issue no policy. There, the court quoted with approval from *Robinson v. United States Ben. Soc.,* 132 Mich. 695, 94 N.W. 211: "The duty of the defendant was to issue the policy in compliance with the terms of the application. If it chose to insert inconsistent provisions, it was its duty to call the attention of the insured to them, so that he might accept or refuse the policy. The insured has the right to assume that his policy will be in accordance with the terms of his application, and he cannot be bound by a different policy until he has had the opportunity to ratify or waive the inconsistent provisions".

In the case at bar, the application, the form of which was prepared by the insurance company, clearly states those things not covered by the policy. The insurance company had no right to add other exclusions to the policy without the approval of the applicant.

Appellee suggests that although the stipulation shows that the insured was injured in a fight, there is no showing that he received an accidental injury within the meaning of the policy. The complaint alleges that the insured was accidentally injured. It is stipulated that he was injured in a fight with a fellow student. The inference is that the in-

jury was accidental. There is no showing that the insured was the aggressor or that he was not acting in self defense. In *Maloney v. Maryland Casualty Co.,* 113 Ark. 174, 167 S.W. 845, the court said: "If an injury occurs without the agency of the insured, it may be logically termed 'accidental,' even though it may be brought about designedly by another person".

There is no dispute about the amount involved, which is $2,454.15. Since it has been decided that the appellant is entitled to recover, it necessarily follows that he is entitled to 12 per cent penalty on the amount sued for and a reasonable attorney's fee. In the circumstances, we believe a $1,000.00 fee would be appropriate.

Reversed.

Questions for Review

1. Why have the courts treated promotional material for group life insurance differently than similar material for individual life insurance?

2. What is meant by *direct response insurance advertising?* Indicate some of the legal hurdles that face an insurer using direct response insurance advertising on an interstate basis.

3. Describe the nature of the authority over insurance advertising each of the following federal agencies possesses:
   a. Federal Trade Commission.
   b. U.S. Postal Service.
   c. Federal Communications Commission.
   d. Internal Revenue Service.
   e. Securities and Exchange Commission.

4. In a state with an unfair trade practices act based on the NAIC model, what legal sanctions can the insurance commissioner impose on an insurer whose advertising practices violate the Unfair Trade Practices Act?

5. How do the model Rules Governing Advertisements of Accident and Sickness Insurance define the terms *exceptions, reductions,* and *limitations?*

6. Define the following:
   a. Institutional advertisements.
   b. Invitations to inquire.
   c. Invitations to contract.
   Which is the most strictly regulated? Why?

7. What must an advertisement that contains a testimonial or endorsement disclose?

8. If a life insurance advertisement uses a term such as *no medical examination required* and policy issuance is not guaranteed upon application, what additional statement must appear?

9. What is a servicemark? How can an insurer protect its servicemarks?

23   PRIVACY AND INSURANCE

Chapter Outline

Privacy is a word with no single commonly accepted definition. The members of the Privacy Protection Study Commission that Congress created in 1974 to recommend privacy legislation could not agree on a definition after two years of studying privacy. The tort of invasion of privacy has not one definition, but four.

    A definition the courts often repeat is that the right to ***privacy*** is "the right to be let alone." However, this definition does not fit well in the context of the right to privacy in insurance transactions. A more workable definition in that context is "the right to fair personal information practices."

    Most people in the United States believe that privacy is a fundamental right. Many are concerned that personal information collected by government, insurers, and other organizations will be misused.[1] A national survey taken in December 1987

---

[1] Robert G. Knowles, *Americans View Privacy as a Fundamental Right,* NAT'L UNDERWRITER, LIFE & HEALTH/FIN. SERVICES EDITION, Nov. 5, 1990, at 27.

showed that only 52 percent of Americans believed insurers would keep acquired immune deficiency syndrome (AIDS) testing data confidential.[2] To increase public confidence in the confidentiality of the personal information in their files, many insurers have created safeguards that go beyond the requirements of the privacy laws.[3]

The recently increased efforts of insurers to reduce insurance fraud, discussed in Chapter 20, "Health Insurance," present another challenge. As an officer of a privacy protection organization noted, "The industry is on the horns of a double dilemma: It not only must figure out how to step up its anti-fraud campaign without stepping on the privacy rights of its customers, but it must also find a way to respect its good premium-paying customers' rights without diminishing the war on fraud."[4]

The History of Privacy Law

The legal right to privacy is of relatively recent origin. It did not exist at English common law. Before 1890, no American court had granted relief for invasion of privacy. In 1890, in a famous and influential article by Samuel D. Warren and Louis D. Brandeis entitled *The Right to Privacy,*[5] the authors argued that the growing excesses of the press made necessary a distinct remedy for invasion of privacy. Thereafter, the right to privacy began to receive protection in statutes and court cases. A body of tort law developed that provided damages for invasion of privacy.

The Tort of Invasion of Privacy

The tort of *invasion of privacy* has taken four distinct forms. The first form is the appropriation of a person's name or likeness by another person for the other person's benefit. For example, ordinarily an invasion of a person's privacy occurs if that person's name or photograph is used for advertising purposes without his consent.

The second form of invasion of privacy is unreasonable intrusion on a person's seclusion or solitude or into the person's private affairs. Invasion of a person's home or eavesdropping on her private conversations by means of a telephone wiretap are examples of unreasonable intrusion.

The third type of invasion of privacy is the public disclosure of private facts about a person. Thus, if one person publishes in a newspaper that another person does not pay his debts, this is an invasion of privacy.

The fourth form of invasion of privacy consists of placing a person in a false light in the public eye. In one case, the court held that the publication of a photograph of an honest waiter to illustrate an article about dishonest waiters was an invasion of privacy.[6]

---

[2]AMERICAN COUNCIL OF LIFE INSURANCE & HEALTH INSURANCE ASSOCIATION OF AMERICA, *Public Attitudes about AIDS and Underwriting Practices Survey Highlights,* Jan. 1988, at 3.

[3]LIFE OFFICE MANAGEMENT ASSOCIATION, INFORMATION PRIVACY: PRINCIPLES AND GUIDELINES, Oct. 1978; *Confidentiality: A Major AIDS Insurance Issue,* RESOURCE, Nov./Dec. 1987, at 64.

[4]Steven Richards, *Privacy Rights Can Survive War on Ins. Fraud,* NAT'L UNDERWRITER, LIFE & HEALTH/FIN. SERVICES EDITION, Sept. 9, 1996, at 52; see also, Stephanie D. Esters, *Fraud Investigators Warned about Going Too Far,* NAT'L UNDERWRITER, LIFE & HEALTH/FIN. SERVICES EDITION, Oct. 21, 1996, at 28.

[5]4 HARV. L. REV. 193 (1890).

[6]Valerni v. Hearst Magazines, 99 N.Y.S.2d 866 (N.Y. Sup. Ct. 1949).

There are several defenses to invasion of privacy lawsuits. First, if the plaintiff consented to the invasion of his privacy, the consent will bar recovery, as is true for other torts. For example, if the waiter in the case discussed above had consented to the use of his photograph in the article about dishonest waiters, he could not have maintained a lawsuit for invasion of privacy.

Second, the mass media have a privilege to report on and discuss public figures or newsworthy people. An ordinary person could be newsworthy if he receives an honor or experiences a calamity. This privilege can bar recovery for public disclosure of private facts.

Third, a defendant has a qualified privilege to further his own legitimate interests. For example, reasonable investigations of insurance applicants or insurance claims are privileged and therefore cannot serve as grounds for a lawsuit based on invasion of privacy.

Although truth is an absolute defense to a defamation lawsuit, it is not a defense to a lawsuit for invasion of privacy. In other words, a public disclosure of private facts, even if the facts are true, may be actionable in a lawsuit for invasion of privacy.

Constitutional Protection of Privacy

The U.S. Supreme Court has held that the federal Constitution provides certain protections against government intrusion into individual privacy. Although the Constitution does not explicitly mention the right to privacy, the Court has held that the right is implied. In *Katz v. United States,*[7] the Court held that although a person's general right to privacy is largely left to state law, various provisions of the federal Constitution protect personal privacy from government invasion. Moreover, the Congress of the United States stated in the Privacy Act of 1974 that "the right to privacy is a personal and fundamental right protected by the Constitution of the United States."[8] Constitutional protection from government intrusion extends to privacy against unreasonable searches and seizures by the police[9]; privacy in marriage,[10] abortion,[11] contraception,[12] the education of children,[13] and family living arrangements[14]; political privacy[15]; and privacy in communications,[16] among others.

The Federal Fair Credit Reporting Act

Public concern over invasions of privacy has increased along with the increase in government regulation and recordkeeping and with the growing impact of computers. The federal government, credit bureaus, insurers, and many other organizations gather and store ever vaster quantities of personal information. The concern that

---

[7]389 U.S. 347 (1967).

[8]Pub. L. 93–579(a)(4).

[9]U.S. Const. amend. IV & amend. XIV, 1.

[10]Boddie v. Connecticut, 401 U.S. 371 (1971); Loving v. Virginia, 388 U.S. 1 (1967).

[11]Roe v. Wade, 410 U.S. 113 (1973).

[12]Carey v. Population Services Internat'l, 431 U.S. 678 (1977); Eisenstadt v. Baird, 405 U.S. 438 (1972); Griswold v. Connecticut, 381 U.S. 479 (1965).

[13]Pierce v. Society of Sisters, 268 U.S. 510 (1925); Meyer v. Nebraska, 262 U.S. 390 (1923).

[14]Moore v. City of East Cleveland, 431 U.S. 494 (1977).

[15]Brown v. Socialist Workers '74 Campaign Committee, 459 U.S. 87 (1982).

[16]Katz v. United States, 389 U.S. 347 (1967).

some of these data may be inaccurate or misused, with harm to the people involved, spurred Congress to enact laws regulating personal information collection, retention, and use. The Fair Credit Reporting Act (FCRA)[17] is the federal privacy law of greatest importance to insurers.

Congress enacted the FCRA in 1970. The FCRA was intended to ensure that credit reporting agencies act "with fairness, impartiality and a respect for the consumer's right to privacy." Insurers and others who use consumer reports also have duties under the FCRA.

A *consumer report* is "any written, oral or other communication of any information by a consumer reporting agency bearing on a consumer's credit worthiness, credit standing, credit capacity, character, general reputation, personal characteristics or mode of living" for use in determining whether the consumer can obtain employment, credit, or insurance to be used primarily for personal or family purposes. A consumer is a natural person under the FCRA. The FCRA does not protect businesses.

An *investigative consumer report,* as opposed to a consumer report, is a report "obtained through personal interviews with neighbors, friends or associates of the consumer reported on or with others with whom he is acquainted or who may have knowledge" about the consumer. Specific factual credit information obtained directly from a credit reporting agency is not considered an investigative consumer report; rather, it is considered a consumer report. The FCRA imposes additional requirements on information seekers if an investigative consumer report is involved. The FCRA requires that the consumer be given both advance notification that such a report might be made and a statement informing the consumer that she can request a disclosure of the nature and scope of the investigation.

A *consumer reporting agency* is any entity that for money, or on a cooperative nonprofit basis, regularly prepares consumer reports and furnishes those reports to others. Consumer reporting agencies must comply with the extensive requirements of the FCRA. A consumer reporting agency can release information only to a person the agency believes has a legitimate business need for the information, on the consumer's request, or on court order. A consumer reporting agency cannot report certain obsolete information. It must maintain reasonable procedures to guard against improper reporting. The consumer reporting agency must disclose to the consumer the nature and substance of all information—except medical information—in its files at the time of the request, certain sources of the information, and the recipients of the information. If a person disputes the information in her file, the information must be either verified or deleted.

Insurers are ordinarily concerned with the FCRA in three situations. First, at the time an insurer assesses a risk, it might obtain consumer reports or investigative consumer reports. Second, an insurer's claims investigations might necessitate obtaining such reports. Third, as employers, insurers might obtain such reports to make employment decisions.

The FCRA requires insurers to make certain reports to consumers. An insurer that makes an adverse decision based on a consumer report must inform the person involved of the decision and, at the same time, supply the name and address of the consumer reporting agency that made the report on which the decision was based. An adverse decision would include denial of insurance or an increase in the charge for insurance.

---

[17]15 U.S.C.A. §§ 1681a–1681t (West 1982 & Supp. 1996).

As of October 2, 1995, an insurer that receives data about an insurance applicant from the Medical Information Bureau (MIB) must inform the applicant if the data are used to alert the underwriter to investigate further and if the MIB information or the reinvestigation results in an adverse underwriting decision. The MIB is a trade association, composed of a large number of insurers, that provides for the exchange of medical information among its insurer members.

It is unlawful under the FCRA for an insurer to obtain information on a consumer from a consumer reporting agency under false pretenses. Any person who knowingly and willfully obtains such information without a legitimate business need, in connection with a business transaction involving the consumer, could be fined up to $5,000, imprisoned up to one year, or both.

State Privacy Laws

As noted at the beginning of this chapter, state tort law protecting people from invasion of privacy has been developing for over a century. In addition, the states have enacted statutes requiring that much of the data held by state agencies be kept confidential. For example, in some states a coroner's report is available only to a person to whom the cause of death is a "material issue." Medical records are usually recognized as personal and private and are protected from public disclosure. State laws often protect adoption records, social service records, educational records, personnel files, and tax returns from disclosure.

State privacy legislation affecting insurance recordkeeping was minimal prior to the development of the NAIC Model Privacy Act. Some states have made use of their Unfair Trade Practices Act to regulate recordkeeping practices to a limited extent. A few states passed laws regulating forms that a person must sign to authorize disclosure of medical information about himself. Some of these laws have precise requirements as to the content of such authorization forms. Insurers have had to develop forms that comply with the various state laws.

Beyond the regulation mentioned above, little state insurance recordkeeping privacy regulation was in place before the NAIC's adoption of the Model Privacy Act. Nevertheless, most insurers have voluntarily instituted measures to safeguard the confidentiality of records, conduct periodic evaluations of recordkeeping practices, allow customers to have access to information collected during a background check, and review the operating practices of the investigative firms the insurers employ.

The NAIC Model Privacy Act

The NAIC adopted the Insurance Information and Privacy Protection Model Act (the Model Privacy Act) in 1979. More than one-third of the states have privacy laws governing insurers, most of which are patterned on the Model Privacy Act.

The Model Privacy Act establishes "standards for the collection, use and disclosure of information gathered in connection with insurance institutions, agents or insurance-support organizations." Insurance-support organizations presumably include the Medical Information Bureau, investigative agencies, claims processing agencies, and credit bureaus. The NAIC stressed the importance of balancing the insurer's need for information with the public's need for fairness in insurance information practices. State laws patterned on the Model Privacy Act protect only a natural person who resides in the state in which the law is enacted and who is the subject of the information collected. These laws do not protect persons obtaining insurance for business purposes.

The Model Privacy Act has five stated purposes: (1) to minimize intrusiveness; (2) to establish a regulatory mechanism to enable natural persons to ascertain what information is being or has been collected about them in connection with insurance transactions; (3) to enable such persons to have access to such information for the purpose of verifying or disputing its accuracy; (4) to limit the disclosure of information collected in connection with insurance transactions; and (5) to enable insurance applicants and policyowners to obtain the reasons for adverse underwriting decisions. The remainder of this section contains a discussion of the requirements of laws patterned on the Model Privacy Act.

Pretext Interviews

A *pretext interview* occurs when an interviewer, in an attempt to obtain information about someone, makes an intentional misrepresentation or refuses to identify himself. The interviewer might pretend to be someone else, pretend to represent someone he does not represent, or misrepresent the purpose of the interview. Under laws patterned on the Model Privacy Act, an insurer, an agent, or an insurance-support organization, such as an investigative or claims processing agency, ordinarily cannot conduct a pretext interview in connection with an insurance transaction.

This rule has one exception. Pretext interviews can be conducted in claims investigations if the insurer has a reasonable basis for suspecting material misrepresentation or material nondisclosure. Such pretext interviews can be conducted with anyone except a person who has a privileged relationship with the person being investigated. Although the term *privileged relationship* is not defined in the Model Privacy Act, privileged relationships probably would include those between husband and wife, doctor and patient, and attorney and client.

Notice of Insurance Information Practices

Under the Model Privacy Act, an insurer or agent must provide notice of insurance information practices to an insurance applicant. With certain exceptions, upon a policy renewal, a reinstatement, or a request for a change in benefits, a policyowner[18] also must be provided with such notice. Exceptions occur if information is collected only from the policyowner or, in the case of renewal, if a similar notice has been given within the past 24 months.

The notice must be given promptly. An applicant must be given the notice when the collection of information from a third person begins. If information is collected only from the applicant, the notice must be given when the policy is delivered.

If notice must be given when a policy is renewed, it must be given by the renewal date. In the case of policy reinstatement or change in insurance benefits, if notice is required, it must be given at the time the insurer receives the request for reinstatement or change in benefits.

The notice of insurance information practices must be in writing and must state whether personal information might be collected from persons other than the proposed insured. The types of personal information that might be collected and the types of sources and investigative techniques that might be used must be disclosed.

---

[18]Group certificateholders are included where the group insurance is individually underwritten.

The notice also must disclose that certain classes of people might receive personal information without prior authorization by the person to whom the information relates. These classes include people who need the information to provide services to the insurer; other insurers or agents who need the information to prevent or detect misrepresentation or nondisclosure or to perform functions in connection with insurance transactions; medical professionals where a medical problem is involved; people conducting certain research or audits; and people who will use the information in marketing. The notice must state the types of personal information that might be disclosed without prior authorization and that the applicant or policyowner can request a description of the circumstances under which such disclosures might occur.

The notice must also state that the person involved has a right of access to the information and the right to correct or amend the information, as well as a right to request a description of the procedures for doing so. Finally, the notice must contain a statement that insurance-support organizations might retain information and disclose it to other people with a need for the information.

Disclosure Authorization Forms

A person signs a disclosure authorization form to indicate consent to disclosure of personal information about him. The Model Privacy Act spells out the required content of disclosure authorization forms. The form must be dated and written in plain language. The form must specify the classes of people authorized to disclose personal information, the nature of the information that can be disclosed, and the classes of people to whom the information can be disclosed. The form must also specify the purpose for which the information is collected.

Disclosure authorizations are not valid after the time indicated in the form, which can be no longer than 30 months according to laws patterned on the Model Privacy Act. The form must provide for the person involved to authorize a shorter period of time if he wishes. Finally, the person involved must be notified that he is entitled to receive a copy of the authorization form.

Investigative Consumer Reports

An investigative consumer report, under laws patterned on the Model Privacy Act, is a report about a person's character, general reputation, personal characteristics, or mode of living obtained from neighbors, friends, associates, acquaintances, or others. When an investigative consumer report is to be prepared, the insurer or agent must inform the person investigated that she can request to be interviewed also. Notice must be given that the person can receive a copy of the investigative report on request if she is not interviewed.

Access to Recorded Personal Information

Under laws patterned on the Model Privacy Act, on request and after proper identification, a person has a right of access to information about himself that is in the possession of an insurer, agent, or insurance-support organization. The person must be informed of the nature and substance of the information and allowed to have a copy on request. She must be informed of the identity of the people or organizations to whom the information has been disclosed, if this has been recorded, or else of the persons to whom such disclosure is normally made. She must also be given a summary of procedures for requesting correction or deletion of information. Institutional sources of the information must be disclosed. A reasonable fee can be charged for providing personal information, except for providing reasons for adverse underwriting decisions.

Medical-record information can be disclosed to the person involved or to a medical professional designated by the person. A medical professional is defined as "any person licensed or certified to provide health care services," including, among others, physicians, dentists, nurses, and optometrists.

Laws patterned on the Model Privacy Act provide the following important exception to the access requirement:

> The rights granted to all natural persons by this subsection shall not extend to information about them that relates to and is collected in connection with or in reasonable anticipation of a claim or civil or criminal proceeding involving them.

This limitation applies to the correction or deletion of information as well.

Correction or Deletion of Information

A person who wishes to correct or delete personal information about himself must send a written request to the insurer, agent, or insurance-support organization holding the information. The holder of the information must either comply with the request or notify the person of its refusal and the reasons for the refusal. The holder must also notify the person that the person has a right to file a supplementary statement.

If the holder of the information complies with the request for correction or deletion, the person involved must be notified of the compliance. The correction or deletion must be furnished to certain others designated by the person and to certain insurance-support organizations.

In the case of a refusal to correct or delete information, the person involved has a right to file with the holder of the information a statement containing information the person believes is correct. This statement must be made available to anyone reviewing the disputed information.

Adverse Underwriting Decisions

Adverse underwriting decisions include an insurer's declinations and terminations of coverage or its offers to insure at higher than standard rates. An insurer responsible for an adverse underwriting decision must provide the applicant, policyowner, or proposed insured with the reason for the decision or with notice that the reason will be given on request. The person involved also has a right to the specific items of personal and privileged information that support the reason for the adverse decision, unless the insurer reasonably suspects criminal activity, fraud, material misrepresentation, or material nondisclosure. Medical record information can be disclosed either to the person involved or to a medical professional the person designates.

When an insurer, agent, or insurance-support organization makes an inquiry to an insurer about a previous adverse underwriting decision, the inquiry must include a request for the reasons for the decision. The same requirement applies to inquiries as to previous coverage through a residual market mechanism. This is an arrangement by which people obtain insurance when they cannot do so through ordinary channels.

An insurer cannot base an adverse underwriting decision solely on a previous adverse underwriting decision or previous coverage through a residual market mechanism. However, an adverse underwriting decision can be based on further information obtained from another insurer responsible for a previous adverse underwriting decision.

An adverse underwriting decision cannot be based solely on personal information received from an insurance-support organization whose primary source of information is insurers. However, an insurer can base an adverse underwriting decision on further personal information, such as a statement by another insurer that its file contains the source of the information supplied by the insurance-support organization, that the information is medical record information or was furnished by the person reported on, and that the information is accurate.

Disclosure Limitations and Conditions

An insurer, agent, or insurance-support organization can disclose personal information to third parties with the written authorization of the person reported on, or under certain conditions without such authorization. As noted above, laws patterned on the Model Privacy Act spell out the required contents of authorization forms. The conditions under which the insurer, agent, or insurance-support organization can disclose personal information without written authorization are also spelled out. They include disclosures to people who need the information to perform a service for the disclosing insurer, agent, or insurance-support organization; disclosures to other insurers, agents, or insurance-support organizations to detect or prevent fraud; disclosures to other insurers, agents, or insurance-support organizations connected with an insurance transaction involving the person reported on; disclosure of a person's medical problem to the person's physician or other medical professional; disclosure to insurance regulatory authorities; disclosures to other government authorities by the insurer to protect itself from illegal activities; disclosure pursuant to a subpoena or search warrant; and certain disclosures in connection with scientific research, audits, and marketing.

Enforcement

State laws patterned on the Model Privacy Act provide that the state commissioner of insurance shall have the power to investigate to determine whether an insurer or agent doing business in the state is complying with the state's privacy act. The commissioner can also investigate an insurance-support organization acting on behalf of an insurer or agent doing business in the state, or if the organization's actions affect a state resident.

If the commissioner's investigation leads to a reasonable belief that a violation of the act has occurred, the commissioner can conduct a hearing at which the person complaining and the insurer, agent, or insurance-support organization can testify and present other evidence. If a violation is found, the commissioner can issue an order requiring the insurer, agent, or insurance-support organization to cease and desist from such conduct. An insurer, agent, or insurance-support organization subject to an order of the commissioner can obtain a court review. Violation of a valid cease and desist order can result in a fine of up to $10,000 for each violation or up to $50,000 for violations constituting a "general business practice."

In addition to this procedure for enforcement, the Model Privacy Act has a section providing for equitable actions (injunctions) to enforce a person's right of access to, or correction of, information, or his right to be given reasons for an adverse underwriting decision. Finally, a person who knowingly and willfully obtains personal information from an insurer, agent, or insurance-support organization under false pretenses can be fined up to $10,000, imprisoned up to one year, or both.

AIDS, Genetic Testing, and Privacy

Some people have voiced concerns about the confidentiality of medical records relating to AIDS and tests for genetic defects. However, the insurance industry has long been committed to keeping medical information confidential, so that only people who have a business need for this knowledge will have access to it. The American Council of Life Insurance (ACLI) and the Health Insurance Association of America (HIAA), in their *Position Paper on AIDS and Insurance,* stated that

> insurers will continue to maintain their excellent record of confidentiality regarding sensitive medical information. After all, this is only sound business practice, since the price of carelessness has always been the loss of consumer confidence. With AIDS, companies have more reason for care.

The absence of reported court cases in which an insurance applicant or an insured has prevailed in an invasion of privacy action against an insurer seems to bear out the claim of the ACLI and HIAA that insurers do protect the confidentiality of medical information.

As one example of insurance industry concern for the privacy of applicants and insureds, the Medical Information Bureau, which had been placing AIDS antibody test results in codes that specifically designated the AIDS antibody test, modified this procedure and now places the test results in a code that designates only general blood abnormalities. Thus, the MIB no longer maintains a specific record of AIDS antibody test results.

The NAIC has attempted to allay privacy concerns of the public regarding underwriting for AIDS. In 1987, the NAIC adopted a bulletin proposed for issuance by insurance departments entitled "Medical/Lifestyle Questions on Applications and Underwriting Guidelines Affecting AIDS and ARC [AIDS-Related Complex]." The statement in the bulletin that "insurance support organizations shall be directed by insurers not to investigate, directly or indirectly, the sexual orientation of an applicant or beneficiary" is directed at concerns about privacy as well as concerns about underwriting discrimination against homosexuals, a group the AIDS epidemic has hit hard. The bulletin also requires that an insurer inform a proposed insured if her blood will be tested for AIDS and obtain her consent to the test.

In the past decade, most states have passed laws mandating that insurers keep AIDS-related information confidential. Some of these laws specify the people or organizations to whom an insurer is permitted to release AIDS test results, such as the applicant's personal physician, a reinsurer, and the insurer's legal counsel. Some laws impose fines for certain disclosures of AIDS test results.[19]

---

[19]Muriel L. Crawford, Eugene Jacobs, & Kathleen R. Schwappach, *Insurance and Employee Benefit Issues,* § 13.17 in Legal Aspects of AIDS, (Donald H. J. Hermann & William P. Schurgin, eds., 1990 & Supp. 1995).

The privacy of information about genetic defects is a more recent concern. As was noted in Chapter 6, "Formation of the Life Insurance Contract," at present insurers rarely do testing to determine whether a proposed insured has a genetic predisposition to disease. However, insurers would like to use any existing genetic information about proposed insureds as part of the underwriting process. Some people are concerned that genetic information will not be kept confidential. Thus, as with AIDS, there are privacy concerns regarding genetic information. About one-third of the states have enacted laws protecting genetic privacy. Some of these laws require that an insurer receive consent from an applicant when the insurer requires a genetic test. Some prohibit health insurers from using genetic tests to select risks.

A spokesperson for an organization promoting genetic privacy stated: "We think that someone's personal genetic makeup is nobody's business but their own. . . . We would certainly consider the use of this predictive technology in the insurance context to be an inappropriate use of this information." However, the medical director of a life insurer pointed out: "We feel that the insurance industry has always dealt responsibly with medical information such as family histories, height, weight, cholesterol, blood pressure . . . [and] all these have a genetic basis, and we've always used them in our underwriting. Just because the tests become more sophistocated in the future . . . we would still want to be able to use the information."[20]

---

[20]Joan Hartnett-Barry, *Massachusetts Weighs Genetic Testing Safeguards*, NAT'L UNDERWRITER, LIFE & HEALTH/FIN. SERVICES EDITION, Oct. 21, 1996, at 49.

Summary

Privacy has no single commonly accepted definition. One definition is "the right to be let alone." As to privacy in insurance transactions, a more workable definition is "the right to fair personal information practices."

The tort of invasion of privacy has four distinct forms. First, appropriation of a person's name or likeness by another person for the other person's benefit can be an invasion of privacy. Second, an unreasonable intrusion on a person's seclusion or solitude or into the person's private affairs can be an invasion of the person's privacy. Third, invasion of privacy can take the form of public disclosure of private facts about a person. Finally, placing a person in a false light in the public eye can constitute an invasion of privacy.

The federal Constitution guards against government intrusions into individual privacy in the areas of unreasonable searches and seizures by the police; privacy in marriage, abortion, contraception, the education of children, and family living; political privacy; and privacy in communications, among others.

Congress has enacted laws regulating personal information collection, retention, and use. The Fair Credit Reporting Act is the federal privacy law of greatest importance to insurers. The purpose of the Fair Credit Reporting Act is to ensure that credit reporting agencies act fairly, impartially, and with a respect for the consumer's right to privacy.

State privacy legislation affecting insurance record-keeping was minimal prior to the development of the NAIC Model Privacy Act. The Model Privacy Act establishes standards for the collection, use, and disclosure of information about applicants and insureds. The Model Privacy Act governs pretext interviews and investigative consumer reports, provides for notice of insurance information practices, and regulates the form and content of disclosure authorization forms. The Model Privacy Act also provides for access to recorded personal information and for correction or deletion of that information. It mandates that an insurer responsible for an adverse underwriting decision provide a reason for the decision. Finally, the Model Privacy Act governs an insurer's disclosure of personal information to third parties. More than one-third of the states now have privacy laws specifically governing insurers, most of which are patterned on the Model Privacy Act.

The AIDS epidemic and genetic testing have raised new public concerns about the confidentiality of the medical information that insurers collect. Most states now have laws mandating that insurers keep AIDS-related information confidential. About one-third of the states have enacted genetic privacy laws.

ILLUSTRATIVE CASE

In this case, the court discusses the right to privacy. The court points out that only unwarranted invasions of privacy are actionable. The right to privacy does not prohibit the communication of matters of a private nature if a person has a duty to communicate such matters.

GALEN D. SENOGLES, Appellant,

v.

SECURITY BENEFIT LIFE INSURANCE COMPANY, Appellee[21]
Supreme Court of Kansas

KAUL, Justice:

This is an appeal from a summary judgment rendered for the defendant-appellee (Security Benefit Life Insurance Company), in an action for damages for invasion of privacy. . . .

The question presented is whether communication to a third party of medical information received by defendant from plaintiff's physicians, under authorization given by plaintiff in connection with an application for life insurance, was made under such circumstances that the transmission thereof was qualifiedly or conditionally privileged.

The facts are not in dispute and are substantially set forth in the trial court's memorandum decision which we quote in pertinent part:

"This is an action to recover $50,000 in damages from the defendant life insurance company, based upon an alleged invasion of the right of privacy of the plaintiff and an alleged breach of the confidential relationship between the plaintiff and defendant, all based upon the transmittal by the defendant of certain medical information applicable to the plaintiff to Medical Information Bureau, an association which provides under certain terms and conditions medical information to member life insurance companies for certain purposes in connection with underwriting risks.

"The facts applicable to defendant's motion for summary judgment are undisputed. On or about February 22, 1972, plaintiff applied to the defendant for a policy of health insurance, application No. 0040037. The application for insurance signed by plaintiff included the following authorization:

" '*I hereby authorize any licensed physician, medical practitioner, hospital, clinic or other medical or medically related facility, insurance company or other organization, institution, or person, that has any records or knowledge of me or my health, to give to the Security Benefit Life Insurance Company any such information.*' "

"As a result of the authorization, the defendant did receive medical information applicable to plaintiff. The information received was to the effect as follows:

"(a) Chest pain, significant but ill defined, no cause indicated, not listed elsewhere—information obtained from attending physician, surgeon, hospital, sanatorium or clinic—within first year, but not known to be present at time of inquiry or application;

"(b) Cardiac arrhythmia, premature contractions or not listed elsewhere (this includes any arrhythmia, not listed elsewhere, except sinus arrhythmia)—information obtained from attending physician, surgeon, hospital, sanatorium or clinic—within first year, but not known to be present at time of inquiry or application.

"(c) Asthma, primary or allergic—information obtained from attending physician, surgeon, hospital, sanatorium or clinic—under treatment, not surgical—within second year.

"Pursuant to its contract with M.I.B., the aforementioned medical information was forwarded to M.I.B. on or about April 10, 1972, in a coded form.

"M.I.B is a nonprofit, unincorporated trade association formed to conduct a confidential exchange of information between offices of about 700 member life insurance companies. All members of the association are required to comply with rules and regulations which include a requirement that all information received through the M.I.B will be held confidential and will be kept in such a manner that its confidential character will be maintained. The rules further provide that a member insurance company can obtain information from M.I.B only after first obtaining medical authorization from their applicant. Pursuant to this rule, Union Central Insurance Company requested medical information applicable to the plaintiff and received the medical information summarized above in a coded form. By reason of the medical information received by the defendant, and pursuant to the terms of the conditional receipt issued by the defendant, the defendant declined to accept plaintiff's application for insurance and returned to plaintiff, the premium paid by the plaintiff at the time of his application. Plaintiff gave no instructions to any representative of the defendant concerning their authority to secure medical information and what defendant could do with such medical information, other than the written instructions set forth in the insurance application. The only information received by the defendant based upon plaintiff's written authorization set forth in the insurance application were the medical reports from Dr. R. M. Brooker dated March 17, 1972, Dr. James K. L. Choy, dated March 2, 1972, and Dr. Horace T. Green, dated March

---

[21]536 P.2d 1358 (Kan. 1975).

27, 1972, copies of which are attached as exhibits herein.'' (Emphasis supplied.)

* * * * *

At oral argument, defendant's counsel, with consent of plaintiff's counsel, agreed to and has supplied us with a copy of the constitution and rules of the Medical Information Bureau, hereafter referred to as M.I.B.

Before dealing with the precise question presented, we should observe that the trial court rendered its judgment solely on the basis of the existence of a qualified privilege. It did not consider whether plaintiff actually had a case for invasion of right of privacy and, if so, whether plaintiff had shown any damages suffered as a result thereof. In this connection defendant says plaintiff was unable to set forth any damages. Plaintiff takes the position that malice is not in the case; that it was neither necessary to plead it nor prove it. In his deposition plaintiff admitted that he had given no written or oral instructions to defendant, or its agents, other than what appears in the authorization included in the application. In this connection we note that in the authorization, heretofore set out verbatim in the trial court's memorandum decision, the plaintiff authorizes *inter alia*[22] an insurance company or other organization to give to defendant any records or knowledge of defendant's health. Neither party attempts to explain the effect, if any, of including ''insurance company or other organization'' in this context within the authorization. We shall give it no significance in our consideration. Neither shall we give consideration to the fact that no express limitation on the use or further communication of medical information was imposed upon defendant by the terms of the authorization.

In view of the posture of the case as presented on appeal we shall confine our decision to the sole question whether, under the particular facts and circumstances shown, the transmission of the medical information to M.I.B. was made in a manner which rendered it qualifiedly privileged. We are not concerned with any question relating to the unauthorized disclosure by a physician concerning a patient which might constitute an actionable invasion of the patient's right to privacy.

Although litigation was scarce until recent times, a citizen's right to privacy has long been recognized in this jurisdiction. Right of privacy was defined in *Johnson v. Boeing Airplane Co.,* supra, wherein we held:

> ''The doctrine of the 'right of privacy' is defined as 'the right to be let alone,' the right to be free from unwarranted publicity, the right to live without unwarranted interference by the public in matters with which the public is not necessarily or legitimately concerned, and the right to be free from unwar-

---

[22]*Inter alia* means ''among other things.''

ranted appropriation or exploitation of one's personality, private affairs and private activities.''

The definition in *Johnson* was quoted with approval in *Munsell* wherein we pointed out the distinction between the torts of defamation and invasion of privacy and set out and adopted what was said to be the general rule concerning invasions of the right to privacy in these words:

> ''. . . It is clear from the decisions that only unwarranted invasions of the right of privacy are actionable. The corollary to this rule is that a 'warranted' invasion of the right of privacy is not actionable. Appellant urges that we recognize and apply here the rule that the right of privacy does not prohibit the communication of any matter though of a private nature, *when the publication is made under circumstances which would render it a privileged communication according to the law of libel and slander.* This rule is recognized in 41 Am.Jur., Privacy, § 20, p. 940; *Brents v. Morgan,* 221 Ky. 765, 299 S.W. 967, 55 A.L.R. 964; and in the first comprehensive article on the subject of the 'Right to Privacy' in 4 Harvard Law Review 193, at page 216 published by Samuel D. Warren and Louis D. Brandeis in 1890. We hold that the rule is sound and should be applied in the case at bar.'' (208 Kan. p. 923, 494 P.2d p. 1075.) (Emphasis supplied.)

Based upon the *Munsell* case the trial court reasoned that under the circumstances attendant herein the communication by defendant to M.I.B. was qualifiedly privileged and, in the absence of an affirmative allegation of malice, entered judgment for the defendant. We believe the reasoning of the trial court was sound and that it made a proper disposition of the case. . . .

In the *Froelich* opinion we reaffirmed what was said in *Munsell* to the effect that the right of privacy does not prohibit communication of a matter of a private nature when the publication is made under circumstances which would render it a privileged communication according to the law of libel and slander.

The principal thrust of plaintiff's argument on appeal is that the *Munsell* case is not on ''all fours'' with the case at bar and that, therefore, the trial judge erred in basing his decision on *Munsell.* From what has been said it is readily apparent that even though *Munsell* may not be on ''all fours'' factually, the principles of law enunciated therein are applicable and control the disposition of the instant case. Concerning an action for invasion of privacy, based upon the communication of matters of a private nature, *Munsell* settled these principles—(1) a warranted invasion of privacy is not actionable; (2) communication or publication of a matter even of a private nature made, under circumstances which would render it a privileged communication according to the law of libel and slander, will not support an action; and (3) generally, the issue whether a publication is qualifiedly privileged is a question of law to be determined by the court.

We turn then to the precise question whether the circumstances under which the instant communication was made were such as to render it qualifiedly privileged. . . .

In the case of *Faber v. Byrle,* 171 Kan. 38, 229 P.2d 718, 25 A.L.R.2d 1379, this court elaborated on the distinction between absolute and qualified privilege and considered the latter in depth. The definition of qualifiedly privileged appearing in 33 Am.Jur., Libel and Slander, § 126, pp. 124–126, was quoted and adopted by this court. It reads:

" '. . . A communication made in good faith on any subject matter in which the person communicating has an interest, or in reference to which he has a duty, is privileged if made to a person having a corresponding interest or duty, even though it contains matter which, without this privilege, would be actionable, and although the duty is not a legal one, but only a moral or social duty of imperfect obligation. The essential elements of a conditionally privileged communication may accordingly be enumerated as good faith, an interest to be upheld, a statement limited in its scope to this purpose, a proper occasion, and publication in a proper manner and to proper parties only. The privilege arises from the necessity of full and unrestricted communication concerning a matter in which the parties have an interest or duty, and is not restricted within any narrow limits.' " (p. 42, 229 P.2d p. 721.)

. . . We believe the communication and the surrounding circumstances under which it was made in the instant case falls within the boundaries of the definition. Defendant had an interest in the medical information which it forwarded to the M.I.B. by reason of which, through its membership, it would receive information pertaining to other applicants for insurance. Defendant had a duty under its contract of membership with M.I.B. M.I.B. had a duty to furnish the information to other members when the requirements of M.I.B. rules were met.

Defendant's counsel vigorously argues that the duty to transmit information was not only required by the contractual relationship between M.I.B. and its members, but was a duty involving the public interest; that it was a legitimate business procedure and vital to the life insurance industry. Defendant's argument is supported by the record.

In the instant case there is no evidence of bad faith on the part of defendant. It is undisputed that the medical information in question was not divulged to the public or to anyone who did not have a legitimate interest in the health of the plaintiff. Our examination of the rules of M.I.B. and affidavits of Joseph C. Wilberding, Executive Director of Medical Information Bureau, indicates the M.I.B. rules are geared to protect against misuse of the information and that it is to be revealed only to home office employees of member companies who directly pass upon the transaction. Medical information is released to a member company only when it has a signed medical authorization from the involved applicant in its home office files.

In this connection Mr. Wilberding stated in his affidavit:

"In order to maintain the strictest security and confidentiality in the exchange of information, M.I.B. had promulgated a number of rules and regulations which must be adhered to by its members. M.I.B. information is not to be made known to insurance agents or anyone else except the member insurance company home office underwriting or claims personnel. General Rules of M.I.B. provide that before a member insurance company can ask for details of medical codes, said member must have in its home office files signed medical authorization from the involved applicant authorizing the member company to obtain information from other insurance companies. . . ."

In addition to the security measures outlined by Mr. Wilberding in his affidavit, rules of M.I.B., which we have examined, provide for strict limitation of the use and possession of code books; that correspondence regarding the meaning of code symbols must be between officers of member companies and the executive director of M.I.B.; and that correspondence regarding medical impairments of applicants may be conducted only by medical directors of other companies.

In a recently published article appearing in Vol. 4 (1974) Rutgers Journal of Computers And The Law, the author makes a comprehensive analysis of the purposes and activities of M.I.B. He concludes:

"The MIB serves an invaluable function in the life insurance industry by meeting underwriters' informational needs. The proved ability to set premiums which result from use of the MIB benefits the policyholders. It is they who bear the burden of increased costs if an applicant is assessed for premiums inadequate to cover the risk of loss he represents."

We are satisfied there is a valid business interest in the communication in question; it was made in good faith; and M.I.B. and member companies had a corresponding interest; and that the information was limited in scope to a proper purpose, published in a proper manner and to proper parties only. In other words, the communication here falls within the definition of qualified privilege adopted by this court in *Faber v. Byrle,* supra and followed in other cases cited.

There is no evidence that the privilege accorded to defendant had been lost by abuse thereof. The record reveals that Union Central Life Insurance Company, a member company, had received in its home office information concerning plaintiff and had contacted plaintiff's physicians. The record further shows, however, that Union Central had previously received an application from plaintiff with the signed medical authorization attached.

We have found no reported decisions involving the activities of M.I.B. However, our attention is directed to *Johns v. Associated Aviation Underwriters,* 203 F.2d 208 (5th Cir. 1953), where, in applying Texas law, the Fifth Circuit Court of Appeals found the existence of a qualified privilege in a libel action based upon a report of an underwriters association concerning a pilot's qualifications. The association performed a service for insurance companies similar to that rendered by M.I.B. to its members. The relationship of the parties and the circumstances surrounding the publication of the report were similar to those shown to exist in the case at bar. The court stated the applicable rule in these words:

"A communication made in good faith on any subject, in which the person reporting has an interest and in reference to which he has a duty, is conditionally or qualifiedly privileged if made to a person having a corresponding interest or duty . . ."

Apparently, California has encoded the rule concerning qualified privilege in such cases. *Mayer v. Northern Life Ins. Co.,* D.C., 119 F.Supp. 536 (1953), was labeled a defamation action. The complaint alleged that defendant (Northern Life) had caused false medical information to be recorded in the records of an agency subscribed to by life insurance companies. The agency is not identified in the opinion, but apparently rendered a service similar to that performed by M.I.B. In applying California law the court said:

"... However, the allegations of the complaint disclose that this is a case of qualified privilege within the provisions of Section 47(3) of the Civil Code of the State of California. . . . (p. 536.)

The section of the California Code (West's Annotated, California Codes [Civil]§ 47), referred to reads:

"A privileged publication or broadcast is one made—

* * * * *

"3. In a communication, without malice, to a person interested therein, (1) by one who is also interested, or (2) by one who stands in such relation to the person interested as to afford a reasonable ground for supposing the motive for the communication innocent, or (3) who is requested by the person interested to give the information."

Since plaintiff had failed to allege malice the court determined that his complaint failed to state a claim upon which relief could be granted and dismissed the action.

We agree with defendant that cases involving agency credit reporting wherein a communication to those with a legitimate business report is generally deemed qualifiedly privileged are analogous in many respects to the case at bar. . . .

The judgment is affirmed.
SCHROEDER, J., dissenting.
FROMME, J., not participating.

Questions for Review

1. What is meant by the term *privacy* as it relates to insurance operations?
2. Describe the different forms of the tort of invasion of privacy.
3. What are the defenses to invasion of privacy lawsuits?
4. How does the Fair Credit Reporting Act relate to the operations of insurers?
5. Suppose an insurer makes an adverse decision based on a consumer report. What rights does the person involved have?
6. Review the purposes of the NAIC Model Privacy Act.
7. What are pretext interviews?
8. Discuss the "notice of insurance information practices" that insurers must provide in states with laws patterned on the Model Privacy Act. Summarize the types of information contained in such notices.
9. How must adverse underwriting decisions be handled in states with privacy laws patterned on the Model Privacy Act?
10. Suppose a person learns that some of an insurer's information about her is false. What can the person do in a state with privacy laws patterned on the Model Privacy Act?

24 INSURERS AND AGENTS AS EMPLOYERS

Chapter Outline

The insurance industry employed over two million people in the United States in 1995.[1] Managers who work for insurers, insurance agencies, and insurance brokerage

---

[1]AMERICAN COUNCIL OF LIFE INSURANCE, LIFE INSURANCE FACT BOOK 111 (1996).

businesses must know how to recognize and avoid employment problems. The purpose of this chapter is to explain some important rules of employment law.

Statutory Protection of Employees from Discrimination

Congress and the great majority of state legislatures have enacted statutes that protect employees from discrimination in employment. The most important of these statutes are outlined in this section.

Federal Employment Statutes

One of the most important employment statutes is the federal Civil Rights Act of 1964. Title VII of this act prohibits employment discrimination based on race, color, religion, sex, or national origin.[2] These are called protected classes. Title VII applies to employers with 15 or more employees.

Other federal statutes also protect people from employment discrimination. Section 1981 of the 1866 Civil Rights Act[3] protects people from race discrimination in employment. The Equal Pay Act of 1963[4] prohibits an employer from paying employees of one sex more than employees of the other sex for the same work unless the pay difference is based on a seniority system, a merit system, or another factor other than sex. The Pregnancy Discrimination Act of 1978[5] protects pregnant women from employment discrimination. The Age Discrimination in Employment Act of 1967[6] and its amendments protect job applicants and employees over the age of 40 from discrimination based on age. The Americans with Disabilities Act of 1990 protects people with disabilities from employment discrimination.[7] These federal statutes are the principal sources of federal antidiscrimination law.

State Statutes and Municipal Ordinances Prohibiting Employment Discrimination

Most states have their own laws that prohibit employment discrimination. The Illinois Human Rights Act[8] is fairly typical of these statutes. It prohibits employment discrimination based on race, color, religion, sex, national origin, ancestry, age, marital status, physical or mental handicap, military status, or unfavorable discharge from military service. The classes of protected persons differ among the states. For example, a New Jersey statute states:

> It shall be an unlawful employment practice, or, as the case may be, an unlawful discrimination . . . [f]or an employer, because of the race, creed, color, national origin, ancestry, age, marital status, affectional or sexual orientation, sex or atypical hereditary cellular or blood trait of any individual, or because of the liability for service in the Armed Forces of

---

[2]42 U.S.C.A. § 2000(e) *et seq.* (West 1994 & Supp. 1996).
[3]42 U.S.C.A. § 1981 (West 1994).
[4]29 U.S.C.A. § 206(d) (West 1978).
[5]42 U.S.C.A. § 2000e(k) (West 1994).
[6]29 U.S.C.A. §§ 621–634 (West 1985 & Supp. 1996).
[7]Pub. L. No. 101–336, 104 Stat. 327 (codified as amended in scattered sections of 2, 29, 42, & 47 U.S.C.).
[8]775 Ill. Comp. Stat. 5/1–101 to 5/10–103 (West 1993 & Supp. 1996).

the United States or the nationality of any individual, to refuse to hire or employ or to bar or to discharge or require to retire, unless justified by lawful considerations other than age, from employment such individual or to discriminate against such individual in compensation or in terms, conditions or privileges of employment.[9]

Many cities and towns have municipal ordinances prohibiting employment discrimination and agencies to enforce those ordinances. The state and municipal laws that apply to an employer depend on the location of the employer's business. Thus, different state and municipal employment laws might apply to an insurer's home office and to each of its branch or field offices. Managers must become familiar with applicable state and municipal antidiscrimination laws as well as with federal antidiscrimination laws.

Disparate Treatment and Disparate Impact Discrimination

The courts have identified two major types of employment discrimination: disparate treatment and disparate impact employment discrimination. These are discussed below.

Disparate Treatment Discrimination

Disparate treatment discrimination occurs when an employer bases an employment decision on a person's race, religion, national origin, sex, age, or other such factor. For example, disparate treatment occurs if an employer refuses to hire a qualified job applicant because the person is a woman, is black, or follows a particular religion. This type of discrimination is clearly unlawful and is easier to identify than disparate impact discrimination.

Disparate Impact Discrimination

Disparate impact discrimination occurs if an apparently nondiscriminatory job requirement has a disproportionately large adverse effect on the opportunities of people in one of the protected classes. The courts have held disparate impact discrimination to exist in a situation in which a job requirement is not closely related to the person's ability to perform the job. Disparate impact discrimination is just as unlawful as disparate treatment discrimination. It is also as damaging to the people it affects.

A review of *Griggs v. Duke Power Co.,*[10] a landmark U.S. Supreme Court case, will provide an understanding of disparate impact discrimination. In that case, Willie S. Griggs and 12 other black employees at Duke Power Company's Dan River Station in Draper, North Carolina, filed a class action against their employer, Duke Power Company, alleging unlawful discrimination on the part of the employer. A *class action* is a lawsuit brought by a representative member, or members, of a large group of persons on behalf of all the members of the group.

Before July 2, 1965, the effective date of the Civil Rights Act of 1964, Duke Power Company employed blacks in only one of its five operating departments at the Dan River Station—the labor department. The wage for the highest-paying job in the labor department was less than the lowest wage paid in the four other operating

---

[9]N. J. Stat. Ann. § 10:5–12 (West Supp. 1996).
[10]401 U.S. 424 (1971).

departments. In 1955, the company began requiring a high school education or its equivalent before it would assign a newly hired person to any operating department other than the labor department or before transferring current employees to the more desirable departments.

In 1965, when blacks were no longer restricted to the labor department, the company instituted a policy of requiring potential transferees from the labor department and from other less desirable jobs to pass two standardized aptitude tests before any transfer would be granted to an employee who did not have a high school education. The two tests were the Wonderlic Personnel Test, which purports to measure general intelligence, and the Bennett Mechanical Comprehension Test. The company also required all newly hired employees to have a high school education or its equivalent and to pass the two tests. The two tests were not designed or intended to measure the ability of an employee to perform a particular job at the Dan River Station. Moreover, the score required for an applicant to be hired or for an employee to be transferred was close to the national median for high school graduates. Approximately one-half of the nation's high school graduates would therefore be unable to achieve a satisfactory score on these tests.

Duke Power Company applied the same testing and education requirements to blacks and whites alike. The trial court found that the tests were "not administered, scored, designed, intended or used to discriminate because of race or color." However, because blacks in North Carolina had been discriminated against in the schools, they had received an education inferior to that received by most whites. The 1960 census statistics indicated that 12 percent of black males in North Carolina had completed high school, whereas 34 percent of white males had done so. Because of their inferior educational opportunities, blacks did worse than whites on the tests, and therefore a greater percentage of blacks than whites was barred from employment opportunities at the Dan River Station.

Finally, the evidence introduced at the trial showed that employees who had not completed high school or taken the aptitude tests continued to perform satisfactorily and to make progress in departments at the Dan River Station for which the high school and test criteria were now prerequisites. In other words, the job requirements were not closely related to a person's ability to perform the job.

In *Griggs,* the U.S. Supreme Court held that Title VII of the Civil Rights Act of 1964 prohibits employment practices that are fair in form but discriminatory in operation if the employment practice is not closely related to job performance. This criterion has been applied to prevent the use of such factors as height and weight requirements, arrest records, and other standards that, even when applied fairly to all, have had the effect of disqualifying more blacks than whites, more women than men, and so forth.

For example, if a job in a factory requires that an object weighing 30 pounds be lifted several times each hour, a height or weight requirement for that job will not ensure that a job applicant will be able to lift the object. The proper method of selecting a qualified employee for this job is to test each applicant's strength directly by having the applicant lift the object.

Bona Fide Occupational Qualifications

In a very few circumstances, age, sex, religion, or national origin can be used to screen job applicants. In such a case, the employer must establish that the use of such a characteristic is a *bona fide occupational qualification.* A **bona fide occupational qualification** is a characteristic that the employee must have to perform a particular job satisfactorily. For example, although an employer usually cannot lawfully base an employment decision on a person's sex, if the job in question is that of locker-room attendant in a women's locker room, sex is a bona fide occupational qualification. The employer can lawfully require that the applicant be female.

As another example, a parochial school seeking a teacher of religious instruction might require applicants to be members of the religious group operating the school. Membership in the religous group would be a bona fide occupational qualification.

Race Discrimination

Under both Title VII of the Civil Rights Act of 1964 and Section 1981 of the Civil Rights Act of 1866, it is unlawful to base employment decisions on an employee's race or color. Race discrimination includes denying a job applicant a job, denying an employee a promotion, assignment, or transfer, and firing an employee on the basis of race or color.

Giving minority employees equipment or training inferior to that given to nonminority employees is racial discrimination. Pay must be the same for similarly situated minority and nonminority employees. For example, minority employees and nonminority employees with the same job title and length of service should be given comparable pay.

Employers must maintain an atmosphere in the workplace that is free of racial bias and racial harassment. Racial epithets, slurs, or jokes directed at or made in the presence of minority employees constitute racial harassment. The consistent use of first names for minority employees, while using Mr., Ms., or Mrs. for nonminority employees, or the use of a term like *boy* for male African-American employees shows racial bias.

An employer may discharge or discipline minority employees for unsatisfactory job performance, an unacceptable number of absences, chronic tardiness, or for other valid reasons, as long as nonminority employees are discharged or disciplined under similar circumstances. Employees in all protected classes can be disciplined or discharged if the employer has a valid reason to do so and treats all employees similarly. Careful documentation of each employee's performance will help the insurer in its defense if an employee files a discrimination charge. This is discussed in the section entitled "Employment Practices and Decisions."

Sex Discrimination

Sex discrimination is forbidden under Title VII of the Civil Rights Act of 1964. As with race discrimination, Title VII prohibits an employer from discriminating on the basis of sex in regard to all the terms and conditions of employment. In addition, as mentioned above, the Equal Pay Act of 1963 prohibits an employer from paying employees of one sex more than employees of the other sex for the same work unless the pay difference is based on a seniority system, a merit system, or another factor other than sex. The Pregnancy Discrimination Act of 1978 protects employees from discrimination related to pregnancy. Sexual harassment is a type of sex discrimination that has created special problems for employers. Sexual harassment and pregnancy discrimination are discussed next.

Sexual Harassment

The Equal Employment Opportunity Commission (EEOC) includes ***sexual harassment*** as a type of sex discrimination barred by Title VII of the Civil Rights Act of 1964. The EEOC's guidelines on sexual harassment provide that "unwelcome sexual advances, requests for sexual favors, and other verbal or physical conduct of a sexual nature" constitute unlawful sexual harassment under certain conditions.[11] Sexual harassment occurs if (1) submission to the sexual conduct is an express or implied condition of the employee's employment; (2) the employee's submission to or rejection of the sexual conduct is the basis for an employment decision, such as a decision to promote or fire the employee; or (3) the sexual conduct substantially interferes with the employee's work performance or creates an intimidating, hostile, or offensive work environment.

Sexual harassment encompasses many types of behavior that can occur in the workplace. For example, a male supervisor who promises to promote a female employee if she has a sexual relationship with him clearly commits sexual harassment. The female employee's opportunity for advancement depends on her submission to her supervisor's request. In such a situation, the employer ordinarily will be held liable for sexual harassment, whether or not the employer knew of the harassment.

Although the clearest cases of sexual harassment involve unwelcome sexual advances of supervisors toward employees who report to them, sexual harassment also can occur between employees of equal rank. Once the employer knows of such behavior by one employee toward another employee, the employer has a duty to investigate and stop the unlawful behavior. An employer who chooses not to investigate and fails to take corrective action could be liable for sexual harassment.

Men as well as women can be victims of sexual harassment. Moreover, sexual harassment can occur between people of the same sex as well as between people of opposite sexes.

Judgment is required to determine whether the behavior of one employee toward another constitutes sexual harassment. An innocent flirtation or a request for a date might not constitute sexual harassment. Repeated unwelcome sexual advances and demands for dates are more likely to constitute sexual harassment. If an employee's supervisor makes sexual advances or demands, a court is even more likely to find sexual harassment.

Where a persistent pattern of sexual conduct of co-workers, or even of nonemployees such as customers or vendors, substantially interferes with an employee's work performance or creates an intimidating, hostile, or offensive work environment, the employer will be liable for sexual harassment. An employer can protect itself by taking immediate and appropriate corrective action as soon as it knows of inappropriate sexual behavior that could lead to a claim of sexual harassment.

Pregnancy Discrimination

Pregnancy must be treated like any other temporary disability. Women who are disabled by pregnancy or medical conditions related to pregnancy must be treated the same as disabled men or disabled nonpregnant women. EEOC guidelines require

---

[11] 29 C.F.R. § 1604.11 (1996).

employers to treat disabilities due to pregnancy the same as other disabilities with respect to all terms and conditions of employment.[12]

A pregnant woman must be allowed to work until her physician determines that she is physically unable to work. The determination of her disability must be based on her actual physical condition. A pregnant woman must not be forced to stop working merely because it is her sixth month of pregnancy or because of some other predetermined factor unrelated to her actual physical condition.

A pregnant woman sometimes becomes disabled for an extended period of time after her child is born if she experienced a complication during childbirth. Alternatively, a woman might be able to resume her job a few days after giving birth. Once her physician finds that she is able to resume her job, she is not entitled to remain at home and return to work whenever she chooses unless the same would be true for a disabled male or nonpregnant female.[13] However, if a disabled male or nonpregnant female can take off additional time after the disability has ended, the woman who has had a disability resulting from pregnancy is entitled to do the same. An employer lawfully can and often does require all employees to return to work as soon as their disabilities have ended. As long as disabilities resulting from pregnancy and pregnancy-related conditions are treated the same as other disabilities with respect to the terms and conditions of employment, ordinarily there is no unlawful discrimination. Some states—California, for example—require special treatment for pregnant employees, such as a right to reinstatement in their jobs.

As an example, suppose a male employee has a back injury that prevents him from performing his job for three months. On his return to work, his employer gives him the seniority he would have had if he had worked those three months. The employer permits him to resume the same position he had before his injury. The employer also pays his medical and hospital bills and gives him disability income payments while he is absent from work.

A woman who works for the same employer becomes pregnant and her physician states that she is unable to perform her job due to the pregnancy. The employer must treat her disability from pregnancy the same as the employer treated the male employee's disability from back injury. The woman would be entitled to payment of medical and hospital bills by her employer and to disability income payments while she is disabled. When the woman's physician says she is no longer disabled, and she returns to work, she is entitled to the same treatment that the male employee with the back injury received. The employer must determine seniority rights, retirement benefits, accrued vacation, and service credit of a woman on disability leave due to pregnancy as if the disability were unrelated to pregnancy.

If an employer does not require a statement from a physician that a male worker or nonpregnant female worker is disabled before that worker is entitled to receive disability benefits, it cannot require such a statement from the pregnant worker. Similarly, if a male worker or nonpregnant female can return to work after a disability without a physician's statement that the disability is no longer present, such a statement cannot be required of an employee disabled by pregnancy.

---

[12]29 C.F.R. § 1604.10(b) (1996).

[13]Certain employees are entitled to unpaid leave under the federal Family and Medical Leave Act of 1993, 29 U.S.C.A. §§ 2601–2654 (West Supp.1996). Laws in some states require an employer to allow an employee maternity leave.

Age Discrimination

The Age Discrimination in Employment Act of 1967 (ADEA) protects people 40 years of age and older from employment discrimination based on age. Under the ADEA, it is unlawful for an employer to

> fail or refuse to hire or to discharge any individual or otherwise discriminate against any individual with respect to his compensation, terms, conditions or privileges of employment, because of such individual's age.

In addition, employees are protected against age harassment, which includes an employer's toleration of an atmosphere in which employees make frequent jokes or comments about older people.

The employer must beware of making subjective hiring decisions based on stereotypes that older workers are not able to learn as well as younger ones or do not take orders as well. The employer's desire to hire workers that will be with the company for a long time might be age discrimination if it results in the exclusion of older applicants. Moreover, refusing to hire an older person because he is "overqualified" might constitute age discrimination. One court noted that

> [d]enying employment to an older job applicant because he or she has too much experience, training or education is simply to employ a euphemism to mask the real reason for refusal, namely, in the eyes of the employer the applicant is too old.[14]

Offering younger employees more training opportunities because the employer assumes that they will be with the company longer is apt to result in age discrimination charges. The same training opportunities and performance standards should be applied to all employees, regardless of age.

Company restructurings, with the consequent firing of many employees, has resulted in a dramatic increase in age discrimination charges. Even if performance evaluations are used as the basis for firings, if a significantly larger number of workers 40 and over than under 40 are fired, a court could decide that the company violated age discrimination laws. Moreover, cost-cutting is not a legitimate reason for firing an older employee and replacing her with an equally proficient younger employee who is paid less.

Most employees 40 and over are protected from mandatory retirement. An employer can entice employees to retire with promises of substantial bonuses, larger pensions, or extended health insurance. As long as the retirement is voluntary, the employer will not have committed age discrimination. However, the employer cannot use any type of threats or coercion to force an older employee to retire.[15]

Discrimination against the Disabled

The Americans with Disabilities Act (ADA) became federal law in 1990. The ADA applies to employers with 15 or more employees.

The purpose of the ADA is to provide "a clear and comprehensive national mandate for the elimination of discrimination against individuals with disabilities." An

---

[14]Taggart v. Time, Inc., 924 F.2d 43 (1991); *but see* EEOC v. Insurance Co. of N. Am., 49 F.3d 1418 (1995).

[15]Moreover, the employer should carefully follow the requirements of the Older Workers Benefit Protection Act of 1990, 29 U.S.C.A. § 626(f) (West Supp.1996).

estimated 43 million Americans have a disability of some kind. The ADA prohibits an employer from discriminating against a qualified person who has a disability with respect to job application procedures, job training, discharge, and other terms, conditions, and privileges of employment. However, an employer is permitted to hire or promote the most qualified candidate, as long as the employer's decision is based on reasons other than the disability.

A disability is any physical or mental impairment that substantially limits a major life activity. Thus, people who are blind, deaf, paralyzed, manic-depressive, diabetic, or afflicted with AIDS are protected. The ADA also protects people with past impairments (such as rehabilitated alcoholics or drug addicts, or people recovered from cancer) and people who are erroneously perceived to have a disability.

Employers must not discriminate against qualified disabled job applicants. A ***qualified job applicant*** is one who can perform the essential functions of a job with or without reasonable accommodation by the employer. Reasonable accommodation could include special keyboards, lighting, or telephones; aisles made wider to accommodate a wheelchair; or a modified work schedule. An employer cannot charge the employee for the cost of an accommodation unless the accommodation creates an "undue hardship" for the employer. An employer is not required to lower quality or quantity standards to make an accommodation.

The ADA prohibits an employer from asking a job applicant about his medical history or possible disability. An employer can ask a job applicant about his ability to perform specific job-related tasks. After the employer has made a conditional offer of employment, it can require the job applicant to submit to a medical examination. A disability revealed by the medical examination will justify the employer's revocation of its offer of employment only if the disability would prevent the job applicant from safely performing essential job functions.

Affirmative Action

The federal regulations augmenting Executive Order 11246[16] require federal contractors and subcontractors having 50 or more employees and a federal contract exceeding $50,000 in a 12-month period to have written affirmative action plans. An employer not subject to Executive Order 11246 is permitted to voluntarily institute an affirmative action plan. Some insurers are federal contractors or subcontractors and have instituted affirmative action plans for that reason. Other insurers and insurance agencies or brokerages have done so voluntarily.

An ***affirmative action plan*** is intended to remedy the effects of past discrimination by requiring the hiring of qualified members of protected classes that have been excluded from fair representation in many types of jobs. Affirmative action plans are meant to bring those who have been unfairly excluded from certain types of jobs into such jobs in numbers that are representative of their membership in the population generally.

An affirmative action plan is a defense to a charge of ***reverse discrimination***—that is, discrimination against persons who are not ordinarily discriminated against,

---

[16]Exec. Order No. 11246, 30 Fed. Reg. 12319 (1965), *reprinted as amended in* 42 U.S.C.A. § 2000e app. at 24–29 (West 1994); 41 C.F.R. 60–1.40 (1996). An ***executive order*** is an order promulgated by the president of the United States that has the force of law when published in the *Federal Register,* an official government publication.

such as young white males. The affirmative action plan must be kept current by annual review and revision. The plan must not create an absolute bar to the hiring or advancement of people it doesn't cover. For example, a training program for minorities and women only is not permitted. Moreover, white employees must not be laid off before minority employees to preserve gains in minority employment.[17]

Retaliation by the Employer

An employer cannot retaliate against an employee who opposes the employer's unlawful employment practices. An employer cannot discipline an employee who has "made a charge, testified, assisted or participated in any manner in an investigation, proceeding or hearing" concerning an employment practice unlawful under Title VII because of such participation.[18]

For example, suppose Larry Henderson reasonably believes that he didn't get the promotion he deserved because of his race. Henderson files a charge of discrimination with the EEOC. Vernon Cook, one of Henderson's associates, assists Henderson in presenting his case to the EEOC by testifying. Connie Walters, Henderson's and Cook's supervisor, is outraged when she learns of the discrimination charge. She believes that she did not discriminate and that Henderson's job performance did not justify a promotion.

Walters must be careful to treat Henderson and Cook the same as other employees. She must not permit their involvement in the discrimination charge to affect her treatment of these two employees. She can discipline either or both for violating a company rule, just as she would have done had there been no discrimination suit. But she cannot retaliate against Henderson or Cook, and she cannot discipline either of them because of his involvement in the discrimination charge.

Even if the allegations in the discrimination charge are untrue, such retaliation itself will be a violation of the law. Suppose Henderson had insufficient evidence to support his claim of discrimination, and Walters is found not to have denied Henderson the promotion because of his race. If Walters treated Henderson or Cook differently from other employees because of their participation in the discrimination charge, she violated Title VII. This violation is separate from the discrimination alleged in the charge.

Thus, managers employed by insurance companies, insurance agencies, or insurance brokerage businesses must take care not to respond emotionally if an employee files a charge of discrimination. Retaliation of any kind will make a successful defense of the charge more difficult and subject the employer to additional liability.

Employment Practices and Decisions

Employment practices and decisions begin with the employer's advertisements for the job and continue throughout employment until after the employee's termination by resignation, discharge, or retirement. With few exceptions, employment practices or decisions cannot lawfully be based on age, religion, national origin, sex, or disability. They can never be based on race or color.

---

[17]Wygant v. Jackson Bd. of Educ., 476 U.S. 267 (1986).
[18]42 U.S.C.A. § 2000e–3(a) (West 1994).

Any test or job requirement must be directly related to determining whether the applicant can perform the duties of the job for which he has applied. Screening devices such as height and weight requirements, education requirements, or required tests that are not directly related to the applicant's abilities to perform the duties of the job might have a disparate impact on minorities, women, and members of other protected classes. Screening devices that have such a disparate impact are unlawful.

Job Advertising

If an insurer, insurance agency, or insurance brokerage business is seeking job applicants, it might advertise in newspapers and trade journals. Any language in the advertisement expressing or implying a preference for applicants of a particular race or color or indicating that applicants of a particular race or color will receive less consideration is always prohibited. The federal regulations that interpret the Age Discrimination in Employment Act prohibit employers from using help-wanted notices or advertisements that "contain terms and phrases such as 'age 25 to 35,' 'young,' 'college student,' 'recent college graduate,' 'boy,' 'girl,' or others of a similar nature, [because] such a term or phrase deters the employment of older persons and is a violation of the Act."[19]

Help-wanted notices or advertisements can specify an age, sex, religion, or national origin requirement only when the requirement meets the strict standards of a bona fide occupational qualification, as described above.

Applications and Interviews

The application and the employment interview are essential tools for gathering information that enables the employer to evaluate the applicant's ability to perform the job. The application and the interview should be designed to elicit only information relating to the applicant's abilities to perform the job. Information not related to the applicant's abilities to perform the job or not required for other legitimate reasons[20] must not be elicited. State employment laws vary as to the information that can be requested on an application or during an interview. The employer's attorney has the responsibility to review hiring procedures and ensure compliance with all applicable laws.

Managers who conduct job interviews should take care to avoid actions that could create liability for the employer. The interviewer must avoid questions to a job applicant eliciting information that might be used as the basis for a discriminatory hiring decision. For example, an interviewer would be unwise to ask an applicant for a word processing job which church he attended. This has nothing to do with the applicant's word processing abilities. Even if the question is a friendly attempt to get acquainted with the applicant, an unsuccessful applicant could view it as the basis of a decision not to hire.

If an interviewer asks a job applicant "What social organizations do you belong to?", this question might elicit the name of a social organization that reveals the applicant's religion or national origin. Except in rare instances, religion or national origin are not related to an applicant's ability to perform a job satisfactorily. More-

---

[19]29 C.F.R. § 1625.4 (1996).

[20]An employer can ask for the person's social security number for F.I.C.A. withholding purposes, for example.

over, if an applicant says she needs Saturdays, Sundays, or holidays off for religious observance, she cannot be discriminated against on that basis unless the employer cannot give the time off without undue hardship.

The question "Are you married?" elicits information that cannot be used to make an employment decision, according to the law of most states. This information has no relationship to the applicant's abilities to perform the job. After the employer makes the hiring decision, the employee can be asked her marital status for insurance or other legitimate purposes.

The question "Have you ever been arrested?" also elicits information an employer cannot use to make an employment decision. The members of several minority groups are arrested at a greater rate than members of nonminority groups. If an employer bases a hiring decision on the number of times an applicant has been arrested, this would adversely affect minorities disproportionately and would therefore be unlawful. However, the employer can inquire about convictions for offenses that adversely reflect on an applicant's ability to perform a job satisfactorily.

The question "How old are you?" should also be avoided. Under federal law, age cannot be considered as a factor in employment decisions if the person is over 40. The only legitimate concerns an employer has with respect to an applicant's age before making the hiring decision is whether the applicant has reached the age of majority (18 to 21, depending on the state). Child labor laws restrict the employment of minors in various ways.

Although the inquiries noted above and others of a similar nature might not be unlawful in themselves, an unsuccessful applicant might convince a court that the information elicited was the basis for an unlawful employment decision. This could happen even if the decision actually was based on job-related criteria. If the employer does not have non-job-related information, such a claim by an unsuccessful applicant will be less likely. In short, the safest procedure is for an employer to ask only for information related to the applicant's abilities to perform the job. If the employer wants to elicit other information, its attorney should assess the situation.

The Immigration Reform and Control Act of 1986

The federal Immigration Reform and Control Act of 1986 (IRCA)[21] makes it illegal for an employer to knowingly employ an illegal alien. In addition, the IRCA imposes on employers the duty of asking certain questions of newly hired persons to determine whether they are illegal aliens.[22] The new employee must sign a form (Form I-9) devised by the Immigration and Naturalization Service (INS) verifying employment eligibility. An employer must verify the new employee's identity and authorization for employment by requiring that the person present one or more documents such as a birth certificate, passport, voter's registration card, driver's license, social security card, or INS employment authorization card. The law spells out which documents or combination of documents the employer must require. It is permissible and advisable for the employer to keep photocopies of the documents that the new employee presents as evidence of compliance with IRCA requirements.

---

[21]Pub. L. No. 99–603, 100 Stat. 3359 (codified as amended in scattered sections of 7, 8, 18, 29, & 42 U.S.C.).

[22]Lance Kaplan, *Verifying Employees' Eligibility—Immigration and Naturalization Service Increases Enforcement Efforts against All Employers,* CAL. B. J., Aug. 1996, at 24.

The IRCA also prohibits discrimination against employees and job applicants because of their national origin or citizenship status, provided they are not illegal aliens. Congress included the antidiscrimination provisions in the act to prevent employers from rejecting job applicants with foreign accents or appearances in order to protect themselves from penalties if the applicant turns out to be an illegal alien. An employer's good faith compliance with the identity and authorization verification procedures described above will protect the employer in such an event.

Job Performance Evaluations

Job performance evaluations, like other employment practices, must not be based on the employee's race, color, sex, age, or other such factor. Such evaluations should be based only on the employee's job performance.

Although periodic job performance evaluations are not required by law, they help to avoid discrimination suits by offering a regularly scheduled opportunity to discuss the employee's job performance. An employee ordinarily files a discrimination charge because he believes an adverse employment decision (that is, a decision not to hire, not to promote, to fire, and so forth) was based on a prohibited criterion, such as the employee's race, national origin, or age. In other words, the employee believes something other than his job performance led the employer to make the adverse employment decision.

One important benefit of periodic job performance evaluations is their role in an employer's defense of a discrimination charge. Periodic written job performance evaluations often aid an employer in demonstrating that an adverse employment decision was not based on race, sex, national origin, age, or disability, but on poor performance. Even if an employee's job performance evaluations reflect good work, but an expected promotion went to another employee, the employer should be able to show why the other employee deserved the promotion.

All employees should receive job performance evaluations and reviews of those evaluations on a regular basis. If an employer evaluates only the poor performers, and some poor performers are members of one or more protected classes, discrimination suits are likely. If the employer evaluates only the good performers, the poor performers might believe discrimination is involved. Thus, the best practice is to evaluate the job performance of all employees.

Managers should strive to make all job performance evaluations accurate and honest. An inaccurate or dishonest job performance evaluation does the employer a disservice. For example, if an employee is given a better rating than she deserves and is later demoted or fired, the documentation of her poor performance won't exist because her manager gave her a "break" rather than an accurate and honest evaluation.

The employer should give an employee a written job performance evaluation at scheduled times, for example every 6 or 12 months, and review the evaluation with the employee. In addition, at the time it makes an employment decision adverse to the employee, the employer should give the employee a written job performance evaluation and review the evaluation with the employee. If an employer writes a job performance evaluation justifying an adverse employment decision after the employee has filed a discrimination complaint about the decision, the administrative agency or court will give no weight to the written job performance evaluation.

The employer should fully document the employee's job performance and should maintain time sheets and written reports on the employee's job performance. Without documentation, it is difficult for an employer to rebut a charge of discrimination.

However, the documentation must be maintained in an evenhanded manner, because a discrimination charge is essentially an allegation that one person was treated differently from others who were similarly situated. For example, if time sheets are kept, they should be kept for all employees similarly situated and not just for some.

Evenhanded treatment and documentation are the keys to the defense of discrimination complaints. Even if adverse actions taken by the employer against an employee were, in fact, nondiscriminatory and completely justified, the employer must have evidence to support its position. The evidence is, in large part, documentation of the reasons the employer took the action.

Uniform Standards for Job Performance

Job performance evaluations will be effective only if the employer establishes uniform standards for job performance. For example, if a manager decides that five instances of unexcused tardiness will put an employee on probation, the manager must apply that standard to all employees in a similar position. The manager who applies different standards to employees in similar positions is more likely to be charged with discriminatory conduct than the manager who applies uniform standards.

For example, suppose Joseph Manning has 10 word processors working for him. Several word processors frequently arrive at work late without satisfactory explanations. Manning informs the employees that from that day forward, any employee who arrives at work late more than twice without a satisfactory explanation will be put on probation. After two weeks, A and B, two of the word processors, have each arrived late twice. Manning likes A but has never had a friendly relationship with B, although B's work is usually better than A's. Manning talks to A about A's tardiness. A and B are each late one more time. Manning puts B on probation but gives A one more chance before putting A on probation.

Here A and B were not treated uniformly, even though each had violated the same rule. If B is a member of a protected class—for example, black, female, or over 40—and A is not, B might be able to convince a court that Manning had unlawfully discriminated, even if that was not Manning's intention. Manning might have treated B differently for reasons unrelated to B's race, sex, or age, but if Manning cannot show a business reason for treating B differently from A, Manning's company might be found liable for discrimination. If a manager treats some employees preferentially, her motive for doing so is irrelevant.

Managers must treat all employees objectively and according to uniform standards. Managers should avoid making exceptions in applying company rules.

Preferences of Co-Workers or Customers

Employment decisions can almost never lawfully be based on the preferences of coworkers or customers for an employee of a certain race, sex, age, or similar non-job-related criterion. For example, if an employer is considering hiring a woman for a job that has previously been held only by men, and the co-workers are all men who would prefer not to have a woman in their group, the employer cannot lawfully consider the co-workers' preferences in making the hiring decision. If the woman is the best-qualified applicant for the job, the employer would illegally discriminate if it did not offer her the job because of the co-workers' preferences.

Similarly, the preferences of customers must not be a factor in an employment decision. Simply because the employer believes that customers would prefer a white, a male, or a Gentile in the job, the employer cannot lawfully base employment decisions on the customers' preferences. Limited exceptions can be made to this rule where personal privacy of customers is a consideration, as when the employer is hiring a locker-room attendant.

Penalties for Employment Discrimination

Employment discrimination can be costly to an employer. For example, an employer could be sued by a group of rejected applicants who were denied employment because of the employer's use of a test or job requirement that was not directly related to ability to do the job. Suppose the job requirements were height and weight requirements that disqualified more women than men and that were unrelated to the job. The employer could be sued by the rejected female applicants. If the women were successful in their suit, each woman who could demonstrate an economic loss might be eligible for back pay. Back pay consists of all the payments, including wages and fringe benefits, that the applicants would have received if the employer had not discriminated against them. The women might also be entitled to have their attorneys' fees and court costs paid by the employer. The judge could order the employer to discontinue the height and weight requirements in its selection process and order that the women be hired.

Moreover, the Civil Rights Act of 1991,[23] allows persons who have been intentionally discriminated against in employment because of their sex, religion, national origin, or disability to be awarded punitive damages. Before the enactment of the Civil Rights Act of 1991, only persons who had been discriminated against because of race could be awarded punitive damages.

The judge has a great deal of discretion and will fashion the remedy to fit the circumstances of each case. Each insurer, insurance agency, or insurance brokerage business would be wise to review its employment practices to make certain that its job requirements are sufficiently related to the job and that they do not result from conscious or unconscious bias.

Wrongful Discharge

One of the most significant developments in employment law in recent years has been the erosion of the employment-at-will rule. The ***employment-at-will rule*** can be defined as follows: An employer can dismiss an employee who was hired for an indefinite period of time without cause and without notice. Although for many years union and government employees have had protection against wrongful discharge, before 1970 a nonunion, private sector employee hired for an indefinite period of time ordinarily could be discharged at the will of the employer. Both contract and tort theories of wrongful discharge of these employees have now developed. A leading case is *Peterman v. Teamsters,*[24] decided in California in 1959. In that case, the employee refused to commit perjury on behalf of the employer. The court held that the employer's discharge of the employee breached a covenant of good faith and fair dealing implied in the at-will employment contract. The term *at-will employment contract* does not necessarily mean a written contract but rather the agreement between the employer and employee as to the terms of the employment. Following

---

[23]Pub. L. No. 102–166, 105 Stat. 1071 (codified as amended in scattered sections of 2, 16, 29 & 42 U.S.C.).

[24]344 P.2d 25 (Cal. Ct. App.1959).

California's lead, courts in other states began to apply the implied covenant of good faith and fair dealing to at-will employment contracts.[25]

Other contract theories also developed. In one case, the court held that employee expectations of employment tenure based on the employer's handbooks and policy statements were enforceable in breach of contract actions.[26] Courts in other states have made similar holdings.[27]

The leading wrongful discharge case using a tort theory is *Nees v. Hocks,*[28] decided in Oregon in 1975. In that case, the employee was discharged for requesting jury duty over his employer's objections. The court held that the employer was liable for tort damages because its actions undermined the public policy in favor of jury service.

Courts in other states have adopted the public policy tort theory. For example, in Connecticut, a quality control supervisor protested deviations from the food labeling required by law. The court held that he could recover tort damages if he could prove that his protests led to his dismissal.[29] Courts have also granted damages for wrongful discharge in cases in which the employer discharged the employee to avoid providing the employee with certain benefits, such as pension benefits that were due to become vested.

Regular job performance evaluations can assist the employer in establishing the reasons for the discharge. Review and revision of employee handbooks and similar materials can be an important preventive measure. Disciplinary and discharge procedures can be scrutinized and changed if necessary. Insurers, insurance agencies, and brokerage businesses can protect themselves from liability for wrongful discharge by giving attention to such preventive measures.

Employees and Independent Contractors

An understanding of the difference between an employee and an ***independent contractor*** is vital to an employer that wishes to avoid violating the law. In recent years, the Internal Revenue Service has investigated businesses to see if they are classifying as independent contractors workers who are actually employees. Because the employer does not withhold income taxes or employment taxes from payments to an independent contractor, but must withhold from the wages of an employee, by classifying as independent contractors workers who are actually employees, many employers have violated federal law with resulting penalties and reclassification of workers by the IRS. Many employers also have violated state laws with resulting penalties.[30]

Determination of Workers' Status.   Unfortunately, it is not always easy to distinguish an employee from an independent contractor. Moreover, a worker may be an employee for some purposes and an independent contractor for others. However, the following are some of the criteria that the courts use in classifying workers:

[25]Kmart v. Ponsock, 732 P.2d 1364 (Nev. 1987); Fortune v. National Cash Register Co., 364 N.E. 2d 1251 (Mass. 1977); Monge v. Beebe Rubber Co., 316 A.2d 549 (N.H. 1974).

[26]Toussaint v. Blue Cross & Blue Shield, 292 N.W. 2d 880 (Mich. 1980).

[27]Duldulao v. St. Mary of Nazareth Hosp. Center, 505 N.E. 2d 314 (Ill. 1987); Aiello v. United Airlines, Inc., 818 F.2d 1196 (5th Cir. 1987); Thompson v. Kings Entertainment Co., 653 F. Supp. 871 (E.D. Va. 1987).

[28]536 P.2d 512 (Ore. 1975).

[29]Sheets v. Teddy's Frosted Foods, Inc., 427 A.2d 385 (Conn. 1980).

[30]Kathy Krawczyk, Lorraine M. Wright & Roby B. Sawyers, *Independent Contractors: The Consequences of Reclassification,* J. ACCOUNTANCY, Jan. 1996, at 47.

Employee versus Independent Contractor

An employee must comply with the employer's instructions about when, where, and how to work; an independent contractor establishes his own hours and has no instructions regarding how the job should be done.

An employee typically has a continuing relationship with the employer; an independent contractor often is retained to complete a particular job.

An employee works on the employer's premises or on a route or site established by the employer; a typical independent contractor works on her own premises and pays rent for those premises.

An employee typically renders services personally; an independent contractor may use others to perform tasks.

An employee is paid by the employer in regular amounts at stated intervals; an independent contractor is paid on the completion of the project in a lump sum or on a commission basis.

An employee is furnished the tools and materials to do the job by the employer; an independent contractor typically furnishes and pays for his own tools and materials.

An employee typically can be fired by the employer at any time; an independent contractor typically is discharged when the job is completed.

An employee can quit at any time, usually without incurring liability; an independent contractor usually is legally obligated to complete a particular job.

An employee typically works for the employer substantially full time; an independent contractor may have several jobs or work for others at the same time.

An employee usually is not known to the general public; an independent contractor often has a business known to the general public.

Respondeat Superior. *Respondeat superior* means "let the master answer."[31] *Respondeat superior* stands for the principle that the employer, as well as the employee, is legally liable for a tort that the employee committed in the course of employment. For example, if a person driving an automobile on business for a corporation negligently collides with a pedestrian, the pedestrian will have a cause of action against the corporation if the driver is an employee. If the driver is an independent contractor, the pedestrian ordinarily will not have a cause of action against the corporation but will have a cause of action against the independent contractor.

A person injured by an employee's negligent act will have grounds to sue the employer, the employee, or both. Ordinarily the plaintiff will have a better chance of recovery from the employer. The employer will have grounds to sue the employee where the employee's negligent act causes the employer to have liability to an injured person.

---

[31]The terms *master* and *servant* are used in older court opinions involving torts against third persons committed by an employee in the course of her employment. The terms *employer* and *employee* are often used today.

Summary

The insurance industry is a major employer in the United States. Managers who work for insurers, insurance agencies, and insurance brokerage businesses need to know how to recognize and avoid employment problems.

Federal, state, and municipal governments have enacted statutes prohibiting employment discrimination. These statutes prohibit discrimination in employment based on race, color, religion, sex, national origin, age, and disability. Some state statutes and municipal ordinances prohibit discrimination in employment based on other criteria such as veteran status, ancestry, marital status, unfavorable discharge from military service, affectional or sexual orientation, or atypical hereditary cellular or blood trait.

Federal law prohibits disparate treatment discrimination and disparate impact discrimination. Disparate treatment discrimination occurs when an employer bases an employment decision on a person's race, religion, national origin, sex, age, or another prohibited criterion. Disparate impact discrimination occurs when a job requirement that is not closely related to a person's ability to perform the job results in a disproportionately large adverse effect on the job opportunities of people in one of the protected classes.

Employers must avoid discrimination charges arising from sexual harassment of employees and pregnancy discrimination. Some employers with federal contracts must have written affirmative action plans to remedy the effects of past discrimination. Employers cannot lawfully retaliate against an employee who has made a charge of discrimination or testified in a discrimination proceeding.

With the exception of situations in which there are bona fide occupational qualifications, employment practices or decisions cannot be based on age, religion, national origin, sex, or disability. They can never be based on race or color. Employment practices and decisions begin with advertisements for the job and involve job applications, interviews, promotions, demotions, raises in pay, probation, job performance evaluations, disciplinary actions, and termination.

Job performance evaluations are an important tool for reducing the likelihood of discrimination complaints. Job performance evaluations give the employer an opportunity to discuss the employee's job performance and thereby eliminate misunderstandings between employer and employee.

Uniform job standards also help to prevent discrimination charges. Uniform job standards assure that employees in the same position will be treated alike.

Employment discrimination can be costly to an employer. Managers can help prevent discrimination charges by avoiding job practices and decisions likely to lead to such charges.

Before 1970, a nonunion, private sector employee hired for an indefinite period ordinarily could be discharged at the will of the employer, without notice and without cause. Both contract and tort theories of wrongful discharge of these employees have now developed.

An understanding of the difference between an employee and an independent contractor is vital to an employer that wishes to avoid violating the law. Misclassification of employees as independent contractors has resulted in penalties imposed by the IRS.

Respondeat superior ("let the master answer") stands for the principle that the employer, as well as the employee, is legally liable for a tort that the employee committed in the course of employment. The employer ordinarily will not be liable for the torts of an independent contractor.

ILLUSTRATIVE CASE

In this case, an employee brought a successful wrongful discharge action against her employer, based on breach of contract.

NORA E. DULDULAO, Appellee,
v.
SAINT MARY OF NAZARETH
HOSPITAL CENTER,
Appellant[32]
Supreme Court of Illinois

Justice THOMAS J. MORAN delivered the opinion of the court:

Plaintiff, Nora E. Duldulao, brought this action in the circuit court of Cook County, alleging that defendant, St. Mary of Nazareth Hospital Center, discharged her from its

employ in violation of the terms of an employee handbook. Plaintiff claimed that the handbook, distributed by defendant, created enforceable contractual rights. Both parties moved for summary judgment. The trial court denied plaintiff's motion but granted defendant's motion, entering judgment in favor of defendant. The appellate court reversed both rulings. This court allowed defendant's petition for leave to appeal.

---

[32]505 N.E.2d 314 (Ill. 1987).

Defendant raises [these] issues for review: (1) Did the employee handbook in this case create contractual terms binding defendant to a particular procedure for terminating plaintiff's employment? (2) Did defendant in fact terminate plaintiff's employment in accordance with the provisions of the employee handbook?

Defendant initially hired plaintiff in 1968, and rehired her in 1970 when she returned from a brief stay in the Philippines. In 1971 she was promoted to head nurse, and in 1972 she was named staff development coordinator of the department of nursing. She served in this position until September 14, 1981, when defendant reorganized several of its departments. Plaintiff became human resources development coordinator, a position which she claims was identical to her previous position. Defendant, however, submitted the affidavits of supervisors who claim that plaintiff's new position included new duties and responsibilities. On December 11, 1981, plaintiff was given a sheet entitled "Probationary Evaluation" and also a "Final Notice" informing her that she was terminated as of the end of the day. Both sheets listed essentially the same alleged infractions:

> "Unsatisfactory performance was demonstrated by the failure to properly monitor the Legal Implications of Documentation seminar and the Patient Education seminar. Further unsatisfactory performance was demonstrated by failure to follow instructions regarding CPR recertification and monitoring of the Patient Education Seminar."

Plaintiff claims that her termination violated procedural rights she had by virtue of an implied contract with defendant. The terms of this contract, plaintiff claims, are to be found in an employee handbook distributed by defendant. Defendant first published an employee handbook before plaintiff was rehired in 1970. The record before us does not reveal the contents of this initial employee handbook other than the fact that it required two weeks' notice for the dismissal of probationary employees. Plaintiff's deposition reveals that she did not discuss the contents of this handbook during her rehiring interview in 1970, although she became aware of it some time after returning to work, and subsequently used it in training sessions for new employees.

In 1975 defendant published a revised employee handbook. At the beginning of this handbook is the following note, signed by Sister Stella Louise, president of the hospital:

> "N.B. The Personnel Policies of Saint Mary of Nazareth Hospital Center are presented in this booklet in a summarized form. Further details regarding any policy may be obtained by consulting the master file in the Personnel Department.
>
> It is then necessary that every employee of Saint Mary of Nazareth Hospital Center be well informed on hospital policy and other pertinent information that will assist him in directing his total efforts toward the best patient care

possible. A booklet containing hospital and personnel policy is given to each employee. As a new policy change is finalized, a copy will be given to every employee to be read and placed in his booklet. If a policy needs clarification, your Supervisor or Department Head will be happy to assist you in its interpretation.

Please take the time to become familiar with these policies. They are designed to clarify your rights and duties as employees. Your observance of these policies will produce a safe and pleasant environment in which to work and assure you a respected place in Saint Mary's family of employees."

Among other things the 1975 handbook modified the previous policy which had required two weeks' notice for dismissal of a probationary employee. The 1975 handbook, as amended by a policy statement finalized on June 18, 1981, provided that "[a]n employee may be terminated without notice but for just cause during the initial probationary period." The probationary period was to last 90 days, unless "extended up to 180 days by the department head for just cause." Once an employee successfully completed the probationary period he or she was to become a "permanent employee." Permanent employees could be terminated only with "proper notice and investigation." The amendments to the handbook provided that "[p]ermanent employees are never dismissed without prior written admonitions and/or investigation that has been properly documented." Except in the case of extremely serious offenses the handbook required three warning notices before a permanent employee could be dismissed.

The contractual status of employee handbooks has been the subject of a great deal of litigation in recent years. Several courts have rejected the notion that an employee handbook or manual can ever create binding contractual obligations. However, the overwhelming majority of courts considering the issue have held that an employee handbook may, under proper circumstances, be contractually binding.

This court has never specifically addressed the issue of employee handbooks. Our appellate court, however, has addressed the issue several times, with conflicting results. In *Carter v. Kaskaskia Community Action Agency* (1974), 24 Ill. App.3d 1056, 322 N.E.2d 574, the court held that an employee manual, which was introduced after the employee began working and was written with input from the employees, created enforceable contractual rights. However, in *Sargent v. Illinois Institute of Technology* (1979), 78 Ill. App.3d 117, 33 Ill. Dec. 937, 397 N.E.2d 443, the court distinguished *Carter* and held that the handbook in question was not binding because it was given to the employee when he first began work and was not specifically "bargained for." Still another appellate decision, *Kaiser v. Dixon* (1984), 127 Ill. App.3d 251, 82 Ill. Dec. 275, 468 N.E.2d 822, rejected *Sargent* and held that an employee manual may be binding notwithstanding that it was not "bargained for."

Federal courts applying Illinois law have reflected the split in our appellate court. Two Federal cases have followed *Sargent.* However, since *Kaiser,* several Federal courts applying Illinois law have followed *Kaiser* as the better reasoned approach.

Nearly all courts agree on the general rule, that an employment relationship without a fixed duration is terminable at will by either party. Those courts which hold that an employee handbook can never create enforceable job security rights appear to apply this general rule as a limit on the parties' freedom to contract. The majority of courts, however, interpret the general "employment-at-will rule" as a rule of construction, mandating only a presumption that a hiring without a fixed term is at will, a presumption which can be overcome by demonstrating that the parties contracted otherwise. We agree with the latter interpretation.

We find particularly persuasive the opinion of the Supreme Court of Minnesota in *Pine River State Bank v. Mettille* (Minn. 1983), 333 N.W.2d 622, which analyzed an employee handbook in terms of the traditional requirements for contract formation: offer, acceptance, and consideration. In *Pine River* an employee handbook was distributed to the plaintiff several months after he began working for defendant. The handbook contained a section entitled "Job Security" which described the generally secure nature of employment in the banking industry. The court held that this section of the handbook did not constitute an offer because it contained no definite promises. The handbook, however, also contained a section entitled "Disciplinary Policy," which stated that "[i]f an employee has violated a company policy, the following procedure will apply ✳✳✳", followed by a step-by-step process of progressive discipline ending with "[d]ischarge from employment for an employee whose conduct does not improve as a result of the previous action taken." The court held this to be a specific offer for a unilateral contract—the bank's promise in exchange for the employee's performance, *i.e.,* the employee's labor. By performing, the employee both accepted the contract and provided the necessary consideration, and thus the bank's dismissal of the plaintiff without the benefit of the progressive disciplinary procedures constituted a breach of the employment contract.

Following the reasoning in *Pine River,* we hold that an employee handbook or other policy statement creates enforceable contractual rights if the traditional requirements for contract formation are present. First, the language of the policy statement must contain a promise clear enough that an employee would reasonably believe that an offer has been made. Second, the statement must be disseminated to the employee in such a manner that the employee is aware of its contents and reasonably believes it to be an offer. Third, the employee must accept the offer by commencing or continuing to work after learning of the policy statement. When these conditions are present, then the employee's continued work constitutes consideration for the promises contained in the statement, and under traditional principles a valid contract is formed.

Applying the above principles to the case at bar it is apparent that the document entitled "Employee Handbook" created an enforceable right to the particular disciplinary procedures described therein. The amended handbook states that "[a]t the end of 90 calendar days since employment the employee becomes a permanent employee and termination contemplated by the hospital *cannot occur* without proper notice and investigation." (Emphasis added.) It states that permanent employees "*are never* dismissed without prior written admonitions and/or an investigation that has been properly documented" (emphasis added), and that "three warning notices within a twelve-month period *are required* before an employee is dismissed, except in the case of immediate dismissal." (Emphasis added.) The reservation as to "immediate dismissal" does not detract from the definiteness of the offer, because that term is well defined. An "immediate dismissal" justifies dismissal "without notice for a grave and valid reason," and the list of examples of grave offenses includes such offenses as "Mistreatment of a patient," "Fighting on hospital premises," "Unauthorized Possession of Weapons," and "Reporting to work under the influence of intoxicants." The handbook also lists offenses which are specifically *not* subject to immediate dismissal, such as "Deliberate Violation of Instructions," "Unwillingness to Render Satisfactory Service," and "Unauthorized Absence." An employee reading the handbook would thus reasonably believe that, except in the case of a very serious offense, he or she would not be terminated without prior written warnings. Furthermore, the handbook creates rights even for probationary employees who may be terminated "without notice but for just cause."

Moreover, the handbook contains no disclaimers to negate the promises made. In fact, the introduction to the handbook states just the opposite, that the policies in the handbook "are designed to clarify your *rights* and duties as employees." (Emphasis added.) Thus, the handbook language is such that an employee would reasonably believe that after the expiration of the initial probationary period the progressive disciplinary procedure would be part of the employer's offer.

Finally, it is undisputed that defendant gave the handbook to plaintiff and intended that plaintiff become familiar with its contents. In fact, a significant part of plaintiff's duties as an employee consisted of instructing new employees on the contents of the handbook. There is no question but that plaintiff continued to work with knowledge of the handbook provisions. Under these circumstances the handbook's provisions became binding on the employer.

A more difficult question is whether or not defendant complied with the provisions of the handbook. It is undisputed that plaintiff had been working for more than 90 days and was receiving benefits only available to "permanent" employees. Defendant, however, claims that plaintiff had been transferred to a new position, and therefore reverted to probationary status. In support of this argument defendant cites an amendment to the handbook, finalized on September 3, 1981, which states that "[a]ll promotions and transferred employees must successfully pass a designated probationary period." This provision means, defendant argues, that once plaintiff had been transferred she could be terminated without the benefit of the progressive disciplinary procedures required for permanent employees.

We disagree. The handbook states that an employee may be terminated without notice during the "*initial* probationary period" (emphasis added), a period which ends "[a]t the end of 90 calendar days since employment." There is nothing in the policy statement on transfers to indicate that an employee serving a "*designated* probationary period" loses the right to progressive disciplinary procedures which vested when the employee successfully passed the "*initial* probationary period." (Emphasis added.) In addition, in distinguishing between "permanent" and "probationary" employees for disciplinary purposes the handbook notes that only "permanent" employees are eligible for employee benefits. It is undisputed that plaintiff continued to receive vacation pay and other benefits after the September 14, 1981, reorganization, as she had following her prior promotions. In fact, plaintiff's supervisors at the hospital claimed in their depositions that plaintiff, upon transfer, had occupied a hybrid "permanent probationary" status.

Moreover, the policy statement on transfers and promotions specifically states that its purpose is to "provide employees with approved promotional or transfer opportunities." The statement provides a procedure which begins with the posting of vacant positions and the employee's filing of a "Request for Transfer Form." The policy statement thus appears to apply only to *voluntary* transfers, and it is undisputed that plaintiff's transfer was not voluntary.

Ambiguous contractual language is generally construed against the drafter of the language, and in the absence of evidence to the contrary we must conclude that the "designated probationary period" does not divest an employee of rights vested at the end of the "initial probationary period." We must also conclude that the designated probationary period applies only to employees who *request* transfer or promotion. It is clear that plaintiff's alleged infractions did not fit into the category of extremely serious offenses warranting "immediate dismissal," and it is undisputed the plaintiff did not receive the progressive disciplinary procedures normally required for permanent employees in a nonimmediate-dismissal situation. Since defendant can point to no reason why plaintiff would not be entitled to the progressive disciplinary procedures, other than the reasons we have rejected above, we must agree with the appellate court that the failure to provide plaintiff with the required process violated her contractual rights.

* * * * *

For the reasons stated above, the judgment of the appellate court is affirmed insofar as it reversed the orders of the circuit court. The cause is remanded to the circuit court of Cook County with directions to enter summary judgment for the plaintiff and for such further proceedings as are consistent with this opinion.

Affirmed in part and remanded, with directions.

Questions for Review

1. List three federal statutes that protect employees against discrimination. Discuss the type, or types, of employment discrimination each statute prohibits.
2. Contrast disparate treatment discrimination and disparate impact discrimination.
3. Define the term *bona fide occupational qualification.*
4. Is it permissible for an advertisement for job applicants:
   a. To imply a preference for applicants of a particular race or color?
   b. To specify that the employer is looking for "a college student"?
5. Why is it inadvisable for an interviewer to elicit information from a job applicant that is not related to the applicant's ability to perform the duties of the job?
6. Describe how the following can help prevent employment discrimination complaints:
   a. Job performance evaluations.
   b. Uniform standards for job performance.

7. The EEOC's guidelines on sexual harassment provide that "unwelcome sexual advances, requests for sexual favors and other verbal or physical conduct of a sexual nature" constitute sexual harassment under three conditions. What are these conditions?

8. Is it unlawful employment discrimination to force a pregnant female employee to stop working because it is her sixth month of pregnancy?

9. Define the terms *reverse discrimination* and *affirmative action.*

10. Under the Americans with Disabilities Act, is an employer permitted to ask a job applicant about her medical history or possible disability?

11. Can an employer lawfully discipline an employee:
    a. For filing an employment discrimination charge against the employer?
    b. For testifying against the employer at a job discrimination hearing?

12. Define the employment-at-will rule. How has this rule been modified in recent years?

ab initio   From the beginning; a contract void *ab initio* is a contract that is void from the beginning.

absolute assignment   The irrevocable transfer of all of the owner's rights in property, such as the transfer of all of a policyowner's rights in a life insurance policy.

acceptance   Assent by an offeree to the terms of an offer.

accident   An unusual, unforeseeable event that happens suddenly and unexpectedly and without the insured's intent.

accidental means clause   A clause requiring both means and result to be accidental if the accidental death benefit is to be payable.

accidental result clause   A clause requiring only the result to be accidental if the accidental death benefit is to be payable.

accord and satisfaction   An agreement between two or more persons to settle a contract dispute between them and the performance of the promises made in the agreement; compromise settlement.

accumulation period   The period during which premium payments are being made and accumulated under a deferred annuity contract.

act   A statute.

actual authority   Authority, express or implied, to act on the principal's behalf that an agent reasonably believes he has been given by the principal.

adhesion contract   Standard contract forms offered on a "take it or leave it" basis.

administrative officer, government   An official belonging to the executive branch of government.

administrative services only contract   A contract under which an insurer assumes no risk for health benefits, pays no premium taxes, and retains no reserves, but makes its exper-

tise in benefit design, actuarial science, and claims handling available to a self-funded employer.

advance   Money paid before the stipulated time of payment.

affirmative action plan   A plan used to remedy the effects of past employment discrimination by requiring the hiring of members of protected classes.

agent   A person who acts for another person, the principal, especially in contractual dealings with third parties.

agent or broker of record   The person whom the insurer recognizes as having earned the commission on the sale of an insurance policy or annuity contract.

aleatory contract   A contract in which the promise by one party is conditioned on the happening of an uncertain event.

A.L.R.   *American Law Reports,* a series of books containing discussions on points of law.

Am. Jur. 2d   *American Jurisprudence Second,* an encyclopedia of law.

annuitant   The recipient of periodic payments made under an annuity contract.

annuity   (1) Periodic payments made under an annuity contract; (2) the annuity contract itself.

annuity contract   An agreement that a person or organization will make periodic payments to an annuitant at regular intervals for a specified period of time.

annuity for life with period certain   An annuity payable for at least a specified number of years and thereafter for as long as the annuitant lives.

answer   A formal written statement by a defendant in which she admits or denies the facts alleged by the plaintiff.

apparent authority   Agency authority a person has because a principal has created the appearance of authority to a third person.

appellate court (1) An intermediate court; (2) a court where appeals are taken.

approval premium receipt A conditional premium receipt under the terms of which temporary life insurance takes effect when the insurer approves the risk.

assignment (1) A property owner's transfer of some or all of his ownership rights in the property to another person; (2) a written document used to effect a transfer of rights in certain kinds of property, usually choses in action.

automatic premium loan provision A life insurance policy provision allowing the insurer to establish a policy loan to pay a premium that remains unpaid at the end of the grace period, if the policyowner has requested it and if the policy has a sufficient net cash value.

bad faith A breach of the covenant of good faith and fair dealing implied in insurance contracts under the laws of many states.

bilateral contract A contract under which promises are made by both parties.

binding premium receipt A premium receipt under which no conditions need be fulfilled and temporary life insurance becomes effective on the date the applicant receives the receipt.

bona fide occupational qualification A characteristic the employee must have to perform a particular job satisfactorily.

breach of contract The failure of a party to perform a contract according to its terms, without a legal excuse.

broker A person who brings buyers and sellers together.

burden of proof (1) The duty of producing evidence; (2) the obligation of the plaintiff in a civil action to present the court with a preponderance of evidence in his favor or, in certain actions, with clear and convincing evidence.

buyer's guide A document describing term life insurance, whole life insurance, and endowment insurance that many states require life insurers to provide to policy applicants.

case law Law contained in reported court decisions.

case management The tailoring of health benefits to individual situations when the patient's illness or injury is severe; also called large case management, catastrophic case management, or individual case management.

cash loan Advances of cash the insurer makes to the policyowner for her to use for whatever purpose she wishes.

cash surrender nonforfeiture benefit The option of a policyowner to surrender the policy to the insurer in return for the policy's cash surrender value.

cash surrender value The amount of cash available to the policyowner on surrender of the policy before the policy matures; net cash value.

center of gravity rule A state conflict of laws rule by which a state applies the law of the state most concerned with the outcome of the litigation; also called grouping of contacts rule, principal contacts rule, most significant relationship rule, governmental interest analysis, and paramount interest rule.

chose in action A right in intangible personal property that can be enforced by legal action or by a suit in equity.

chose in possession Something tangible of which the owner has actual possession, such as a chair, a bracelet, or money.

civil law (1) Law derived from the law of the Roman empire; (2) the body of law that determines private rights and liabilities.

C.J.S. *Corpus Juris Secundum,* an encyclopedia of law.

class action A lawsuit brought by a representative member, or members, of a large group of persons on behalf of all members of the group.

class beneficiary designation A beneficiary designation that names several people as a group, without listing them individually, such as "children of the insured."

code (1) The published statutes of a jurisdiction; (2) a part of the statutes of a jurisdiction, as an insurance code.

collateral assignment A temporary transfer of some, but not all, life insurance policy rights to a lender as security for a loan.

collusion A secret agreement between two or more persons to do some act to defraud a third person.

Commerce Clause A clause in the federal Constitution that reads, in part, "The Congress shall have Power . . . To regulate Commerce with foreign Nations, and among the several States, and with the Indian Tribes."

common disaster A single catastrophe in which two or more people lose their lives, such as a fire, airplane accident, or flood.

common law (1) A heritage of general principles involving custom, public policy, and ideas of justice that are followed by courts of common-law countries, states, and provinces; (2) a system of law followed by England and by nations that derive their law from English law, as contrasted with civil law; (3) decisions of the courts.

community property Certain property that a husband and wife residing in a community property state own.

compensatory damages The money a court awards a plaintiff to compensate for a wrong done to him.

competent party A person competent to enter into a valid contract because she is of legal age and without mental infirmity or other incapacity.

complaint A formal written statement of a plaintiff's cause of action.

compromise settlement   An agreement between two or more persons to settle a matter in dispute between them and the performance of the promises made in the agreement; accord and satisfaction.

condition precedent   An uncertain event that must occur before a right arises.

condition subsequent   An event that cancels an existing right.

conditional premium receipt   A premium receipt that will not provide temporary life insurance unless specified conditions occur.

conflict of laws   That part of the law of each state or nation that determines whether, in dealing with a legal situation, the law of some other state or nation will be recognized, be given effect, or be applied.

consideration   The thing of value that a promisor requested that is given to him in exchange for his promise; any benefit to the promisor or detriment to the promisee.

constitution   The general principles that form the legal foundation of a government.

constructive delivery   A policy delivery that occurs when an insurer releases the policy with intent to be bound by it.

construe   Interpret.

consumer report   "Any written, oral or other communication of any information by a consumer reporting agency bearing on a consumer's credit worthiness, credit standing, credit capacity, character, general reputation, personal characteristics or mode of living" for use in determining whether the consumer can obtain employment, credit, or insurance.

consumer reporting agency   Any entity that for money, or on a cooperative nonprofit basis, regularly prepares consumer reports and furnishes the reports to others.

contest, policy   A court action challenging the validity of a policy.

contract   An agreement enforceable at law; a promise or set of promises for breach of which the law gives a remedy or the performance of which the law recognizes as a duty.

contract damages   In a lawsuit on an insurance contract, the amount of money, equal to the insurance proceeds, that the insurer must pay to the plaintiff if the plaintiff wins the lawsuit.

contract fee   A flat dollar amount the insurer charges annually or once at the time an annuity contract is issued.

contract performance   Completion of the act or acts required by the contract.

contributory policy   Group policy paid for jointly by employer and employees.

conversion   An unauthorized act that deprives an owner of her property; one type of tort.

corporation   A legal entity authorized by law to carry on a business of a specific nature.

counteroffer   A rejection of an offer and making of a new offer.

court of original jurisdiction   A court where a case is first brought; a trial court.

courts of equity   The courts that arose in England because of the inadequacy of legal remedies.

creditor beneficiary   A person whom the policyowner names as beneficiary because the policyowner owes a debt to that person.

crime   Conduct causing harm to the public; a felony or misdemeanor.

criminal law   Law that prohibits and punishes conduct causing harm to the public.

damages   The sum of money that the law awards as compensation for a legal wrong to the plaintiff.

declaratory judgment   A judgment that declares the rights and duties of the parties involved in the suit but does not require either of the parties to take any action or to pay any money to the other.

defamation   A false communication that tends to harm the reputation of a person so as to lower that person in the estimation of others and deter others from associating or dealing with the defamed person; one type of tort.

default judgment   A judgment, usually in favor of the plaintiff, entered without the defendant's being heard in his own defense, because of the defendant's failure to answer the complaint or to appear at trial.

defendant   The person being sued in a lawsuit or suit in equity.

deferred annuity contract   An annuity contract, usually purchased to supplement retirement income, under the terms of which periodic payments are to begin at an agreed time in the future.

deferred fixed annuity contract   A deferred annuity contract with premiums that are accumulated at rates of interest set by the insurer.

demurrer   A method of raising an objection to a pleading.

deposition   The oral testimony under oath of a witness, taken somewhere other than the courtroom.

direct response insurance solicitation   A solicitation for the sale of, or inquiry about, an insurance policy without the use of a soliciting agent; also called mail order solicitation, direct mail solicitation, or mass merchandising.

discovery   The determination of facts and issues by means of pretrial devices such as depositions, interrogatories, subpoenas, and medical examinations.

disparate impact discrimination   Discrimination that occurs when an apparently nondiscriminatory job requirement has a disproportionately large adverse impact on the opportunities of people in a protected class, such as blacks or women.

disparate treatment discrimination Discrimination in which an employer bases an employment decision on a person's race, religion, national origin, sex, age, or other such factor.

district court A first-level federal court; a federal trial court.

diversity of citizenship Domicile in different states by parties on opposite sides of a lawsuit; one of the grounds to invoke jurisdiction of a U.S. district court.

dividends, policyowners' The refund of excess premium to the owner of a participating policy; a premium abatement.

dividends, stockholders' The money paid to the owners of corporate stock, usually out of the accumulated earnings of the corporation.

donee A person who receives a gift.

donee beneficiary A person whom the policyowner names as the beneficiary but who gives no consideration to the policyowner in return.

duress An inducement to make or modify a contract against a person's will by the wrongful act or threat of another.

election of remedies, doctrine of The court doctrine that a person with two or more inconsistent remedies available for the enforcement of a single right must elect one remedy and forgo the others.

employment-at-will rule The rule that an employer can dismiss an employee who was hired for an indefinite period of time without notice or cause.

equitable remedy A court of equity's enforcement of a right or redress of a wrong.

escheat The reversion of ownership of property to the state in the absence of persons legally entitled to take claim to the property.

estop A legal term meaning to stop, bar, prevent, or preclude.

estoppel, equitable A court's bar to a party from exercising a right or from asserting a fact because of something the party said or did that misled a second party to act so that harm resulted to the second party.

evidence of insurability An application form with questions pertaining to the proposed insured's health; health certificate.

exception A provision in an accident and sickness insurance policy whereby the insurer entirely eliminates coverage for a specific hazard; a statement of risk not assumed under a policy.

exclusive provider organization (EPO) A type of managed care organization that is essentially the same as an HMO.

executive branch The branch of government empowered to carry out laws.

executive order An order promulgated by the president of the United States that has the force of law when published in the *Federal Register,* an official government publication.

exemption A right given by law to a debtor to retain certain property free from seizure by his creditors.

exoneration statutes Statutes in community property states that make payment of a death benefit, in good faith and without knowledge of an adverse claim, sufficient to discharge the insurer of liability.

expire To cease to provide insurance coverage. An insurance policy expires when it ceases to provide insurance coverage.

express authority Oral or written authority to act that a principal gives to an agent.

express waiver An oral or written waiver.

Expressio unius est exclusio alterius A Latin phrase meaning "the expression of one thing means the exclusion of another thing."

extended term insurance nonforfeiture benefit The policyowner's option to choose insurance for the face amount of the life insurance policy, less any unpaid policy loan and unpaid interest, extended for such period as the net cash value will provide.

extra-contract damages In a lawsuit on an insurance contract, awards of money in addition to the amount payable under the contract. See *contract damages.*

external means A term used in accidental means clauses referring to an agency external to the insured that results in bodily injury to the insured.

facility-of-payment clause A policy clause that permits the insurer to choose as beneficiary a person appearing to the insurer to be equitably entitled to part or all of the death benefit because that person has incurred expenses of the insured's last illness or burial.

facts Actions that were taken, events that occurred, or circumstances that existed.

felony A serious crime for which the punishment can be imprisonment in a state or federal penitentiary, or even death.

fiduciary A person who occupies a position of special trust and confidence in handling the affairs or funds of another person.

flexible premium annuity contract An annuity contract that allows the contract holder to pay whenever and in whatever amount she wishes, within specified limits.

forgery   The signing of another person's name to a document with the intention of deceitfully and fraudulently presenting the signature as genuine.

formal contract   A contract binding because of its form.

401(k) plan   A profit-sharing or stock bonus plan under which an employee can choose to receive an amount in the form of currently taxable compensation or to defer receipt of this amount so that it will be taxed at a future time; a cash or deferred arrangement (CODA).

fraud   An intentional misrepresentation of a material fact communicated to another person who is injured as a result of reasonably relying on the misrepresentation.

garnishment   A remedy a court can impose at the request of a creditor to obtain property that belongs to a debtor but is in the hands of a third person.

gift   A voluntary transfer of property to another person, made without receiving consideration in return.

grantor   One who creates a trust by transferring property to a trustee; also called a settlor, trustor, donor, or creator of the trust.

group annuity contract   An annuity contract providing periodic payments, usually at retirement, to each person in a group of covered persons.

health certificate   An application form with questions pertaining to the proposed insured's health; evidence of insurability.

health maintenance organization (HMO)   A prepaid health care delivery system in which subscribers pay an enrollment fee in exchange for medical care and usually are restricted to obtaining health care from the health maintenance organization's physicians.

heirs   Those persons entitled to inherit the property of a person who has no will.

immediate annuity contract   An annuity contract under the terms of which the insurer begins making periodic payments to the annuitant one period after the contract holder pays the insurer the purchase price for the annuity contract.

implied waiver   A waiver that can be clearly inferred from a party's words or conduct when the party does not express an intention to waive a right.

incidental authority   Implied authority of an agent to do all the things normally incident to carrying out the agency.

incidental beneficiary   A person who benefits from a contract but who has no rights under it.

income for a fixed period settlement option   A settlement option in a life insurance policy under which the insurer

agrees to retain policy proceeds and make regular payments in equal amounts for a period specified by the policyowner or by the beneficiary if the beneficiary chooses the option.

income for life settlement option   A settlement option in a life insurance policy under which the insurer retains the proceeds and pays them out to a named payee in an income of a guaranteed amount for the entire lifetime of that payee.

income for life with refund annuity contract   An annuity contract that guarantees periodic payments for the lifetime of the annuitant and guarantees that the insurer will pay out at least the purchase price of the annuity.

income of a fixed amount settlement option   A settlement option in a life insurance policy under which the insurer retains the policy proceeds and pays them out in regular payments of a specified amount until the fund is exhausted.

income period   The period during which an insurer is making periodic payments to an annuitant; also called the payout period.

incorporation by reference   A rule of contract law that permits contracting parties to incorporate into a written contract any other document by referring to it in the contract.

independent contractor   A person who has a distinct business, is hired to do a particular job, is paid for that job at stated intervals rather than in regular amounts, uses her own tools, and follows her own discretion in carrying out the job.

indicia of authority   Indications, signs, or evidence of agency authority such as credentials or documents used in carrying out the agency.

individual annuity contract   An annuity contract between an individual purchaser and an insurer in which the insurer agrees to make periodic payments to the purchaser or another person.

informal contract   A contract that creates legal duties because the parties have met requirements that relate to the substance rather than to the form of the transaction.

installment premium annuity contract   An annuity contract under which the contract holder pays a series of premiums rather than a single premium.

institutional advertisement   An advertisement that has as its sole purpose the promotion of the insurer or of the reader's, viewer's, or listener's interest in the concept of accident and sickness insurance.

insurability premium receipt   A conditional premium receipt under the terms of which temporary life insurance takes effect if the insurer determines that the proposed insured was insurable on the date of the receipt, of the application, or of a required examination, depending on the language in the receipt.

insurable interest   An interest that takes an insurance contract out of the class of wager contracts; in life insurance, any reasonable expectation of benefit or advantage from the continued life of another person.

insurance advertisement Written or spoken material designed to promote public interest in life or health insurance or annuity contracts or to induce the purchase of such contracts.

insurance consultant A person who receives fees from clients for rendering advice about insurance contracts.

intended beneficiary A person whom the parties to a contract intended to benefit from the performance of the contract.

interest income settlement option A settlement option in a life insurance policy under which the insurer pays interest of at least a guaranteed rate at intervals agreed on between the insurer and the policyowner or beneficiary.

interpleader An equitable action brought by a disinterested holder of property to which there are conflicting claims. The holder deposits the property with the court and is dismissed from the case, leaving the claimants to litigate.

interrogatories A series of written questions drawn up by one party to a lawsuit and given to the other party, or to a witness, to answer within a fixed period of time.

inter vivos trust A trust that takes effect during the lifetime of the grantor.

intestate A person who dies without a valid will.

invasion of privacy A tort taking four forms: (1) appropriation of a person's name or likeness for another's benefit; (2) unreasonable intrusion into a person's seclusion, solitude, or private affairs; (3) public disclosure of private facts about a person; (4) placing a person in a false light in the public eye.

investigative consumer report A report "obtained through personal interviews with neighbors, friends, or associates of the consumer reported on, or with others with whom he is acquainted or who may have knowledge" about the consumer.

invitation to contract An advertisement for an accident and sickness insurance policy containing the terms and cost of the policy advertised.

invitation to inquire An advertisement for an accident and sickness insurance policy designed to create a desire to inquire further about the policy advertised.

issue (1) Lineal descendants such as children, grandchildren, great-grandchildren and so forth; (2) a material point of fact or of law that is affirmed by one party to a lawsuit and denied by the other; (3) a question.

issue of fact A material fact alleged by one party to a lawsuit and denied by the other.

issue of law A material point of law, the application of which the parties to a lawsuit disagree.

joint and survivor annuity contract An annuity contract providing periodic payments during two annuitants' lifetimes and continuing the payments, in whole or in part, after one annuitant's death to the surviving annuitant for the surviving annuitant's lifetime.

joint tenancy A form of property ownership in which two or more persons hold property with equal rights to share in its enjoyment during their lives and with rights of survivorship.

judicial branch The branch of government empowered to interpret laws.

jurisdiction of the subject matter The power of a court to hear and make an enforceable decision in a case.

jurisdiction over the person The jurisdiction of a court over the person sued because of compliance by the court with certain constitutional requirements.

laches In equity, an unreasonable delay by a plaintiff that harms the defendant.

lapse A default in premiums before a life insurance policy has a nonforfeiture value.

late remittance offer An insurer's offer to extend the time for payment of an overdue premium.

law A system of rules governing human conduct that are enforceable by a controlling authority.

legislative branch The branch of government empowered to make laws.

libel Written or pictorial defamation.

liberty of contract The freedom to contract as a person wishes as to contract terms, the people with whom she is willing to contract, and adequacy of the consideration.

lien A right to retain another person's property as security for a debt.

life income with period certain A form of income for life settlement option under which the primary payee receives payments for life, but if the primary payee dies before a specified period of time has elapsed, payments will continue to a contingent payee until the end of the specified period.

limitation Any provision that restricts accident and sickness insurance coverage but is not an exception or reduction.

loan The transfer of money from one person, the creditor, to another person, the debtor, on agreement that the debtor will return to the creditor an equivalent sum at a later date, usually plus interest.

malice Conduct intended to cause injury or despicable conduct carried on with a willful and conscious disregard of the rights of others.

managed care organization A health maintenance organization or preferred provider arrangement.

mandatory injunction A court of equity's command that a person do a specified thing.

material fact   A fact that, if known to a party to a contract, would have caused that party not to have entered into the contract.

means   Cause.

minimum premium plan   A plan under which an employer purchases a group health insurance policy from an insurer, but employees' health claims are paid up to the annual expected claims liability with the employer's own funds, and the insurer pays additional claims, if any, from its funds.

misdemeanor   A crime less serious than a felony, usually punishable by fine or by imprisonment other than in a penitentiary, as, for example, in a county jail.

model law   An act or regulation proposed by experts in a particular field for adoption by the states; a uniform law.

moral turpitude   Baseness, vileness, or depravity in the private or social duties that a person owes to other people or to society in general.

motion   An application by a party to a lawsuit to the judge for a ruling favorable to the applicant.

necessaries   Things reasonably necessary for a minor's or mentally infirm person's maintenance, considering his social position and financial status.

net cash value   A life insurance policy's cash value, minus any unpaid policy loans and unpaid loan interest, plus any dividends, any interest on dividends, and the net cash value of any paid-up additions.

noncontributory policy   A group insurance policy the premiums of which are paid by the employer.

nonqualified annuity contract   An annuity contract not purchased for tax-qualified plan purposes.

non resident license   A license that a state issues to an insurance agent who is a resident of another state authorizing the agent to sell insurance in the licensing state.

nonwaiver clause   A clause in an application or policy giving notice of limitations on an agent's authority to waive the insurer's rights.

offer   A proposal that, if accepted by the offeree according to its terms, will create a contract.

offeree   A person to whom an offer to enter into a contract is made.

offeror   A person who makes an offer to enter into a contract.

operation of law   The determination of rights and obligations through the automatic effects of the law and not by any act of an affected party.

oppression   Despicable conduct that subjects a person to cruel and unjust hardship in conscious disregard of that person's rights.

oral testimony   Testimony given under oath in a deposition or at trial.

overinsurance   Insurance in an amount that is excessive in relation to the loss insured against.

ownership clause   A clause in a life insurance policy that describes the policyowner's rights, and that the policyowner must comply with to make an absolute assignment of the policy that will be binding on the insurer.

parol evidence   Oral evidence (testimony) given by a witness in court.

parol evidence rule   The rule that, when parties put their contract into an unambiguous writing, all previous oral agreements merge into the written contract and that parol evidence is not admissible to add to, detract from, or alter the contract as written.

partnership   An association of two or more persons to carry on an unincorporated business.

payee   A person receiving life insurance proceeds under a settlement agreement.

per capita   (1) By head or by individual; (2) to share equally.

percentage of premium charge   A specified percentage of the annuity premium that the insurer deducts from each annuity premium paid.

personal property   A right over that which is not land or something attached to land, such as a bracelet, a racehorse, money, or shares of stock.

personal representative   The executor or administrator of a deceased person's estate.

per curiam   By the court; used to distinguish an opinion of the whole court from an opinion written by any one judge.

per stirpes   By family branches. A per stirpes beneficiary designation is a method of dividing benefits among living members of a class of beneficiaries and the descendants of deceased members.

plaintiff   A person who brings a lawsuit or a suit in equity; the person suing.

pleadings   The formal written statements of the respective claims and defenses of the parties to a court action.

point-of-service option   An option that allows HMO subscribers to use health care providers outside the HMO's provider network and have the HMO pay part of the charges, although a subscriber typically will have to pay 20 to 30 percent herself.

policy date   Date written on the policy, often the same as the date the insurer issued the policy.

policy loan   An advance to the policyowner of money the insurer must eventually pay out under a life insurance policy.

policy summary   A document disclosing detailed financial data with respect to a particular life insurance policy.

preauthorized check plan   An agreement under which a policyowner authorizes an insurer to draw checks to the insurer's own order on the policyowner's bank account to pay insurance premiums.

preauthorized electronic fund transfer   Electronic transfer of funds to pay a premium from the policyowner's bank account to the bank account of the insurer with the policyowner's authorization.

precedent   A previous decision by the court deciding a case, or by a higher court of the same jurisdiction, on the same question and involving the same general set of facts as the case being decided, which previous decision will be followed unless there is a strong reason to depart from it.

preexisting condition   A physical or mental condition of the insured that manifested itself prior to the effective date of the insured's individual health insurance policy or group health insurance coverage.

preferred provider network   A group of physicians or hospitals, or both, that offers a system of health care through contracts with insurers or self-funded employers.

preferred provider organization (PPO)   An arrangement in which an insurer, employer, or other organization enters into contracts with physicians, hospitals, and other health care providers to provide health care services to a defined group of patients on a predetermined, discounted, fee-for-service basis.

premium loan   Advances of policy cash values the insurer makes to the policyowner for the purpose of paying the premium.

premium refund   Return of premium where the insurer is a stock company.

presumption   A conclusion that the law requires to be drawn from a given set of facts, which conclusion will stand until adequate evidence to the contrary is presented to the court.

pretext interview   An interview in which the interviewer, in an attempt to obtain information about someone, makes a misrepresentation or refuses to identify herself.

prima facie case   A set of facts established by evidence sufficient to entitle the party presenting the evidence to a verdict in her favor if the other party does not refute the evidence.

primary beneficiary   The person who will receive the death benefit if he is living at the time of the insured's death, or living at the expiration of the time period specified in a survivorship clause.

principal   One for whom an agent acts, especially as to contractual dealings with third persons.

private annuity   An annuity that a natural person sells or gives to another person.

privacy   (1) The right to be let alone; (2) in insurance contexts, the right to fair personal information practices.

probate   To prove the validity of a will in court.

procedural law   Law that provides a structure and set of rules for the enforcement of the rights and duties created by substantive law.

prohibitory injunction   A court of equity's command that a person stop doing a specified thing.

promissory note   A written promise to pay a stated sum of money.

property   (1) Rights of possession, use, control, and disposition; (2) popularly, that which is owned.

proximate cause   A cause that is either directly responsible for a death or injury or that initiates an unbroken chain of events, each causing the next, that leads to and brings about the death or injury.

punitive damages   The damages awarded to a plaintiff or given to the state to punish and make an example of the defendant; exemplary damages.

qualified annuity contract   An annuity contract used to fund or distribute, or both fund and distribute, a tax-qualified pension or profit-sharing plan.

qualified assignment   Under federal law, any assignment of a liability to make periodic payments as tort damages on account of physical injury or physical sickness, whether the liability arises by lawsuit or agreement.

qualified job applicant   An applicant who can perform the essential functions of a job with reasonable accommodation by the employer if necessary.

Qui facit per alium facit per se   A Latin phrase meaning "he who acts through another acts himself."

ratification   The validation by a principal of an unauthorized act done by his purported agent.

real property   A right over land and that which is attached to the land, such as a house and trees; real estate.

reasonable expectations doctrine   The doctrine that the reasonable expectations of policyowners and beneficiaries will be honored, even though the strict terms of the policy do not support those expectations.

rebating   An inducement by an insurer or its agent to the purchase of insurance by giving the purchaser part of the agent's commission, a deduction from the stipulated premium, or some other thing of value.

rebuttable presumption   A presumption that a party can overturn by showing the court proof to the contrary.

reduced paid-up insurance nonforfeiture benefit   The policyowner's option to choose paid-up life insurance of the kind and for the duration provided by the life insurance policy immediately prior to lapse, in whatever amount the cash surrender value will purchase.

reduction   A provision that reduces the amount of an accident and sickness insurance benefit.

reformation   An equitable remedy by which a written contract is revised or interpreted to express the original intent of the parties.

release   The giving up of a right or claim, ordinarily in exchange for consideration.

remedy   A court's enforcement of a right or redress of a wrong.

renewal premiums   All premiums paid after the initial premium.

representation   An applicant's statement of facts on which the insurer bases its decision whether or not to issue the policy applied for.

rescission   An equitable remedy in which a court declares a contract void because of material misrepresentation or mistake.

respondeat superior   "Let the master answer"; the principle that an employer is responsible for the wrongful act (tort) of an employee committed in the course of the employee's employment.

reverse discrimination   Discrimination against persons who are not ordinarily discriminated against, such as young white males.

revised statutes   A code based on a prior code with alterations and additions necessary to bring the code up to date.

rights of survivorship   The rights of a joint tenant, or joint tenants, on the death of another joint tenant, to the deceased tenant's share of the property.

risk classification   An insurer's identification of people with similar loss potential and placement of those people in the same risk group for the purpose of setting premium rates.

risk selection   An insurer's choice from among its proposed insureds of those persons it is willing to insure.

rule against accumulations   The rule of law that prohibits one person from leaving property to another person to accumulate income for the other person too far into the future.

rule against perpetuities   The rule of law aimed at preventing remoteness of vesting, which is stated "No interest is good, unless it must vest, if at all, not later than 21 years after some life in being at the creation of the interest."

rules of jurisdiction   Rules for determining which cases are properly heard by each court.

scheduled premium annuity contract   An annuity contract that specifies the amount and time of the premium payments.

secondary beneficiary   The person who will receive the death benefit if he is living at the time of the insured's death and no primary beneficiary is living; first contingent beneficiary.

self-funded plan   A plan under which an employer pays for the health claims of its employees out of its own funds; also called a self-insured plan.

separate account   A pool of investments that an insurer establishes and maintains without consideration of the investment results of the insurer's other assets.

separation of powers   The division of a government into branches, as the executive, legislative, and judicial branches.

servicemark   A letter, word, phrase, number, design, or combination thereof that a service company, such as an insurer, uses to identify its services; similar to a trademark.

sexual harassment   Unwelcome sexual advances, requests for sexual favors, and other unwelcome verbal or physical conduct of a sexual nature.

simultaneous death act   A state law providing that, unless there is a clause in the policy to the contrary, if an insured and beneficiary die simultaneously, or if it is impossible to tell who died first, it will be deemed that the beneficiary died first.

single premium annuity contract   An annuity contract under the terms of which the contract holder pays one premium.

slander   Spoken defamation.

sole proprietorship   An unincorporated business owned by one person.

specific performance   An equitable remedy requiring that a contract be carried out as promised.

spendthrift trust   A special type of trust that provides a fund for the benefit of a person other than the grantor, secures the fund against the improvidence of the trust beneficiary, and places it beyond the reach of the trust beneficiary's creditors. **Spendthrift clauses** in life insurance policies derive from spendthrift trusts.

standing to sue   A person's right to maintain a legal action because the person has a legally protectible interest at stake in the controversy.

Stare decisis   The courts' practice of following previous court decisions (precedents) on the same question.

statute   An act of the legislature declaring, commanding, or prohibiting something; a particular law enacted and established by the will of the legislative department of government; an act.

Statute of Frauds   A statute originally enacted in England, since enacted in the states, requiring that certain informal contracts be evidenced by a writing.

Statute of Wills   Portion of a state's probate code that prescribes the formalities of execution of wills.

stop-loss contract   Contract under which an insurer provides a self-funded employer with protection against catastrophic occurrences.

straight life annuity contract   An annuity contract under which the insurer makes periodic payments during the annuitant's lifetime only.

structured settlement   An agreement to pay specified sums of money over time, ordinarily to a person claiming tort damages because of personal injury or the wrongful death of a close family member, or to an employee claiming worker's compensation benefits.

subagent   A person employed by an agent to assist in performing functions for the principal.

subpoena   A command to a witness to appear at a certain place and time to give testimony.

subpoena duces tecum   A subpoena requiring that a witness provide documents or other physical evidence.

substantial compliance rule   The rule of law that, when a policyholder has done everything possible to comply with the beneficiary change procedure set forth in the policy, but has failed because of circumstances beyond her control, the change will be effective.

substantive law   An area of law that creates rights and duties, such as contract law or tort law.

succession beneficiary designation provision   A beneficiary designation provision, included in some life insurance policies, that lists classes of persons (such as, in order of preference, the insured's surviving spouse, child or children, parent or parents, and executors or administrators) who will receive the benefits if no named beneficiary survives the insured.

summons   A notice to a defendant that an action has been filed against him and that a judgment will be granted unless he files an answer within a specified period of time.

surrender charge   A percentage of the annuity premiums paid or of the annuity contract value, made when the annuity contract holder surrenders the annuity contract.

survivorship clause   A clause that requires that the beneficiary survive the insured for a specified length of time before becoming entitled to the insurance proceeds; also called a time clause or delay clause.

tender   An unconditional and timely offer to pay a sum due (for example, a premium due) in a medium of payment acceptable to the payee (for example, an insurer).

tertiary beneficiary   The person who will receive the death benefit if she is living at the time of the insured's death and no primary or secondary beneficiary is living; second contingent beneficiary.

testamentary trust   A trust created by a will and that takes effect at the testator's death.

testator   A deceased person who died leaving a valid will.

tort   A violation of a duty to another person imposed by law, rather than by contract, causing harm to the other person and for which the law provides a remedy.

transaction fee   A flat dollar amount an insurer charges per annuity premium payment.

trial   A judicially supervised investigation and determination of the issues between the parties to a lawsuit or a suit in equity.

trust   An arrangement whereby property is transferred to a trustee, who has legal title to the property, with the intention that the property be administered for the benefit of someone other than the trustee (the trust beneficiary), who has equitable title.

trust beneficiary   One who has equitable title to trust property.

trustee   One who holds legal title to trust property, subject to an obligation to manage the property for the benefit of the trust beneficiary, who has equitable title.

twisting   An insurance agent's attempt through misrepresentation to induce a policyowner to replace his policy.

undue influence   The misuse of a position of confidence or dominion to overcome the will of another person.

uniform law   See *model law.*

unilateral contract   A contract having promises by one party only.

universal life insurance   An individual life insurance policy under the provisions of which separately identified interest credits and mortality and expense charges are made to the policy.

utilization review   The process of examining the health care given by physicians, hospitals, and other health care providers to detect and eliminate unnecessary or inappropriate care.

vacate   To annul, as to vacate (annul) a judgment of a lower court.

valid contract   A contract that is enforceable in either a lawsuit or in a suit in equity, depending on the remedy sought.

variable annuity contract   An annuity contract under the terms of which the value of the accumulated premiums paid depends on the investment results of a separate account.

variable life insurance   A level premium, cash value, whole life insurance contract with premiums that are credited to investment accounts separate from the insurer's other investment accounts.

violent means   A term used in accidental means clauses referring to a physical force that produces a harmful result to the insured.

void contract   An agreement that is unenforceable by court action. *Void contract* is a contradiction in terms.

voidable contract   A contract that is enforceable until a party who has the right to do so (such as a minor) takes some action to disaffirm the contract.

wagering agreement   A type of aleatory agreement that is often illegal.

waiver   The voluntary and intentional giving up of a known right.

warranty   A statement guaranteed to be true in all respects, and if the statement is untrue in any respect, even if the statement is not material, the contract of which the statement is a part can be rescinded.

will   A document directing the disposition of property after the death of the owner (the testator).

writ of certiorari   One way in which a party to a court action can obtain appellate review of the case.

wrongful death statute   A statute that gives the executor, administrator, or heirs of a deceased person a cause of action for injuries to the deceased that resulted from the wrongful acts of another.

FIGURE 1

washington national INSURANCE COMPANY

A Washington National Corporation Financial Service Company

APPLICATION FOR LIFE/HEALTH/ANNUITY - PART I

- PLEASE PRINT -

☐ MEDICAL
☐ NON-MEDICAL

1. Proposed Insured/Annuitant

John   A.   Doe
First   Middle   Last

☐ Single ☒ Married ☐ Widowed ☐ Divorced ☐ Separated

Birthplace (State)	Birthdate			Age	Sex	Height	Weight
Illinois	M	D	Y				
SS#	05	05	63	34	M	5'11'	180

2. Address   Number and Street

7900 Airport Dr.

Previous Address (within 2 years)

City	State	Zip Code
Peoria	Illinois	61605

3. Name of Employer

XYC Company, Inc.

a. Address - No. and St.	City	State	Zip Code
16 Oak St.	Peoria	IL.	61600

b. Occupation	**c. Duties**	**d. How Long Employed?**	**e. Former Occupation**
Salesman	Sales	15 Yrs. Mos.	Student

f. Avg. Mo. Earned Income	**g. Avg. Mo. Unearned Income**	**4. Address premium notices and correspondence to:**
$ 2,500.	$ None	☒ Insured/Annuitant ☐ Owner ☐ Employer ☐ Payor

5. LIFE INSURANCE

Basic Plan of Insurance   Amount

a. Whole Life   b. $ 100,000.

c. ☒ WP   e. ☐ Payor Benefits
d. ☒ ADB f. ☐ Guaranteed Insurability g. $ _____

Additional Rider Benefits   **Amount/Units**

h. _____ i. _____

j. _____ k. _____

l. _____ m. _____

n. Shall Automatic Premium Loan provision be operative if available in basic plan of insurance? ☒ Yes ☐ No

Amount Paid $ ___COD___

6. ANNUITY   ☐ Annuity Contract   ☐ Annuity Rider

a. Deferred
   ☐ Single Purchase   Amount $ _____
   ☐ Periodic Purchase   Amount $ _____
     Maturing at Age _____
     ☐ Waiver of Payment
b. ☐ Single Purchase Immediate - Amount $ _____

     Plan _____

     Amount Paid $ _____

7. Is this Policy/Contract being applied for under a Tax Qualified Retirement Plan? ☐ Yes ☐ No

If yes, indicate type ☐ TDA ☐ 401 Corp. ☐ 403a ☐ HR-10 Keogh ☐ IRA ☐ Deferred ☐ Other Comp.

Purchase Payment Allocation:

Employer _____ % Employee _____ %

8. HEALTH INSURANCE   Occupational Class _____

☐ Disability Income Form _____ Monthly Benefit _____ Max. Ben. Period _____ Elim. Period _____

   Rider _____ Benefit _____ Rider _____ Benefit _____ Rider _____ Benefit _____

☐ Business Expense Form _____ Monthly Benefit _____ Elimination Period _____
(Submit Business Expense Questionnaire)

☐ Major Med. Policy Form _____ Deductible _____ Maximum Benefit _____
   ☐ In-Full Hospital Rider ($100 Deductible only)   ☐ Rider _____

☐ Hospital Indemnity Form _____ Daily Hosp. Ind. $ _____ Elimination Period _____

☐ Other (Specify Form and Benefits) _____ Amount Paid $ _____

9. Present Coverage on Proposed Insured - List all Life/Health/Annuity coverage in force. ☐ ✓ if none

Company or Service Plan	Year of Issue	Amt. of Life Ins.	Amt. of Annuity	Amt. of ADB	Benefits: Indicate Mo./Wkly			Hospitalization		Major Medical	
					Dis. Inc.	Bus. Exp.	Ben. Per.	Rm. Ben.	Surgery	Deductible	Max. Ben.
ABC Ins.	1983	$10,000	–	$10,000							

Is this coverage to replace any Insurance or Annuity? ☐ Yes ☒ No   If replacing Life Insurance or Annuity, complete Replacement Proposal. If replacing Health Insurance, termination date of such insurance is _____

10. MODE: ☒ ANN ☐ SA ☐ QR ☐ PAC ☐ MDO
☐ MDH ☐ GA ☐ SD - No. of Payments _____

11. Total Amount Paid in Exchange for Receipt $ _____

O2336   (1-83)

FIGURE 1

(continued)

PART I - CONTINUED

12. **Beneficiaries** Primary	Relationship	Contingent	Relationship
Jane Margaret Doe	Wife	James Mark Doe	Son

COMPLETE FOR FAMILY COVERAGE AND CHECK TYPE OF COVERAGE DESIRED ☐ **Life Ins.** ☐ **Health Ins.**

13. **Full names** of dependents proposed for coverage	Relationship	Birthplace (State)	Birthdates M	D	Y	Age	Height/ Weight	Present Life Ins.
	Spouse							$
Children		XXX					XXX	XXX
		XXX					XXX	XXX
		XXX					XXX	XXX
		XXX					XXX	XXX

14. **a.** Spouse's occupation, duties	**b.** Spouse's other health coverage	**c.** Avg. Mo. Inc. $	**d.** SS#

COMPLETE QUESTIONS 15 AND 19—27 FOR PAYOR BENEFITS

15. **a.** Full name of proposed payor. Please print.	Birthplace (State)	Birthdate M	D	Y	Age	Sex	Height	Weight	Relationship to Insured

b. Payor's occupation	**c.** Mailing Add. No., Street, City, State, Zip Code	**d.** SS#

COMPLETE IF APPLICANT/OWNER IS NOT PROPOSED INSURED/ANNUITANT

16. Proposed ownership designation applies to ☐ Life ☐ Annuity - Please print full names		Relationship to Insured/Annuitant
Owner	SS#	
Contingent	SS#	

Proposed Insured/Annuitant, if a minor, is to become Owner: ☐ At Owner's death ☐ At age 21 or upon prior death of the Owner

Owner's mailing address: Number and Street	City	State	Zip Code

17. **SPECIAL REQUESTS:** Identify Life/Health/Annuity	18. **HOME OFFICE ENDORSEMENTS:**

Questions 19—24 must be answered if applying for Life or Health Coverage or WP on an Annuity Contract.

Has **any person** proposed for insurance, so far as you know or believe:	Yes	No	**Identify question and individual to whom details apply.**
19. Any income payable during disability other than policies listed under question no. 9?	☐	☒	22a - Sports pilot; 600 hours per year.
20. Been refused new insurance or reinstatement or had insurance postponed, limited, offered, or quoted on a substandard or rated basis?	☐	☒	
21. Any other application for personal Life or Health Insurance pending with this or any other company?	☐	☒	
22. In the past two years, participated in: (If yes, attach questionnaire).			
a) Aviation activities as pilot or crew member?	☒	☐	
b) Hazardous activities, sports, avocations, hobbies?	☐	☒	
23. Smoked cigarettes within the past year? If so, indicate quantity per day	☐	☒	
24. Used narcotics, barbiturates, amphetamines, psychedelic drugs, frequently or been treated for drug usage or alcoholism?	☐	☒	

Questions 25—27 should be answered if applying for Life or Health Coverage or WP on an Annuity Contract.

ANSWER THE FOLLOWING QUESTIONS AND GIVE FULL DETAILS — NAMES; AILMENTS; TREATMENT; DATES; PHYSICIANS' NAMES AND ADDRESSES; RECOVERY DATES; ETC.

Has **any person** proposed for insurance, so far as you know or believe:	Yes	No	**Identify question and individual to whom details apply.**
25. Ever had symptoms or been diagnosed as having disorder, disease, or persistent discomfort of —			
a) Respiratory System (lungs, bronchi, trachea, etc) such as TB, asthma, emphysema, bronchitis?	☐	☒	

FIGURE 1

(continued)

PART I - CONTINUED

                                          Yes No

b) Circulatory System (heart, blood, arteries, veins, etc) such as high blood pressure, heart attack, murmur, rheumatic fever? .... ☐ ☒   27a – Dr. Jones – checkups each year

c) Digestive System (esophagus, stomach, intestine, liver, gall bladder, etc) such as ulcer, cirrhosis, hemorrhoids, bleeding? .... ☐ ☒   15 Main St.

d) Nervous System (brain, nerves, etc) such as paralysis, fainting, epilepsy, convulsions, mental or nervous disorders? .... ☐ ☒   Peoria, IL. 61600

e) Muscular and Skeletal Systems (muscles, bones, joints, spine, etc) such as neck or back problems, fracture, arthritis? .... ☐ ☒

f) Genito-urinary System (kidney, bladder, reproductive organs, etc) such as infection, bleeding, male or female disorders? .... ☐ ☒

g) Glandular System (thyroid, pancreas, adrenal, lymph glands, etc) such as diabetes, or abnormal growth or function? .... ☐ ☒

h) Breast disorder or menstrual irregularity? .... ☐ ☒

26. Ever had impaired sight or hearing, cancer or growth, venereal disease, hernia, or skin disease? ☐ ☒

27. Within the past five years:

a) Been treated by or consulted any physician, health practitioner or psychologist?............ ☒ ☐

b) Had surgery or operation?   Has either been advised, or is either contemplated? .... ☐ ☒

c) Been on, or now on, prescribed diet or medication? ☐ ☒

d) Received disability, Worker's Compensation or pension benefits? .... ☐ ☒

Give name and address of personal or family physician(s).

Dr. M.D. Jones, 15 Main St., Peoria, IL. 61600

The undersigned represent(s) and agree(s), to the best of his (her) knowledge or belief, that the foregoing statements and answers are complete, true and correctly recorded and agree(s) to be bound by all statements and answers made or to be made in this application consisting of Part I and Part II (if said Part II is required by the Company). The undersigned further expressly agree(s) as follows: 1. This application and any policy issued in consequence thereof shall constitute the entire Contract. No agent is authorized to make or modify contracts, to waive any of the Company's rights or requirements or to bind the Company by making or receiving any promise, representation or information, unless the same be in writing, submitted to the Company, and made a part of such contract. 2. Except as otherwise provided in the Conditional Receipt bearing the same date as this application, the insurance applied for shall not become effective until the policy is delivered to and accepted by the Owner and the entire first premium is actually paid while all of the answers in Part I and Part II of this application continue to be complete and true answers. 3. The Company is authorized to amend any portion of this application pertaining to Life Insurance/Annuity by making an appropriate notation of any corrections or changes in the space designated "Home Office Endorsements," and the acceptance of any policy issued on this application shall constitute a ratification of any such amendment; provided, in those States where it is required by Statute, regulation or Insurance Department Ruling, any amendment as to amount, classification, plan of insurance or benefits shall be made only with written consent of the undersigned. 4. Unless otherwise stated in Question 16, the Proposed Insured/Annuitant will be the Owner of any policy issued on this application.

Signed At _Peoria_   _IL_   _John A Doe_
           City   State   Proposed Insured/Annuitant

Date _Nov._   _20_   19 _97_   Spouse (If coverage applied for)

Witnessed By _Sarah Smith_
                    Writing Agent   Applicant/Owner if other than Proposed Insured/Annuitant

FIGURE 1
(continued)

SUPPLEMENTAL APPLICATION FOR LIFE/HEALTH INSURANCE — Part 1

Your application for Life or Health Insurance is hereby amended to include the following questions. This Supplemental Application will be attached to, and made a part of your policy, if issued.

In the past 5 years did you, any member of your family, or co-habitant:

    a. Have a fever of more than three weeks duration, weight loss of more than 15 pounds in two months, diarrhea of more than one months duration, skin rash or oral lesions (infections or sores of the mouth)? *No*

        If yes, please explain.

    b. Have Acquired Immune Deficiency Syndrome (AIDS), AIDS-Related Complex (ARC) or any other immunological deficiency? *No*

        If yes, please explain.

Signed At *Peoria*   *IL*   *John A. Doe*
           City   State   **Proposed Insured**

Date *Nov. 20*   19*97* _____
                                   Spouse (If coverage applied for)

Witnessed By *Sarah Smith*
                 Writing Agent   **Applicant/Owner if other than Proposed Insured**

FIGURE 1

(continued)

AGENT'S/AGENCY REPORT

1. Did you personally see the person(s) proposed for coverage? Were all questions answered and the application signed in your presence? .... ☐ Yes ☐ No
2. Did Proposed Insured come to you for coverage? .... ☐ Yes ☐ No
3. Did you provide the Proposed Insured with the Notice of Information Practices and all other required Disclosure Information? ☐ Yes ☐ No
4. To the best of your knowledge, is the policy for which application is being made to Washington National Insurance Company to replace any existing Life Insurance, Health Insurance, or Annuity in this or any other Company? (If answer is "Yes", for Life Insurance or Annuity, complete proposal for policy replacement) .... ☐ Yes ☐ No
5. Does Proposed Insured intend to change his/her occupation? ☐ Yes ☐ No
6. Do you have any information not included in the application which might affect the insurability of any person to be covered? ☐ Yes ☐ No
7. Have standard premium rates been quoted? .... ☐ Yes ☐ No
8. If Family coverage applied for, are there any family members on whom coverage is not requested? .... ☐ Yes ☐ No
9. If Health Insurance application includes a family member age 19 and over, other than the spouse, is such member enrolled as a full-time student in a college or university? .... ☐ Yes ☐ No
10. How long have you known Proposed Insured/Annuitant? _____
11. Proposed Insured's Business/Daytime telephone number _____
12. What is purpose of Life Insurance/Annuity? _____
    (Details/Explanation of above answers, where applicable, are to be recorded below under "Additional Information".)

REQUEST FOR ALTERNATE OR ADDITIONAL LIFE POLICY

Check one: ☐ Alternate (only one policy to be delivered)
            ☐ Additional

Basic Plan	Amount
	$
Rider	
	$
Rider	
	$
Rider	
	$

☐ Waiver of Premium   ☐ Accidental Death Benefit   ☐ APL

Premium   ☐ Ann.   ☐ S.A.   ☐ PAC
$ ☐ Q.R.   ☐ S.D.   ☐ G.A.

DISTRICT OFFICE REPORT
Issue to the credit of: (Please Print)

Name of District		District No.
Agent's Name	Code No.	Account No.

PREMIUM INFORMATION

1. Premium Quoted on _____ Mode.

	LIFE	HEALTH	ANNUITY
Basic Policy	$_____	$_____	$_____
WP	$_____	$_____	$_____
ADB	$_____	$_____	$ XXX
Riders _____	$_____	$_____	$ XXX
	$_____	$_____	$ XXX
	$_____	$_____	$ XXX
_____	$_____	$_____	$ XXX
Modal Adjust./Policy Size Factor	$_____	$_____	$ XXX
TOTAL Mode Premium	$_____	$_____	$_____

2. Who will pay the premiums? _____

GENERAL AGENCY REPORT
Issue to the credit of: (Please Print)
(If a Joint Sales Policy, provide name and code number, if known, of Group Office.)

General Agent	Code
Writing Agent	Code
Writing Agent	Code
JSP - Group Office	Code

WRITING AGENTS RECEIVING LESS THAN 50% CREDIT. I AGREE TO ACCEPT THE ABOVE COMMISSION ARRANGEMENT.

_____   _____
Signature   Date

COMPLETE IF SALARY DEDUCTION MODE

1. Total amount to be deducted each pay period $ _____
2. Amount to be applied toward Life Insurance (Includes Modal Adjustment Factor) $ _____
3. Amount to be applied toward Health Insurance (Includes Policy Size Factor) $ _____
4. Amount to be applied toward Annuity (Includes Waiver of Payment) $ _____
5. Date deductions to begin _____
6. Policy(s) to be dated _____

CHECK THE APPROPRIATE DEDUCTION AND BILLING METHOD:

☐ Monthly (12 pays) - Bill monthly
☐ Semi-Monthly (24 pays) - Bill monthly
☐ *Semi-Monthly (24 pays) - Bill twice monthly
☐ *Bi-Weekly (26 pays) - Bill twice monthly with a third Billing to be sent the months of _____
   and _____
☐ *Bi-Weekly (26 pays) - Bill monthly with the extra Billing to be sent the month of _____
☐ Bi-Weekly (26 pays) - FESAP. Not Billed
   *Not Applicable to Health Insurance

ADDITIONAL INFORMATION/INSTRUCTIONS

_____   _____
Writing Agent's Signature   Date

FIGURE 1

(continued)

| Adult
Application
Part 2 | **WASHINGTON NATIONAL INSURANCE COMPANY**
EVANSTON, ILLINOIS 60201
Declarations to Medical Examiner |

Proposed Insured...... JOHN .... A. .... DOE
First Name / Middle initial / Last name

Birth Date:
Month **5** Day **5** Year **63**   Insurance Applied For: ☒ Life ☐ Health   Amount $ **100,000.** Monthly Indemnity $

1. a. Name and address of your personal physician? DR. M.D. JONES 15 MAIN ST.
   (If none, so state)   PEORIA, IL.
   b. If consulted within the last five years give date, reason, and treatment prescribed. CHECKUPS EACH YEAR

2. Have you ever been treated for or ever had any known indication of:	Yes	No
a. Disorder of eyes, ears, nose, or throat?	☐	☒
b. Dizziness, fainting, convulsions, headache; speech defect, paralysis or stroke; mental or nervous disorder?	☐	☒
c. Shortness of breath, persistent hoarseness or cough, blood spitting; bronchitis, pleurisy, asthma, emphysema, tuberculosis or chronic respiratory disorder?	☐	☒
d. Chest pain, palpitation, high blood pressure, rheumatic fever, heart murmur, heart attack or other disorder of the heart or blood vessels?	☐	☒
e. Jaundice, intestinal bleeding; ulcer, hernia, appendicitis, colitis, diverticulitis, hemorrhoids, recurrent indigestion, or other disorder of the stomach, intestines, liver or gallbladder?	☐	☒
f. Sugar, albumin, blood or pus in urine; venereal disease; stone or other disorder of kidney, bladder, prostate or reproductive organs?	☐	☒
g. Diabetes; thyroid or other endocrine disorders?	☐	☒
h. Neuritis, sciatica, rheumatism, arthritis, gout, or disorder of the muscles or bones, including the spine, back, or joints?	☐	☒
i. Deformity, lameness or amputation?	☐	☒
j. Disorder of skin, lymph glands, cyst, tumor, or cancer?	☐	☒
k. Allergies; anemia or other disorder of the blood?	☐	☒
l. Excessive use of alcohol, tobacco, or any habit-forming drugs?	☐	☒
3. Are you now under observation or taking treatment?	☐	☒
4. Have you had any change in weight in the past year?	☐	☒
5. Other than above, have you within the past 5 years:		
a. Had any mental or physical disorder not listed above?	☐	☒
b. Had a (checkup) consultation, illness, injury, surgery?	☒	☐
c. Been a patient in a hospital, clinic, sanatorium, or other medical facility?	☐	☒
d. Had electrocardiogram, (X-ray) other diagnostic test?	☒	☐
e. Been advised to have any diagnostic test, hospitalization, or surgery which was not completed?	☐	☒
6. Have you ever had military service deferment, rejection or discharge because of a physical or mental condition?	☐	☒
7. Have you ever requested or received a pension, benefits, or payment because of an injury, sickness or disability?	☐	☒
8. Family History: Tuberculosis, diabetes, cancer, high blood pressure, heart or kidney disease, mental illness or suicide?	☐	☒

DETAILS of "Yes" answers. (IDENTIFY QUESTION NUMBER, CIRCLE APPLICABLE ITEMS: Include diagnoses, dates, duration and names and addresses of all attending physicians and medical facilities.)

5(b) AND (d) - DR. JONES
CHECKUPS EACH YEAR

	Age if Living?	Cause of Death?	Age at Death?
Father	60		
Mother	59		
Brothers and Sisters No. Living 2 No. Dead			

9. Females only:	Yes	No
a. Have you ever had any disorder of menstruation, pregnancy or of the female organs or breasts?	☐	☐
b. To the best of your knowledge and belief are you now pregnant?	☐	☐

The undersigned represents that the foregoing statements and answers are complete, true and correctly recorded, and shall form a part, designated as Part 2, of the application for insurance.

Signed at **Peoria IL** on **Nov 20** 19**97** **John A. Doe**
                                                    Signature of Proposed Insured

Witnessed by *Julia Hershal, M.D.*
                Medical Examiner

O1033-4   (6-74)

FIGURE 1

(concluded)

PART 3   MEDICAL EXAMINER'S REPORT

10a. Height (In Shoes) ft. in.	Weight (Clothed) lbs.	Chest (Full Inspiration) in.	Chest (Forced Expiration) in.	Abdomen, at Umbilicus in.	Details of "Yes" answers. (Identify item.)

b. Did you weigh? ☐ Yes ☐ No   Did you measure? ☐ Yes ☐ No
c. Is appearance unhealthy or older than stated age? ☐ Yes ☐ No

11, Blood Pressure (Record ALL readings)

Systolic

Diastolic { 4th phase
        5th phase

12. Pulse:	At Rest	After Exercise	3 Minutes Later
Rate			
Irregularities per min.			

13. Heart: Is there any:
Enlargement ☐ Yes ☐ No   Dyspnea ☐ Yes ☐ No
Murmur(s) ☐ Yes ☐ No   Edema ☐ Yes ☐ No
(describe below — if more than one, describe separately)

Location ☐ ☐

Indicate:

Constant	☐ ☐	Apex by X
Inconstant	☐ ☐	
Transmitted	☐ ☐	Murmur area by ⊘
Localized	☐ ☐	
		Point of greatest intensity by O
Systolic	☐ ☐	
Presystolic	☐ ☐	Transmission by ◊
Diastolic	☐ ☐	
Soft (Gr. 1-2)	☐ ☐	
Mod. (Gr. 3-4)	☐ ☐	For comments and your impression?
Loud (Gr. 5-6)	☐ ☐	

After exercise:
Increased ☐ ☐
Absent ☐ ☐
Unchanged ☐ ☐
Decreased ☐ ☐

14. Is there on examination any abnormality of the following:
(Circle applicable items and give details.)   Yes No
(a) Eyes, ears, nose, mouth, pharynx?...................................... ☐ ☐
    (If vision or hearing markedly impaired, indicate degree and correction.)
(b) Skin (incl. scars); lymph nodes; varicose veins or
    peripheral arteries? .... ☐ ☐
(c) Nervous system (include reflexes, gait, paralysis)?................. ☐ ☐
(d) Respiratory system? .... ☐ ☐
(e) Abdomen (include scars)? .... ☐ ☐
(f) Genitourinary system? .... ☐ ☐
(g) Endocrine system (include thyroid and breasts)?..................... ☐ ☐
(h) Musculoskeletal system (include spine, joints, amputations,
    deformities)? .... ☐ ☐
15. (a) Are there any hernias?... ☐ ☐
16. Are you aware of additional medical history?........................... ☐ ☐
    (A confidential report may be sent to the Medical Director)

17. Urinalysis   **Mail Current Urine Specimen to Home Office If**

Specific Gravity   ....   1. Applicant's age is 60 or over.

Albumin   ....   2. Insurance applied for is $300,000 or more.

Sugar   ....   3. If albumin, sugar, hypertension (past or present)
                                ☐ Yes   is found.
Are you mailing a specimen to the Home Office? ☐ No   4. History of prostatic or urinary tract disease found.

I certify that I have carefully examined...whose signature is affixed to the foregoing

declaration, and that the examination was made in private at { my office.
                                             applicant's residence.
                                             applicant's place of business.

At..this.........day of................................, 19.......... at............ ☐ A.M.
      (City)   (State)   ☐ P.M.

....M.D.   ....
     (Medical Examiner)   (Address)

F<small>IGURE</small> 1

Whole Life Insurance Policy

If the Insured dies while this Policy is in force, we will pay the Sum Insured to the Beneficiary, when we receive at our Home Office due proof of the insured's death, subject to the provisions of this Policy.

Right to Examine and Return Policy Within 20 Days

You may, at any time within 20 days after receipt of this Policy, return it to us at our Home Office or to the Agent through whom it was purchased, and we will cancel it. The return of the Policy will void it from the beginning and any premium paid will be refunded to the owner.

Secretary	President

Signed for the Company at Evanston, Illinois, on the Policy Date.

WHOLE LIFE INSURANCE POLICY

Premium Payable for A Stated Period
or Until Prior Death of Insured

Sum Insured Payable at Death

Non-Participating

Washington National®
INSURANCE COMPANY

EVANSTON, ILLINOIS 60201

A Washington National Corporation Financial Service Company

OP 868   Page 1   **10-88**

FIGURE 2
(continued)

```
INSURED:                   JOHN A DOE

AGE AND SEX:               34 MALE

POLICY NUMBER:             2 222 299

POLICY DATE:       DECEMBER  01, 1997

SUM INSURED:               $100,000

PREMIUM CLASS:             STANDARD
```

FIGURE 2
(continued)

POLICY SPECIFICATIONS

INSURED	JOHN A DOE	AGE 34	SEX MALE
POLICY DATE	DECEMBER 01, 1997	2 222 299	POLICY NUMBER
SUM INSURED	$100,000		
PREMIUM CLASS	STANDARD		

SCHEDULE OF BENEFITS AND PREMIUMS

BENEFIT DESCRIPTION	SUM INSURED	BENEFIT TERMINATES	ANNUAL PREMIUM	PREMIUM PERIOD
WHOLE LIFE	$100,000	LIFE	$1,277.00	66 YEARS
DISABILITY PREMIUM WAIVER		DEC 01, 2028	$67.00	31 YEARS
ACCIDENTAL DEATH BENEFIT	$100,000	DEC 01, 2033	$100.00	36 YEARS

TOTAL PREMIUM $1,444.00

FIGURE 2
(continued)

INSURED   JOHN A DOE   2 222 299   POLICY NUMBER

SCHEDULE OF TOTAL PREMIUMS

	BEGINNING					
MONTH	DAY	YEAR	ANNUAL	SEMIANNUAL	QUARTERLY	MONTHLY
DEC	01	1997	$ 1,444.00	$ 741.00	$ 378.00	$ 130.00
DEC	01	2028	$ 1,377.00	$ 707.00	$ 360.00	$ 124.00
DEC	01	2033	$ 1,277.00	$ 656.00	$ 334.00	$ 115.00
DEC	01	2063	PAID-UP			

FIGURE 2
(continued)

```
                                          2 222 299    POLICY NUMBER

      INSURED    JOHN A DOE                   AGE 34      SEX  MALE

                     TABLE OF GUARANTEED VALUES
                              WHOLE LIFE
                     SUM INSURED $  100,000
```

END OF POLICY YEAR	CASH OR LOAN VALUE	PAID-UP INS. VALUE	EXTENDED INSURANCE YEARS	DAYS
1	$ 0.00	$ 0	0	0
2	541.00	2,300	1	359
3	1,626.00	6,500	5	117
4	2,742.00	10,600	7	348
5	3,888.00	14,600	10	43
6	5,062.00	18,300	11	335
7	6,264.00	22,000	13	140
8	7,495.00	25,500	14	218
9	8,756.00	28,800	15	229
10	10,047.00	32,000	16	187
11	11,369.00	35,100	17	91
12	12,723.00	38,100	17	304
13	14,110.00	41,000	18	101
14	15,530.00	43,800	18	223
15	16,984.00	46,400	18	314
16	18,472.00	49,000	19	14
17	19,992.00	51,500	19	57
18	21,545.00	53,900	19	78
19	23,127.00	56,200	19	77
20	24,738.00	58,400	19	55
@60	34,782.00	69,500	17	278
@62	38,382.00	72,700	17	34
@65	43,905.00	77,000	15	360

```
    NON-FORFEITURE FACTOR     FIRST YEAR      2670.47900
                              ULTIMATE *      1203.68200

     * INTERMEDIATE NON-FORFEITURE FACTORS AVAILABLE UPON REQUEST.
     POLICY LOAN INTEREST RATE IS 8% (PAID IN ARREARS) COMPOUNDED ANNUALLY
```

FIGURE 2
(continued)

SPECIAL ENDORSEMENTS

INSURED   JOHN A DOE   2 222 299   POLICY NUMBER

OPRS 80. ALL INTEREST SHALL ACCRUE ON THE PROCEEDS PAYABLE
           BECAUSE OF THE DEATH OF THE INSURED, FROM THE DATE OF
           DEATH, AT THE RATE OF 6 % ON THE TOTAL AMOUNT PAYABLE OR
           THE FACE AMOUNT, IF PAYMENTS ARE TO BE MADE IN
           INSTALLMENTS UNTIL THE TOTAL PAYMENT OR FIRST
           INSTALLMENT IS PAID, UNLESS PAYMENT IS MADE WITHIN
           FIFTEEN (15) DAYS FROM THE DATE OF RECEIPT BY THE
           COMPANY OF DUE PROOF OF LOSS.

Secretary

FIGURE 2
(*continued*)

Alphabetical Guide To Your Policy

Provision	Page
Automatic Premium Loan	7
Beneficiary	5
Cash Values*	3A (B-C)
Change of Beneficiary	5
Collateral Assignment	6
Common Disaster	5
Computation of Guaranteed Values	8
Definitions	5
Entire Contract	5
Extended Term Insurance*	7
Grace Period	6
Incontestability	6
Incorrect Age or Sex	6
Indebtedness	6
Loans	7
Nonforfeiture Benefit Options*	7
Non-Participating	6
Ownership	5
Paid-up Insurance	7
Premiums	6
Premium Refund at Death	6
Reinstatement	6
Right to Examine Contract	1
Settlement Options	9
Suicide	6
Table of Guaranteed Values	8

*Pages 3B and C are not included if your policy does not contain additional benefit rider(s) with cash value(s).

Additional Benefits

The additional benefits, if any, listed on page 3 are described in the additional benefit agreements that follow page 11.

FIGURE 2

(continued)

1. Definitions

We, our, us – The Washington National Insurance Company.

You, your – the owner of this Policy.

Policy Date – the effective date of coverage under the Policy and the date from which policy anniversaries, policy years, policy months and premium due dates are determined. The Policy Date is also the Date of Issue of this Policy.

Policy Anniversary – the same day and month as the Policy Date for each succeeding year this policy remains in force.

Attained age – the Insured's age at issue plus the number of years and completed months from the Policy Date.

Written request – in a written form satisfactory to us, signed by you and filed in our Home Office at Evanston, Illinois.

Indebtedness – unpaid policy loans and unpaid loan interest.

In force – the Insured's life remains insured under the terms of this Policy.

Insured – the person whose life is insured under this Policy as shown on page three.

Beneficiary – the person or entity to receive the proceeds in the event of the Insured's death.

Proceeds – the amount we are obligated to pay under the terms of this Policy when it is surrendered, matures or when the Insured dies.

2. Entire Contract

We have issued this Policy in consideration of the application and payment of the premiums. A copy of the application is attached and is a part of this Policy. The Policy with the application makes the entire contract. All statements made by or for the Insured will be considered representations and not warranties. We will not use any statement in defense of a claim unless it is made in the application and a copy of the application is attached to this Policy when issued.

Only our President, one of our Vice Presidents, our Secretary or our Actuary has the authority to modify or waive any provision in this Policy, and then only in writing. No Agent or other person has the authority to change or waive any provision of this Policy.

3. Ownership

You, as the owner of this Policy, are named as owner in the application. You may exercise all the rights and options that this Policy provides, while the Insured is living, subject to the rights of any irrevocable beneficiary. If you are not the Insured and you die before the Insured, your estate will become the owner unless you have made a written request naming a contingent owner.

You may name a new owner or contingent owner at any time while the Insured is living by filing a written request with us. Your written request will not be effective until it is recorded in our Home Office. Once recorded, the change will be effective as of the date you signed the request whether or not you or the Insured is alive when we record the change. However, the change will be subject to any payments made or other action taken by us before your request was recorded in our Home Office.

4. Beneficiary

The beneficiary named in the application will receive the death proceeds unless you name a new beneficiary. In that event, we will pay the death proceeds to the beneficiary named in your last change-of-beneficiary request as provided in this Policy.

You may name a new beneficiary by filing a written request with us. The written consent of any irrevocable beneficiary will be required. Your change-of-beneficiary request will not be effective until recorded by us at our Home Office. Once recorded, the change will be effective as of the date you signed the request whether or not you or the Insured is alive when we record the change. However, the change will be subject to any payments made or other action taken by us before your request was recorded in our Home Office.

Unless otherwise provided in the application or in a written request, if more than one primary beneficiary is named in the application, death proceeds will be paid in equal shares to the primary beneficiaries who survive the Insured. If none survive, death proceeds will be paid in equal shares to the contingent beneficiaries who survive the Insured. If no beneficiary survives the Insured, death proceeds will be paid to you, if you are living, otherwise to your estate.

If any beneficiary dies simultaneously with the Insured or during the 14 days immediately following the date of death of the Insured, the proceeds of this Policy shall, unless otherwise provided in the application or in a written request, be paid to the same payee or payees and in the same manner as if the deceased beneficiary had died before the Insured. Any reference in this Policy to a beneficiary living or surviving shall mean living on the 15th day immediately following the date of death of the Insured.

FIGURE 2

(continued)

5. Collateral Assignment

You may assign this Policy as collateral for a loan without the consent of any revocable beneficiary. We are not bound by any assignment unless it is in writing and recorded at our Home Office. We are not responsible for the validity of any assignment. The rights of an assignee will at all times be subject to any indebtedness to us at the time the assignment is recorded by us, and, if applicable, to loans granted at anytime by us under the automatic premium loan provision of the Policy.

6. Incorrect Age or Sex

This Policy is issued at the age shown on page three, which should be the age attained by the Insured on the last birthday prior to the Policy Date. If the Policy Date falls on the Insured's birthday, the age should be the Insured's attained age on the Policy Date.

If the Insured's age or sex is incorrectly shown on page three, we will adjust the proceeds payable under this Policy to the proceeds the premium would have purchased at the correct age and sex based upon our rates in effect when this Policy was issued.

7. Premiums

The first premium is due on the Policy Date. Future premium due dates are determined by the frequency of payment you selected in the application. The amount of premiums, their due dates, and the period of years for which they are payable are shown on page three.

You may change the frequency of premium payment on any premium due date so that the interval between premium due dates is exactly twelve, six or three months. Other intervals may be permitted with our consent. The premium for any frequency will be based on our rates in effect on the Policy Date.

Each premium must be paid on or before its due date, or within the grace period. Premiums can either be mailed to us at our Home Office or paid to an authorized agent. Upon request, we will give you a receipt signed by our President or Secretary.

8. Grace Period

We will allow a period of 31 days after the premium due date for payment of each premium after the first. This is the grace period. If the Insured dies during the grace period before the premium is paid, we will deduct one month's premium from the death proceeds of this Policy.

If any premium is not paid on or before its due date, that premium is in default. If that premium is still unpaid at the expiration of the grace period, this Policy terminates except for any nonforfeiture benefits.

9. Premium Refund at Death

Any portion of a paid premium which applies to a period beyond the end of the policy month of the Insured's death will be added to the proceeds payable under this Policy.

Premiums waived under any disability rider attached to this Policy will not be refunded.

10. Suicide

If the Insured dies by suicide, while sane or insane, within two years from the Policy Date, our liability will be limited to the amount of the premiums paid, less any indebtedness.

11. Incontestability

We will not contest the validity of this Policy, except for nonpayment of premiums, after it has been in force during the Insured's lifetime for two years from the Policy Date. This provision does not apply to any rider providing accidental death or disability benefits.

12. Non-Participating

The premium rates for this Policy are guaranteed. Therefore, the Policy will not participate in any surplus earnings of the Company.

13. Indebtedness

Indebtedness will be deducted in any settlement under this Policy.

14. Reinstatement

If this Policy lapses due to an unpaid premium, it may be reinstated subject to the following conditions:

1) The Insured must be alive and still insurable by our standards; and

2) Any indebtedness which existed at the time of termination must either be paid or reinstated with interest compounded annually at the loan interest rate shown on page three; and

3) Each unpaid premium must be paid, with interest of 6% per annum compounded annually, from its due date to the reinstatement date; and

4) The request for reinstatement must be made by you in writing and submitted to our Home Office within 5 years after the date the Policy lapses; and

5) If you are not the Insured, the request for reinstatement must also be signed by the Insured if age 15 or older, last birthday, on the reinstatement date.

A Policy which has been surrendered for its cash value may not be reinstated.

FIGURE 2

(continued)

15. Policy Loans

You may obtain a loan from us whenever this Policy has a loan value. The loan value is the amount which, with interest at the loan interest rate stated on page three computed to the next premium due date, or to the next Policy anniversary if no further premiums are payable, will equal the cash surrender value on such date or anniversary. Any premium due and unpaid at the time the loan is made will be deducted from the loan proceeds. You cannot obtain a loan if this Policy is in force as Extended Term Insurance. This Policy is the sole security for any loan.

We have the right to postpone your loan for up to six months unless the loan is to be used to pay premiums on any policies you have with us.

We will charge daily interest on policy loans at the rate stated on page three. Interest is payable on each policy anniversary. Any interest not paid when due is added to the loan.

If this Policy is in force and not on Extended Term Insurance, your loan can be repaid in full or in part at any time before the Insured's death. However, any loan repayment must be at least $20 unless the balance due is less than $20, in which case the loan repayment must be for the full amount of the loan.

Any indebtedness will be deducted from any proceeds paid under this Policy.

Whenever the indebtedness on this Policy is more than the Policy's guaranteed cash surrender value, this Policy terminates. We will mail a notice to your last known address, and to that of any assignee whose interest we have recorded, at least 31 days before such termination.

16. Automatic Premium Loan

This provision will be in effect only if you have requested it in the application or in a written request at a time when no premium is unpaid beyond its grace period. You may cancel the effect of this provision in the same manner.

If this provision is in effect, any premium which remains unpaid at the end of a grace period will be paid by automatic loan. We may change the frequency of premium payment so that the interval between premium due dates is three, six, or twelve months after the first premium has been paid by automatic loan. If the loan value of this Policy is not sufficient to pay the premium due, the Nonforfeiture Benefit Options will apply.

Any automatic loan will be subject to the Policy Loan provisions.

17. Nonforfeiture Benefit Options

If you discontinue premium payments after this Policy has a cash value, you may, subject to the following conditions and limitations, choose one of these Options:

(a) Cash Surrender. You may surrender the Policy to us for its cash surrender value. Once the Policy is surrendered, it is no longer eligible for reinstatement.

(b) Paid–Up Insurance. You may apply the cash surrender value to purchase a fully paid whole life policy for a reduced amount of insurance. The amount of such insurance will be that amount which the cash surrender value will buy when applied as a net single premium at the Insured's then attained age as of the due date of the first unpaid premium. Reduced Paid–Up Insurance has cash and loan values.

(c) Extended Term Insurance. If the Premium Class shown on page three is "Standard," you may continue the Policy as paid–up term insurance. The amount of such term insurance will be the Sum Insured less any indebtedness. The term period will begin on the due date of the first unpaid premium and will be such as the cash surrender value will provide as a net single premium at the Insured's then attained age. At the end of the term period all insurance under this Policy will terminate.

You may elect a Nonforfeiture Benefit Option within 60 days of the due date of the first unpaid premium. Your written election should be sent to us at our Home Office. If no election is made during this period, we will

1) If the Premium Class shown on page three is other than "Rated," automatically continue this Policy as Extended Term Insurance under Option (c); or

2) If the Premium Class shown on page three is "Rated", automatically continue this Policy as Paid–Up Insurance under Option (b).

Any insurance provided under Option (b) or (c) may be surrendered at any time for its then present value. If surrendered within 30 days after a policy anniversary, the present value will not be less than the value on that anniversary.

The term "cash surrender value" as used in this Policy means the cash value shown in the Table of Guaranteed Values on page three, less any existing indebtedness.

We may delay paying the cash surrender value for up to six months from the date surrender is requested.

FIGURE 2

(continued)

18. Table of Guaranteed Values

This Policy's guaranteed values are shown in the table on page three. The table assumes that premiums have been paid to the end of the policy year indicated and that there is no indebtedness. We will determine the cash value at any time within a policy year, with allowance for the time elapsed in such year and for the period premiums have been paid. We will furnish values upon request for policy years not shown.

19. Computation of Guaranteed Values

Reserves, cash values, and net single premiums are calculated on the basis of the Commissioner's 1980 Standard Ordinary Mortality Table except that calculations for Extended Term Insurance are based on the Commissioner's 1980 Extended Term Insurance Table. Both tables assume continuous functions, age last birthday, with interest at the rate of 4% compounded annually. Computations are made on the assumption that death benefits are paid immediately upon death. In making these calculations the premium for, or the value of, any additional benefit provided by rider is excluded.

Cash values are calculated by the Standard Non-Forfeiture Value Method, using the non-forfeiture factor or factors shown in the Table of Guaranteed Values. The amount of Paid-Up Insurance or the term of Extended Insurance which could be purchased at any time is that which the cash surrender value would purchase when applied as a net single premium at the Insured's attained age.

The cash values and non-forfeiture benefits provided by this Policy equal or exceed those required by the laws of the state governing this Policy. A detailed statement of the method of computation of non-forfeiture values has been filed with the insurance supervisory official of such state.

FIGURE 2

(continued)

Settlement Options

Election of Options

You may elect to have all or part of the proceeds of this Policy applied under one of the following settlement options. You may cancel or change a previous election, but only if you do so prior to the death of the Insured or the endowment maturity date of the policy, if applicable. If you do not elect a settlement option prior to the Insured's death, the beneficiary may do so provided the election is made within one year after the date of death of the Insured. Any settlement option election will be subject to the limitations and conditions set forth below.

Any election or cancellation of a settlement option must be in writing in a form satisfactory to us. At the time an option is elected, we will prepare an agreement to be signed which will state the terms and conditions under which payments will be made. Any change of beneficiary will cancel any previous election of a settlement option.

OPTION 1 – Income for a Fixed Period

We will pay the proceeds in equal installments over a period of from one to thirty years. The amount of each installment will be based upon the period and the frequency of the installments selected from Table 1 on page 10. Higher payments may be made at our discretion.

OPTION 2 – Income for Life

We will pay a monthly income during a person's lifetime. The monthly income may be a life annuity only – Option 2(A), a life annuity with a minimum guaranteed period of 5, 10, or 20 years – Option 2(B), or an installment refund life annuity – Option 2(C), as shown in Table 2 on page 10. Payments will be at least equal to the amount shown in Table 2. Higher payments may be made at our discretion.

OPTION 3 – Income of a Fixed Amount

We will pay the proceeds in equal installments in the amount and at the intervals agreed upon until the proceeds applied under this option, with interest of at least 3% per annum, are exhausted. The final installment will be for the then remaining balance only.

OPTION 4 – Interest Income

We will hold the proceeds on deposit and pay or credit interest at the rate of at least 3% per annum. Payment of interest will be at such times and for such periods as are agreeable to you and us.

OPTION 5 – Joint and Survivor Income for Life

We will pay an income during the lifetime of two payees, and continuing until the death of the survivor. This option includes a minimum guaranteed period of 10 years. Payments will be at least equal to the amount shown in Table 3. Higher payments may be made at our discretion. On request, we will furnish minimum income information for age combinations not shown in the table.

OPTION 6 – Joint and Two-thirds Survivor Income for Life

We will pay an income (the "original amount") during the time two persons both remain alive, and two-thirds of the original amount during the remaining lifetime of the survivor. Payments during the time both payees are alive will be at least equal to the amount shown in Table 3. Higher payments may be made at our discretion. On request, we will furnish minimum income information for age combinations not shown in the table.

Limitations/Conditions

1. The amount applied under any Settlement Option must be at least $2,000 and must be sufficient to provide a periodic installment or interest payment of at least $20.

2. An Option will be available without our consent only if the proceeds are payable to a natural person receiving for his or her own benefit.

3. We may require proof of the age of any payee under Option 2, 5, or 6. We also may require evidence that the payee is living at the time any payment is due.

4. The first payment under an Option will be due on the date proceeds are applied, except under Option 4 it will be due at the end of the first payment interval.

Death of Payee

If the last surviving payee dies while receiving payments under an Option, we will pay as follows:

1. If Option 1 was elected, an amount equal to the commuted value of any unpaid installments.

2. If Option 2(B) or 5 was elected, an amount equal to the commuted value of any unpaid installments for the guaranteed period.

3. If Option 2(C) was elected, an amount equal to the commuted value of any unpaid installments required to equal the amount of proceeds applied under the Option.

FIGURE 2

(continued)

4. If option 3 or 4 was elected, an amount equal to any proceeds still on deposit plus accrued interest.

5. If Option 2A or 6 was elected, an amount equal to any unpaid installment due prior to the death of the payee under Option 2A or the last survivor under Option 6.

Commuted values under Option 1 will be calculated by us using 3% interest per year, compounded annually. Commuted values under Options 2(B), 2(C), or 5 will be calculated by us using interest compounded annually at the rate of 3% per year, or the rate of interest used in the calculation of the amount of the monthly installments, whichever is higher. Unless we have agreed otherwise in writing, payment shall be made in one sum to the payee's estate.

Surrender of Benefits

Unless the right was reserved in the Settlement Option election, no payee is allowed to (a) assign or borrow against the proceeds of an Option', (b) receive any installment payments in advance, or (c) make any changes in the provisions elected. All benefits shall be exempt from the claims of creditors to the maximum extent permitted by law.

Excess Interest

We may pay or credit excess interest of such amount and in such manner as we determine.

Settlement Option Tables

Monthly installments are shown per $1,000 of proceeds and are calculated using a minimum guaranteed interest rate of 3% per year, compounded annually. Installment amounts under Options 2, 5, and 6 depend on the age last birthday of the payee or payees on the date the first installment is due. Installments for any age or combination of ages not shown in Table 2 or 3 (Minimum age 59) will be furnished by us on request.

TABLE 1 -- Income for a Fixed Period

(Annual, semiannual, or quarterly installments shall be determined by multiplying the monthly installment by 11.839, 5.963, or 2,993 respectively.)

Years	Monthly Installment	Years	Monthly Installment	Years	Monthly Installment	Years	Monthly Installment	Years	Monthly Installment	Years	Monthly Installment
1	$84.47	6	$15.14	11	$8.86	16	$6.53	21	$5.32	26	$4.59
2	42.86	7	13.16	12	8.24	17	6.23	22	5.15	27	4.47
3	28.99	8	11.68	13	7.71	18	5.96	23	4.99	28	4.37
4	22.06	9	10.53	14	7.26	19	5.73	24	4.84	29	4.27
5	17.91	10	9.61	15	6.87	20	5.51	25	4.71	30	4.18

TABLE 2 -- Income for Life

Age of Payee	2A Life Annuity	2B Guaranteed Period 5 Years	2B Guaranteed Period 10 Years	2B Guaranteed Period 20 Years	2C Installment Refund	Age of Payee	2A Life Annuity	2B Guaranteed Period 5 Years	2B Guaranteed Period 10 Years	2B Guaranteed Period 20 Years	2C Installment Refund
46	$4.36	$4.35	$4.31	$4.14	$4.14	66	$7.34	$7.16	$6.66	$5.29	6.21
47	4.45	4.44	4.39	4.20	4.20	67	7.61	7.40	6.83	5.32	6.38
48	4.54	4.52	4.47	4.26	4.27	68	7.90	7.65	7.00	5.36	6.56
49	4.63	4.62	4.56	4.32	4.34	69	8.20	7.92	7.18	5.39	6.75
50	4.73	4.71	4.65	4.38	4.42	70	8.54	8.20	7.36	5.41	6.95
51	4.84	4.01	4.74	4.44	4.49	71	8.90	8.50	7.54	5.44	7.17
52	4.95	4.92	4.83	4.50	4.57	72	9.28	8.82	7.71	5.45	7.39
53	5.06	5.03	4.93	4.56	4.66	73	9.70	9.15	7.89	5.47	7.63
54	5.18	5.15	5.04	4.62	4.74	74	10.15	9.50	8.06	5.48	7.89
55	5.31	5.27	5.14	4.69	4.84	75	10.63	9.87	8.23	5.49	8.16
56	5.44	5.40	5.26	4.75	4.93	76	11.15	10.26	8.40	5.50	8.45
57	5.58	5.53	5.37	4.81	5.03	77	11.72	10.65	8.55	5.50	8.75
58	5.73	5.67	5.49	4.87	5.14	78	12.33	11.07	8.70	5.51	9.08
59	5.89	5.82	5.62	4.93	5.25	79	13.00	11.49	8.84	5.51	9.43
60	6.06	5.98	5.75	4.99	5.37	80	13.72	11.93	8.96	5.51	9.79
61	6.24	6.15	5.89	5.05	5.49	81	14.50	12.38	9.08	5.51	10.19
62	6.43	6.33	6.04	5.10	5.62	82	15.34	12.83	9.18	5.51	10.61
63	6.63	6.52	6.18	5.15	5.75	83	16.26	13.28	9.27	5.51	11.06
64	6.85	6.72	6.34	5.20	5.90	84	17.27	13.74	9.34	5.51	11.54
65	7.09	6.93	6.50	5.25	6.05	85 and over	18.35	14.18	9.41	5.51	12.06

FIGURE 2

(continued)

TABLE 3 -- Joint and Survivor Life Income

OPTION 5 — Joint Life Income with Installments Guaranteed for 10 Years

Age of Payee	50	55	57	58	59	60	62	65	70
50	4.19	4.37	4.44	4.47	4.50	4.53	4.59	4.66	4.76
51	4.23	4.42	4.49	4.53	4.56	4.60	4.66	4.74	4.85
52	4.26	4.47	4.55	4.59	4.63	4.66	4.73	4.82	4.94
53	4.30	4.52	4.61	4.65	4.69	4.73	4.80	4.90	5.03
54	4.34	4.57	4.66	4.71	4.75	4.79	4.87	4.98	5.12
55	4.37	4.62	4.72	4.77	4.81	4.86	4.94	5.06	5.22
56	4.41	4.67	4.77	4.83	4.87	4.92	5.02	5.14	5.32
57	4.44	4.72	4.83	4.88	4.94	4.99	5.09	5.23	5.42
58	4.47	4.77	4.88	4.94	5.00	5.06	5.16	5.32	5.52
59	4.50	4.81	4.94	5.00	5.06	5.12	5.24	5.40	5.63
60	4.53	4.86	4.99	5.06	5.12	5.19	5.31	5.49	5.74
61	4.56	4.90	5.04	5.11	5.18	5.25	5.38	5.58	5.85
62	4.59	4.94	5.09	5.16	5.24	5.31	5.46	5.66	5.96
63	4.61	4.98	5.14	5.22	5.29	5.37	5.53	5.75	6.07
64	4.64	5.02	5.19	5.27	5.35	5.43	5.60	5.83	6.18
65	4.66	5.06	5.23	5.32	5.40	5.49	5.66	5.92	6.29
66	4.68	5.10	5.27	5.36	5.45	5.54	5.73	6.00	6.41
67	4.71	5.13	5.31	5.41	5.50	5.60	5.79	6.08	6.51
68	4.72	5.16	5.35	5.45	5.54	5.65	5.85	6.15	6.62
69	4.74	5.19	5.39	5.49	5.59	5.69	5.91	6.23	6.72
70	4.76	5.22	5.42	5.52	5.63	5.74	5.96	6.29	6.82
71	4.77	5.24	5.45	5.56	5.67	5.78	6.01	6.36	6.92
72	4.79	5.27	5.48	5.59	5.70	5.82	6.06	6.42	7.01
73	4.80	5.29	5.51	5.62	5.74	5.86	6.10	6.48	7.10
74	4.81	5.31	5.53	5.65	5.77	5.89	6.14	6.53	7.18
75	4.82	5.32	5.55	5.67	5.79	5.92	6.18	6.58	7.25

OPTION 6 — Joint Life Income with Two-thirds to Survivor

Age of Payee	50	55	57	58	59	60	62	65	70
50	4.70	4.96	5.06	5.12	5.17	5.23	5.35	5.52	5.82
51	4.75	5.02	5.13	5.19	5.24	5.30	5.42	5.61	5.92
52	4.80	5.08	5.19	5.25	5.31	5.37	5.50	5.69	6.02
53	4.85	5.14	5.26	5.32	5.39	5.45	5.58	5.78	6.12
54	4.90	5.20	5.33	5.39	5.46	5.53	5.66	5.87	6.23
55	4.96	5.27	5.40	5.47	5.53	5.60	5.75	5.96	6.34
56	5.01	5.33	5.47	5.54	5.61	5.68	5.83	6.06	6.46
57	5.06	5.40	5.54	5.61	5.69	5.76	5.92	6.16	6.57
58	5.12	5.47	5.61	5.69	5.77	5.85	6.01	6.26	6.70
59	5.17	5.53	5.69	5.77	5.85	5.93	6.10	6.37	6.82
60	5.23	5.60	5.76	5.85	5.93	6.02	6.20	6.47	6.96
61	5.29	5.67	5.84	5.93	6.02	6.11	6.29	6.58	7.09
62	5.35	5.75	5.92	6.01	6.10	6.20	6.39	6.70	7.23
63	5.40	5.82	6.00	6.09	6.19	6.29	6.49	6.81	7.38
64	5.46	5.89	6.08	6.18	6.28	6.38	6.59	6.93	7.53
65	5.52	5.96	6.16	6.26	6.37	6.47	6.70	7.05	7.68
66	5.58	6.04	6.24	6.35	6.46	6.57	6.80	7.17	7.84
67	5.64	6.11	6.32	6.44	6.55	6.67	6.91	7.30	8.00
68	5.70	6.19	6.41	6.52	6.64	6.76	7.02	7.42	8.16
69	5.76	6.27	6.49	6.61	6.73	6.86	7.12	7.55	8.33
70	5.82	6.34	6.57	6.70	6.82	6.96	7.23	7.68	8.50
71	5.88	6.42	6.66	6.79	6.92	7.05	7.34	7.81	8.67
72	5.94	6.49	6.74	6.87	7.01	7.15	7.45	7.94	8.84
73	6.00	6.57	6.82	6.96	7.10	7.25	7.56	8.07	9.02
74	6.06	6.64	6.91	7.05	7.19	7.35	7.67	8.20	9.20
75	6.12	6.71	6.99	7.13	7.28	7.44	7.78	8.33	9.37

FIGURE 2
(concluded)

```
WASHINGTON NATIONAL INSURANCE COMPANY      FOR MORE INFORMATION ABOUT THIS POLICY PLEASE CONTACT:
ORDINARY LIFE DEPARTMENT                        12/15/97              HOME OFFICE
1630 CHICAGO AVENUE                         POLICY NUMBER             HOME OFFICE
EVANSTON, ILLINOIS  60201                     2 222 299               WASHINGTON NATIONAL INS CO
                                                                      1630 CHICAGO AVENUE
                                                                      EVANSTON IL  60201
                    STATEMENT OF POLICY COST AND BENEFIT INFORMATION
                            PREPARED FOR: DOE,JOHN A

                         AGE BASIS: 34  ISSUE BASIS: STANDARD
```

	BASIC POLICY	WHOLE LIFE					
POL		------------ANNUAL PREMIUMS------------			GUAR AMT(2)	GUARANTEED CASH	
YR	COVERAGE	PRM WV	A D B	TOTAL	PAYABLE	SURRENDER VALUE	
		(1)			ON DEATH	TOTAL	INCR
01	1277.00	67.00	100.00	1444.00	100,000	0	0
02	1277.00	67.00	100.00	1444.00	100,000	541	541
03	1277.00	67.00	100.00	1444.00	100,000	1,626	1,085
04	1277.00	67.00	100.00	1444.00	100,000	2,742	1,116
05	1277.00	67.00	100.00	1444.00	100,000	3,888	1,146
10	1277.00	67.00	100.00	1444.00	100,000	10,047	6,159
20	1277.00	67.00	100.00	1444.00	100,000	24,738	14,691
31	1277.00	67.00	100.00	1444.00	100,000	43,905	19,167

(AGE 65)

```
                                    EFFECTIVE POLICY LOAN INTEREST RATE IS 8.00% PAID IN ARREARS.
          SURRENDER         NET PAYMENT
          COST INDEX        COST INDEX           AN EXPLANATION OF THE INTENDED USE OF
                                                 EACH OF THESE INDEXES IS PROVIDED IN
YEAR 10     5.162              12.770            THE LIFE INSURANCE BUYER'S GUIDE.
YEAR 20     5.644              12.770
```

(1) PREMIUM PAYMENTS ARE WAIVED IN THE EVENT OF TOTAL DISABILITY.
(2) DEATH BENEFITS ARE DOUBLED IN THE EVENT OF DEATH DUE TO ACCIDENTAL DEATH.
(3) THE INFORMATION CONTAINED IN THIS POLICY SUMMARY IS GENERAL IN NATURE. A COMPLETE STATEMENT OF
    COVERAGE CAN ONLY BE FOUND IN THE POLICY.
(4) ALL FIGURES ASSUME RENEWAL OF THE RENEWABLE TERM COVERAGES, WHEN APPLICABLE.

THIS POLICY MAY AT ANY TIME WITHIN TWENTY (20) DAYS AFTER ITS RECEIPT BE RETURNED TO THE COMPANY.
UPON ITS RETURN THE POLICY WILL BE CONSIDERED VOID FROM ITS INCEPTION AND THE PREMIUM WILL BE
REFUNDED TO THE OWNER.

Figure 3

PRINTED IN U.S.A.

DIVIDEND PROVISIONS———————————————————————————————————

Annual Dividends. Dividends such as the company may apportion shall be payable at the end of each policy year after the first while this policy is in force other than as extended term insurance. The Owner may elect in writing to have each dividend applied under one of the following methods:

1. Premium Payment. Used toward the payment of premiums.

2. Paid-Up Additions. Used to buy a participating paid-up life insurance addition to this policy. The net value of each paid-up life insurance addition shall not be less than the dividend used to purchase that addition. Paid-up additions may be surrendered at any time.

3. Dividend Accumulation. Left on deposit with the company to earn interest at a rate not less than 3.5% per year. Any dividend accumulations not applied under the Credits to Avoid Lapse provision will be added to the sum payable at the death of the Insured or upon surrender for cash. Dividend accumulations may be withdrawn at any time.

4. Cash. Paid in cash.

The company will change the dividend method for any dividends payable after the company receives a written request for such change. If no election has been made, method 3 shall apply.

Dividend Credits. Dividend Credits are any dividend accumulations and any current dividend payable under dividend methods 1 or 3.

Dividend At Death. The company will pay a portion of the dividend which would have been paid if the Insured had lived to the end of the policy year in which the Insured died. If such a dividend is paid, the company will also pay a portion of the interest on any dividend accumulations which would have been payable if the Insured had lived to the end of such policy year. This dividend and interest on any dividend accumulations payable at the time the Insured dies will be based on the dividend scale in effect at the time the company receives notice of the Insured's death.

Election of Paid-Up Policy. The company will, upon receipt of a written election and the surrender of dividend credits, endorse this policy as a participating paid-up policy. The dividend credits surrendered must be equal to the net single premium increased by 3% for an amount of paid-up insurance equal to the difference between the Amount of Basic Plan insurance and the amount of reduced paid-up insurance then available under the Non-Forfeiture Provisions. Such paid-up insurance shall be payable under the same conditions as the insurance under the Basic Plan.

Election of Matured Endowment. The company will, upon receipt of a written election and the surrender of this policy and dividend credits, mature this policy as an endowment. This election may be made when the sum of the dividend credits and the cash surrender value are equal to the amount of insurance then in force under the Basic Plan.

FIGURE 4

WASHINGTON NATIONAL INSURANCE COMPANY
EVANSTON, ILLINOIS 60201

ACCIDENTAL DEATH BENEFIT RIDER

THIS RIDER IS A PART OF THE POLICY TO WHICH IT IS ATTACHED

Benefit

We will pay the Accidental Death Benefit when we receive due proof of the accidental death of the Insured. The amount payable is shown on page three of the policy. We will pay the Beneficiary. Any payment is subject to the provisions of the Policy and this Rider.

Proof of the accidental death must show that death resulted solely and directly from: 1) an accidental bodily injury; or 2) an accidental drowning. Such death must occur on or after the effective date of this Rider:

1. while this Rider was in force with no premium more than 31 days overdue; and

2. within 90 days after the accidental injury; and

3. on or after the Policy anniversary on which the Insured's age is five; and

4. before the Policy anniversary on which the Insured's age is 70.

Definition of Accidental Death

Accidental death means death resulting directly and solely from:

(a) an accidental bodily injury visible on the surface of the body or disclosed by an autopsy;

(b) a disease or infection resulting from ptomaine poisoning or from an accidental bodily injury as described and beginning within 30 days after the date of the injury; or

(c) an accidental drowning.

Risks Not Covered

Certain risks are not covered. We will not pay an Accidental Death Benefit if the Insured's death results from any of the following causes:

1. Intentionally self-inflicted injury while sane; or

2. Self-inflicted injury while insane; or

3. Participation in an assault; or

4. Participation in a felony; or

5. Travel or flight in or descent from any kind of aircraft: (a) on which the Insured is a pilot, officer or member of the crew; or (b) on which the Insured has duties aboard; or

(c) which is being operated for any training or instructional purpose; or (d) on which the Insured is being flown for the purpose of descent while in flight; or

6. Any bodily or mental infirmity existing before or beginning after the accident; or

7. Any infection or disease existing before or beginning after the accident, except a disease or infection as provided in the definition of "accidental death"; or

8. Any drug, medication or sedative voluntarily taken unless: (a) administered by a licensed physician; or (b) taken as prescribed by a licensed physician; or

9. Alcohol in combination with any drug, medication or sedative; or

10. Suicide, whether sane or insane; or

11. Any poison, gas or fumes voluntarily taken, absorbed or inhaled; or

12. War or any act of war, whether or not the Insured is in military service. The term "war" includes war declared or undeclared. It also includes armed aggression resisted by: (a) the armed forces of any country; and (b) any international organization or combination of countries.

Termination

This Rider shall terminate upon the earliest of:

1. The Policy anniversary on which the Insured's age is 70; or

2. When any premium for the Policy or this Rider is in default beyond the end of its grace period; or

3. The date the Policy terminates; or

4. The date the Policy matures; or

5. The date the Policy is surrendered; or

6. The date the Policy is continued under a nonforfeiture benefit option.

Any termination shall not affect an existing claim.

Benefits Suspended

This Rider shall automatically be suspended during any period for which premiums are being waived under a Disability Benefit Rider attached to the Policy.

FIGURE 4

(concluded)

Cancellation

You may cancel this Rider on the due date of any premium. Your written request should be sent to our Home Office. The Policy should accompany your request.

Right of Autopsy

We shall have the right to examine the Insured's body. We shall have the right to perform an autopsy. However, our right expires 30 days after we receive due proof of the Insured's accidental death. Our right to an autopsy is subject to local law.

Consideration

This Benefit is granted in consideration of: 1) the application; and 2) the payment of the additional premium stated on page three of the Policy. Such payment is subject to the same conditions as the Policy's premiums. The additional premium shall cease to be payable when: 1) this Rider terminates; or 2) the Rider is cancelled.

Effective Date

The effective date of this Rider shall be the policy date of the Policy; unless otherwise specified on page three.

Nonforfeiture Benefit Limitations

Any nonforfeiture benefit option provisions in the Policy apply only to the Policy. Such provisions shall not include these Rider benefits.

WASHINGTON NATIONAL INSURANCE COMPANY

Secretary

FIGURE 5

WASHINGTON NATIONAL INSURANCE COMPANY

EVANSTON, ILLINOIS 60201

WAIVER OF PREMIUM DISABILITY BENEFIT RIDER

THIS RIDER IS A PART OF THE POLICY TO WHICH IT IS ATTACHED

Benefit

We will waive premiums for the Policy while the Insured is totally disabled. However, the Insured must be totally disabled for six consecutive months to qualify for this benefit. Waiver of any premium is subject to the terms of this Rider and the Policy.

Disability must commence:

1) on or after the effective date of this Rider; and

2) while this Rider is in force with no premium more than 31 days overdue; and

3) on or after the policy anniversary on which the Insured's age is 5; and

4) before the policy anniversary on which the Insured's age is 65.

Definition of Total Disability

Total disability is defined as follows. It is the Insured's inability to:

1) engage in an occupation for remuneration; or

2) engage in an occupation for profit.

The inability must result from:

    (a) in injury; or

    (b) a sickness.

Occupation is defined as follows:

1) It is any occupation for which the Insured is qualified by reason of:

    (a) an education; or

    (b) some training; or

    (c) some experience.

2) It is also any occupation for which the Insured could become qualified by reason of:

    (a) an education; or

    (b) some training; or

    (c) some experience.

Engaging in an occupation for remuneration; or engaging in one for profit, include:

1) being a homemaker; and

2) attending school as a full-time student;

if that is the Insured's principal occupation at the time total disability begins.

Total disability shall also include the following. If the Insured has totally lost:

1) the sight of both eyes; or

2) the use of both hands; or

3) the use of both feet; or

4) the use of one hand and one foot;

then the Insured is totally disabled. We will waive premiums as long as:

1) such loss of sight continues; or

2) such loss of use continues.

Risks Not Covered

Certain risks are not covered. They are as follows. We will not waive premiums if total disability results from:

1) intentionally self-inflicted injury while sane; or

2) self-inflicted injury while insane; or

3) war, or any act of war; whether or not the Insured is in military service. The term "war" includes armed aggression resisted by:

    (a) the armed forces of any country; or

    (b) any international organization; or

    (c) any combination of countries.

Notice of Claim

Written notice of claim must be received:

1) at our Home Office; and

2) during the Insured's lifetime; and

3) during the continuance of total disability;

unless it can be shown that such notice was given as soon as reasonably possible.

Proof of Disability

We must receive due proof of total disability before we will waive any premium. Afterwards, we may ask for proof that total disability continues. This will be done at reasonable intervals. After two years, "reasonable intervals" shall mean annually; or less often at our option. As part of due proof, we may require the Insured to be examined by a medical examiner of

FIGURE 5
(concluded)

our choice. We will pay for the examination. We will advise you of this requirement. We will do so in writing.

Commencement of Benefits

We will waive premiums beginning with the first premium due after the date total disability begins. If any such premium has been paid, we will refund it to you. However, no premium which became due more than one year prior to the time we receive written notice of disability will be waived or refunded. If disability begins during the Grace Period or a premium in default, we will not waive the payment of that premium. Premiums will be waived in accordance with the mode of payment in effect at the time disability begins. Any premium we waive will not be deducted in any settlement under the Policy.

Discontinuance of Benefits

You must again pay premiums beginning with the policy month following the earliest of:

1) termination of the Insured's total disability; or

2) failure of the Insured to have a medical exam when we request one; or

3) failure to furnish due proof that the Insured is still totally disabled when we request it; or

4) upon the waiver of the last premium due prior to the policy anniversary on which the Insured's age is 70, if disability begins on or after the policy anniversary on which the Insured's age is 60.

We will advise you of the premium due date. We will do so in writing.

Termination of Rider

This Rider shall terminate upon the earliest of:

1) the anniversary of the Policy on which the Insured's age is 65; or

2) when any premium: (a) for the Policy; or (b) for this Rider is in default beyond the end of its grace period; or

3) the date the Policy matures; or

4) the date the Policy terminates; or

5) the date the Policy is surrendered; or

6) the date the Policy is continued under a nonforfeiture benefit option, if any.

Any termination of this Rider will be without prejudice to any existing claim.

Cancellation

You may cancel this Rider by written request. This can be done on the due date of any premium. The Policy must be sent to us.

Consideration

This Disability Benefit is granted in consideration of:

1) the application; and

2) the payment of the additional premium specified on page three of the Policy.

Payment of the additional premium is subject to the same conditions as the premium for the Policy. However, the additional premium shall cease to be payable whenever this Rider terminates or is cancelled.

Effective Date

Unless otherwise specified on page three of the Policy, the effective date of this Rider shall be the policy date of the Policy.

Nonforfeiture Benefit Limitations

If the Policy to which this Rider is attached contains nonforfeiture values, any insurance contained under the nonforfeiture value provisions in the basic Policy shall not include the benefits provided by this Rider.

WASHINGTON NATIONAL INSURANCE COMPANY

Secretary

FIGURE 6

WASHINGTON NATIONAL INSURANCE COMPANY
EVANSTON, ILLINOIS 60201

GUARANTEED INSURABILITY RIDER

THIS RIDER IS A PART OF THE POLICY TO WHICH IT IS ATTACHED

Option Dates

Each policy anniversary on which the Insured's age is 25, 28, 31, 34, 37, 40, or 43, and which occurs after the Effective Date of this Rider shall be an Option Date. However, any Option Date shall be canceled if the right to purchase additional insurance on that date is previously exercised under an "Advance Purchase Privilege."

Benefit

You may purchase a new policy on the life of the Insured on each Option Date if the Policy and this Rider are in force. However, your purchase will be subject to the provisions of the Policy and this Rider. Evidence of insurability will not be required.

Your written request for a new policy must be received by us on or within 60 days before the Option Date. Payment of the first premium must also be made on or before that date. The Option Date shall be the policy date of the new policy. The new policy will be effective on that date if the Insured is living and the first premium has been paid.

The new policy may be any form of Life or Endowment policy we then issue. The premium for the new policy will be based on the same risk classification as this Policy. It will be calculated using our rates then in use for the plan elected and for the then attained age of the Insured. If this Policy on the Option Date contains a disability benefit provision, a similar provision may be included in the new policy without evidence of insurability. However, the disability benefit will be included only if the Insured is not then totally disabled as defined in such provision. We will require evidence of insurability if any additional benefits are to be included in the new policy. We will also require an additional payment for such benefits.

The maximum amount of insurance you may purchase on any Option Date is the option amount shown on page three of this Policy. The minimum amount is the amount we will issue based on our rules in effect on the Option Date. However, the maximum amount may be increased as described in "Advance Purchase Privilege."

The incontestability and suicide provisions in the new policy shall be operative from the policy date of this Policy.

If you do not exercise your option to purchase a new policy on an Option Date, the option expires on that date.

Advance Purchase Privilege

Your right to purchase insurance on a future Option Date may be exercised immediately upon the happening of any of the following events:

1. the Insured's marriage; or

2. each birth of a living child to the Insured and his or her spouse; or

3. each legal adoption of a child by the Insured.

"Marriage" means a marriage ceremony legally performed by a third person.

The maximum amount of insurance you may purchase increases if there is a multiple birth or if more than one child is adopted on the same day. The maximum amount is the option amount shown on page three of the Policy multiplied by the number of children liveborn or adopted.

We must receive within 90 days of the event:

1. your written application for the new policy; and

2. proof satisfactory to us that the event happened.

The policy date of the new policy shall be the date of your application. The new policy shall be effective on the policy date or the date we receive the first premium, whichever is later, provided the Insured is then living.

The exercise of this Advance Purchase Privilege shall automatically cancel the next Option Date. If you do not exercise the privilege, it shall expire on the 90th day following the event.

Consideration

The consideration for this Rider is the application for the Policy and this Rider and the payment of the additional premium shown on page three of the Policy. Payment of the additional premium is subject to the same conditions as

O 2363

(10-82)

FIGURE 6
(concluded)

the premium for the Policy. However, the additional premium shall cease to be payable whenever this Rider terminates.

General Provisions

The payment of premiums for this Rider shall not increase the cash, loan or non-forfeiture values under the Policy.

This Rider is subject to all of the terms and conditions contained in the Policy insofar as such terms and conditions are applicable to and not in conflict with this Rider.

If the Policy to which this Rider is attached contains non-forfeiture values, any insurance contained under the non-forfeiture value provisions in the basic Policy shall not include the benefits provided by this Rider.

Effective Date

The effective date of this Rider shall be the policy date of the Policy.

Termination

This Rider shall terminate upon the earliest of:

1. the termination date shown on page three of the Policy; or

2. when any premium for the Policy or this Rider is in default beyond the end of its grace period; or

3. the date the Policy matures, terminates, is surrendered or continued under a non-forfeiture benefit option; or

4. upon cancellation or expiration of all Option Dates.

Cancellation

You may cancel this Rider on the due date of any premium by written request accompanied by the Policy for endorsement.

WASHINGTON NATIONAL INSURANCE COMPANY

Muriel L. Crawford

SECRETARY

FIGURE 7

PROVIDENT MUTUAL LIFE INSURANCE COMPANY OF PHILADELPHIA

RIDER
ACCELERATED DEATH BENEFIT

INSURED   **POLICY NUMBER**

EFFECTIVE DATE   **RIDER ISSUE DATE**

If Accelerated Death Benefits are advanced under the terms of this Rider, their payment will reduce the amount of death benefits, surrender benefits and loan value that may subsequently be paid under this Policy.

Receipt of Accelerated Death Benefits under this Rider may or may not be taxable. Whether or not the Owner or Beneficiary incurs a tax liability when benefits are paid depends on how the IRS interprets applicable provisions of the Internal Revenue Code. As with all tax matters, the Owner should consult his or her personal tax adviser to assess the impact of receiving Accelerated Death Benefits under this Rider.

Receipt of Accelerated Death Benefits may adversely affect eligibility for Medicaid or other government benefits or entitlements.

This Rider is not a long term care rider as defined in the statutes of the state where the Policy is delivered.

This Rider is a part of the Policy to which it is attached. All definitions, provisions, conditions and limitations of the Policy apply to this Rider, unless changed by this Rider. The Effective Date and Rider Issue Date are the same as the Issue Date shown in the Policy Specifications, unless another Effective Date and Rider Issue Date are shown above.

DEFINITIONS

Due Proof of Eligibility - Certification in a written form satisfactory to us by a Physician treating the Insured stating that the Insured has a Terminal Illness or is expected to be Permanently Confined in a Nursing Care Facility. This Certification must include a diagnosis of the Terminal Illness or of the disease or disorder resulting in Permanent Confinement in the Nursing Care Facility.

Eligible Death Benefit - The Insurance Proceeds payable at death as of the date we approve payment of the Accelerated Death Benefit less:
1. any dividend accumulations;
2. any dividends due and not paid;
3. any dividend payable at death;
4. any Premium Refund at Death;
5. any insurance payable under the terms of any rider attached to this policy.

Nursing Care Facility - A facility which meets all of the following standards:

1. it is licensed and operated to provide skilled, intermediate or custodial care according to the laws of the state in which it is located;
2. its primary function is:
   (a) to provide nursing and/or custodial care and room and board to individuals who are not able to care for themselves and who require nursing care; and
   (b) to charge a fee for facility confinement and services rendered. Care must be provided under the direction of: a Physician; a registered nurse (RN); a licensed practical nurse (LPN); or a licensed vocational nurse (LVN);
3. it is not a hospital, a home for the aged, a retirement home, a rest home, a community living center, or a place mainly for the treatment of alcoholism, mental illness or drug abuse. It is a separate facility or a distinct part of another facility which is physically separate from that facility.

FIGURE 7

(continued)

Permanently Confined - The Insured:

1. has resided in a Nursing Care Facility for at least 180 consecutive days; and
2. has a disease or disorder which, with reasonable medical certainty, necessitates the Insured's continued residence in a Nursing Care Facility until the time of such Insured's death.

Physician - A person who is licensed to practice medicine in the state in which treatment is received and who is acting within the scope of that license. The Physician may not be the Owner, Insured or a spouse, parent, child, brother or sister of either the Owner or Insured.

Terminal Illness - A noncorrectable medical condition which, with reasonable medical certainty, can be expected to result in the Insured's death within twelve months from the date of certification given to us as Due Proof of Eligibility for this benefit.

DESCRIPTION OF
ACCELERATED DEATH BENEFIT

Amount of Benefit. Upon receipt at our Home Office of Due Proof of Eligibility, we will pay you an Accelerated Death Benefit while this Policy is in force and the Insured is living. The amount of your Accelerated Death Benefit request must be for at least $10,000; the maximum available amount is equal to 75% of the Eligible Death Benefit less 25% of any outstanding policy loans and accrued interest (if any). The total of the Accelerated Benefits paid from all your Policies issued by us and our subsidiaries cannot exceed $250,000.

The $250,000 maximum limitation will be adjusted at the beginning of each calendar year by the CPI Factor. The CPI Factor is based upon the Consumer Price Index for All Urban Consumers, United States City Average, All Items, as published by the U.S. Department of Labor (or other nationally published index which is comparable in scope and purpose to this index). This CPI Factor is the percentage equivalent of the difference between C and D divided by D. ("C" is the CPI Factor for the October preceding the year the claim is approved; "D" is the CPI Factor for October 1992.)

You may request only one Accelerated Death Benefit from this Policy. After receiving the Accelerated Death Benefit, you may request additional Accelerated Death Benefits to pay premiums and policy loan interest which are due for this Policy. There are no restrictions on the use of the Accelerated Death Benefit.

Means of Payment. Once we have approved payment of the Accelerated Death Benefit, we will make a loan in accordance with the Policy's Loan Provisions (if any). The amount of the loan will be the lesser of the maximum loan available under the Policy and the amount of the Accelerated Death Benefit payment. If the amount of the Accelerated Death Benefit payment is greater than the amount of such loan, we will pay the remaining amount to you and place a Death Benefit Lien against the Policy's Death Benefit for such remaining amount.

Payment Method. You may choose to have the Accelerated Death Benefit amount paid under one of the following methods:

1. Lump Sum - the Accelerated Death Benefit amount will be paid in one sum.
2. Monthly Installment - the Accelerated Death Benefit amount will be paid in 12 or 24 equal monthly installments. Monthly payments will be calculated using interest of at least 3% per annum. If the Insured dies before the full number of payments has been made, the present value of the remaining payments will be paid to the named Beneficiary in a lump sum. We will compute the lump sum based on the interest rate we used to determine the monthly payments.

INTEREST PAYABLE

Policy Loan Interest. Interest is payable on the outstanding policy loan at the rate of interest specified in the Policy.

Death Benefit Lien Interest. Interest accrues daily on the amount of the Death Benefit Lien from the date the Accelerated Death Benefit payment is made until the date of the Insured's death. The lien interest rate is the rate in effect on the first day of the calendar quarter in which the claim is approved. The lien interest rate is determined as follows:

To determine the lien interest rate per annum for any calendar quarter, we will compare the lien interest rate for the previous calendar quarter with a Maximum Interest Rate prescribed by law and defined below. If there is a difference of 1/2% or more and the Maximum Interest Rate is higher, the lien interest rate may be increased by at least 1/2% but not higher than the Maximum Interest Rate; if it is lower, the lien interest rate will be reduced to be the same as or less than the Maximum Interest Rate.

FIGURE 7

(continued)

Maximum Interest Rate. The Maximum Interest Rate is the greater of:

1. Moody's Corporate Bond Yield Average - Monthly Average Corporates, as published by Moody's Investors Services, Inc., or any successor thereto, for the calendar month ending two months before the date on which the rate is determined. (If the bond average is no longer published, a similar average will be established by law or regulation issued by the insurance commissioner); and

2. the rate used to compute the cash surrender value under the Policy during the applicable period plus 1% per annum.

We will notify you at the time a lien is made of the interest rate applicable to such lien.

EFFECT ON EXISTING POLICY

Insurance Proceeds at Death. The Insurance Proceeds at Death otherwise payable under the Policy at the time of the Insured's death will be reduced by the amount of any outstanding Death Benefit Lien and accrued interest thereon.

Surrender Value and Loan Value. If you make a request for a surrender, a policy loan or a withdrawal, the Policy's Surrender and Loan Value (if any) will be reduced by the amount of any outstanding Death Benefit Lien and accrued interest thereon as of the date of receipt of your written request for the surrender, loan or withdrawal.

Premiums and Policy Loan Interest. Premiums and policy loan interest must be paid when due. However, if elected at the time the claim form is completed, you may change the premium frequency to yearly and pay future premiums and policy loan interest through additional Accelerated Death Benefit payments. If this Policy is a flexible premium policy, the Planned Periodic Premium will be considered due for the purposes of this provision.

Dividends. Since the amount of dividends payable reflects policy loan activity, additional policy loan amounts incurred due to payment of the Accelerated Death Benefit will affect the amount of dividends payable for the Policy.

Policy Termination and Reinstatement. The Policy will terminate on the Policy Anniversary when the Insurance Proceeds at Death on such Policy Anniversary is less than or equal to zero. We will have no further obligations under this Policy.

If the Policy terminates while subject to a Death Benefit Lien, we will extinguish the Death Benefit Lien without further recourse. If the Policy is reinstated, the Death Benefit Lien must also be reinstated with accrued interest as if the Policy had never terminated.

GENERAL PROVISIONS

Conditions for Payment of Accelerated Benefits. Your right to receive the Accelerated Death Benefit payment is subject to the following conditions:

1. The Policy must be in force other than as Extended Term Insurance;

2. Due Proof of Eligibility and a properly completed claim form must be received at our Home Office prior to payment of the Accelerated Death Benefit. We may request additional medical information from your Physician. We reserve the right to require an independent physical examination at our expense;

3. We reserve the right to charge an Administrative Fee at the time of payment of the Accelerated Death Benefit. It will not exceed $250 and will be deducted from the amount of the Accelerated Death Benefit payment;

4. The Accelerated Death Benefit amount requested must be for at least $10,000;

5. The Accelerated Death Benefit paid may not exceed 75% of the Eligible Death Benefit for this Policy less 25% of outstanding Policy loans and accrued interest (if any);

6. The total of the Accelerated Death Benefits paid by us and our subsidiaries for all of your policies may not exceed $250,000. (This cumulative maximum will be adjusted yearly as described above);

7. The Policy may not be assigned in whole or in part except to us as security for the Death Benefit Lien; therefore, we must receive a signed release of interest from any assignee and a signed consent from any irrevocable beneficiary authorizing payment of Accelerated Death Benefits. At our discretion, before we pay the Accelerated Death Benefit, we may require written authorization from any other party whom we believe has a potential interest in the proceeds of this Policy;

544

Appendix

FIGURE 7

(concluded)

8. No benefit is available if the Terminal Illness or Permanent Confinement is the result of intentionally self-inflicted injuries;

9. This Rider provides for the accelerated payment of the death benefit of your life insurance policy. It is not meant to cause you to involuntarily access proceeds ultimately payable to the named Beneficiary. Accelerated Death Benefits will be made available to you on a voluntary basis only. Therefore you are not eligible for this benefit if:

    (a) you are required by law to use this benefit to meet the claims of creditors, whether in bankruptcy or otherwise;

    (b) you are required by a government agency to use this benefit in order to apply for, obtain, or otherwise keep a government benefit or entitlement.

TERMINATION OF RIDER

This Rider will terminate on the earliest of:

1. Receipt of your written request for termination of this Rider; or

2. Policy termination or maturity; or

3. The Policy Anniversary when the Insurance Proceeds payable at Death on such Policy Anniversary is less than or equal to zero.

Signed for the Company at Philadelphia, Pennsylvania on the Rider Issue Date.

L. J. Rowell, Jr.

President and Chief Executive Officer

FIGURE 8

WASHINGTON NATIONAL INSURANCE COMPANY

Evanston, Illinois

Attached to and Forming a   Issued on the Life of...

Part of Policy No......................................   Effective Date...

AVIATION AND WAR RISK EXCLUSION PROVISION

The term "Home Area" as used in this provision means only the fifty states of the United States, the District of Columbia, Canada, Canal Zone, Puerto Rico and the Virgin Islands; "war service" means being in the military, naval or air forces or any civilian force auxiliary thereto of any country (a) at war, declared or undeclared, or (b) involved in any conflict between the armed forces of countries, international organizations, or combinations thereof.

The liability under this Policy shall be limited to the amount specified below if the death of the Insured:

1. occurs as a result of an act of war, declared or undeclared, if such act occurs outside the Home Area while the Insured is in war service and if death occurs while the Insured is in war service outside the Home Area or within 6 months after his return to the Home Area or within 6 months after his termination of service in such forces, whichever is the earlier date; or

2. occurs within 2 years after the date of issue of this Policy as a result of an act of war, declared or undeclared, if such act occurs outside the Home Area while the Insured is not in war service, and death occurs outside the Home Area or within 6 months after returning to the Home Area; or

3. occurs inside or outside the Home Area whether or not the Insured is in war service and as a result of operating or riding in or descending from any kind of aircraft if the Insured is a pilot, officer or member of the crew of such aircraft or is giving or receiving any kind of training or instruction or has any duties aboard such aircraft or requiring descent therefrom.

In event the Insured's death should occur under any of the conditions defined above, the Company's liability shall be limited to the payment of a single sum equal to the greater of (a) the premiums paid on this Policy, decreased by any indebtedness on or secured by this Policy, or (b) the reserve under this Policy, less any indebtedness on or secured by this Policy; provided, however, that in no event shall such liability be greater than the amount payable in the absence of this provision. If no basis for the computation of reserves is specified in this Policy, reserves shall be computed according to the Commissioners 1941 Standard Ordinary Mortality Table, with 3% interest and on the basis of the Commissioners Reserve Valuation Method.

The limitations of liability contained herein shall also apply to any reduced paid-up insurance or extended term insurance put in force in accordance with any non-forfeiture provisions contained in this Policy, and shall be included in any Policy to which this Policy may be changed or converted.

If this Policy has attached thereto any supplementary contract for an additional benefit in event of accidental death, the conditions and exceptions contained therein shall not be affected by this provision.

The provision of this Policy entitled "Incontestability" is hereby amended to read as follows:

.his Policy shall be incontestable after 2 years from its date of issue except (a) for non-payment of premiums, (b) as to any provision for an additional benefit in the event of accidental death, (c) as to any provision for benefits in the event of total and permanent disability and (d) for the limitation of benefits contained in the provision entitled Aviation and War Risk Exclusion Provision.

AMENDMENT OF APPLICATION

It is agreed and understood that my original application for insurance under the above designated Policy is hereby amended to permit the inclusion in such Policy of the foregoing Aviation and War Risk Exclusion Provision and that such provision shall be attached to and made a part of such Policy.

Dated at...this..................day of..., 19.........

....

The foregoing Aviation and War Risk Exclusion Provision shall become operative as of the Effective Date shown above.

WASHINGTON NATIONAL INSURANCE COMPANY

Muriel L. Crawford

SECRETARY

O 1105

FIGURE 9

WASHINGTON NATIONAL INSURANCE COMPANY
Evanston, Illinois

Attached to and Forming a   Issued on the Life of __John A. Doe__

Part of Policy No. __2 222 299__   Effective Date __December 1, 1997__

AVIATION EXCLUSION PROVISION

The liability under this Policy shall be limited to the amount specified below if the death of the Insured occurs as a result of travel or flight in any kind of aircraft while the Insured (1) is a pilot, officer or member of the crew of such aircraft, or (2) is participating in aeronautic or aviation training during such flight, or (3) is in a military, naval or air force aircraft while under flight orders or on flying status in the military, naval or air forces of any country. Descent from or with any kind of aircraft in flight shall be deemed to be part of such flight.

In event the Insured's death should occur under any of the conditions defined above, the Company's liability shall be limited to the payment of a single sum equal to the greater of (a) the premiums paid on this Policy, decreased by any indebtedness on or secured by this Policy, or (b) the reserve under this Policy, less any indebtedness on or secured by this Policy; provided, however, that in no event shall such liability be greater than the amount payable in the absence of this provision. If no basis for the computation of reserves is specified in this Policy, reserves shall be computed according to the Commissioners 1941 Standard Ordinary Mortality Table, with 3% interest and on the basis of the Commissioners Reserve Valuation Method.

The limitations of liability contained herein shall also apply to any reduced paid-up insurance or extended term insurance put in force in accordance with any non-forfeiture provisions contained in this Policy, and shall be included in any policy to which this Policy may be changed or converted.

If this Policy has attached thereto any supplementary contract for an additional benefit in the event of accidental death, the conditions and exceptions contained therein shall not be affected by this provision.

The provision of this Policy entitled "Incontestability" is hereby amended to read as follows:

This Policy shall be incontestable after 2 years from its date of issue except (a) for non-payment of premiums, (b) as to any provision for an additional benefit in the event of accidental death, (c) as to any provision for benefits in the event of total and permanent disability and (d) for the limitation of benefits contained in the provision entitled Aviation Exclusion Provision.

AMENDMENT OF APPLICATION

It is agreed and understood that my original application for insurance under the above designated Policy is hereby amended to permit the inclusion in such Policy of the foregoing Aviation Exclusion Provision and that such provision shall be attached to and made a part of such Policy.

Dated at __Peoria IL__   this __20th__ day of __Nov.__ , 19__97__

__John A. Doe__

The foregoing Aviation Exclusion Provision shall become operative as of the Effective Date shown above.

WASHINGTON NATIONAL INSURANCE COMPANY

Gary R. Edwards
Secretary

O 1109   *Detach This Portion and Return to the Home Office*   (1-69)

FIGURE 10

LIFE INSURANCE BUYER'S GUIDE

Prepared by the National Association of Insurance Commissioners

Contents

Prepared by the National Association of Insurance Commissioners

FIGURE 10
(continued)

LIFE INSURANCE BUYER'S GUIDE

This guide can show you how to save money when you shop for life insurance. It helps you to:

- Decide how much life insurance you should buy

- Decide what kind of life insurance policy you need, and

- Compare the cost of similar life insurance policies

BUYING LIFE INSURANCE

When you buy life insurance, you want a policy which fits your needs without costing too much. Your first step is to decide how much you need, how much you can afford to pay and the kind of policy you want. Then, find out what various companies charge for that kind of policy. You can find important differences in the cost of life insurance by using the life insurance cost indexes which are described in this guide. A good life insurance agent or company will be able and willing to help you with each of these shopping steps.

If you are going to make a good choice when you buy life insurance, you need to understand which kinds are available. If one kind does not seem to fit your needs, ask about the other kinds which are described in this guide. If you feel that you need more information than is given here, you may want to check with a life insurance agent or company or books on life insurance in your public library.

CHOOSING THE AMOUNT

One way to decide how much life insurance you need is to figure how much cash and income your dependents would need if you were to die. You should think of life insurance as a source of cash needed for expenses of final illnesses, paying taxes, mortgages or other debts. It can also provide income for your family's living expenses, educational costs and other future expenses. Your new policy should come as close as you can afford to making up the difference between (1) what your dependents would have if you were to die now, and (2) what they would actually need.

CHOOSING THE RIGHT KIND

All life insurance policies agree to pay an amount of money if you die. But all policies are not the same. There are three basic kinds of life insurance.

Figure 10
(continued)

1. *Term insurance*

2. *Whole life insurance*

3. *Endowment insurance*

Remember, no matter how fancy the policy title or sales presentation might appear, all life insurance policies contain one or more of the three basic kinds. If you are confused about a policy that sounds complicated, ask the agent or company if it combines more than one kind of life insurance. The following is a brief description of the three basic kinds:

TERM INSURANCE

Term insurance is death protection for a "term" of one or more years. Death benefits will be paid only if you die within that term of years. Term insurance generally provides the largest immediate death protection for your premium dollar.

Some term insurance policies are "renewable" for one or more additional terms even if your health has changed. Each time you renew the policy for a new term, premiums will be higher. You should check the premiums at older ages and the length of time the policy can be continued.

Some term insurance policies are also "convertible". This means that before the end of the conversion period, you may trade the term policy for a whole life or endowment insurance policy even if you are not in good health. Premiums for the new policy will be higher than you have been paying for the term insurance.

WHOLE LIFE INSURANCE

Whole life insurance gives death protection for as long as you live. The most common type is called "straight life" or "ordinary life" insurance, for which you pay the same premiums for as long as you live. These premiums can be several times higher than you would pay initially for the same amount of term insurance. But they are smaller than the premiums you would eventually pay if you were to keep renewing a term insurance policy until your later years.

Some whole life policies let you pay premiums for a shorter period such as 20 years, or until age 65. Premiums for these policies are higher than for ordinary life insurance since the premium payments are squeezed into a shorter period.

Although you pay higher premiums, to begin with, for whole life insurance than for term insurance, whole life insurance policies develop "cash values" which you may have if you stop paying premiums. You can generally either take the cash, or use it to buy some continuing insurance protection. Technically speaking, these values are called "nonforfeiture benefits". This refers to benefits you do not lose (or "forfeit") when you stop paying premiums. The amount of these benefits depends on the kind of policy you have, its size, and how long you have owned it.

FIGURE 10

(continued)

A policy with cash values may also be used as collateral for a loan. If you borrow from the life insurance company, the rate of interest is shown in your policy. Any money which you owe on a policy loan would be deducted from the benefits if you were to die, or from the cash value if you were to stop paying premiums.

ENDOWMENT INSURANCE

An endowment insurance policy pays a sum or income to you - the policyholder - if you live to a certain age. If you were to die before then, the death benefit would be paid to your beneficiary. Premiums and cash values for endowment insurance are higher than for the same amount of whole life insurance. Thus endowments insurance gives you the lease amount of death protection for your premium dollar.

FINDING A LOW COST POLICY

After you have decided which kind of life insurance fits your needs, look for a good buy. Your chances of finding a good buy are better if you use two types of index numbers that have been developed to aid in shopping for life insurance. One is called the "Surrender Cost Index" and the other is the "Net Payment Cost Index". It will be worth your time to try to understand how these indexes are used, but in any event, use them only for comparing the relative costs of similar policies. LOOK FOR POLICIES WITH LOW COST INDEX NUMBERS.

WHAT IS COST?

"Cost" is the difference between what you pay and what you get back. If you pay a premium for life insurance and get nothing back, your cost for the death protection is the premium. If you pay a premium and get something back later on, such as a cash value, your cost is smaller than the premium.

The cost of some policies can also be reduced by dividends; these are called "participating" policies. Companies may tell you what their current dividends are, but the size of future dividends is unknown today and cannot be guaranteed. Dividends actually paid are set each year by the company.

Some policies do not pay dividends. These are called "guaranteed cost" or "nonparticipating" policies. Every feature of a guaranteed cost policy is fixed so that you know in advance what your future cost will be.

The premiums and cash values of a participating policy are guaranteed, but the dividends are not. Premiums for participating policies are typically higher than for guaranteed cost policies, but the cost to you may be higher or lower, depending on the dividends actually paid.

WHAT ARE COST INDEXES?

In order to compare the cost of policies, you need to look at:

FIGURE 10

(continued)

1. *Premiums*

2. *Cash values*

3. *Dividends*

Cost indexes use one or more of these factors to give you a convenient way to compare relative costs of similar policies. When you compare costs, an adjustment must be made to take into account that money is paid and received at different times. It is not enough to just add up the premiums you will pay and to subtract the cash values and dividends you expect to get back. These indexes take care of the arithmetic for you. Instead of having to add, subtract, multiply and divide many numbers yourself, you just compare the index numbers which you can get from life insurance agents and companies:

1. LIFE INSURANCE SURRENDER COST INDEX - This index is useful if you consider the level of the cash values to be of primary importance to you. It helps you compare costs if at some future point in time, such as 10 or 20 years, you were to surrender the policy and take its cash value.

2. LIFE INSURANCE NET PAYMENT COST INDEX - This index is useful if your main concern is the benefits that are to be paid at your death and if the level of cash values is of secondary importance to you. It helps you compare costs at some future point in time, such as 10 or 20 years, if you continue paying premiums on your policy and do not take its cash value.

There is another number called the Equivalent Level Annual Dividend. It shows the part dividends play in determining the cost index of a participating policy. Adding a policy's Equivalent Level Annual Dividend to its cost index allows you to compare total costs of similar policies before deducting dividends. However, if you make any cost comparisons of a participating policy with a nonparticipating policy, remember that the total cost of the participating policy will be reduced by dividends, but the cost of the nonparticipating policy will not change.

HOW DO I USE COST INDEXES?

The most important thing to remember when using cost indexes is that a policy with a small index number is generally a better buy than a comparable policy with a larger index number. The following rules are also important:

(1) Cost comparisons should only be made between similar plans of life insurance. Similar plans are those which provide essentially the same basic benefits and require premium payments for approximately the same period of time. The closer policies are to being identical, the more reliable the cost comparison will be.

(2) Compare index numbers only for the kind of policy, for your age and for the amount you intend to buy. Since no one company offers the lowest cost for all amounts of insurance, it is important that you get the indexes for the actual policy, age and amount which you intend to buy. Just because a "shopper's guide" tells you that one company's policy is a good buy for a particular age and amount,

FIGURE 10
(continued)

you should not assume that all of that company's policies are equally good buys.

(3) Small differences in index numbers could be offset by other policy features, or differences in the quality of service you may expect from the company or its agent. Therefore, when you find small differences in cost indexes, your choice should be based on something other than cost.

(4) In any event, you will need other information on which to base your purchase decision. Be sue you can afford the premiums, and that you understand its cash values, dividends and death benefits. You should also make a judgment on how well the life insurance company or agent will provide service in the future, to you as a policyholder.

(5) These life insurance cost indexes apply to new policies and should not be used to determine whether you should drop a policy you have already owned for awhile, in favor of a new one. If such a replacement is suggested, you should ask for information from the company which issued the old policy before you take action.

IMPORTANT THINGS TO REMEMBER - A SUMMARY

The first decision you must make when buying a life insurance policy is choosing a policy whose benefits and premiums most closely meet your needs and ability to pay. Next, find a policy which is also a relatively good buy. If you compare Surrender Cost Indexes and Net Payment Cost Indexes of similar competing policies, your chances of finding a relatively good buy will be better if you do not shop. **REMEMBER, LOOK FOR POLICIES WITH LOWER COST INDEX NUMBERS.** A good life insurance agent can help you to choose the amount of life insurance and kind of policy you want and will give you cost indexes so that you can make cost comparisons of similar policies.

Don't buy life insurance unless you intend to stick with it. A policy which is a good buy when held for 20 years can be very costly if you quit during the early years of the policy. If you surrender such a policy during the first few years, you may get little or nothing back and much of your premium may have been used for company expenses.

Read your new policy carefully, and ask the agent or company for an explanation of anything you do not understand. Whatever you decide now, it is important to review your life insurance program every few years to keep up with changes in your income and responsibilities.

FIGURE 10
(concluded)

■ The National Association of Insurance Commissioners is an association of state insurance regulatory officials. This association helps the various Insurance Departments to coordinate insurance laws for the benefit of all consumers. You are urged to use this Guide in making a life insurance purchase.

– This Guide Does Not Endorse Any Company Or Policy

FIGURE 11

LIJashington
national
INSURANCE COMPANY
EVANSTON-ILLINOIS 60201

Request for Change of Beneficiary and Election of Settlement Option

Policy No(s).	Insured	Owner, if designated

A. BENEFICIARY DESIGNATION

All previous beneficiary designations and any previous election of a settlement option under the above numbered policy are hereby revoked and the beneficiary designation is hereby changed to:

Primary

_____

Contingent

_____

Tertiary

_____

B. ELECTION OF SETTLEMENT OPTION

The undersigned hereby requests that in the event the above numbered policy shall become a death claim while any of the above named Primary or Contingent Beneficiaries are living and entitled to the proceeds thereunder, and not otherwise, the proceeds of said policy shall be retained by the Company and applied as indicated by an "X" or a checkmark in the box beside each applicable provision. (Payment to any Tertiary Beneficiaries shall be in one sum, as provided below.)

Section I — Single Sum Payment

☐ Pay $_____ in one sum, or the entire proceeds if less, to _____

Section II — Settlement for Primary Beneficiary

The entire proceeds, or any proceeds remaining after any single sum payment required under Section I, shall be apportioned into equal shares for each Primary Beneficiary who survives the Insured and paid as follows:

☐ Pay proceeds in one sum.

☐ Option 1 — Fixed Period Income. Pay proceeds in equal _____ instalments for a fixed period of _____ years.

☐ Option 2 — Life Income. Pay proceeds in equal monthly instalments.

    ☐ as a life annuity for the lifetime of the payee.

    ☐ as a life annuity with payments guaranteed for _____ years and continuing thereafter during the remaining lifetime of the payee.

    ☐ as an instalment refund annuity with payments guaranteed until the sum of the instalments paid equals the share of the proceeds applied under the option for the payee, and continuing thereafter during the remaining lifetime of the payee.

☐ Option 3 — Fixed Amount Income. Pay proceeds in equal _____ instalments of $_____ each until such proceeds and interest thereon are exhausted, the final instalment to be the balance of the proceeds and interest.

☐ Option 4 — Interest Income. The proceeds shall be retained by the Company and interest thereon shall be paid _____

    ☐ the proceeds shall be retained by the Company only until the _____ birthday of the payee when the proceeds in the Company's hands, with any accrued interest, shall be paid in one sum to the payee.

Section III — Settlement for Contingent Beneficiary

If no Primary Beneficiary survives the Insured, or if the last surviving Primary Beneficiary dies while receiving payment under Options 1, 3 or 4, the entire proceeds (less any single sum payment required under Section I) or the unpaid balance then being held by the Company under Options 1, 3 or 4 shall be apportioned into equal shares for each then living Contingent Beneficiary and paid as follows:

☐ Pay proceeds in one sum.

☐ Option 1 — Fixed Period Income. Pay proceeds in equal _____ instalments for a fixed period of _____ years.

☐ Option 2 — Life Income. Pay proceeds in equal monthly instalments.

    ☐ as a life annuity for the lifetime of the payee.

    ☐ as a life annuity with payments guaranteed for _____ years and continuing thereafter during the remaining lifetime of the payee.

    ☐ as an instalment refund annuity with payments guaranteed until the sum of the instalments paid equals the share of the proceeds applied under the option for the payee, and continuing thereafter during the remaining lifetime of the payee.

☐ Option 3 — Fixed Amount Income. Pay proceeds in equal _____ instalments of $_____ each until such proceeds and interest thereon are exhausted, the final instalment to be the balance of the proceeds and interest.

☐ Option 4 — Interest Income. The proceeds shall be retained by the Company and interest shall be paid _____

    ☐ the proceeds shall be retained by the Company only until the _____ birthday of the payee when the proceeds in the Company's hands with any accrued interest, shall be paid in one sum to the payee.

Section IV — Settlement for Tertiary Beneficiary

If no Primary or Contingent Beneficiary survives the Insured, or if the last surviving Primary or Contingent Beneficiary dies while receiving payment under Options 1, 3, or 4, the entire proceeds (less any single sum payment required under Section I) or the unpaid balance then being held by the Company under Options 1, 3, or 4 shall be apportioned into equal shares for each living Tertiary Beneficiary and paid in one sum to such Tertiary Beneficiary.

Section V — Right to Withdraw, Commute and Change Options

The following provisions shall be included in this settlement option election.

Withdrawal Privilege. Unless otherwise indicated below, each Beneficiary while entitled to receive instalments under Options 3 or 4 shall have the right to withdraw all or any portion (not less than $250.00) of his or her share of the proceeds then being held by the Company.

Primary Beneficiary   ☐ Limit withdrawal to $_____ per year, non-cumulative.   ☐ No right to withdraw.

    ☐ Right to withdraw only after _____, 19_____.

    ☐ Limit withdrawal per year to an amount not exceeding _____% of the original share of the proceeds, non-cumulative.

Contingent Beneficiary   ☐ Limit withdrawal to $_____ per year, non-cumulative.   ☐ No right to withdraw.

    ☐ Right to withdraw only after _____, 19_____.

    ☐ Limit withdrawal per year to an amount not exceeding _____% of the original share of the proceeds, non-cumulative.

Commutation Privilege. Unless otherwise indicated below, each Beneficiary while entitled to receive instalments under Option 1 shall have the right to elect to receive in a single sum the commuted value of any unpaid instalments due such Beneficiary under said Option.

Primary Beneficiary   ☐ Right to commute only after _____, 19_____.   ☐ No right to commute.

Contingent Beneficiary   ☐ Right to commute only after _____, 19_____.   ☐ No right to commute.

Privilege to Change Options. Unless otherwise indicated below, any beneficiary who is entitled to receive a share of the proceeds hereunder may, with the consent of the Company, elect to apply such share under any other settlement option contained in the policy. Any such election must be made in writing on forms satisfactory to the Company and shall be effective only when accepted by the Company.

Primary Beneficiary   ☐ Right to change only after _____, 19_____.   ☐ No right to change.

Contingent Beneficiary   ☐ Right to change only after _____, 19_____.   ☐ No right to change.

FIGURE 11

(continued)

Section VI – Special Provisions

The following provisions shall be included in this settlement option election only if the box ☐ preceding such provision is marked with an "X" or a checkmark.

☐ **PAYMENT TO CHILDREN OF DECEASED BENEFICIARIES**

Notwithstanding any provision in this settlement option election to the contrary, if any _____ beneficiary shall be deceased at the time he would otherwise be entitled to have a share of the proceeds apportioned to him or interest thereon paid to him or any instalment or refund paid to him, if living, such share or the share from which such interest was derived or the commuted value of any instalments or refund remaining unpaid shall be apportioned in equal parts to (a) the then living children of such beneficiary, or if none be living, to (b) the then living Primary Beneficiaries, or if none be living, to the then living Contingent Beneficiaries, or if none be living, to the then living Tertiary Beneficiaries, provided, that if any such Primary or Contingent Beneficiary shall be then deceased leaving a child or children then living, the share which the deceased beneficiary would have received, if living, shall be apportioned in equal parts to the then living children of such deceased beneficiary. Any share apportioned to the children of a deceased beneficiary shall be paid in one sum. Any share apportioned to a living Primary or Contingent Beneficiary shall (a) if such beneficiary is then entitled to receive payment under Option 2, be paid in one sum, or (b) if such beneficiary is then entitled to receive payment under Options 1, 3, or 4, be added to and paid in the same manner as provided for the amount then being held under such option. Any share apportioned to a living Tertiary Beneficiary shall be paid in one sum.

☐ **PAYMENT TO INDIVIDUALS FOR THE BENEFIT OF CHILDREN**

Any payment hereunder which becomes due to a child under the age of ____ years shall be paid not to said child but to _____ _____ of the Insured, or _____, _____ of the Insured, as Trustee for said child. If more than one Trustee is designated, said Trustees shall serve in the order named. In the event of the death, inability or refusal of the Trustee to act, the Successor-Trustee shall be Trustee hereunder. In the event of the death, inability, or refusal to act of all Trustees, then payment shall be made to said child. Said Trustee and said Successor-Trustee, if any, are hereby appointed and designated as such with full power and authority to receive, hold and disburse any proceeds in their absolute discretion for the use and benefit of said child, and may, on behalf of said child, exercise any rights which may be available to the child hereunder. Any payment made to said Trustee or said Successor Trustee pursuant hereto shall fully and finally discharge the Company from any further liability for the amount so paid.

Section VII – General Provisions

The following provisions shall apply to this Change of Beneficiary and Settlement Option Election:

1. **Payment to Beneficiary.** Payment of any amount, when due, shall be paid to the Primary Beneficiary, if living, otherwise to the Contingent Beneficiary, if living, otherwise to the Tertiary Beneficiary, if living. If two or more Primary, Contingent, or Tertiary Beneficiaries are designated, the proceeds or any specified amount payable to such beneficiaries shall be applied in equal shares for the beneficiaries living when they become entitled to share in the proceeds as beneficiary, unless otherwise provided. A provision for changing or terminating payments in certain events other than death, or granting a right or privilege shall apply to each beneficiary individually.

If any beneficiary dies after becoming entitled to payment, the commuted value or the unpaid portion of the deceased beneficiary's share shall be apportioned equally to the surviving Primary Beneficiaries, or if none be living, to the then living Contingent Beneficiaries, or if none be living, to the then living Tertiary Beneficiaries, and paid as follows:

(1) Any such surviving Primary or Contingent Beneficiary then entitled to receive payment under Option 2 shall receive his share in one sum.

(2) All other such surviving Primary or Contingent Beneficiaries shall be paid in the same manner as provided for payment of their respective shares.

(3) Any such surviving Tertiary Beneficiary shall receive his share in one sum.

2. **Minimum Amounts and Payments.** If at any time the amount to be applied or held under a settlement option for any beneficiary is less than the minimum amount specified in the policy, the option will not be available and payment will be made to such beneficiary in one sum, provided that if no minimum amount is specified in the policy, such minimum amount shall be $2,000. Unless otherwise provided in the Policy, at any time an interest or instalment payment to a beneficiary shall amount to less than $20.00 the Company reserves the right to make payment thereof in equivalent amounts quarterly, semiannually or annually, so that no such payment shall amount to less than $20.00.

3. **Withdrawal or Commutation Privilege.** Any withdrawal or commutation privilege granted to a beneficiary may be exercised only upon written request satisfactory to the Company at its Home Office, accompanied by the policy or such other instrument as the Company may require. No withdrawal shall be made for less than $250.00 and the Company reserves the right to limit the number of withdrawals made by any beneficiary to four per calendar year.

4. **Proceeds.** As used in this settlement option election, the term "Proceeds" shall be the net amount due under any policy included hereunder as a death benefit, and shall include any proceeds payable under any rider, provision or additional benefit, unless otherwise provided. However, the term "Proceeds" shall not include benefits payable under any Family Term or Children's Term Insurance Rider. If the policy by its terms, or by the terms of any family income or income replacement rider attached thereto, shall provide for instalments or deferred payments, the present value thereof, commuted on the basis provided in such policy or rider, shall be included in the proceeds in lieu of such instalments or deferred payments.

Any payment due to an assignee under a policy included hereunder shall be made in one sum and the proceeds of such policy shall be reduced by the amount of the payment.

If more than one policy is payable hereunder, the proceeds of each policy shall contribute pro rata to any division into parts and to any withdrawal and to any payments under Option 3.

5. **Final Beneficiary.** Any amount payable upon the death of the last survivor among the Insured, the Primary Beneficiary, the Contingent Beneficiary, and the Tertiary Beneficiary shall be paid in one sum to the estate of such last survivor.

6. **Rights of Creditors.** The proceeds and all payments hereunder shall be exempt from the claims of creditors to the maximum extent permitted by law and may not be assigned or withdrawn before coming payable except as expressly authorized by the provisions herein.

7. **Definitions.** The words "Insured," "policy," "insurance" and "payee" shall mean "Annuitant," "annuity policy," "annuity" and "payee," if appropriate. The word "child" or "children" shall include legally adopted children unless otherwise provided. Whenever applicable the singular shall include the plural and the plural singular, and all pronouns of either masculine or feminine gender shall include the opposite gender. The words "effective date of settlement" shall mean the date of death of the Insured.

8. **Miscellaneous.** All decisions upon questions of fact in the determination of unnamed beneficiaries or in the determination concerning any beneficiary made by the Company in good faith and based upon any affidavit or other proof satisfactory to the Company shall be conclusive, and any payment made in reliance thereon shall fully discharge the liability of the Company for the amount so paid. No elective instruction or direction designated or preceded by a box ☐ shall be a part of this settlement option election unless the applicable box is marked with an "X" or checkmark and the pertinent information required, if any, has been inserted. The Owner shall have the right, prior to the effective date of settlement, to change any beneficiary designation and/or settlement option election, unless otherwise provided herein.

If there is a provision in said policy requiring that it must accompany any request for change of beneficiary or that such change shall not take effect until endorsed on the policy by the Company, the undersigned hereby request(s) that said policy be amended so that the person or persons having the right to change the beneficiary may designate a new beneficiary at any time while the Insured is living, subject to the rights of any assignee, by filing with the Company a written request for change of beneficiary in form satisfactory to the Company, such change to be effective when it is recorded by the Company, but upon such recording the change will be deemed to have been made as of the date such person or persons signed said written request for change of beneficiary, whether or not the Insured be living at the time of such recording, subject to any payment made or action taken by the Company before such recording.

The foregoing Change of Beneficiary and Election of Settlement Option is subject to the Change of Beneficiary and Settlement Option provisions contained in said policy and the General Provisions contained in this Section VII.

If a trustee is designated as beneficiary and the trust is not in force at the Insured's death, then unless otherwise provided in the beneficiary designation, the proceeds will be paid as though a natural beneficiary predeceased the Insured. The Company will not be responsbile for the failure of any trustee to perform the duties of trustee, nor for the application or disposition of any money paid to a trustee, and any such payment shall fully discharge the liability of the Company for the amount so paid.

If a Trustee under a Will is designated as beneficiary, unless otherwise provided in the beneficiary designation, the Trust so indicated shall be the Trust created in the instrument admitted to Probate as the Insured's Last Will and Testament. If the Last Will and Testament of the Insured is admitted to Probate within 60 days after the death of the Insured and the Trusteeship is accepted by said Trustee within the aforesaid period, the proceeds shall be payable to said Trustee as beneficiary, otherwise the proceeds shall be paid as though a natural beneficiary predeceased the Insured. The Company reserves the right to declare this form void and of no effect if it is incomplete or completed in an unsatisfactory manner.

Date_____
Witness:

_____   Signature of Authorized Person:

_____   _____

_____   _____

HOME OFFICE USE ONLY	The foregoing Change of Beneficiary and Election of Settlement Option is hereby recorded by and filed with the Company and, where applicable, the Company has amended the policy as requested above.
Date_____	*George R. Lambert* X **SECRETARY** By:

DISTRICT OFFICE ENTRY ONLY	District		Agency	Register Page	P.T.D.

FIGURE 12

Front of Late Remittance Offer Form

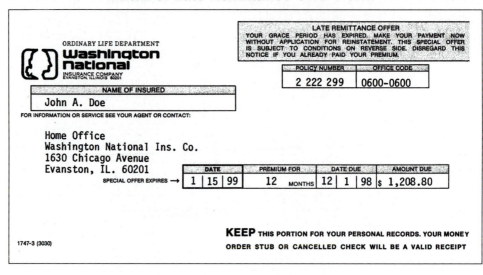

Back of Late Remittance Offer Form

CONDITIONS OF SPECIAL OFFER

This policy terminated at the expiration of the grace period, except as the Automatic Premium Loan or non-forfeiture provision may apply. This offer to accept a late remittance without evidence of insurability is made subject to the following conditions:

1. Payment must be made on or before expiry date of special offer shown on reverse.

2. Payment must be made within the lifetime of the person or persons covered under the policy on date of default.

3. The grace period provided in the policy is not extended by this offer and this offer applies to this premium only.

4. This voluntary offer to waive evidence of insurability is a special offer and will not apply to any future premium.

5. Checks and drafts will be accepted subject to collection.

WASHINGTON NATIONAL INSURANCE COMPANY

FIGURE 12
(concluded)

CONSERVATION NOTICE - **AGENCY COPY**

ORDINARY LIFE DEPARTMENT

Washington National

INSURANCE COMPANY
EVANSTON, ILLINOIS 60201

A LATE REMITTANCE OFFER HAS BEEN SENT TO THE INSURED. CONTACT THE POLICYOWNER IN ORDER TO CONSERVE THIS BUSINESS.

POLICY NUMBER	OFFICE CODE
77-2000000	0600-0600

NAME OF INSURED
John A. Doe

FOR INFORMATION OR SERVICE SEE YOUR AGENT OR CONTACT:

Home Office
Washington National Ins. Co.
1630 Chicago Avenue
Evanston, IL. 60201

SPECIAL OFFER EXPIRES →

DATE			PREMIUM FOR		DATE DUE			AMOUNT DUE
12	1	92	12 MONTHS		10	15	92	$ 1,208.80

01747-3 (3030)

THIS POLICY NEEDS ATTENTION!

FIGURE 13

Form No. 10—LIFE INSURANCE ASSIGNMENT

ASSIGNMENT OF LIFE INSURANCE POLICY AS COLLATERAL

A.　　*For Value Received* the undersigned hereby assign, transfer and set over to _____

_____ of _____

its successors and assigns, (herein called the "Assignee") Policy No. _____ issued by the

_____

(herein called the "Insurer") and any supplementary contracts issued in connection therewith (said policy and contracts being

herein called the "Policy"), upon the life of _____

of _____ and all claims, options, privileges, rights, title and interest therein and thereunder (except as provided in Paragraph C hereof), subject to all the terms and conditions of the Policy and to all superior liens, if any, which the Insurer may have against the Policy. The undersigned by this instrument jointly and severally agree and the Assignee by the acceptance of this assignment agrees to the conditions and provisions herein set forth.

B.　　It is expressly agreed that, without detracting from the generality of the foregoing, the following specific rights are included in this assignment and pass by virtue hereof:
1.　The sole right to collect from the Insurer the net proceeds of the Policy when it becomes a claim by death or maturity;
2.　The sole right to surrender the Policy and receive the surrender value thereof at any time provided by the terms of the Policy and at such other times as the Insurer may allow;
3.　The sole right to obtain one or more loans or advances on the Policy, either from the Insurer or, at any time, from other persons, and to pledge or assign the Policy as security for such loans or advances;
4.　The sole right to collect and receive all distributions or shares of surplus, dividend deposits or additions to the Policy now or hereafter made or apportioned thereto, and to exercise any and all options contained in the Policy with respect thereto; provided, that unless and until the Assignee shall notify the Insurer in writing to the contrary, the distributions or shares of surplus, dividend deposits and additions shall continue on the plan in force at the time of this assignment; and
5.　The sole right to exercise all nonforfeiture rights permitted by the terms of the Policy or allowed by the Insurer and to receive all benefits and advantages derived therefrom.

C.　　It is expressly agreed that the following specific rights, so long as the Policy has not been surrendered, are reserved and excluded from this assignment and do not pass by virtue hereof:
1.　The right to collect from the Insurer any disability benefit payable in cash that does not reduce the amount of insurance;
2.　The right to designate and change the beneficiary;
3.　The right to elect any optional mode of settlement permitted by the Policy or allowed by the Insurer;
but the reservation of these rights shall in no way impair the right of the Assignee to surrender the Policy completely with all its incidents or impair any other right of the Assignee hereunder, and any designation or change of beneficiary or election of a mode of settlement shall be made subject to this assignment and to the rights of the Assignee hereunder.

D.　　This assignment is made and the Policy is to be held as collateral security for any and all liabilities of the undersigned, or any of them, to the Assignee, either now existing or that may hereafter arise in the ordinary course of business between any of the undersigned and the Assignee (all of which liabilities secured or to become secured are herein called "Liabilities").

E.　　The Assignee covenants and agrees with the undersigned as follows:
1.　That any balance of sums received hereunder from the Insurer remaining after payment of the then existing Liabilities, matured or unmatured, shall be paid by the Assignee to the persons entitled thereto under the terms of the Policy had this assignment not been executed;
2.　That the Assignee will not exercise either the right to surrender the Policy or (except for the purpose of paying premiums) the right to obtain policy loans from the Insurer, until there has been default in any of the Liabilities or a failure to pay any premium when due, nor until twenty days after the Assignee shall have mailed, by first-class mail, to the undersigned at the addresses last supplied in writing to the Assignee specifically referring to this assignment, notice of intention to exercise such right; and
3.　That the Assignee will upon request forward without unreasonable delay to the Insurer the Policy for endorsement of any designation or change of beneficiary or any election of an optional mode of settlement.

F.　　The Insurer is hereby authorized to recognize the Assignee's claims to rights hereunder without investigating the reason for any action taken by the Assignee, or the validity or the amount of the Liabilities or the existence of any default therein, or the giving of any notice under Paragraph E (2) above or otherwise, or the application to be made by the Assignee of any amounts to be paid to the Assignee. The sole signature of the Assignee shall be sufficient for the exercise of any rights under the Policy assigned hereby and the sole receipt of the Assignee for any sums received shall be a full discharge and release therefor to the Insurer. Checks for all or any part of the sums payable under the Policy and assigned herein, shall be drawn to the exclusive order of the Assignee if, when, and in such amounts as may be, requested by the Assignee.

G.　　The Assignee shall be under no obligation to pay any premium, or the principal of or interest on any loans or advances on the Policy whether or not obtained by the Assignee, or any other charges on the Policy, but any such amounts so paid by the Assignee from its own funds, shall become a part of the Liabilities hereby secured, shall be due immediately, and shall draw interest at a rate fixed by the Assignee from time to time not exceeding 6% per annum.

H.　　The exercise of any right, option, privilege or power given herein to the Assignee shall be at the option of the Assignee, but (except as restricted by Paragraph E (2) above) the Assignee may exercise any such right, option, privilege or power without notice to, or assent by, or affecting the liability of, or releasing any interest hereby assigned by the undersigned, or any of them.

I.　　The Assignee may take or release other security, may release any party primarily or secondarily liable for any of the Liabilities, may grant extensions, renewals or indulgences with respect to the Liabilities, or may apply to the Liabilities in such order as the Assignee shall determine, the proceeds of the Policy hereby assigned or any amount received on account of the Policy by the exercise of any right permitted under this assignment, without resorting or regard to other security.

J.　　In the event of any conflict between the provisions of this assignment and provisions of the note or other evidence of any Liability, with respect to the Policy or rights of collateral security therein, the provisions of this assignment shall prevail.

K.　　Each of the undersigned declares that no proceedings in bankruptcy are pending against him and that his property is not subject to any assignment for the benefit of creditors.

Signed and sealed this _____ day of _____. 19_____

_____　　_____(L.S.)
　　　　　　　　Witness　　　　　　　　　　　　　　　　　　　Insured or Owner

_____　　_____
　　　　　　　　　　　　　　　　　　　　　　　　　　　　　　　Address

_____　　_____(L.S.)
　　　　　　　　Witness　　　　　　　　　　　　　　　　　　　Beneficiary

_____　　_____
　　　　　　　　　　　　　　　　　　　　　　　　　　　　　　　Address

FIGURE 13
(concluded)

INDIVIDUAL ACKNOWLEDGMENT

STATE OF _____

COUNTY OF _____ }ss:

On the _____ day of _____ 19 _____, before me personally came

_____ to me known to be the individual _____ described in and who

executed the assignment on the reverse side hereof and acknowledged to me that _____ he _____ executed the same.

_____
Notary Public

My commission expires_____

CORPORATE ACKNOWLEDGMENT

STATE OF _____

COUNTY OF _____ }ss:

On the _____ day of _____ 19_____, before me personally came _____

_____, who being by me duly sworn, did depose and say that he resides in _____

that he is the _____ of _____, the corporation described in and which executed the assignment on the
reverse side hereof; that he knows the seal of said corporation; that the seal affixed to said assignment is such corporate seal; that
it was so affixed by order of the Board of Directors of said corporation, and that he signed his name thereto by like order.

_____
Notary Public

My commission expires_____

• • • • •

Duplicate received and filed at the home office of the Insurer in _____. this _____ day of _____ 19_____

_____

By_____
Authorized Officer

NOTE: When executed by a corporation, the corporate seal should be affixed and there should be attached to the assignment a certified copy of the resolution of
the Board of Directors authorizing the signing officer to execute and deliver the assignment in the name and on behalf of the corporation.

BMC 136-6-1941

FIGURE 14

Washington National
INSURANCE COMPANY
EVANSTON, ILLINOIS 60201

APPLICATION FOR REINSTATEMENT
LIFE AND/OR HEALTH INSURANCE

If District Agency, specify
Family Account No.

Insured's Name (Please print full name)	Date of Birth
Mary Roe	January 1, 1958

Mailing Address	Policy Number
1234 Main Street Peoria, IL. 60615	77-2300000

Occupation	Amount Paid with this Application $	Premium Due Date
Lawyer	30.00	March 12, 1995

The undersigned hereby declare(s) that the following statements and answers are complete and true and are made to induce the Company to reinstate the above numbered policy.

I. Since the date of the Application for the policy, have:

1. The INSURED

2. The Other Insured(s) (if this is a Universal Life Policy which includes one or more Other Insured Riders)

3. The Insured Spouse (if Family Plan or Family Term benefits are included in this Policy)

4. The Insured CHILD or CHILDREN (if Family Plan, Family Term, or Childrens Term benefits are included in this Policy)

5. The PURCHASER (if the Policy is a Juvenile Policy which includes Purchaser Waiver of Premium benefits)

Explain "Yes" answers. Include names, dates, disorders and physicians.

ALL QUESTIONS MUST BE ANSWERED

	Yes	No
a. Had any injury or change in health?	☐	☒
b. Been a patient in a hospital, clinic or sanitorium?	☐	☒
c. Had any treatment or examination or been a patient of any physician or practitioner?	☐	☒
d. Smoked cigarettes within the past year? If so, indicate quantity per day	☐	☒
e. Used narcotics, barbiturates, amphetamines, psychedelic drugs, marijuana or been treated for drug habit or alcoholism?	☐	☒
f. Participated in any hazardous sport or flown other than as a fare paying passenger?	☐	☒
g. Applied for any life or health insurance with this or any other company?	☐	☒
h. Been declined, postponed or rated for insurance or for reinstatement in this or any other company?	☐	☒

II. INSURED'S Height: 5 ft. 5 in. Weight 125

The undersigned expressly agree(s) as follows: (1) the policy shall not be reinstated until the Company has received payment of all arrears and has approved this application at its Home Office; (2) the terms and conditions of the incontestable provision in said policy shall apply to a reinstatement thereof made upon this application, but the period of time specified in said provision shall run from the date of approval of this application by the Company; and (3) if said reinstatement application is approved the Company shall be under no liability nor shall any insurance be restored with respect to any person now deceased or with respect to any person who would not be covered under said policy on the date of this application had there been no default in premium payment.

AUTHORIZATION

To: Any licensed physician, medical practitioner, hospital, clinic or other medically related facility, the Veterans Administration, insurance or reinsurance company, consumer reporting agency, government agency, Medical Information Bureau, Inc., benefit plan administrator, employer, and the agent through whom application is being made.

(1) I authorize you to release the following to Washington National Insurance Company or its reinsurers for purposes of determining eligibility for insurance benefits under an existing policy or claims for benefits:

Full information including copies of records concerning medical examinations, history and treatment, character and general reputation, habits, occupation, income, finances, aviation activities, and hazardous activities of the undersigned and all minor children proposed for coverage.

(2) I authorize Washington National Insurance Company or its reinsurers to release any information to the Medical Information Bureau, Inc., to a benefit plan administrator, to other insurance or reinsurance companies and to persons or organizations performing business or legal services in connection with my application, or as may be otherwise lawfully required.

(3) I know that I may receive a copy of this authorization upon request. I agree this authorization shall be valid for two and one-half years from its date and that a photographic copy of it shall be as valid as the original. I acknowledge receipt of the Notice of Information Practices, which includes the Fair Credit Reporting Act Notice and Medical Information Bureau Notice.

(4) ☐ I elect to be interviewed if an investigative consumer report is prepared in connection with this application.

Dated June 17 , 19 97

James Smith
Witness

Mary Roe
Signature of Insured

Check if Applicable

Signature of ☐ SPOUSE (Family Term)
☐ PURCHASE (Juvenile) ☐ OWNER, if other than Insured ☐ Other Insured (UL Policy)

Name of Owning Corporation, Partnership, ect., if applicable

Agency/District	Agent	Code/Agency	Mode of Payment

B394-1

FIGURE 14

(concluded)

NOTICE OF INFORMATION PRACTICES

In addition to the information provided by you, we may also obtain information from physicians or other medical professionals; from hospitals or other medical-care institutions; from the Medical Information Bureau, the Veterans Administration, government agencies, public records, insurance or reinsurance companies, agents, consumer reporting agencies and financial institutions. We may also obtain information from your friends, neighbors, associates, and past and present employers, either directly or through an investigative consumer report.

FAIR CREDIT REPORTING ACT NOTICE

If an investigation is conducted in connection with your application, you are entitled, under the Federal Fair Credit Reporting Act, to disclosure of the nature and scope of that investigation. If a consumer investigative report is prepared, you may obtain a copy of such report as provided in the section, entitled "Your Right To Information In Our Files". Further information regarding the investigation and any investigative consumer reports may be obtained by mailing your request to the office identified at the end of this notice. The type of information we may obtain includes any which relates to your mental and physical health, character and general reputation, habits, finances, occupation, income, insurance coverage, and participation in aviation and other hazardous activities. If insurance is sought for members of your family, similar information may be requested about them.

As permitted by law, Washington National Insurance Company or our agent may disclose personal information about you without your authorization when such disclosure is necessary to conduct our business.

MEDICAL INFORMATION BUREAU NOTICE

We or our reinsurers may make a brief report regarding your insurability to the Medical Information Bureau, a non-profit membership organization of life insurance companies, which operates an information exchange on behalf of its members. If you apply for life or health insurance coverage, or submit a claim for benefits to a Bureau member company, the Bureau, upon request, will supply such company with the information it may have in its file.

Upon receipt of a request from you, the Bureau will arrange disclosure to you of any information it may have in your file. (Medical information will be disclosed only to your attending physician.) If you question the accuracy of the information contained in the Bureau's file, you may contact the Bureau and seek a correction in accordance with the procedures set forth in the Federal Fair Credit Reporting Act. The address of the Bureau's information office is Post Office Box 105, Essex Station, Boston, Massachusetts 02110; telephone number (616) 426-3660.

We or our reinsurers may also release information in our file to other life insurance companies to whom you may apply for life or health insurance, or to whom a claim for benefits may be submitted.

OTHER DISCLOSURES

There are other circumstances in which disclosure of personal information may be made:

• to persons or organizations which perform a business or professional function for us;

• to other insurers, agents or insurance-support organizations to enable them to perform their function in connection with an insurance transaction involving you, or to detect or prevent insurance fraud or other misrepresentation;

• to a medical professional for the purpose of informing you of a medical problem of which you may not be aware;

• to an insurance regulatory authority;

• to a law enforcement or other government authority to prevent or prosecute fraud or other unlawful activities;

• for the purpose of conducting scientific research, including actuarial or underwriting studies;

• to our affiliated companies in connection with the marketing of an insurance product or service; and

• to a group policyholder for the purpose of reporting claims experience or conducting an audit of the Company's or the agent's operations.

In each case, only that personal information which is reasonably necessary to accomplish the business purpose will be disclosed. Information obtained by an insurance-support organization may be retained by it and disclosed to other persons as permitted by the Federal Fair Credit Reporting Act and other applicable laws.

YOUR RIGHT TO INFORMATION IN OUR FILE

You have a right of access to recorded personal information about you which we have in our files and which is reasonably locatable and retrievable. Within 30 business days after we receive your request for access, we will inform you of the nature and substance of the recorded personal information and the name of any institutional source of such information. You may come to the Company and photocopy the information, or if you prefer, we will photocopy and mail it to you. We may ask you to pay a reasonable charge to cover the cost of providing the copies.

We will also provide the identitiy, if recorded, of those persons to whom we have disclosed the information in the two years preceding the date of your request. If the identity of those persons is not recorded, we will provide you with the names of those persons and organizations to whom such information is normally disclosed.

Your right of access includes any medical information we may have about you, but we will disclose medical information only to the medical professional you designate, providing he or she is licensed to provide medical care with respect to the condition to which the information relates. Your right of access does not include any information which relates to and is collected in connection with or in reasonable anticipation of a claim or civil or criminal proceeding.

DISPUTED INFORMATION

You may request, in writing, that recorded personal information be corrected, amended, or deleted from our files. We will notify you if we comply with your request. If we do not comply we will notify you within 30 business days after we receive your written request and will provide the reasons for our refusal. You will then have the opportunity to file with us a concise statement of your position regarding the disputed personal information. We will include your statement in our files and will provide it with any subsequent disclosure of recorded personal information.

If we correct, amend, or delete disputed personal information from our records, or if we refuse and you file a concise statement with us, we will furnish the additional information or fact of deletion to any insurance support organization that furnished the disputed information to us and to any person you designate who may have received the disputed information within the preceding two years.

Please send any questions concerning our information practices or your access to information in our files to:

Director of Public Affairs
Washington National Insurance Company
1630 Chicago Avenue
Evanston, Illinois 60201

THIS NOTICE MUST BE GIVEN TO THE PROPOSED INSURED(S)/POLICYHOLDER

Washington National
INSURANCE COMPANY
EVANSTON ILLINOIS 60201

REINSTATEMENT CONDITIONAL RECEIPT

Ordinary Department

This form is to be used only as a conditional receipt for the deposit on an application for reinstatement of a lapsed Ordinary Policy.

_____, 19____

RECEIVED from _____, the sum of

_____ Dollars, as a deposit on account of

premium on Policy No. _____ issued or assumed by WASHINGTON NATIONAL INSURANCE COMPANY

upon the life of _____, application for

reinstatement of which has this day been made.

The above amount is received by me merely for transmittal to and subject to acceptance and approval by the Company at its Home Office, and such tender of payment shall not revive or restore said policy or constitute payment of all or any protion of any premium thereunder unless so accepted and approved. This receipt is issued upon the express understanding that if the Company declines to approve such application it shall have the right to reject said payment, in which case the above amount will be refunded and this receipt shall become null and void.

_____ Agent

FIGURE 15

Washington National INSURANCE COMPANY

APPLICATION FOR ANNUITY

1. Proposed Annuitant's Name:
   PUBLIC (Last)   JOHN (First)   Q (Initial)

2. Address:
   2525 AMERICA WAY, HOUSTON, TX (Zip) 9999

3. Proposed Annuitant's Soc. Sec. No.:
   999-99-9999

4. Age: 37   5. Date of Birth: 5-14-39   6. Birthplace: HOUSTON   7. Sex: M

8. Citizenship: USA   Marital Status: M

9. Owner's Name (If other than Annuitant):

10. Address: (Zip)

11. Owner's Soc. Sec. No. or Tax I.D. No.:

12. Is Owner: ☐ Trustee ☐ Corporation ☐ Individual ☐ Partnership

13. Address for Contract Communications:
    ☒ Annuitant ☐ Employer ☐ Owner ☐ Other
    Name _____
    City _____ State _____ Zip _____
    Phone ( ) _____

14. Successor Owner's Name:

15. Address: (Zip)

16. Successor Owner's Soc. Sec. No. or Tax I.D. No.:

17. Will the contract applied for replace other insurance ☐ Yes ☒ No
    or annuties: If Yes, give name of company being replaced _____

18. Type of contract:
    ☒ Single purchase: ☒ WN Plan I   ☐ WN Plan III
    ☐ Periodic purchase: ☐ WN Plan II   ☐ WN Plan II +

19. Age at maturity: 65

20. Purchase payment amount:
    Periodic ...... $ _____   Total amount paid
    Single .... $ 10,000.00 $ 10,000.00

21. Type of plan:
    ☒ Non-Qualified   ☐ TDA [403(b)]
    ☐ IRA   ☐ 401 Corporate
    ☐ IRA (Spousal)   ☐ 403 A
    ☐ IRA (Rollover)   ☐ Def. Comp. (Private)
    ☐ SEP   ☐ Def. Comp. (Public)
    ☐ HR10 KEOGH   (I.R.C. Sec. 457)
    ☐ Other

22. Payment Frequency: Type of payment
    ☐ ANN.   ☐ PAC   ☐ Military Allotment
    ☐ SA.   ☐ FESAP
    ☐ QR.   ☐ SD.   1
    ☐ MO.   No. of payments _____

23. Annuitant's Occupation: MANAGER   Empl. Date: 5-7-72
    Employer: JACK-IN-THE-BOX
    Address: 123 HUNGRY WAY
    HOUSTON TX 99999 (Zip)

24. Purchase payment allocation:
    Employer _____ %   Employee 100 %

25. Beneficiary - print full name, relationship and social security no.:
    Primary SUSAN A. PUBLIC, WIFE
    999-99-9999
    Contingent
    ESTATE

26. H.O. Endorsement

27. Special Request/Rollover of matured policy (Dist.)

The undersigned represent(s) that the foregoing statements and answers are complete, true and correctly recorded and agree(s) to be bound by all statements and answers made or to be made in this application. The undersigned further expressly agree(s) as follows: 1. This application and any contract issued in consequence thereof shall constitute the entire annuity contract. No agent is authorized to make or modify contracts, to waive any of the Company's rights or requirements or to bind the Company by making any promise, representation or information, unless the same be in writing, submitted to the Company, and made a part of such contract. 2. The Company is authorized to amend this application by making an appropriate notation of any corrections or changes in the space designated "Home Office Endorsements Only", and the acceptance of any contract issued on this application shall constitute a ratification of any such amendment; provided, in those states where it is required by statute, regulation or Insurance Department Ruling, any amendment as to amount, plan or annuity or benefits shall be made only with the written consent of the undersigned.

Signed at HOUSTON   TX (State)

Date 8-9-76   19

Witnessed by Washington National (Writing Agent)

Signature of Proposed Annuitant   John Q. Public

Signature of Applicant If Not Proposed Annuitant _____

(Name of Corporation, Partnership, Trustee, etc., if any)

ED 31-3   All checks are to be made Payable to: WASHINGTON NATIONAL INSURANCE COMPANY   (2-85)

FIGURE 15
(continued)

Washington National
INSURANCE COMPANY
EVANSTON, ILLINOIS 60201

CONTRACT NUMBER

ANNUITANT

AGE AND SEX

MATURITY DATE

CONTRACT DATE

PLAN

Washington National Insurance Company of Evanston, Illinois, agrees:

to apply the proceeds of this Contract to pay to the Owner, commencing on the maturity date, subject to the terms of this Contract, annuity payments for a period of 10 years and for the remaining lifetime of the Annuitant. Payments thereafter will be paid in accordance with the Settlement Options Provisions of this Contract.

If the Annuitant dies prior to the maturity date, the Company agrees to pay to the Beneficiary the accumulated value of this Contract on the date written notice of death is received, and to make such payment upon receipt of due proof of death at its Home Office.

George P. Kendall Jr.
PRESIDENT

Thomas Pontarell
SECRETARY

**SINGLE PURCHASE PAYMENT
DEFERRED LIFE ANNUITY**

DEATH BENEFIT PAYABLE IN EVENT OF DEATH PRIOR TO THE MATURITY DATE.

SURRENDER BENEFIT PAYABLE BEFORE MATURITY. NON-PARTICIPATING SCHEDULE OF CONTRACT SPECIFICATIONS AND PURCHASE PAYMENTS ARE SHOWN ON PAGE THREE.

ED 28A-1   PAGE ONE

FIGURE 15
(continued)

ALPHABETICAL INDEX

FIGURE 15
(continued)

CONTRACT SPECIFICATIONS   FA   99999

JOHN Q PUBLIC

37   MALE

AUGUST 15, 1976

AUGUST 15, 2004

SINGLE PURCHASE PAYMENT: $10,000,00   SINGLE PAY DEFERRED ANNUITY

SCHEDULE OF GUARANTEED INTEREST RATES

PERIOD	RATES
FIRST CONTRACT YEAR	9.25%
THEREAFTER	4.00%

FIGURE 15
(continued)

ENTIRE CONTRACT

This Contract is issued in consideration of the application and the payment of a single purchase payment. The Contract and the application, a copy of which is attached and made a part of this contract, shall constitute the entire contract between the parties.

All statements made in applying for this Contract shall, in the absence of fraud, be deemed representations and not warranties. No statement shall avoid this Contract or be used in defense of a claim thereunder unless it is contained in the application, and a copy of the application is attached to this Contract when issued.

No condition, provision or privilege of this Contract can be waived or modified in any case except by an endorsement or an amendment signed by either the President, a Vice-President, the Secretary or the Actuary of the Company. No agent has the power in behalf of the Company to make or modify this or any other contract, to waive any forfeiture, or to bind the Company by making any promise, or by making or receiving any representation or information.

CONTRACT DATE

The Contract Date is the date shown in the Contract Specifications and from which contract years and anniversaries referred to in this Contract shall be determined.

INCONTESTABILITY

This Contract shall be incontestable from the contract date.

AGE OR SEX

This Contract is issued at the Annuitant's age last birthday on the contract date. If the contract date falls on a birthday of the Annuitant, the age last birthday shall be deemed to be the age attained by the Annuitant on the contract date.

If prior to the commencement of annuity payments, it is found that the age or sex of the Annuitant has been misstated, the benefits provided under this Contract shall be that which would have been provided at the correct age or sex. If after the commencement of annuity payments, it is found that the age or sex of the Annuitant has been misstated, any overpayment by the Company will be charged against the then current or next succeeding annuity payment or payments with compound interest at the effective rate of 6% per annum, and any underpayment by the Company shall be made up immediately with compound interest at the effective rate of 6% per annum.

NON-PARTICIPATING

This Contract is issued on the non-participating plan and is not entitled to participate in the profits or divisible surplus of the Company.

OWNERSHIP

Owner. The Owner is as designated in the application for this Contract unless subsequently changed as provided below. Unless otherwise provided in the ownership designation in effect under this Contract, if an Owner other than the Annuitant dies during the Annuitant's lifetime, ownership shall pass to any successor Owner, if living, otherwise to the estate of the Owner.

FIGURE 15

(continued)

BENEFICIARY

Owner's Rights. All benefits, rights and privileges under this Contract which are available while the Annuitant is living are vested in the Owner and may be exercised without the consent of the Annuitant, any Beneficiary or any Successor Owner.

When a trustee is the Owner, the Company may deal with such trustee, or any successor trustee, proof of whose appointment as such has been duly filed with the Company at its Home Office, in accordance with the terms of this Contract without regards to the provisions of any trust instrument, or any modification or amendment thereof, or any supplemental agreement thereto. Nothing in any such trust or other agreement shall be construed to enlarge, change, vary, or in any way affect the obligations of the Company under this Contract, nor shall the Company be responsible for the failure of a trustee to perform the duties of trustee, nor for the application or disposition of any money paid to a trustee, and such payment to a trustee shall fully discharge the Company with respect to the amounts paid.

Transfer or Change of Ownership. The Owner may transfer this Contract to a new Owner or otherwise change the ownership designation at any time while the Annuitant is living, subject to the rights of any assignee, by filing with the Company a written instrument of transfer or change satisfactory to the Company. No such transfer or change shall be effective until it is recorded by the Company, but upon such recording the transfer or change will be deemed to have been made as of the date the Owner signed said written instrument of transfer or change, whether or not the Annuitant be living at the time of such recording, subject to any payment made or action taken by the Company before such recording.

Beneficiary Designation. The Beneficiary is as designated in the application for this Contract unless subsequently changed as provided below. Unless otherwise provided in the beneficiary designation in effect under this Contract, death proceeds shall be payable in equal shares to the primary beneficiaries who survive the Annuitant or, if none survives, to the contingent beneficiaries who survive the Annuitant. If no beneficiary survives the Annuitant, the proceeds shall be payable to the Owner, if living, otherwise to the Owner's estate.

Simultaneous Death. Unless otherwise provided in the beneficiary designation in effect under this Contract, if any Beneficiary dies simultaneously with the Annuitant or during the 14 days immediately following the date of death of the Annuitant, the proceeds of this Contract shall be paid to the same payee or payees and in the same manner as if the deceased Beneficiary had died before the Annuitant. Any reference in the beneficiary designation to a Beneficiary living or surviving shall mean living on the 15th day immediately following the death of the Annuitant.

Change of Beneficiary. The Owner may designate a new Beneficiary at any time while the Annuitant is living, subject to the rights of any assignee, by filing with the Company a written request for change of Beneficiary in form satisfactory to the Company. No such change shall be effective until it is recorded by the Company, but upon such recording the change will be deemed to have been made as of the date the Owner

FIGURE 15

(continued)

signed the written request for change of Beneficiary, whether or not the Annuitant be living at the time of such recording, subject to any payment made or action taken by the Company before such recording.

SINGLE PURCHASE PAYMENT

The Single Purchase Payment for the Contract is payable during the lifetime of the Annuitant on or before delivery of this Contract as consideration for the benefits provided herein.

The Single Purchase Payment is payable either at the Home Office of the Company or to an authorized agent of the Company, in exchange for the Company's official receipt signed by the President or Secretary and duly countersigned by an authorized agent.

NET SINGLE PURCHASE PAYMENT

The Net Single Purchase Payment is the balance of the single purchase payment after the deduction of any immediate premium taxes.

PREMIUM TAXES

In the event that a premium tax is imposed upon the Single Purchase Payment paid for this Contract as of the effective date of the Contract such premium tax will be deducted from the Single Premium and calculations will be on the basis of the Net Single Purchase Payment. In the event that a premium tax is imposed at any time subsequent to the contract date, such premium tax will be deducted from the accumulated value of the Contract.

BASIS OF ACCUMULATED VALUE

The Accumulated Value is the Net Single Purchase Payment accumulated daily at interest rates which are equivalent to guaranteed annual rates. The guaranteed annual rate for the first contract year is shown in the Contract Specifications. Guaranteed annual rates applicable to contract years after the first will be furnished to the contract owner prior to each subsequent contract year.

ACCUMULATED VALUE

The Accumulated Value as of any date prior to the maturity date, is the Net Single Purchase Payment credited to this Contract, increased by the total sum of all interest credits made to this Contract, and reduced by the total sum of any amounts withdrawn and any applicable withdrawal charges.

ANNUAL NOTICE

The Company will send to each Owner at least once each contract year a statement as to the amount of the Contract's then accumulated value. In addition, the Company will advise the Owner the amount of the Contract's then accumulated value at any time upon request.

PARTIAL WITHDRAWAL

At any time while the Annuitant is living and prior to the maturity date, the Owner, upon written request in form satisfactory to the Company at its Home Office, may withdraw a portion of the accumulated value of this Contract. However, a partial withdrawal may not be made for less than $100. The amount of such withdrawal will be deducted from

FIGURE 15
(continued)

the accumulated value as of the date of withdrawal and a withdrawal charge shall be deducted from the funds so withdrawn on the following basis:

Contract Year of Withdrawal	Withdrawal Charge (Percentage of Amount Withdrawn)
1st through 5th	5%
Thereafter	-0-

The Owner may, withdraw an amount of up to 6% of the accumulated value during any contract year, on a noncumulative basis, without incurring a withdrawal or surrender charge.

The Owner has the right to repay amounts so withdrawn at any time, and such repayments will be added to the accumulated value of this Contract; provided however, that such repayments cannot be made in an amount less than $25.00.

CASH
SURRENDER

The Owner may at any time during the lifetime of the Annuitant and prior to the maturity date of this Contract, upon written request to the Company at its Home Office, surrender this Contract for its net accumulated value. The net accumulated value on any such date will be the accumulated value of the Contract on said date reduced by applicable premium taxes and surrender charges as of such date. In no event, however, will the net accumulated value be less than the Net Single Purchase Payment paid in consideration of this Contract. Surrender charges will be computed on the following basis:

Contract Year of Surrender	Surrender Charge (Percentage of Accumulated Value)
1st through 5th	5%
Thereafter	-0-

DEFERMENT
OF PAYMENT

The Company at its discretion may defer the payment of any amount to be withdrawn or any surrender benefit for a period not exceeding six months after a request, in accordance with the provisions of this contract, is received by the Company at its Home Office.

TABLE OF GUARANTEED MINIMUM VALUES

The guaranteed minimum values applicable to this Contract appear in the table which follows and are determined by the number of full contract years from the Contract Date. The values shown in the table are based on a contract with a Net Single Purchase Payment of $1,000.00. The values for a contract with a Purchase Payment of greater amount shall be proportionate. The table shows

FIGURE 15

(continued)

the minimum values available at the end of various contract years. The value at any time during a contract year will be calculated with allowances for the time elapsed in that year. The table is based on the assumption that no withdrawals have been made.

End of Contract Year	Minimum Value	End of Contract Year	Minimum Value	End of Contract Year	Minimum Value	End of Contract Year	Minimum Value	End of Contract Year	Minimum Value
1	$1,040.00	15	$1,716.00	29	$2,595.60	43	$3,926.07	57	$5,938.52
2	1,081.60	16	1,767.48	30	2,673.47	44	4,043.85	58	6,116.67
3	1,124.86	17	1,820.51	31	2,753.67	45	4,165.16	59	6,300.17
4	1,169.86	18	1,875.12	32	2,836.28	46	4,290.12	60	6,489.18
5	1,216.65	19	1,931.37	33	2,921.37	47	4,418.82	61	6,683.85
6	1,265.32	20	1,989.31	34	3,009.01	48	4,551.38	62	6,884.37
7	1,315.93	21	2,048.99	35	3,099.28	49	4,687.92	63	7,090.90
8	1,368.57	22	2,110.46	36	3,192.25	50	4,828.56	64	7,303.62
9	1,423.31	23	2,173.78	37	3,288.02	51	4,973.42	65	7,522.73
10	1,480.24	24	2,238.99	38	3,386.66	52	5,122.62	66	7,748.41
11	1,524.65	25	2,306.16	39	3,488.26	53	5,276.30	67	7,980.86
12	1,570.39	26	2,375.34	40	3,592.91	54	5,434.58	68	8,220.29
13	1,617.50	27	2,446.60	41	3,700.69	55	5,597.62	69	8,466.90
14	1,666.02	28	2,520.00	42	3,811.71	56	5,765.55	70	8,720.90

COLLATERAL ASSIGNMENT

The Owner may assign this Contract as collateral at any time prior to the effective date of settlement without the consent of the Annuitant, any Beneficiary or any successor Owner, by filing with the Company duplicate copies of a form of assignment satisfactory to the Company, and the interest of the Annuitant, any Beneficiary or successor Owner shall be subordinate to the interest of any assignee of record. No assignment shall bind the Company until it has been recorded by the Company at its Home Office. The Company assumes no responsibility for the validity or sufficiency of any assignment and may rely solely on the assignee's statement as to the amount of the assignee's interest. An assignment shall not be construed as a transfer of ownership within the meaning of this Contract.

OPTIONAL MATURITY DATE

While this contract is in force, the Owner may elect to have annuity payments commence at an Optional Maturity Date, which may be any contract anniversary, subsequent to the filing of such election, at which the Annuitant's age last birthday is any age from 55 through 75 years. An annuity commencing at an Optional Maturity Date shall be of the same form and shall be payable in the same manner as the annuity described on the first page. The amount of the monthly annuity payments commencing at an Optional Maturity Date shall be an amount for each $1,000 of proceeds paid as a Single Sum Settlement (defined below) determined according to the applicable table which appears in the Settlement Option provision. Prior to the due date of the first annuity payment,

FIGURE 15

(continued)

the Owner may change a previously elected Optional Maturity Date to another Optional Maturity Date. Any election or request for change must be in writing and shall not take effect until recorded by the Company at its Home Office.

The Maturity Date referred to in this contract is the Normal Maturity Date unless an Optional Maturity Date is elected, in which event the Maturity Date shall be the Optional Maturity Date.

SINGLE SUM
SETTLEMENT

While it is in force, the Owner, by surrendering this contract and filing written notice with the Company at its Home Office within thirty days prior to the Maturity Date, may elect to receive a Single Sum Settlement at the Maturity Date equal to the accumulated value of this contract at that date, less any applicable surrender charges and premium taxes existing at that date. Such election shall take effect as of the Maturity Date if the Annuitant is then living and, in such event, the annuity payments that would otherwise have commenced at the Maturity Date will not be made.

SETTLEMENT OPTIONS

DESCRIPTION
OF OPTIONS

Upon written election made to and accepted by the Company, all or a part of the amount payable in settlement of this Contract will be paid out in accordance with one of the following options:

Option 1. *Income for a Fixed Period.* Equal annual, semi-annual, quarterly, or monthly instalments shall be paid for a specified number of years, not to exceed 30, in accordance with the Option 1 table on the following page.

Option 2. *Life Income.* Equal monthly instalments shall be paid (A) as a life annuity for the lifetime of the payee, or (B) as a life income with payments guaranteed for a fixed period and continuing thereafter during the remaining lifetime of the payee, or (C) as an instalment refund annuity with payments guaranteed until the sum of the instalments paid equals the proceeds applied under this option and continuing thereafter during the remaining lifetime of the payee.

The amount of each instalment under (A), (B), or (C) above shall be determined from the Option 2 table on the following page, based on the payee's sex and age last birthday on the effective date of settlement.

Option 3. *Income of a Fixed Amount.* Equal annual, semi-annual, quarterly, or monthly instalments of a specified amount as approved by the Company shall be paid until the proceeds applied under this option, with interest at the effective rate of 3% per annum on the unpaid balance, are exhausted; the final instalment to be the balance of the proceeds and interest.

Option 4. *Interest Income.* Interest on proceeds left on deposit with the Company shall be paid at the effective rate of 3% per annum in annual, semi-annual, quarterly, or monthly instalments. The guaranteed interest payment for each $1,000 of proceeds retained by the Company shall be $30.00

FIGURE 15

(continued)

annually, \$14.89 semi-annually, \$7.42 quarterly, or \$2.47 monthly, depending on the frequency of payment elected. The maximum period for which the Company will retain proceeds under this option and the payee's withdrawal privileges shall be as approved by the Company at the time the option is elected.

Option 5. *Joint and Survivor Life Income.* Monthly instalments shall be paid during the joint lifetime of two designated payees either (A) with instalments guaranteed for 120 months and continuing thereafter as long as either payee is living, or (B) with instalments reduced one-third upon the death of either payee and continuing thereafter during the remaining lifetime of the survivor.

The amount of each instalment under (A) or (B) above shall be determined from the Option 5 table on the following page, based on the payees' sex and age last birthday on the effective date of settlement. Both the designated payees must be named when the Option is elected and both must be age 50, last birthday, or older on the effective date of settlement. If the proceeds to be applied under this Option on the effective date of settlement are not sufficient to provide an initial instalment of \$30.00 or more, the Option shall not be available and the proceeds shall be paid in one sum to the joint order of the designated payees.

EFFECTIVE DATE OF SETTLEMENT

The effective date of any settlement shall be the date of death of the Annuitant, or the maturity date, or the effective date of surrender, or such other date as may be mutually agreed upon, whichever is applicable. The first instalment under an option will be payable on the effective date except that under Option 4 it will be payable at the end of the first payment interval.

ELECTION OF OPTIONS

The Owner may elect that any death benefit or surrender benefit be applied under a settlement option, or he may revoke or change a previous election provided the election, revocation or change is made prior to the effective date of any settlement.

If no election is in effect when this Contract matures by the death of the Annuitant or on its maturity date, the payee otherwise entitled to receive payment of the proceeds in a single sum may elect a settlement option provided the election is made before any payment is made under this Contract. In the case of death of the Annuitant, no surrender charge will be deducted for election of an option.

If this Contract is surrendered for its net accumulated value, the Owner may elect a settlement option by written notice, in form satisfactory to the Company, upon surrender of the Contract, provided the proceeds have not been paid. If the Owner does not qualify as a payee under these Settlement Option provisions, or if the Owner so requests, the Annuitant shall be the payee.

Any such election, request for revocation, or change must be made in writing in form satisfactory to the Company and shall be effective only when accepted by the Company. Such election, revocation or change shall take effect as of the date of the request, whether or not the Annuitant is living at the time of acceptance by the Company, subject to any payment

Figure 15

(continued)

made or other action taken by the Company before such acceptance. Any change of beneficiary under this contract or a change of election of a settlement option shall revoke any option previously elected.

DEATH OF PAYEE

Unless otherwise directed in the settlement option election, upon the death of the payee the Company shall pay in one sum to the payee's estate any proceeds and accrued interest then remaining on deposit under Option 3 or 4, or the then commuted value of any unpaid instalments (a) for the fixed period under Option 1, or (b) for the guaranteed period under Option 2(B) or 5(A), or (c) as may be required to complete the payments which would equal the total proceeds applied under Option 2(c). Such commuted value shall be the amount calculated by the Company on the basis of compound interest at the effective rate of 3% per annum, provided that if such commutation is applicable to instalments payable under the alternate life income provision, the rate of interest used in such commutation shall be the rate applicable to the single premium immediate annuity rates in use by the Company on the effective date of settlement.

Under Option 2(A) or 5(B), the Company's liability shall terminate entirely with the last instalment due prior to the death of the payee under Option 2(A) or the last survivor under Option 5(B).

LIMITATIONS

A settlement option will be available only with the consent of the Company if the proceeds of this Contract are payable to a corporation, partnership, association, assignee, trustee or estate.

If the amount to be applied under a settlement option for any payee is less than $2,000, the option will not be available and payment will be made to such payee in one sum.

If at any time an interest or instalment payment to a payee shall amount to less than $20.00, the Company reserves the right to make payment thereof in equivalent amounts quarterly, semi-annually, or annually, so that no such payment shall amount to less than $20.00.

If a settlement option is elected during the lifetime of the Annuitant prior to this Contract being in effect for five (5) years, a surrender charge will be assessed against the accumulated cash value used to compute the settlement option.

PROOF OF AGE
AND SURVIVAL

Before making any payments under Option 2 or 5, the Company will require satisfactory evidence of the age of the payee or payees. If any instalment under an Option depends on the survival of any payee, the Company will require satisfactory evidence that such payee is living when the payment becomes due.

PAYMENTS TO
ANNUITANT

If the Owner is other than the Annuitant, the Company will, upon receipt of written request by the Owner satisfactory to it, not later than 30 days before the due date of the first annuity payment, make such payments becoming due thereafter while the Annuitant is living payable to the Annuitant instead of the Owner. Any such request will be subject to the

FIGURE 15

(continued)

rights of any assignee and, unless otherwise specified by the Owner in such request, will be irrevocable after payments to the Annuitant have commenced. If an irrevocable request has been made, no payments available to or being paid to the Annuitant during his lifetime will be transferable or subject to commutation, anticipation or encumbrance. Upon any permitted revocation, payments thereafter becoming due will be made in accordance with the terms of this policy.

ANNUITY PAYMENTS AFTER ANNUITANT'S DEATH

During the lifetime of the Annuitant but not later than 30 days before the due date of the first annuity payment, the Owner may make a designation, of a person or persons to receive any annuity payments due after the death of the Annuitant, subject to these Settlement Options Provisions and subject to the rights of any assignee. A designation or change in designation may be effected by filing at the Home Office of the Company, written request satisfactory to the Company. No designation or change of designation will take effect unless request is so filed, but if filed it will be effective as of the date signed subject to any payment made or action taken by the Company before such filing. If a payee was not the Owner of the contract at the death of the Annuitant, no payments available to or being paid to such payee during his lifetime will be transferable or subject to commutation, anticipation or encumbrance, unless otherwise specified in the designation of such payee.

If at the later of the death of the Annuitant and the death of any designated payee for annuity payments payable after the death of the Annuitant, there is no designated person then living who is entitled to receive any remaining annuity payments certain, such payments will be commuted on the basis of 3% per annum compound interest and paid in a single sum to the estate of the payee under the contract immediately prior to such later death.

ASSIGNMENT

If this Contract is assigned, the Company shall have the right to pay to the assignee in one sum the amount to which he shall be entitled, but the balance of the net proceeds, if any, shall be paid in accordance with the terms of the mode of settlement in effect under this Contract. A payee who, under the terms of a mode of settlement, does not have the right to surrender the benefits under such mode of settlement, may not assign or encumber such benefits or any payment thereunder.

SURRENDER OF BENEFITS

Unless otherwise directed in the settlement option election, the payee shall have the right to receive the withdrawal value of any proceeds being held by the Company under Option 1, 3, or 4. Under Option 1 the withdrawal value shall be the commuted value of any unpaid instalments calculated on the basis of compound interest at the effective rate of 3% per annum. Under Option 3 or 4, the withdrawal value shall be any unpaid balance of proceeds, with accrued interest.

RIGHTS OF CREDITORS

All benefits shall be exempt from the claims of creditors to the maximum extent permitted by law.

FIGURE 15

(continued)

EXCESS INTEREST

The Company at its sole discretion may declare the payment of additional interest under Option 1, 3 and 4 and during the fixed period of Option 2(B), 2(C), and 5(A). Such additional interest will be computed at a rate determined by the Company in excess of the rate used in the computation of said options and will be paid in a single sum on the anniversary of the effective date of the option elected. The instalment payments in the following tables for Options 1, 2 and 5 are computed with interest at the effective rate of 3% per annum.

CONTRACT ENDORSEMENT

In case one of the foregoing settlement options is elected, this Contract must be surrendered at the time of settlement for endorsement of the option elected.

SETTLEMENT OPTION TABLES

Monthly instalments are shown for each $1,000 of proceeds applied under the option. Instalment amounts under Options 2 or 5 depend on the age last birthday and sex of the payee or payees on the date the first instalment is payable. Amounts for any age not shown in the Option 2 table or combination of ages not shown in the Option 5 table (minimum age 50) will be furnished by the Company upon request.

Option 1—Income for a Fixed Period

(Annual, semiannual, or quarterly instalments shall be determined by multiplying the monthly instalment by 11.839, 5.963, or 2.993 respectively.)

Years	Monthly Instalment	Years	Monthly Instalment	Years	Monthly Instalment	Years	Monthly Instalment	Years	Monthly Instalment	Years	Monthly Instalment
1	$84.47	6	15.14	11	$ 8.86	16	6.53	21	$ 5.32	26	4.59
2	42.86	7	13.16	12	8.24	17	6.23	22	5.15	27	4.47
3	28.99	8	11.68	13	7.71	18	5.96	23	4.99	28	4.37
4	22.06	9	10.53	14	7.26	19	5.73	24	4.84	29	4.27
5	17.91	10	9.61	15	6.87	20	5.51	25	4.71	30	4.18

Option 2—Life Income

Age of Payee Male	Age of Payee Female	2A Life Annuity	2B Guaranteed Period 5 Years	2B Guaranteed Period 10 Years	2B Guaranteed Period 20 Years	2C Instalment Refund	Age of Payee Male	Age of Payee Female	2A Life Annuity	2B Guaranteed Period 5 Years	2B Guaranteed Period 10 Years	2B Guaranteed Period 20 Years	2C Instalment Refund
46	51	4.36	4.35	4.31	4.14	4.14	66	71	7.34	7.16	6.66	5.29	6.21
47	52	4.45	4.44	4.39	4.20	4.20	67	72	7.61	7.40	6.83	5.32	6.38
48	53	4.54	4.52	4.47	4.26	4.27	68	73	7.90	7.65	7.00	5.36	6.56
49	54	4.63	4.62	4.56	4.32	4.34	69	74	8.20	7.92	7.18	5.39	6.75
50	55	4.73	4.71	4.65	4.38	4.42	70	75	8.54	8.20	7.36	5.41	6.95
51	56	4.84	4.01	4.74	4.44	4.49	71	76	8.90	8.50	7.54	5.44	7.17
52	57	4.95	4.92	4.83	4.50	4.57	72	77	9.28	8.82	7.71	5.45	7.39
53	58	5.06	5.03	4.93	4.56	4.66	73	78	9.70	9.15	7.89	5.47	7.63
54	59	5.18	5.15	5.04	4.62	4.74	74	79	10.15	9.50	8.06	5.48	7.89
55	60	5.31	5.27	5.14	4.69	4.84	75	80	10.63	9.87	8.23	5.49	8.16
56	61	5.44	5.40	5.26	4.75	4.93	76	81	11.15	10.26	8.40	5.50	8.45
57	62	5.58	5.53	5.37	4.81	5.03	77	82	11.72	10.65	8.55	5.50	8.75
58	63	5.73	5.67	5.49	4.87	5.14	78	83	12.33	11.07	8.70	5.51	9.08
59	64	5.89	5.82	5.62	4.93	5.25	79	84	13.00	11.49	8.84	5.51	9.43
60	65	6.06	5.98	5.75	4.99	5.37	80	85 and over	13.72	11.93	8.96	5.51	9.79
61	66	6.24	6.15	5.89	5.05	5.49	81	82		14.50	12.38	9.08	5.51	10.19
62	67	6.43	6.33	6.04	5.10	5.62	82		15.34	12.83	9.18	5.51	10.61
63	68	6.63	6.52	6.18	5.15	5.75	83		16.26	13.28	9.27	5.51	11.06
64	69	6.85	6.72	6.34	5.20	5.90	84		17.27	13.74	9.34	5.51	11.54
65	70	7.09	6.93	6.50	5.25	6.05	85 and over		18.35	14.18	9.41	5.51	12.06

FIGURE 15

(concluded)

Option 5—Joint and Survivor Life Income

5A
Joint Life Income with Instalments Guaranteed for 10 Years

Age of Payee M F	F50	M50 F55	M55 F60	M57 F62	M58 F63	M59 F64	M60 F65	M62 F67	M65 F70	M70 F75
50 55	3.85	4.02	4.18	4.24	4.27	4.30	4.32	4.38	4.44	4.53
55 60	3.96	4.18	4.41	4.49	4.53	4.58	4.62	4.69	4.80	4.94
56 61	3.98	4.21	4.45	4.54	4.59	4.63	4.67	4.76	4.87	5.03
57 62	4.00	4.24	4.49	4.59	4.64	4.69	4.73	4.82	4.95	5.12
58 63	4.02	4.27	4.53	4.64	4.69	4.74	4.79	4.89	5.03	5.22
59 64	4.03	4.30	4.58	4.69	4.74	4.80	4.85	4.96	5.10	5.31
60 65	4.05	4.32	4.62	4.73	4.79	4.85	4.91	5.02	5.18	5.41
61 66	4.07	4.35	4.65	4.78	4.84	4.90	4.96	5.09	5.26	5.51
62 67	4.08	4.38	4.69	4.82	4.89	4.96	5.02	5.15	5.34	5.61
63 68	4.10	4.40	4.73	4.87	4.94	5.01	5.08	5.21	5.42	5.72
64 69	4.11	4.42	4.76	4.91	4.98	5.06	5.13	5.28	5.49	5.82
65 70	4.12	4.44	4.80	4.95	5.03	5.10	5.18	5.34	5.57	5.92
66 71	4.13	4.46	4.83	4.99	5.07	5.15	5.23	5.40	5.64	6.02
67 72	4.14	4.48	4.86	5.03	5.11	5.19	5.28	5.45	5.72	6.13
68 73	4.16	4.50	4.89	5.06	5.15	5.24	5.33	5.51	5.79	6.23
69 74	4.16	4.52	4.92	5.09	5.18	5.28	5.37	5.56	5.86	6.33
70 75	4.17	4.53	4.94	5.12	5.22	5.31	5.41	5.61	5.92	6.42

5B
Joint Life Income with Two-thirds to Survivor

Age of Payee M F	F50	M50 F55	M55 F60	M57 F62	M58 F63	M59 F64	M60 F65	M62 F67	M65 F70	M70 F75
50 55	4.26	4.47	4.70	4.79	4.84	4.89	4.94	5.04	5.20	5.47
55 60	4.45	4.70	4.97	5.09	5.15	5.21	5.27	5.39	5.59	5.93
56 61	4.49	4.75	5.03	5.15	5.21	5.28	5.34	5.47	5.67	6.03
57 62	4.53	4.79	5.09	5.21	5.28	5.34	5.41	5.55	5.76	6.13
58 63	4.57	4.84	5.15	5.28	5.35	5.41	5.48	5.62	5.85	6.23
59 64	4.61	4.89	5.21	5.34	5.41	5.48	5.56	5.70	5.94	6.34
60 65	4.65	4.94	5.27	5.41	5.48	5.56	5.63	5.79	6.03	6.46
61 66	4.69	4.99	5.33	5.48	5.55	5.63	5.71	5.87	6.12	6.57
62 67	4.73	5.04	5.39	5.55	5.62	5.70	5.79	5.96	6.22	6.69
63 68	4.78	5.10	5.46	5.62	5.70	5.78	5.87	6.04	6.32	6.82
64 69	4.82	5.15	5.52	5.69	5.77	5.86	5.95	6.13	6.42	6.95
65 70	4.86	5.20	5.59	5.76	5.85	5.94	6.03	6.22	6.53	7.08
66 71	4.91	5.26	5.66	5.83	5.92	6.02	6.11	6.31	6.64	7.22
67 72	4.95	5.31	5.72	5.90	6.00	6.10	6.20	6.41	6.74	7.35
68 73	5.00	5.36	5.79	5.98	6.08	6.18	6.28	6.50	6.85	7.50
69 74	5.04	5.42	5.86	6.05	6.16	6.26	6.37	6.60	6.97	7.64
70 75	5.09	5.47	5.93	6.13	6.23	6.34	6.46	6.69	7.08	7.79